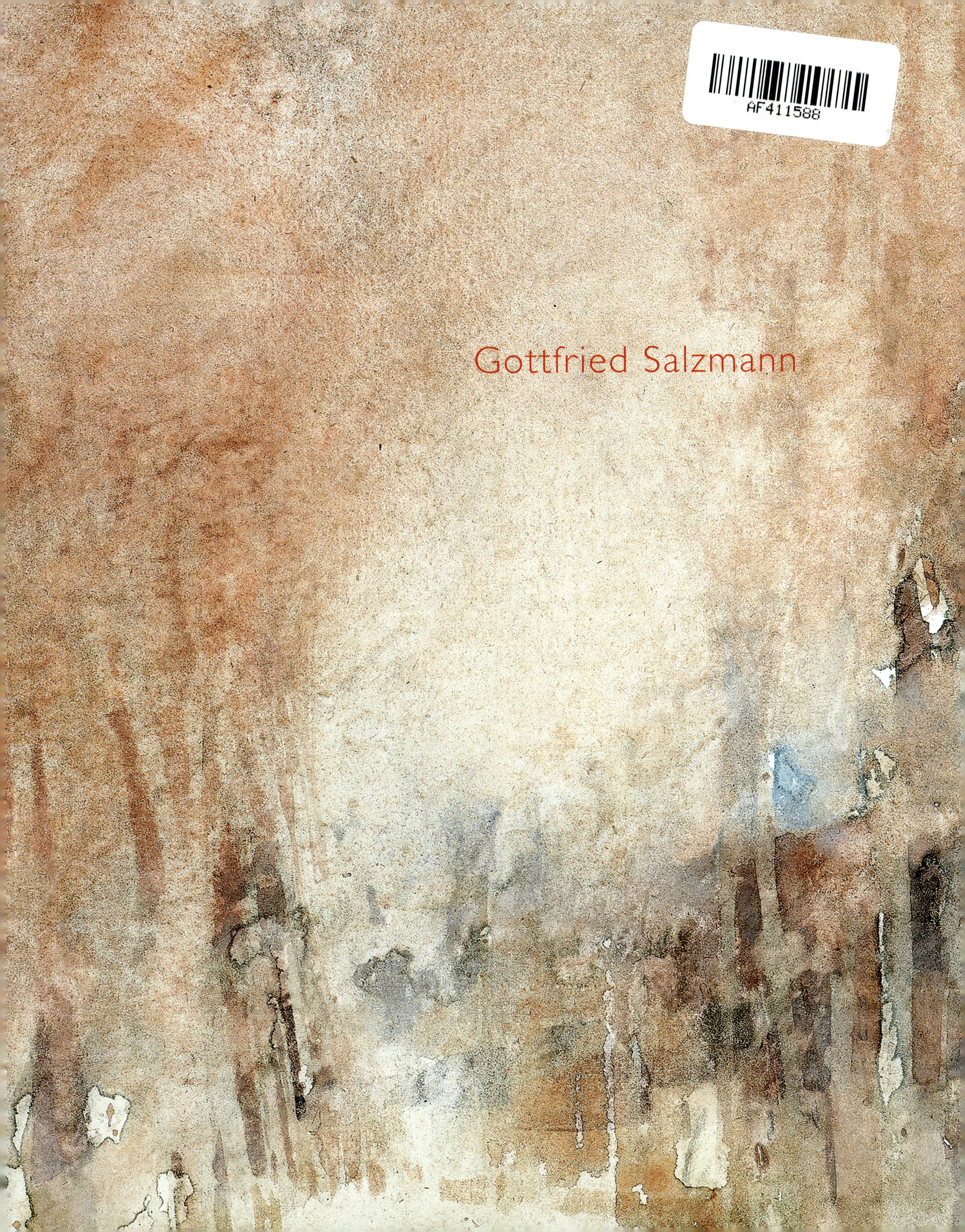
Gottfried Salzmann

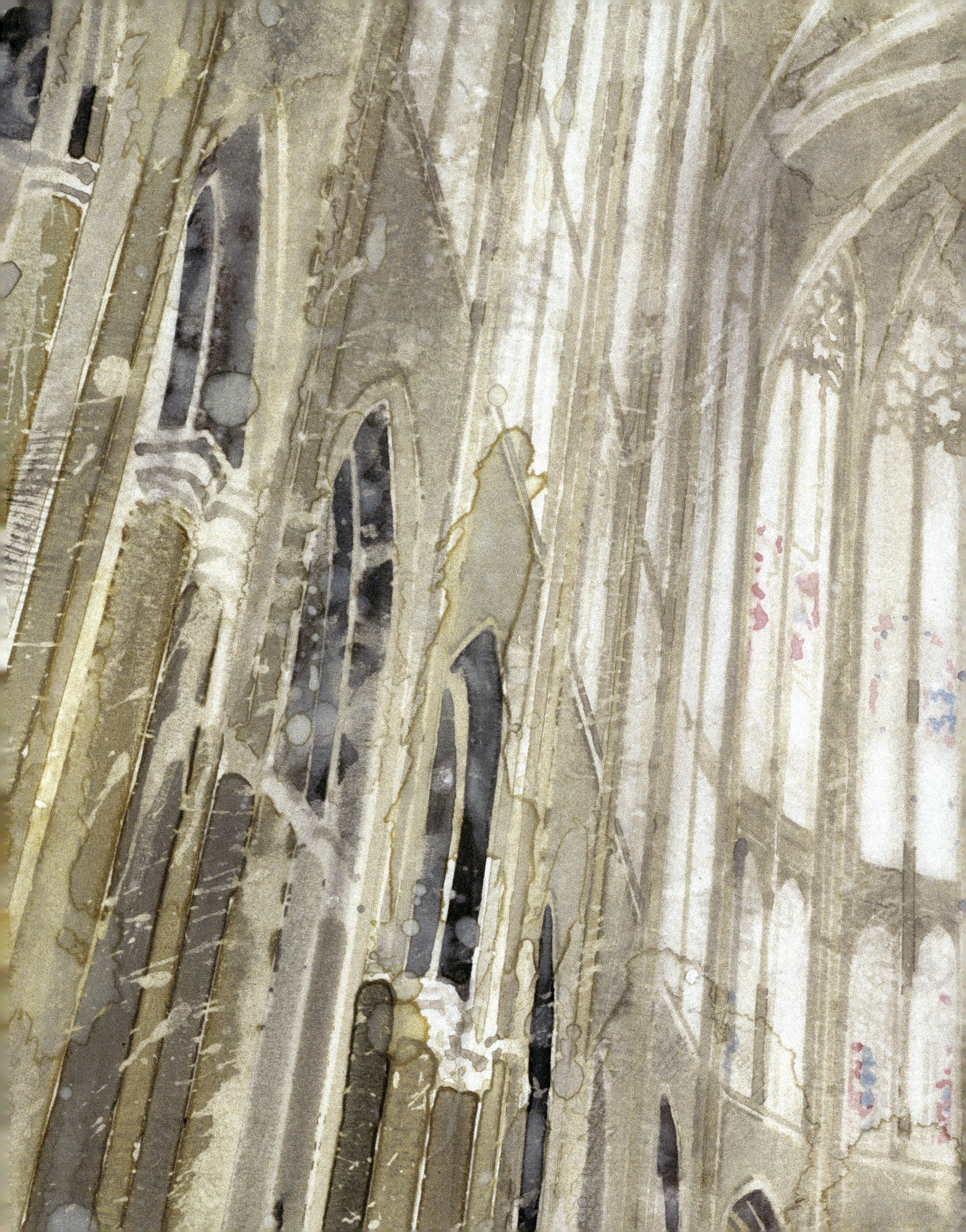

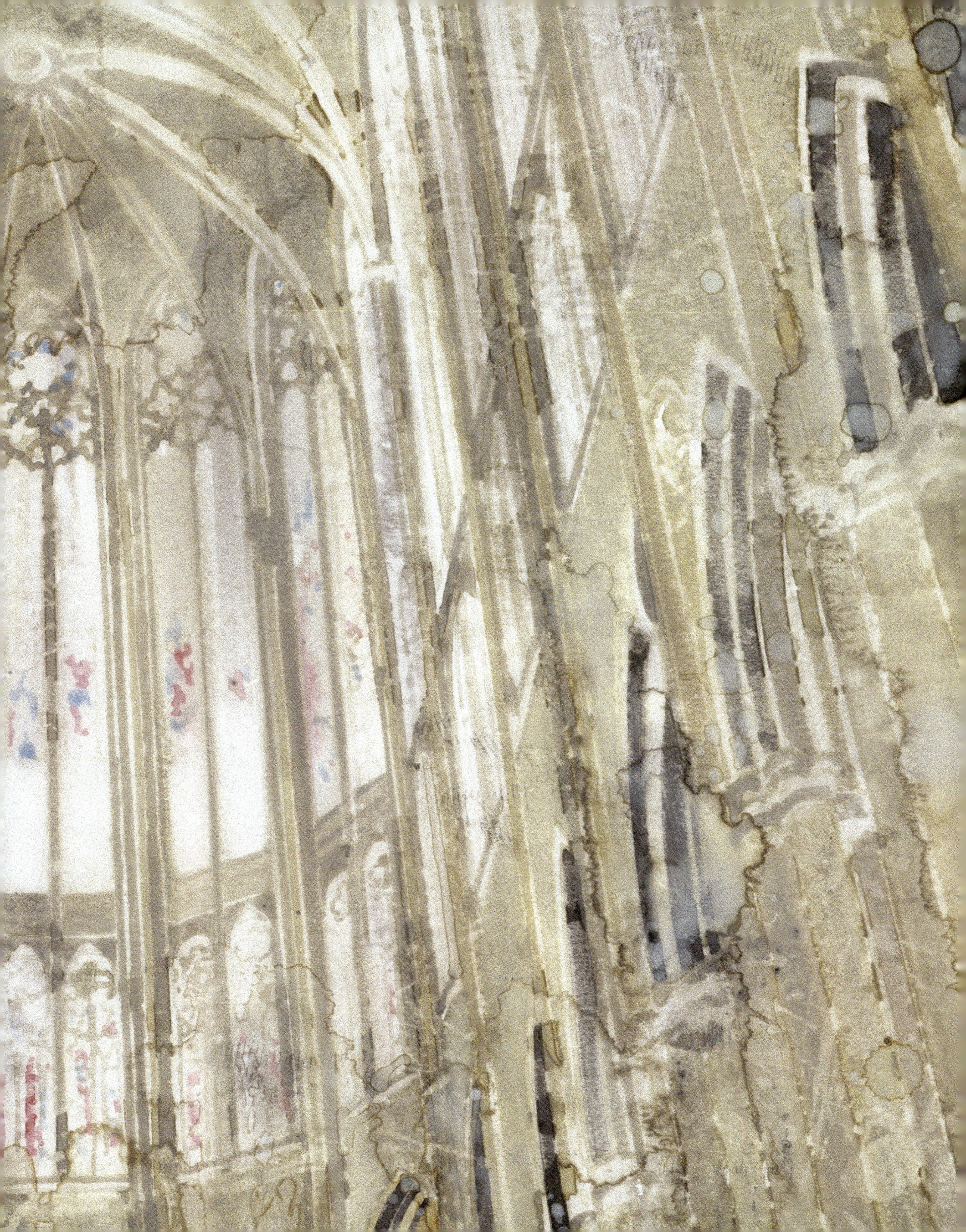

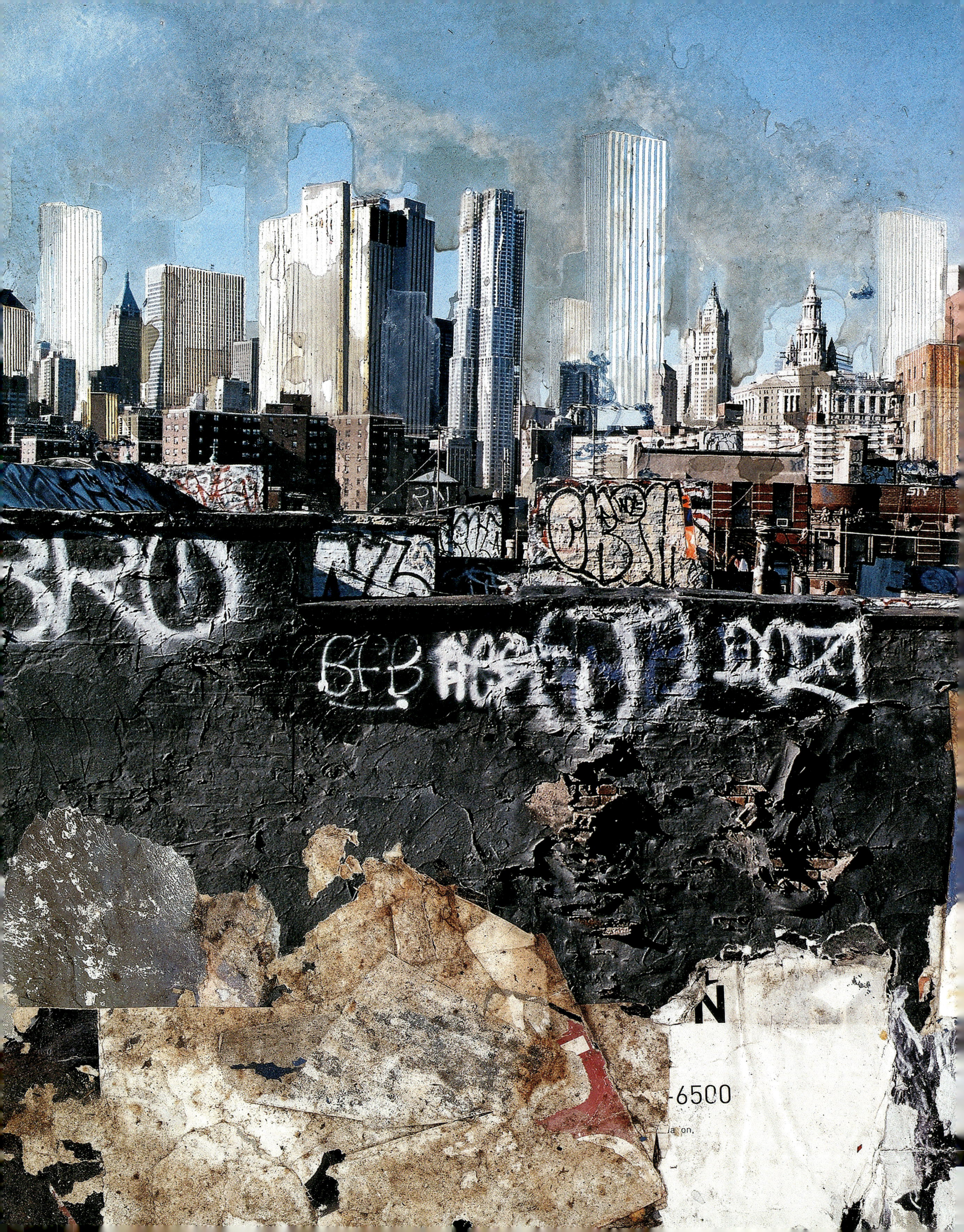

BRO
NZ
CBS
6500

Cityscapes
Stadtlandschaften
Paysages urbains

From Paris to New York

Gottfried Salzmann

PRESTEL

Munich London New York

Foreword

This publication, issued in the summer of 2013, is the most comprehensive documentation of the artistic oeuvre of Gottfried Salzmann ever compiled. Featuring works selected with great care by the artist himself, the book offers truly unique insights into his life and work.

Gottfried Salzmann was born in Saalfelden, Austria, in 1943. He studied in Vienna, Austria and Paris during the 1960s and succeeded relatively soon in positioning himself as an internationally recognized representative of the newly established genre of the watercolor. Viewed in retrospect, his watercolors, the technical brilliance and fascinating motifs of which are widely acclaimed, have always engaged in fascinating dialogue with other groups of works—his early collages and charcoal drawings, as well as his later photographs, which he also incorporated masterfully into his pictorial concept.

All of Salzmann's works can be placed within a biographical and artistic context, regardless of the medium in which they were created. This publication calls attention to the authentic relationships that exist between the various work groups and specific life experiences, such as his emigration to France, for example. Other travels and working visits also reveal Salzmann's natural inclination to respond to specific situations with personal artistic considerations. We repeatedly encounter fields of tension between urban and natural landscapes, which he renders in nuanced gradations and atmospheric soft focus in some cases, and highly charged color spaces and dynamic imagery in others. Salzmann loves to experiment with distinctive concepts of reality in his art. What is actually

Vorwort

Die vorliegende Publikation erscheint im Sommer 2013 und erweist sich als die bislang umfangreichste Dokumentation des künstlerischen Schaffens von Gottfried Salzmann. Durch die vom Künstler persönlich und mit großer Sorgfalt getroffene Bildauswahl vermag das Buch einen speziellen Einblick in sein Leben und Werk zu geben.

Gottfried Salzmann wurde 1943 in Saalfelden in Österreich geboren. Er studierte in den 1960er-Jahren in Wien und Paris und konnte sich relativ rasch als ein international rezipierter Vertreter einer neu etablierten Kunst des Aquarells positionieren. Retrospektiv stehen die durch ihre technische Brillanz und ihre spannungsvolle Motivwelt erfolgreich wahrgenommenen Aquarelle stets in spannungsvollen Dialogsituationen zu anderen Werkgruppen: zu frühen Collagen und Kohlezeichnungen sowie zu den sich anschließenden Fotografien, die er ebenfalls in ganz besonderer Weise in sein Bildkonzept zu integrieren vermochte.

Salzmanns Kunst lässt sich unabhängig vom jeweils verwendeten Medium immer in einem biografischen und künstlerischen Zusammenhang verorten. So wird durch diese Publikation auch deutlich, wie authentisch sich einzelne Werkgruppen mit unterschiedlichen Lebenserfahrungen, etwa der Übersiedelung nach Frankreich, in Verbindung bringen lassen. Auch andere Reisen bzw. Arbeitsaufenthalte zeigen Salzmanns Neigung, auf konkrete Situationen mit eigenen künstlerischen Überlegungen zu reagieren. Immer wieder trifft man auf Spannungsfelder zwischen Stadt- und Naturlandschaften, die er teils in nuancierten Abstufungen und atmosphärischen Unschärfen, teils in aufgela-

Avant-propos

La présente publication doit paraître à l'été 2013 et constituera la plus importante à ce jour sur le travail artistique de Gottfried Salzmann. Les illustrations, sélectionnées avec le plus grand soin et conformément à la volonté personnelle de l'artiste, offrent un regard inédit sur sa vie et son œuvre.

Gottfried Salzmann est né en 1943 à Saalfelden, en Autriche. Il étudie à Vienne et Paris dans les années 1960, et ne tardera pas à s'établir à l'échelon international comme le représentant d'un nouvel art de l'aquarelle. Rétrospectivement, on constate du reste combien ses aquarelles, remarquables tant par leur technique que par leurs motifs, ont toujours entretenu un dialogue vivifiant avec d'autres groupes d'œuvres, qu'il s'agisse des collages et des dessins au fusain des débuts ou des photographies qui viendront par la suite et qui trouveront, là aussi, à s'intégrer de façon particulière dans son univers artistique.

Le travail de Salzmann, indépendamment du procédé utilisé, s'inscrit toujours dans un contexte biographique et artistique. Cette publication veille ainsi à mettre en lumière les liens authentiques qui rattachent chaque groupe d'œuvres à un épisode de vie, comme par exemple celui de son installation en France. Mais les voyages aussi, de même que les séjours de travail, montrent comment Salzmann réagit à des situations concrètes par des réflexions artistiques qui lui sont propres. Les vues urbaines, d'une part, et les paysages, de l'autre, sont autant de champs de tension qui s'expriment tantôt dans des nuances vaporeuses, tantôt dans des aplats colorés et dynamiques. Salzmann aime à jouer avec toutes sortes de notions de la réalité. Le regard réel, l'œil photographique,

seen, what is captured photographically, what is perceived in mirror images, what is experienced dynamically, and what is registered emotionally are concentrated by the artist within the system of the visual work of art. Yet this great diversity notwithstanding, each work appears as a very personal natural, urban, landscape, and sensory experience that is rendered masterfully and with considerable aesthetic intelligence.

Following the many publications issued for national and international exhibitions, in which Gottfried Salzmann has dealt as a matter of preference with individual work groups, techniques, and realms of imagery, this book makes a particularly important contribution to the critical reception of his various positions by consolidating the diverse narrative strands and fields of activity. Moreover, in combination with the essay by Nikolaus Schaffer, it enriches our understanding of the visual worlds the artist has pursued with admirable rigor for nearly fifty years. The Prestel Verlag in Munich deserves thanks for taking on this project in honor of the artist's seventieth birthday and for realizing it as a sincere gesture of tribute to Gottfried Salzmann.

Martin Hochleitner

denen Farbräumen und dynamischen Bildwelten künstlerisch umsetzt. Salzmann liebt in seiner Arbeit das Spiel mit differenzierten Wirklichkeitsbegriffen. Das real Geschaute, das fotografisch Erfasste, das in Spiegelungen Wahrgenommene, das dynamisch Erlebte, das emotional Empfundene werden vom Künstler im System Bild verdichtet. Bei aller Vielfalt erweist sich jedoch auch jede Arbeit als ein ganz persönliches Natur-, Stadt-, Landschafts- und Sinneserlebnis, das der Künstler virtuos und mit hoher ästhetischer Intelligenz umzusetzen vermag.

Nach vielen Einzelpublikationen zu nationalen und internationalen Ausstellungen, in denen Gottfried Salzmann bevorzugt einzelne Werkgruppen, künstlerische Techniken und Motivwelten behandelte, leistet das aktuelle Buch gerade durch die Zusammenführung der vielfältigen Erzählstränge und Arbeitsfelder einen besonders wichtigen Beitrag für die Rezeption seiner Positionen und – in Verbindung mit dem Essay von Nikolaus Schaffer – für das Verständnis der mit großer Konsequenz in knapp fünfzig Jahren verfolgten Bildwelten. Dem Prestel Verlag in München gilt der Dank, dieses Projekt anlässlich des 70. Geburtstages des Künstlers in Angriff und mit großer Wertschätzung für Gottfried Salzmann umgesetzt zu haben.

Martin Hochleitner

la perception des reflets, le vécu actif, les émotions et le ressenti – c'est tout cela que l'artiste fait interférer et concentre dans l'image. Mais, au-delà de cette pluralité, chaque œuvre s'avère comme une expérience tout à fait personnelle de la nature, de la ville, des paysages, comme une expérience sensorielle que l'artiste traduit brillamment, avec une grande intelligence esthétique.

Après plusieurs publications individuelles, parues lors d'expositions nationales ou internationales, et dans lesquelles Gottfried Salzmann avait préféré aborder chaque fois des groupes d'œuvres, techniques artistiques et univers motiviques différents, le présent ouvrage choisit au contraire de réunir les multiples fils narratifs et champs de travail. Il offre ainsi une contribution importante à la réception des positions de l'artiste et – grâce également au texte de Nikolaus Schaffer – une meilleure compréhension de cet univers pictural construit en quelque cinquante années avec rigueur et persévérance. Que les Éditions Prestel à Munich soient ici remerciées d'avoir soutenu la réalisation de ce projet et qu'un bel hommage soit ainsi rendu à Gottfried Salzmann pour ses 70 ans.

Martin Hochleitner

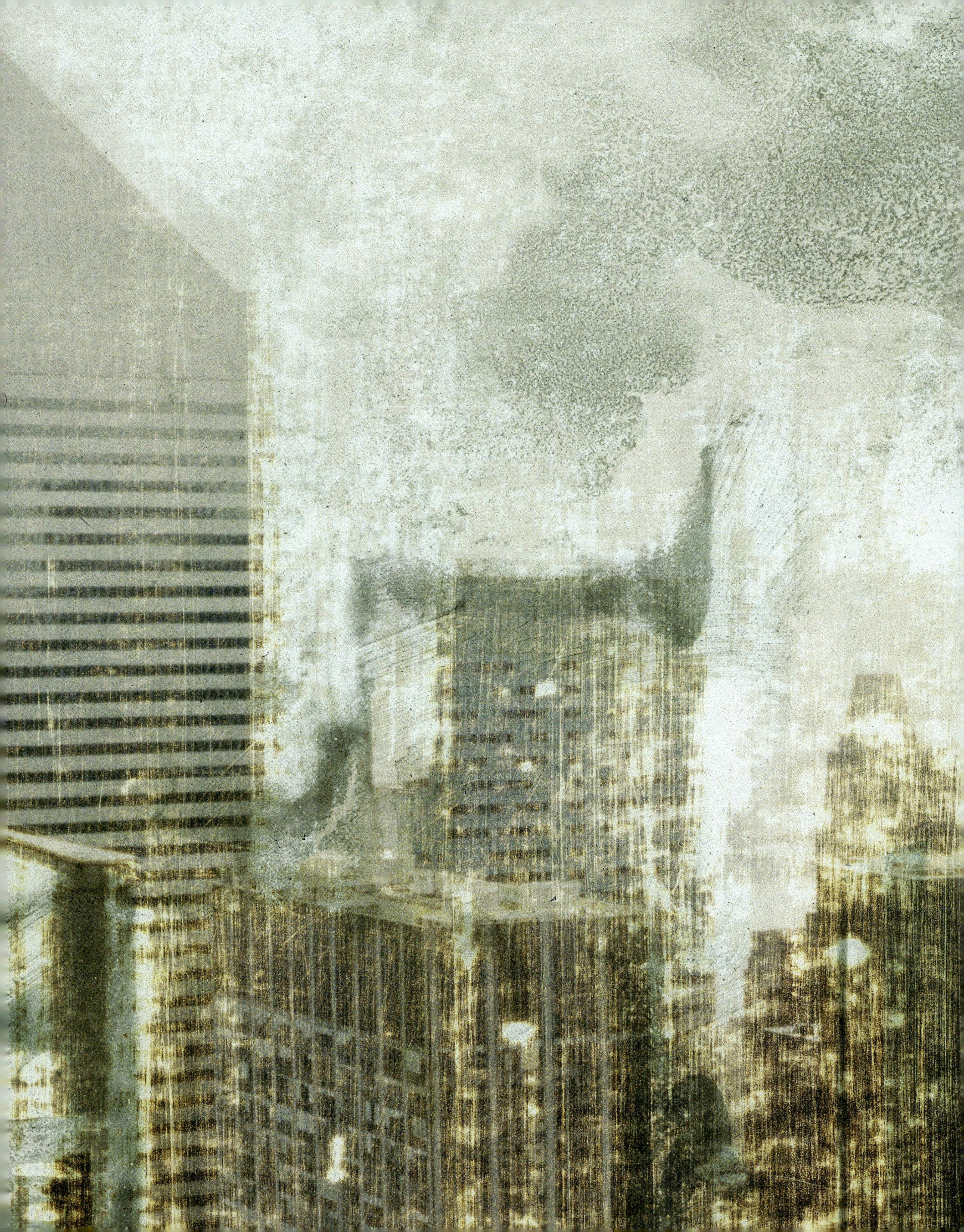

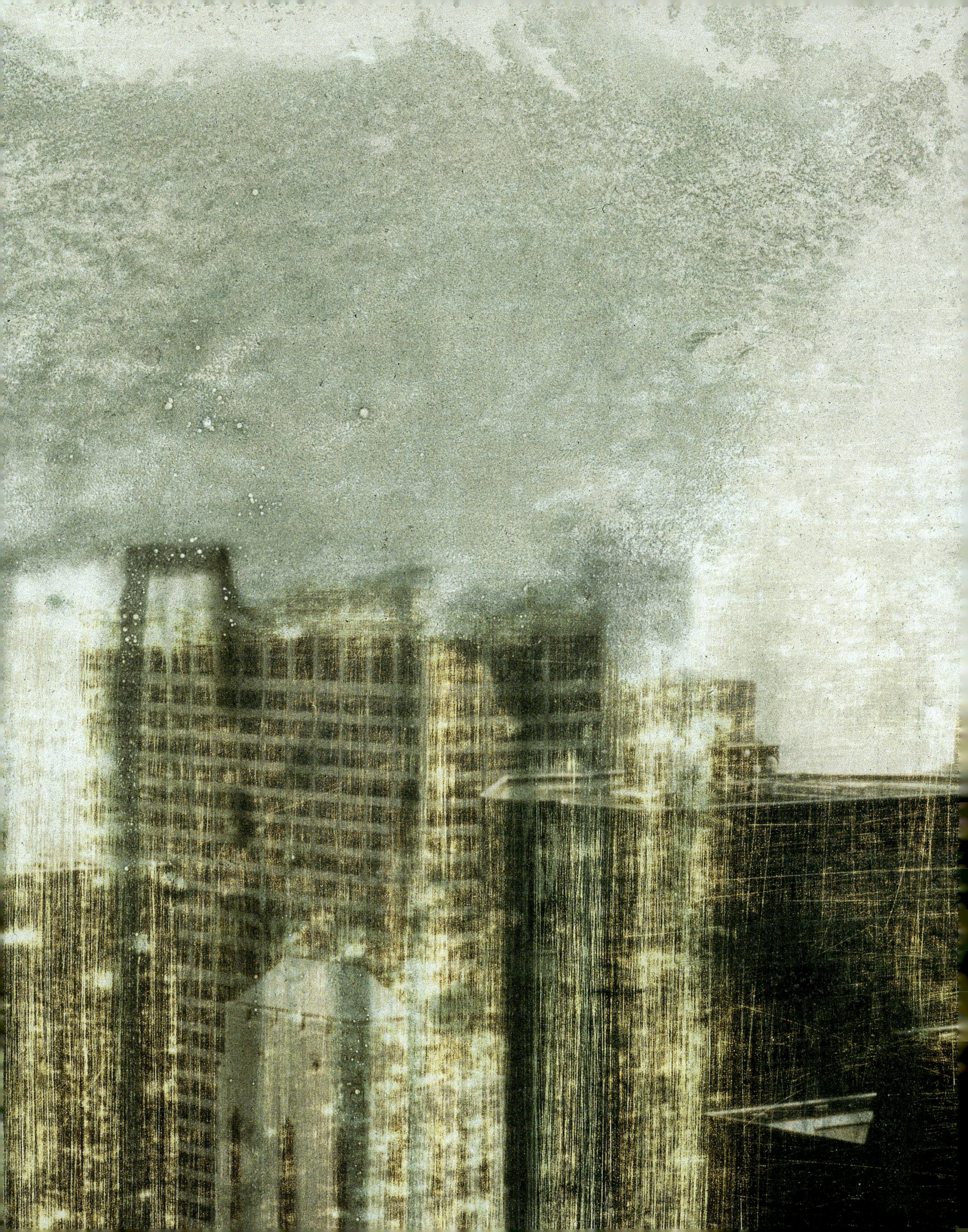

Nikolaus Schaffer
Gottfried Salzmann
A Dreamer in the Here and Now

Gottfried Salzmann is no friend of grand and verbose utterances, especially when it comes to his own art. He also sees little need for explanation, since he regards his works as readily understandable and true to life, as they are based on fundamental principles of sense perception. He exhibits an almost naive sense of self and reacts incredulously and with a hint of protest to the suggestion that anyone could regard his paintings as daringly divorced from reality or extremely complicated—as a kind of visual puzzle.

On only one occasion have I known Salzmann, who otherwise responds to all ventures into interpretation with benevolent interest or simple amazement, to react with something close to outrage: when I asked him about a very intense shade of color, suggesting that its boldness might be attributable to an exquisite artistic mood. "No, no," he hastened to insist. It was precisely the color of the sky—or whatever it was—at the time.

It was now my turn to be astonished in the face of his resolute dismissal of any suspicion of willfulness and his insistence on authenticity in an age that had long since tossed the pact of loyalty with nature onto the scrap heap. Evidently still at work here is something of the ethos of an era for which there were still limits to artistic freedom. Yet as devoted as an artist like Salzmann may be to the empirical world and as much as he may strive to evade the speculative possibilities of art—in his results he is nevertheless in many ways more fantastic than a declared fantasist

Nikolaus Schaffer
Gottfried Salzmann
Ein Träumer im Jetzt

Gottfried Salzmann ist kein Freund großer und vieler Worte, erst recht nicht, wenn es um sein eigenes künstlerisches Schaffen geht. Auch schätzt er diesbezüglichen Erklärungsbedarf als gering ein, denn er hält seine Bilder für mühelos verständlich und wirklichkeitsnah, weil sie auf den Grundgegebenheiten der sinnlichen Wahrnehmung basieren. Er legt dabei ein fast naives Selbstverständnis an den Tag, reagiert ungläubig und leicht protestierend darauf, dass man seine Bilder auch als halsbrecherisch abgehoben und hoch kompliziert, als ein visuelles Verwirrspiel empfinden kann.

Ein einziges Mal hat er sich, der sonst allen interpretatorischen Bemühungen ein wohlwollendes bis verwundertes Interesse entgegenbringt, mir gegenüber nahezu empört gezeigt: Als ich ihn wegen eines sehr intensiven Farbtons angesprochen habe, dessen Gewagtheit ich mir aus einer exquisiten künstlerischen Laune entstanden erklären wollte. Nein, nein, genau diese Farbe habe der Himmel – oder was es nun war – damals gehabt, wurde ich unverzüglich korrigiert.

Dieses entschiedene Zurückweisen jeglichen Verdachts auf Willkür und stattdessen Beharren auf Authentizität in einer Zeit, die den Treuepakt mit der Natur längst zum alten Eisen gelegt hat, erstaunte nun wiederum mich. Hier wirkt offensichtlich etwas vom Ethos einer Epoche nach, für die es noch Grenzen künstlerischer Freiheit gegeben hat. Doch so stark sich ein Künstler wie Salzmann auch der Empirie verpflichtet fühlt und den spekulativen Möglichkeiten des Kunstschaf-

Nikolaus Schaffer
Gottfried Salzmann
Un rêveur du présent

Gottfried Salzmann n'aime pas les profusions de grands mots, encore moins lorsqu'il est question de son propre travail artistique. Il ne fait pas grand cas des explications. Selon lui, ses toiles sont aisément compréhensibles et proches de la réalité, dans la mesure où elles relèvent des fondements de la perception sensorielle. Il affiche une évidence presque naïve, réagit avec incrédulité et proteste légèrement à l'idée que l'on puisse ressentir ses toiles comme dangereusement coupées du réel et hautement compliquées ou comme un imbroglio visuel.

Une fois, et une seule, il s'est presque emporté devant moi, lui qui, d'ordinaire, montre un intérêt bienveillant ou étonné à tous les efforts d'interprétation : c'était à propos d'une tonalité très intense dont je pensais pouvoir mettre l'audace sur le compte d'un trait artistique plein d'allant. J'ai été repris sur-le-champ. Non et non, cette couleur est bel et bien celle que le ciel – ou autre, peu importe – avait alors.

Refuser catégoriquement tout ce qui soupçonne l'arbitraire et insister au contraire sur l'authenticité, en un temps qui a relégué depuis longtemps le pacte de fidélité avec la nature – cela m'a laissé pantois. Là-dedans résonne manifestement la déontologie d'une époque qui considérait que la liberté artistique avait ses limites. Or Salzmann a beau être redevable de l'empirie et faire fi des possibilités spéculatives de la création artistique, ce qu'il produit est pourtant à bien des égards plus fantastique que la fantaisie proclamée, et plus abstrait que l'abstraction « pure et

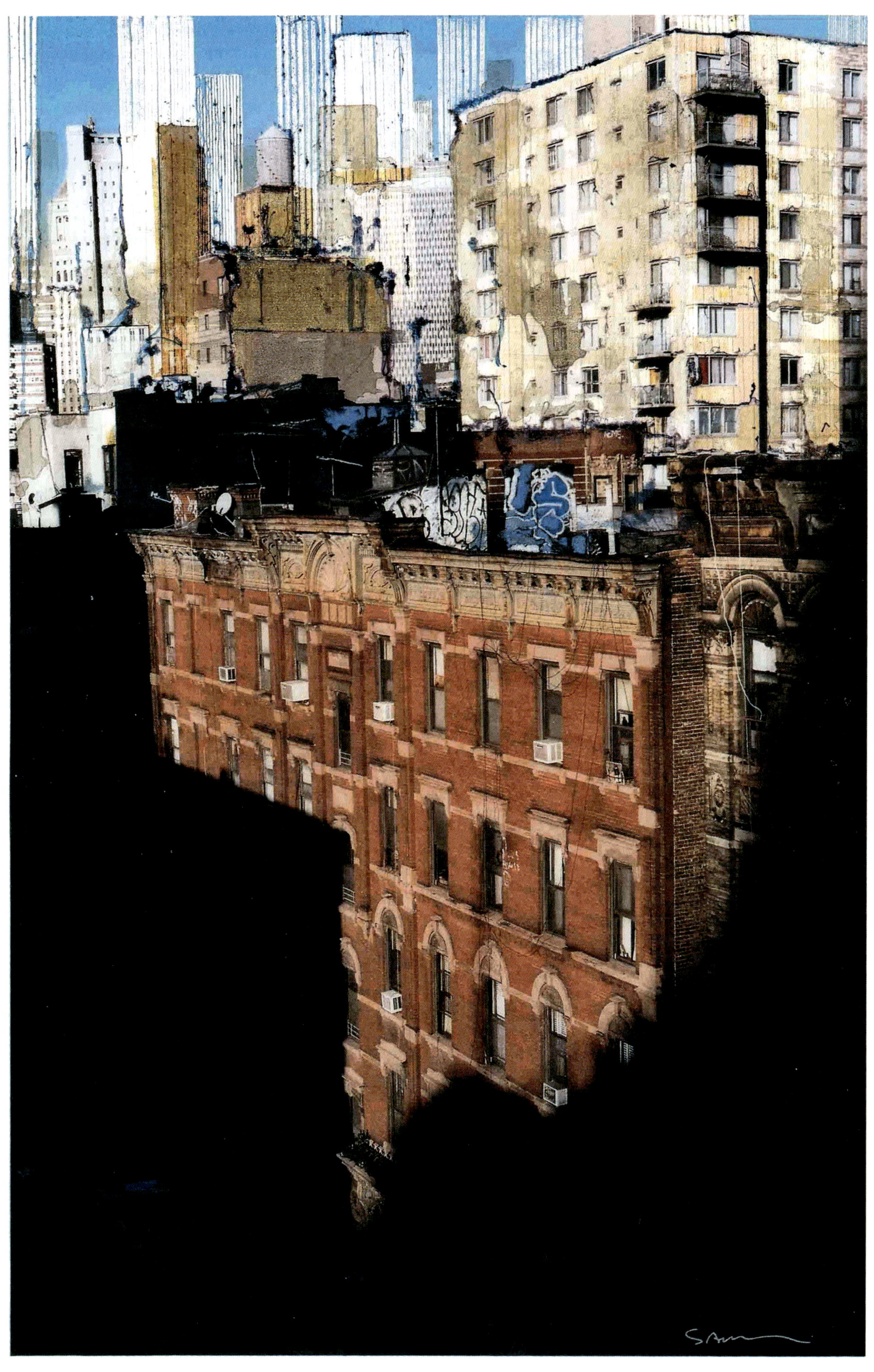

Shadow | Schatten | Ombre
2011, 81 × 54 cm

and more abstract than many "dyed-in-the-wool" abstractionists. He has become a true poet and visionary solely through the processes of seeing and observing. Those who enter his visual world are immediately swept away, although no leap into the realm of thoughts, dreams, or hallucinations need follow. And his abstract quality is derived from the precision with which he observes the objective world around him.

Thus this artist paints precisely what appears before his eyes, adding nothing from his own imagination to what he sees. Instead, he demands the utmost from the eye's sensual capacity. The artist becomes inventive in the manner in which he incorporates his formal ideas and his material, the more or less formless content of perception, in the ways in which he tames and drives it forward, in the perspectives he develops and the strategies he employs to make the visual experience more conscious, more astonishing, and more fantastic. That has little in common with conventional visual access. Deformations, metamorphoses, and estranged variations of customary images are the order of the day. Yet the need for transfiguration and atmospheric balsam is also essential to Salzmann's program. Today, he often employs the tactic of combating the overwhelming flood of images with its own weapons.

Constantly Underway

Salzmann harvests all of his impressions and visual ideas on the go—that is, through visual resourcefulness and sensitivity rather than conceptual brooding. In a certain sense he is a descendant of outdated plein-air painting, which is celebrated with the opportunism typical of the historical disciplines as the crowning achievement of the Impressionists—but only to file it away once and for all, or to bequeath it tax-free to hobby painters. With his subjects from rural and urban landscapes, Salzmann has always stood apart as a somewhat anachronistic figure, yet he has succeeded in overcoming this flaw with his innovative interventions into a tradition-laden terrain that has long since been aban-

fens aus dem Weg geht – in seinen Resultaten ist er dennoch in vieler Hinsicht fantastischer als ein erklärter Fantast, abstrakter als so mancher „waschechte" Abstrakte. Einzig und allein durch das Sehen und Betrachten wird er zum hochgradigen Poeten und Visionär. Wer in seine Bildwelt einsteigt, wird stante pede entrückt, ohne dass ein Sprung ins Reich der Gedanken, Träume oder Halluzinationen erfolgen müsste. Und auch seine Abstraktheit gewinnt er aus dem Sinn für Genauigkeit im Wahrnehmen der ihn umgebenden Dingwelt.

Hier wird also dezidiert nur das gemalt, was dem Künstler tatsächlich vor Augen tritt, er fügt nichts aus seiner Vorstellung hinzu. Dagegen wird der Sensualität des Auges ein Höchstmaß abverlangt. Erfinderisch wird der Künstler darin, wie er seine Formvorstellungen einbringt und sein Material, den mehr oder weniger formlosen Inhalt der Wahrnehmung, aufzäumt, wie er es bändigt und ankurbelt, welche Vorkehrungen er trifft, welche Sichtweisen er entwickelt und welche Strategien er anwendet, um das Seherlebnis bewusster, überraschender, fantastischer zu machen. Das hat mit einem herkömmlichen visuellen Zugriff nicht mehr viel zu tun. Deformationen, Metamorphosen, Verrückungen des gewohnten Sehbildes stehen an der Tagesordnung, aber auch das Bedürfnis nach Verklärung und atmosphärischem Balsam kommt bei Salzmann auf seine Rechnung. Heute geht er vielfach dazu über, die sich überstürzende Bilderflut mit ihren eigenen Waffen zu schlagen.

Unentwegt unterwegs

Salzmann gewinnt alle seine Eindrücke und Bildideen unterwegs, das heißt: nicht durch gedankliches Ausbrüten, sondern durch visuelle Findigkeit und Spürsinn. Er ist in gewissem Sinn ein Nachfahre der überkommenen Freilichtmalerei, die mit dem für die historischen Wissenschaften bezeichnenden Opportunismus als Großtat der Impressionisten gefeiert wird, aber anscheinend nur zu dem Zweck, sie ein für alle Mal ad acta zu legen bzw. taxfrei den Hobbymalern zu überlassen.

dure ». Il lui suffit de voir et d'observer pour devenir poète et visionnaire. Quiconque pénètre dans son univers sera aussitôt emporté, sans avoir eu à plonger dans l'univers des pensées, des rêves ou des hallucinations. Et même ce qui est abstrait chez lui est le fruit d'un sens de l'exactitude dans la perception des choses matérielles environnantes.

L'artiste ne peint donc délibérément que ce qu'il a devant les yeux, rien ne s'y ajoute qui serait le fruit de son imagination. Mais l'œil se doit en revanche d'être extrêmement sensible. L'inventivité de l'artiste réside dans la manière dont il présente ses conceptions formelles et contient son matériau, teneur plus ou moins informe de sa perception, comment il l'apprivoise et le stimule – quelles mesures il prend, selon quels modes il regarde, quelles stratégies il applique pour rendre l'aventure du regard plus consciente, plus surprenante, plus fantastique. Il n'est plus tellement question d'approche visuelle habituelle. C'est de déformations, métamorphoses et décalages de l'image coutumière qu'il s'agit, mais le besoin de transfiguration et de baume atmosphérique y trouve aussi son compte. Aujourd'hui, Salzmann s'en prend souvent aux déferlements d'images en leur rendant la pareille.

Par monts et par vaux

Toutes ses impressions, images et idées, Salzmann les acquiert en marchant. Autrement dit, non pas en mûrissant ses pensées, mais en dénichant des trouvailles visuelles. En un certain sens, il descend de la peinture de plein air traditionnelle, avec cet opportunisme caractéristique des sciences historiques (mais apparemment seulement pour qu'elle soit classée une bonne fois pour toutes ou abandonnée gratuitement aux peintres amateurs). Avec ses sujets empruntés au monde rural ou aux paysages urbains, Salzmann a toujours été et reste quelque peu anachronique, mais il a pu compenser ce défaut en se montrant novateur sur le terrain chargé de traditions et depuis longtemps récusé par les tenants de la modernité. Cette disposition à innover, à

doned by modernists. Salzmann remains as eager as ever to innovate, constantly driving and elaborating his basic ideas.

This unhindered movement from place to place is an inseparable element of Salzmann's art and always evident in his paintings. The clearly defined and stable vantage point in conventional views, which have recognizably originated in the presence of the motif in the green outdoors or at the drawing board, has given way to a flow of perceptions that suggests an unbounded process of observation that is open in all directions. A sense of boundlessness is evoked, as if we were in the midst of the space. Employing sophisticated montage and cross-fading techniques, Salzmann succeeds in heightening this spatial feeling; he links multiple visual levels together to form a panoramic spread, often exhibiting a tendency toward the unreal. At first entirely concrete and realistic, the perspective gives way to a broad and widely branching total view.

Why Salzmann felt drawn from the outset to the aesthetic culture of France, which is generally associated with a specific concept of form, is also immediately evident in his paintings. One need only consider the formal garden, the austere elegance of the building facades, and the axial clarity of the grounds, the squares—there is something of this concept of form in every one of Salzmann's paintings. That is the one side of his art—the rational and intellectual side. Yet there is also an equally strong counterforce in his art, an irrational, fantastical aspect, a romantic striving for the infinite. The dreamlike imagery of things liberated from all ties to the earth and the strict regulation of forms—it is from this mixture that Salzmann develops his typical, unique blend of technoid precision and lyrical-poetic vision.

Of crucial importance is the spatial experience that is transformed in Salzmann's art into spatial fantasy. We associate that concept above all with the graphic architectural visions of Piranesi. In Piranesi's case, they are interior fantasies, whereas Salzmann succeeds like no other artist in communicating to us the phenomenon of outdoor space, of the exterior, of boundlessness in all direc-

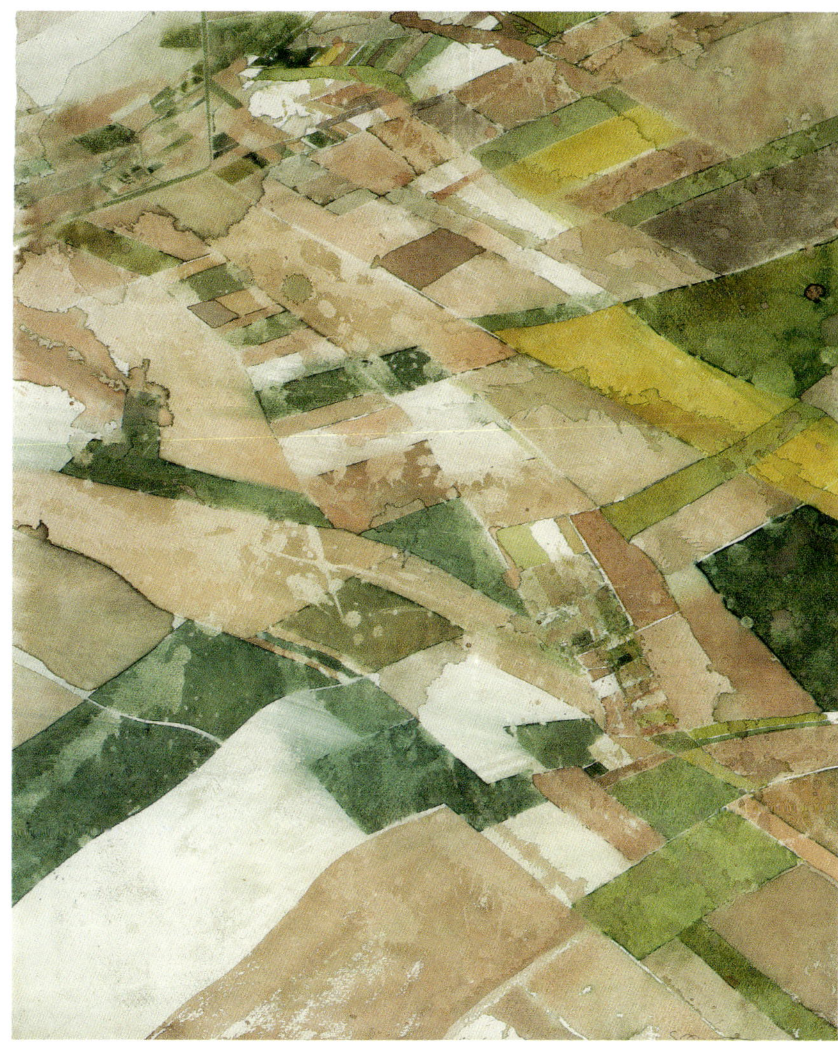

développer sans cesse ses idées, ne connaît chez lui aucun répit.

Marcher librement d'un lieu à l'autre est indissociable de l'art de Salzmann et transparaît d'ailleurs partout dans ses toiles. Le point de vue, net et arrêté, de celui qui regarde traditionnellement, et qui – on le sent – se trouve devant le motif dans une verte prairie ou à son chevalet, est relayé ici par un flot de sensations qui suggère l'infinitude du regard tourné dans toutes les directions. Un sentiment de détachement se communique, comme si l'on se trouvait au beau milieu de l'espace. Par des techniques raffinées de montage et de fondu enchaîné, Salzmann parvient à renforcer encore cette notion d'espace ; il combine ainsi plusieurs niveaux de représen-

Carpet of Fields | Felderteppich | Le tapis des champs   1995, 57,2 × 45,5 cm

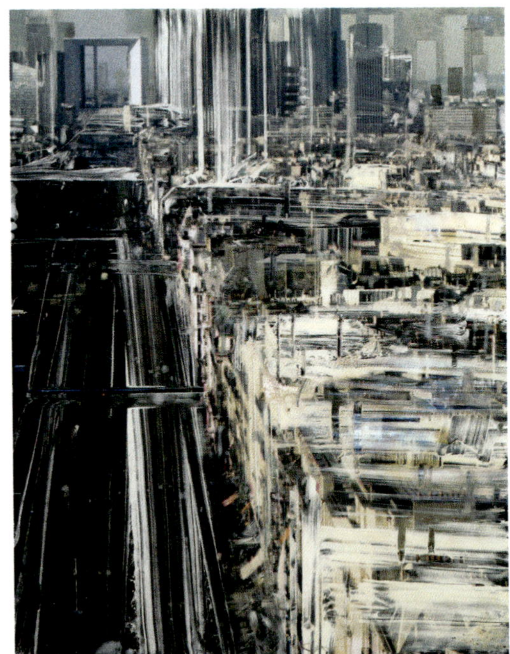

L'arche II   2008, 51 × 38 cm

tions. In contrast to the confining interior worlds of Piranesi, Salzmann's paintings not only give us a feeling of physical lightness, they also liberate us from physical ballast. The effect is the opposite of that evoked by expressive works that cry out for viewer involvement. These are not impressions that bind us to an object or otherwise attempt to take us under their spell. We become creatures of the air, travelers without baggage.

It would be wrong to evoke the impression that these visual adventures are entirely harmless and that they engender only pleasant states of mind, like fairy-tale journeys on a flying carpet. Salzmann does not release the viewer into a void filled with harmless allures. There is, in the heightened possibility of spatial penetration, also something dizzyingly irritating in which somber intimations too may emerge. We must relinquish some of the certainty that we are at home on this planet, and the immeasurable vastness of urban sprawl does not necessarily make us feel more secure. An impenetrable mantle of silence lies over these megacities, which appear to be bursting with energy nonetheless.

In his earlier works, Salzmann is underway in the horizontal, moving over land or gliding in low-altitude flight, and this specific form of mobility is incorporated into many

bundenheit teilt sich mit, als würden wir uns mitten im Raum befinden. Durch raffinierte Montage- und Überblendungstechniken versteht Salzmann dieses Raumgefühl noch zu potenzieren, er koppelt mehrere Schau-Ebenen zu panoramaartiger Auffächerung, vielfach mit einem Zug ins Irreale. Die Perspektive, die ganz konkret und realistisch ansetzt, hebt ab in eine weit gestreute und weit verzweigte Totale.

Warum sich Salzmann von Anfang an zur ästhetischen Kultur Frankreichs hingezogen fühlte, die man mit einem besonderen Formbewusstsein assoziiert – auch das kann man an seinen Bildern unmittelbar ablesen. Man denke nur an den Formalgarten, an die strenge Eleganz der Gebäudefronten und die axiale Klarheit der Anlagen, die Carrés – etwas von diesem Formempfinden ist in jedem Salzmann-Bild. Das ist die eine, rationale und intellektuelle Seite seiner Kunst. Aber es gibt eine genau so starke Gegenkraft, einen irrationalen, fantastischen Zug in seinem Werk, einen romantischen Unendlichkeitsdrang. Die träumerische, bodenferne Sicht der Dinge und das strenge Reglement der Formen – aus dieser Mischung ergibt sich die für Salzmann typische einzigartige Verbindung von technoider Präzision und lyrisch-poetischer Schau.

Entscheidend ist das Raumerlebnis, das bei Salzmann sogleich zur Raumfantasie wird. Das ist ein Begriff, den wir in erster Linie mit den gezeichneten Architekturvisionen von Piranesi verbinden. Bei diesen handelt es sich um Innenraumfantasien, während uns Salzmann gerade das Phänomen des Außenraumes, des Exteriers, des nach allen Richtungen hin Unbegrenzten wie kein anderer zu vermitteln versteht. Im Gegensatz zu den beklemmenden Innenwelten Piranesis verleihen uns Salzmanns Bilder nicht nur ein Gefühl physischen Leichtwerdens, sie befreien uns auch von psychischem Ballast. Die Wirkung ist derjenigen von expressiver, nach Beteiligung heischender Kunst entgegengesetzt. Es sind keine Eindrücke, die uns an ein Objekt fesseln oder uns auf eine andere Weise vereinnahmen. Wir werden zu Luftgeschöpfen, zu Reisenden ohne Gepäck.

Es soll indes nicht der Eindruck entstehen,

tation en éventail panoramique, souvent avec quelque chose d'irréel. La perspective, dans une approche d'abord concrète et réaliste, s'envole vers une totalité se multipliant au loin.

La raison pour laquelle Salzmann fut d'emblée attiré par la culture esthétique de la France – que l'on associe à une conscience particulière des formes – se traduit elle aussi directement dans ses toiles. Que l'on pense seulement au jardin à la française, à l'élégance rigoureuse des façades architecturales, à la géométrie des espaces publics, aux carrés – cette sensibilité pour la forme se retrouve un peu dans chaque toile de Salzmann. C'est là le côté rationnel et intellectuel de son art. Mais il y a aussi tout le contraire, un élan irrationnel et fantastique, un besoin compulsif et romantique d'infini. Vision onirique-éthérée des choses et agencement rigoureux des formes : c'est ce mélange qui donne cette association caractéristique de Salzmann entre précision technicisante et représentation poétique.

L'expérience de l'espace est décisive, et, chez Salzmann, elle devient aussitôt imagination de l'espace. Nous pensons aussitôt aux visions architecturales dessinées par Piranesi. Or il s'agit là d'évocations d'espaces intérieurs, tandis que Salzmann, de manière inégalée, nous présente le phénomène de l'espace extérieur, le dehors multidirectionnel et sans limites. Contrairement aux intérieurs oppressants de Piranesi, les toiles de Salzmann nous donnent un sentiment de légèreté physique, et elles nous libèrent aussi d'un poids psychique. On est aux antipodes d'un art expressif sollicitant l'implication. Ce ne sont pas des impressions qui nous enchaînent à l'objet, ni qui nous accaparent d'une manière ou d'une autre. Nous devenons des créatures aériennes, des voyageurs sans bagages.

Mais il ne faut pas non plus imaginer que ces aventures visuelles seraient totalement sans risque et ne produiraient que des agréments, comme un voyage de rêve sur un tapis volant. Salzmann ne délaisse pas le spectateur dans un néant de stimuli anodins. Cette possibilité accrue de traverser l'espace a aussi quelque chose de troublant, de vertigineux –

of his paintings, namely, as the forward motion of the artist, as a reflection of his experience of speed, or as a traffic situation. Fractions of a second are recorded on paper as trace impressions on the boundary of what is capable of being recorded at all. The tumultuous character of a street scene inspires him, yet the absence of people shifts everything into the unreal realm of slow motion, a state of dreamlike wandering.

This aspect is well suited to watercolor, and thus Salzmann's fascination with cloud formations, fog, and even industrial smoke and smog is understandable. He dissolves solid, earthbound formations into veils of air and vapor, and the weather helps him achieve such cloudy moods. More astonishing is the fact that this inclination toward soft-focus is matched by an equally rigorous use of oversharpness. The so-called middle road appears nowhere in Salzmann's art. The same can be said of his palette, which is either extremely intense or rather more dusky and pallid.

With the emergence and eventually the nearly total dominance of skyscrapers in Salzmann's paintings, which represent one of the most significant shifts of emphasis in his art, vertical motion takes the place of horizontal progress. The fantastic, towering architecture of New York inspired him to a kind of paradigm shift in his art. Presumably, he had always been a kind of closet high-altitude flyer and urban climber, and now he had discovered an ideal field of endeavor.

Salzmann arrived at his eccentric perspectives in several ways, for example by setting his own eye level at a very low—or very high—point, almost at the edge of the sheet. At first, his geographic reach encompassed only northern France, Paris, Bourges (his first French home), and Salzburg. Even the rooftop regions were still relatively low-lying terrain. The positions of his "tours en l'air" then grew progressively more daring and less constrained by human limitations, soaring from the bird's-eye view to practically stratospheric heights.

One is occasionally tempted to think that the painter is striving for an extraterrestrial vantage point. Consequently, the distance that has always characterized his mode of

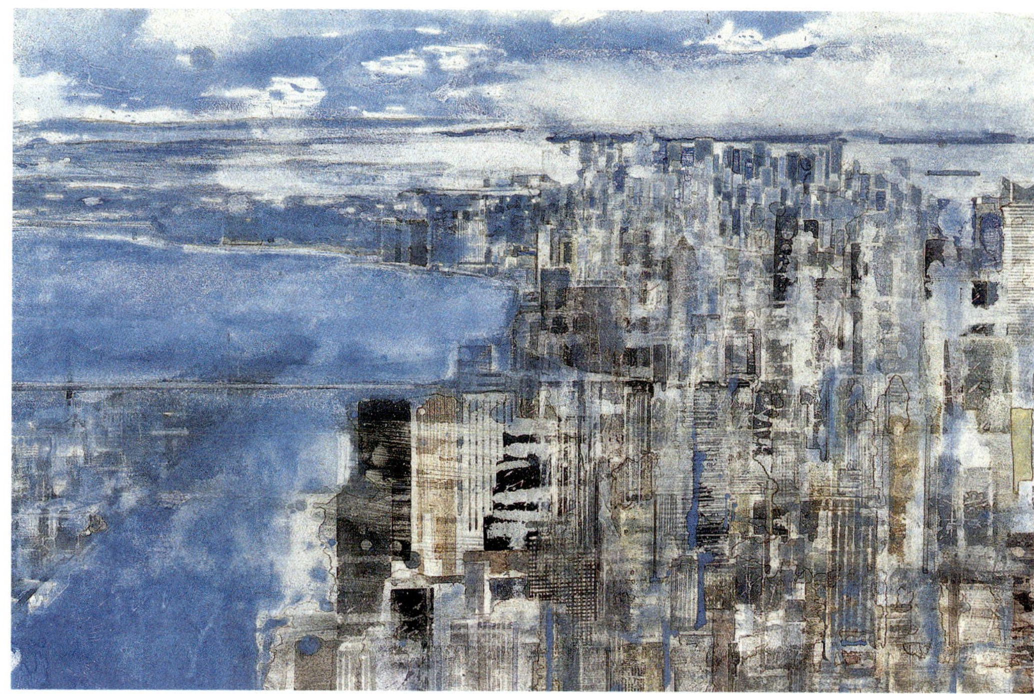

dass diese visuellen Abenteuer ganz gefahrlos wären und nur angenehme Zustände hervorrufen, so wie eine Märchenreise auf einem fliegenden Teppich. Salzmann entlässt den Betrachter nicht in eine von unverfänglichen Reizen erfüllte Leere. Es liegt in der gesteigerten Möglichkeit des räumlichen Durchdringens auch etwas schwindelerregend Irritierendes, in dem auch düstere Ahnungen aufsteigen können. Wir müssen etwas von der Sicherheit preisgeben, dass wir auf diesem Planeten heimisch sind, und auch die Unermesslichkeit der urbanen Ausdehnung trägt nicht unbedingt zur Geborgenheit bei. Es liegt ein undurchdringlicher Mantel des Schweigens über diesen Megastädten, die doch gleichzeitig vor vitaler Energie zu bersten scheinen.

In den frühen Arbeiten ist Salzmann in der Horizontalen, auf dem Landwege, im niederen Gleitflug unterwegs, und diese spezielle Bewegtheit findet vielfach Eingang in die Bilder, nämlich als Fortbewegung des Künstlers, als Reflex der von ihm erfahrenen Geschwindigkeit, als Verkehrssituation. Sekundenbruchteile werden als Eindrucksspuren an der Grenze des Festhaltbaren auf dem Papier erfasst. Das Tumultartige eines Straßenbildes regt ihn an, aber durch die Abwesenheit des Menschen ist alles ins Unwirkliche,

les sombres présages n'en sont pas exclus. Nous devons abandonner un peu de nos certitudes selon lesquelles nous sommes chez nous sur cette planète. L'incommensurabilité de l'extension urbaine ne contribue pas non plus forcément à sécuriser. Une chape impénétrable de silence repose sur ces mégalopoles qui, pourtant, semblent regorger d'énergie vitale.

Dans ses travaux des débuts, Salzmann se déplace dans l'horizontalité, sur la route ou comme dans un vol plané à basse altitude. Cette mobilité particulière se retrouve fréquemment dans ses toiles. C'est le déplacement de l'artiste, le réflexe de la vitesse vécue, une situation de transport. Des fragments de secondes sont fixés sur le papier comme des empreintes à la limite du saisissable. Le tumulte d'une rue certes le stimule, mais l'absence humaine fait que tout devient irréel, comme une déambulation onirique filmée au ralenti.

Cet aspect est parfaitement adapté à l'aquarelle. La fascination que Salzmann a très tôt éprouvée pour les nuages, le

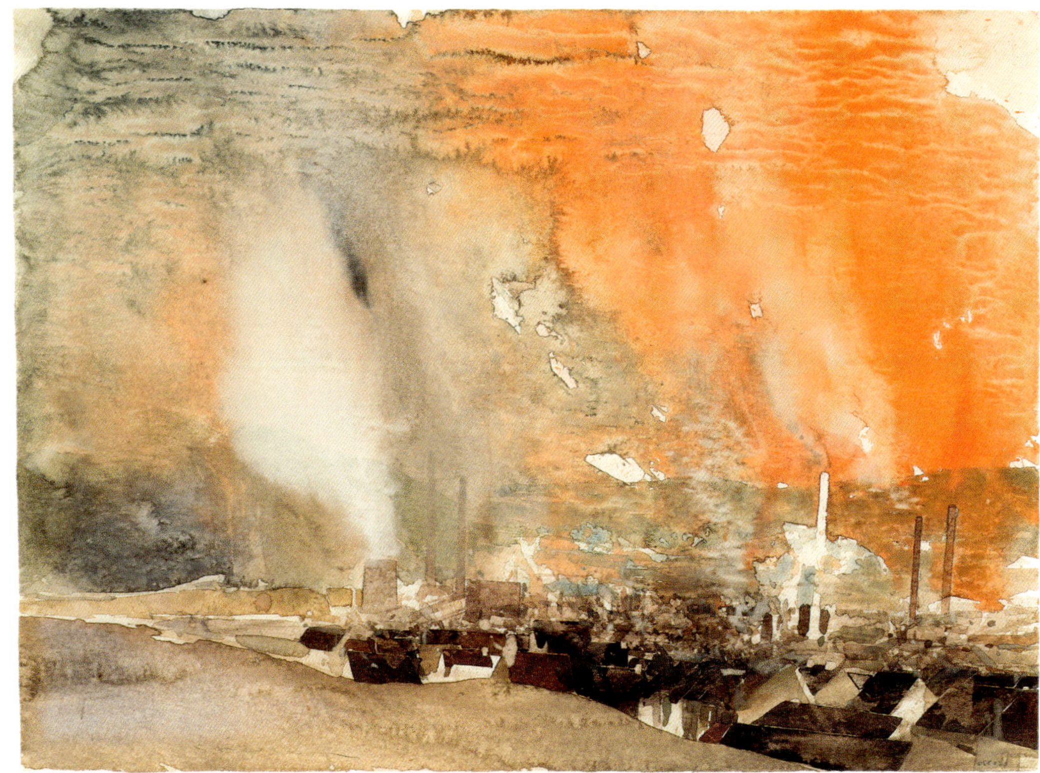

Longwy 1980, 37,5 × 49,7 cm

observation has become entirely nonsubjective. He sees even what is close as if from afar. More recently, the artist has taken to frequenting the roofs and towers of Gothic cathedrals. His art would be quite different if he suffered from fear of heights. He has always been interested in Gothic architecture—because of its steep proportions, on the one hand, and because of the complicated, flamboyant world of forms that challenges his creative capacities, on the other.

From Nature to Architecture

Everything happens underway. Salzmann does not think things up, but instead draws inspiration from what he sees. Travel and work are one and the same for him. He is on the go from morning till night, spending his days collecting impressions. Leaps in the development of his art have always been triggered by travels, the most enduring of them by his trip to New York in 1983 on the occasion of his first exhibition in the United States. Feeling as if he were about to experience an artistic fiasco, Salzmann ended his stay in New York firmly resolved never to set

Zeitlupenhafte gewendet, in ein träumerisches Umherschweifen verwandelt.

Dieser Aspekt ist dem Aquarell durchaus gemäß, und so ist Salzmanns frühe Faszination für Wolkenballungen, Nebel, sogar für industriellen Rauch und Qualm auch wieder naheliegend. Er löst feste und bodennahe Formationen in Luftschleier und Dämpfe auf, und die Meteorologie verhilft ihm zu solchen verhangenen Stimmungen. Erstaunlicher ist schon, dass dieser Hang zur Unschärfe in einer ebenso konsequent eingesetzten Überschärfe seine Entsprechung findet. Die sogenannte mittlere Lage kommt bei Salzmann hingegen niemals vor. Das gilt auch für seine Palette, die entweder äußerst intensiv oder eher dämmerig und fahl ist.

Mit dem Auftauchen und schließlich fast ausschließlichen Dominieren von Wolkenkratzern in Salzmanns Werk, das eine der wichtigsten Zäsuren in seinem Schaffen bedeutet, setzt sich gegenüber der horizontalen Bewegungsrichtung die Vertikale durch. Die fantastisch ragende Architektur von New York hat ihn bewogen, in seinem Schaffen so etwas wie einen Paradigmenwechsel zu vollziehen. Vermutlich hat schon immer ein Höhenjäger und urbaner Kletterer in ihm

brouillard, et même les fumées et émanations industrielles, est donc à nouveau compréhensible. Il désagrège les formations solides et terrestres dans des brumes et voiles de vapeur, incité en ce sens par la météorologie à créer des ambiances couvertes. Il est plus étonnant que ce penchant pour le flou trouve sa correspondance dans une acuité extrême et aussi systématique. C'est le registre intermédiaire, en revanche, qui ne figure jamais chez Salzmann. Et cela vaut aussi pour sa palette, qui est soit extrêmement intense soit plutôt pâle et crépusculaire.

Lorsque surgissent les gratte-ciel dans l'œuvre de Salzmann et qu'ils finissent par presque exclusivement dominer – c'est là une des césures majeures dans son travail –, la direction verticale l'emporte sur l'horizontale. L'architecture new-yorkaise, fantastique et toute en hauteur, l'a poussé à ce changement de paradigme. Le chasseur d'altitude et varappeur urbain, qui sommeillait sans doute en lui, trouvait là soudain son champ d'action idéal.

Pour arriver à ces perspectives excentriques, Salzmann place son regard très bas – parfois aussi très haut, presque sur le bord de la toile. Il a commencé d'abord à ne rayonner que dans le Nord de la France, à Paris, Bourges (sa première ville d'adoption en France) et à Salzbourg. Même les toits constituaient encore un terrain relativement bas. Les positions de ses « tours en l'air » deviennent ensuite de plus en plus risquées et dégagées des restrictions humaines, et vont de la vue surplombante jusqu'à des altitudes quasiment stratosphériques.

On a parfois le sentiment que le peintre voudrait pouvoir adopter un point de vue supraterrestre ; le recul, dans son mode d'observation, perd ainsi toute subjectivité. Même ce qui est proche apparaît comme lointain. Ces derniers temps, l'artiste se balade aussi sur les toits et les tours des cathédrales gothiques. S'il était sujet au vertige, son art serait tout autre. L'architecture gothique lui va depuis toujours : l'aplomb des propor-

foot in the city again. He was convinced that his artistic means, which had previously developed rather more on the horizontal plane, were totally out of place there. Yet after returning home he discovered that the yield was not as useless as he had thought. His doubts and fears of failure have since given way to a burning hunger. Salzmann never tires of portraying New York, again and again, and actually succeeds in harvesting new facets from this "Venice of the air." He sees the city as a quarry that continues to produce more and more, although he has also turned his attention to other megacities, such as Hong Kong, Rio de Janeiro, and Tokyo. His decision to abandon the natural landscape is irreversible. His path had led him from the idyllic, enclosed rural setting to a sprawling architectural landscape.

Although Gottfried Salzmann began drawing city buildings very early in his career, those images were more closely associated with the irregularity of nature. Aside from uniform, anonymous cities, unusual historical views of cities have always been a part of his repertoire. With unconventional details and complicated perspectives, he succeeds in imbuing even cities that have virtually been painted to death—Paris, Arles, Vienna, and Salzburg, for example—with a quality that practically ensures that they have never been seen in quite this way before. From a familiar context, Salzmann filters out aesthetic structures that make the motif appear significantly more abstract to us than it is ordinarily perceived to be. The view from above is ideally suited to this approach. A rooftop landscape exhibits an intricate, abstract pattern that cannot be produced in any other way, as it still contains so much meaning as motif and spatial fluidity that it cannot be confused with a uniform pattern; abstract intrinsic vitality and objective association intensify each other. And a sense-specific local flair is always present.

The shift from rural to urban landscapes included a phase marked by landscapes dominated by water and featuring extremely steep or extremely flat coastlines. Salzmann did a series showing bunkers in Normandy in which rugged terrain and exploded architec-

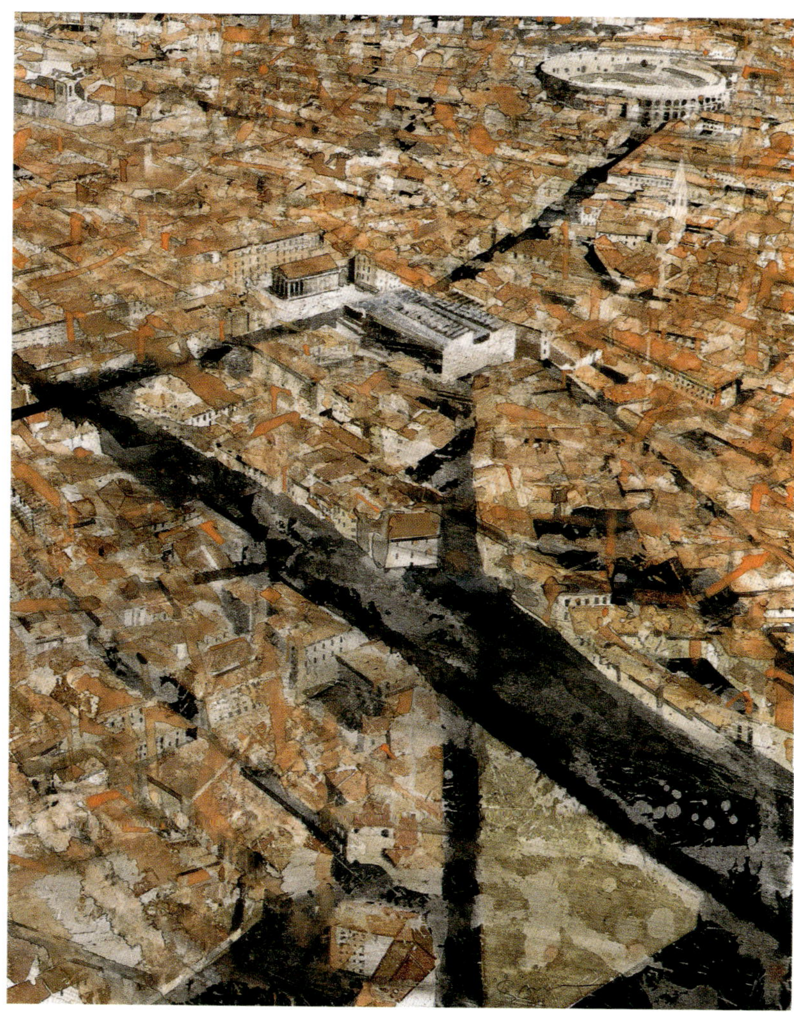

gesteckt, der nun auf ein ideales Aktionsfeld gestoßen ist.

Salzmann kam zu seinen exzentrischen Perspektiven beispielsweise dadurch, dass er seinen Augpunkt sehr tief – oder auch sehr hoch, fast am Blattrand – ansetzte. Sein geografischer Radius umfasste anfangs nur Nordfrankreich, Paris, Bourges (seine erste französische Heimat) und Salzburg. Auch die Dächerregionen waren noch ein relativ niederes Gelände. Die Positionen seiner „tours en l'air" werden danach immer waghalsiger und unabhängiger von menschlichen Einschränkungen, stoßen von der Vogelschau bis in geradezu stratosphärische Höhen vor.

Manchmal hat man das Gefühl, der Maler strebe einen außerirdischen Standpunkt an; das schon immer sehr Distanzierte seiner Betrachtungsweise wird dadurch vollends entsubjektiviert. Er sieht auch das Nahe wie von ferne. Neuerdings treibt sich der Künstler auf den Dächern und Türmen gotischer Kathe-

tions, mais aussi le vocabulaire formel compliqué et flamboyant qui sont un défi aux aptitudes du peintre.

De la nature à l'architecture

Tout se passe en route. Salzmann ne conçoit rien à l'avance, il se laisse inspirer par les sensations. Déambuler revient pour lui à travailler. Du matin au soir, il se déplace, il passe ses journées à recueillir des impressions. Les voyages ont toujours déclenché des sursauts dans son évolution, notamment celui qu'il fit à New York en 1983, à l'occasion de sa première exposition en Amérique. Salzmann se sentait au bord du marasme artistique et il acheva son séjour là-bas avec la ferme inten-

Nîmes, La Maison Carrée   2007, 74 × 61 cm

ture merge to the point of indistinguishability. The perspectives in these works literally plunge into the depths.

Salzmann works with the resources of formal alienation, which he applies with considerable imagination and which enable him, for example, to transform a shopping mall into an archaeological site displaced in time, in one case, and to make a venerable monument perform a Saint Vitus' dance, in another. Typical of the emphatic view from below are stairways, which interest Salzmann much more than the famous buildings to which they lead. Urban images are automatically associated with a heightened interest in architecture, which certainly relates to the fact that Salzmann's watercolor style has grown increasingly precise and ostensibly more objective. In his views of New York, the geometric structures of the steel-skeleton highrise buildings protrude so prominently into the foreground that we feel as if we are gazing at a complicated electrical circuit plan. In addition to the bird's-eye view, which is often directed vertically into the depth—in which case the city appears as a teeming mosaic divided by more or less regular bands—it is the breathtaking canyons and vistas that are so fascinating to the eye. Here, we recognize the workings of a law that applies in the early landscapes as well: the view from all sides in contrast to the extreme narrow field of view.

In these works, the human being appears only as a billboard figure or is represented by vehicles. Yet one hardly feels lost in this fascinating show. There is no sentimentality, although there are very different atmospheres. In one case, the sea of skyscrapers appears extinct and ruined, like an archaeological site, or burned to the ground as if after a disaster; in another, it is filled with pulsating life, bathed in high gloss and metallic luster. The stacked high-rises leap forward and back, form walls and passages, a towering labyrinth, and even taller new, imaginary cities tower on the horizon.

The progression "from nature to architecture" is also reflected in aspects of style. The natural, flowing, picturesquely unconstrained has shifted progressively toward a constructive, screen-patterned, strict draw-

dralen herum. Seine Kunst wäre ganz anders geworden, würde er Schwindelgefühle kennen. Die gotische Architektur war ihm schon immer gelegen: einerseits wegen der Steilheit ihrer Proportionen, andererseits wegen der komplizierten, flamboyanten Formenwelt, die sein Leistungsvermögen herausfordert.

Von der Natur zur Architektur

Alles passiert unterwegs. Salzmann denkt sich nichts aus, sondern lässt sich von den Wahrnehmungen anregen. Reisen ist für ihn gleich arbeiten, er ist dann von früh bis spät auf den Beinen, verbringt den Tag mit dem Sammeln von Eindrücken. Entwicklungsschübe wurden bei ihm immer von Reisen ausgelöst, am nachhaltigsten der von jener nach New York im Jahr 1983 – Anlass war die erste Ausstellung, die er in Amerika hatte. Salzmann fühlte sich einem künstlerischen Fiasko nahe, er beendete diesen Aufenthalt mit dem festen Entschluss, diese Stadt nie mehr sehen zu wollen. Er glaubte seine künstlerischen Mittel, die sich bisher eher in der Horizontalen entfaltet hatten, hier absolut fehl am Platz. Zu Hause erwies sich die Ausbeute dann doch nicht als so unbrauchbar. Die Skrupel und Versagensängste haben sich inzwischen in einen Heißhunger verwandelt. Salzmann wird nicht müde, New York immer und immer wieder zu konterfeien, und gewinnt diesem „Venedig der Lüfte" tatsächlich immer neue Facetten ab. Die Stadt ist für ihn ein Steinbruch, der an Ergiebigkeit immer noch zunimmt, doch nahm er auch andere Megacities wie Hongkong, Rio de Janeiro und Tokio ins Visier. Die Abkehr von der Naturlandschaft ist unwiderruflich, sein Weg führte von einer idyllenhaft umschlossenen Ländlichkeit zur ausufernden Architekturlandschaft.

Salzmann hat bereits in frühester Zeit Stadthäuser gezeichnet, doch diese waren mehr der Unregelmäßigkeit der Natur verwandt. Neben den uniformen, anonymen Metropolen stehen historische Stadtansichten der ungewöhnlichen Art nach wie vor im Repertoire von Gottfried Salzmann, längst zu Tode gemalten Städten wie Paris, Arles, Wien

tion de ne plus jamais y remettre les pieds. Sa facture artistique, qui s'était jusque-là déployée plutôt dans l'horizontalité, lui parut alors totalement inopportune. Cependant, de retour chez lui, la récolte s'avéra finalement moins mauvaise. Les craintes et les hésitations se muent alors en avidité. Désormais, Salzmann ne se lasse de représenter New York, trouvant dans cette « Venise des airs » des facettes sans cesse nouvelles. La ville est pour lui une mine de plus en plus rentable, et dans son viseur, il a aussi des mégalopoles comme Hongkong, Rio de Janeiro ou Tokyo. Fini le paysage naturel, il quitte la ruralité circonscrite et idyllique pour les gigantesques panoramas architecturaux.

Très tôt déjà, Salzmann avait dessiné des immeubles urbains, mais ils s'apparentaient davantage à l'irrégularité de la nature. Outre les métropoles uniformes et anonymes, les vues citadines historiques et insolites figurent aussi dans le répertoire de Gottfried Salzmann, au même titre que des villes peintes à foison comme Paris, Arles, Vienne ou Salzbourg, sur lesquelles il a réussi, en choisissant des fragments inhabituels ou des perspectives extravagantes, à laisser une telle empreinte personnelle que l'on peut être sûr de ne les avoir jamais vues ainsi. À partir d'un système familier, Salzmann extrait des structures esthétiques qui révèlent le motif comme autrement plus abstrait qu'il ne l'est dans la perception quotidienne. Pour voir ainsi, c'est le regard d'en haut qui est tout indiqué : un paysage de toits donne alors un motif abstrait et gracile qui ne pourrait être produit d'aucune autre manière, dans la mesure où il renferme encore tant de signification motivique et de fluide spatial qu'il ne peut être confondu avec un rendu à l'identique ; une vie intrinsèque et abstraite corrobore l'association concrète et vice-versa. Même le cachet local reste toujours sensible.

Entre les paysages ruraux et urbains, il y a eu une phase de paysages dominés par l'eau, les côtes y sont extrêmement accidentées ou plates. Naît alors la série avec les blockhaus de

Reflection 7th Avenue | Spiegelung 7th Avenue | Reflet 7th Avenue   2012, 64,8 × 50,8 cm

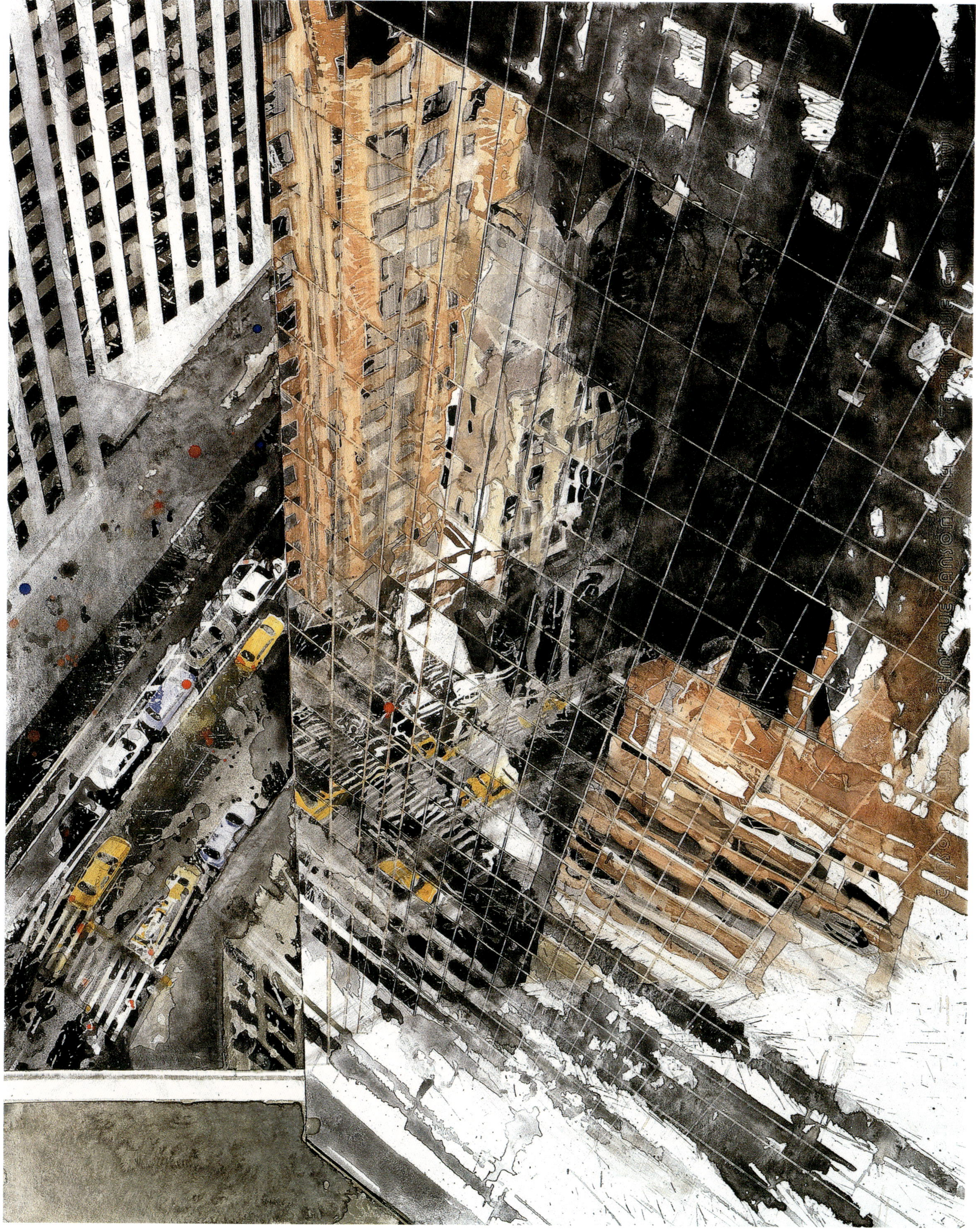

ing style, whereby the various modes are set differently. In essence, it is evident that what is strictly regulated is always counteracted in an opposite sense, while, on the other hand, the diffuse and blurred always have a strict formal counterpart. Salzmann's contemporary works look considerably more exact than those of earlier years, which evoke the impression of perfectly balanced random formations—and which presupposes an equally keen sense of precision.

Eccentric Strategies

Salzmann's approach to watercolor cannot be reduced to a single common denominator, as he covers the entire spectrum from maximum precision to flowing improvisation, from photo-realistic illusion to informal lyricism. It has practically nothing to do with the mostly pale, blurry, spontaneously recorded impressions that viewers tend to regard as typical of the genre. Salzmann's tacit goal has always been to combine the fantastical imaginative effects of a William Turner with the discerning sense of reality and the flexible technique of a Rudolf von Alt. Today, he commands a number of different registers and refuses above all to be limited to a single approach. He is capable of shifting maximum possible sharpness to extreme soft-focus. The only difficulties he encounters have to do with watercolor paper, the quality of which has been deteriorating for some time, as he notes.

Precisely because of his affinity for watercolor, Salzmann would be the last artist in the world to insist on the constantly cited purist ideal of the "pure" watercolor that is painted in a single sitting and regarded among specialists as the ne plus ultra. Of course we find plenty of examples of this "classical" type of watercolor art in his oeuvre, yet when it comes to his preferences, he finds it lacking in both technical and iconographic depth and complexity. He ordinarily employs systematic procedures when producing his watercolors, ranging from the use of hot air to accelerate the drying process to multiple washes—a practice demonstrated by his teacher Sergius

oder Salzburg versteht er durch ausgefallene Ausschnitte und vertrackte Blickwinkel einen Stempel aufzudrücken, der als Garant dafür genommen werden kann, dass sie so noch nicht gesehen worden sind. Salzmann filtert aus einem vertrauten Zusammenhang ästhetische Strukturen heraus, die uns das Motiv wesentlich abstrakter erscheinen lässt, als es in der alltäglichen Wahrnehmung ist. Prädestiniert für diese Sicht ist der Blick von oben: Eine Dachlandschaft ergibt ein feingliedriges abstraktes Muster, das auf keine andere Weise herstellbar ist, da es immer noch so viel motivische Bedeutung und räumliches Fluidum enthält, dass es nicht mit einem gleichförmigen Rapport verwechselt werden kann; abstraktes Eigenleben und gegenständliche Assoziation steigern einander. Auch das lokale Flair bleibt immer spürbar.

Zwischen ruraler und urbaner Landschaft gab es eine Phase vom Wasser dominierter Landschaften mit extrem steilen oder extrem flachen Küsten. Es entstand beispielsweise die Serie mit Bunkern der Normandie, wo schroffes Gelände und geborstene Architektur bis zur Ununterscheidbarkeit ineinander übergehen. Die Perspektiven stürzen sich hier förmlich in die Tiefe.

Salzmann arbeitet mit Mitteln der formalen Verfremdung, die er mit großem Einfallsreichtum bewerkstelligt und die es zuwege bringt, uns das eine Mal beispielsweise eine Shoppingmall in die zeitentrückte Schau einer archäologischen Stätte zu versetzen, das andere Mal ein ehrwürdiges Monument einen Veitstanz vollführen zu lassen. Für die betonte Untersicht sind Treppenanlagen bezeichnend, die Salzmann viel mehr interessieren als die berühmten Bauwerke, zu denen sie führen. Mit den Städtebildern verbindet sich automatisch ein gesteigertes Interesse für die Architektur, was sicherlich damit im Zusammenhang steht, dass Salzmanns Aquarellstil immer präziser und vordergründig gegenständlicher wird. In den New-York-Ansichten schieben sich die geometrischen Strukturen der Stahlskelett-Hochbauten so sehr in den Vordergrund, dass man vor einem komplizierten elektrischen Schaltplan zu stehen vermeint. Neben der Vogelschau, die oft ganz senkrecht in die Tiefe zielt – dann ist die

Normandie, où le terrain âpre et l'architecture rebondie se mêlent jusqu'à devenir impossibles à distinguer. Les perspectives basculent ici littéralement dans la profondeur.

Salzmann travaille avec les procédés de la distanciation formelle qu'il manie avec une grande ingéniosité et qui parvient aussi bien à transformer un centre commercial en spectacle atemporel d'un site archéologique, qu'à faire s'agiter un monument imposant. Les escaliers sont caractéristiques de cette vue d'en bas et ils intéressent Salzmann d'ailleurs davantage que les édifices célèbres auxquels ils conduisent. Les peintures de villes vont automatiquement de pair avec un intérêt poussé pour l'architecture ; ce qui explique aussi que le style de Salzmann, à l'aquarelle, devient de plus en plus précis, de plus en plus d'abord figuratif. Dans les vues de New York, les structures géométriques des gratte-ciel avec leur ossature métallique sont tellement en avant qu'on se croirait face à un curieux schéma de montage électrique. Outre la vue aérienne, souvent à la verticale et toute en profondeur (la ville devient alors une mosaïque foisonnante, répartie en bandes plus ou moins régulières), c'est la frénésie des artères et voies passantes qui accroche l'œil. On retrouve ici une antinomie que l'on connaît déjà des premiers paysages : le regard panoramique face à l'exiguïté extrême.

L'être humain n'apparaît là que comme personnage de publicité ou remplacé par les moyens de locomotion. Et pourtant, dans ce spectacle fascinant, la solitude ne se ressent guère. Il n'y a pas de sentimentalité, mais des atmosphères très diverses. Tantôt le flot de gratte-ciel semble tomber en ruines, comme un site archéologique ou anéanti après une catastrophe, puis le voilà de nouveau, brillant et irisé, regorgeant de vitalité. Les immeubles superposés avancent et reculent, ils forment des murailles et des trouées, labyrinthe s'élevant en hauteur, et, à l'horizon, s'empilent d'autres villes encore plus hautes, nouvelles et imaginaires.

Le passage évoqué « de la nature vers l'architecture » transparaît aussi dans le style. Ce qui est naturel, fluide, libre et pittoresque se transforme progressivement en quelque

Pauser at the Vienna Academy. This work with material also encompasses technical experimentation and the application of several different techniques or media in a single work, which can be observed to an increasing extent in recent years. In this way, he frees himself progressively from the odious label of the specialist, with which he has never been entirely happy despite his eminent achievements as a watercolorist.

Salzmann leaves no room for doubt that atmospheric transparency and spatial openness are guiding principles that govern his work as an artist, and since a strong spatial quality cannot be achieved with any single technique, watercolor was and has remained his natural point of departure. He made numerous attempts in his early years to find a comfort level in oil painting, and one could observe that the atmospheric magic that detests all that is ponderous and awkward drifted progressively toward the dark and melancholy. A turpentine allergy was not the only thing that kept him from pursuing this direction. Salzmann had always been intent upon elevating watercolor from the status of a hastily executed trifle to the aesthetic level of painting, as is evident in the multilayered application of paint and his heightened interest in pictorial structure and compositional integrity.

Such a pictorial plan also underlies the watercolor landscapes in his early creative phase—with their close affinities to the "lyrical informality" of abstract painting—which were largely responsible for the spectacular start of Salzmann's career as an artist in 1969. What appears to have taken shape by chance also exhibits stability and structure. The veils of color with their branching patterns form an artful, precious-looking web with insular extensions on the white paper. Every spot of paint is incorporated into this intricate network. And the jewel-like intensity of the colors eliminates any hint of mere impressionistic, hasty improvisation. An almost piercing yellowish green that looks as if it is covered with liquid gold came to be known as "Salzmann green."

The fact that the painting can be seen as an abstract, flat composition as well as an expan-

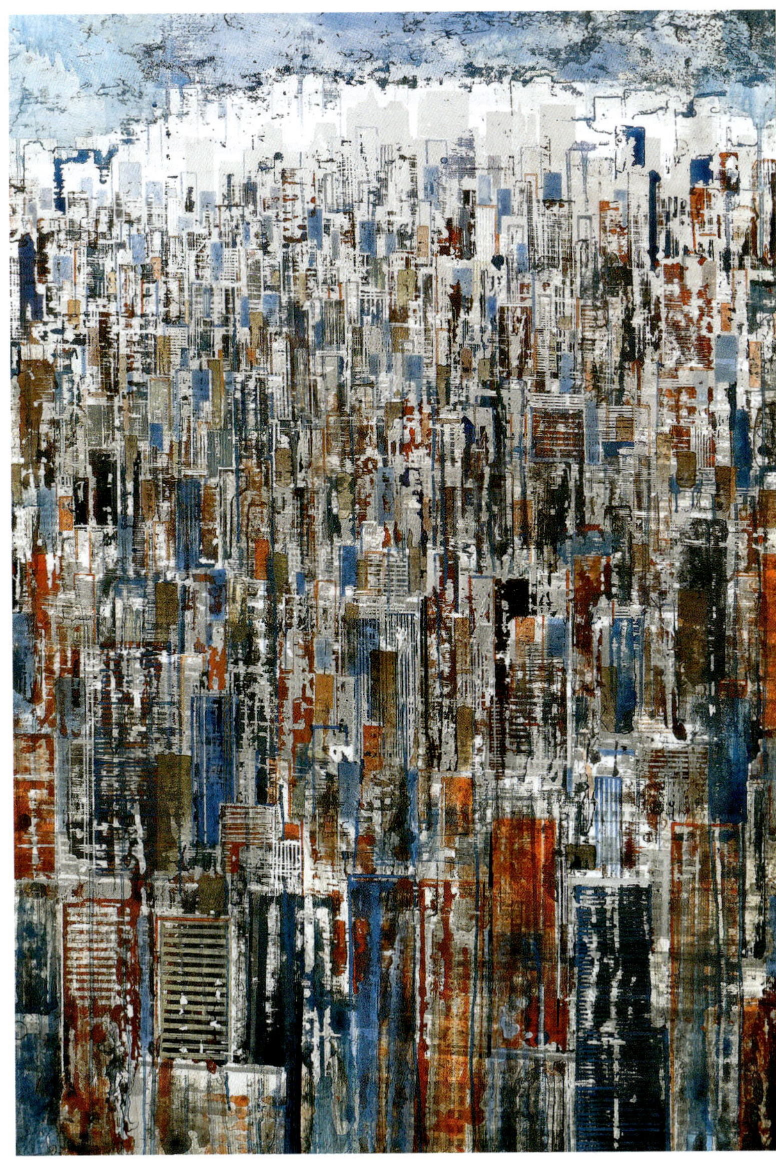

Stadt ein wimmelndes Mosaik, von mehr oder weniger regelmäßigen Bändern unterteilt –, sind es die rasanten Straßenschluchten und Schneisen, die das Auge besonders fesseln. Hier kommt wiederum ein Gegensatz zum Tragen, den wir schon in den frühen Landschaften finden: die allseitige Sichtweise gegenüber der extremen Engführung.

Der Mensch tritt hier nur als Reklamefigur in Erscheinung oder wird durch seine Fahrzeuge vertreten. Ein Gefühl der Verlorenheit kommt in dieser faszinierenden Schau dennoch kaum auf. Es gibt keine Sentimentalitäten, aber sehr unterschiedliche Atmosphären. Einmal wirkt das Wolkenkratzermeer ausgestorben und ruinös wie eine archäologische Stätte oder ausgebrannt wie nach einer Katastrophe, dann wieder von pulsierendem Le-

chose de construit, de quadrillé, de graphique et rigoureux – les modalités étant chaque fois différentes. On constate en principe que ce qui est réglementé est toujours contrecarré pour aller dans le sens contraire, et, inversement, ce qui est flou et diffus appelle la rigueur d'un contraste formel. Les œuvres que Salzmann réalise aujourd'hui révèlent autrement plus d'exactitude que celles des débuts, lesquelles donnent plutôt l'impression de formations aléatoires en parfait équilibre – ce qui suppose d'ailleurs un sens non moindre de la minutie.

NY Puzzle   2008, 130 × 89 cm

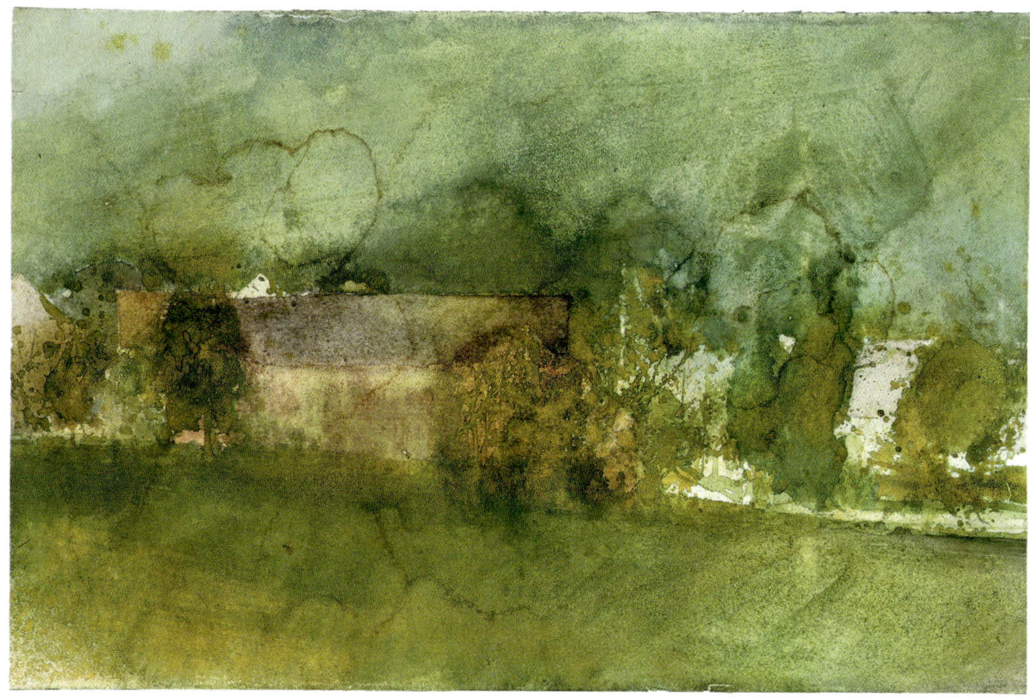

Stratégies excentriques

L'aquarelle, chez Salzmann, ne peut être réduite à une seule approche : de la suprême méticulosité à l'improvisation évanescente, du trompe-l'œil hyperréaliste au lyrisme informel, l'éventail est multiple et n'a plus grand-chose à voir avec ces impressions souvent pâles et diffuses couchées sur le papier avec force spontanéité et que le public considère comme l'expression typique du genre. Le but non avoué de Salzmann a toujours été d'associer le côté fantastique-imaginatif d'un William Turner avec le sens nuancé de la réalité et la souplesse technique d'un Rudolf von Alt. Il maîtrise aujourd'hui de nombreux registres et n'entend surtout pas être confiné dans un seul mode ; il varie de la netteté extrême jusqu'au flou total. C'est tout au plus la qualité du papier à aquarelle qui lui pose problème et il constate d'ailleurs qu'elle empire depuis quelque temps.

sive landscape doubles the forcefulness of the work. Groups of houses are literally spun into the web of meadows and trees. The representational is concealed, so to speak, within the complex interplay between fields of color, streaks of water, spots, and splashes. Individual axial ordering elements provide—unobtrusively yet undeniably—for stability and order. Characteristics of the American Color Field painting of Mark Rothko and others are certainly in evidence in these works.

In many of the watercolors of this type, the exposed white of the ground is incorporated deliberately into the overall pictorial effect, forming an autonomous, fragmented pictorial plane. Although Salzmann dispensed with conventional landscape scenes, his paintings exhibit a certain poetic flair. He discovered many of his motifs in the highly industrialized provinces of northern France, the effluvium of which contributed as much to a sense of atmospheric enchantment as the natural precipitation of the region did.

During his early years, when he studied the cloud-filled sky systematically and spent considerable time working outdoors, Salzmann adopted a kind of "espressivo" style that betrayed not least of all his admiration for Nolde. This emotional spontaneity eventually gave way to a rational, carefully calculated

ben erfüllt, in Hochglanz und Métallisée gebadet. Die übereinandergestaffelten Hochhäuser springen vor und zurück, bilden Wände und Durchlässe, ein emporragendes Labyrinth, und am Horizont türmen sich noch höhere neue, imaginäre Städte auf.

Die angedeutete Entwicklungslinie „von der Natur zur Architektur" wirkt sich auch in stilistischer Hinsicht aus. Das Natürliche, Fließende, malerisch Freizügige wandelt sich kontinuierlich zum Konstruktiven, Gerasterten, zeichnerisch Strengen hin, wobei die Modalitäten ganz unterschiedlich gesetzt sind. Prinzipiell stellt man fest, dass das Reglementierte immer in einem gegenläufigen Sinn konterkariert wird, und umgekehrt hat das Diffuse und Verwischte immer einen strengen formalen Gegenpart. Salzmanns heutige Arbeiten wirken ungleich exakter als die seiner frühen Jahre, die den Eindruck perfekt ausponderierter Zufallsbildungen erwecken – was einen nicht minder ausgeprägten Sinn für Genauigkeit voraussetzt.

Exzentrische Strategien

Salzmanns Verständnis vom Aquarell lässt sich nicht auf einen einfachen Nenner bringen, denn seine Bandbreite reicht von der

pictorial concept that responds to the finest vibrations. Gradually, Salzmann developed strategies that enabled him to gain more complete control of his unconventional points of view. The imponderable mélange is tamed by a strict pictorial structure. The middle of the painting is often left blank, and the eye is deliberately drawn to the edges in order to avoid the formation of a focal point in the sense of a central perspective. But Salzmann also employs rigorous frontality as well as extreme vanishing lines—the all-encompassing pull into the depth, whether it be represented in an allée in Normandy or a perfectly straight avenue in Manhattan. He also used the expansive diagonal with increasing boldness—nearly approaching the steepness of a "nosedive."

Formal processes of this kind were combined in many cases with specific pictorial motifs to form groups of works that kept the artist occupied for considerable periods of time. Salzmann consistently employed a wall-like arrangement parallel to the pictorial plane in the *Tree Curtains*, the *Passages*, and the facades sprayed with graffiti, for example.

höchsten Präzisionsarbeit bis zur verfließenden Improvisation, von fotorealistischem Augentrug zum informellen Lyrismus. Am wenigsten hat es zu tun mit jenen möglichst spontan zu Papier gebrachten, meist blässlichen und verschwommenen Impressionen, die das Publikum für die typischen Vertreter der Gattung hält. Salzmanns unausgesprochenes Ziel war es immer, das Fantastisch-Imaginative eines William Turner mit dem differenzierten Wirklichkeitssinn und der flexiblen Technik eines Rudolf von Alt zu verbinden. Heute beherrscht er viele Register und lässt sich vor allem nicht auf eine einzige Spielart festnageln, er kann die Einstellung vom höchsten Schärfegrad bis zum extremen Weichzeichnen variieren. Schwierigkeiten bereitet ihm höchstens die Qualität des Aquarellpapiers, dessen Verschlechterung Salzmann seit einiger Zeit konstatiert.

Salzmann ist gerade wegen seiner Äffinität zum Aquarell der Letzte, der auf dem immer wieder heraufbeschworenen puristischen Idealbild des „reinen" Aquarells besteht, das in einem Arbeitsgang geschaffen wird und in Spezialistenkreisen als das non plus ultra gilt. Selbstverständlich finden wir auch von dieser „klassischen" Sorte von Aquarellkunst in seinem Schaffen Beispiele zur Genüge, doch ist sie ihm, wenn wir nach seinen Vorlieben fragen, technisch wie inhaltlich zu wenig vielschichtig und komplex. In der Regel unterzieht er das Aquarell gezielten Prozeduren, die von einer durch Heißluft herbeigeführten Beschleunigung des Trocknungsvorganges bis zum mehrfachen Auswaschen der Farbe reicht – eine Praxis, die schon sein Lehrer Sergius Pauser an der Wiener Akademie demonstrierte. Diese Arbeit am Material findet ihre Fortsetzung im technischen Experimentieren und Zusammenführen unterschiedlicher Techniken bzw. Medien in einem Werk, wie wir es im Schaffen der letzten Jahre zunehmend beobachten. Damit spielte er sich immer mehr frei vom Odium des Spezialisten, mit dem er trotz seiner eminenten Erfolge als Aquarellist nie ganz glücklich war.

Freilich lässt Salzmann keinen Zweifel daran, dass atmosphärische Transparenz und räumliche Offenheit die sein künstlerisches Tun beherrschenden Leitgedanken sind, und

Compte tenu justement de son affinité pour l'aquarelle, Salzmann est le dernier à s'attacher au canon puriste – celui, si souvent invoqué, de l'aquarelle « idéale » réalisée en une seule étape et que les cercles de spécialistes prennent pour le nec plus ultra. Bien sûr que son œuvre foisonne d'exemples relevant de l'aquarelle « classique », mais elle est pour lui – l'interroge-t-on sur ses préférences – trop peu complexe en terme de technique et de contenu. En règle générale, il fait subir à l'aquarelle des méthodes spéciales, allant du séchage accéléré à l'air chaud jusqu'au lavage répété de la couleur ; son professeur Sergius Pauser les avait déjà pratiquées à l'École des Beaux-Arts de Vienne. Ce travail sur le matériau se prolonge dans les différents procédés qu'il expérimente et combine, toujours plus présents chez lui ces dernières années. Chemin faisant, il s'affranchit de plus en plus du côté négatif du spécialiste avec lequel, malgré ses éminents succès en tant qu'aquarelliste, il n'avait jamais été très heureux.

Bien sûr Salzmann ne laisse aucun doute sur le fait que la transparence de l'atmosphère et l'ouverture de l'espace marquent fortement son travail artistique, et qu'aucune autre technique que l'aquarelle ne permet d'atteindre à une telle profondeur ; celle-ci a donc toujours été sa base naturelle et l'est restée jusqu'à aujourd'hui. Au début, il a tenté de se familiariser avec la peinture à l'huile. On observe alors que la magie atmosphérique, hostile à toute pesanteur, se mue en quelque chose de sombre et mélancolique. L'allergie à la térébenthine n'explique pas à elle seule pourquoi l'artiste n'a pas poursuivi dans cette direction. Au contraire, Salzmann s'est toujours efforcé d'ériger l'aquarelle du statut de bagatelle fugace au rang de tableau. On le voit aussi bien à la complexité dans l'application de la couleur qu'à son goût prononcé pour la construction de l'image et l'agencement de la composition.

Cette conception – qui sous-tend précisément les aquarelles de paysage proches de l'« informel lyrique » de la peinture abstraite

Évecquemont   1971, 30,8 × 50 cm

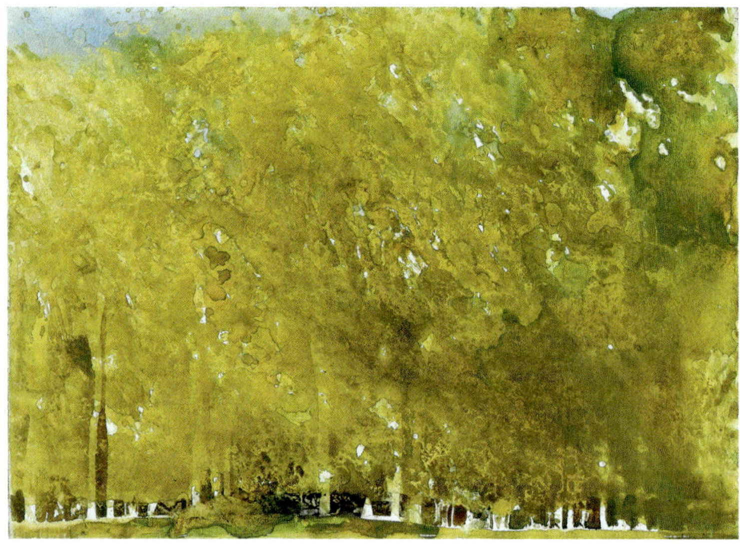

Curtain of Trees | Baumvorhang | Rideau d'arbres   ca. | ca. | vers 1980, 54 × 73,5 cm   Hedge II | Hecke II | Haie II   1974, 32,7 × 48 cm

The seeing eye is by no means repelled in these works, but rather carried through and distributed over the entire surface. And that applies as well to the graffiti transcribed with meticulous philological precision—including even the structure of the masonry. The artist was equally interested in the aggressive formal language and the stages of its fading. Yet by rendering them in fragmentary form, he alienated them from their original context and altered them in aesthetic terms—they became floating signs, and who is to say that he did not invent them himself?

Wherever Salzmann puts up barriers to vision, they prove upon closer examination to be anything but impermeable. They often consist of semitransparent or reflective material, as in the series of *Jalousies.* In the more recent photographic works, tarpaulins and sheeting of the kind used to cover scaffolding perform a similar function. We often encounter unexpected reverse effects—the narrowed view turns out to be an expansion. And wherever the view is blocked, new "windows" are opened. The view from above that tips over into the abstract plane is one of his favorite devices, which he employs artfully and with considerable variation in such works as the *Canola Fields.* Salzmann's *Logbooks* are particularly interesting—each one a mosaic composed of individual miniature images that are joined together by a checkerboard matrix.

da mittels keiner Technik ein stärkerer Raumgehalt zu erzielen ist, war das Aquarell seine natürliche Ausgangsbasis und ist es bis heute geblieben. Es hatte anfänglich nicht an Versuchen gefehlt, im Ölbild heimisch zu werden, und es war dabei zu beobachten, dass sich der allem Schwerfälligen abholde atmosphärische Zauber ins Düstere und Schwermütige umbildete. Eine Terpentin-Allergie war nicht der einzige Grund, warum er sich in diese Richtung nicht mehr weiterbewegte. Stattdessen war Salzmann immer bestrebt, das Aquarell vom Status einer flüchtig hingeworfenen Bagatelle auf die gestalterische Höhe eines Gemäldes zu heben, das kann man an der Mehrschichtigkeit des Farbauftrags ebenso wie an dem gesteigerten Interesse für Bildaufbau und kompositorischen Zusammenhalt ablesen.

So ein Bildplan liegt gerade auch den dem „lyrischen Informel" der abstrakten Malerei nahestehenden Landschaftsaquarellen der frühen Schaffensphase zugrunde, welche 1969 für den spektakulären Start von Salzmanns Künstlerlaufbahn sorgten. Was wie zufällig so geronnen scheint, weist doch auch Festigkeit und Struktur auf. Die Farbschleier mit ihren Verästelungen bilden auf dem weißen Papier ein kunstvolles, kostbar wirkendes Gespinst mit inselhaften Erweiterungen aus. Jeder Farbspritzer wird sogleich in dieses feine Netz einbezogen. Auch dass die Farbe zu juwelenhafter Intensität gesteigert ist,

des débuts – a valu à Salzmann de connaître en 1969 un envol spectaculaire en tant qu'artiste. Ce qui semble couler par hasard s'avère pourtant ferme et structuré. Les voiles de couleur avec leurs ramifications forment sur le papier blanc un lacis tout en finesse qui se prolonge en sorte d'îles. Chaque éclaboussure de couleur s'intègre ensuite dans ce délicat réseau. Et si la couleur gagne en intensité, telle un joyau, tout cela agit comme une vague impression d'improvisation et de fugacité. Un vert vif tirant sur le jaune, comme recouvert d'or, a d'ailleurs donné le fameux « vert Salzmann ».

On ressent avec plus d'insistance encore que la toile peut être vue aussi bien comme une composition abstraite en aplat que comme un immense paysage. Les blocs de maisons sont littéralement étreints par les prés et les arbres, le figuratif se dissimule en quelque sorte dans la corrélation nuancée des pans de couleurs, des rainures, taches et giclées. Mine de rien, quelques éléments linéaires assurent résolument la stabilité et l'orientation de l'ensemble. On retrouve ici sans nul doute les principes, alors très en vogue, du all-over américain tel que celui de Mark Rothko, par exemple.

Dans bon nombre d'aquarelles de ce genre, le blanc du fond laissé en l'état contribue délibérément à l'impact de la toile, en formant une strate autonome, transpercée. Même si Salzmann s'abstient de représenter

White Jalousie | *Weiße Jalousie* | Store blanc   1983, 77,5 × 57 cm

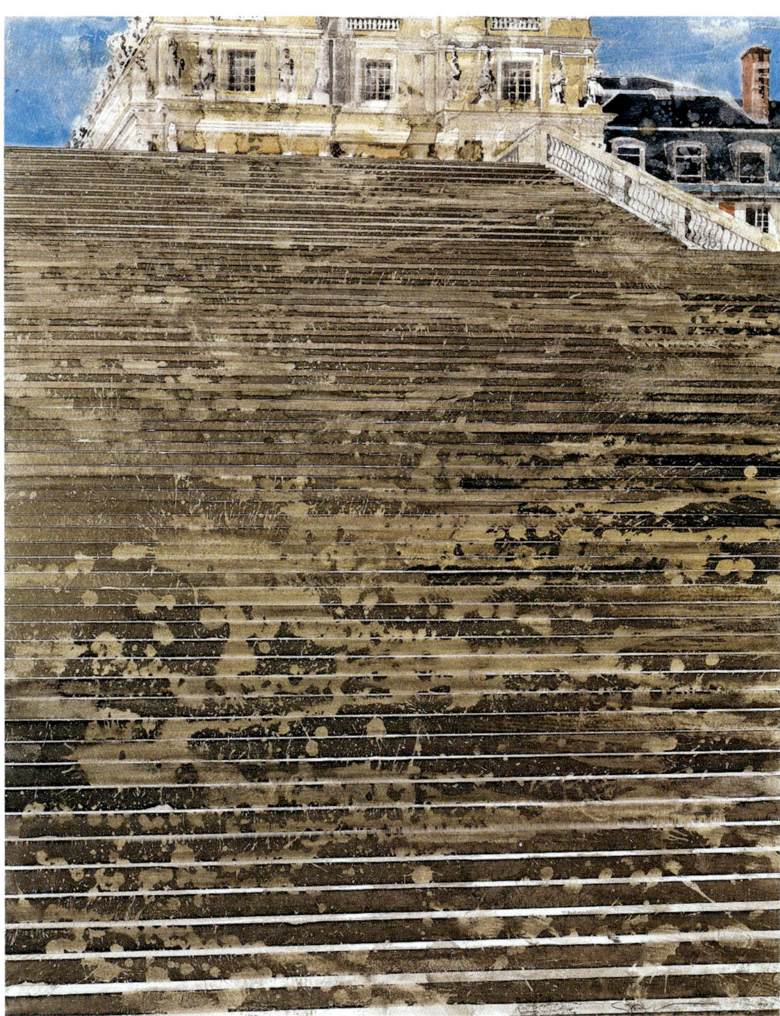

Stairs at Versailles I | *Treppen in Versailles I* | *Escaliers à Versailles I*   2010, 64,8 × 50 cm

His use of reflections, one of his greatest discoveries in the realm of visibility, began quite harmlessly at calm park lakes, and Salzmann was content to turn what is seen upside down in a slightly blurry presentation. The reflections in rearview mirrors or the hoods of cars were a further step into this sphere of absolute inconsistency. The subjective point of view from inside a car had previously inspired Salzmann to create a series of windshield-wiper paintings. He raised this ordinarily ignored peripheral zone of perception, which resists capture and approaches the state of a liquid element, into the brightly illuminated consciousness of precise articulation, much as the Impressionists once fell upon colored shadows and light reflexes. The world in the mirror appeared more real to him than his palpable surroundings, and it assumed increasingly bold dimensions and

wirkt einem bloß Eindruckshaften und flüchtig Improvisierten entgegen. Ein fast stechendes, wie von Gold übergossenes Gelbgrün wurde als „Salzmann-Grün" sprichwörtlich.

Es verdoppelt die Eindringlichkeit, dass das Bild als abstrakte Flächenkomposition ebenso wie als weitläufige Landschaft gesehen werden kann. Die Häusergruppen sind von den Wiesen und Bäumen förmlich eingesponnen, das Gegenständliche versteckt sich gewissermaßen in dem differenzierten Zusammenspiel der Farbflächen, Wasserschlieren, Flecken und Spritzer. Einzelne axiale Ordnungselemente sorgen unaufdringlich, aber doch entschieden für Stabilität und Orientierung. Zweifellos sind hier Eigenschaften der damals ganz aktuellen amerikanischen Farbflächenmalerei etwa eines Mark Rothko eingegangen.

des scènes bucoliques à proprement parler, l'ambiance poétique est là. Il a puisé quantité de ses motifs dans les grands bassins industriels du Nord de la France, les effluves lui inspirant autant de magie que les précipitations naturelles.

À ses débuts, alors qu'il en était encore à l'étude systématique du ciel nuageux et au travail répété en plein air, Salzmann s'est laissé tenter par un « espressivo », qui trahissait d'ailleurs aussi son admiration pour Nolde. Cette sensibilité instinctive s'affina avec la recherche d'une approche plus calculée et rationnelle réagissant aux vibrations les plus infimes. Salzmann développa alors progressivement des stratégies lui permettant de maîtriser encore mieux son mode d'observation inhabituel. L'amas impénétrable est domestiqué par les strictes segmentations de l'image. Le centre de la toile est

bizarre forms. Even such famous monuments as the Brandenburg Gate, St. Stephen's Cathedral, the Eiffel Tower, and the facades at the Place de la Concorde were subjected to such disrespectful deformations.

Mirrored high-rise facades are an ideal course for such visual high-wire acrobatics, which negotiate even multiple bent, curved, and prismatic surfaces with total ease. In the process, they unleash a tumultuous rush of images that one might otherwise experience only in a state of intoxication. The sources of even the most bizarre of these images lie nowhere else than in precise observation.

Testing Technical Boundaries

Salzmann is and remains a watercolorist, even when he makes use of other techniques, which he does more and more frequently today, if only to avoid being labeled too hastily. Watercolor provides him with a terrain of practically unlimited opportunities, not only because it can be employed so flexibly, but also because it is constantly reaching out into neighboring areas. The artistic gesture, the characteristic artist's hand, the motion of the brush, which are largely responsible for significant visual effects, play a relatively minor role in comparison. The fact that results comparable to those achieved in watercolor can also be achieved in etching and that a liquid element plays a similarly crucial role in both techniques appears to have inspired his keen interest in this graphic technique. Salzmann proceeds as an unorthodox border-crosser when he ignores narrow-minded concepts of "the language of material." He allows the techniques to flow together. With his technical inventiveness and love of experimentation, he takes possession of new fields of application, building bridges to other areas of visual art. Although his thematic interest is narrowly defined, he possesses the ability of a master of all classes.

Charcoal drawings occupy a special position in his oeuvre. Salzmann originally devel-

In vielen Aquarellen dieser Richtung wird das ausgesparte Weiß des Grundes gezielt in die Bildwirkung einbezogen, es bildet eine eigenständige, durchbrochene Bildebene. Auch wenn Salzmann auf einschlägige Landschaftsszenerien verzichtet, stellt sich ein poetisches Flair ein. Viele seiner Motive fand er in der hoch industrialisierten nordfranzösischen Provinz, deren Ausdünstungen ihm ebenso zu einer atmosphärischen Verzauberung dienten wie die natürlichen Niederschläge.

In seiner Frühzeit, als er systematisch den Wolkenhimmel studierte und viel im Freien arbeitete, ließ sich Salzmann zu einem „Espressivo" hinreißen, das nicht zuletzt seine Bewunderung für Nolde verriet. Diese spontane Emotionalität klärte sich im Sinne eines rationalen Bildkalküls, das auf feinste Schwingungen reagiert. Nach und nach entwickelte Salzmann Strategien, mit denen er seine ausgefallenen Sichtweisen noch stärker in den Griff bekam. Das undurchschaubare Vielerlei wird durch strikte Bildteilungen gebändigt. Die Bildmitte wird gerne leer belassen und das Augenmerk bewusst an die Ränder gelenkt, um keine Schwerpunktbildung im Sinn der Zentralperspektive aufkommen zu lassen. Salzmann kennt aber auch die konsequente Frontalität sowie die extreme Raumflucht, den alles erfassenden Sog in die Tiefe, wobei es sich genauso gut um eine Allee in der Normandie wie um eine der schnurgeraden Avenues von Manhattan handeln kann. Ebenso setzte er die raumgreifende Diagonale mit zunehmender Kühnheit – bis hin zum „Sturzflug" – ein.

Vielfach verbanden sich formale Prämissen dieser Art mit bestimmten Bildmotiven zu Werkgruppen, die den Künstlern jeweils für eine geraume Zeit beschäftigten. Eine bildparallele, wandhafte Anordnung hat er beispielsweise rigoros in den „Baumvorhängen", den „Passagen" oder den mit Graffiti besprühten Fassaden durchgezogen. Das Sehen prallt hier keineswegs ab, sondern wird hindurchgeführt und über die ganze Fläche gestreut. Das gilt auch für die mit geradezu philologischer Akribie – bis hin zur Struktur des Mauerwerks – übertragenen Graffiti. Die aggressive Formensprache samt Wortlaut interessierte den Künstler genauso wie die Sta-

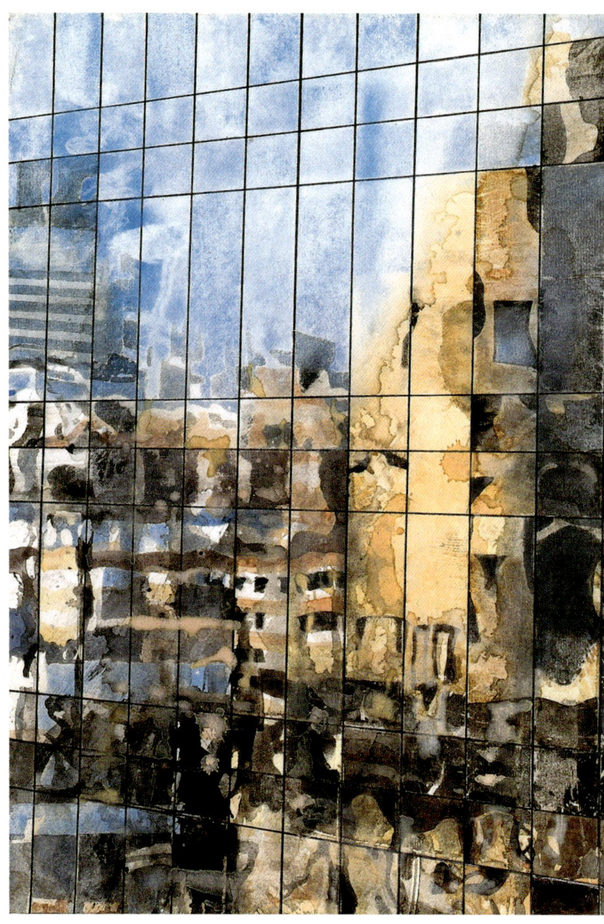

volontiers laissé vide, l'attention est consciemment dirigée vers les bords pour éviter toute accentuation de la perspective centrale. Salzmann connaît cependant aussi la frontalité systématique, tout comme les points de fuite extrêmes qui aspirent vers le fond, que ce soit une allée en Normandie ou une grande avenue à Manhattan. Avec une audace croissante, il recourt aussi à la diagonale qui envahit l'espace, et jusqu'à la « descente en piqué ». Ce genre de principes formels associés à certains motifs picturaux a donné à plusieurs reprises des groupes d'œuvres qui ont occupé l'artiste pendant longtemps. Dans les *Rideaux d'arbres*, les *Passages* ou les façades bombées de graffitis, il a respecté de façon rigoureuse l'agencement parallèle, à la manière d'un mur. Le regard ne s'y heurte pourtant en aucun cas, au contraire, il est conduit sur toute la surface. Pareil avec les graffitis très minutieusement écrits, ou la structure de l'ouvrage maçonné. Le langage agressif des formes, y compris ce qu'il énonce, intéresse l'artiste autant que les différents stades de

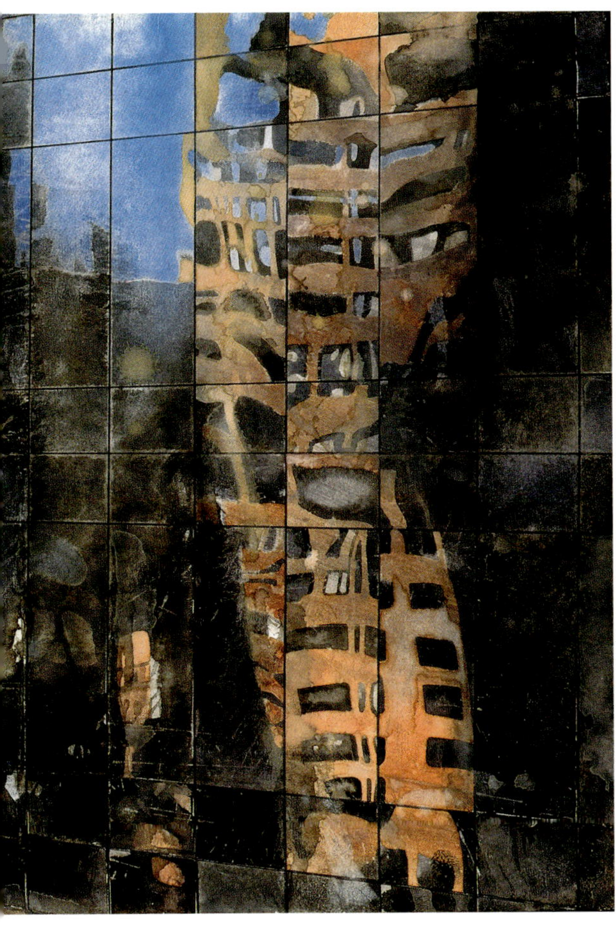

oped this medium into a second domain alongside his watercolor landscapes, although it plays no role at all in his current constellation of works. It is perhaps the most personal side of his art, though that can be said of the graphic genre in general, however. There is always something particularly suggestive about black and white, since reduction and the absence of color demand more of the viewer's imagination and because the emotions are automatically involved to a greater extent. In these drawings, some of which are very large, Salzmann works with the opposition of dark, formless agglomerations and a sparse, carefully configured framework of lines. Large fields are deliberately left empty, accentuated with brittle single lines and spots of black.

The juxtaposition of diffuse darkness and light, formally strict line structures creates a unique atmospheric tension. Salzmann has succeeded in translating some of that into his lithographs and etchings. They are encounters involving the precisely calculated and the

dien des Verblassens. Andererseits hat er sich durch ausschnitthafte Wiedergabe von ihrem ursprünglichen Zusammenhang gelöst und ästhetisch verfremdet – sie werden zu schwebenden Zeichen, und wer sagt, dass er sie nicht auch selbst erfunden hat?

Wenn Salzmann Blicksperren einbaut, so erweisen sie sich beim zweiten Hinsehen keineswegs als undurchlässig; oft sind sie aus halb transparentem oder reflektierendem Material, so in seinem Zyklus mit „Jalousien". In den neueren Fotoarbeiten übernehmen Planen und Plachen, die zum Einhüllen von Baugerüsten dienen, eine ähnliche Aufgabe. Es gibt häufig unerwartete Umkehreffekte, die Engführung des Blicks erweist sich als Erweiterung; auch wo der Blick verstellt ist, öffnen sich neue „Fenster". Die Aufsicht, die in die abstrakte Fläche kippt, ist einer seiner beliebtesten Kunstgriffe, sehr kunstvoll und abwechslungsreich etwa in den „Rapsfeldern" eingesetzt. Etwas Besonderes sind Salzmanns „Logbücher" – jedes ein Mosaik aus miniaturhaften Einzelbildchen, die von einem Schachbrett-Raster zusammengefasst werden.

Die Spiegelungen, eine seiner größten Entdeckungen im Reich der Sichtbarkeit, begannen ganz harmlos an ruhigen Parkgewässern und begnügten sich damit, das Gesehene leicht verwackelt auf den Kopf zu stellen. Die Reflexionen auf Rückspiegeln oder Kühlerhauben waren ein weiterer Schritt in diese Sphäre der absoluten Inkonsistenz. Die subjektive Perspektive vom Auto aus hatte Salzmann schon zu einer Serie mit Scheibenwischer-Bildern angeregt. Er hebt diese ignorierte Randzone der Wahrnehmung, die sich dem Festgehaltenwerden entzieht und fast einem flüssigen Element gleichkommt, ins helle Bewusstsein klarster Artikulation, so wie sich die Impressionisten einst über farbige Schatten und Lichtreflexe hergemacht hatten. Die gespiegelte Welt scheint ihm realer als die handgreifliche Umgebung, sie nahm immer tollere Ausmaße und bizarrere Gestalt an. Auch berühmte Monumente wie das Brandenburger Tor, der Stephansdom, der Eiffelturm oder die Fassaden der Place de la Concorde mussten sich derlei despektierliche Deformation gefallen lassen.

l'estompage. Mais d'un autre côté, en restituant des fragments, il se détache de leur contexte d'origine et pratique une distanciation esthétique – ces signes deviennent fluctuants et qui sait d'ailleurs s'il ne les a pas lui-même inventés ?

Lorsque Salzmann entrave la vue, il s'avère au deuxième regard que l'on peut tout à fait passer au travers ; le matériau est alors souvent à moitié transparent ou réfléchissant, comme dans son cycle *Jalousies*. Dans les tout récents travaux photos, des bâches servant à recouvrir les échafaudages ont une fonction semblable. Fréquemment, et de manière inattendue, l'effet inverse se produit, l'exiguïté du champ visuel devient élargissement ; et même là où le regard est brouillé, de nouvelles « fenêtres » s'ouvrent. La vue qui bascule dans la surface abstraite est l'une de ses astuces préférées, et il l'utilise avec beaucoup d'habileté dans les *Champs de colza*. Ses *Livrets de bord* ont quelque chose de tout à fait particulier – ils sont chacun une mosaïque d'images miniatures enchâssées dans un quadrillage de type échiquier.

Les reflets, une de ses plus grandes découvertes, ont commencé tout simplement en observant dans les parcs de paisibles flaques d'eau dans lesquelles miroitait la nature à l'envers.

Les reflets sur des rétroviseurs ou des capots constituent une étape supplémentaire dans la sphère de l'inconsistance absolue. La perspective subjective depuis la voiture avait déjà inspiré à Salzmann une série de peintures « essuie-glace ». Cette zone marginale et ignorée de la perception, qui échappe à la tangibilité et équivaut presque à un élément liquide, il l'amène à la conscience vive où les choses s'articulent clairement, comme naguère les impressionnistes avec les ombres colorées et les reflets de lumière. Le monde reflété lui paraît plus réel que l'environnement concret et prend alors des dimensions de plus en plus exagérées, des contours de plus en plus bizarres. Même les monuments célèbres, comme la Porte de Brandebourg, la cathédrale Saint-Étienne de Vienne, la Tour Eiffel ou la Place de la Concorde ont dû subir ce genre de déformations irrespectueuses.

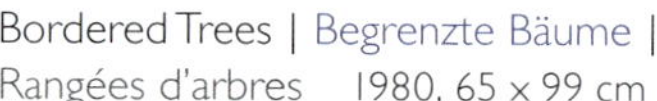

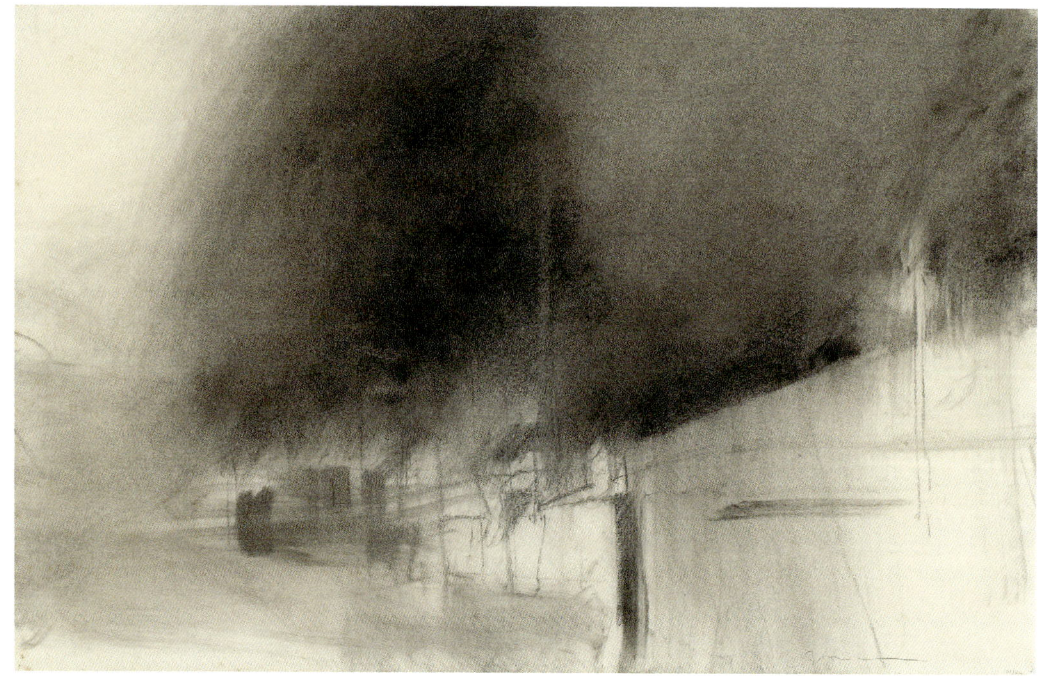

shapeless in the form of experiments with light and shadow captured by a highly sensitive lens, which represents a first point of contact with photography. In this case, one is reminded of the results achieved by the earliest photographers with the aid of extremely long exposure times.

In adapting various techniques to suit his intentions, Salzmann does not focus on their differences but rather on a common denominator, whereby he is constantly expanding his basis of watercolor and drawing—sometimes to the point of indistinguishability. Is it photography or photo-realistic watercolor? The purpose of everything he does is to enrich perception by adding new facets, to conquer new terrain for the experience of seeing. Thus he incorporated photography, which may also be regarded as a form of graphic art, into his technical repertoire without dramatic drumrolls and almost as a given. By no means does he emphasize the aspect of difference, as he does not ordinarily proceed on the basis of theoretical considerations, but instead treats it as an alternative possibility, although he found it easier to do so in the case of immaterial photographs than with oil paintings. Photography is also concerned primarily with the traces of light and shadow; it is a surface seismograph that registers the outer skin of perception. Even in his early years, long

Verspiegelte Hochhausfassaden sind ein idealer Parcours für diese visuelle Hochseilakrobatik, die auch mit vielfach geknickten, gekrümmten und prismatischen Oberflächen spielend fertigwird. Er entfesselt damit einen Bilderwirbel, wie man ihn sonst allenfalls in einem psychedelischen Rauschzustand erleben könnte. Die Quelle auch dieser abenteuerlichsten Formerfindungen liegt nirgendwo anders als in der genauen Beobachtung.

Technische Grenzgänge

Salzmann bleibt Aquarellist, auch wenn er sich anderer Techniken bedient, und das tut er immer häufiger, schon um einer vorschnellen Etikettierung aus dem Weg zu gehen. Für ihn ist das Aquarell ein Terrain der fast unbegrenzten Möglichkeiten, nicht nur weil es sich so flexibel anwenden lässt, sondern weil es ständig in Nachbargebiete ausgreift. Das Gestische, die Handschrift, der Pinselschwung, die in erster Linie verantwortlich sind für expressive Bildwirkungen, spielen hingegen eine untergeordnete Rolle. Dass man beim Radieren vergleichbare Ergebnisse erzielen kann wie mit dem Aquarell und dass hier das flüssige Element eine ähnlich bestimmende Rolle spielt, hat ihn wohl

Les parois vitrées des grands immeubles offrent un parcours idéal à cette haute voltige visuelle qui affronte, comme en jouant, les surfaces concaves, convexes et prismatiques. Un tourbillon d'images se déchaîne, que l'on ne connaîtrait autrement tout au plus que dans un état d'ivresse psychédélique. Ces intrépides trouvailles formelles ne puisent pourtant nulle part ailleurs que dans l'observation exacte.

Aux limites de la technique

Salzmann reste un aquarelliste, même s'il se sert d'autres techniques, ce qu'il fait d'ailleurs de plus en plus fréquemment, déjà pour éviter tout étiquetage hâtif. Pour lui, l'aquarelle est le champ des possibilités presque illimitées, non seulement parce qu'elle permet de la souplesse dans l'application, mais aussi

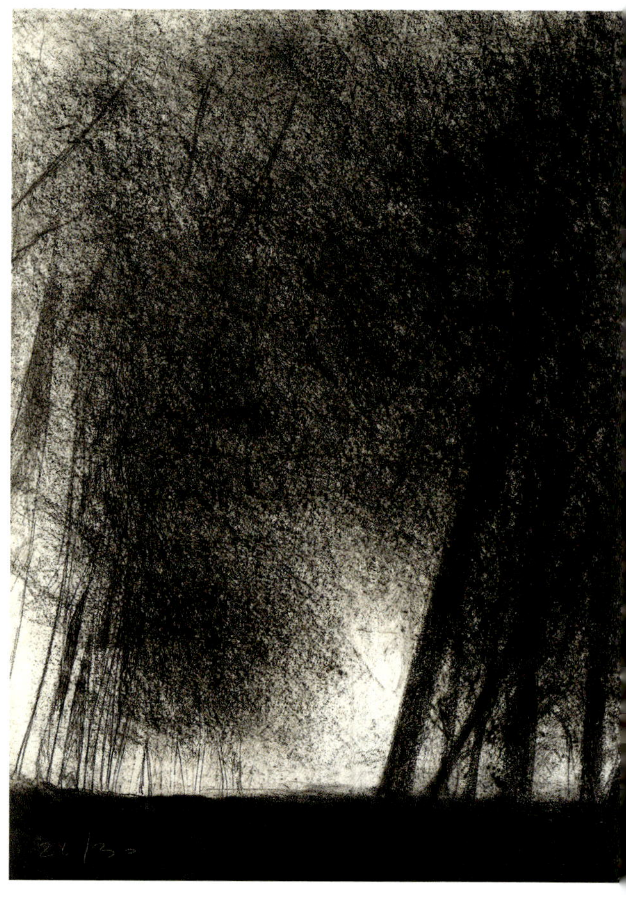

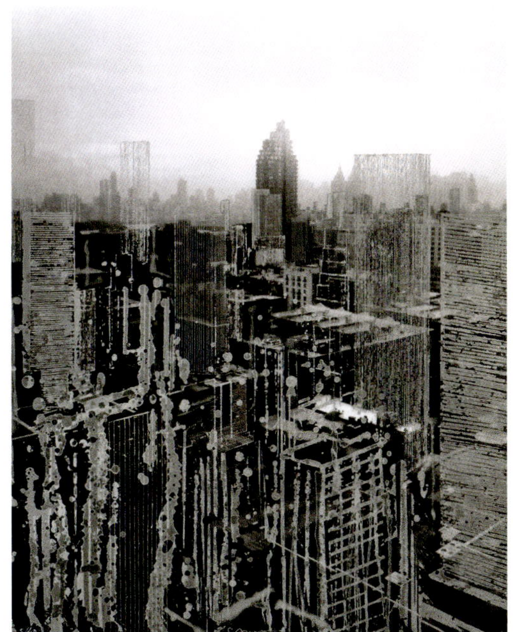

Silver Buildings   2011, 65 × 50 cm

Trees | Bäume | Arbres   1987, 80 × 119,5 cm

für diese druckgrafische Technik besonders eingenommen. Salzmann agiert wiederum als unorthodoxer Grenzgänger, wenn er sich über engstirnige Vorstellungen von „Materialsprache" hinwegsetzt. Er lässt die Techniken ineinanderfließen. Mit seiner technischen Findigkeit und Experimentierfreude erobert er sich neue Anwendungsgebiete, schlägt er Brücken in andere Bereiche der Bildkunst. Obwohl sein thematischer Bereich eng gesteckt ist, hat er doch die Anlage zum Meister aller Klassen.

Eine Sonderstellung kommt den Kohlezeichnungen zu, die Salzmann ursprünglich neben den Landschaftsaquarellen zu seiner zweiten Domäne entwickelte, die in der derzeitigen Werkkonstellation allerdings keine Rolle mehr spielen. Es ist vielleicht die persönlichste Seite seiner Kunst, was allerdings für die zeichnerische Gattung generell gilt. Schwarz-Weiß hat immer etwas besonders Suggestives, da durch die Reduktion und den Farbentzug die Fantasietätigkeit des Betrachters mehr gefordert und das Emotionale automatisch stärker beteiligt wird. Salzmann arbeitet in diesen teilweise sehr großen Zeichnungen mit dem Gegensatz von dunklen, formlosen Ballungen und einem spärlichen, sorgfältig gesetzten klaren Liniengerüst. Große Flächenstücke werden gezielt leer gelassen, mit spröden Einzellinien und Schwärzen akzentuiert.

Das Gegeneinander von diffuser Dunkelheit und hellen, formenstrengen Lineamenten erzeugt eine besondere atmosphärische Spannung. Etwas davon vermochte Salzmann auch in Lithografie und Radierung zu übertragen. Es sind Begegnungen des Abgezirkelten und des Ungestalten in Form von mit hochsensibler Linse festgehaltenen Licht-Schatten-Spielen, was einen ersten Berührungspunkt mit der Fotografie ergibt. In diesem Fall fühlt man sich an die mittels extrem langer Belichtungszeit zustande gekommenen Ergebnisse der frühesten Fotografen erinnert.

In der Adaption verschiedener Techniken für seine Intentionen sucht Salzmann nicht den Unterschied, sondern den gemeinsamen Nenner, wobei er seine Basis, Aquarell und Zeichnung, ständig erweitert. Manchmal bis

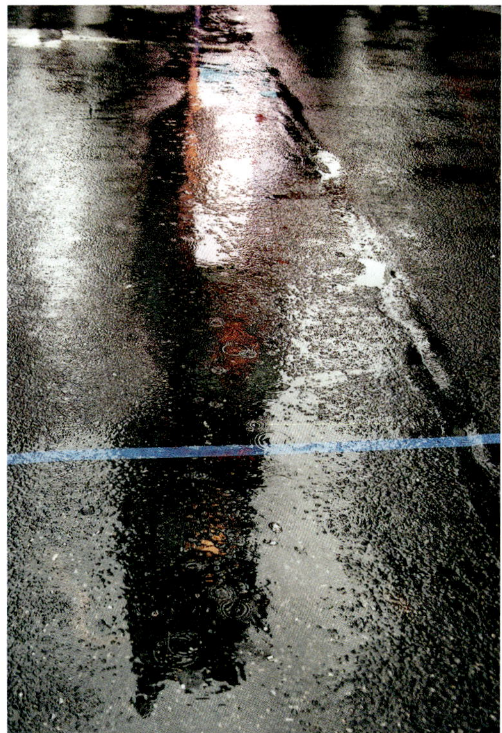

Times Square V   2009

parce qu'elle empiète constamment sur d'autres territoires avoisinants. La gestuelle, le style, le coup de pinceau, qui font au premier plan l'impact et l'expressivité de la toile, jouent en revanche un rôle secondaire. La technique de la gravure permet d'obtenir des résultats comparables à ceux de l'aquarelle, et l'élément liquide y est également déterminant. Salzmann agit de nouveau en anticonformiste lorsqu'il récuse la notion étriquée de « langage du matériau ». Pour lui, les techniques se fondent les unes aux autres. Avec son ingéniosité technique et son plaisir de l'expérimentation, il conquiert de nouveaux domaines d'application et lance des passerelles vers d'autres secteurs des arts plastiques. Bien que son champ thématique soit restreint, il est potentiellement un maître toutes catégories.

Une position particulière revient au fusain, dont Salzmann avait fait initialement son deuxième domaine, avec l'aquarelle, mais qui ne joue actuellement plus aucun rôle. C'est peut-être l'aspect le plus personnel de son art, qui vaut toutefois pour le genre du dessin en général. Le noir et blanc a toujours quelque chose de suggestif, dans la mesure où la réduction et la suppression de la couleur

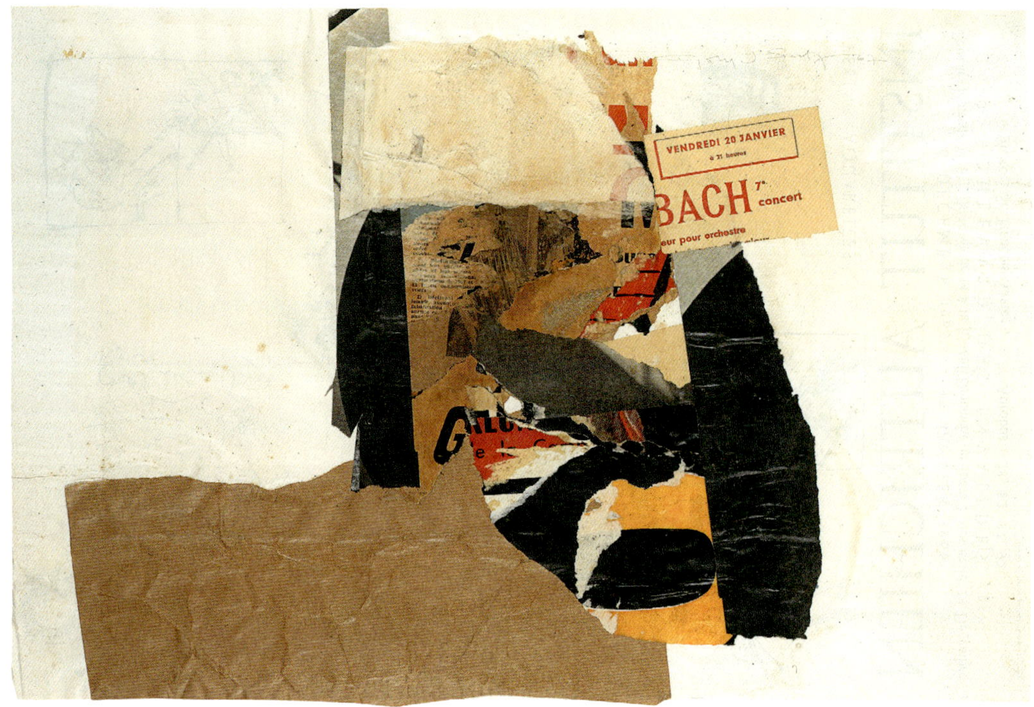

Bach   1967, 42,2 × 50 cm

stimulent l'imagination de l'observateur et, de ce fait, impliquent davantage la sensibilité. Dans ces dessins, parfois très grands, Salzmann travaille sur l'antinomie entre les concentrations sombres et informes d'une part, et la trame linéaire, claire et discrète. Des pans entiers, volontairement laissés vides, sont accentués par l'âpreté du noir ou des lignes individuelles.

L'obscurité diffuse ainsi apposée aux linéaments clairs et précis crée une tension d'ensemble particulière. Salzmann a essayé de reporter un peu de cette ambiance dans la lithographie et la gravure. C'est la rencontre du circonscrit et de l'informe dans un jeu d'ombres et de lumière captées par une lentille à haute sensibilité qui amorce le contact avec la photographie. On ne peut s'empêcher de penser ici à des clichés très anciens pris avec une durée d'exposition particulièrement longue.

before the onset of the photo boom in the visual arts, Salzmann experimented with cameras and even presented exhibitions at which only photographs were shown. Today, his ambitions as a photographer are once again on the verge of assuming a life of their own.

Initially, Salzmann employed black-and-white photographs developed in his own darkroom as grisailles or foundations that required alterations and offered themselves as material for further processing. He could now realize works in larger formats than were possible in finely articulated watercolor. Salzmann achieved a kind of aesthetic concentration with the aid of overpainting, in some cases expansive and energetic, in others with a more detailed, graphic character. He also combined or overlaid photographs with printing plates, which led to the *photeauforte* technique and provided new types of material stimulus: surface luster could be heightened by metallic effects or roughed with artificially induced corrosion.

Yet Salzmann also succeeded in integrating the collage—an entirely different type of work—into such environments. He now began to resort increasingly to this method, with which he had already worked in the

Vente sur saisie (Le trou des Halles)
1978, 43,7 × 48,8 cm

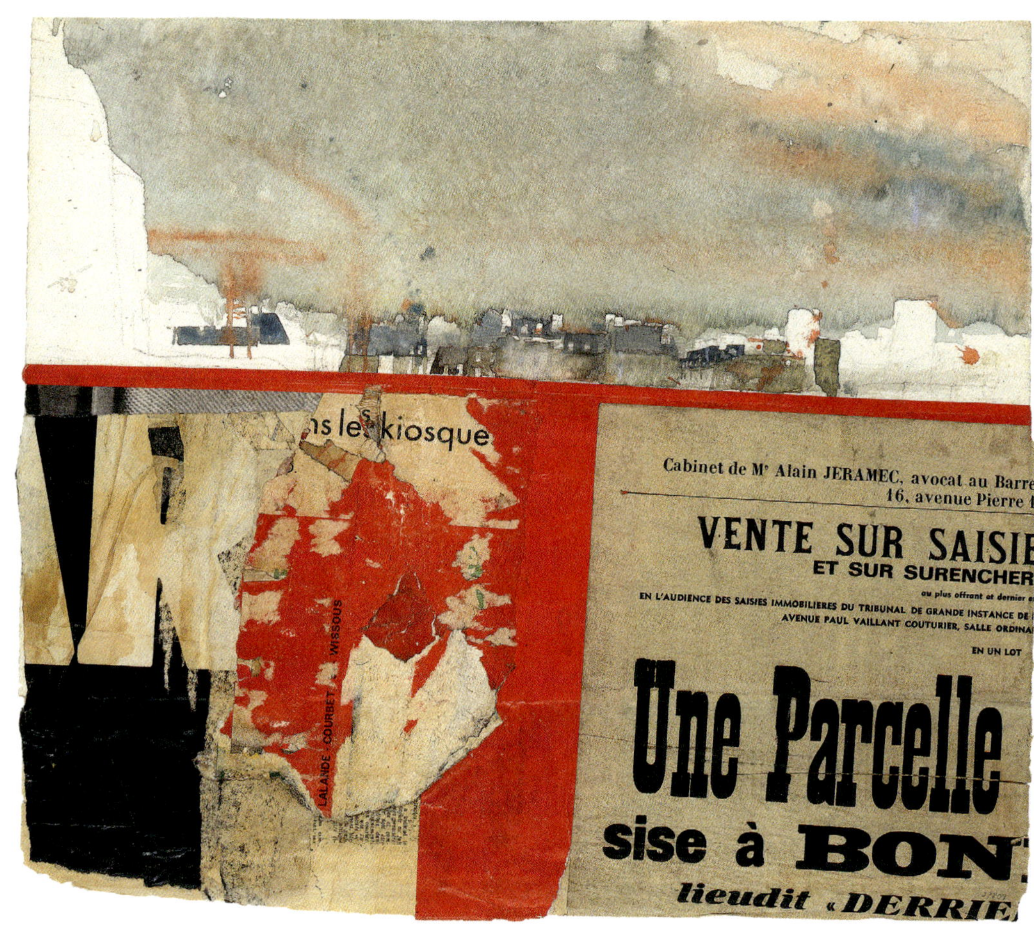

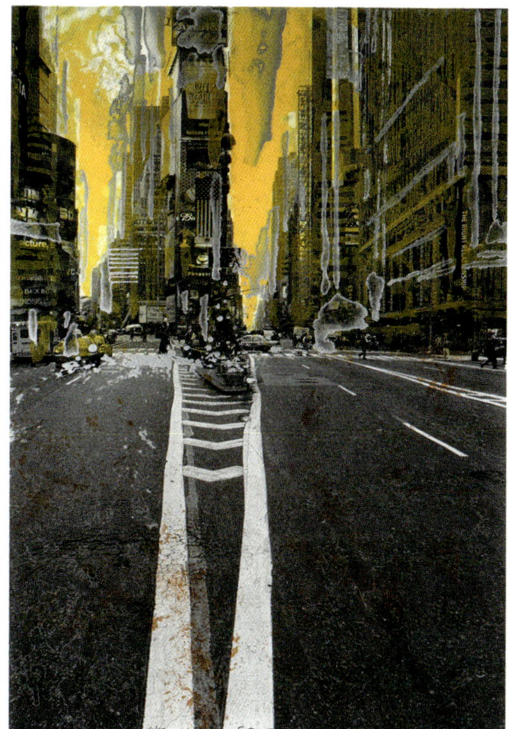

Yellow Times Square | Gelber Times Square | Times Square jaune   2005, 73,5 × 49,3 cm

1960s. To be precise, it was the *décollage* or "tear-off" picture that enjoyed a triumphant entry into the French art scene at the time. Salzmann was fascinated by the ravaged billboards, as he was with other phenomena associated with ruin and shabbiness—the detritus of civilization, the automobile cemeteries, the back sides of magnificent facades, which he never tired of gazing at in wonder. This was his way of approaching the world of consumption and merchandise that American Pop Art elevated to the status of a major subject for art. In his earliest watercolors, we encounter weathered advertisements and pictures on building walls, which assumed the character of mysterious and melancholy tidings in the context of the time.

It is typical of Salzmann that he combined *décollage* with collage, thus transforming them into a "recollage," and that he proceeded immediately to process the ravaged image. In other words, he subjected found objects to aesthetic calculation. Often layered with centimeters of paper, the billboards of Paris, on which the torn patches left huge gaps or hung like tongues, were a phenomenon that Salzmann had never encountered in quite the

zur Ununterscheidbarkeit. Ist es Fotografie oder fotorealistisches Aquarell? Alles dient dem Ziel, die Wahrnehmung um weitere Facetten zu bereichern, dem Seherlebnis Neuland zu erschließen. So vollzog sich die Aufnahme der Fotografie, die man auch als eine Form der Grafik ansehen kann, in sein technisches Repertoire ohne Paukenschlag und fast selbstverständlich. Er betont keineswegs das Andersartige, weil er nicht von theoretischen Erwägungen auszugehen pflegt, sondern behandelt sie als eine Spielart, wobei er sich im Fall des immateriellen Lichtbildes leichter tat als mit dem Ölbild. Auch in der Fotografie geht es in erster Linie um die Spuren von Licht und Schatten, sie ist ein Oberflächenseismograf, erfasst die äußerste Haut der Wahrnehmung. Bereits in jungen Jahren, also lange vor Ausbruch des Foto-Booms in den bildenden Künsten, hat Salzmann mit der Kamera experimentiert und sogar Ausstellungen gehabt, auf denen nur Fotografien gezeigt wurden. Auch jetzt sind seine Ambitionen als Fotograf wieder nahe daran, sich zu verselbstständigen.

Zunächst setzte Salzmann die von ihm selbst entwickelte Schwarz-Weiß-Fotografie als Grisaille bzw. Fond ein, die sich als ergänzungsbedürftig erwies und zur Weiterbearbeitung anbot. Es konnten nun auch größere Formate als im feingliederigen Aquarell realisiert werden. Gestalterische Verdichtung erreichte Salzmann mittels einer teils großflächigen und schwungvollen, teils detaillierten und eher grafischen Übermalung. Weiters kombinierte bzw. überblendete er Fotos mit Druckplatten, was zur Photeauforte-Technik führte und neuartige Materialreize ergab. Der Glanz der Oberfläche kann durch metallische Wirkungen gesteigert oder durch eine künstlich herbeigeführte Korrosion aufgeraut werden.

Aber auch die ganz anders geartete Collage versteht Salzmann in ein solches Umfeld zu integrieren. Er greift jetzt wieder verstärkt auf diese künstlerische Methode zurück, mit der er sich schon in den Sechzigerjahren beschäftigt hat. Genau genommen war es die Decollage, das Abriss-Bild, die damals in der französischen Kunstszene ihren großen Auftritt hatte. Die verwüsteten Plakatwände interes-

En variant les techniques selon ses intentions, Salzmann ne cherche pas la différence mais le dénominateur commun, tout en ne cessant d'élargir la base que constitue pour lui l'aquarelle. Parfois jusqu'à rendre les techniques indissociables. Tout doit concourir à enrichir le champ de la perception, à explorer des zones visuelles inconnues. La photographie, qui peut être considérée comme une forme graphique, apparaît donc tout naturellement dans son répertoire technique, sans en faire cas. Peu coutumier des conjectures théoriques, il n'y voit du reste aucune différence, seulement une variante. Cela dit, l'aspect immatériel de la photographie lui est plus commode que la peinture à l'huile. En photographie, là aussi, jouent avant tout les empreintes de l'ombre et de la lumière. Le procédé, à la manière d'un sismographe des surfaces, saisit l'ultime strate de la perception. Dès ses jeunes années, bien longtemps avant l'essor de la photo dans les arts plastiques, Salzmann a expérimenté ce domaine et se produisit dans des expositions ne montrant que des photographies. Ses ambitions de photographe sont de nouveau sur le point de s'affirmer en tant que telles.

Pour commencer, Salzmann a utilisé la photographie en noir et blanc (qu'il développe lui-même) comme grisaille ou arrière-plan demandant à être complété et remanié. Il peut ainsi réaliser des formats plus grands que même la finesse de l'aquarelle ne le permet. Pour densifier la forme, il peint pardessus soit des aplats dans un geste plein d'entrain, soit plutôt des éléments graphiques et détaillés. Par ailleurs, il combine ou superpose des photos avec des plaques de gravure, il renouvelle cette technique en inventant la « photeauforte ». L'éclat de la surface est rehaussé par des effets métallisés ou rendu rugueux par une corrosion artificielle.

Dans un genre tout autre, Salzmann fait également intervenir le collage, méthode artistique à laquelle il recourt désormais davantage après l'avoir déjà pratiquée dans les années 1960. Il s'agit plus exactement de « décollage », alors très prôné par la scène artistique française. Salzmann s'intéresse au délabrement des murs affichés, mais aussi à d'autres apparences miteuses et dégradées,

same form in Vienna. In this way, an originally cohesive image could be transformed into a fragmented landscape that produced an entirely new kind of random beauty and directed the imagination toward new relationships. The torn, lacerated edges had a great deal in common with the arbitrary boundaries of a watercolor landscape.

As an impoverished student, Salzmann occasionally took jobs mounting posters on billboards himself. He was particularly receptive to such thin-skinned surfaces and saw them as seismographs of rapid change and thus as materialized time. He began collecting these torn scraps of paper and putting them together according to a new set of rules. Representational motifs were rigorously avoided, while typography was welcomed—as in the classical collages of a Picasso or Braque.

In a work realized in 1976, we find an unconventional combination of different, apparently mutually exclusive techniques that would play a determining role in his work thirty years later. A typical village rooftop landscape appears behind or above a billboard. We recognize shared characteristics in this combination of filtered real and emphatically abstract levels. The collage does not form a static surface but lives instead from spatial complexity, from the "insights" offered by the superimpositions, tears, and gaps visible on the poster-bearing wall, and thus presents itself as a kind of landscape.

The advertising world has become more aggressive and shrill in the interim, and Salzmann does not shy away from even the gaudiest scenes or the crudest headlines. In fact, one senses that this tactic enables him to steer away from what one might refer to as aesthetic "splendid isolation"—even though this may seem an affront to some admirers of his earlier refined watercolors. At the same time, however, we find elements of a familiar poetry in the neon-colored dance of light in such nightlife ads.

sierten Salzmann, wie so manche Phänomene des Ruinösen und Schäbigen, der Zivilisationsmüll, die Autofriedhöfe, die Kehrseiten der glanzvollen Fassaden, die zu bestaunen er gleichfalls nicht müde wird. Es ist seine Form der Annäherung an die Konsum- und Warenwelt, welche die amerikanische Pop-Art zu einem Hauptthema der Kunst machte. Bereits in seinen allerfrühesten Aquarellen gab es halb verwitterte Reklameschriften oder -bilder an Hauswänden, die im damaligen Kontext etwas von geheimnisvollen und melancholischen Botschaften annahmen.

Typisch für Salzmann ist, dass er die Decollage mit der Collage kombinierte und damit in eine „Recollage" verwandelte, dass er sich also unverzüglich an die Bearbeitung des geschundenen Bildes machte, d.h. er ordnete das Vorgefundene seinem ästhetischen Kalkül unter. Die oft zentimeterdick beklebten Pariser Plakatwände, auf denen die abgerissenen Stellen große weiße Lücken rissen oder wie Zungen herabhingen, waren ein Phänomen, das Salzmann von Wien her in dieser Form unbekannt war. Eine ursprünglich zusammenhängende Darstellung konnte sich auf diese Weise in eine Splitterlandschaft verwandeln, die eine ganz neue Art von zufälliger Schönheit hervorbrachte und die Fantasie auf neue Zusammenhänge kommen ließ. Die abgerissenen, zerfransten Ränder hatten durchaus etwas Gemeinsames mit den zufälligen Begrenzungen seiner Landschaftsaquarelle.

Als armer Student betätigte sich Salzmann sogar gelegentlich selbst als Plakatierer. Er war für diese Art dünnhäutiger Oberflächen besonders empfänglich, sah in ihnen Seismografen für den raschen Wandel, also materialisierte Zeit. Er begann solche abgerissenen Papierfetzen zu sammeln und setzte sie nach neuen Spielregeln zusammen. Gegenständliche Motive wurden strikt vermieden, hingegen war – wie bei den klassischen Collagen eines Picasso und eines Braque – die Typografie willkommen.

In einer Arbeit von 1976 finden wir bereits eine unkonventionelle Kombination verschiedener, sich gegenseitig scheinbar ausschließender Techniken, wie sie dreißig Jahre später für seine Schaffensweise bestimmend

les rebuts de notre civilisation, les casses automobiles – l'envers des décors rutilants, que jamais il ne se lasse de contempler avec stupeur. C'est là sa manière d'aborder le monde de la consommation et des marchandises dont le pop art américain a fait un des grands thèmes de l'art. Dans ses toutes premières aquarelles déjà, on trouve des pancartes et enseignes publicitaires à moitié détruites sur les murs des maisons qui, dans le contexte de l'époque, revêtaient ainsi un tour mystérieux et mélancolique.

Geste typique de Salzmann, il combine décollage et collage pour donner un « recollage » ; autrement dit, en remaniant aussitôt l'image décrépite, il soumet la chose trouvée à son calcul esthétique. Les murs de Paris, avec leurs épaisses couches d'affiches superposées, déchirées, en lambeaux, étaient un phénomène que Salzmann n'avait jamais rencontré à Vienne. Une représentation initialement cohérente pouvait de cette manière se transformer en paysage éclaté, faisant émerger un tout nouveau genre de beauté aléatoire et permettant à l'imagination d'établir des rapports inédits. Les bords déchiquetés ont du reste quelque chose en commun avec les délimitations hasardeuses de ses aquarelles de paysages.

Alors qu'il était encore étudiant dans le besoin, Salzmann fut d'ailleurs lui-même colleur d'affiches à ses heures. Il avait une sensibilité particulière pour ces fines pellicules, comme l'expression, à ses yeux, des oscillations rapides du temps matérialisé. Il se mit donc à rassembler des bouts de papier déchirés pour recomposer quelque chose selon de nouvelles règles. Les motifs figuratifs étaient rigoureusement évités ; en revanche, comme dans les collages classiques de Picasso ou Braque, la typographie était bienvenue.

Un travail de 1976 montre déjà une combinaison inhabituelle de diverses techniques, s'excluant mutuellement en apparence, et qui allait devenir trente ans plus tard déterminante pour son mode de création. Derrière ou au-dessus d'un mur d'affiches surgit un de ses paysages de toits campagnards caractéristiques. Il y a d'ailleurs des points communs entre le niveau épuré, réel, et celui qui est délibérément abstrait. Car le collage ne forme

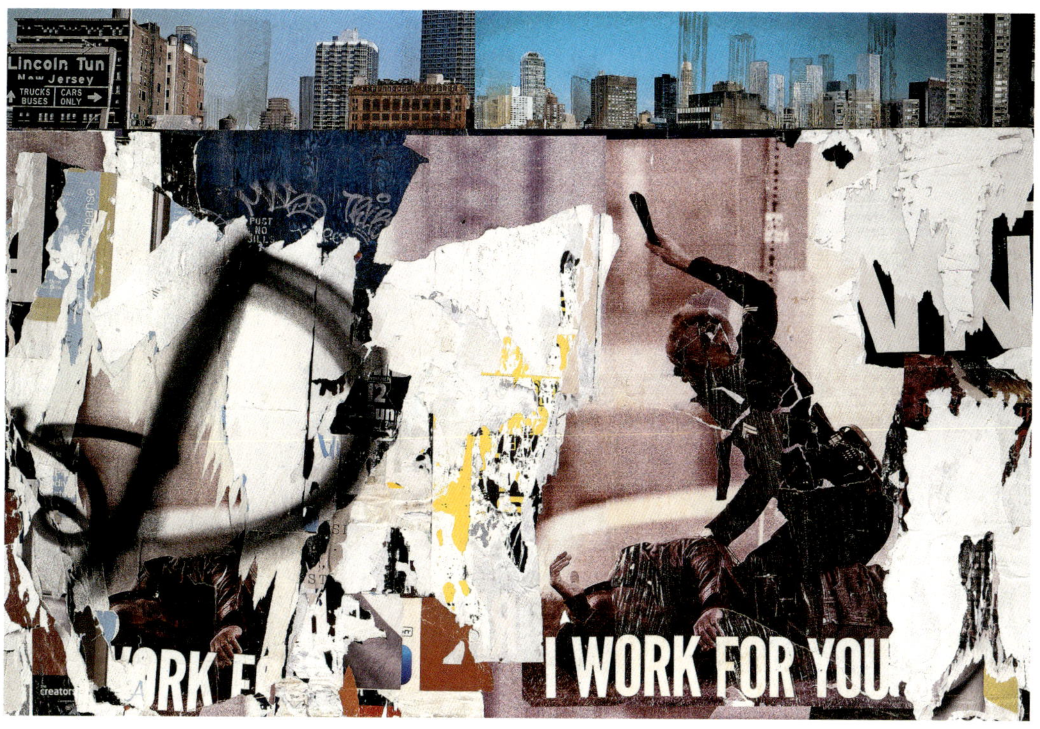

I work for you II   2012, 114 × 162 cm

Collages and Cathedrals

Most of Salzmann's recent works combine color photographs with collages, each of which usually occupies a separate area of the picture, although they may also be artfully blended and interwoven. There is always something unifying and dividing, a surprising correspondence that is evident, for example, in surface structures or the details of a motif. Salzmann enjoys contrasting the demolition of old brick buildings with the erection of new glass palaces, patina with polished gloss, and thus introduces an aspect of urban *vanitas* into his world of images.

The photographs Salzmann took as an "urban tramp" and attentive daydreamer on marches lasting for days are cut up and set in new visual contexts through the process of montage. The artist refuses to work with Photoshop or other nonmanual processing methods, and no photograph is used more than once. We encounter "leitmotifs" that are familiar to us from the realm of watercolor, such as window shutters, steps, banners, or ugly containers with interesting surfaces that disguise most of the surface area. Light and shadow contribute to the impression of spatial depth and often evoke a mysterious sense of alienation. The penetration of semitrans-

Collagen und Kathedralen

Die aktuellen Arbeiten kombinieren vorzugsweise Farbfotos mit Collagen, die meist separierte Bildbereiche einnehmen, aber sich werden sollte. Hinter oder über einer Plakatwand taucht eine seiner typischen dörflichen Dachlandschaften auf. Es gibt auch Gemeinsamkeiten in dieser Koppelung einer gefilterten realen und einer betont abstrakten Ebene. Denn die Collage bildet keine starre Fläche, sondern lebt von der räumlichen Vielschichtigkeit, den „Einblicken", die sich aus den Überschneidungen, Rissen und Klüften auf der beklebten Wand ergeben, und stellt sich somit ebenfalls als eine Art Landschaft dar.

Mittlerweile ist die Reklamewelt aggressiver und schriller geworden, und Salzmann hat keine Scheu vor den knalligsten Kulissen und krudesten Schlagzeilen. Man hat sogar das Gefühl, dass er auf diese Weise der Gefahr einer ästhetischen „splendid isolation" bewusst entgegensteuert – auch wenn er damit so manchen Verehrer seiner verfeinerten Aquarelle von einst verstört. Umgekehrt findet man auch noch im neonbunten Lichtertanz der Nightlife-Reklamen Elemente einer wohlvertrauten Poesie.

pas un plan figé, il vit de la multiplicité des volumes, des « aperçus » que permettent les recoupements, les encoches et les fentes sur le mur recouvert ; le collage représente lui-même une sorte de paysage.

Entre-temps, le monde de la publicité est devenu plus agressif, plus incisif, mais Salzmann ne redoute la violence ni des décors ni des slogans. On a même le sentiment que, de cette façon, il se prémunit consciemment de la « splendide isolation » esthétique – au risque d'en chagriner quelques-uns parmi ceux qui admirent ses aquarelles raffinées de jadis. Inversement, on trouve encore dans la valse des réclames bariolées et lumineuses les éléments d'une poésie familière.

Collages et cathédrales

Les travaux actuels marient de préférence photos couleur et collages, qui, généralement, occupent sur l'image des zones à part. Mais il arrive aussi qu'elles soient habilement imbriquées les unes dans les autres. Il y a toujours quelque chose qui associe et qui sépare, une correspondance surprenante, par exemple dans la structure des surfaces ou le détail d'un motif. Salzmann aime à créer le contraste, démolition d'un vieux bâtiment en briques vs surgissement de nouveaux gratte-ciel en verre patiné, lisse et poli. Son univers acquiert ainsi la dimension de vanités urbaines.

Les photos que Salzmann prend au cours de ses longues journées d'« errance » et de déambulation sont ensuite découpées puis remontées dans un contexte visuel nouveau. L'artiste refuse de travailler avec Photoshop ou autre procédé non-manuel ; chaque photo n'est utilisée qu'une fois. Nous retrouvons parfois des « leitmotivs » que nous connaissons de ses aquarelles – des volets, des escaliers, des pancartes ou de vilains containers à la surface intéressante qui brouillent la majeure partie de la superficie. Les ombres et la lumière contribuent à donner une impres-

parent areas—the appearance of shadowy forms shining through a surface layer—is another artistic resource that is playing an increasingly important role.

Thanks to the techniques of photograph and collage, which enable the artist to work with large pictorial fields, Salzmann has finally conquered the large format and now feels entirely at home in that dimension. These works are given added aesthetic polish through partial overpainting with watercolor or acrylic paint or pens, which often goes into considerable detail and remains in the background in terms of overall impression.

The collages now almost assume the dimensions of real billboards. Salzmann digs through the mass of paper like a geologist, exposing older layers that were covered over as much as a year before. From this colorful confusion of paper scraps emerge landscapes and mountain ranges, a rutted landscape for the wanderings of a moving eye. Casual coordinates emerge, and the torn spots serve a function similar to that of the uncovered white spaces in the watercolors.

Rudimentary representational elements frequently intrude into the pictorial mix, deliberately hidden in some cases, impacting significantly on the overall impression in others. Salzmann now even seizes opportunities to offer ironic or sarcastic comments on contemporary life. He recently compiled a series entitled *You are observed*, which responds to the fact of inescapable surveillance in everyday life in a playful yet perhaps for that very reason all the more urgent way. It is reasonable to expect that the traditional billboard will disappear progressively from our increasingly "clean" and nonsensual environment, and thus there is already a hint of nostalgia in these works.

The montages are literally consolidated in agglomerations. Their arrangements are based on the principles of unfolding and depth layering, which produce an equally confusing and stimulating variety of insights, perspectives, and overviews—all in all a panorama of contemporary urban civilization. Yet what is most astonishing of all is the sensitivity with which the artist transforms this garishly colorful and abstruse mélange,

auch kunstvoll verschränken und vermischen können. Es gibt immer etwas Verbindendes und Trennendes, eine überraschende Korrespondenz, beispielsweise in der Struktur der Oberflächen oder im Motivdetail. Gerne kontrastiert Salzmann den Abbruch von alten Ziegelbauten mit dem Aufschießen neuer Glaspaläste, die Patina mit der polierten Glätte, und bringt sozusagen eine urbane Vanitas-Dimension in seine Bildwelt ein.

Die Fotos, die Salzmann als „Stadtstreicher" und hellwacher Tagträumer auf tagelangen Märschen aufgenommen hat, werden zerschnitten und durch Montage in einen neuen visuellen Kontext gestellt. Photoshop oder ähnliche nicht-händische Bearbeitung lehnt der Künstler ab, jedes Foto wird nur einmal verwendet. Wir begegnen mitunter „Leitmotiven", die wir aus der Aquarell-Sphäre kennen, wie Rollläden, Stufen, Transparenten oder hässlichen Containern mit interessanten Oberflächen, die den Großteil der Fläche verstellen. Licht und Schatten tragen zum Eindruck der räumlichen Tiefe bei und bewirken oft eine geheimnisvolle Entrücktheit. Das Durchdringen von halb transparenten Flächen bzw. das schemenhafte Durchscheinen ist ein weiteres, an Wichtigkeit zunehmendes Kunstmittel.

Dank der ein großflächiges Arbeiten erlaubenden Techniken der Fotografie und Collage hat sich Salzmann endgültig das große Bildformat erobert und fühlt sich äußerst wohl in dieser Dimension. Ästhetischen Schliff bekommen diese Arbeiten durch partielle Übermalung in Aquarell- und Acrylfarbe oder mit Stiften, die oft sehr ins Detail geht und sich hinsichtlich des Gesamteindrucks im Hintergrund hält.

Die Collage nimmt nun fast die Ausmaße von realen Plakatwänden an, Salzmann gräbt sich wie ein Geologe durch den Papierwust, holt ältere Schichten hervor, die schon vor Jahr und Tag zugewachsen sind. Aus dem bunten Gewirr der Papierreste ergeben sich Landschaften und Gebirge, ein zerklüftetes Gelände für die Wanderungen eines schweifenden Auges. Es formieren sich zwanglose Koordinaten, wobei die aufgerissenen Stellen eine ähnliche Funktion haben wie die weiß belassenen Partien in den Aquarellen.

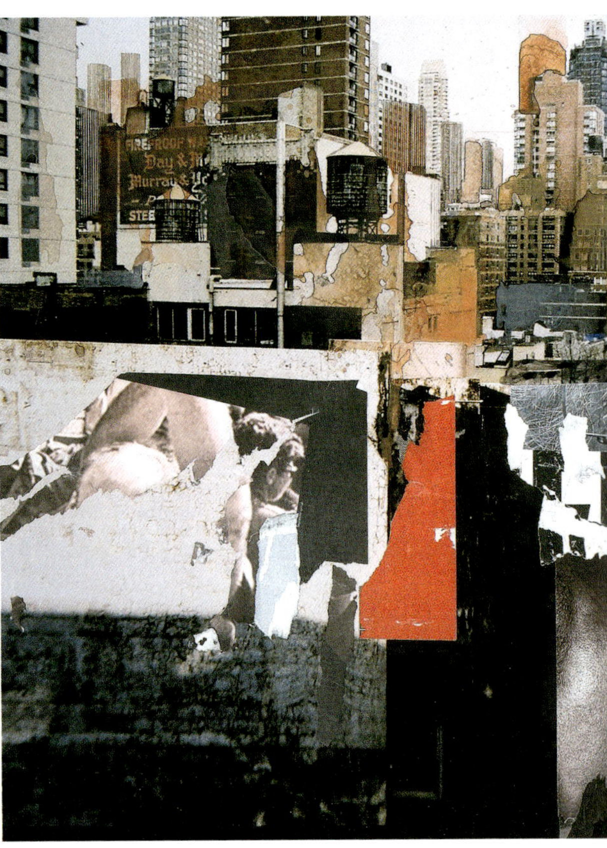

You are observed II   2012, 73 × 116 cm

sion de profondeur, dégageant souvent quelque chose de mystérieux et décalé. Un autre procédé joue de plus en plus, le travail sur la transparence et ses effets presque irréels.

Grâce aux techniques de la photographie et du collage, qui lui permettent de travailler à plus grande échelle, Salzmann conquiert définitivement les grands formats et s'y sent d'ailleurs parfaitement à l'aise. Pour les parfaire, esthétiquement parlant, ces travaux sont partiellement repeints, à l'aquarelle, à l'acrylique ou au crayon, souvent jusque dans le moindre détail, mais tout en retenue par rapport à l'impression d'ensemble.

Le collage occupe presque autant de place que les vrais murs affichés. Salzmann creuse comme un géologue dans la masse de papier, met au jour les couches plus anciennes qui ont été ensevelies depuis longtemps. Cet embrouillamini de morceaux de papier donne des paysages et des montages, des terres escarpées à travers lesquelles le regard

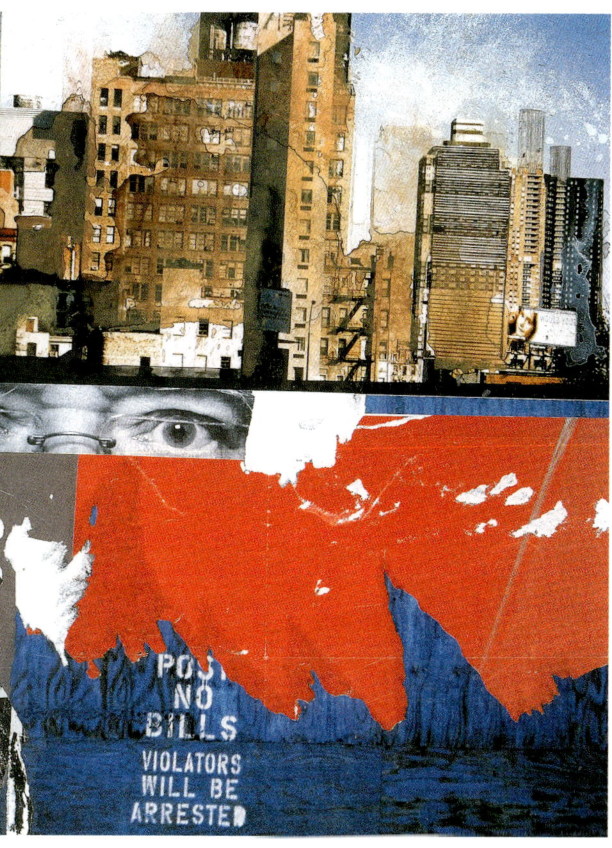

which guides the eye farther and farther on, into an aesthetic experience of the highest order.

In Salzmann's case, technical exploration has served as a driving force in his development as an artist. Expressed in exaggerated terms, he changes techniques more often than motifs, for he is not a painter who pursues variety of motif at all cost, although he is a painter who loves variation. He has never gotten stuck in one place. His path of development proceeds from the essentially homogeneous watercolor to the mixed-media picture to the combination and interplay of different techniques that once followed different paths and are now employed alongside and over each other. Salzmann produces reciprocal effects between technical production methods, aspects of motif, and formal strategies, weaving these components into a tension-laden web of relationships in which one can easily get lost, but from which one always emerges having gained something in the bargain.

Salzmann has avoided stagnation in his favorite discipline, watercolor painting, as

Es mischen sich nun häufig gegenständliche Rudimente ins Bildgeschehen, manchmal absichtsvoll versteckt, manchmal ganz vordergründig den Eindruck bestimmend. Salzmann nützt jetzt sogar die Gelegenheit für ironische und sarkastische zeitkritische Kommentare. So hat er jüngst einen Zyklus unter dem Titel „You are observed" zusammengestellt, der das Faktum des unentrinnbaren Überwachtseins auf spielerische, aber deswegen vielleicht umso eindringlichere Weise einfließen lässt. Im Übrigen ist es absehbar, dass die traditionellen Plakatwände mehr und mehr aus unserer immer „cleaner" und unsinnlicher werdenden Umwelt verschwinden werden, und so liegt schon jetzt der Hauch des Nostalgischen auf diesen Arbeiten.

Die Montagen sind förmlich zu Agglomerationen gebündelt. Ihre Anordnung folgt dem Prinzip der räumlichen Auffächerung und Tiefenstaffelung, die eine ebenso verwirrende wie anregende Vielfalt von Ein-, Durch- und Überblicken ergibt, in der Gesamtheit ein Panorama der heutigen urbanen Zivilisation. Am erstaunlichsten ist aber doch, mit welch sensiblem Gespür der Künstler dieses grellbunte und abstruse Vielerlei, das das Auge weiter und immer weiter führt, zu einem hochästhetischen Erlebnis werden lässt.

Die technische Exploration wirkt sich bei Salzmann stark als Antrieb für seine künstlerische Entwicklung aus. Sehr überspitzt ausgedrückt: Er wechselt die Techniken öfter als die Motive, denn er ist kein Maler, der auf motivische Abwechslung um jeden Preis aus ist, er ist eher einer, der die Variation liebt. Aber er ist nie stecken geblieben. Vom in sich homogenen Aquarell geht die Entwicklung zum Mixed-Media-Bild, zur Kombination und Verschränkung verschiedener Techniken, die vorher getrennte Wege gingen und die jetzt neben- und übereinander eingesetzt werden. Salzmann stellt Wechselwirkungen zwischen technischen Herstellungsverfahren, motivischen Gegebenheiten und formalen Strategien her und verwebt diese Komponenten zu einem spannungsvollen Beziehungsgeflecht, in dem man sich verirren kann, aber mit Gewinn auch wieder herausfindet.

peut randonner. De vagues repères se forment, les passages béants ayant une fonction comparable aux parties laissées en blanc dans les aquarelles.

Des rudiments de figuration s'invitent désormais fréquemment dans l'image, parfois intentionnellement cachés, parfois au tout premier plan. Salzmann profite même de l'occasion pour apporter quelques commentaires critiques et moqueurs sur notre époque. Tout récemment, il a réalisé un cycle intitulé *You are observed* qui évoque de manière ludique, mais d'autant plus percutante, le fait d'être constamment sous surveillance. On peut d'ailleurs prévoir que les murs d'affiches traditionnels vont peu à peu disparaître de notre environnement toujours plus aseptisé. En ce sens, un souffle de nostalgie enveloppe ces travaux.

Les montages sont littéralement des agglomérats. Ils s'organisent selon le principe de la répartition en profondeur. La diversité troublante et stimulante de la perception de l'ensemble offre un panorama de la civilisation urbaine d'aujourd'hui.

Mais on reste ébahi par la sensibilité avec laquelle l'artiste parvient à transformer en expérience esthétique suprême cette kyrielle de choses clinquantes et absurdes qui emmènent l'œil plus loin, toujours plus loin.

L'exploration des techniques a eu chez Salzmann un impact fort sur son évolution artistique. De façon caricaturale, on pourrait dire qu'il change de techniques plus souvent que de motifs. Il n'est pas un peintre à alterner les motifs à tout prix, il préfère au contraire la variation. Mais il n'est jamais non plus resté immobile. Depuis l'aquarelle, en soi homogène, son évolution le conduit à la technique mixte, autrement dit à l'association de différentes techniques qui auparavant allaient chacune dans une voie et qui désormais se juxtaposent ou se superposent. Salzmann crée des interactions entre des procédés techniques, des motifs donnés et des stratégies formelles ; ainsi entremêlés, ces composants donnent un labyrinthe captivant dans lequel on peut se perdre, mais dont on ressort aussi grandi.

Même dans sa discipline de référence qu'est l'aquarelle, Salzmann n'a jamais

well, and has recalled his passion for French cathedral architecture. While studying in Paris, he developed the habit of acquainting himself with one of the readily accessible architectural jewels in the area every week-end. While he never seriously considered using these beloved show objects as a motif for his art, Salzmann has since embraced this subject matter with a vengeance, and has produced a steadily growing group of works. He has now taken possession of Amiens, Senlis, Chartres, Bourges, Rouen, and Clermont-Ferrand, focusing on a variety of architectural and spatial aspects and in some cases visiting perilous sites.

The expanse of the heavenly vault, the compact vanishing lines of naves, and the vistas or the patterns of floors as they appear succinctly before the eye correspond to consistent visual approaches with which Salzmann has experimented with reference to an entirely different world of motifs. The palette takes each type of stone in a building into account; the monochrome appearance is highlighted with a delicate sprinkling that covers the surface. Other accents are provided by the shimmering windows, whose light Salzmann brings to the fore by breaking it down into tiny splinters of color.

The execution of such works in finely painted watercolor technique is worthy of admiration as an architectural image alone, whereby the artistic interventions in the spatial construct are handled with utmost discretion, as Salzmann does not wish to achieve an intensification of impression at the price of falsifying facts or exaggerating proportions in an obvious way. Yet he succeeds in expanding space imaginatively, in conveying a sense of the experience of space of which the "mortal" observer can only dream and which surpasses the reach of customary vision in every conceivable sense.

Auch in seiner Leibdisziplin, dem Aquarell, hat Salzmann keine Stagnation aufkommen lassen und sich seiner Passion für die französische Kathedralarchitektur erinnert. Als er in Paris studierte, hatte er es sich zur Gewohnheit gemacht, jedes Wochenende eine andere der von da aus erreichbaren Architektur-Juwele kennenzulernen. Nachdem er es als junger Künstler noch nicht ernsthaft erwogen hatte, diese bevorzugten Schauobjekte als Darstellungsproblem in Angriff zu nehmen, griff Salzmann die Thematik nun mit vollem Nachdruck auf. Eine ständig wachsende Werkgruppe ist entstanden. Amiens, Senlis, Chartres, Bourges, Rouen, Clermont-Ferrand hat er inzwischen erobert, wobei er verschiedene architektonische bzw. räumliche Aspekte ins Visier nahm und teilweise waghalsige Standorte aufsuchte.

Die Himmelsweite des Gewölbes, die geballten Fluchten der Schiffe und die Durchblicke oder die lapidar vor das Auge gerückte Musterung des Fußbodens entsprechen konstanten Sichtweisen, die Salzmann anhand einer ganz anderen Motivwelt erprobt hat. Die Palette nimmt auf die jeweils verbaute Steinsorte Rücksicht, das monochrome Erscheinungsbild wird mit einer die Fläche überziehenden zarten Sprenkelung hinterlegt. Weitere Akzente bilden die flimmernden Fenster, deren Lichtgehalt Salzmann zur Geltung bringt, indem er sie in winzige Farbsplitter zerlegt.

Die Ausführung in feinmalerischer Aquarelltechnik ist allein schon als Architekturaufnahme bewundernswürdig, wobei die künstlerischen Eingriffe in das Raumgefüge mit besonderer Distinktion gesetzt sind, da Salzmann keine Eindruckssteigerung auf Kosten einer Verfälschung der Gegebenheiten oder offensichtlichen Übertreibung der Proportionen erzielen möchte. Und dennoch: Er schafft es, den Raum imaginär zu erweitern, vermittelt ein Raumerlebnis, von dem der „sterbliche" Betrachter nur träumen kann und das den Radius des gewohnten Sehens in jeder Hinsicht übersteigt.

stagné ; il s'est adonné à sa passion pour l'architecture française des cathédrales. Du temps de ses études à Paris, il s'était fixé de découvrir chaque fin de semaine un autre joyau architectural. Le jeune artiste n'envisageait pas encore sérieusement de se mettre à la difficile représentation de ce thème, ce qu'il fit plus tard avec d'autant plus de force. Des groupes d'œuvres de plus en plus importants finissent par voir le jour : Amiens, Senlis, Chartres, Bourges, Rouen, Clermont-Ferrand – autant de lieux qu'il a conquis en choisissant parfois des angles risqués pour mieux cerner les différents aspects de l'architecture et de l'espace.

L'immensité céleste des voûtes, la profondeur des nefs ou le motif minimaliste du sol correspondent à des perspectives que Salzmann a inlassablement éprouvées dans des motifs très différents. La palette tient compte de la pierre du lieu, l'apparence monochrome est légèrement jaspée. Un accent supplémentaire provient du chatoiement des fenêtres dont Salzmann met la luminosité en valeur en la décomposant en de minuscules éclats de couleur.

Exécuter aussi finement une vue architecturale à l'aquarelle est en soi admirable. Les incursions artistiques dans ce tout spatial se font avec d'autant plus de délicatesse que Salzmann ne voudrait en aucun cas en augmenter l'effet par une falsification des données ou une exagération des proportions. Et pourtant, il réussit à élargir l'espace de l'imaginaire et à transmettre une notion d'espace dont tout observateur « mortel » ne peut que rêver – le rayon du regard habituel est, à tout point de vue, dépassé.

Rouen Cathedral I | Kathedrale von Rouen I | Cathédrale de Rouen I   2011, 92 × 63,3 cm

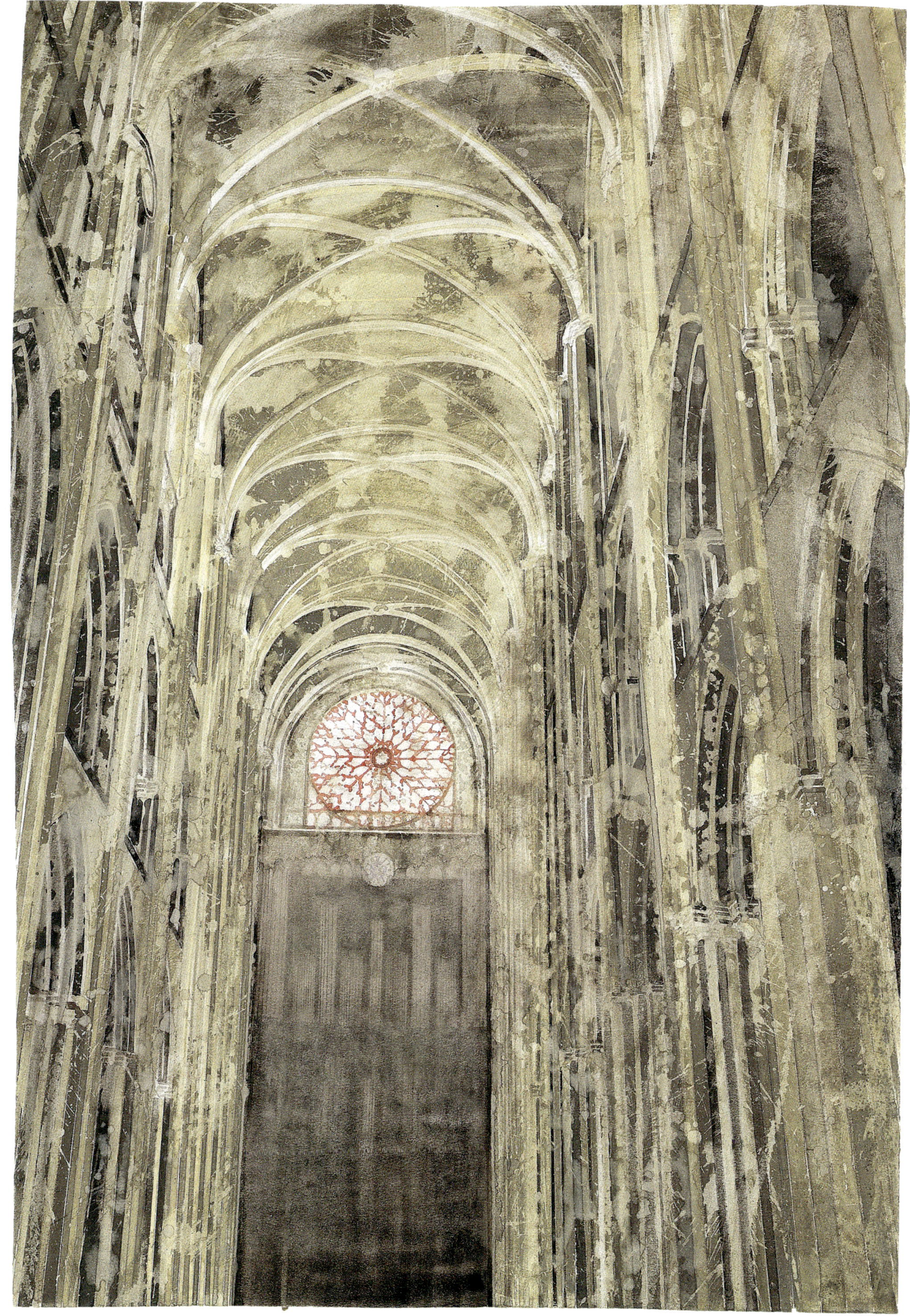

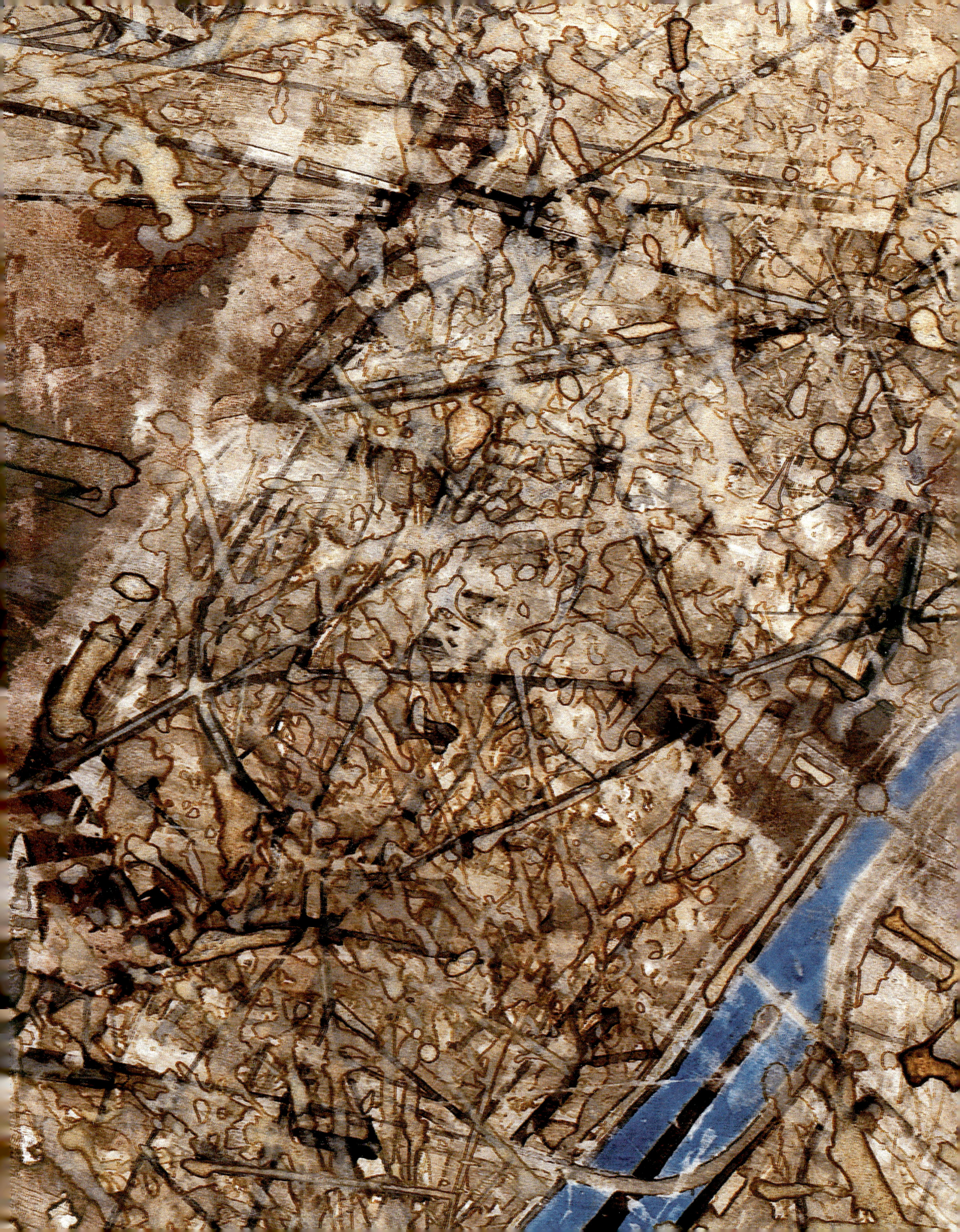

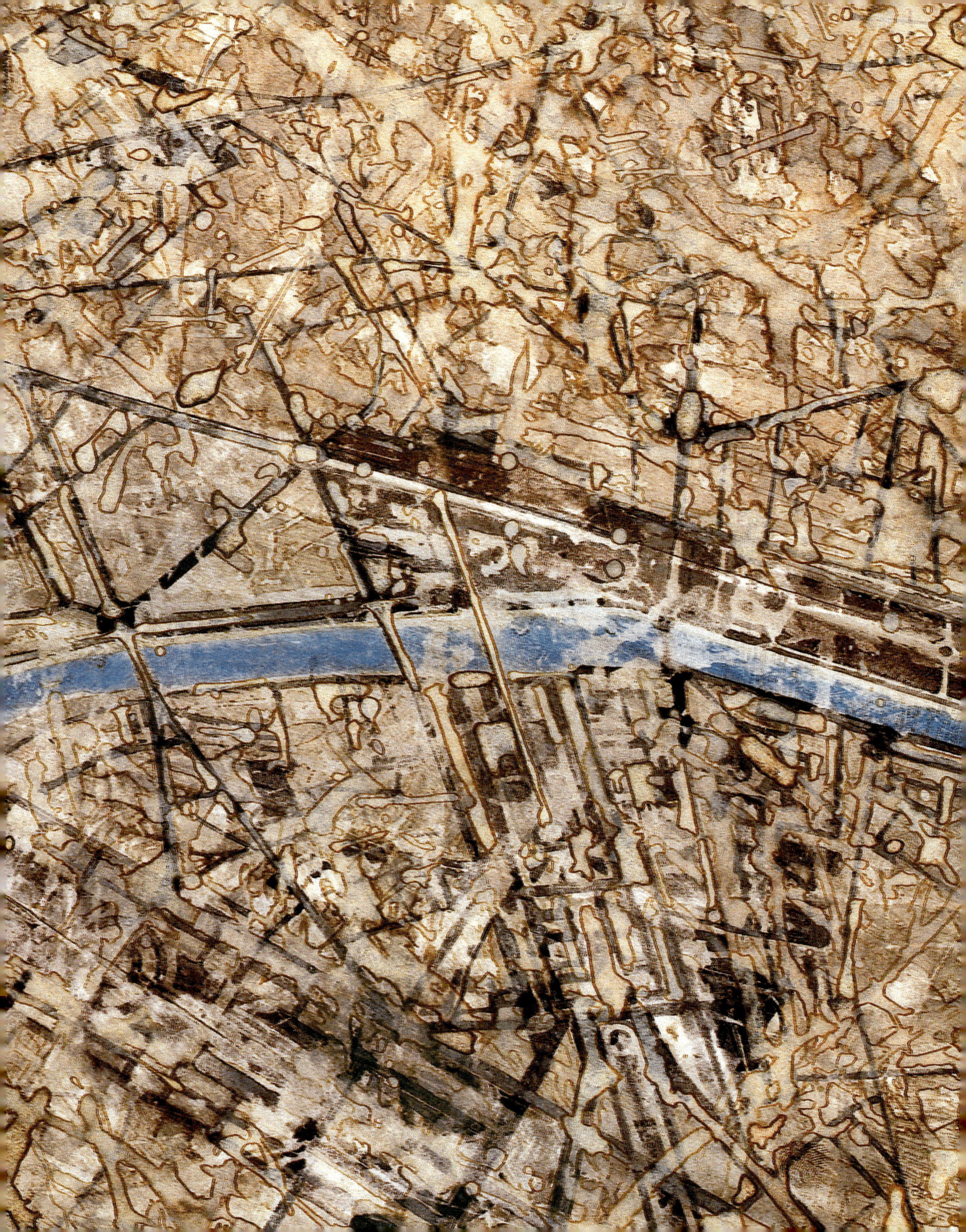

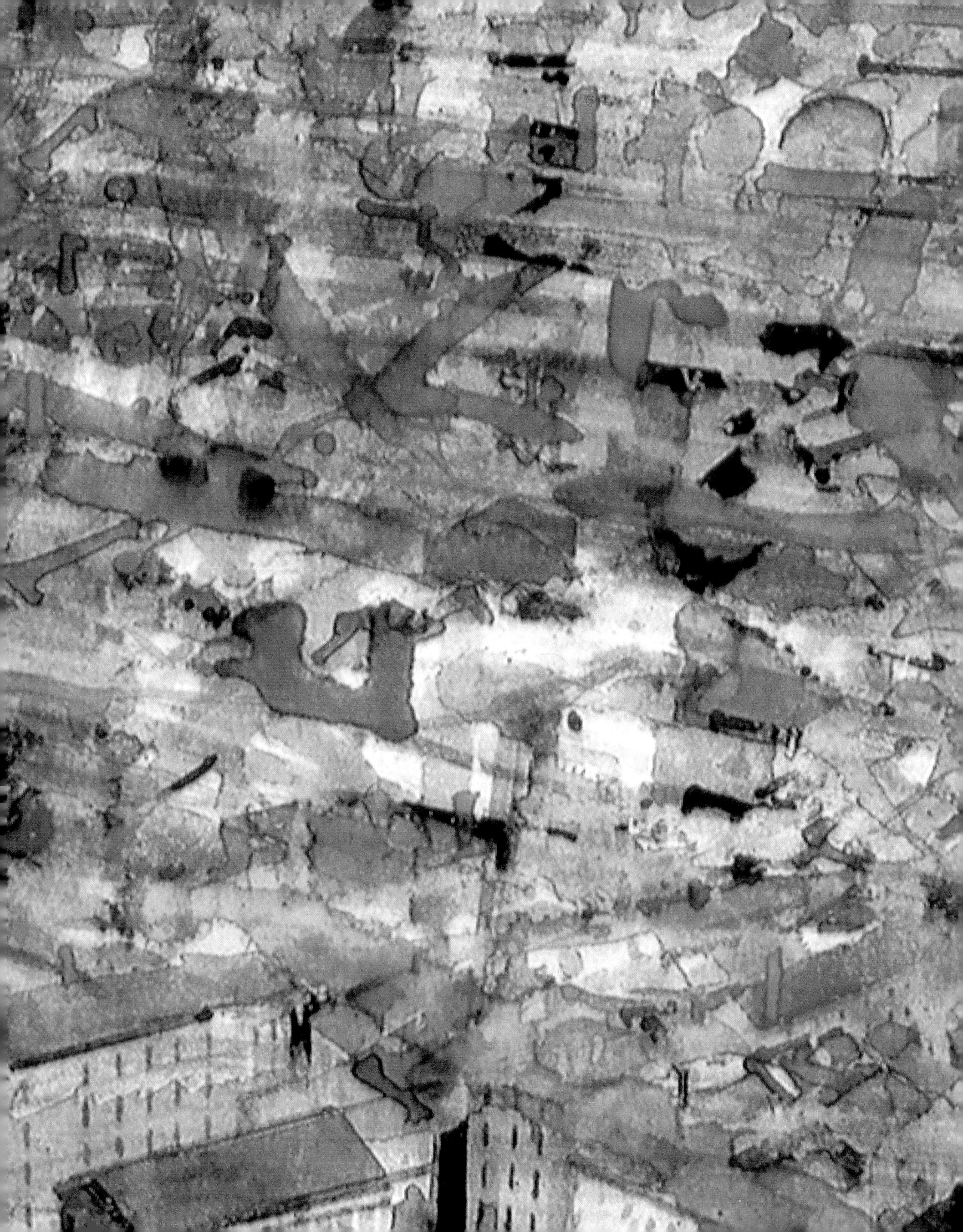

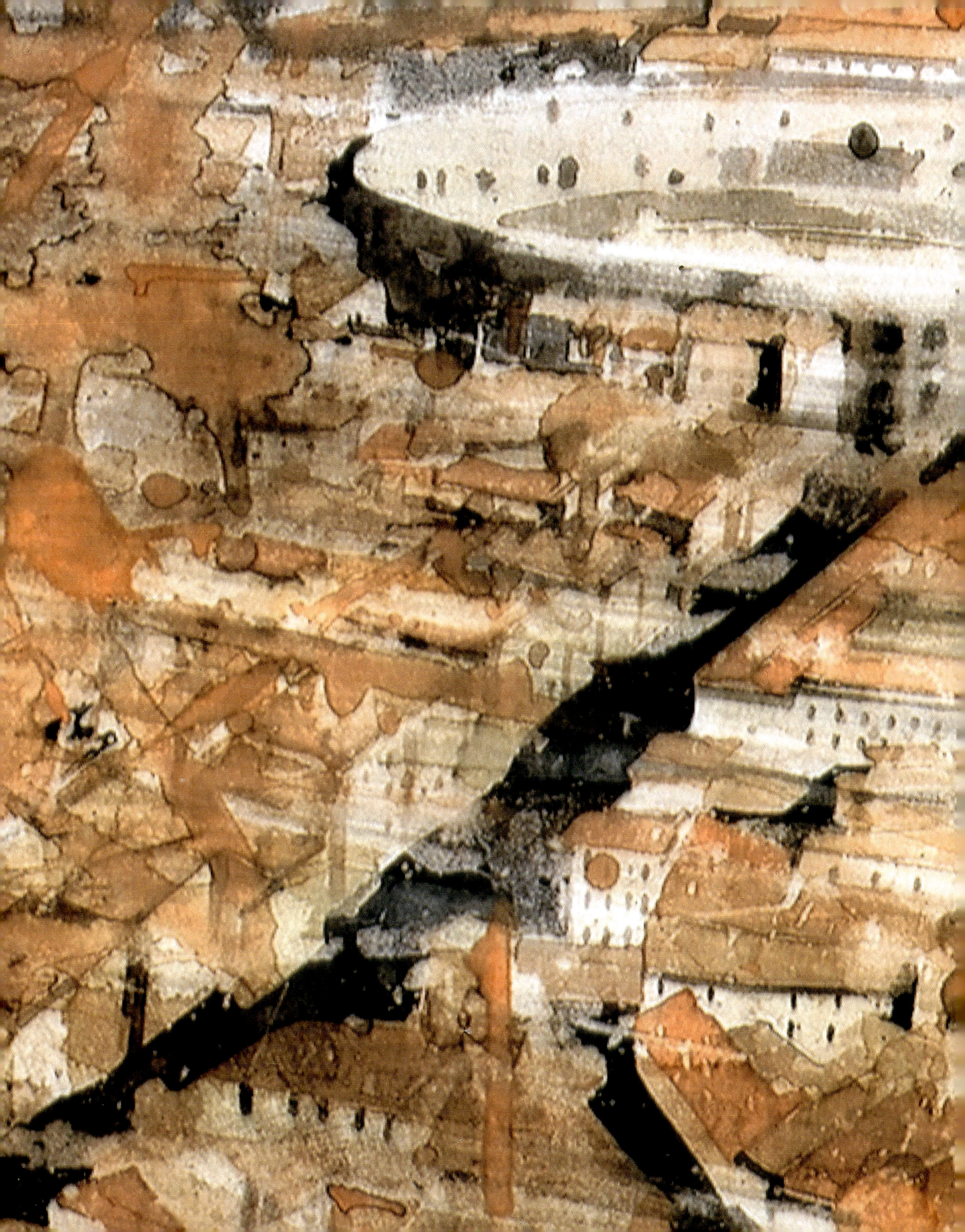

Landscapes
Landschaften
Paysages

Neither the traditional opposition between the city and the countryside nor the recognition that urbanization swallows up "beautiful" landscapes at a frightening, rapidly accelerating pace played a part in Gottfried Salzmann's decision to turn away from the natural landscape in the mid-1980s and concentrate exclusively on urban landscapes—preferably those of huge mega-cities.

Salzmann is first and foremost an explorer of spatial dimensions, a hunter of heights and distances. Anything that narrows the field of perception and fixes it at a single point is eliminated from consideration. Everything becomes transparent.

He appears to penetrate even solid bodies effortlessly—on the wings of light. He is equally adept at artfully instrumentalizing the processes of veiling and blurring. Unlike artists of the nineteenth century, who depended on optimum weather conditions, Salzmann capitalizes aesthetically on gloomier atmospheric situations. He makes use of clouds, fog, and mist, as well as smoke and industrial smog—albeit less as conveyors of mood in the traditional sense, as they tend instead to represent the visual bridge to an abstract pictorial concept and thus establish a new level of imagination in the landscape picture. That applies as well to water surfaces, which have a life of their own but also exhibit a more or less distorted image. They can be seen as interestingly structured fields, yet they also contribute to the expansion of pictorial space.

Der traditionelle Gegensatz zwischen Stadt und Land oder die Tatsache, dass die Urbanisierung in atemberaubendem Tempo immer mehr „schöne" Landschaft verschlingt, spielten keine Rolle bei der Entscheidung, dass sich Gottfried Salzmann Mitte der 1980er-Jahre von der Natur-Landschaft abkehrte und seitdem nur mehr Stadt-Landschaften, vorzugsweise riesige Mega-Cities, aufsucht.

Salzmann ist in erster Linie ein Eroberer räumlicher Dimensionen, ein Höhen- und Weitenjäger. Alles, was die Wahrnehmung einengt und auf einen Punkt fixiert, setzt er außer Kraft. Alles wird durchsichtig, auch feste Körper scheint er – auf den Schwingen des Lichts – mühelos zu durchdringen. Ebenso kunstvoll versteht er das Verhüllen, die Verunklärung zu instrumentieren. Im Gegensatz zu den Künstlern des 19. Jahrhunderts, die sich von der besten Wetterlage abhängig machten, schlägt Salzmann ästhetisches Kapital aus den Eintrübungen der Atmosphäre. Wolken, Nebel und Dunst, aber auch Rauch und Industriedämpfe werden eingesetzt; allerdings nicht so sehr als Stimmungsträger im herkömmlichen Sinn, schlagen sie doch optisch vielmehr die Brücke zu einem abstrakten Bildbegriff und etablieren damit eine neue Vorstellungsebene im Landschaftsbild. Das gilt auch für die Wasseroberflächen, die einerseits ein eigenständiges Leben aufweisen, andererseits ein mehr oder weniger verzerrtes Abbild zeigen. Man kann sie als interessant strukturierte Flächen sehen, ebenso viel tragen sie aber auch zur Erweiterung des Bildraumes bei.

L'antinomie habituelle entre ville et campagne ou le fait que l'urbanisation engloutit de plus en plus, et de plus en plus vite, de beaux paysages n'interviennent nullement dans la décision que Gottfried Salzmann a prise au milieu des années 1980 : là, il s'éloigne des paysages naturels pour se tourner vers les paysages urbains, de préférence même ceux des gigantesques mégalopoles.

Salzmann est d'abord et avant tout un conquistador des dimensions spatiales, un explorateur des hauteurs et de l'infini. Ce qui restreint la perception et la réduit à un point, il l'annihile. Tout devient transparent, même les corps compacts semblent aisément transpercés par les vibrations de la lumière. Et c'est avec autant d'adresse qu'il parvient à instrumentaliser la dissimulation, la déformation. Contrairement aux artistes du XIXe siècle, qui se rendaient tributaires des meilleures conditions climatiques qui fussent, Salzmann met son capital esthétique dans les perturbations atmosphériques. Nuages, brumes et brouillard ont toute leur place ici, au même titre d'ailleurs que les fumées industrielles ; non pas cependant pour créer de l'ambiance, au sens habituel, mais pour établir un lien optique avec l'abstraction artistique et définir un nouveau plan de représentation dans le paysage. Cela vaut aussi pour les surfaces de l'eau qui, d'une part, révèlent leur vie autonome, mais d'autre part reproduisent une image plus ou moins distordue. Elles peuvent être vues comme des plans habilement structurés, qui contribuent en même temps à élargir l'espace pictural.

    Tagtägliches (detail | Detail | détail)   1982, 84,1 x 59,3 cm

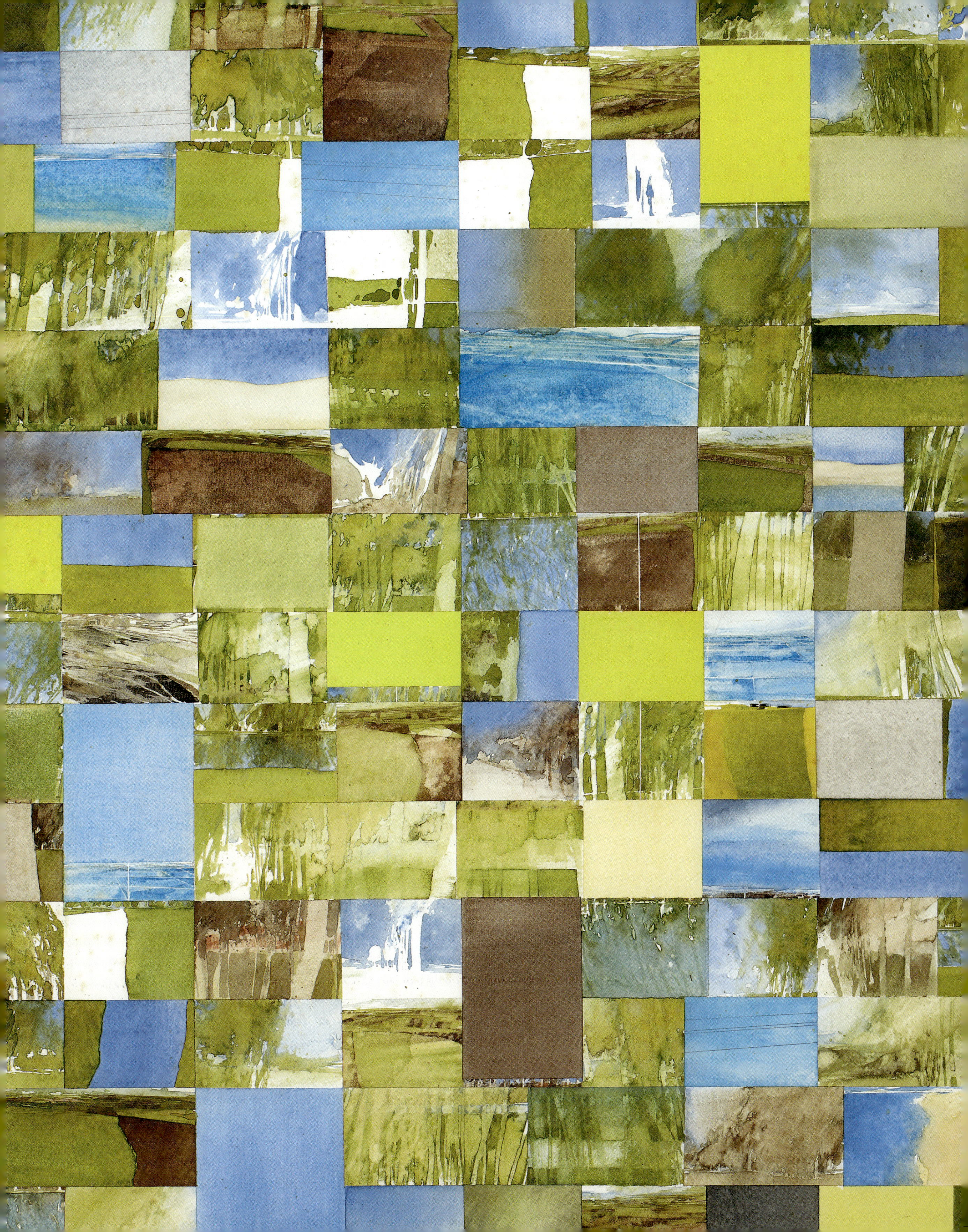

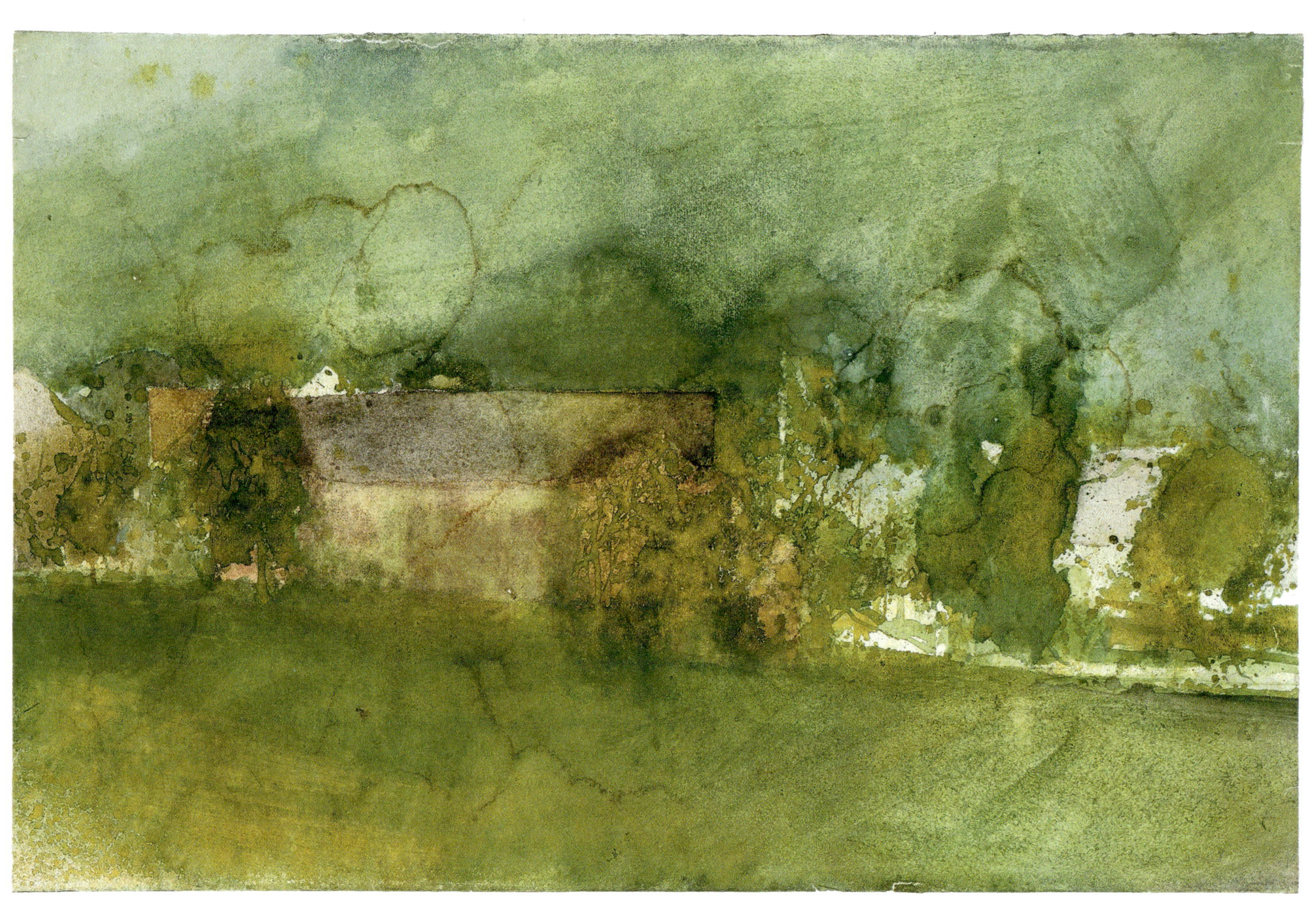

   Saint-Palais   1972, 32,3 × 47,6 cm

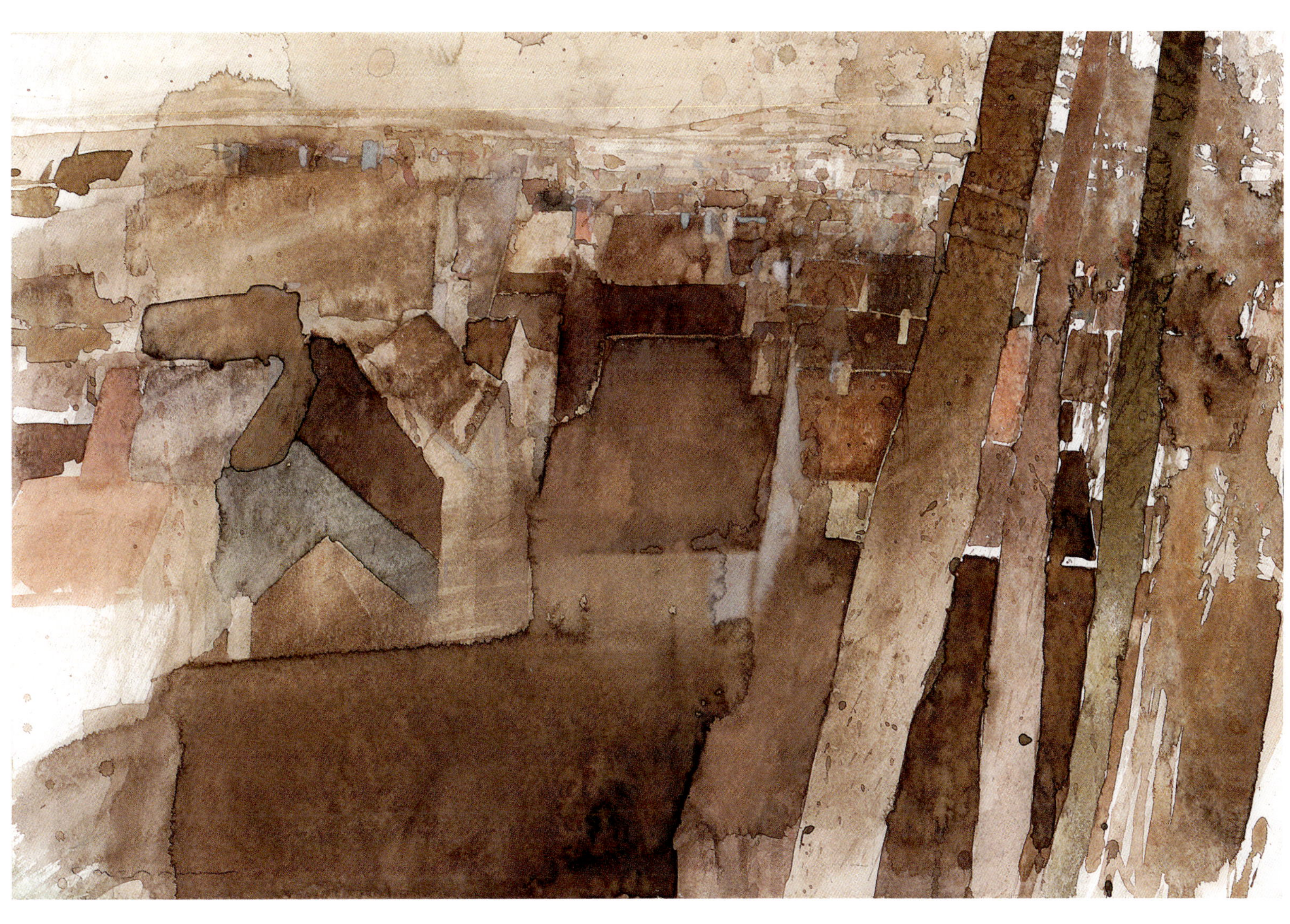

Le Brun des Toits   1977, 33 × 48 cm

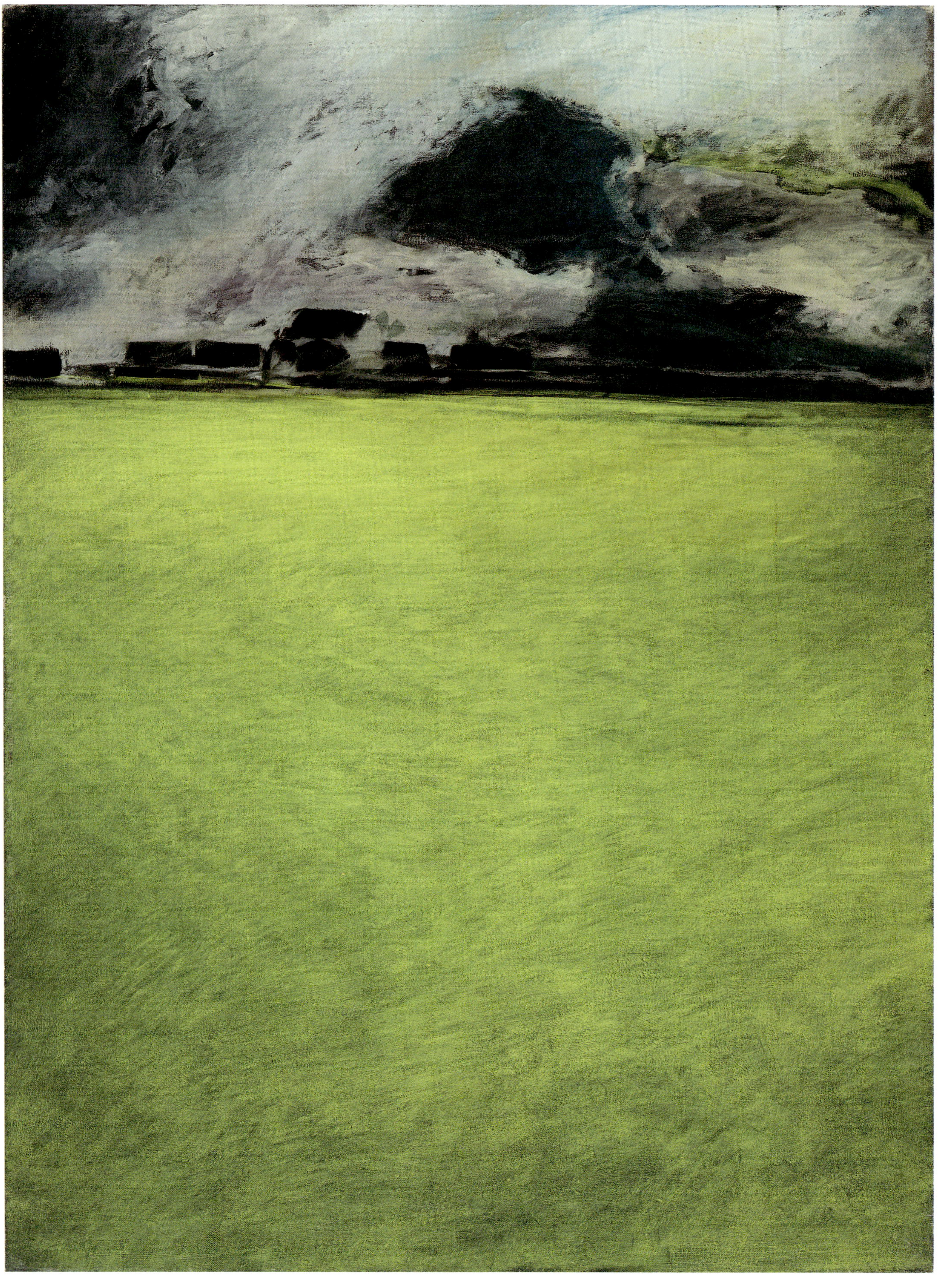

 Landscape with Railroad | Landschaft mit Eisenbahn | Paysage avec voie ferrée   ca. | ca. | vers 1972, 100 × 73 cm

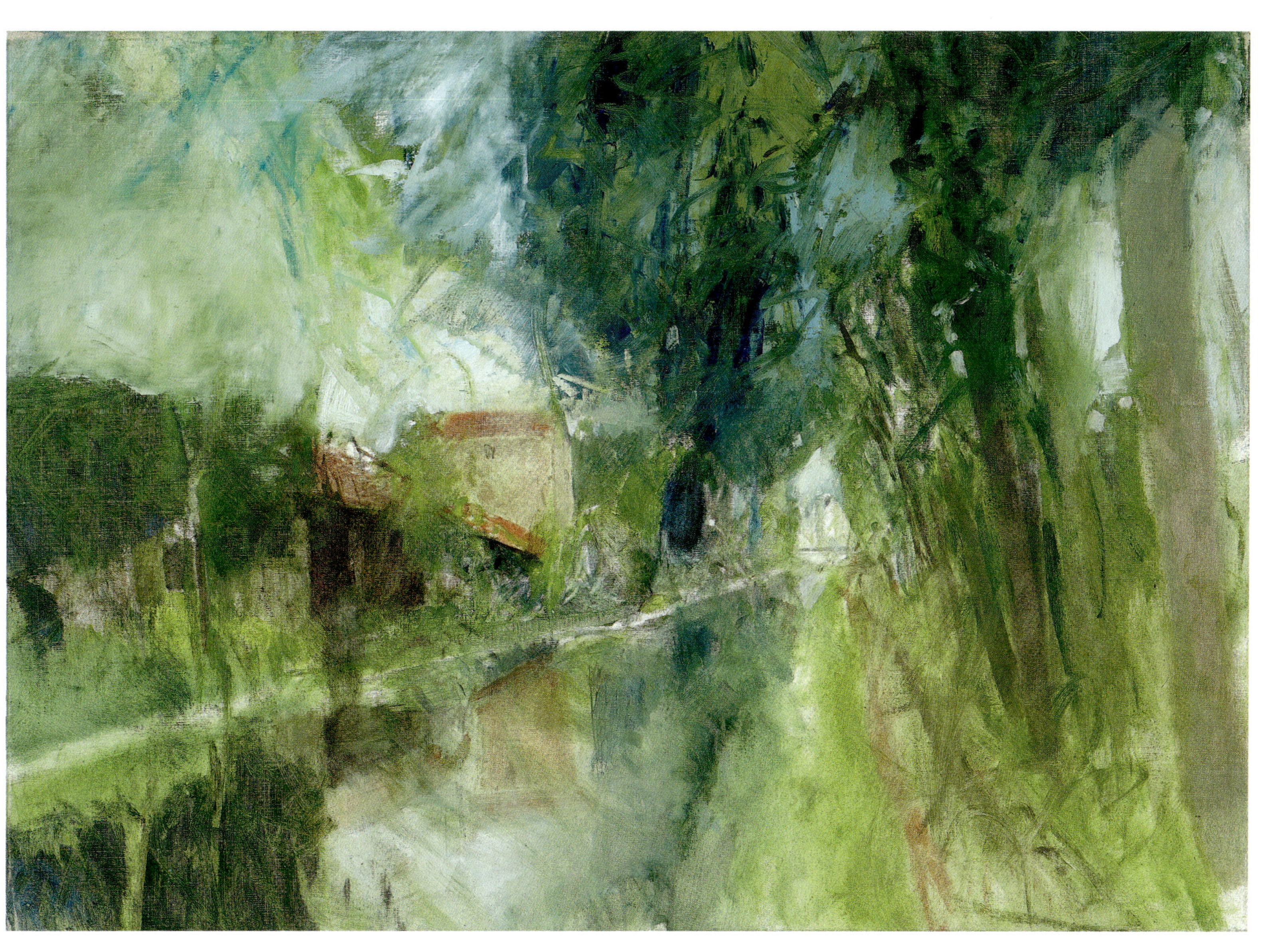

Canal d'Auron   ca. | ca. | vers 1970, 54 × 72,5 cm

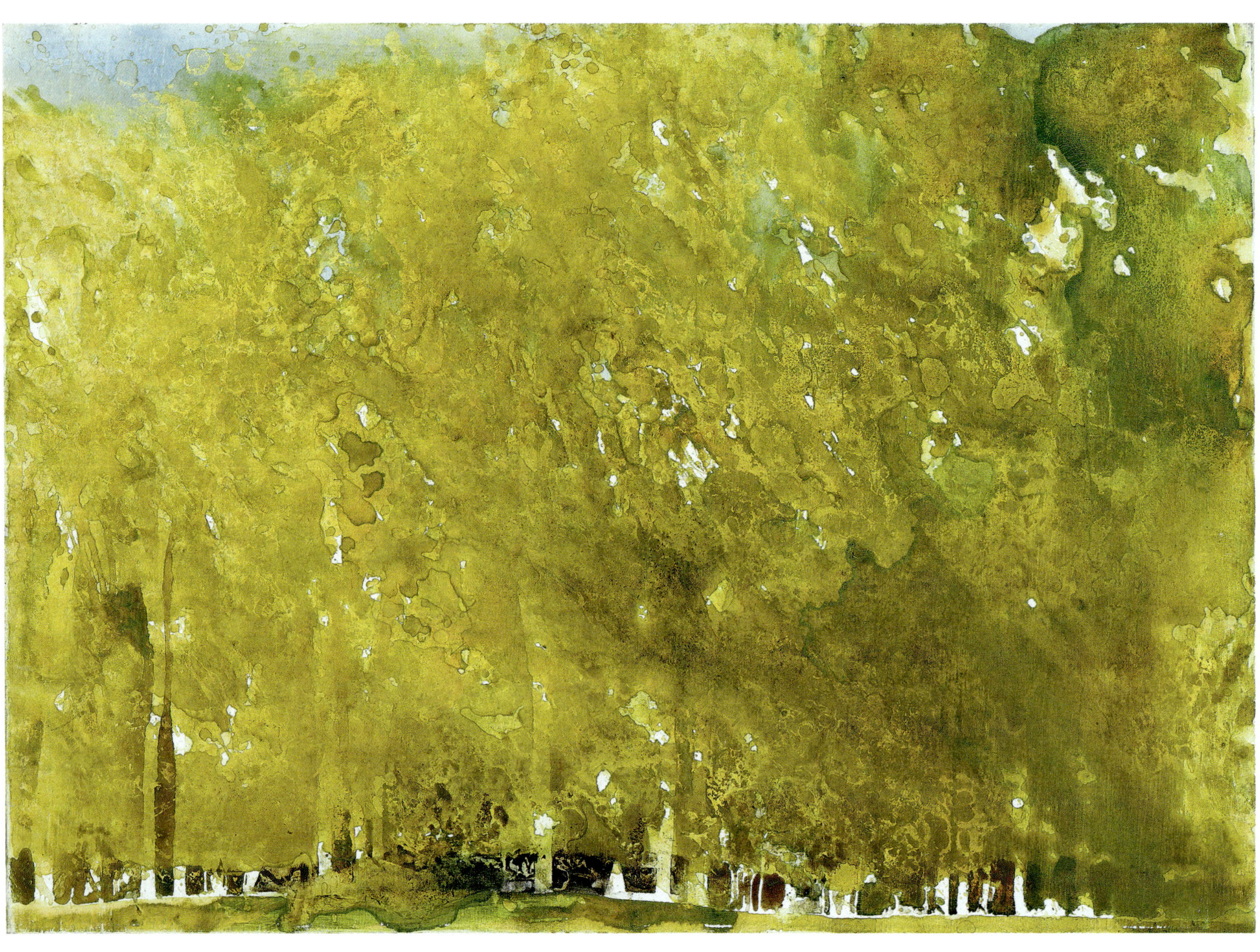

48   Curtain of Trees | Baumvorhang | Rideau d'arbres   ca. | ca. | vers 1980, 54 × 73,5 cm

Les Abbés   1972, 30 x 47 cm

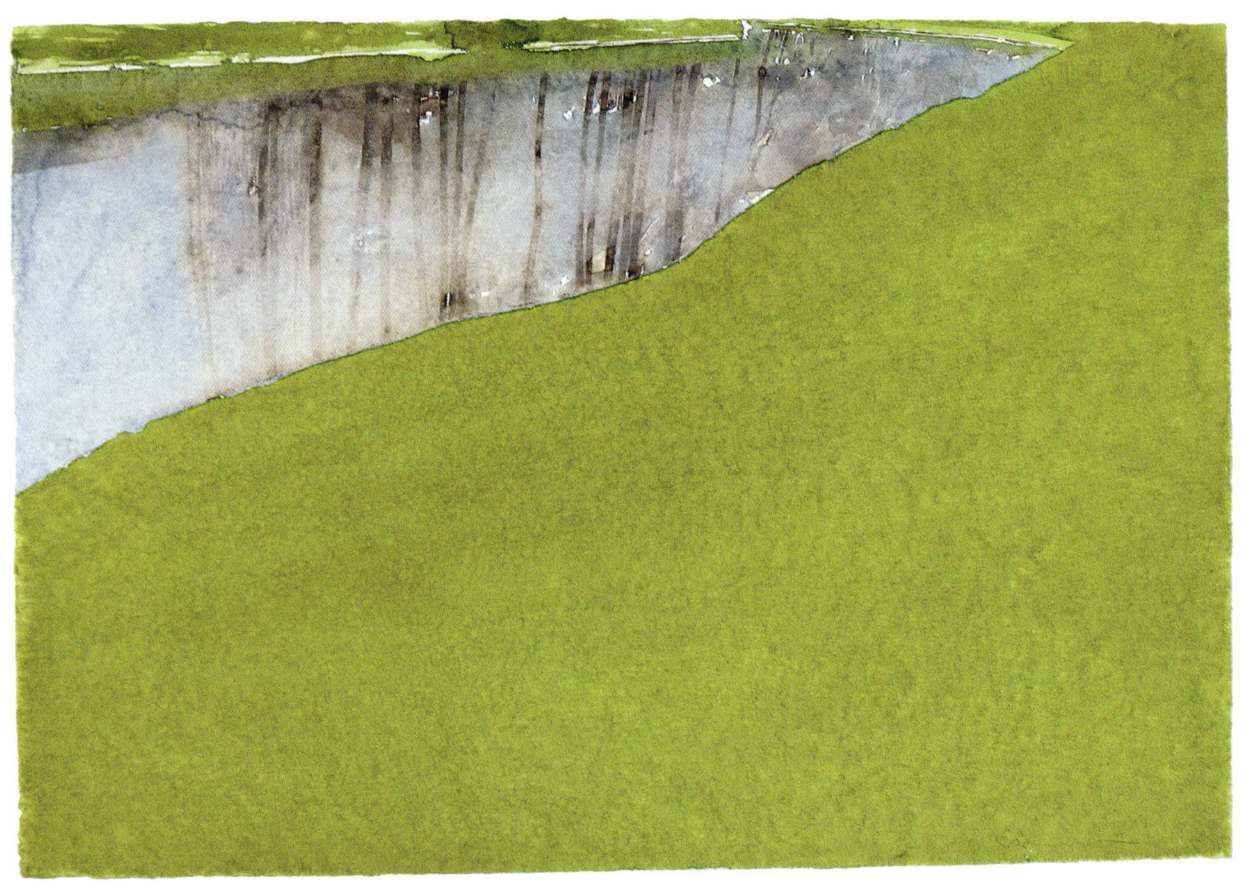

Triangular Reflection | Dreieckspiegelung | Reflet triangulaire   1980, 35 × 49,8 cm

  Hedge II | Hecke II | Haie II   1974, 32,7 × 48 cm

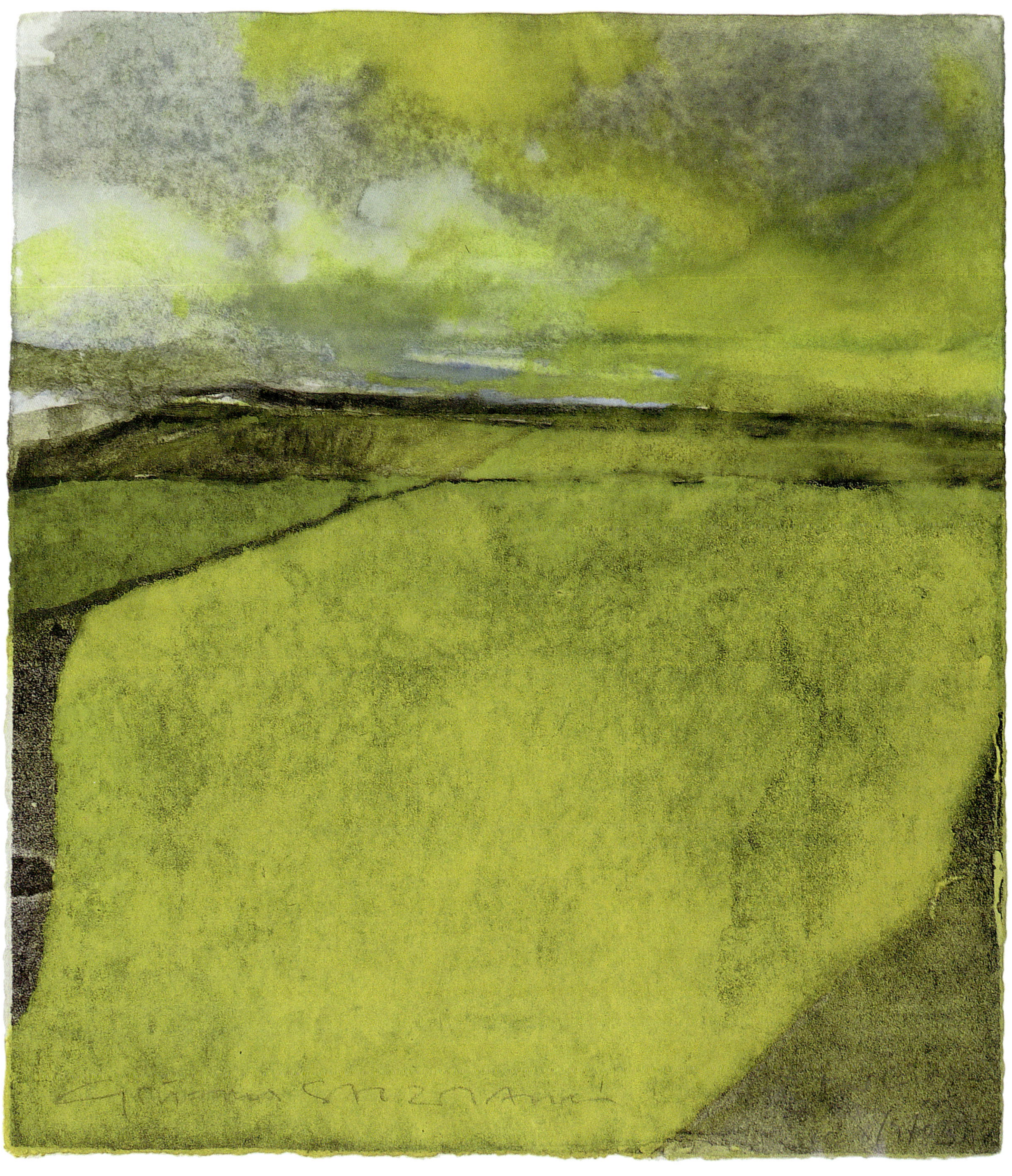

Saint-Martin d'Auxigny   1972, 22,2 × 19,1 cm

   Évecquemont   1971, 30,8 × 50 cm

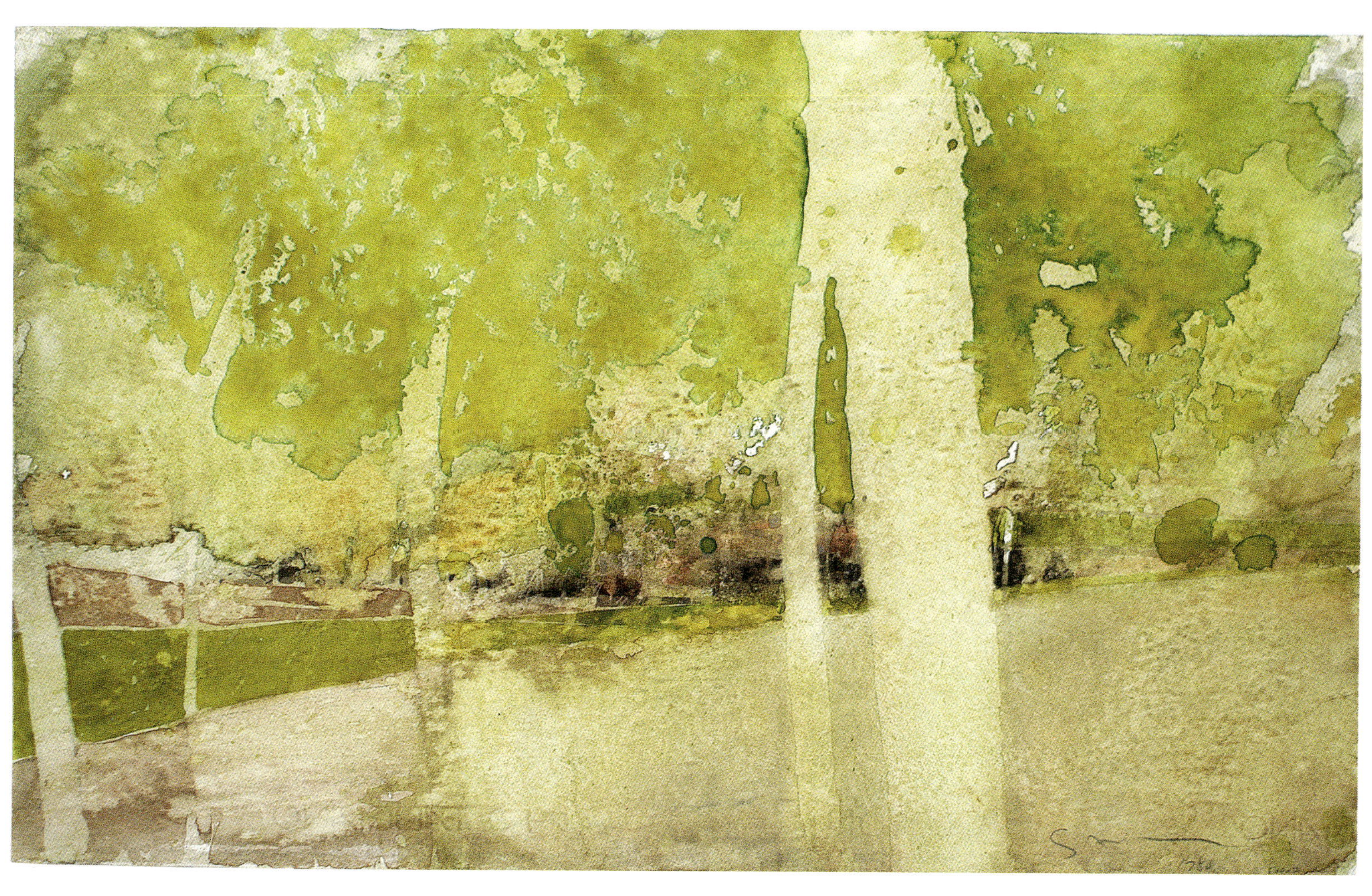

Near Orgeval | Bei Orgeval | Près d'Orgeval   1972, 31 × 50 cm

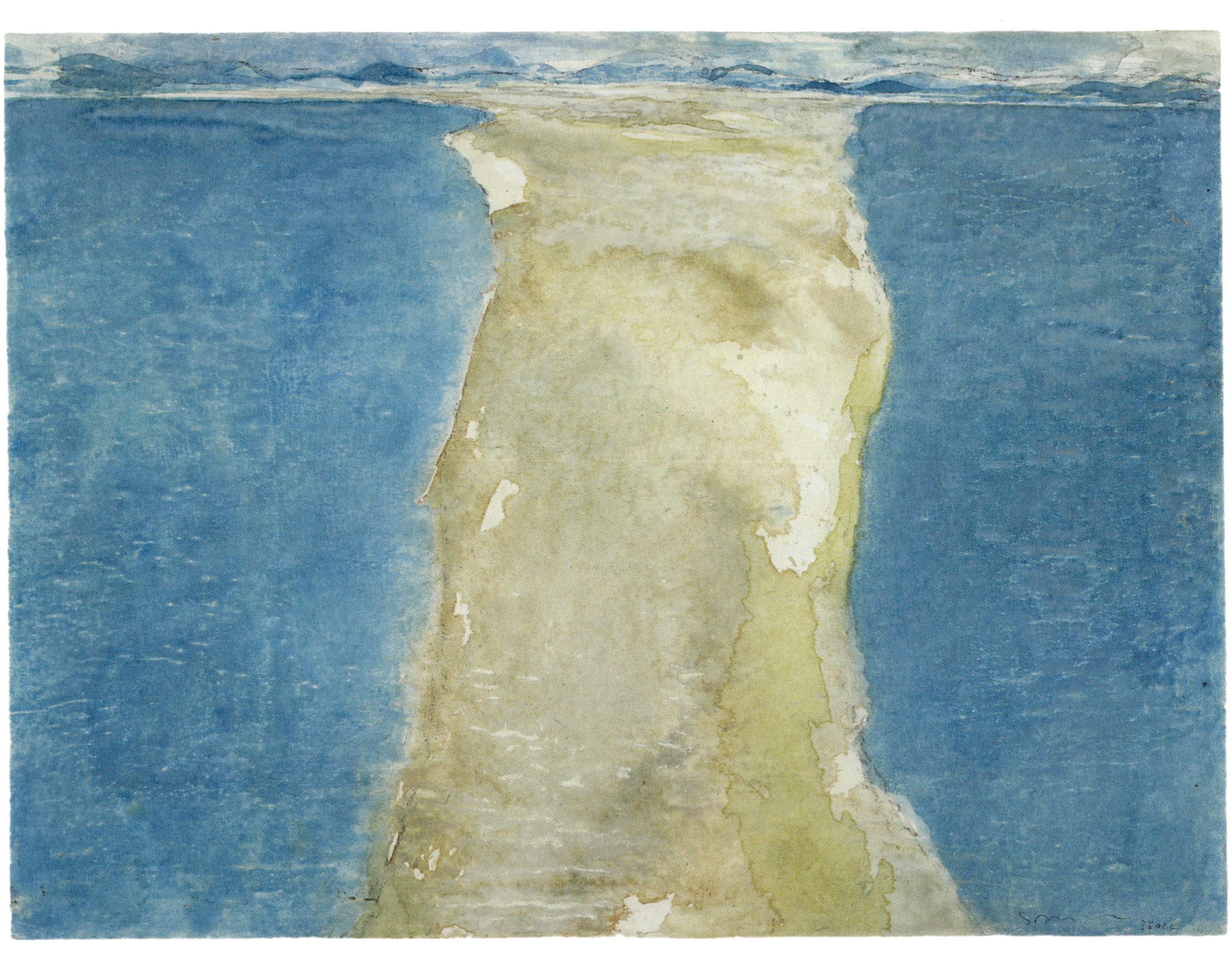

  Las Illetas   1980, 37,5 × 49,8 cm

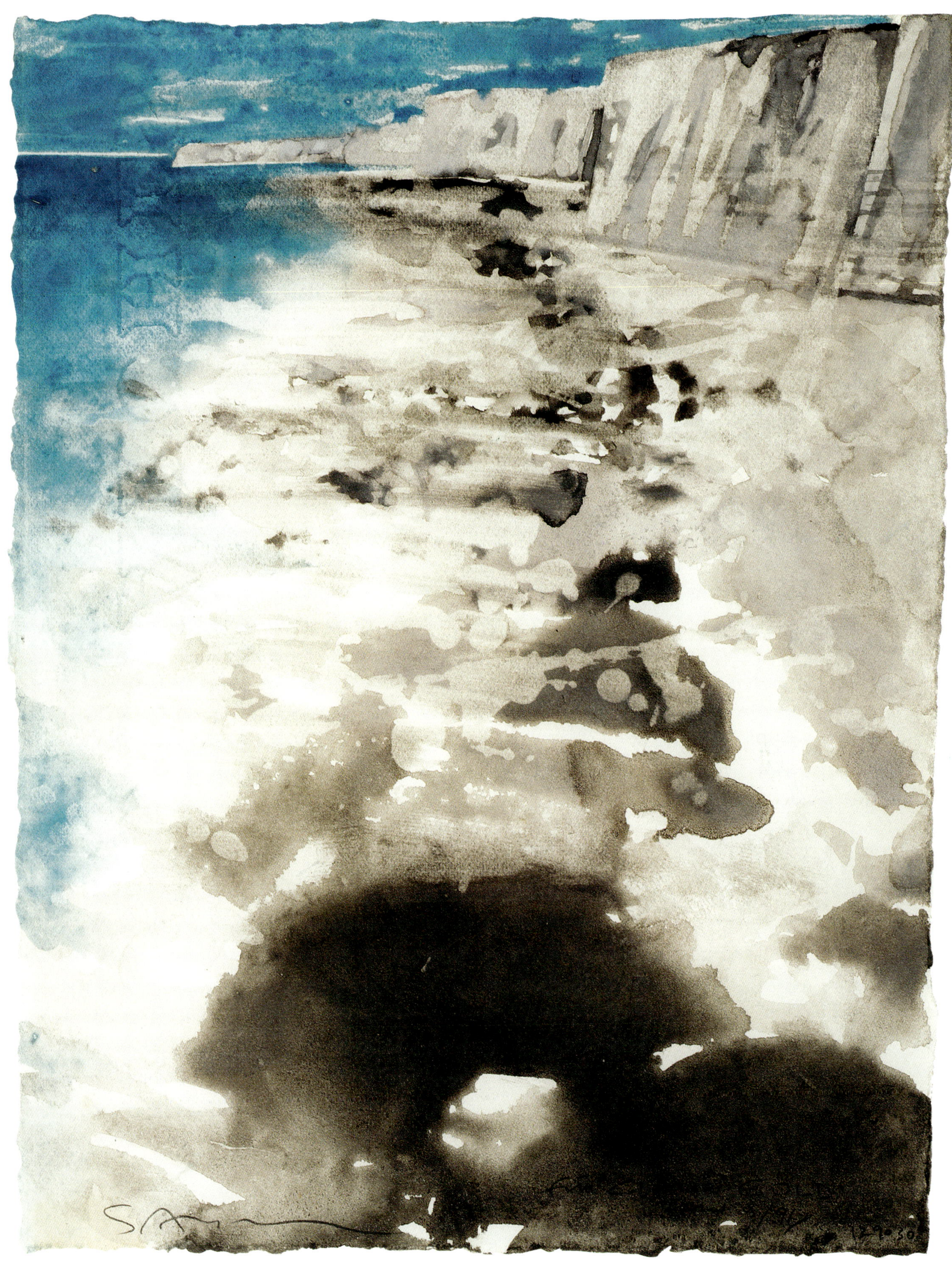

Seacoast Cliffs | Steilküste am Meer | Falaise du littoral   1990, 19 × 15 cm

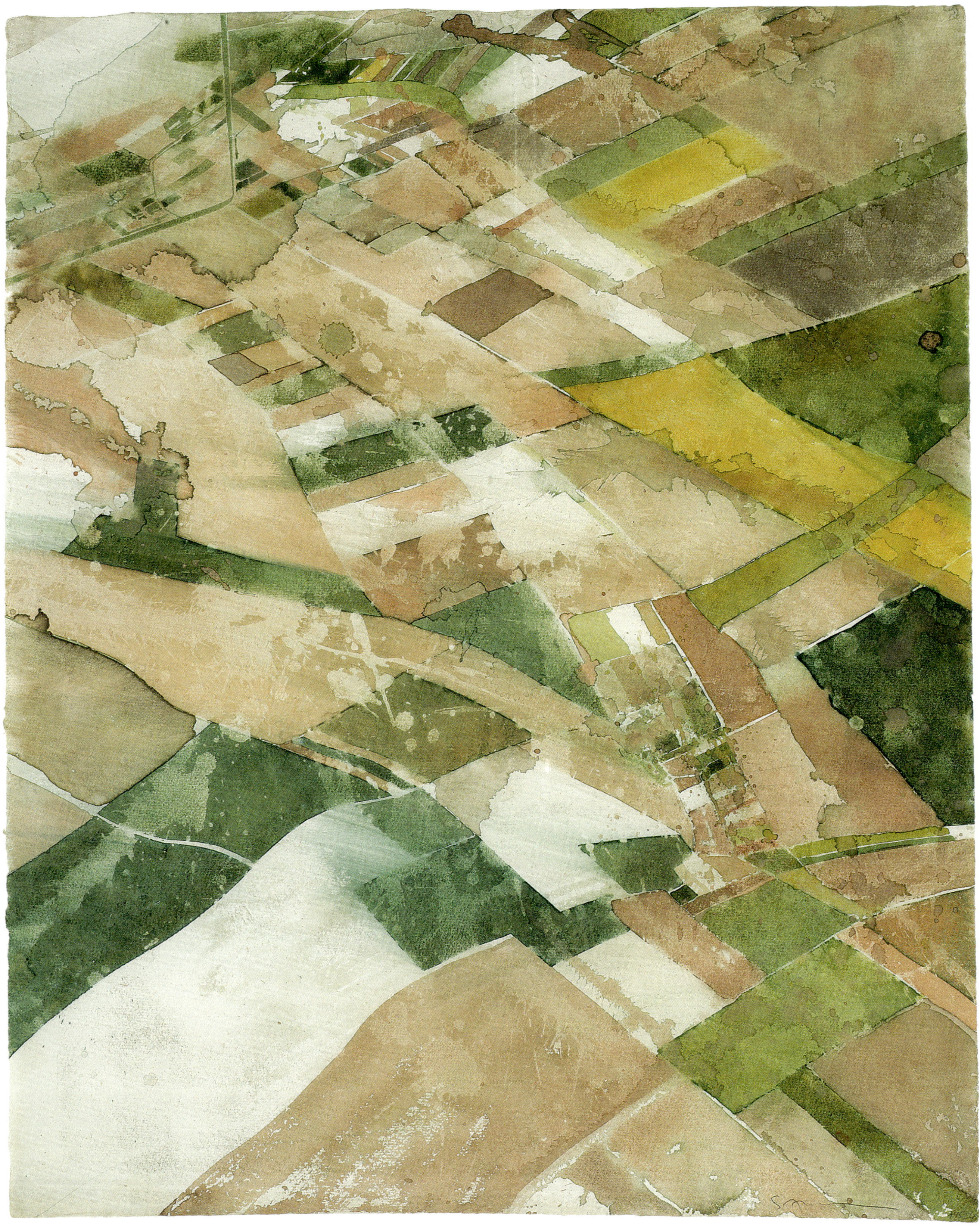

Carpet of Fields | Felderteppich | Le tapis des champs   1995, 57,2 × 45,5 cm

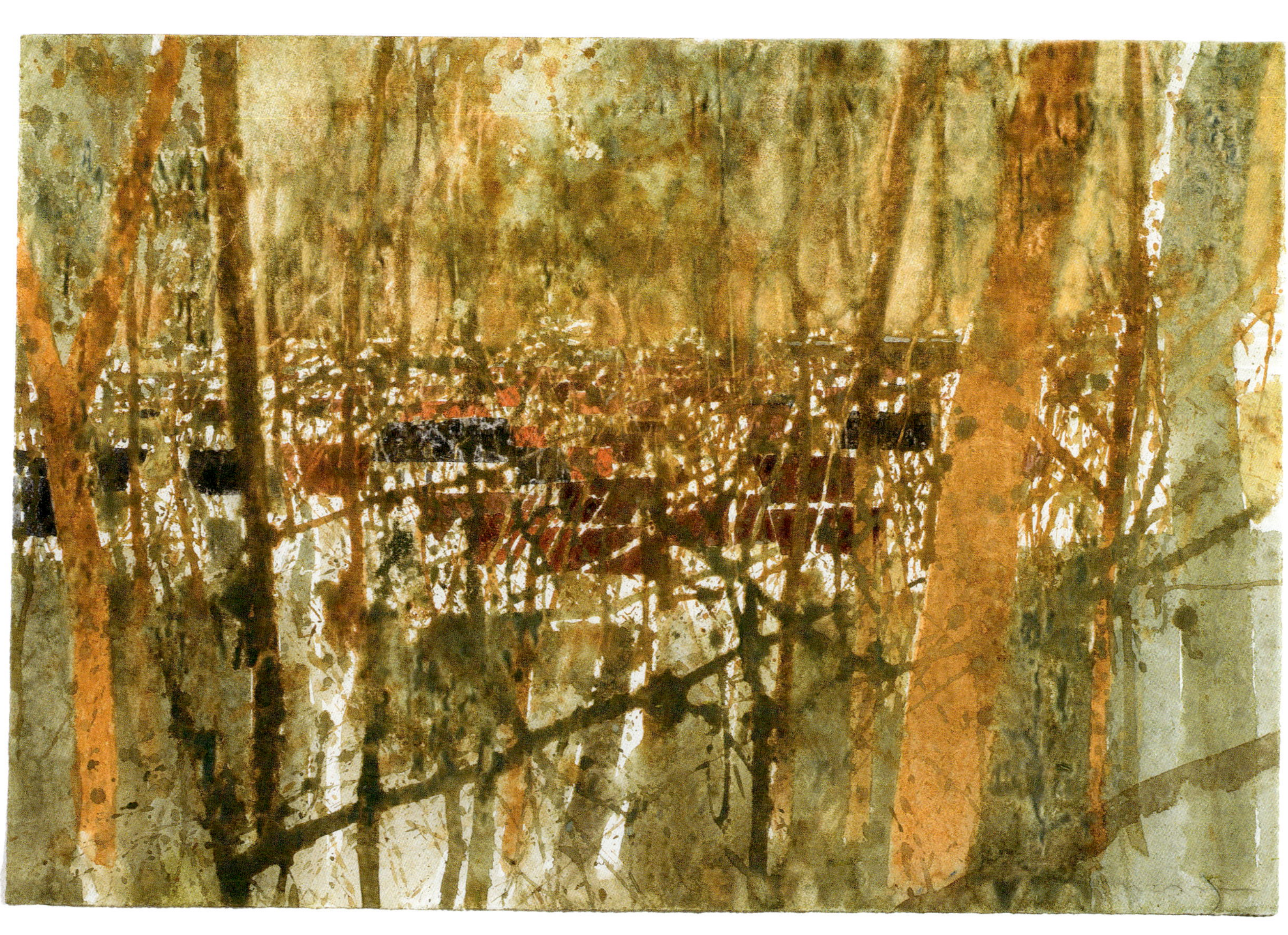

Rooftop Landscape | Dachlandschaft | Paysage de toits   1975, 33,3 × 47,7 cm

Reflections
Spiegelungen
Reflets

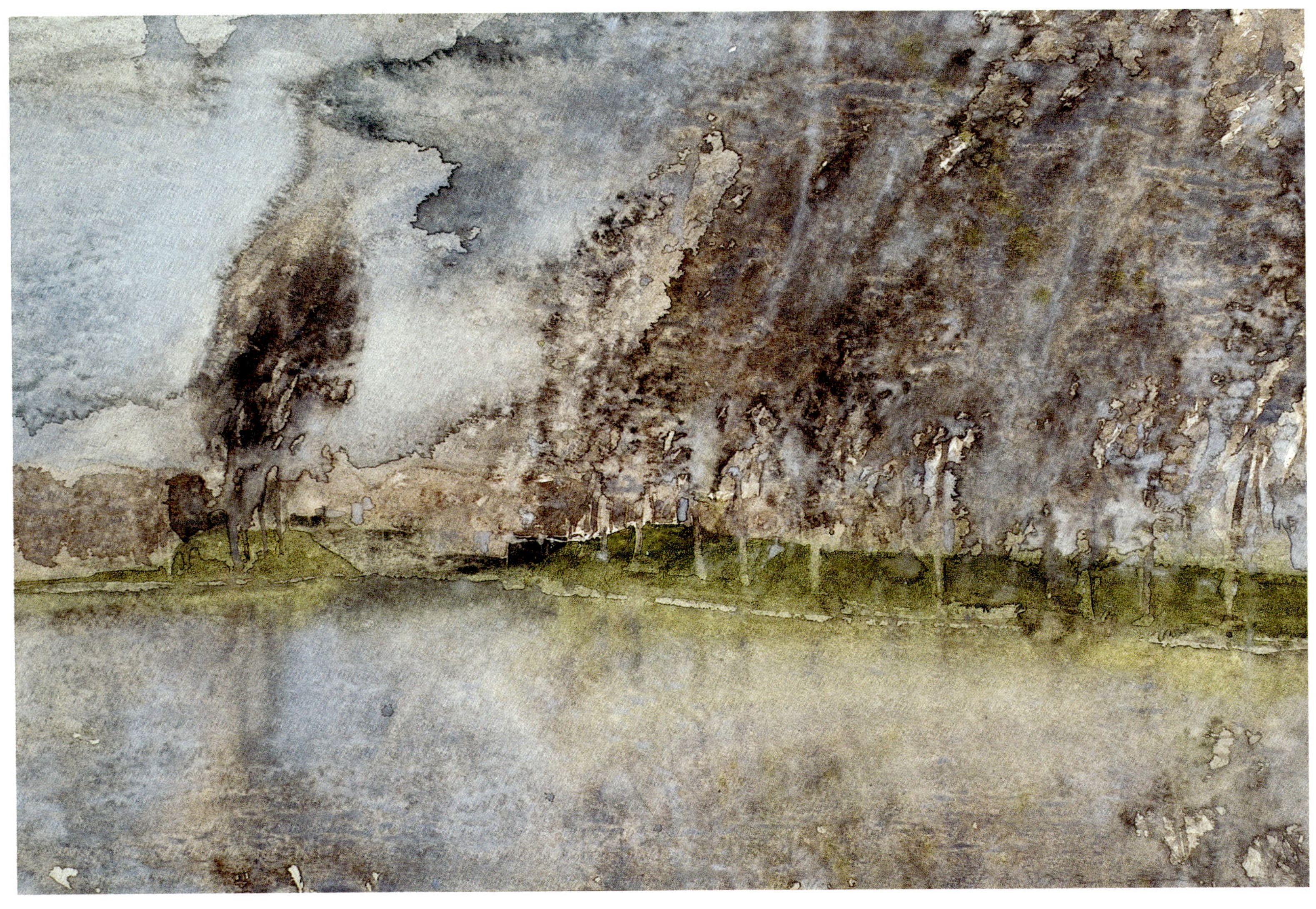

    Troncos Morado   1972, 38,4 × 58,4 cm

Reflections of Boats in Dieppe | Bootspiegelung in Dieppe | Reflets de bateaux à Dieppe   1985, 23 × 15 cm

Clouds, fog

Nuages, brouillard

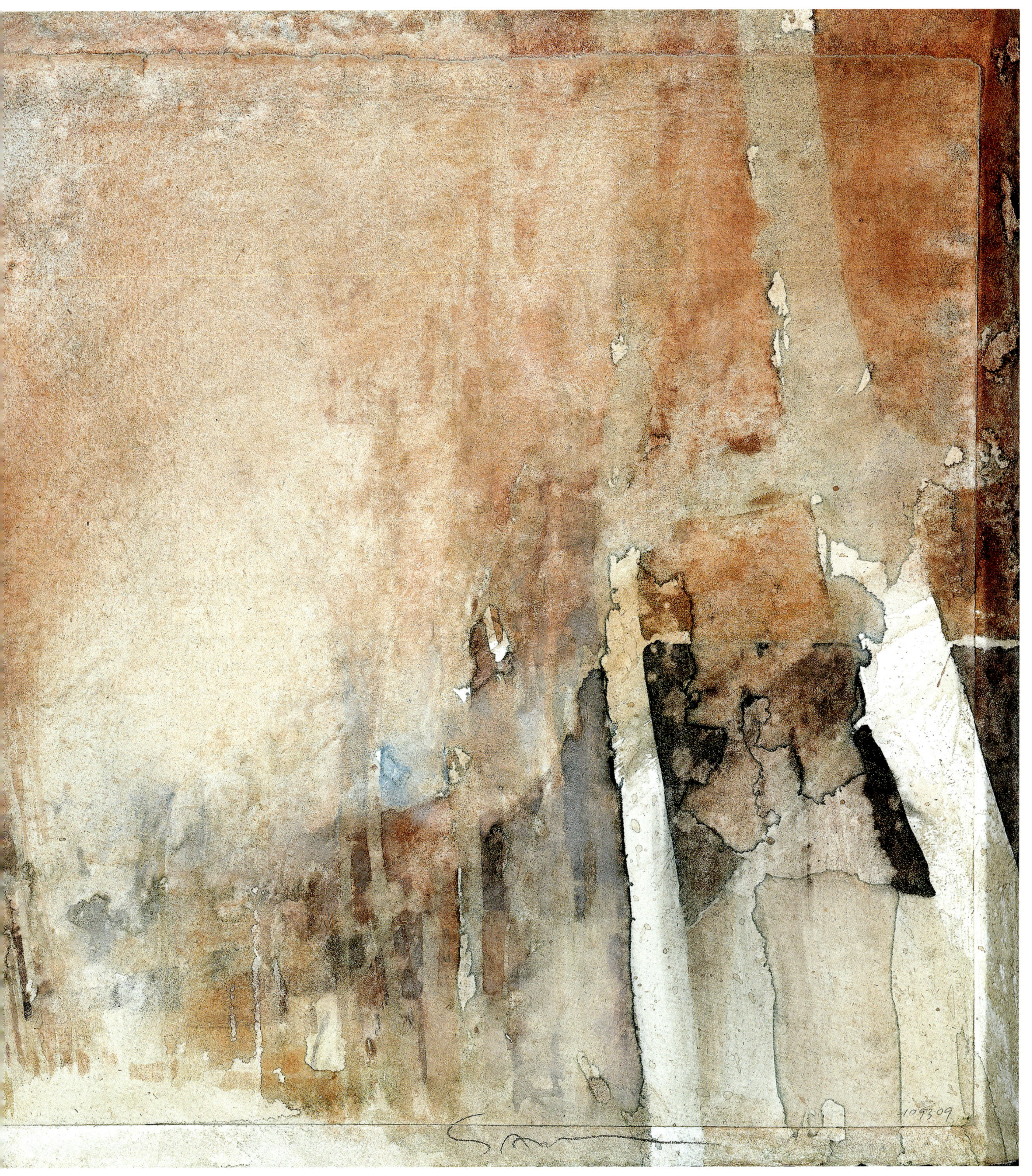

Brouillard IV   1982, 26,2 × 37,3 cm

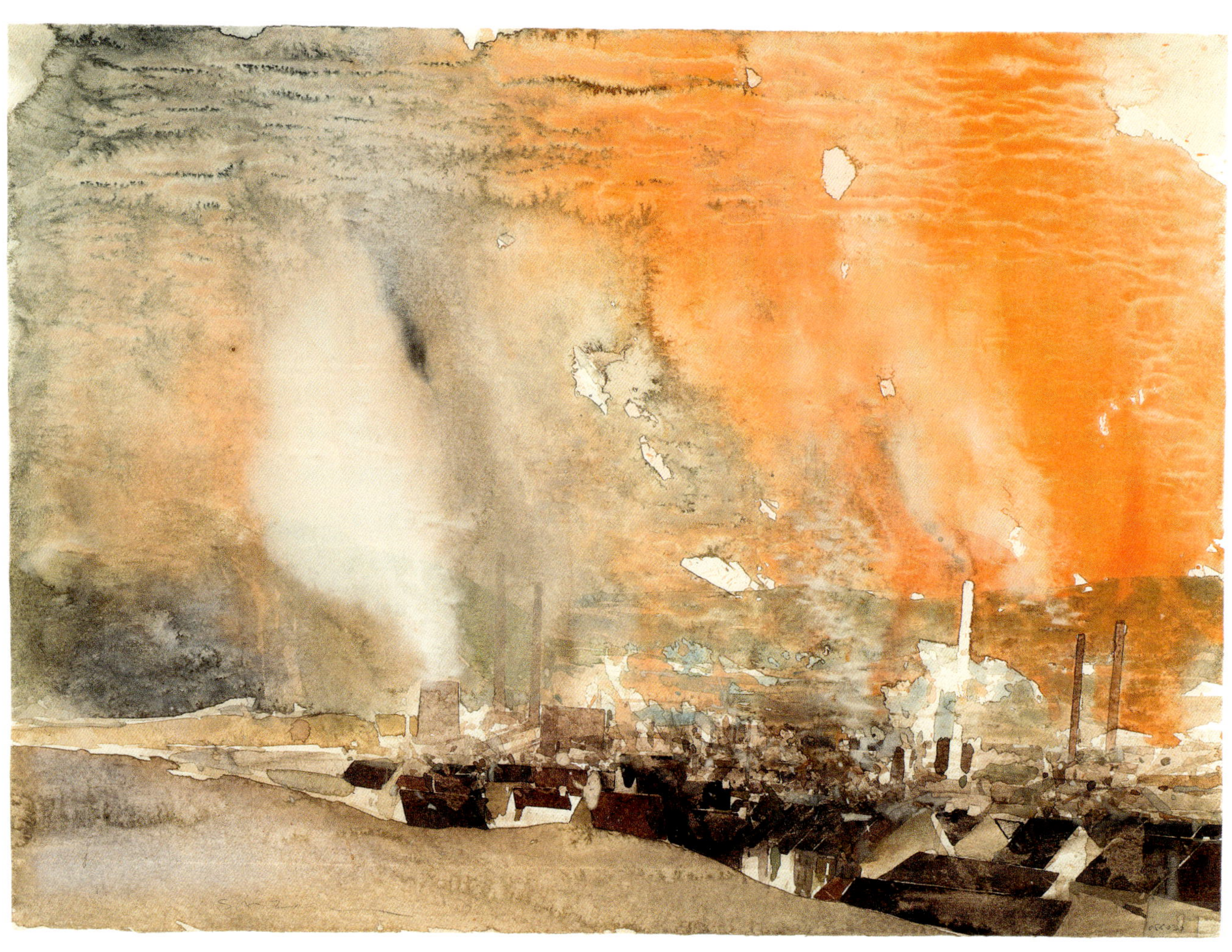

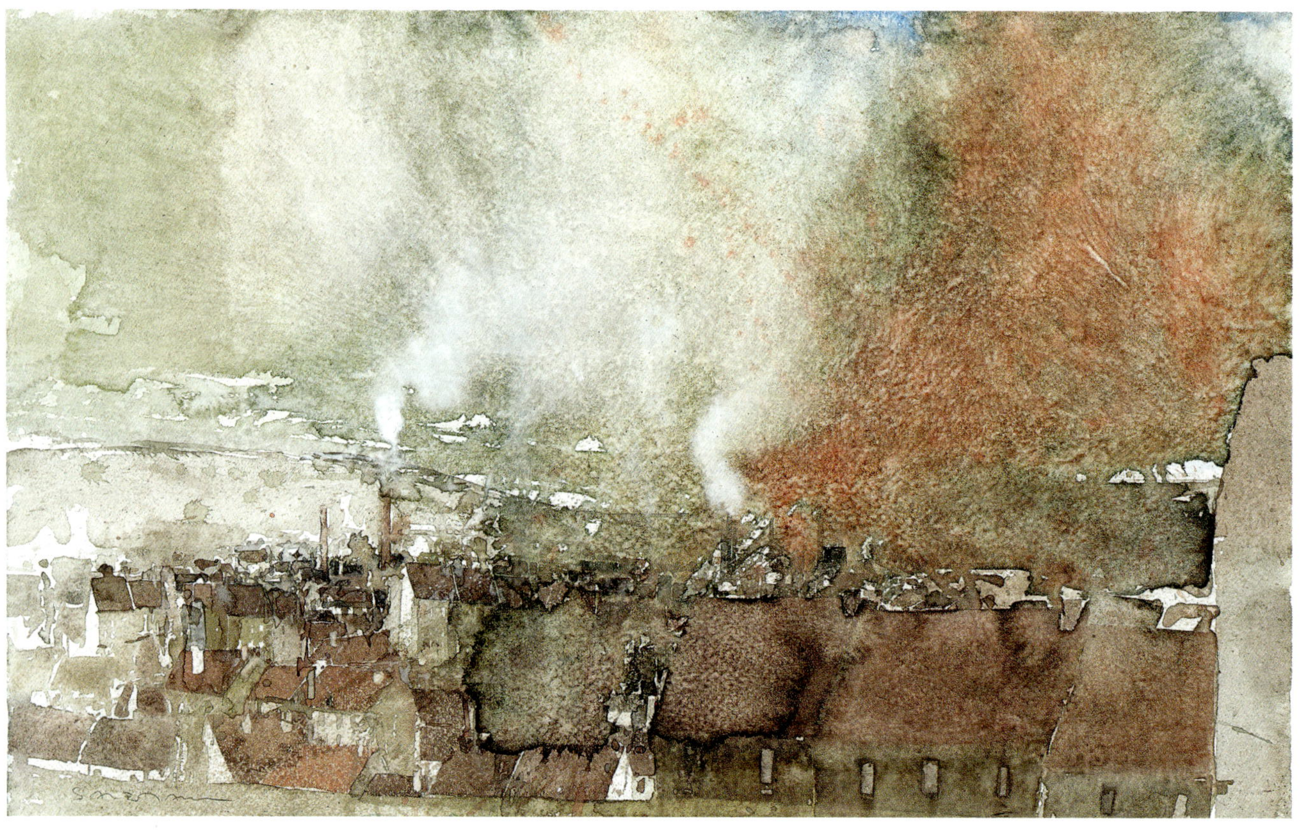

Longwy   1980, 37,5 × 49,7 cm
Carling   1979, 30,7 × 48,2 cm

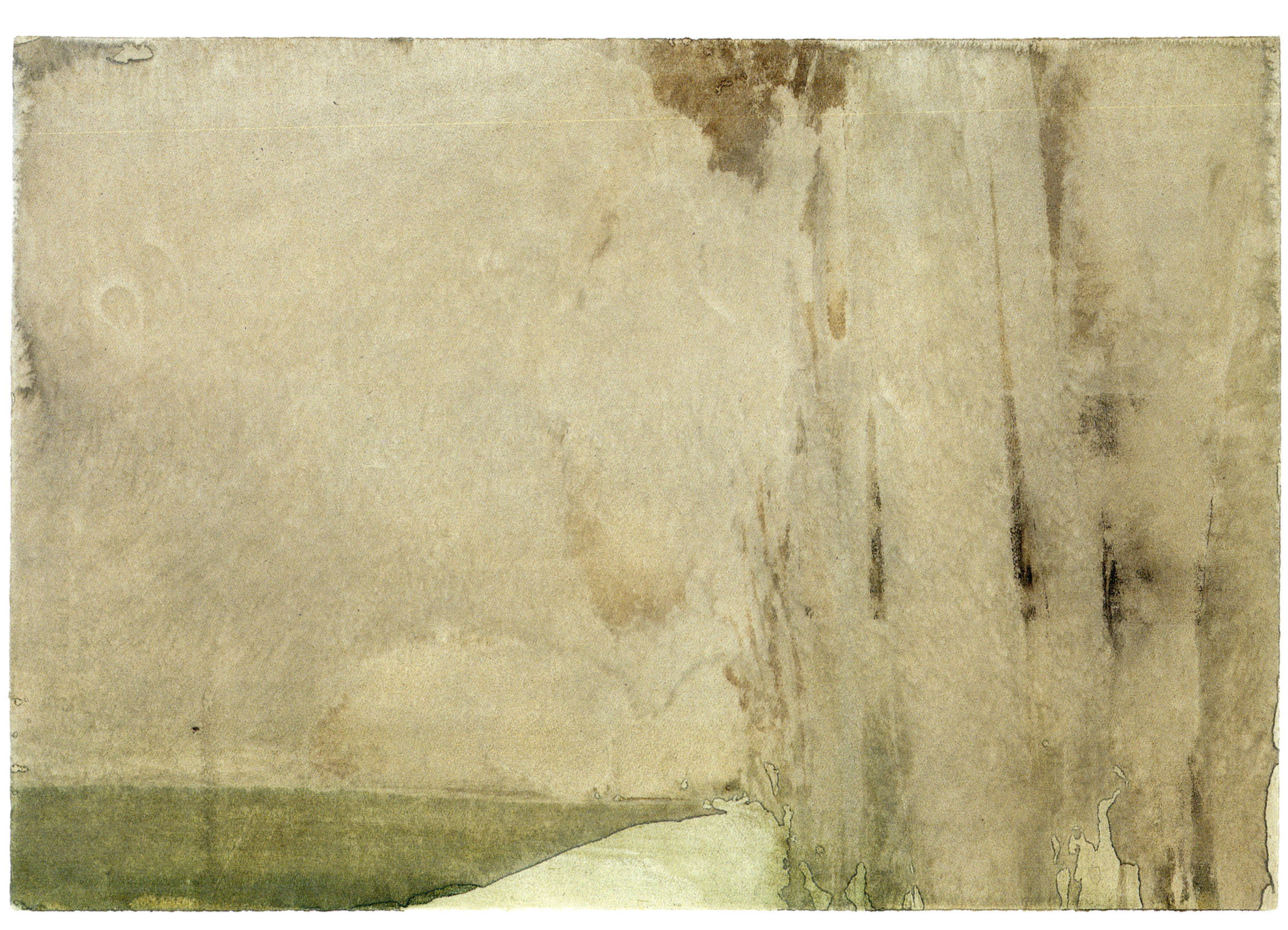

Brouillard III   1982, 35 × 50,2 cm

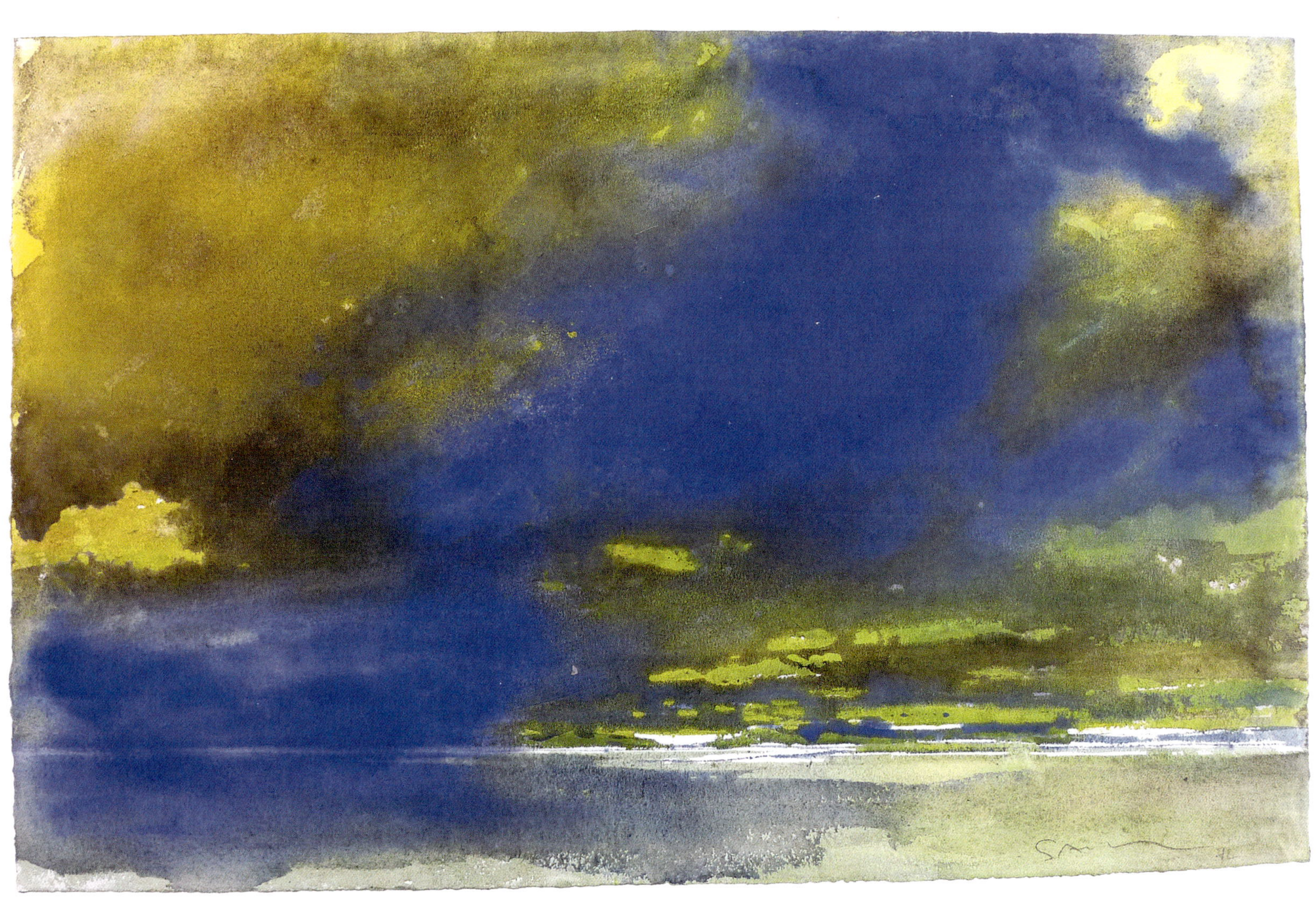

64   Golden Blue | *Goldblau* | *Bleu or*   1972, 38,4 × 58,4 cm

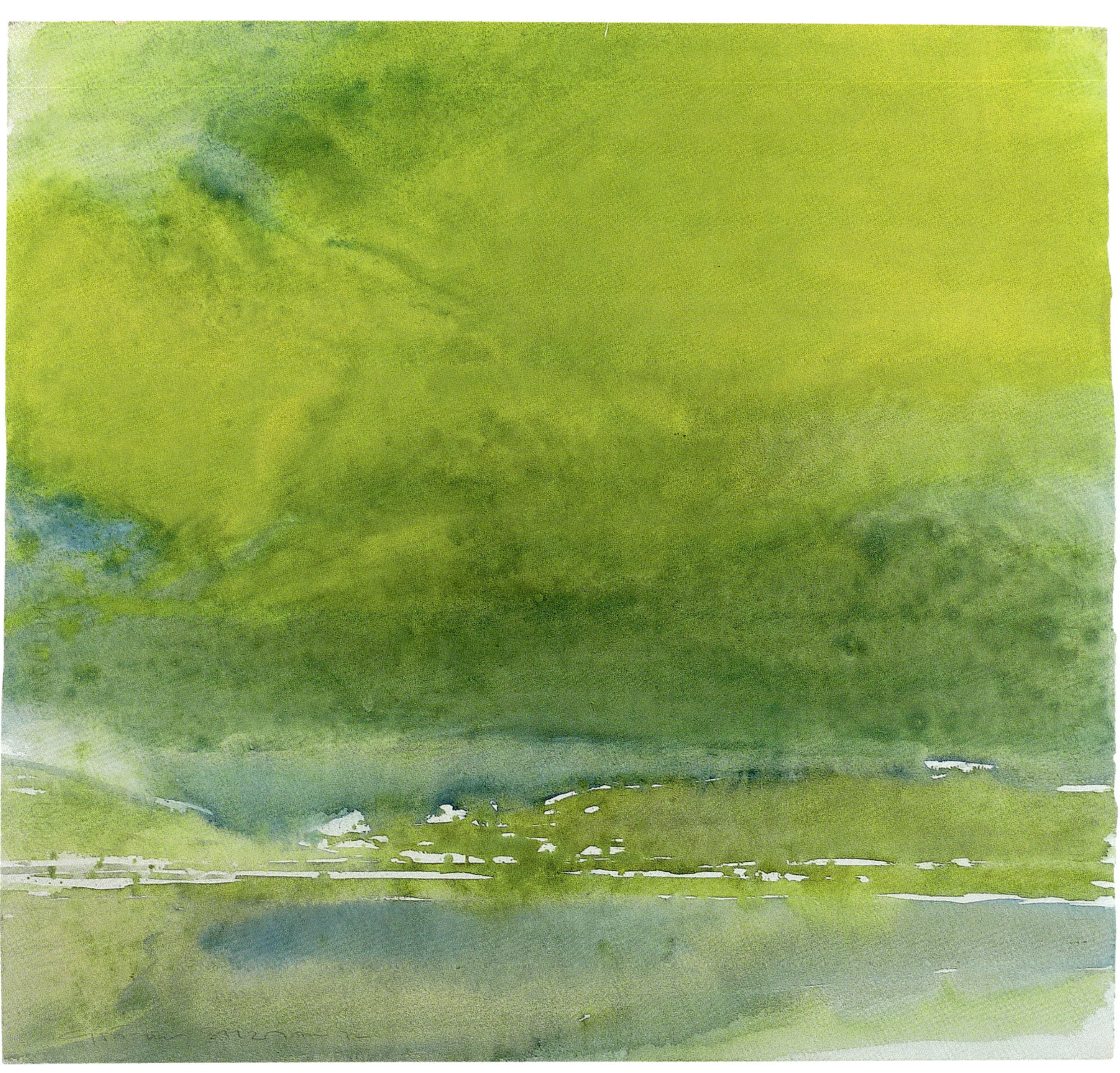

Cities
Städte
Villes

New York, San Francisco, Berlin, Hamburg, Salzburg, Vienna

New York, San Francisco, Berlin, Hamburg, Salzburg, Wien

New York, San Francisco, Berlin, Hambourg, Salzbourg, Vienne

After having measured out the countryside on the horizontal plane and at ground level in accordance with all of the rules of his art, Salzmann's encounter with the high-rise metropolis of New York led to a radical, steeply upward-oriented change of direction. From that point on, his beloved bird's-eye view, which found a welcome sphere of activity in the richly structured rooftop landscapes of the Old World, knew no bounds. While atmospheric phenomena play only a secondary role in the urban context, they offer plenty of new avenues of approach, all of which have in common the use of aesthetic interventions to transform the banal into events of significance. Salzmann developed an interest in billboards in Paris, particularly those from which the poster paper hung in strips and scraps. Today, he collects these fragments more often than ever before, often transporting them over great distances to his studio, where he combines them on the basis of new ideas. These re-collages open up new perspectives for the eye, perspectives an intact poster would never have brought to mind. The pictorial field unfolds like a rugged, fissured landscape, forming gorges, craters, and plains. The viewer is at once very close to and very far from everyday events.

In his wall pictures, Salzmann works as a "tracker" who transposes older and more recent layers of graffiti into his format, thereby imbuing them with something of the aura of mysterious hieroglyphs. His penchant for reflections also finds abundant nourishment in megacities, where many buildings are constructed with smooth, reflective materials. In these works, the rug is pulled rather abruptly from beneath the feet of conventional habits of perception.

Nachdem er die Lande in horizontaler Richtung und in Bodennähe nach allen Regeln seiner Kunst durchmessen hatte, führte Salzmanns Begegnung mit der Wolkenkratzer-Metropole New York zu einer einschneidenden, steil nach oben zeigenden Richtungswende. Seiner Vorliebe für die Vogelschau, die in den reich gegliederten Dachlandschaften der alten Welt ein dankbares Tätigkeitsfeld fand, waren jetzt keine Grenzen mehr gesetzt.

Die atmosphärischen Phänomene spielen im urbanen Kontext eine geringere Rolle, dafür bieten sich genügend neue Ansatzpunkte, denen gemeinsam ist, dass Banales durch ästhetische Eingriffe zum Ereignis wird. Bereits in Paris hatte sich Salzmann für Plakatwände zu interessieren begonnen, besonders für solche, von denen das Papier bereits in Fetzen herunterhing. Mehr denn je sammelt er heute diese Fragmente auf, transportiert sie oft über weite Distanzen ins Atelier und setzt sie nach neuen Gesichtspunkten zusammen. Diese Re-Collagen öffnen Perspektiven für das Auge, an die bei einem intakten Plakat nicht zu denken wäre. Wie eine zerklüftete Landschaft faltet sich die Bildfläche auseinander, bildet Schluchten, Krater und Ebenen. Der Betrachter befindet sich sehr nah und gleichzeitig sehr fern vom Geschehen des Alltags.

In den Mauerbildern betätigt sich Salzmann als „Spurensucher", der ältere und neuere Schichten von Graffiti in sein Format überträgt und ihnen damit etwas von der Aura geheimnisvoller Hieroglyphen verleiht. Auch sein Faible für Spiegelungen findet in den Millionenstädten reichlich Nahrung, da hier vorzugsweise mit glatten, reflektierenden Materialien gebaut wird. Der Wahrnehmung wird, auf ziemlich unsanfte Weise, quasi der Boden unter den Füßen weggezogen.

Une fois qu'il eut arpenté les terres à l'horizontale, près du sol et dans toutes les règles de son art, Salzmann découvrit New York, la métropole, les gratte-ciel. Un changement de direction décisif s'opère. Sa prédilection pour les vues plongeantes, qui avait trouvé un champ d'action idéal dans les paysages de toits de l'ancien monde, ne connaît désormais plus aucune limite.

Dans l'environnement urbain, les phénomènes atmosphériques jouent un rôle moindre, mais les nouveaux angles d'approche ne manquent pas et tous ont en commun de transformer la banalité en événement grâce à l'intervention artistique. À Paris, déjà, Salzmann avait commencé à s'intéresser aux murs jonchés d'affiches, surtout quand celles-ci étaient en lambeaux. Aujourd'hui, plus que jamais, il en collectionne des fragments qu'il transporte jusque dans son atelier, sans craindre les longues distances, et les réassemble ensuite selon des aspects différents. Ces re-collages offrent au regard des perspectives qu'une affiche intacte n'aurait jamais suggérées. Tels des paysages escarpés, la surface de l'image se flétrit, forme des ravines, des cratères, des plaines. Le spectateur se trouve à la fois très près et très loin des épisodes quotidiens.

Avec ses représentations de murs, Salzmann devient « archéologue » ; des strates de graffiti anciennes et plus récentes acquièrent un autre format, évoquant de mystérieux hiéroglyphes. De même, son penchant pour les reflets a dans la grande ville de quoi se nourrir en abondance, ne serait-ce qu'avec les matériaux de construction lisses et réfléchissants. C'est comme si, de façon presque gênante, la perception se mettait alors à tanguer.

New York, 8th Avenue (detail | Detail | détail)   2006, 50,6 x 75,8 cm

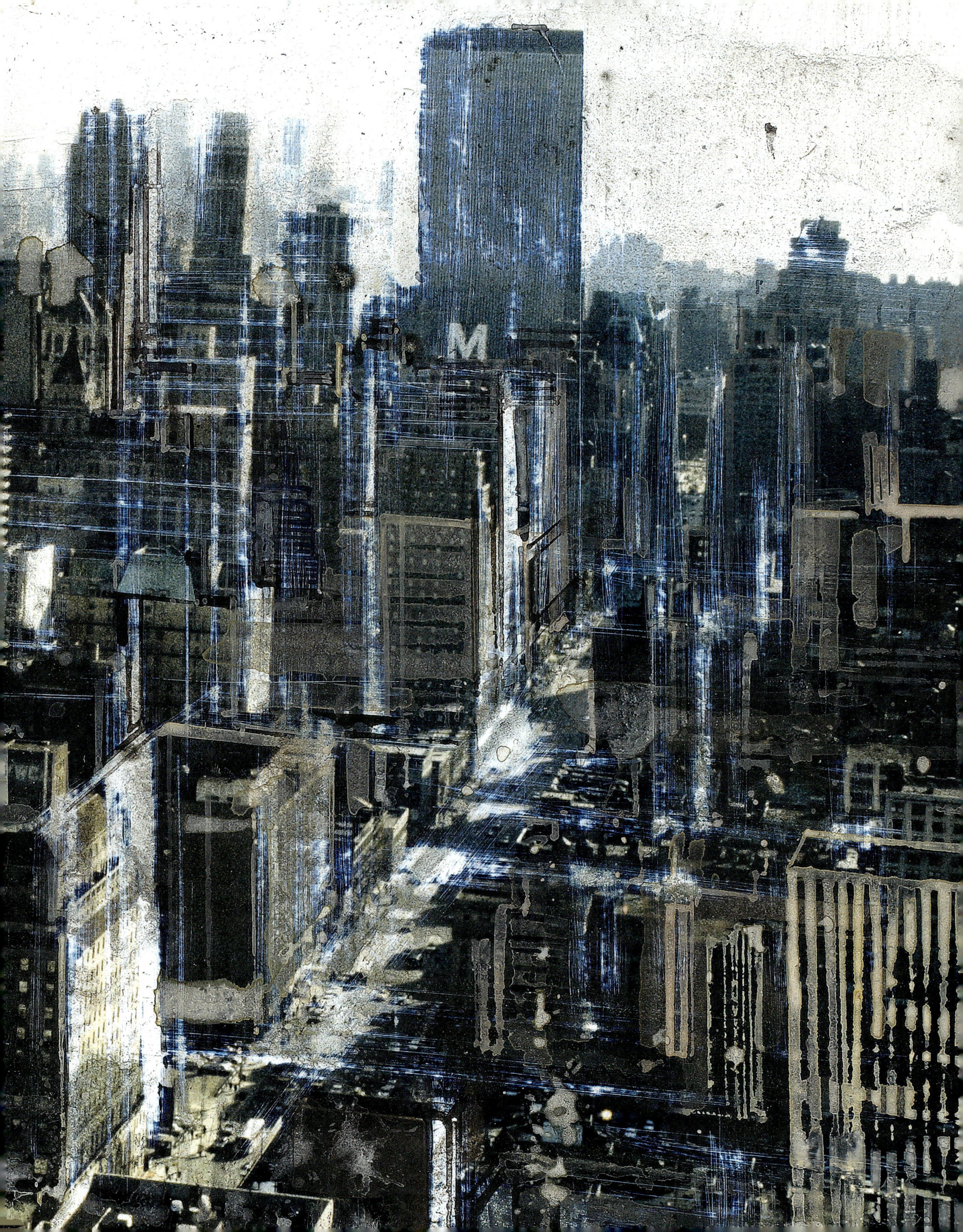

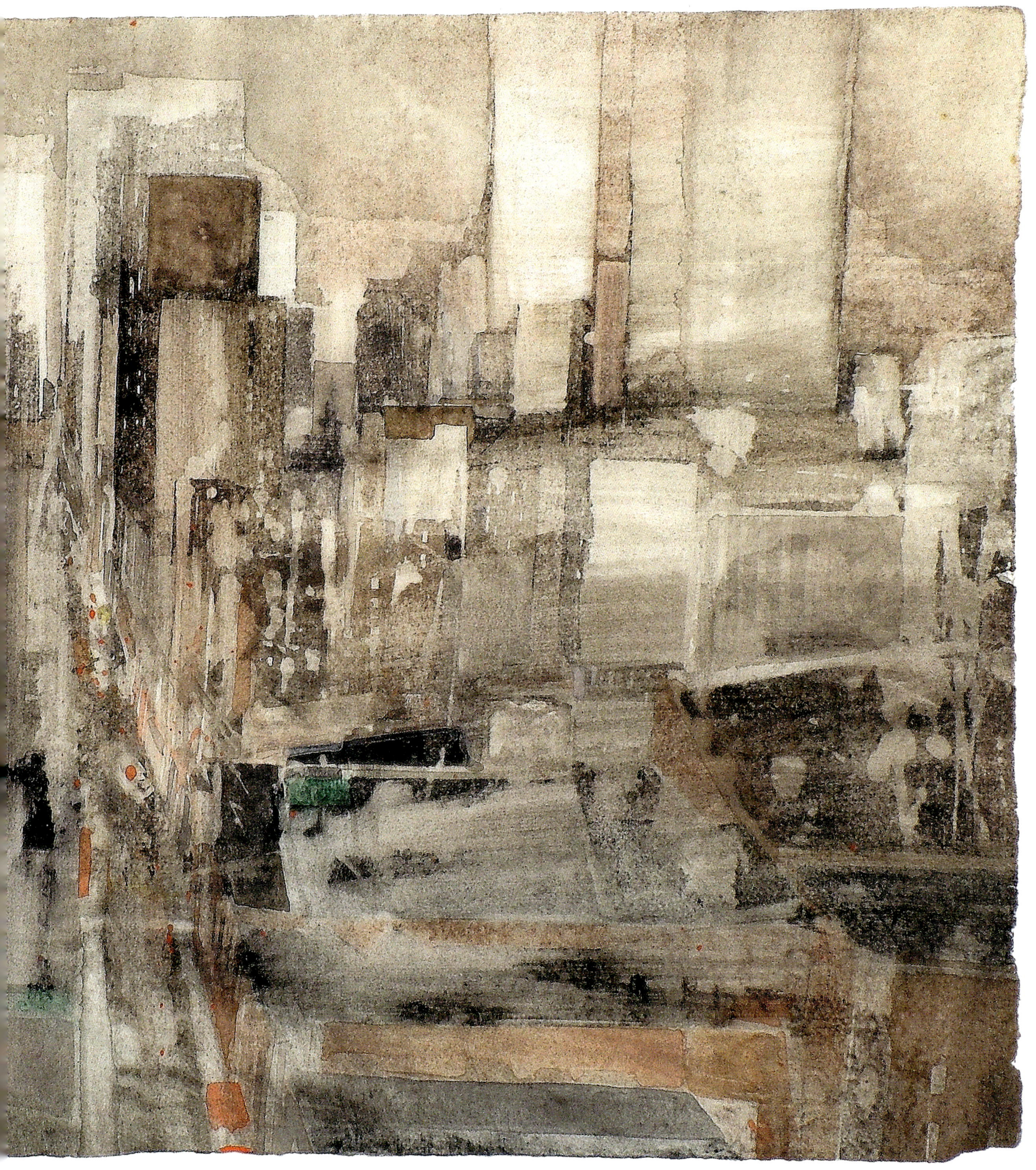

NY 56th Street   1983, 29,2 × 46,7 cm

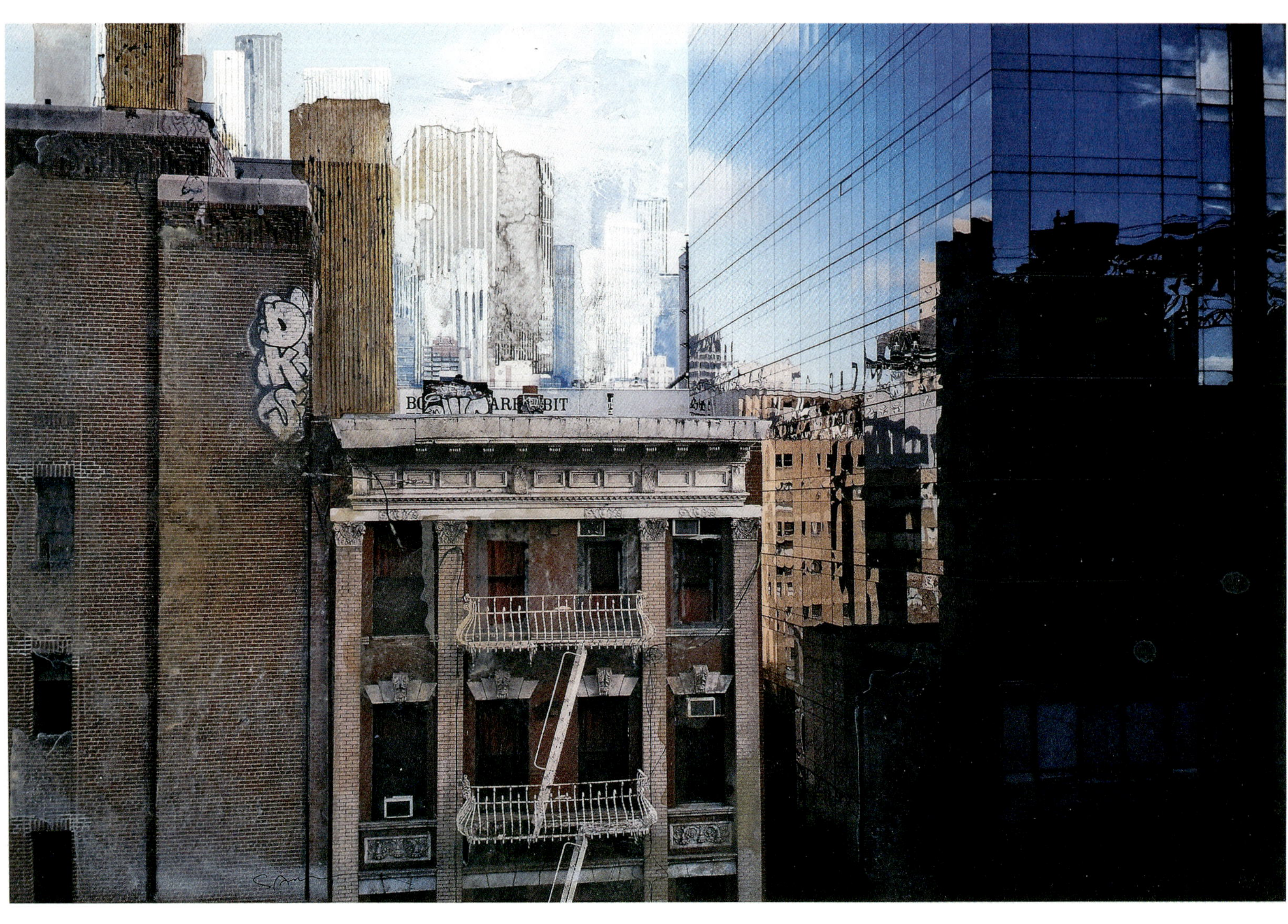

   DKS   2010, 60 × 81 cm

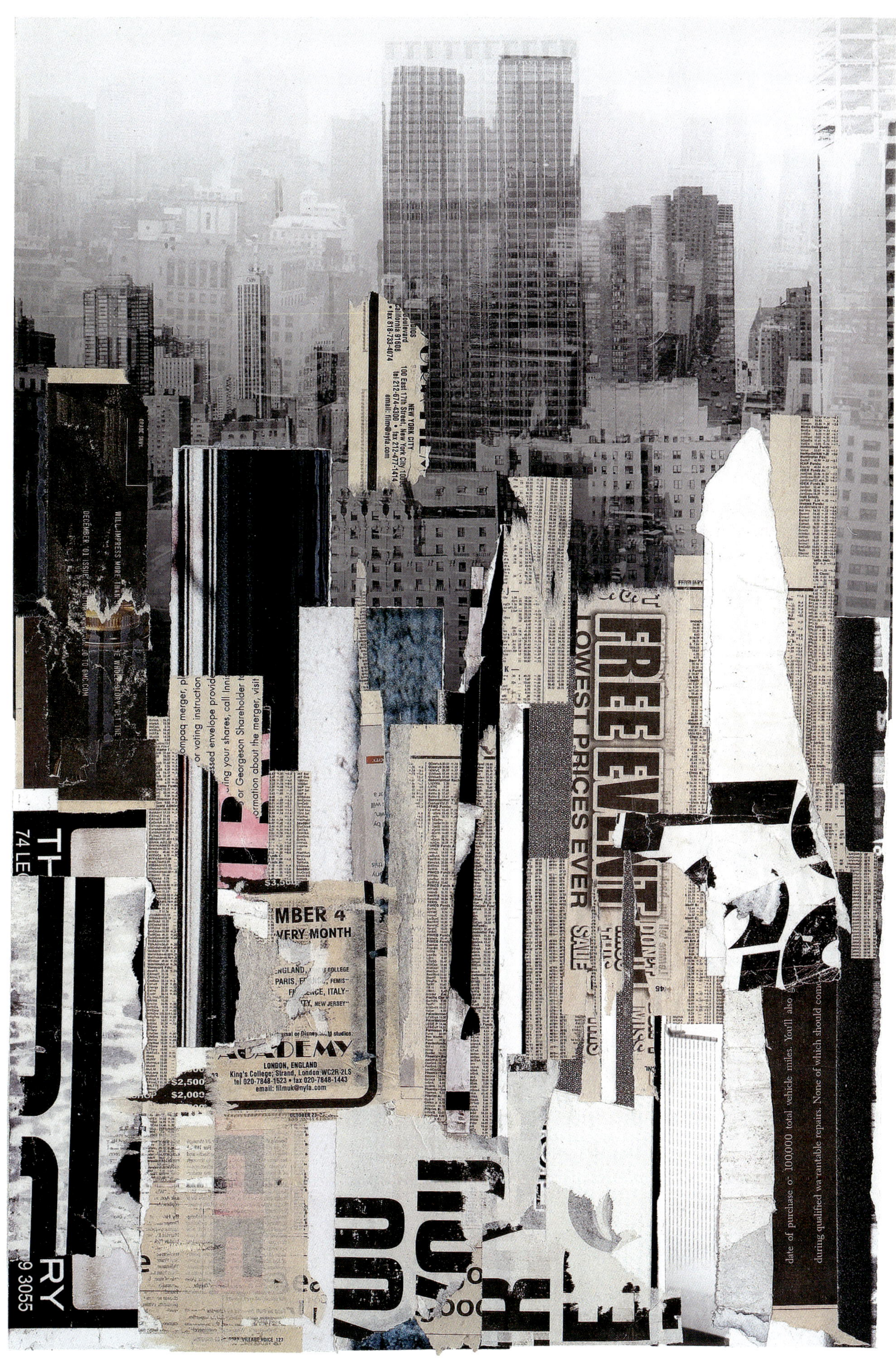

Free Event, The Cathedral | Free Event, Der Dom | Free Event, La cathédrale   2011, 81 × 54 cm

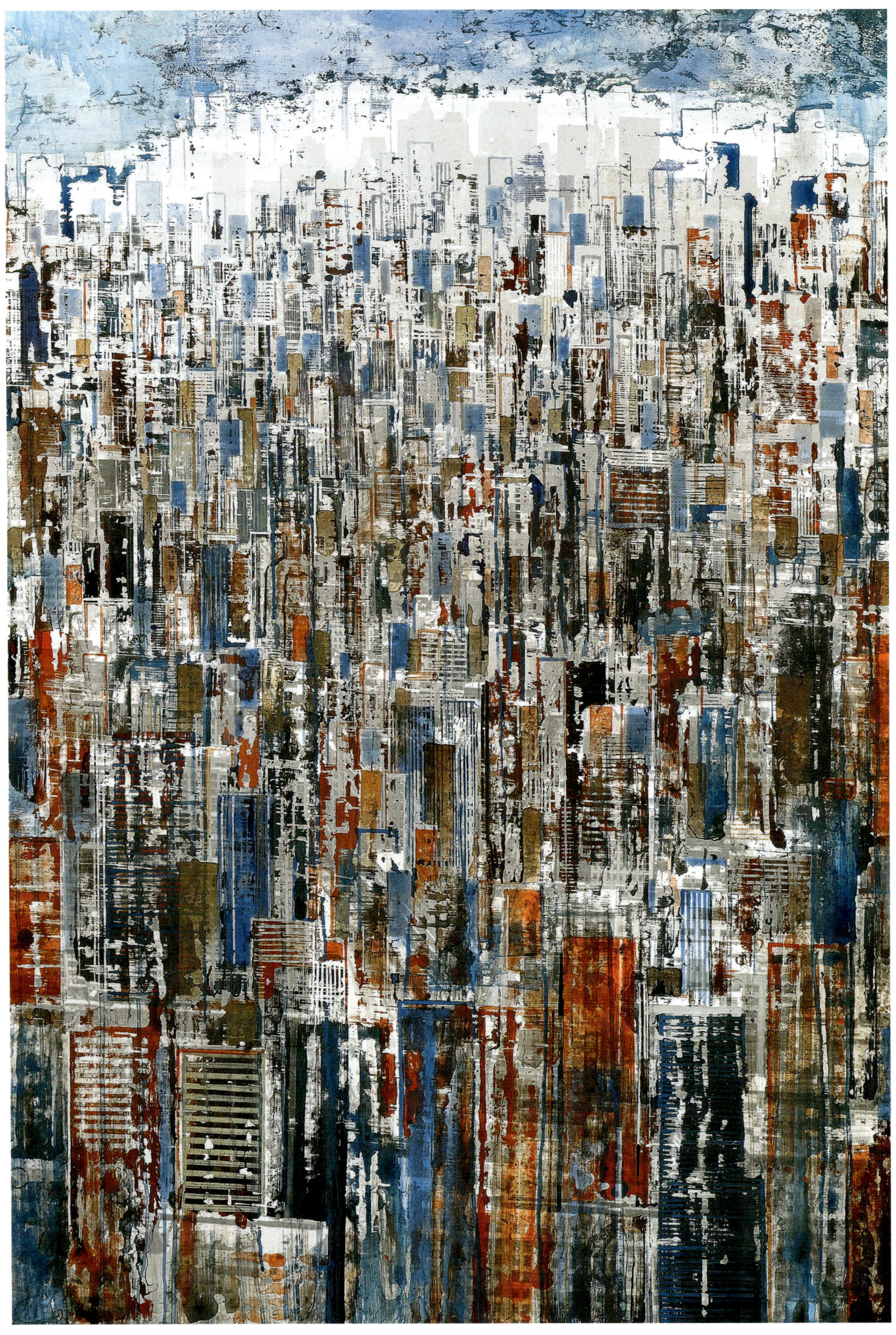

   NY Puzzle   2008, 130 × 89 cm

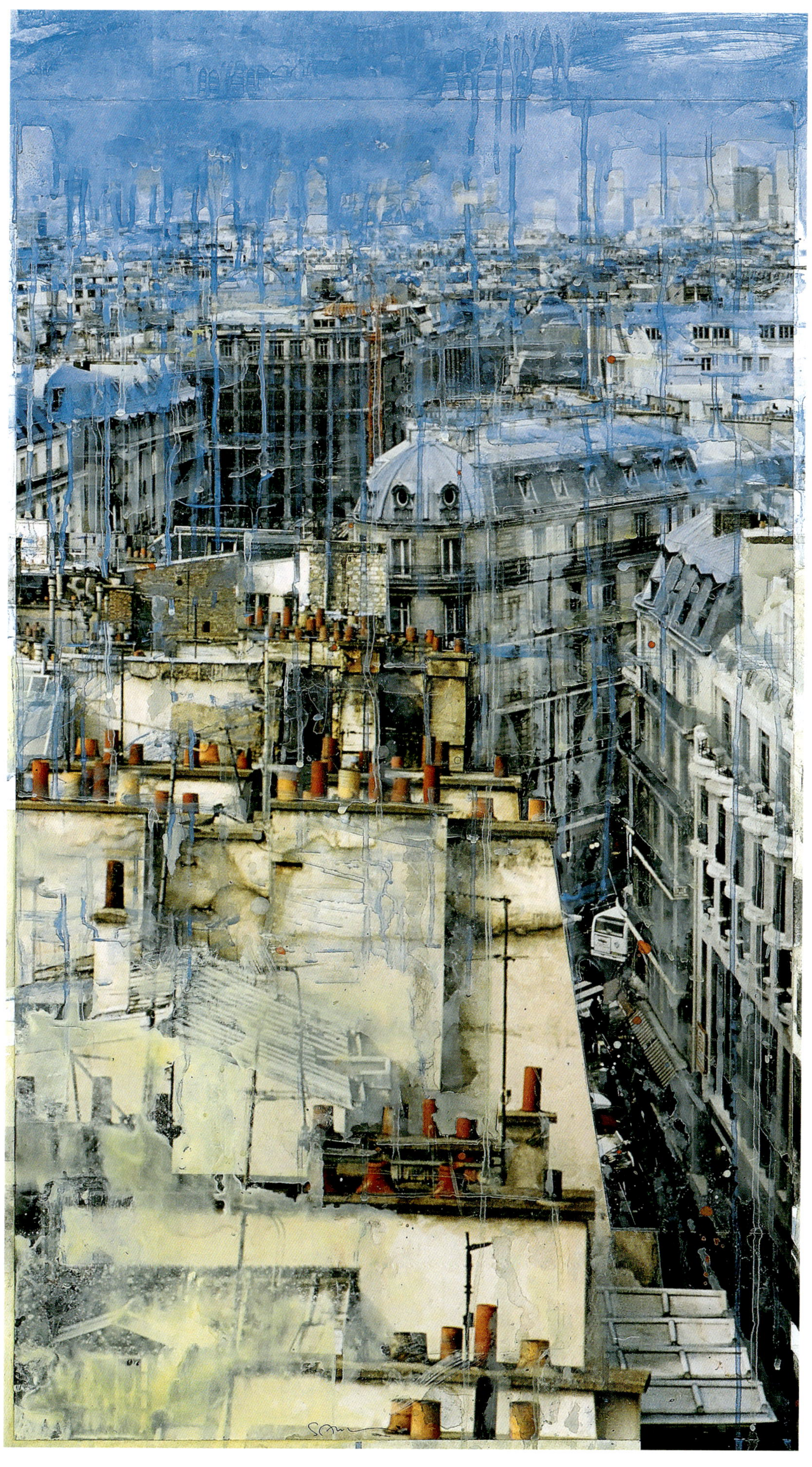

Paris, Chimneys | Paris, Die Kamine | Paris, Les Cheminées   2008, 95 × 52 cm

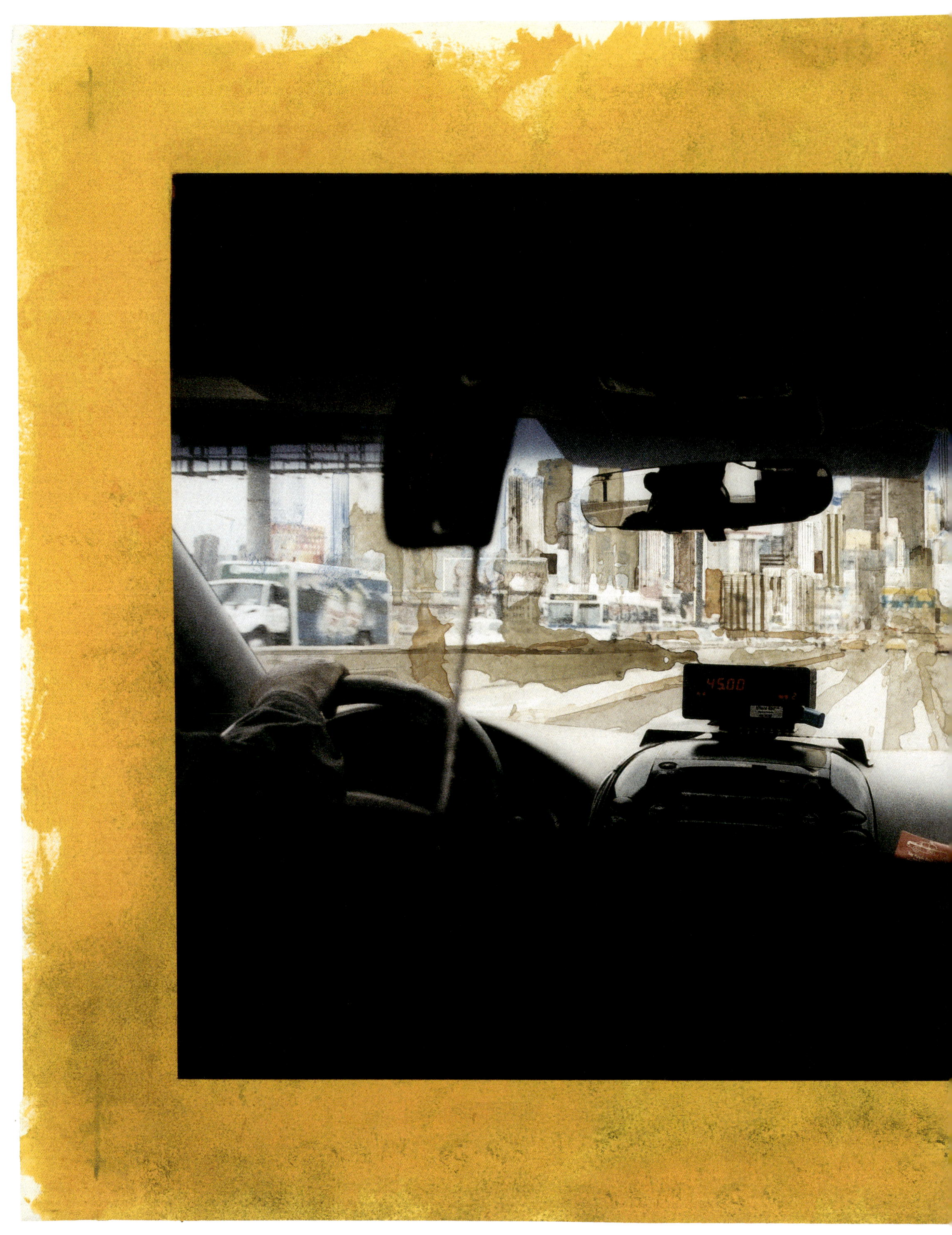

5E31 CON   2009, 60 × 81 cm

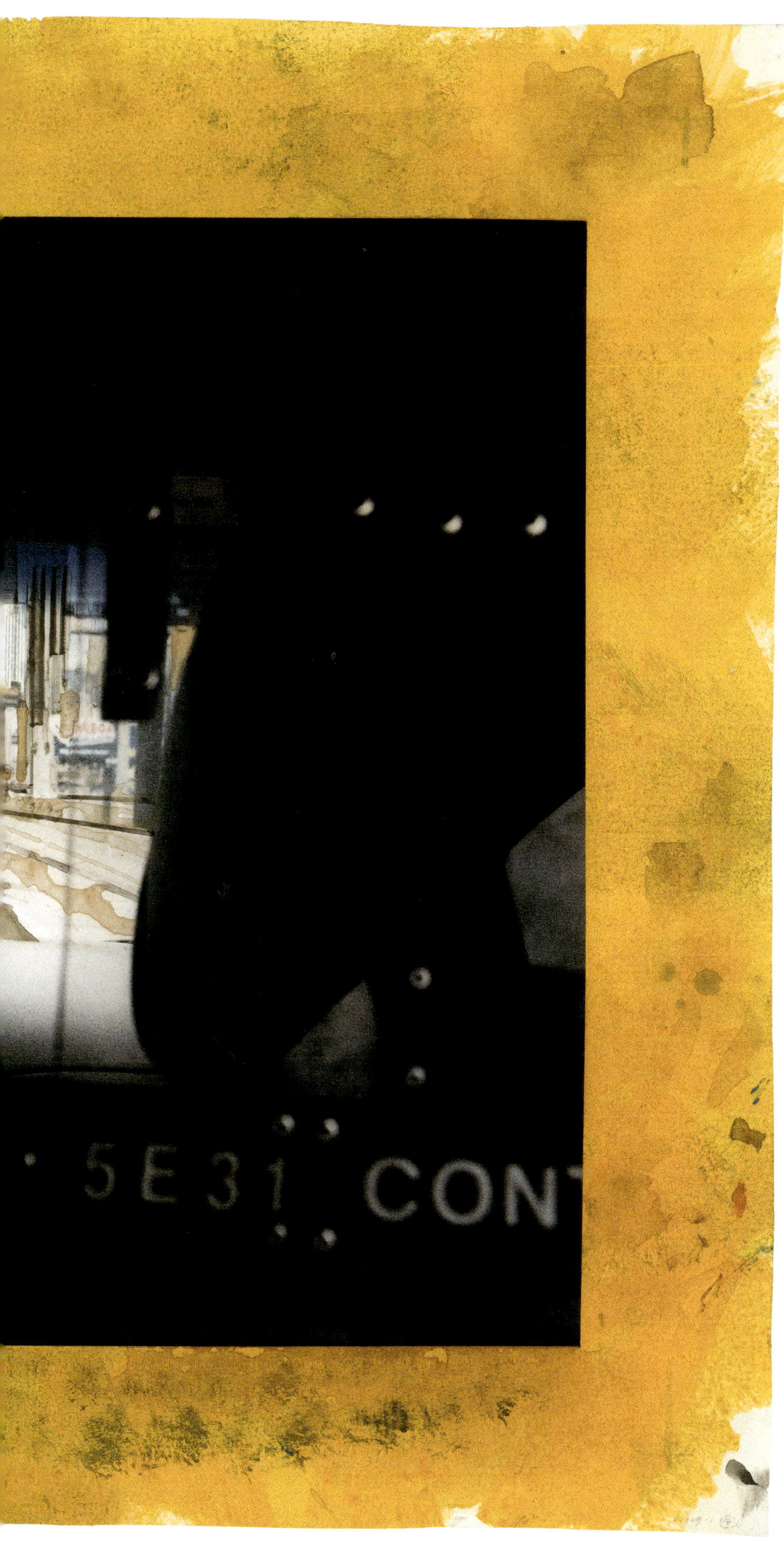
5E31 CONT

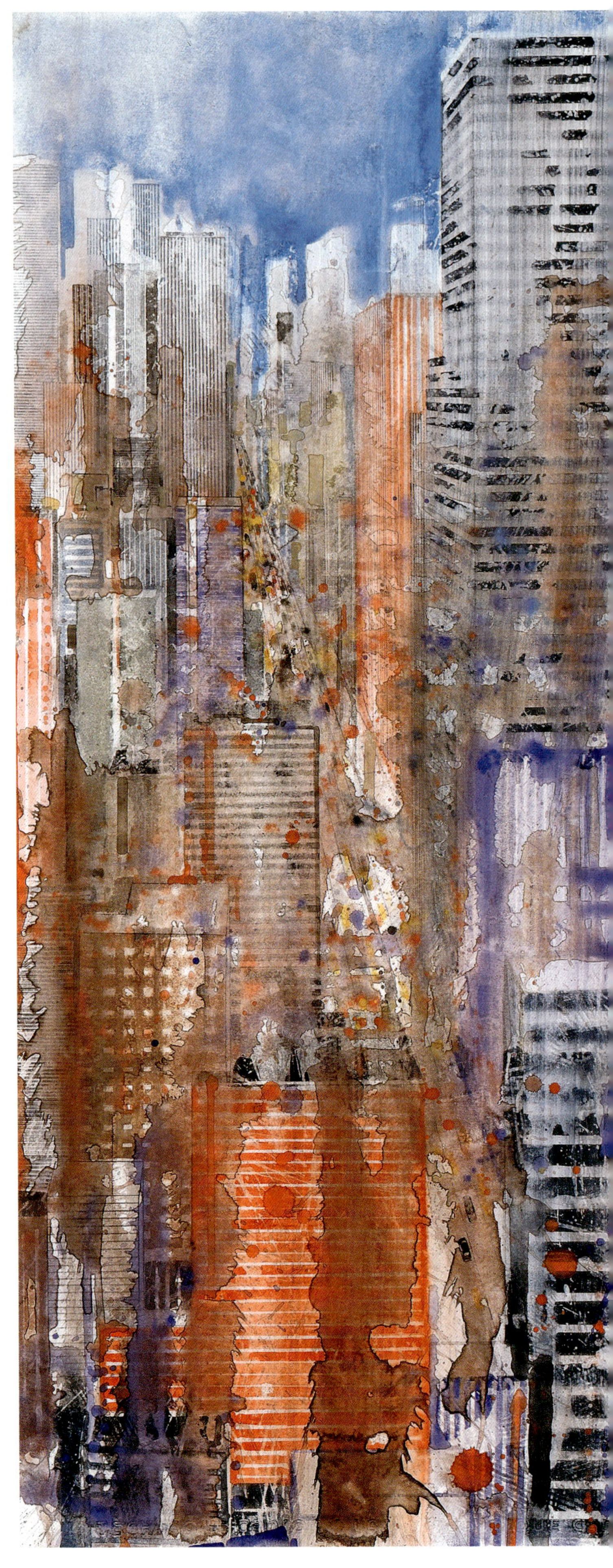

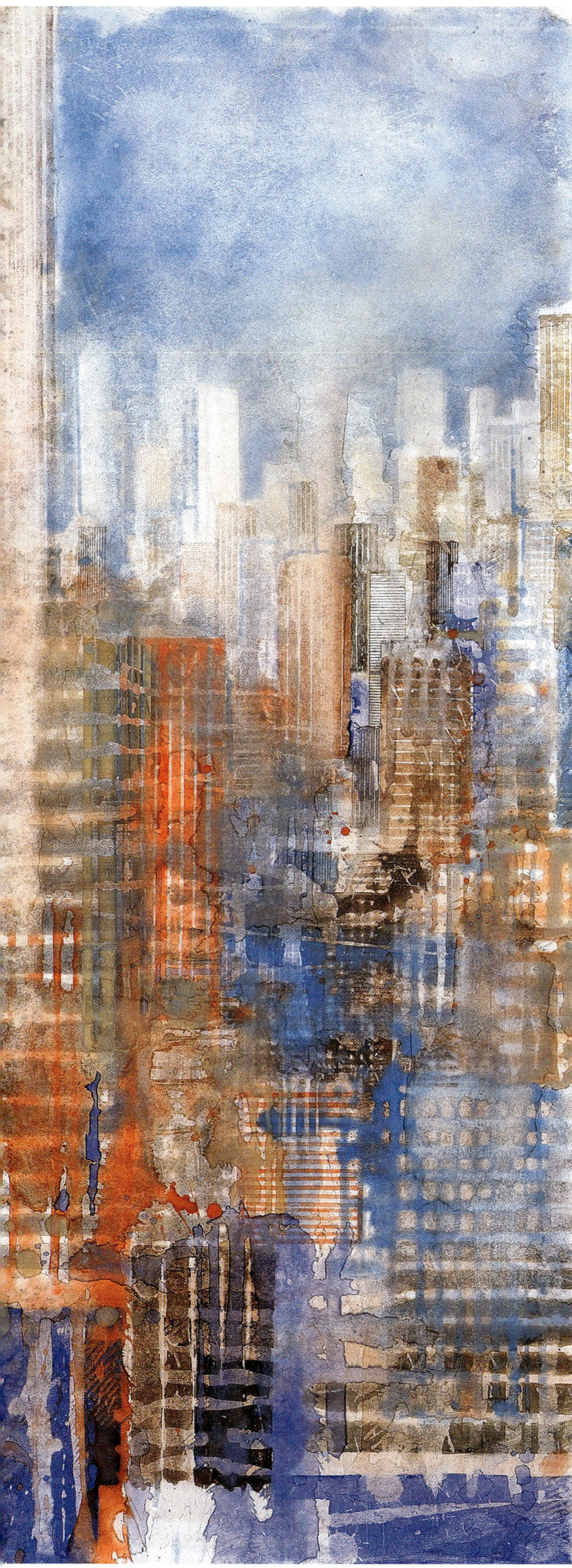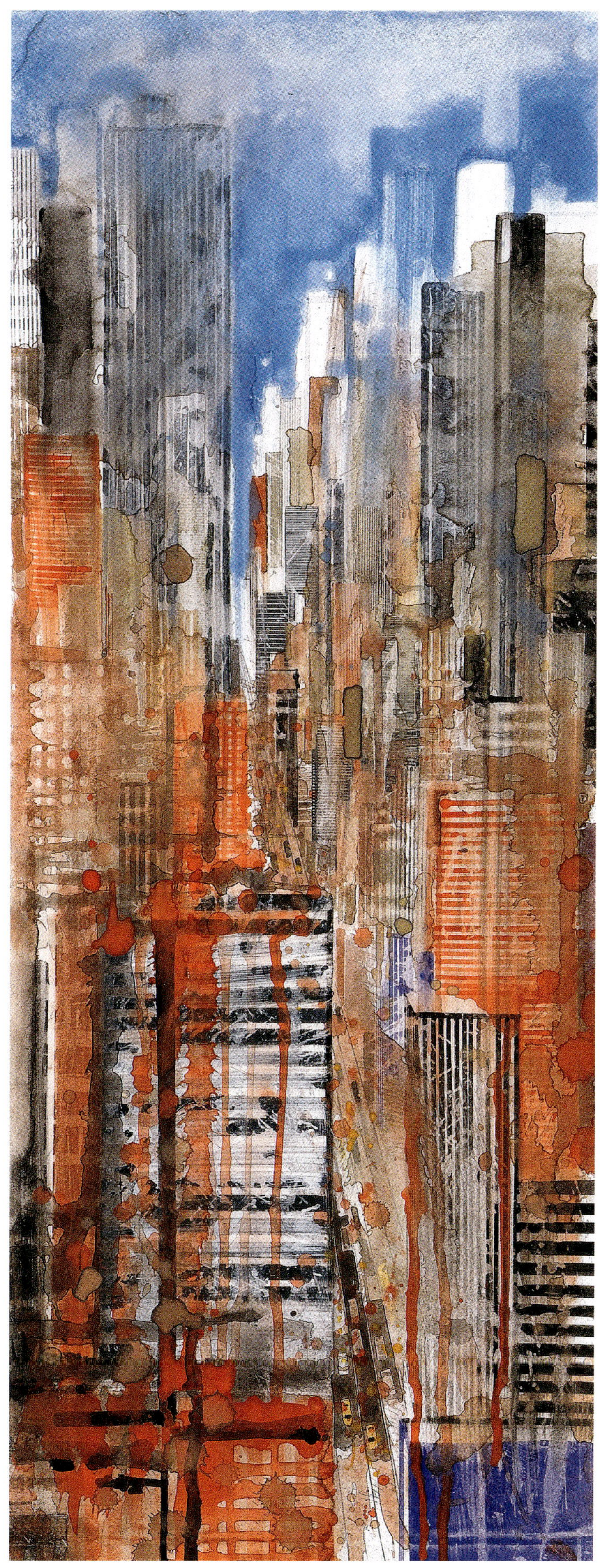

NY I   2012, 74,3 × 29,3 cm   NY II   2012, 76 × 28 cm   NY III   2012, 75,8 × 28 cm

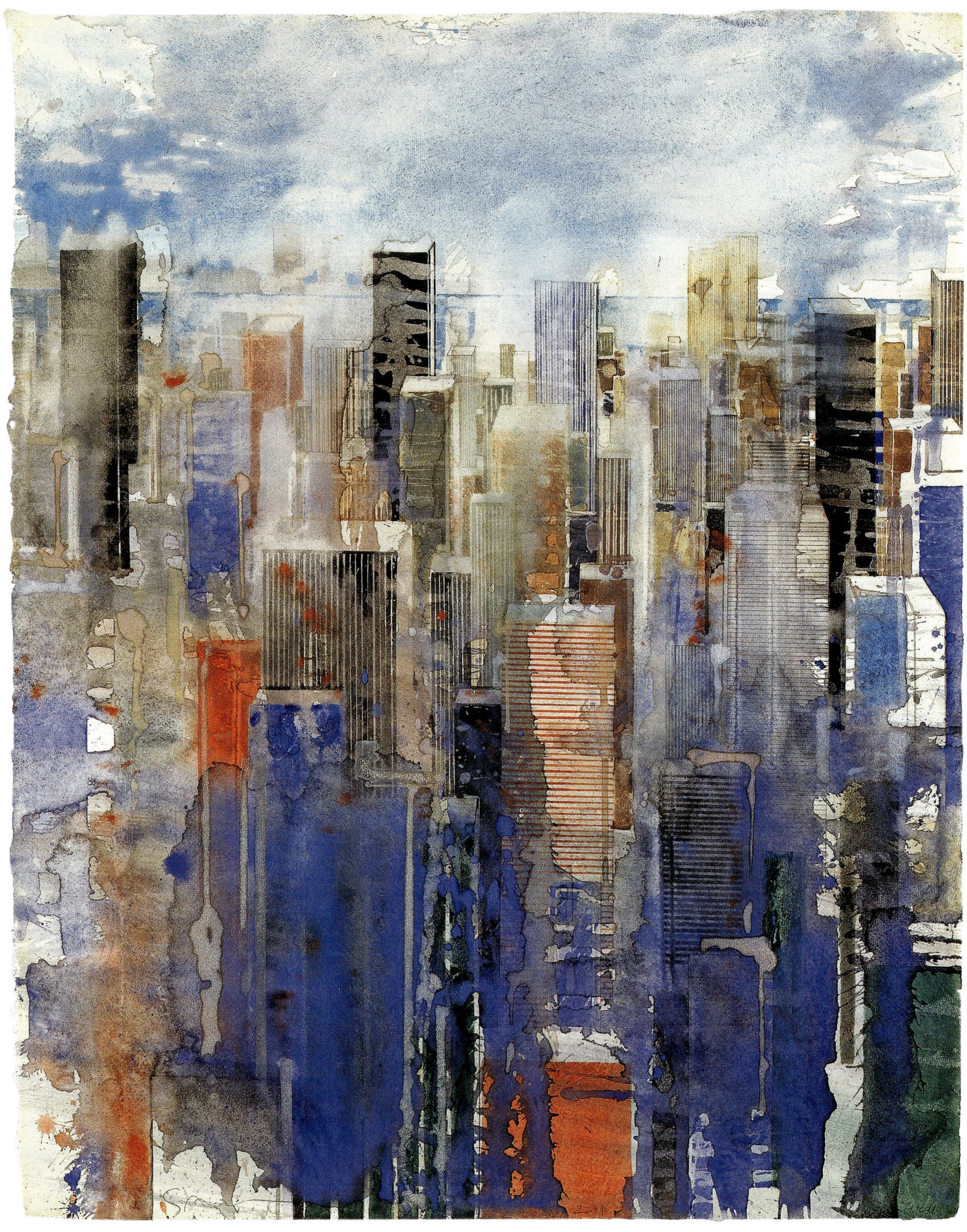

     NY, Blue Red Green | NY, Blau Rot Grün | NY, bleu rouge vert   2010, 59,5 × 47,2 cm

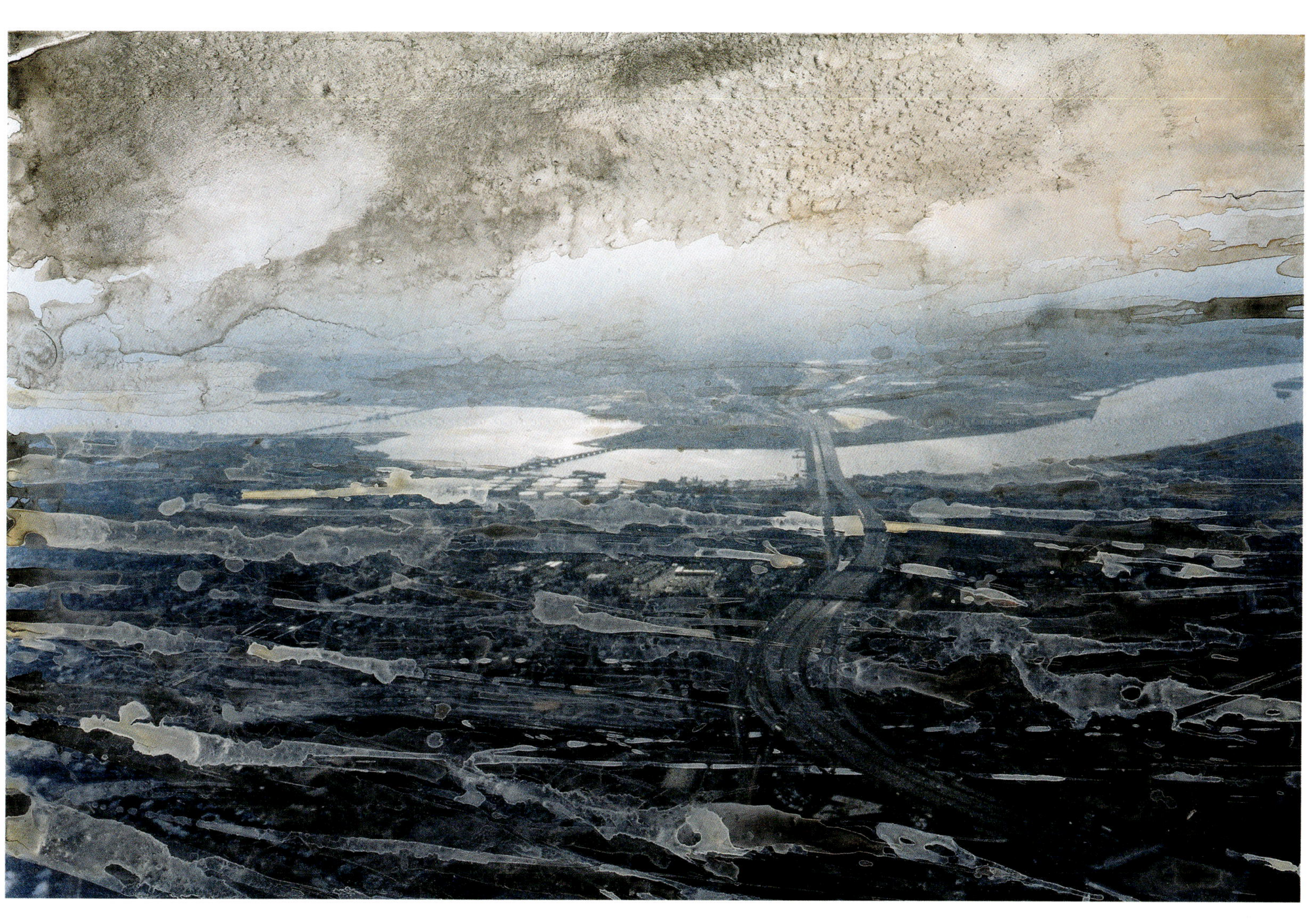

Hamburg over the Elbe | Hamburg über der Elbe | Hambourg au-dessus de l'Elbe   1999, 50,5 × 75 cm

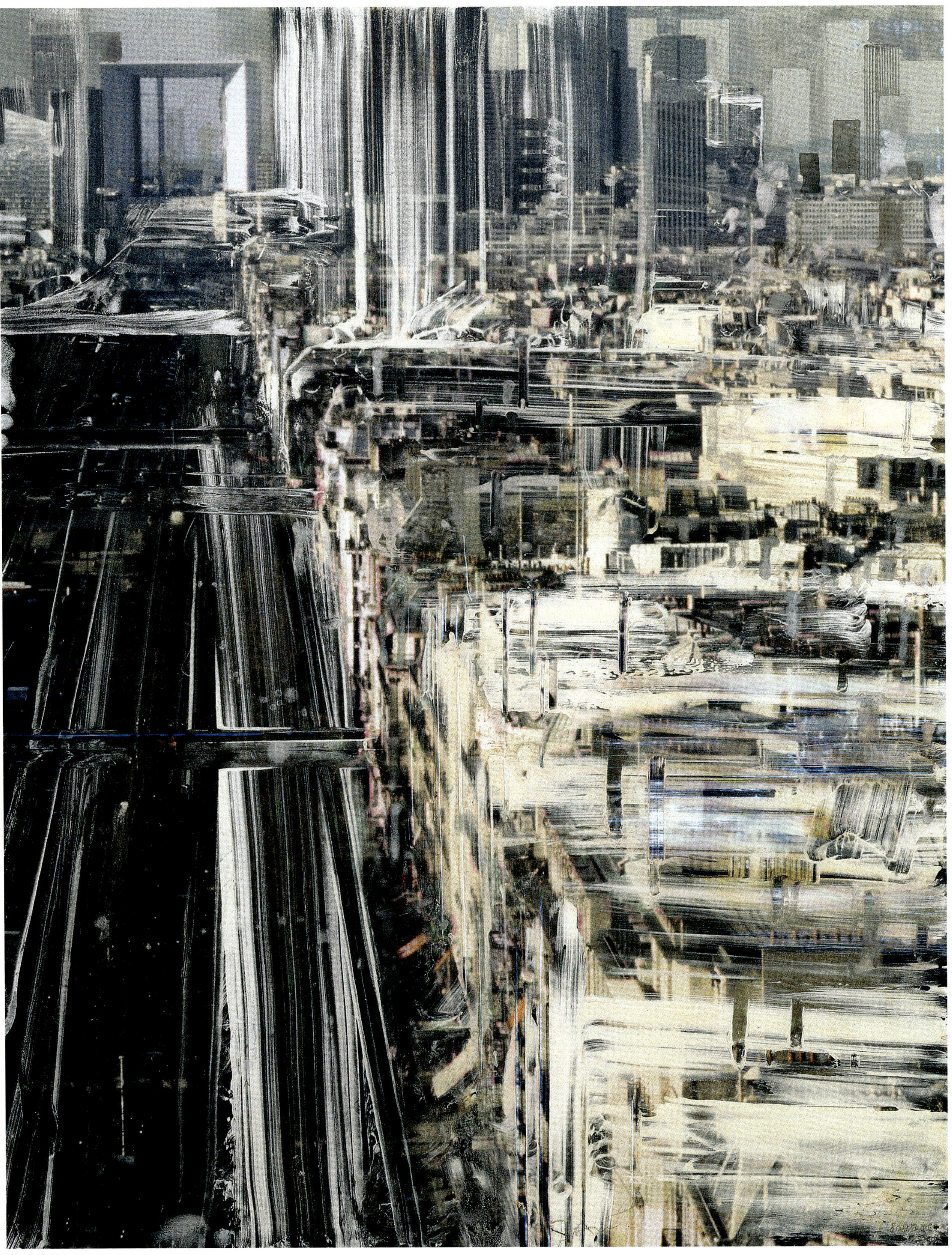

L'arche II   2008, 51 × 38 cm

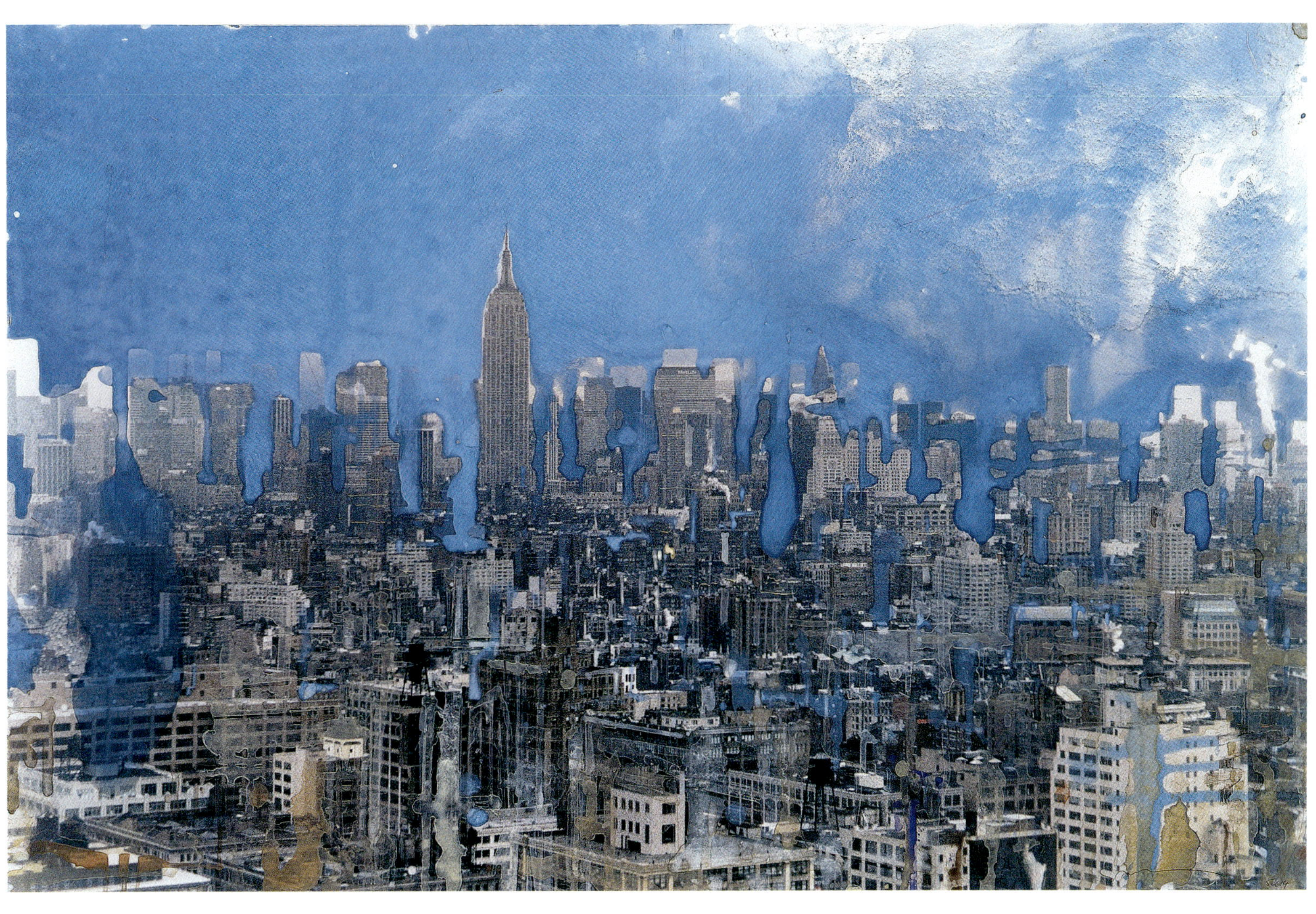

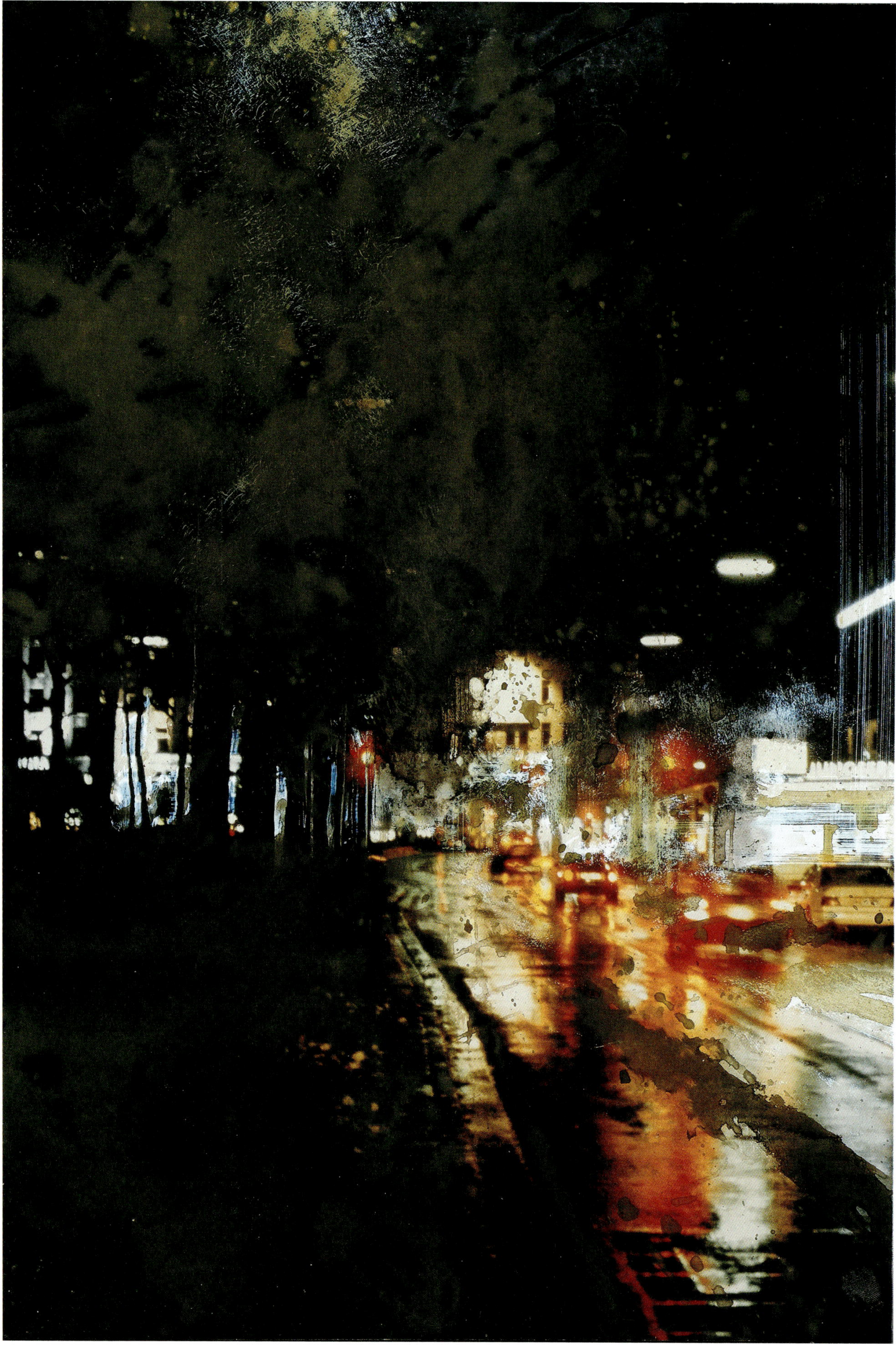

 Hamburg by Night | Hamburg bei Nacht | Hambourg la nuit   2007, 46 × 30,5 cm

NY by Night | NY bei Nacht | NY la nuit   2004, 60 × 26 cm

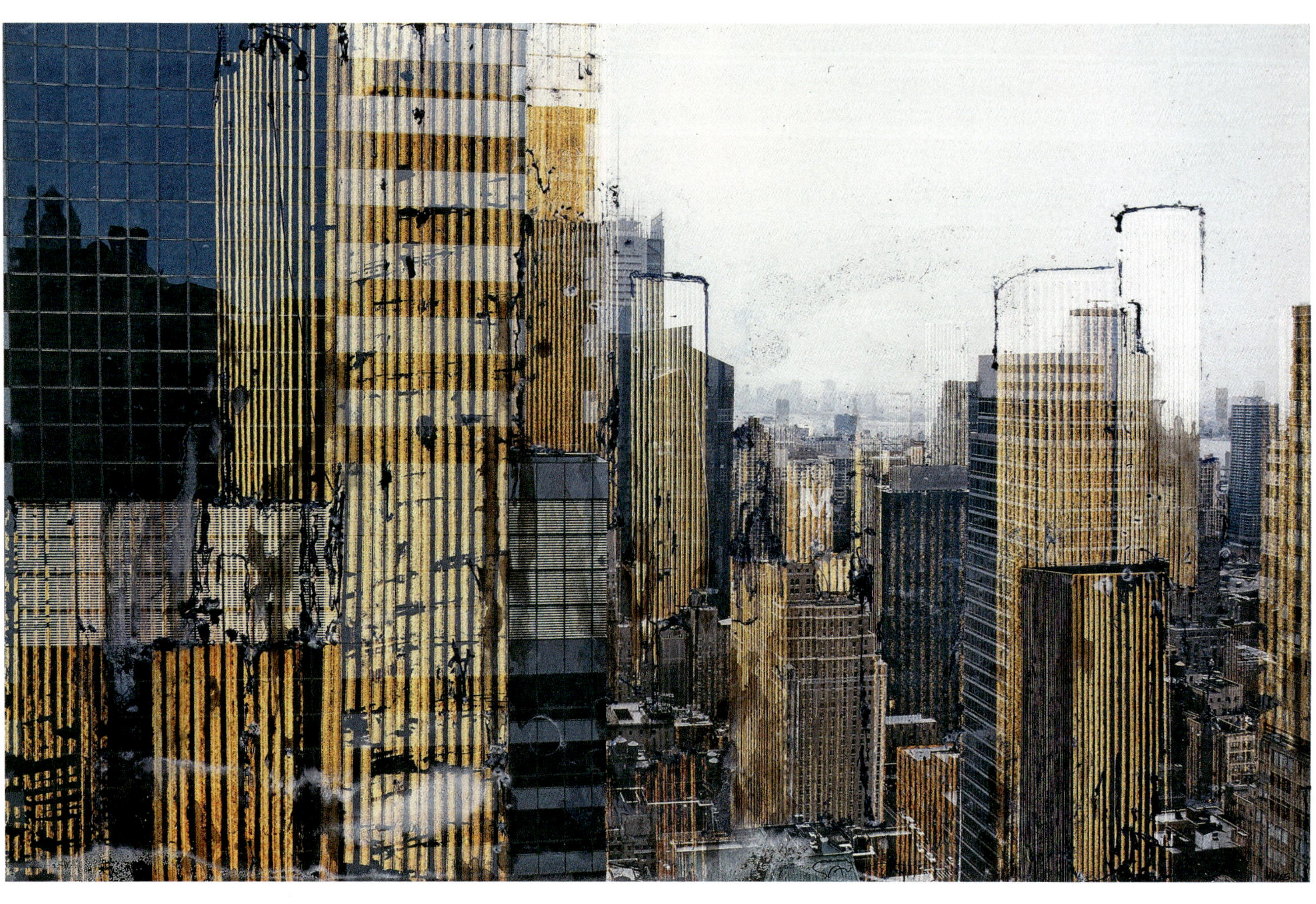

Yellow Buildings   2009, 50,5 × 75,3 cm

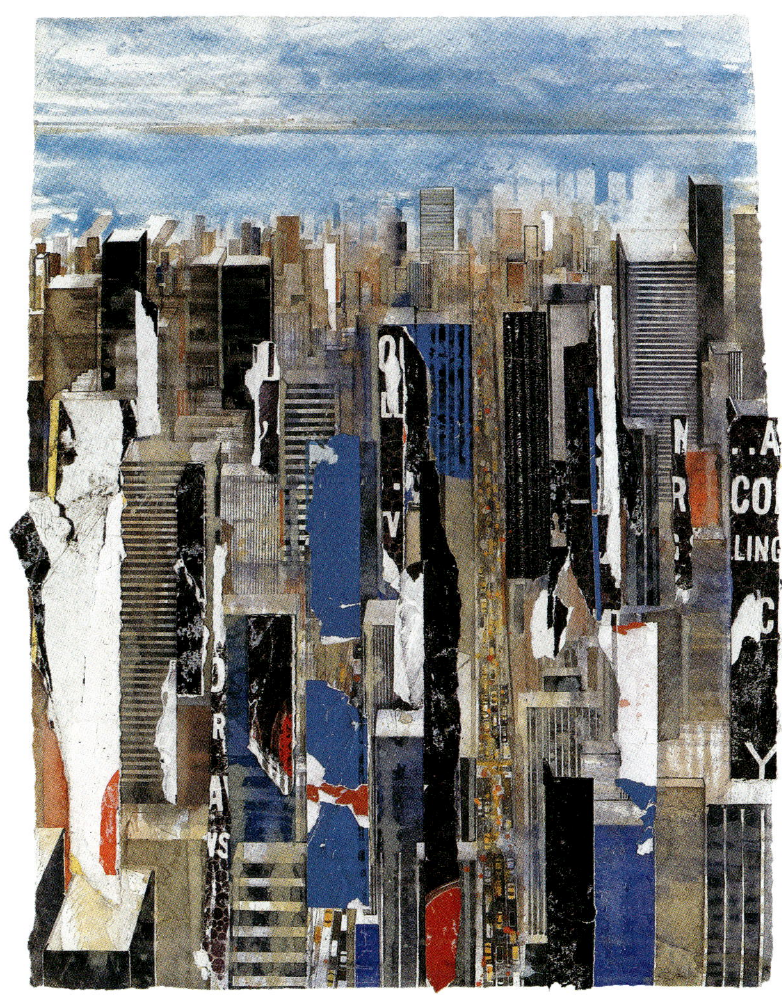 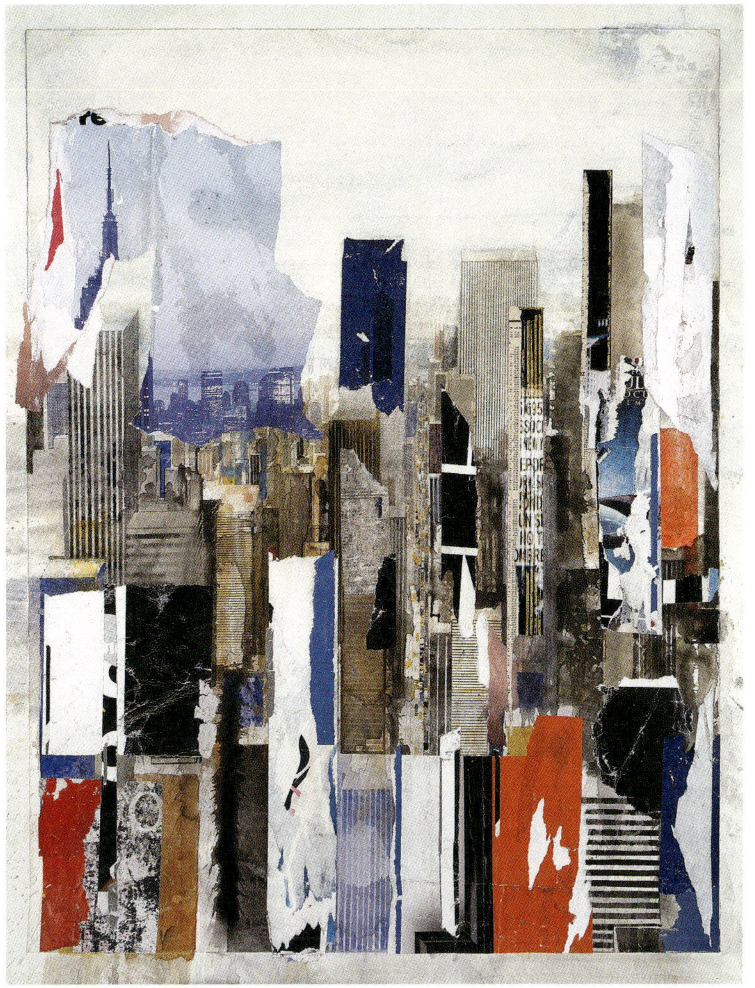

NY Aquacollage   2011, 76,8 × 59,2 cm
NY LM   2012, 76 × 57,5 cm

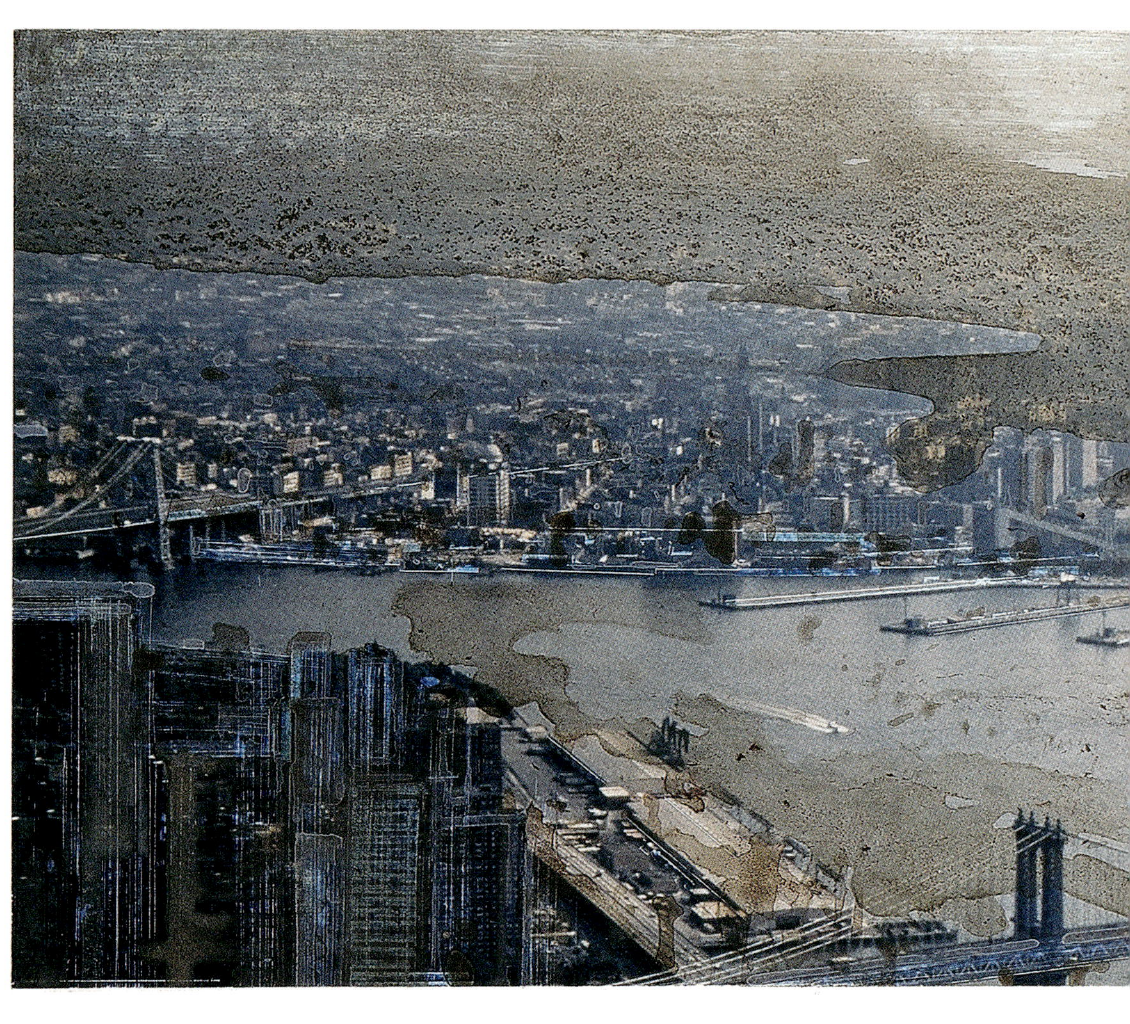

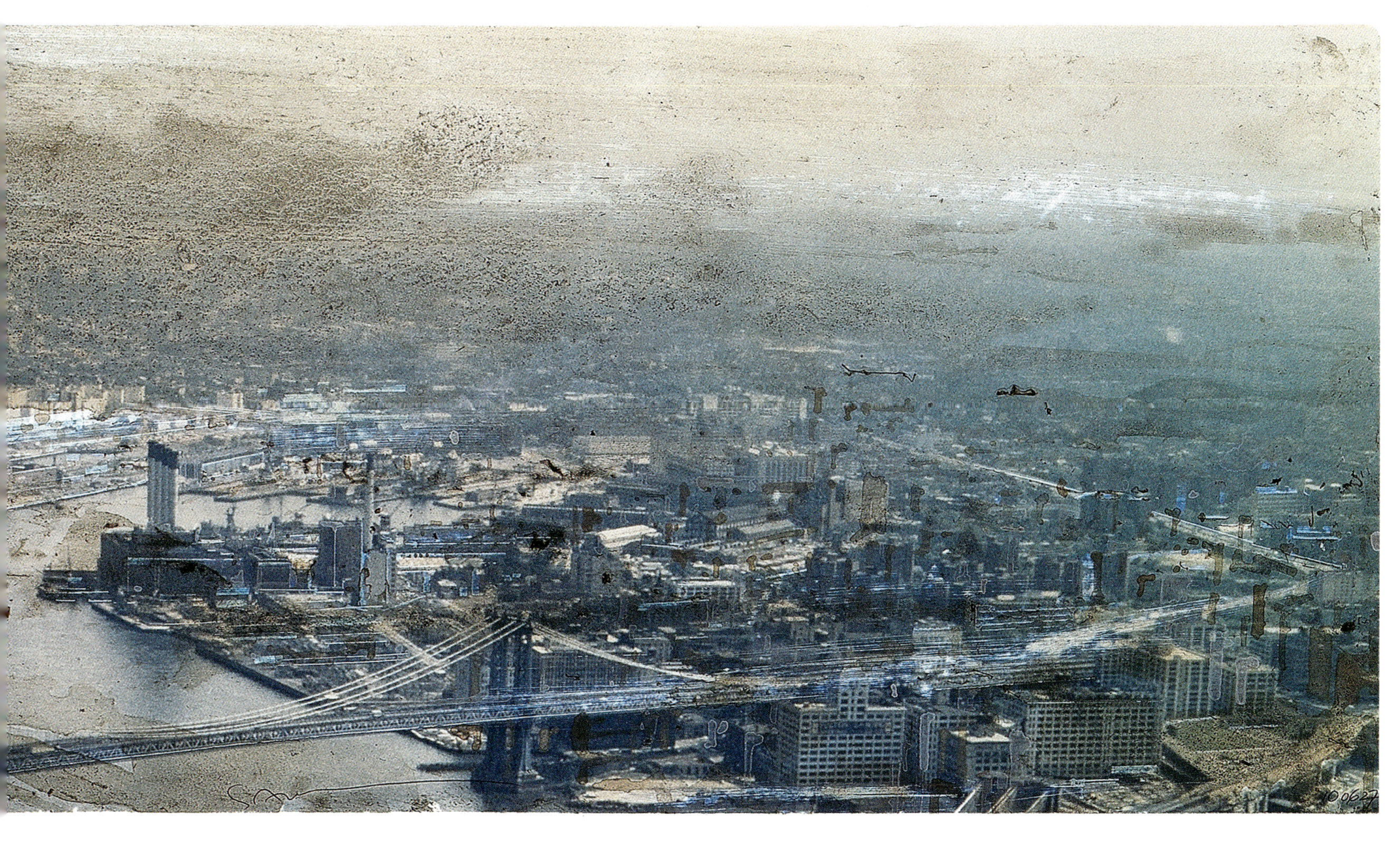

NY East River   2006, 25,3 × 76 cm

Under the Sky | Unterm Himmel | Sous le ciel   2012, 500 × 75 cm

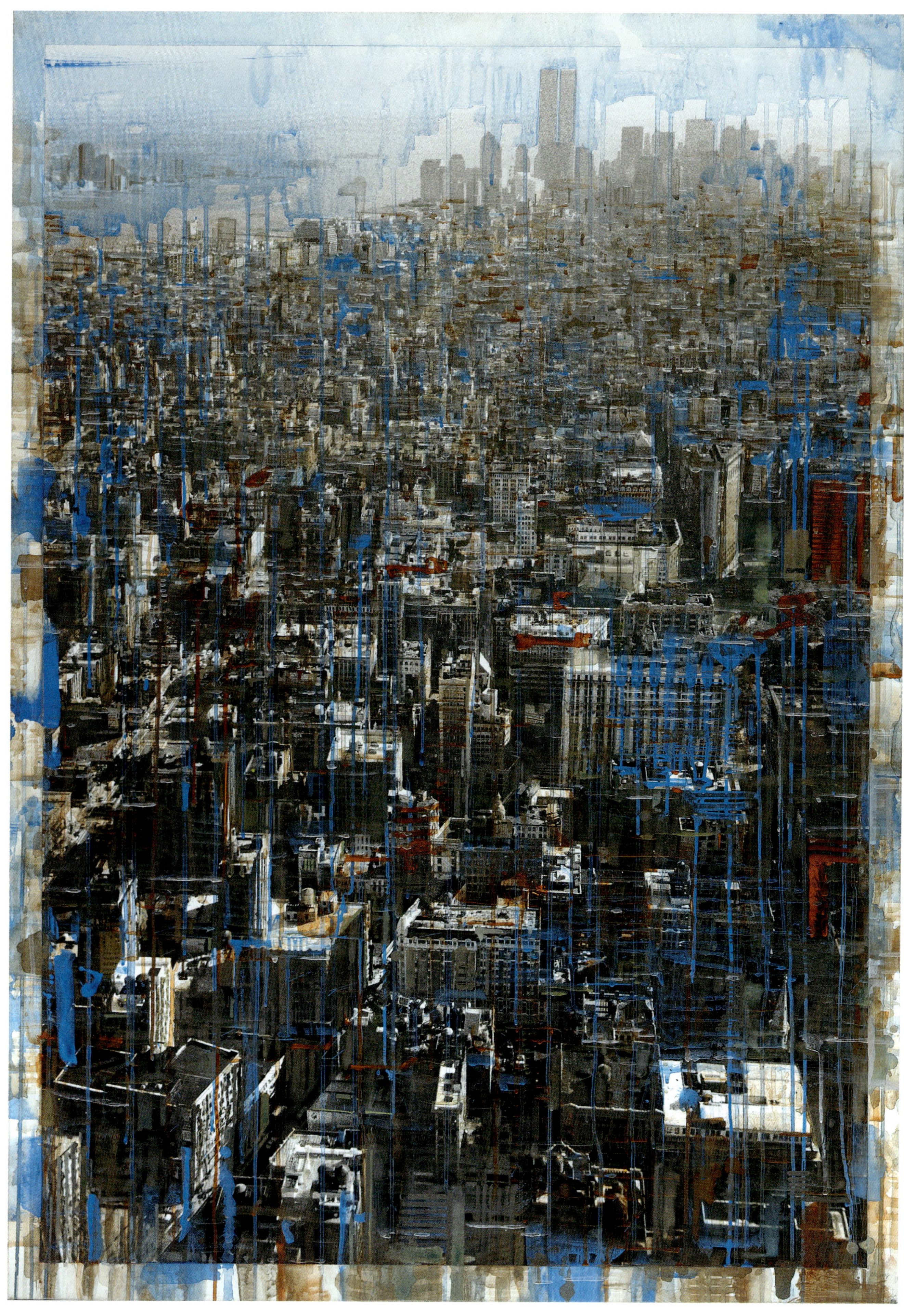

New York, Midtown I   2001, 131 x 89 cm

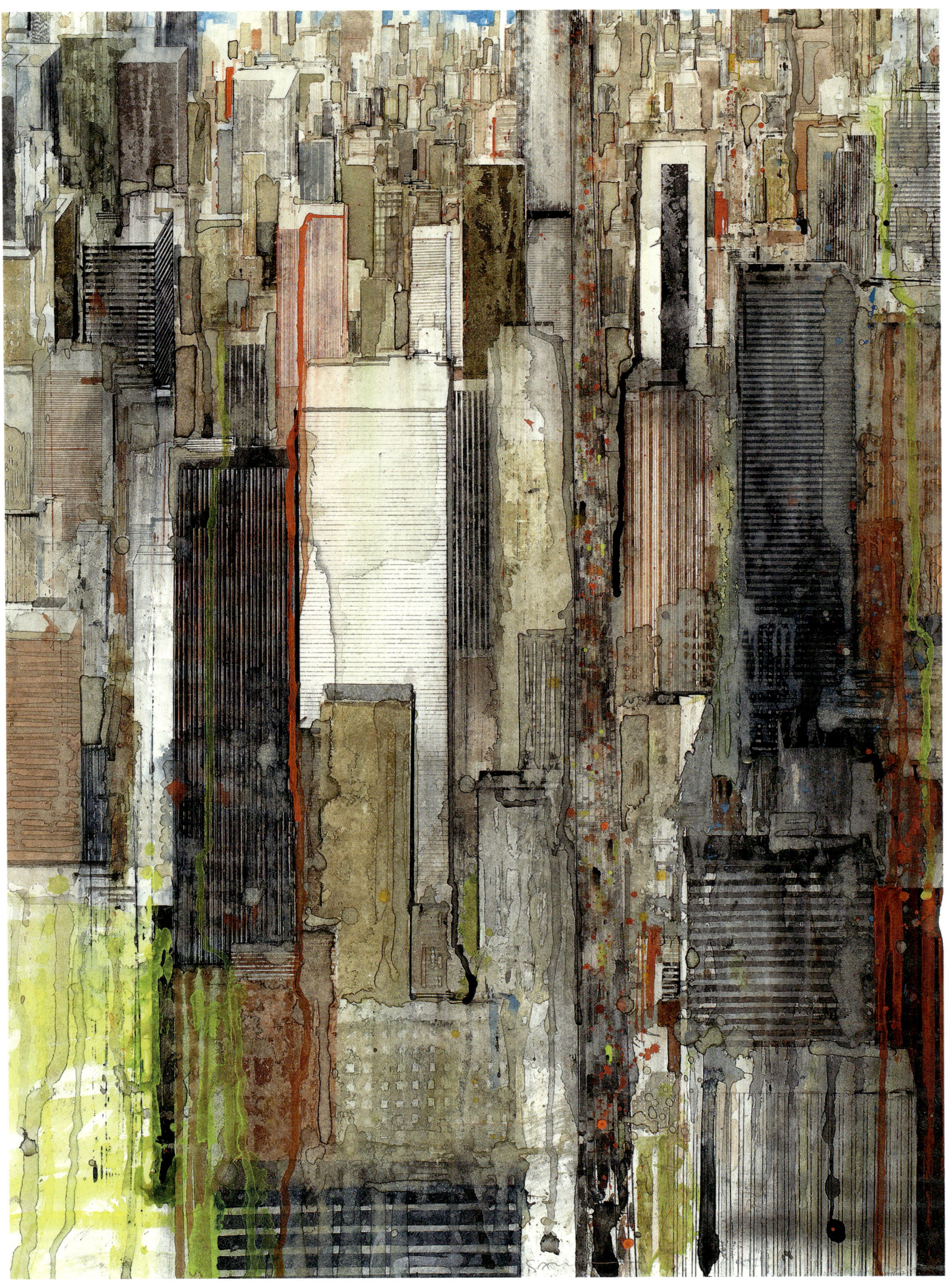

  New York, Midtown II   1995, 74,8 × 55,1 cm

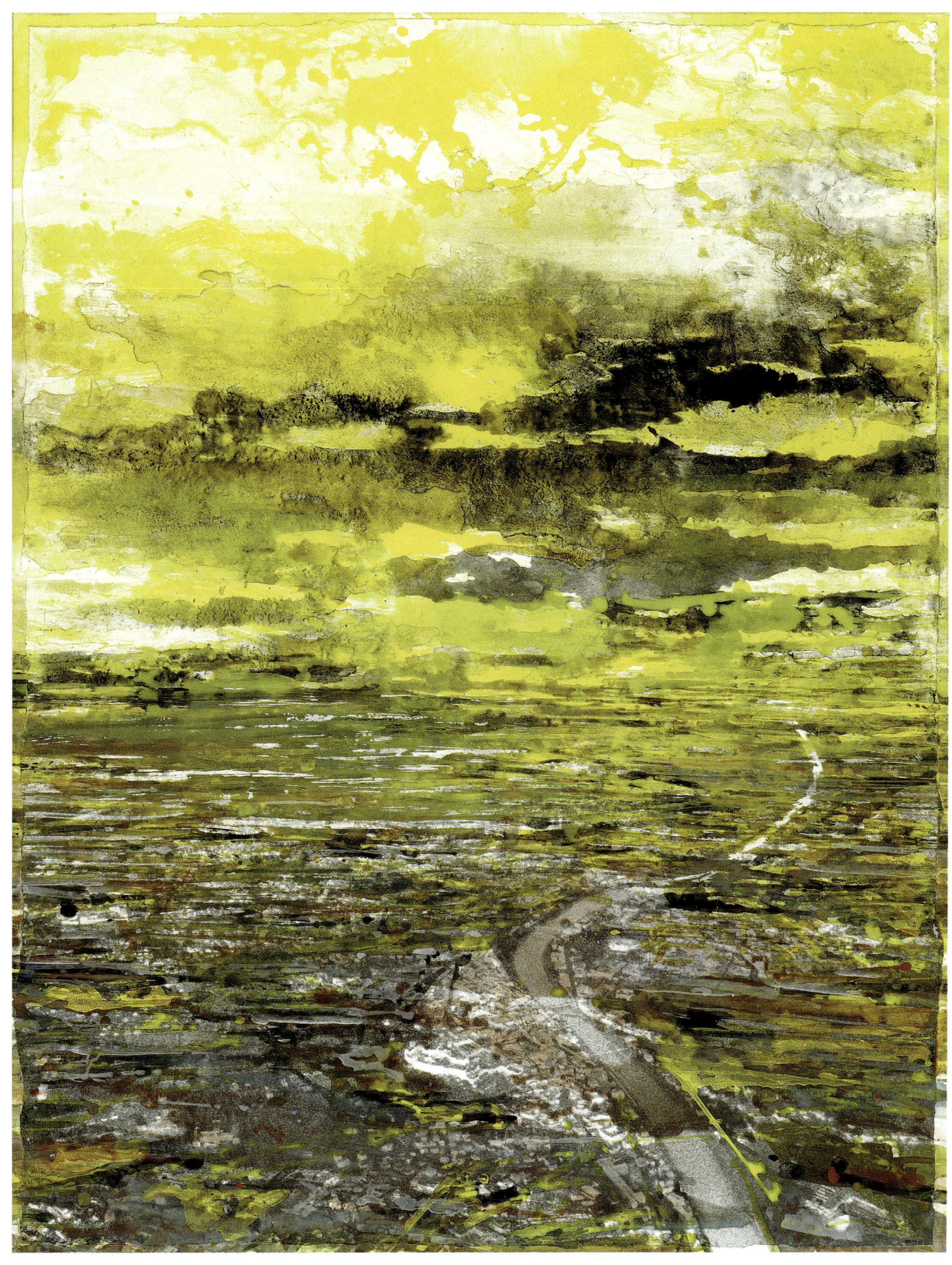

Salzburg from the Air | *Salzburg aus der Flugperspektive* | Salzbourg, perspective aérienne   2004, 124 × 94 cm

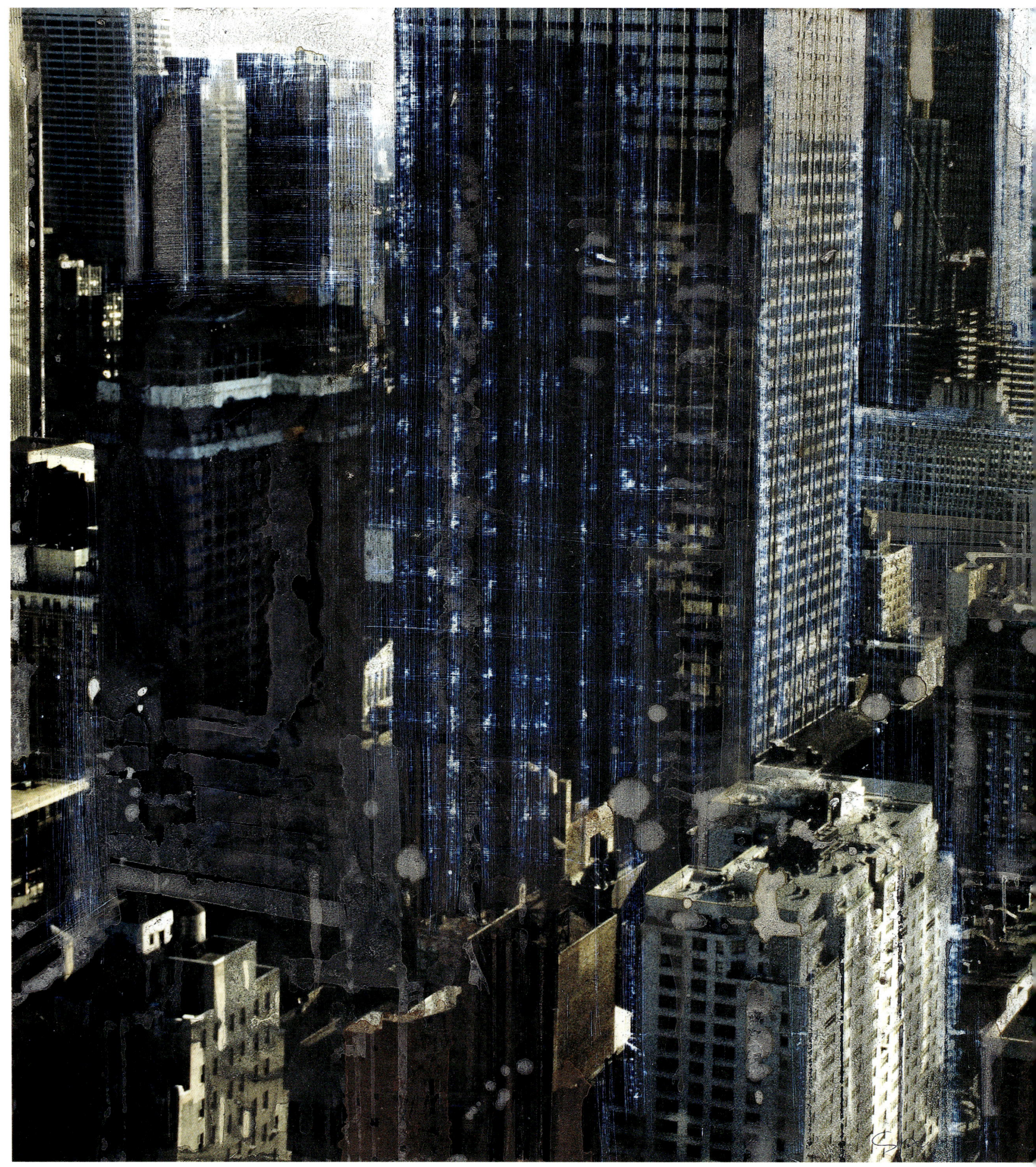

   New York, 8th Avenue   2006, 50,6 × 75,8 cm

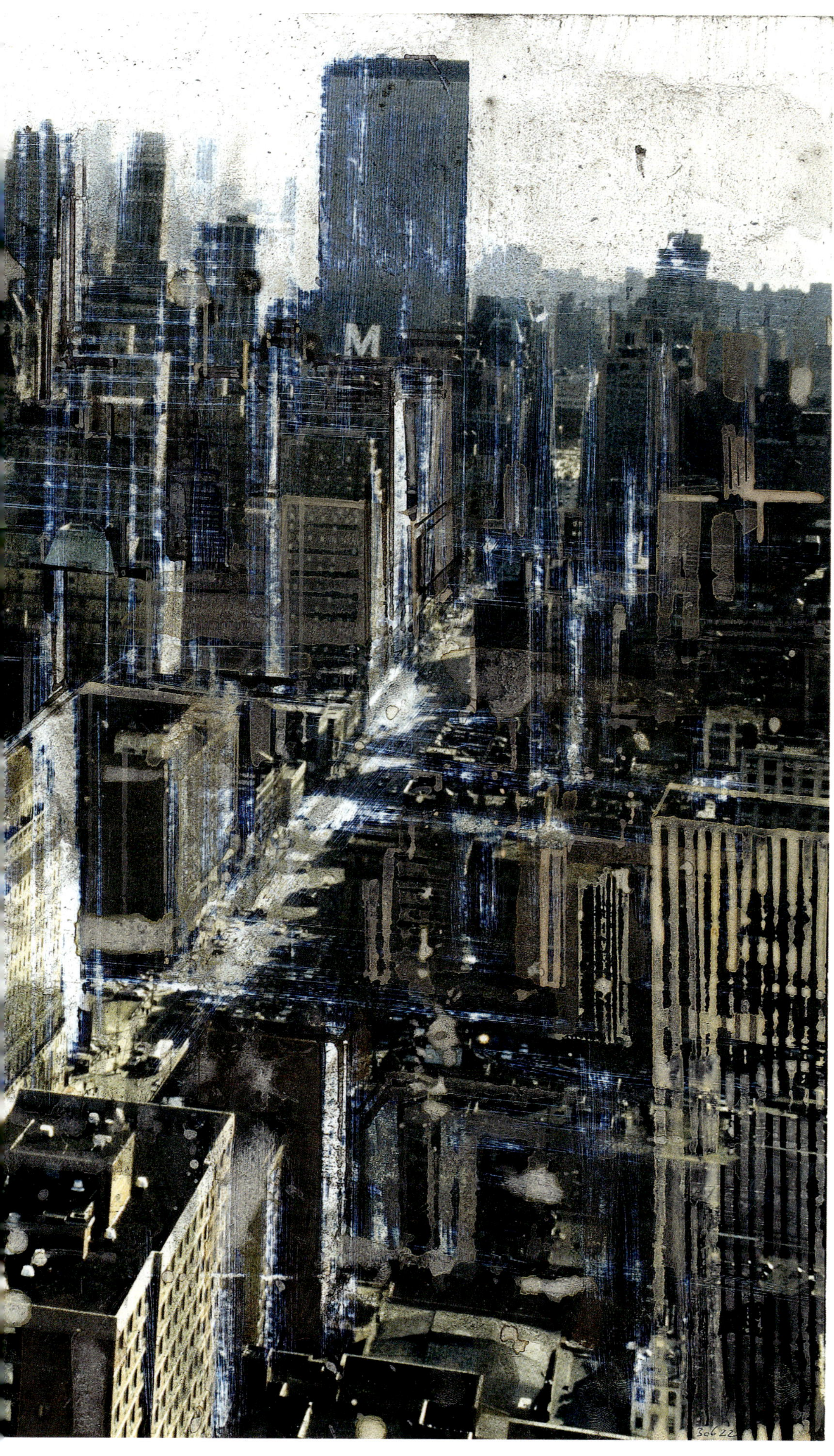

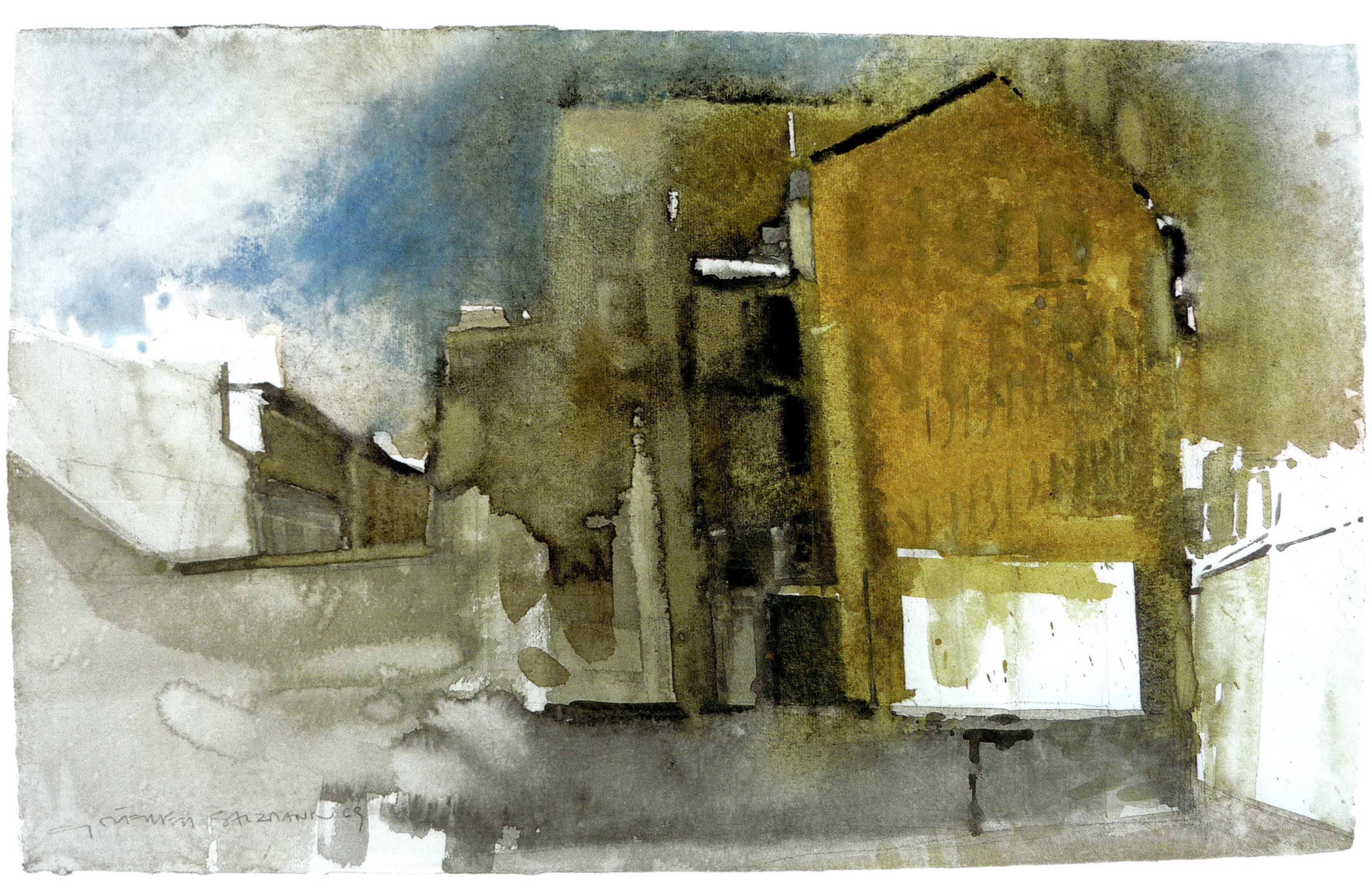

   Lion noir   1969, 30,5 × 49,2 cm

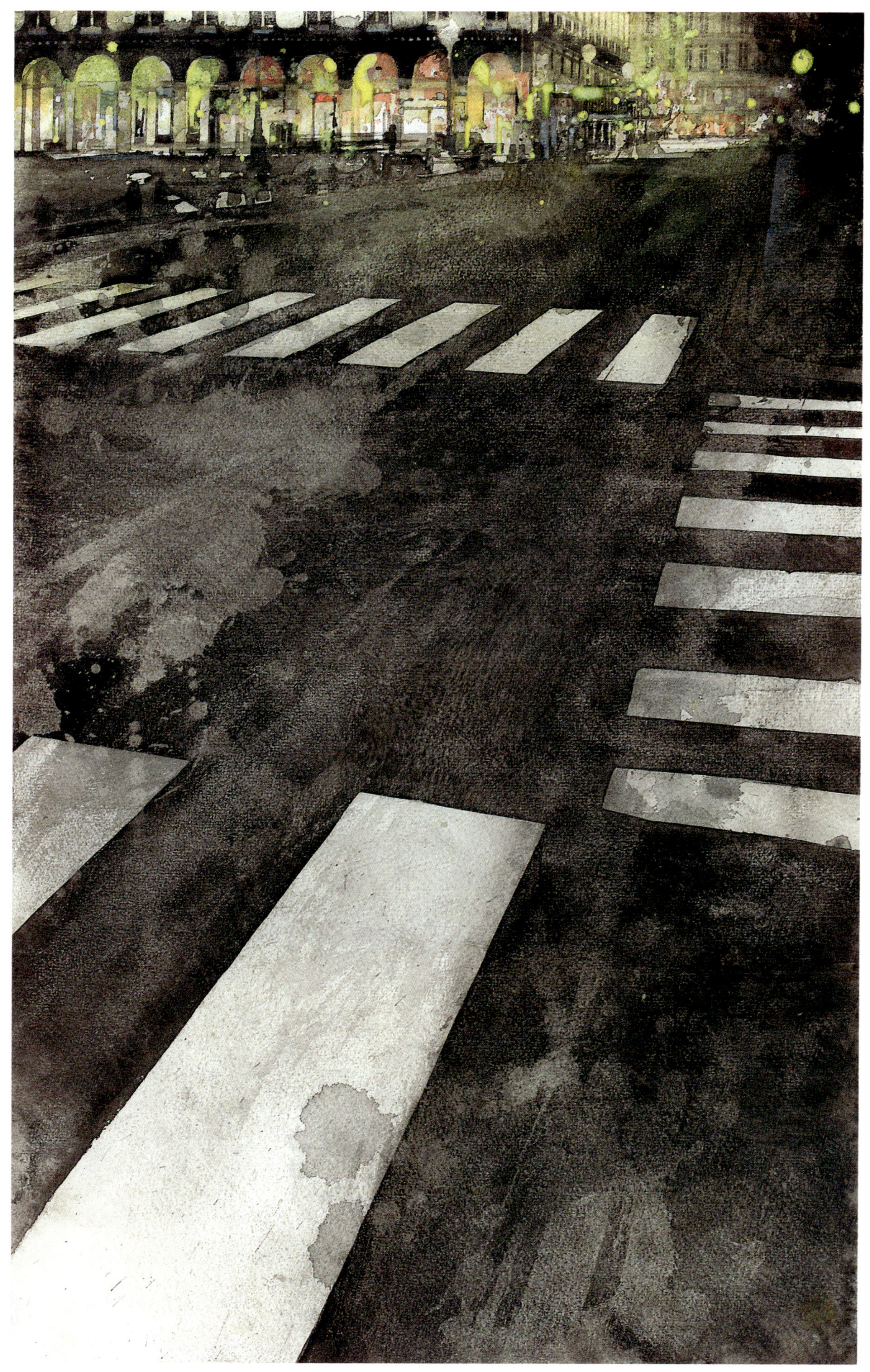

Crosswalk, Paris | Zebrastreifen Paris | Passage piéton, Paris   1999, 49,5 × 30,7 cm

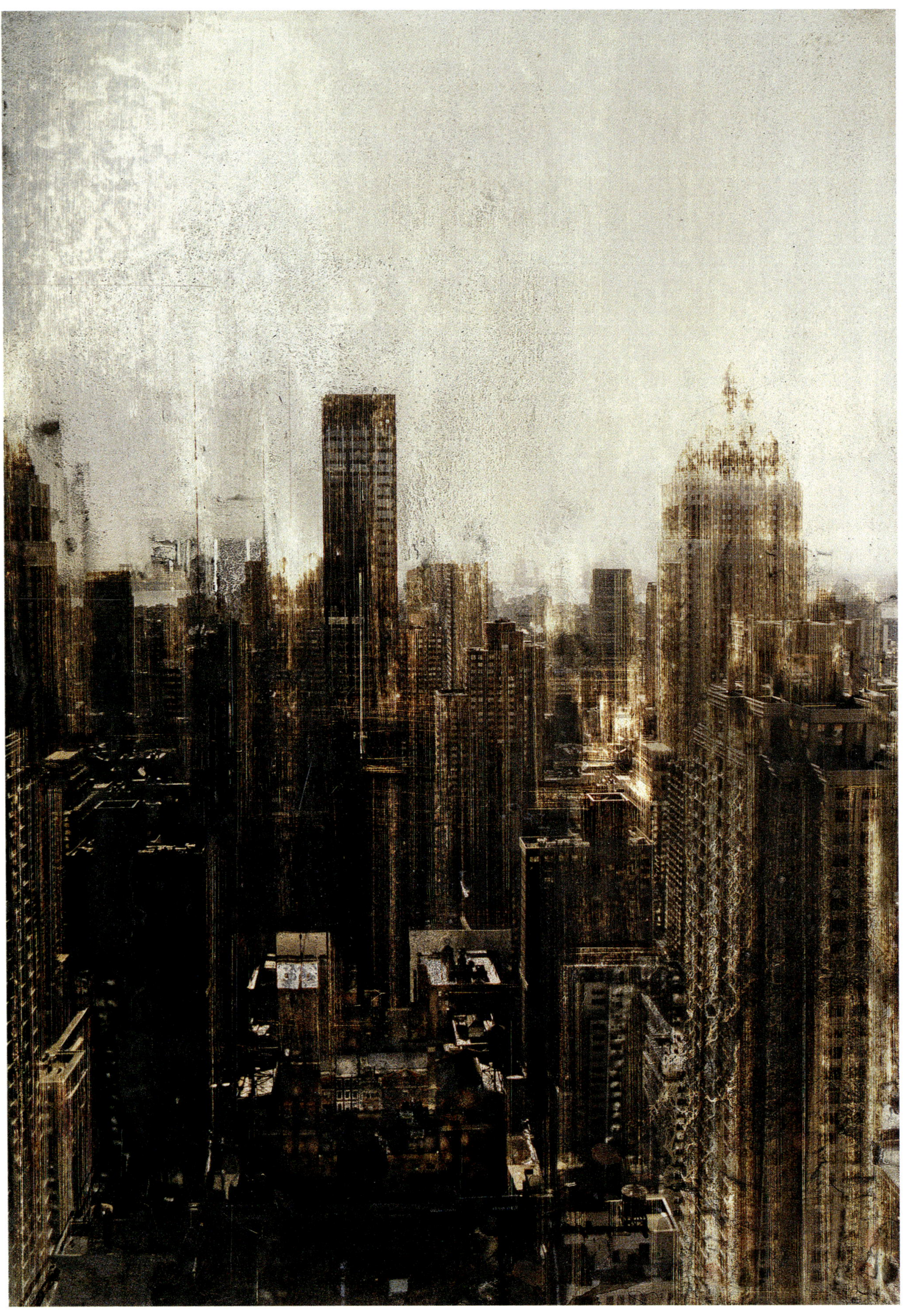

   New York, Midtown III   2006, 75,5 × 50,5 cm

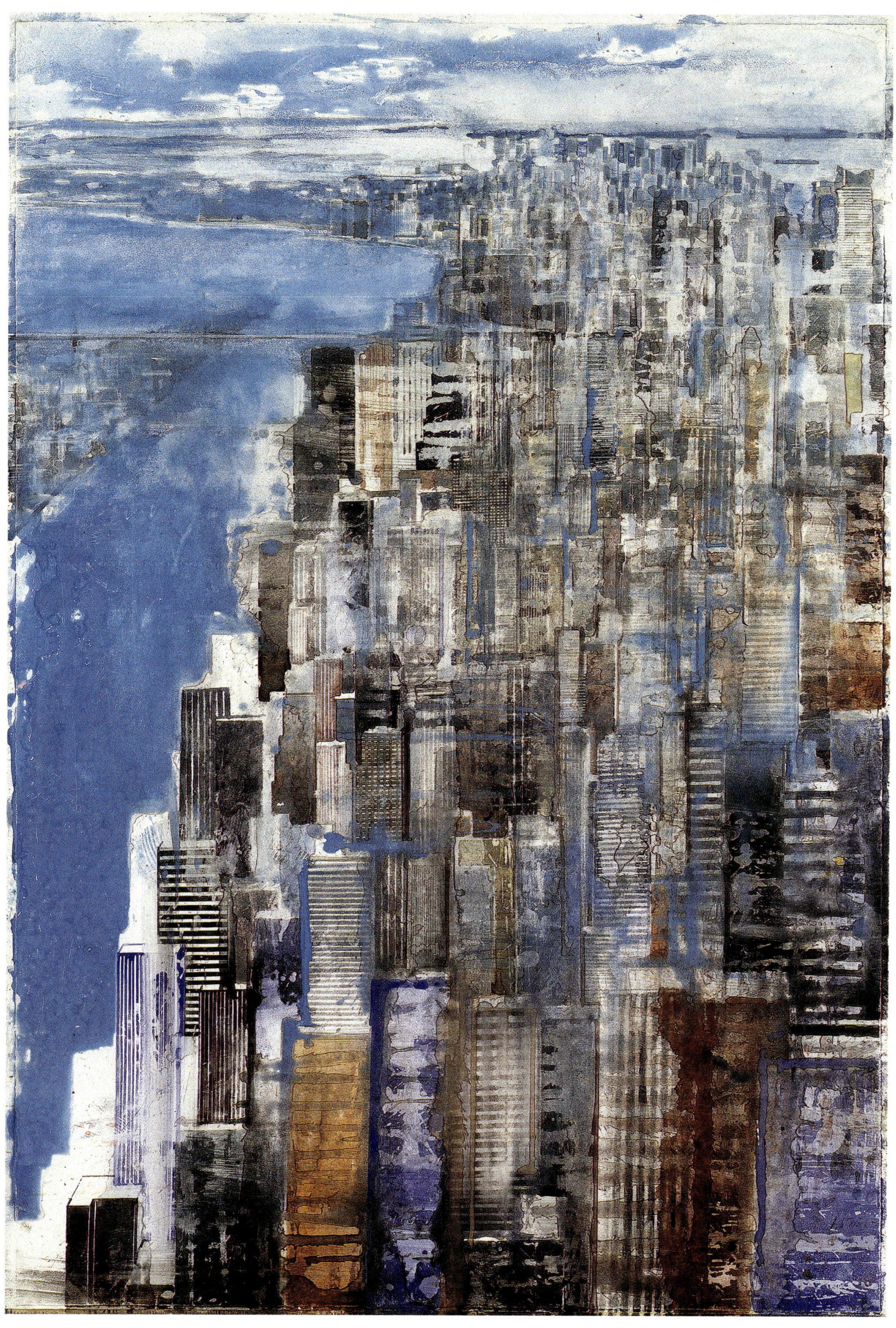

New York: Another Blue Day | New York: Noch ein blauer Tag | New York : encore un jour bleu   2006, 109 x 73 cm

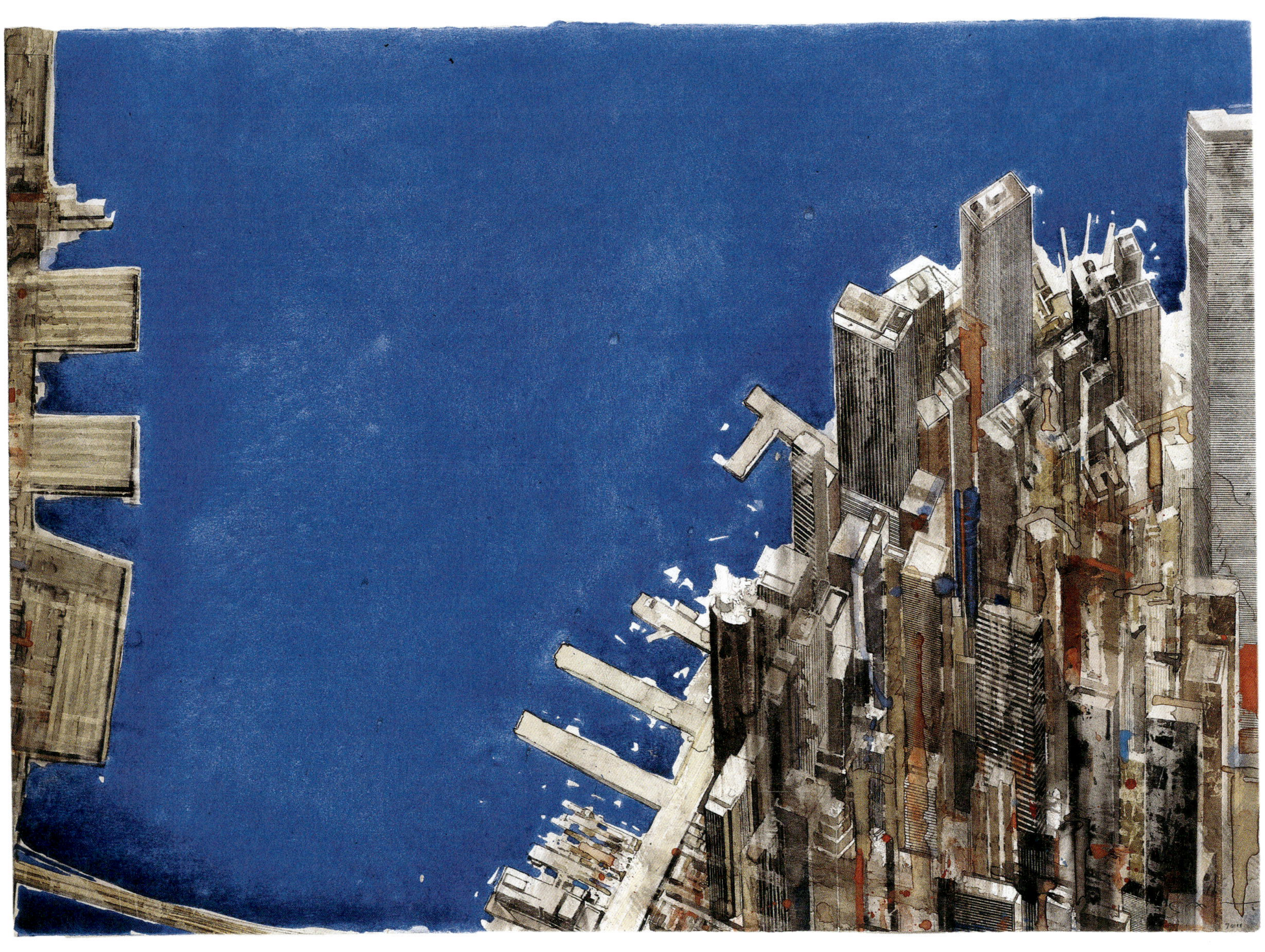

New York before September 11 | New York vor dem 11. September | New York avant le 11 septembre   1998, 47 × 60 cm

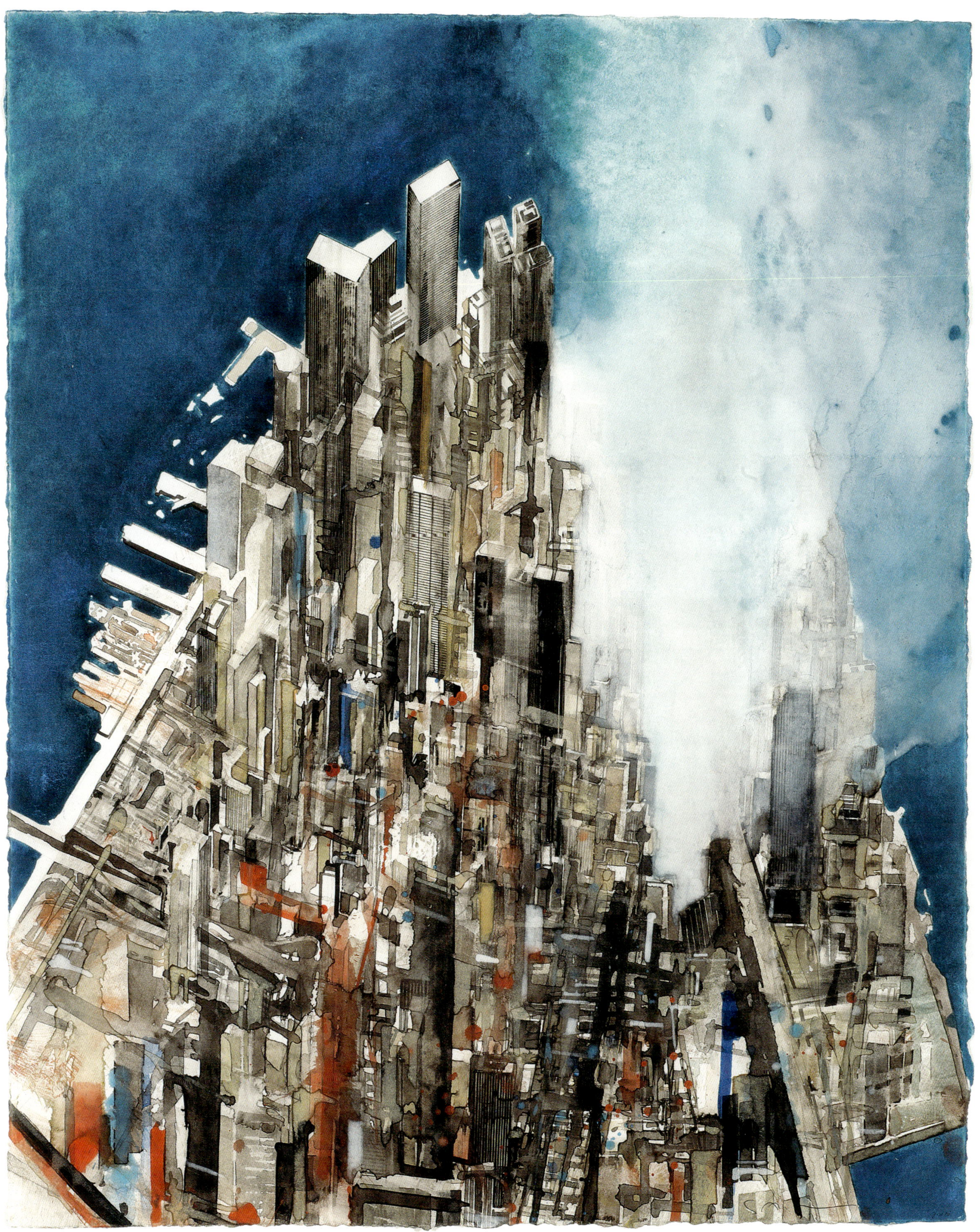

New York, September 11 | New York 11. September | New York 11 septembre   2001, 90 × 72 cm

Billboards, graffiti, walls
Plakatwände, Graffiti, Mauern
Affiches, graffiti, murs

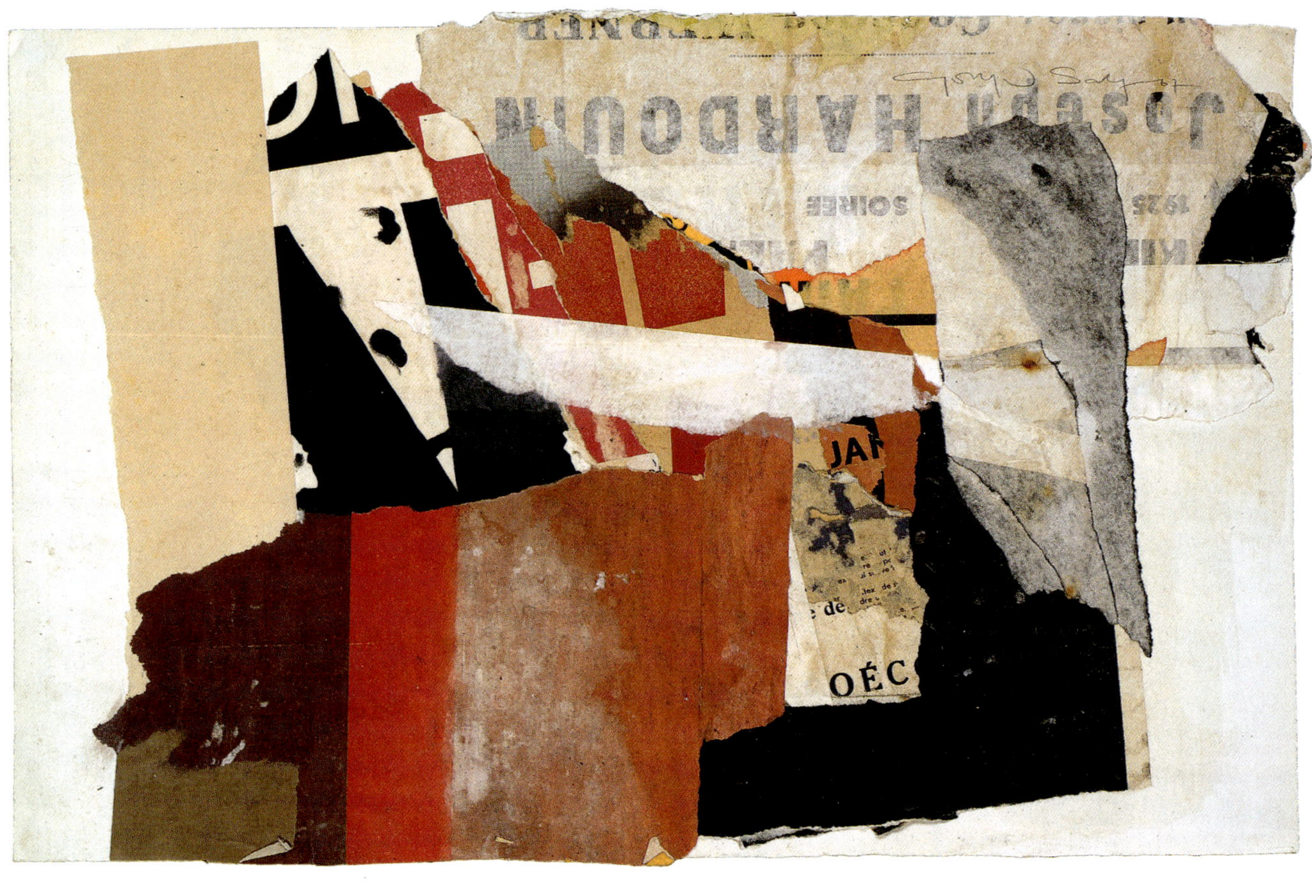

    Hardouin   1967, 32,5 × 50 cm

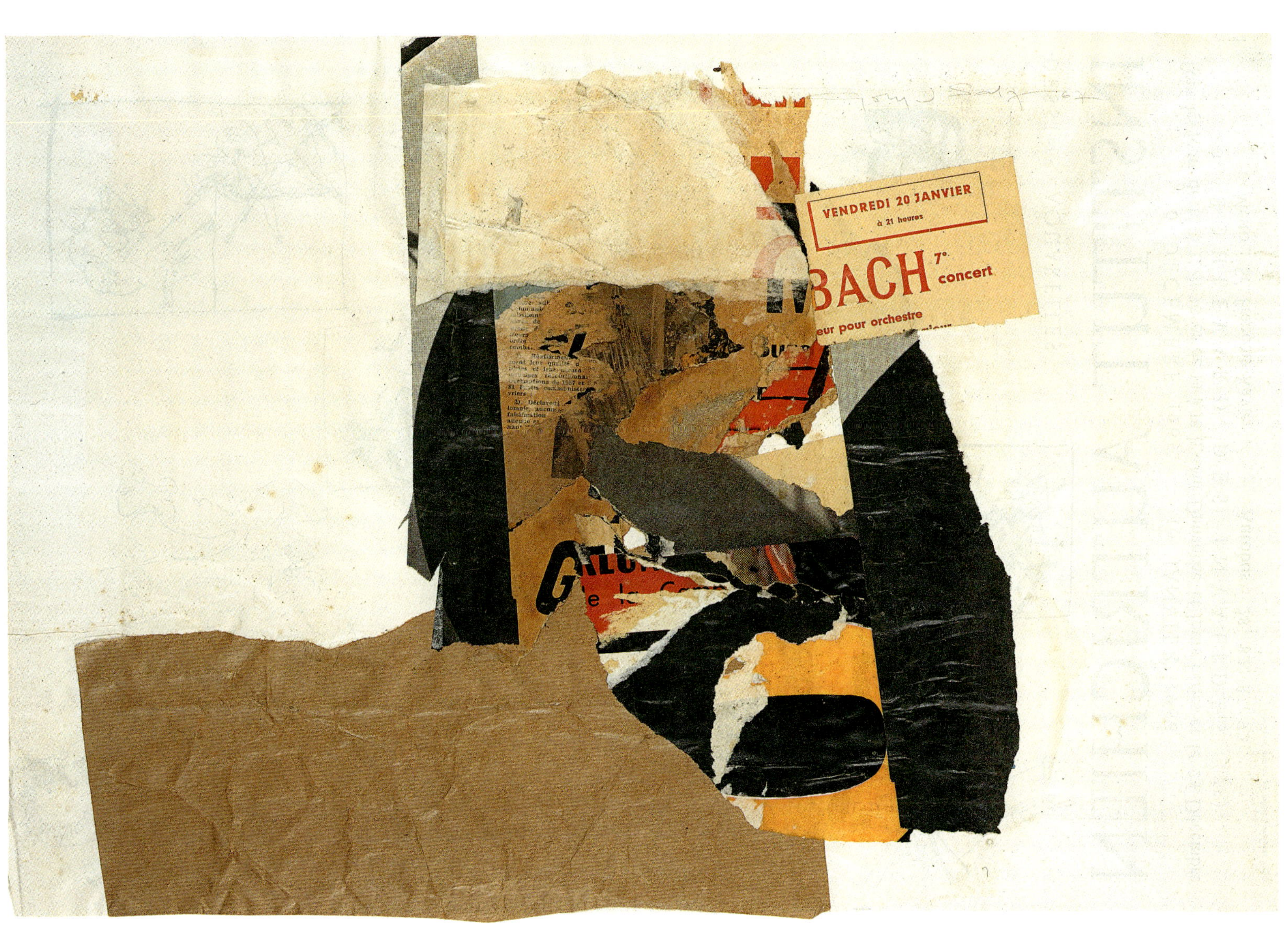

Bach   1967, 42,2 × 50 cm

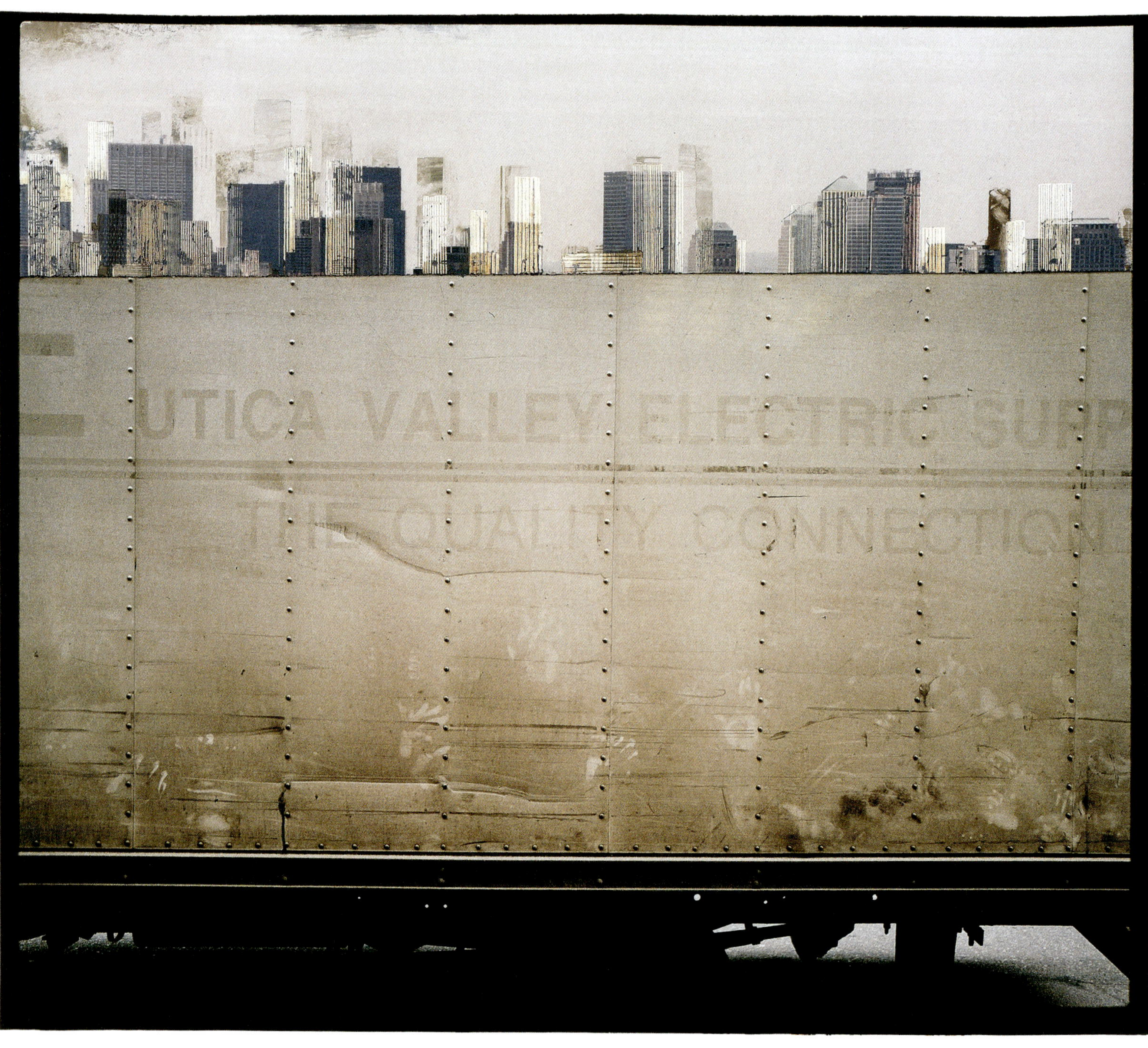

     Utica   2009, 118 × 131 cm

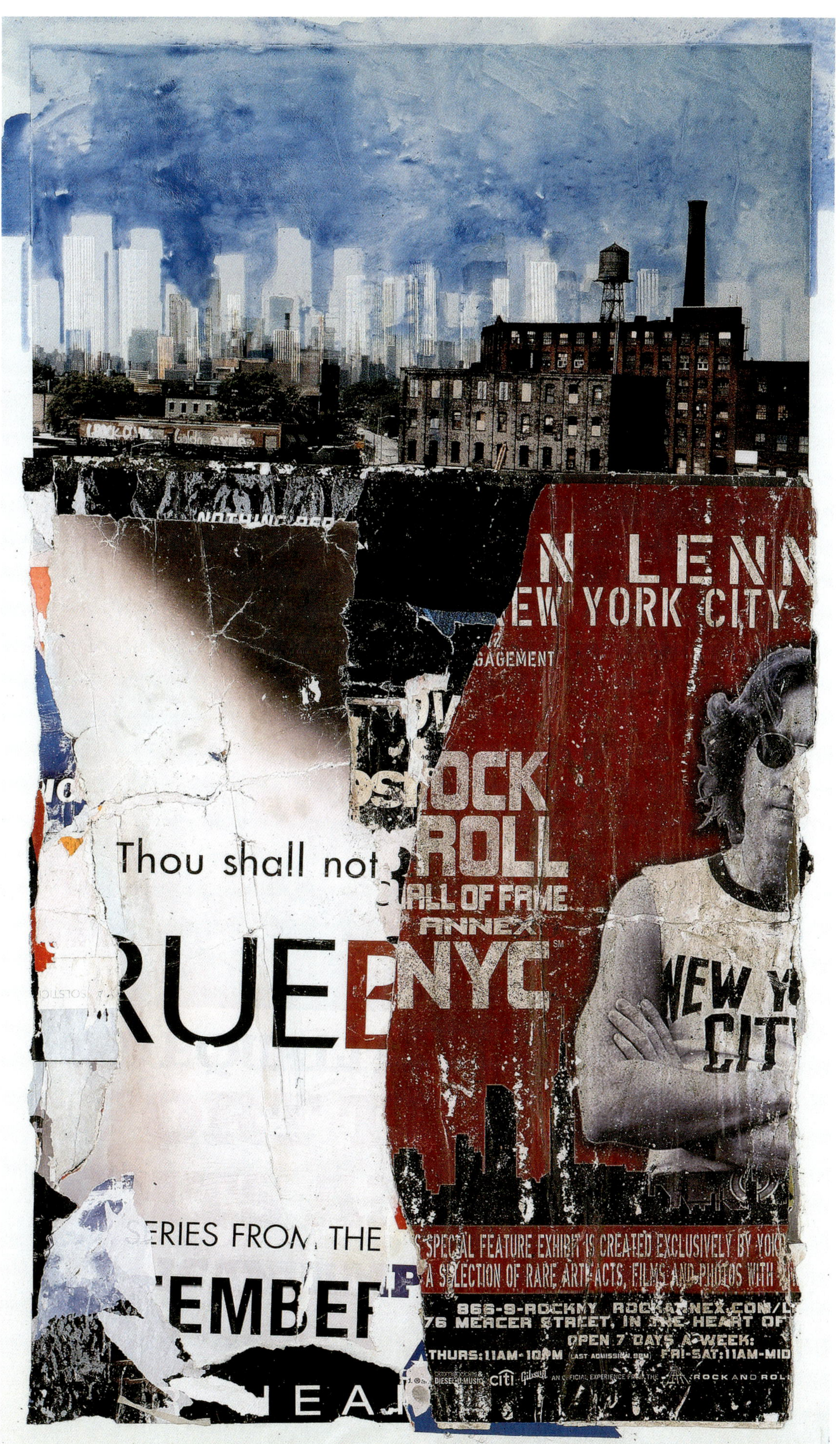
N LENN
EW YORK CITY
GAGEMENT
ROCK
ROLL
HALL OF FAME
ANNEX
NYC
NEW YORK CITY
Thou shall not
RUEB
SERIES FROM THE
TEMBEF
EA
THIS SPECIAL FEATURE EXHIBIT IS CREATED EXCLUSIVELY BY YOKO
A SELECTION OF RARE ARTIFACTS, FILMS AND PHOTOS WITH
866-9-ROCKNY ROCKANNEX.COM/L
76 MERCER STREET, IN THE HEART OF
OPEN 7 DAYS A WEEK:
THURS:11AM-10PM FRI-SAT:11AM-MID
ROCK AND ROLL

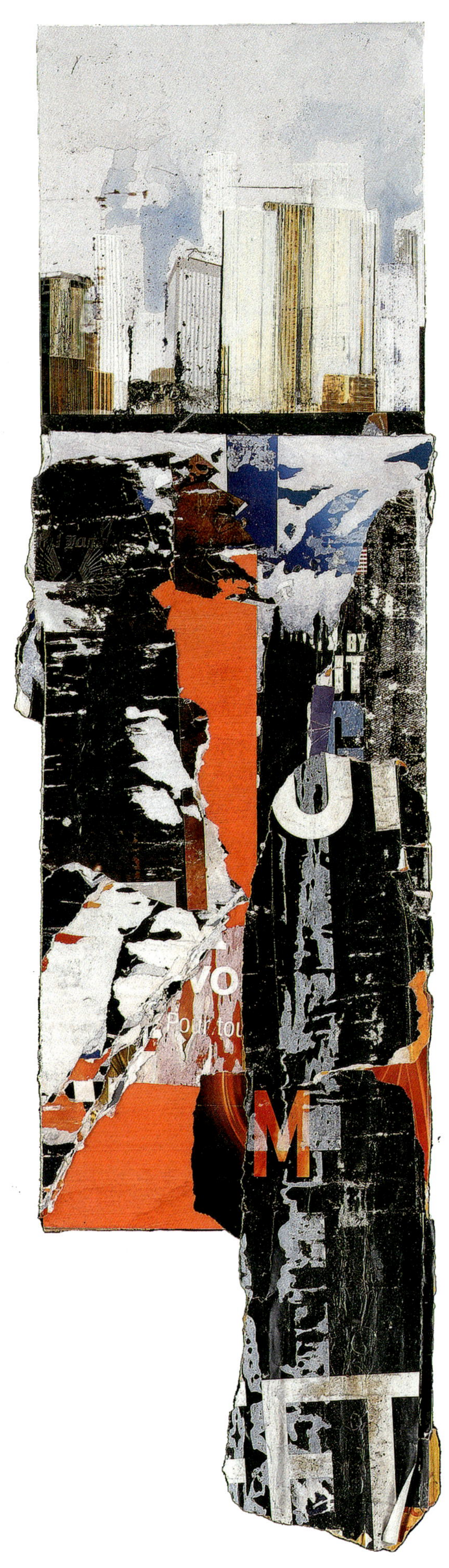

   BY   2011, 106 × 29 cm

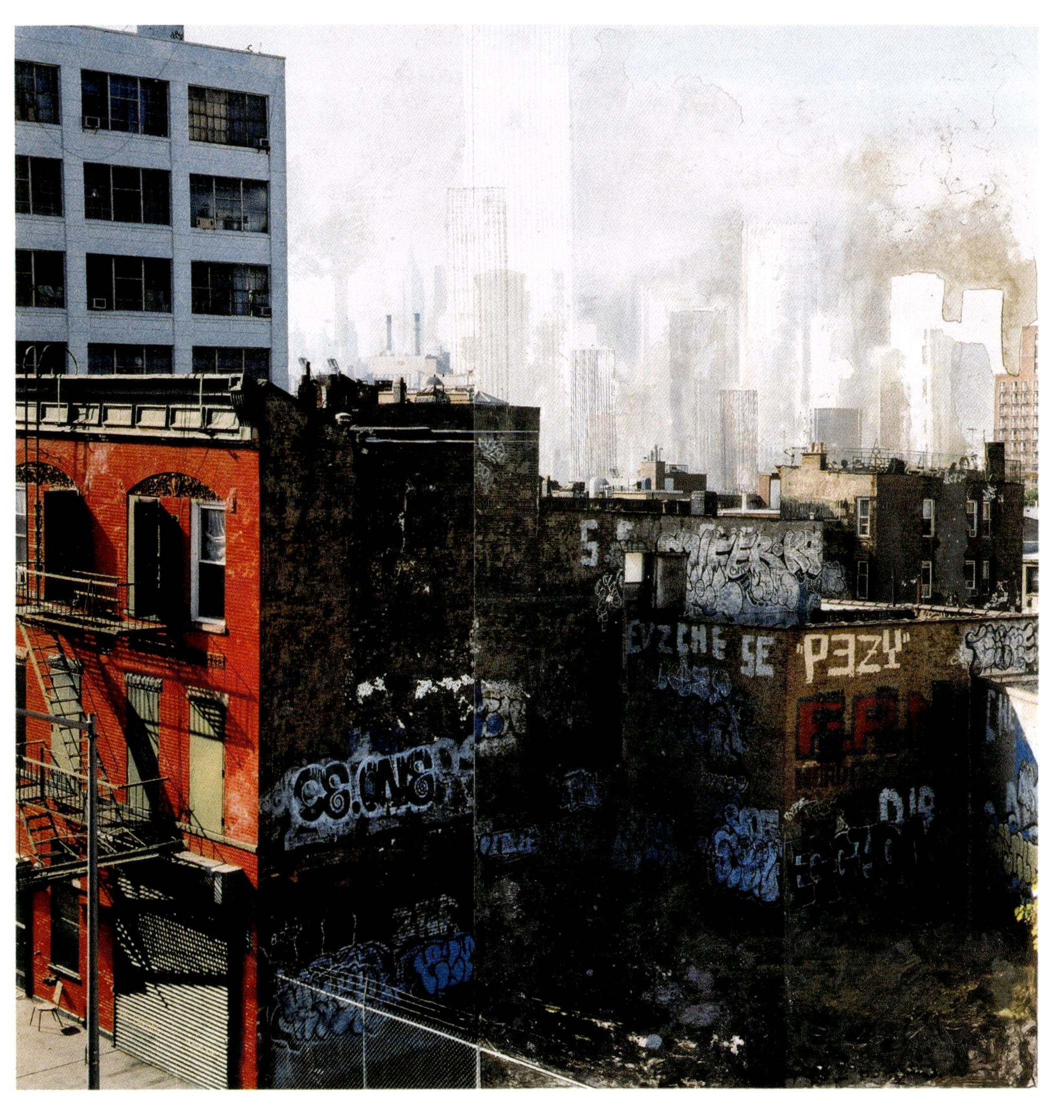

Pezy   2010, 78 × 74 cm

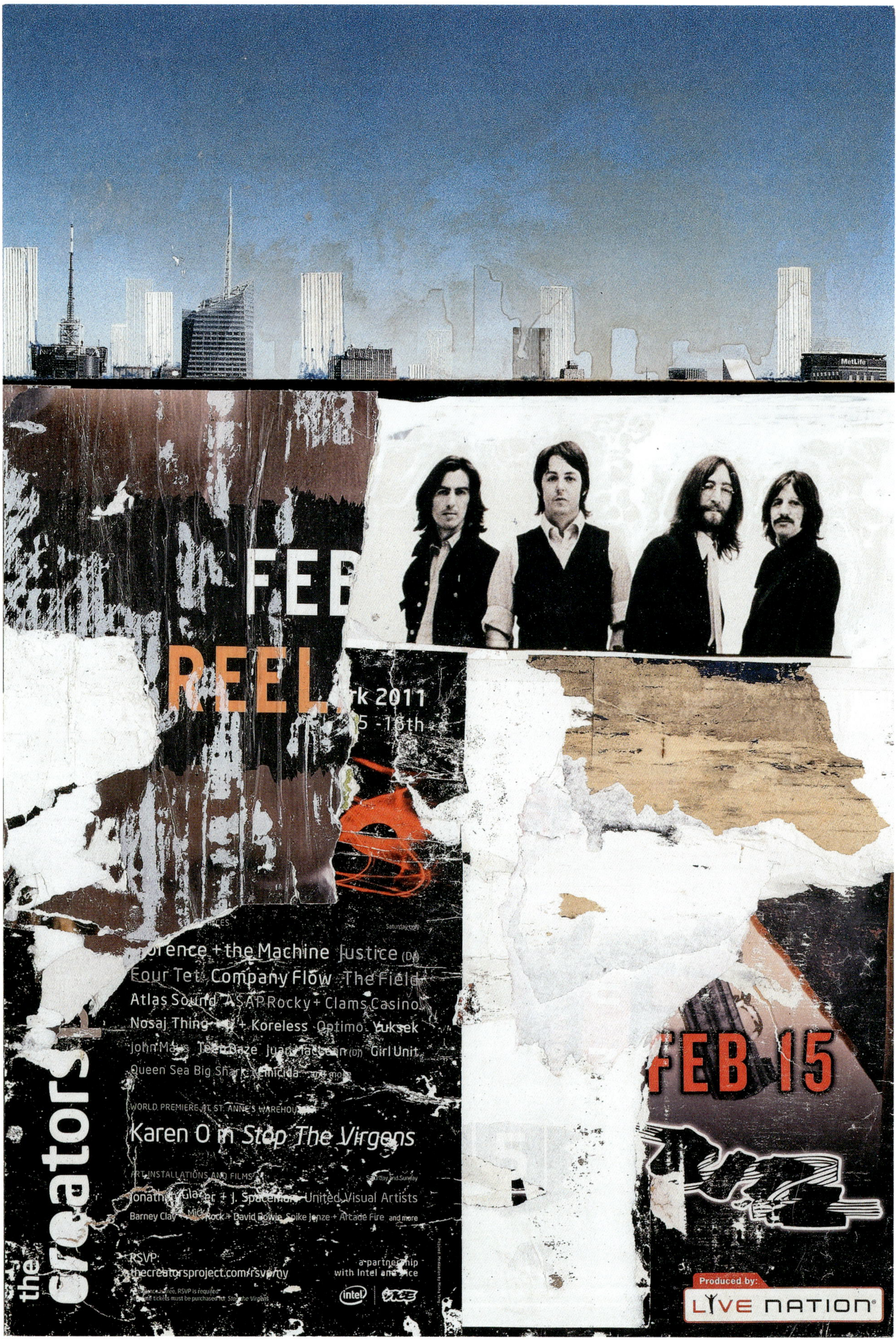

Creators February 15   2012, 81 × 54 cm

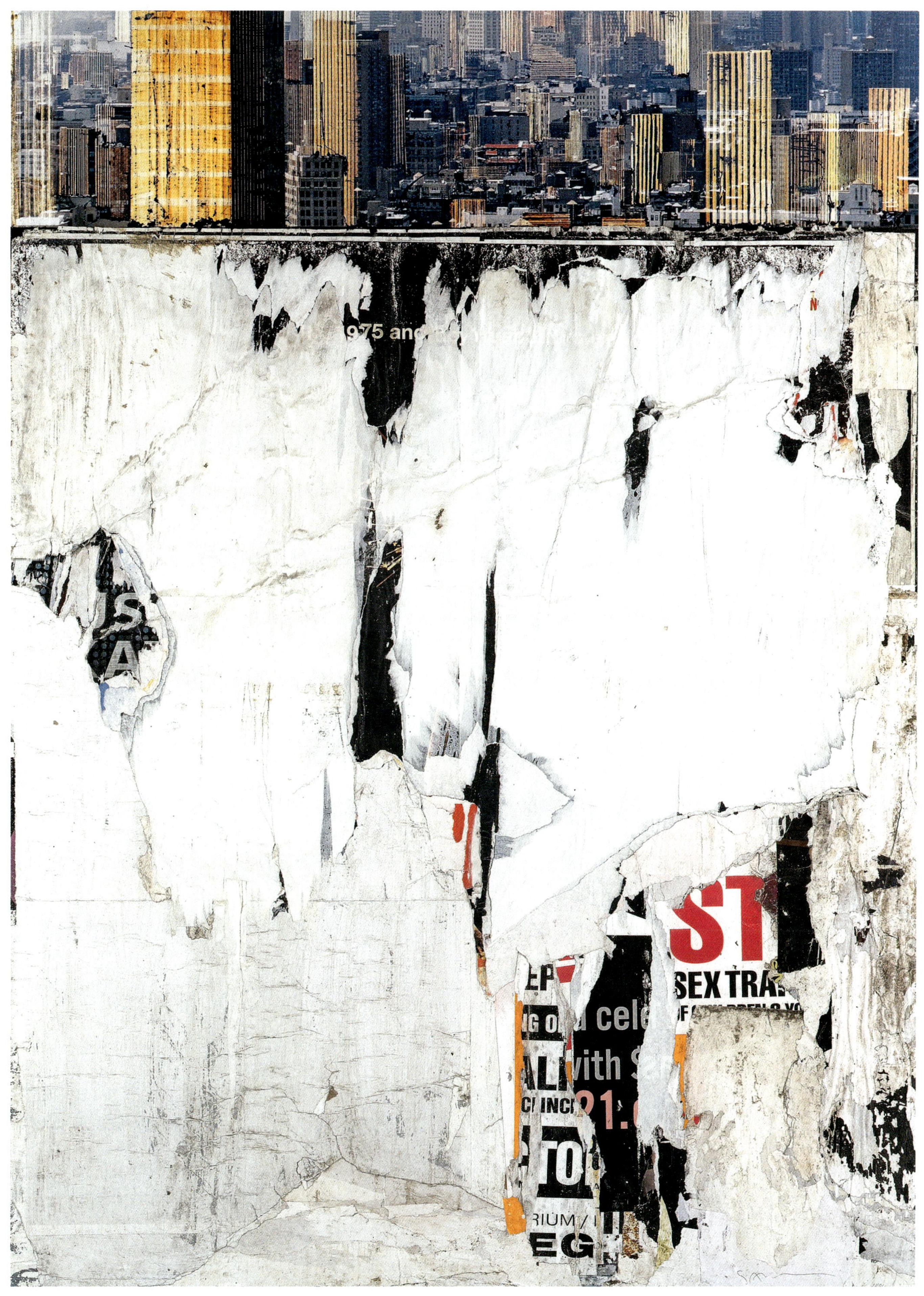

Sextra   2011, 162 × 114 cm

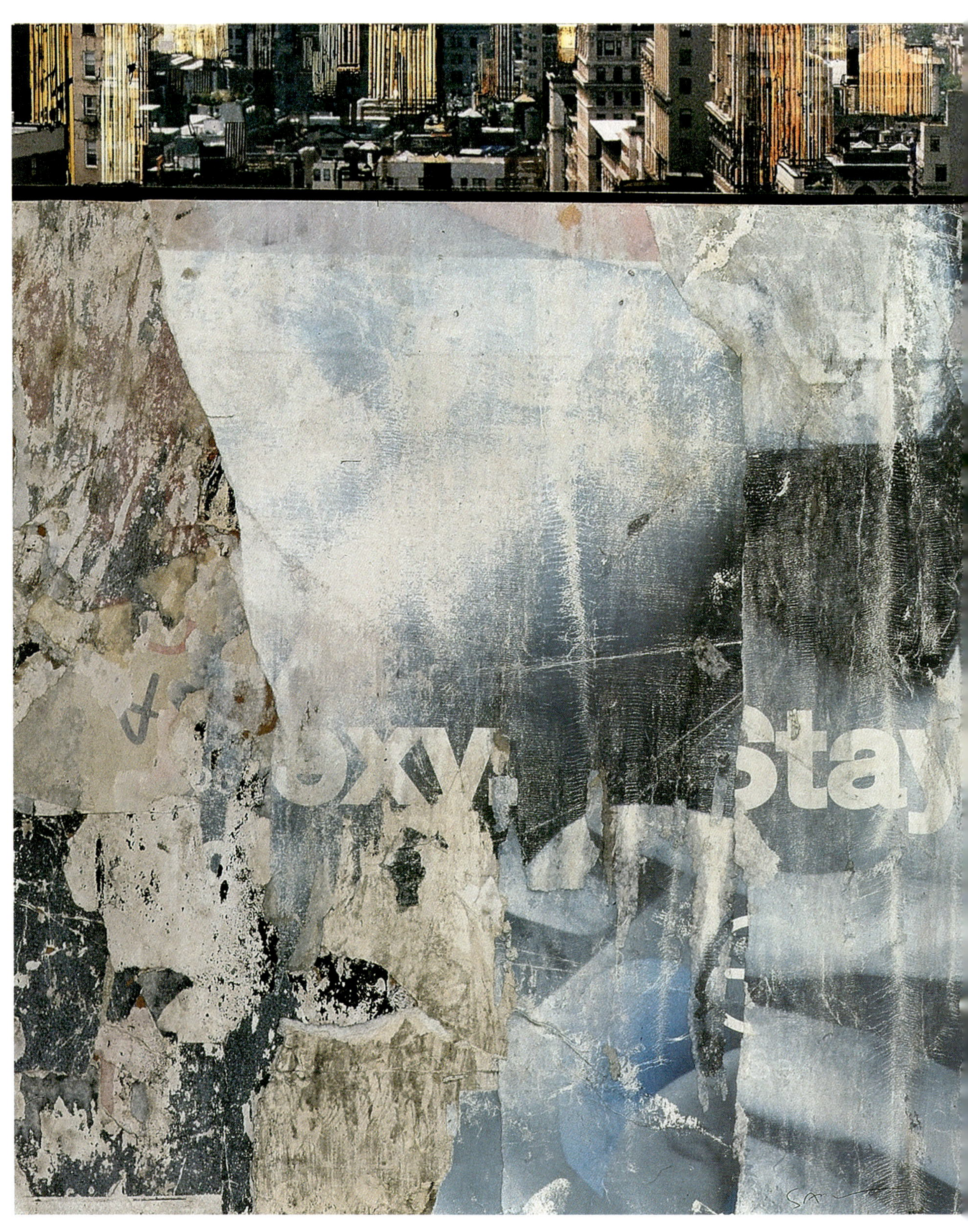

oxy
Sta

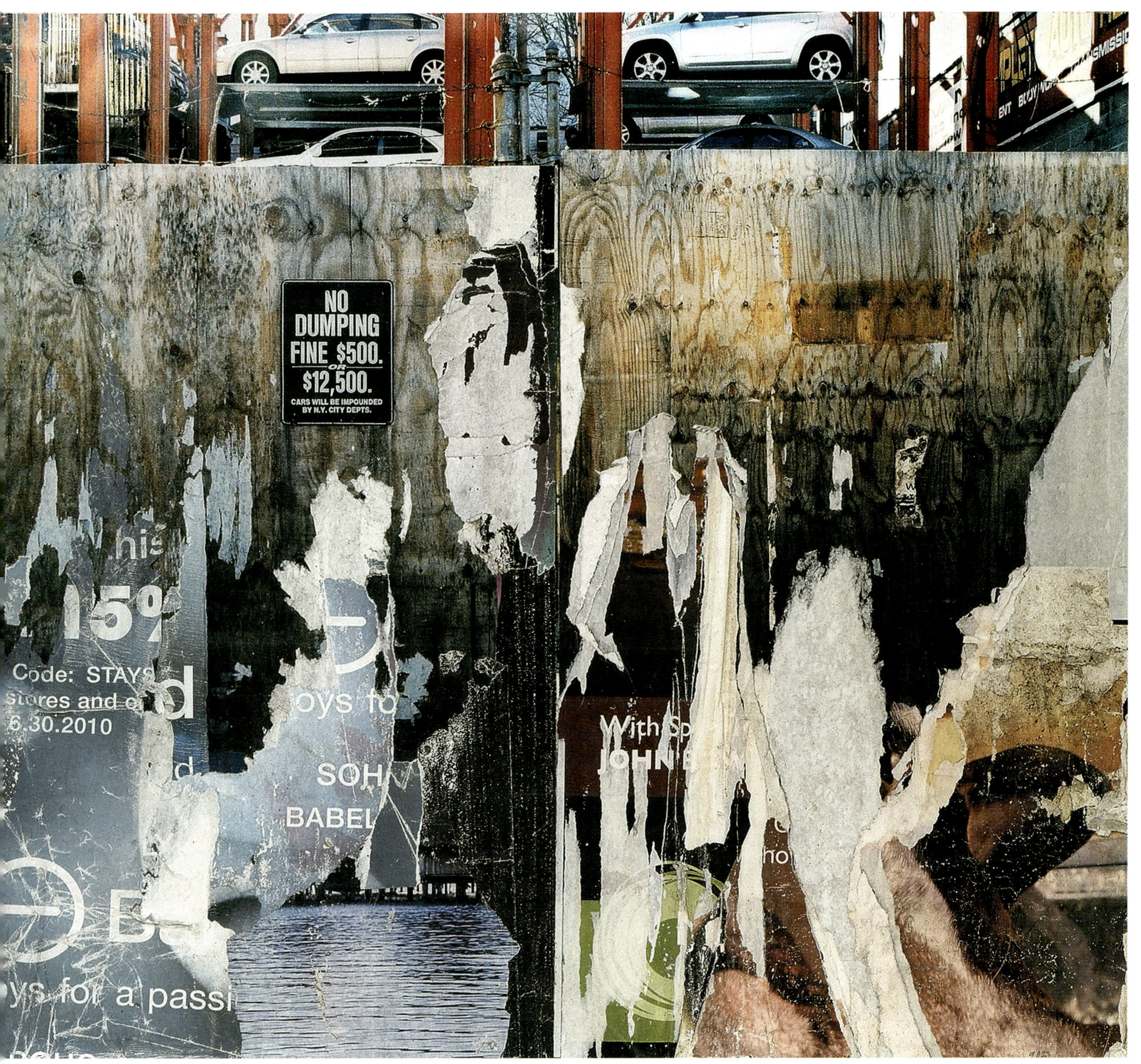

No Dumping   2010, 68 × 130 cm

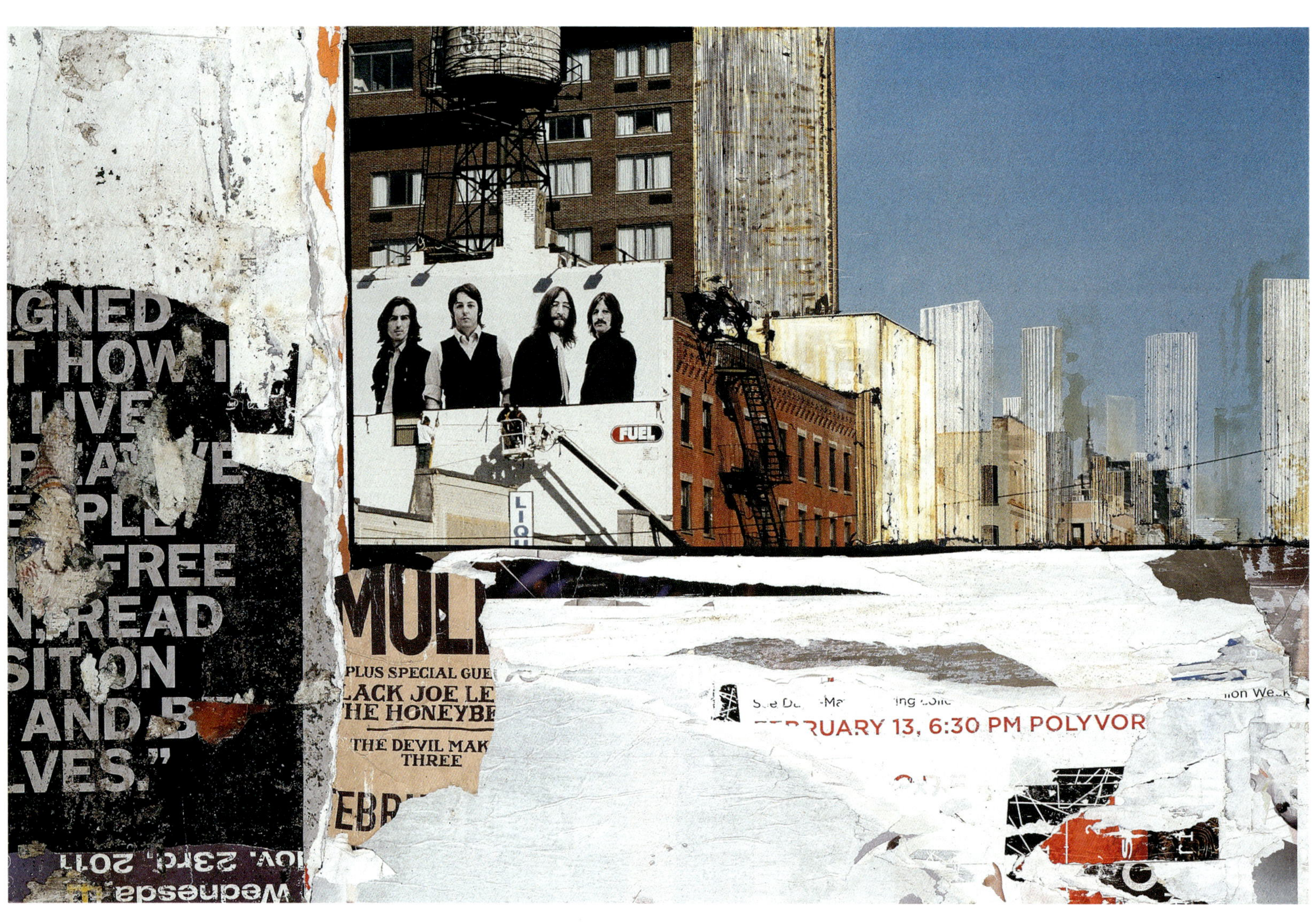

 Feb 13, 6:30 pm (The Beatles)   2012, 89 × 130 cm

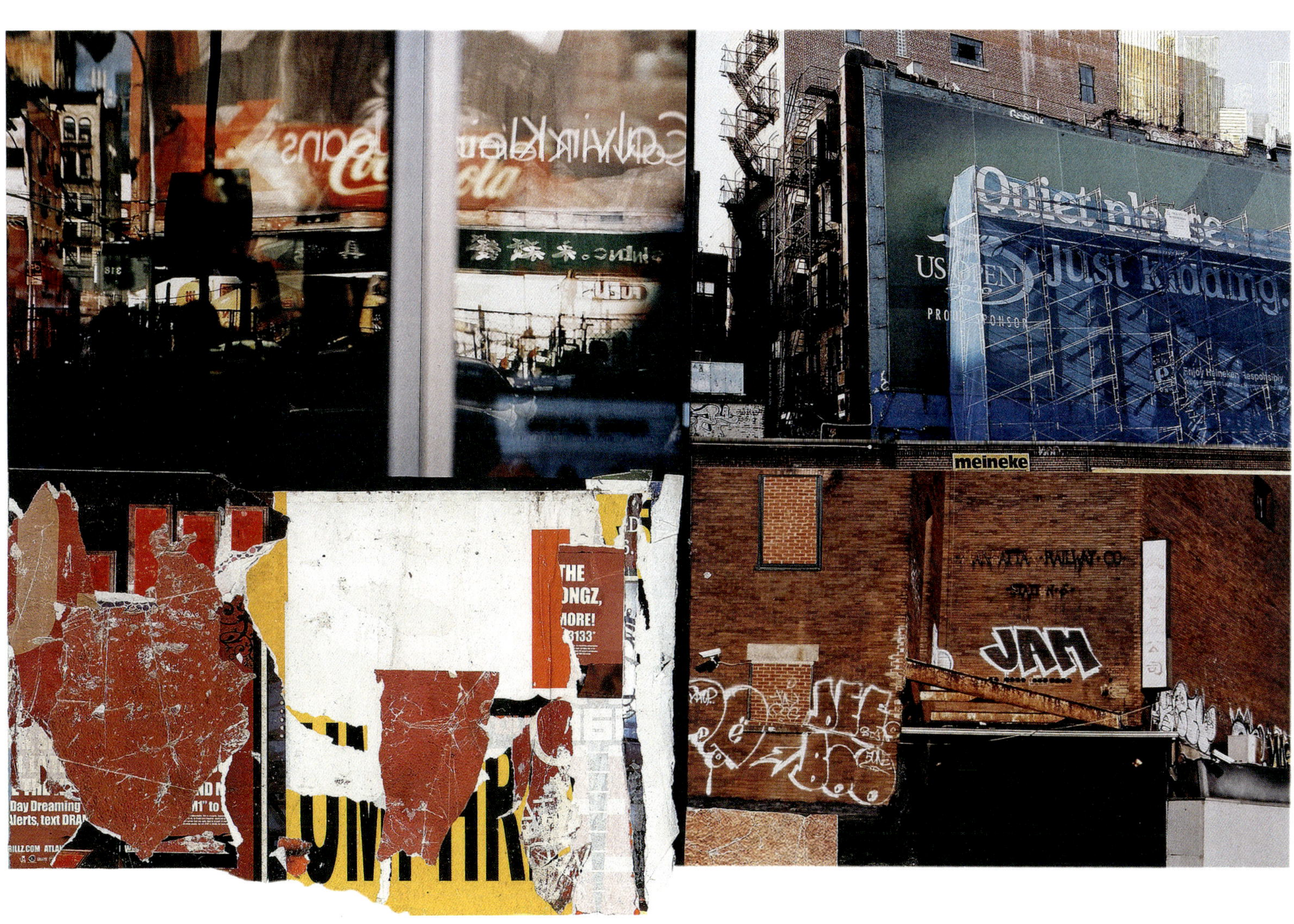

Calvin Klein
Coca-Cola
Quiet please.
Just kidding!
US OPEN
PROUD SPONSOR
meineke
JAM
THE
ONGZ,
MORE!

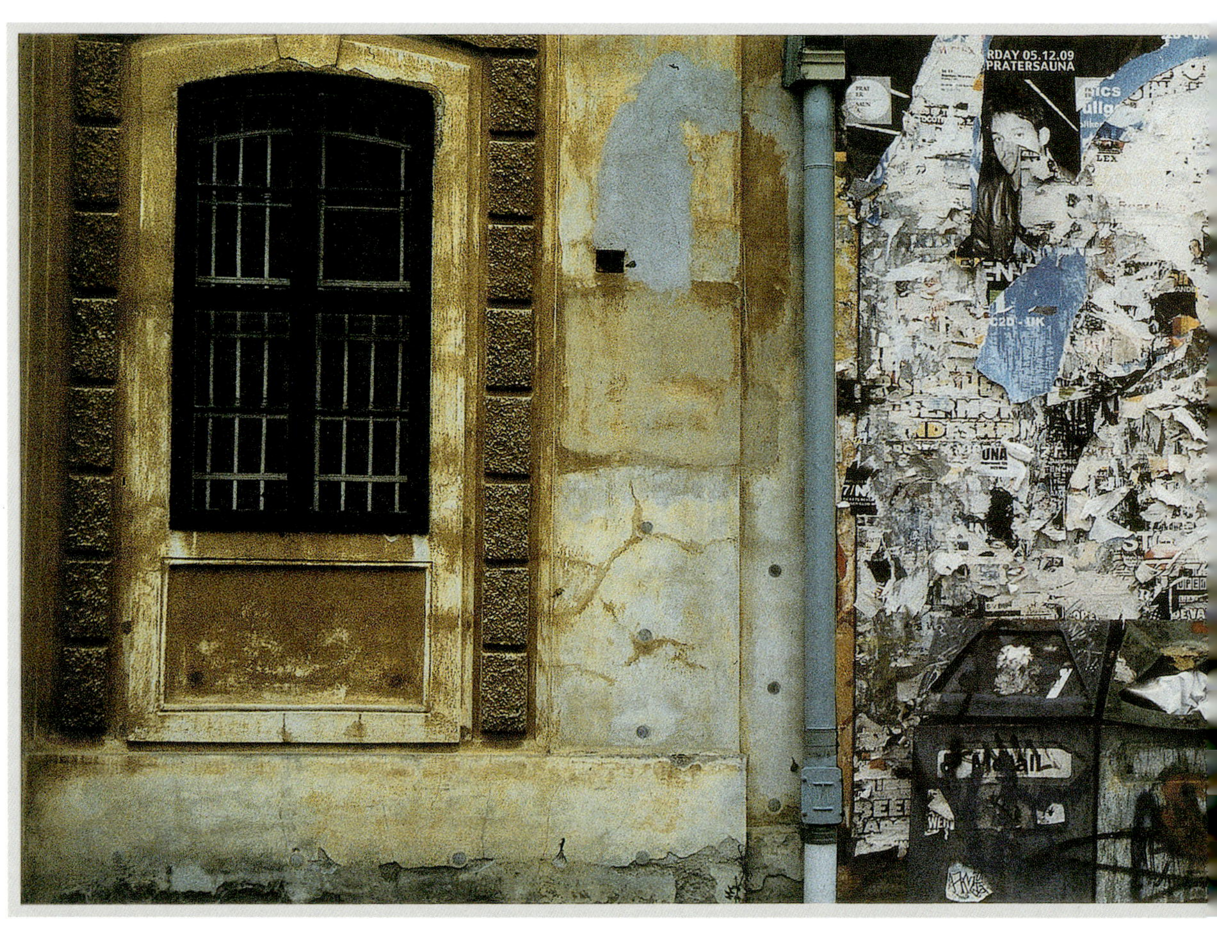

RDAY 05.12.09
PRATERSAUNA

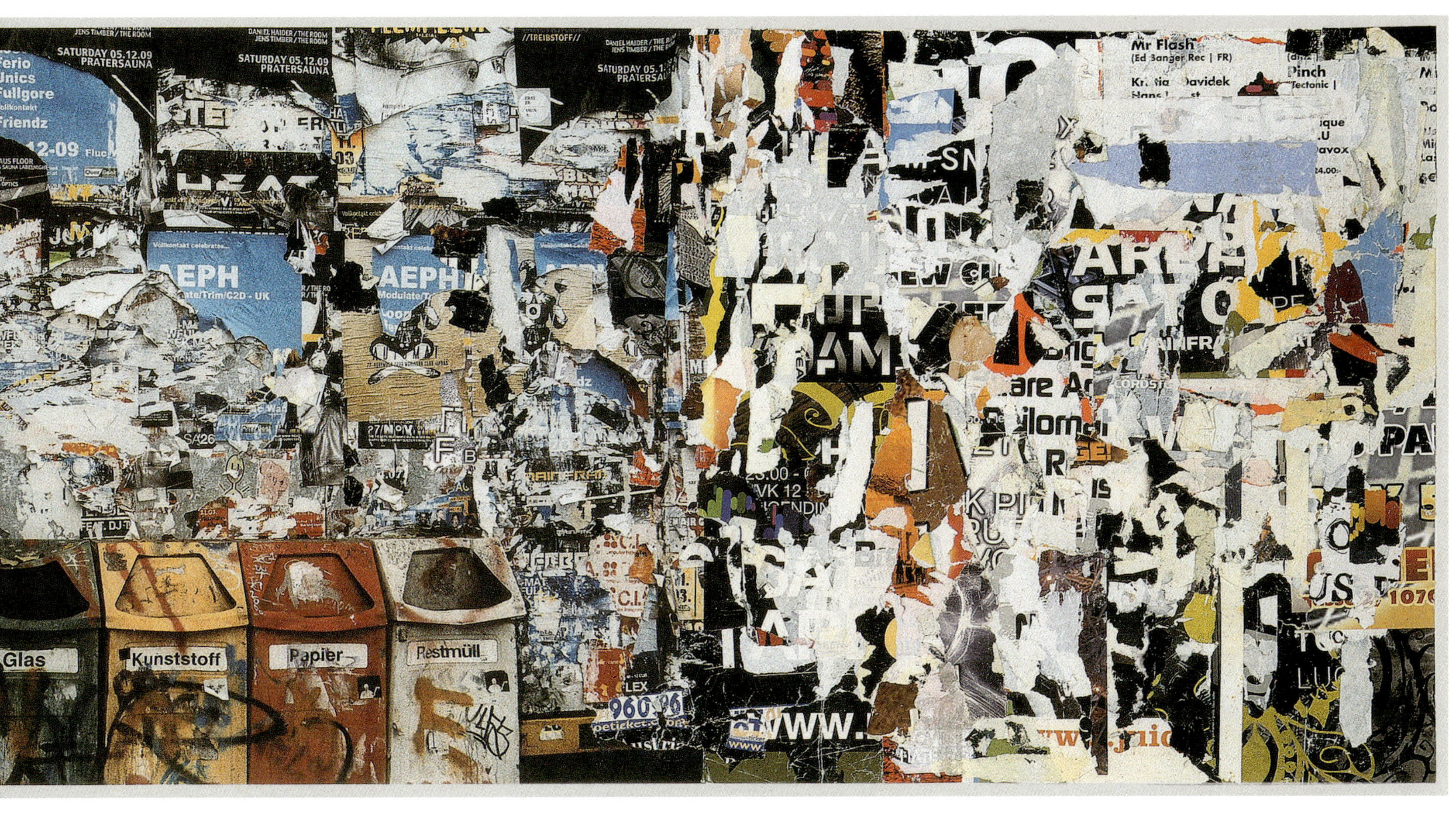

Vienna, Restmüll | *Wien, Restmüll* | Vienne, Restmüll   2009, 57 × 178 cm

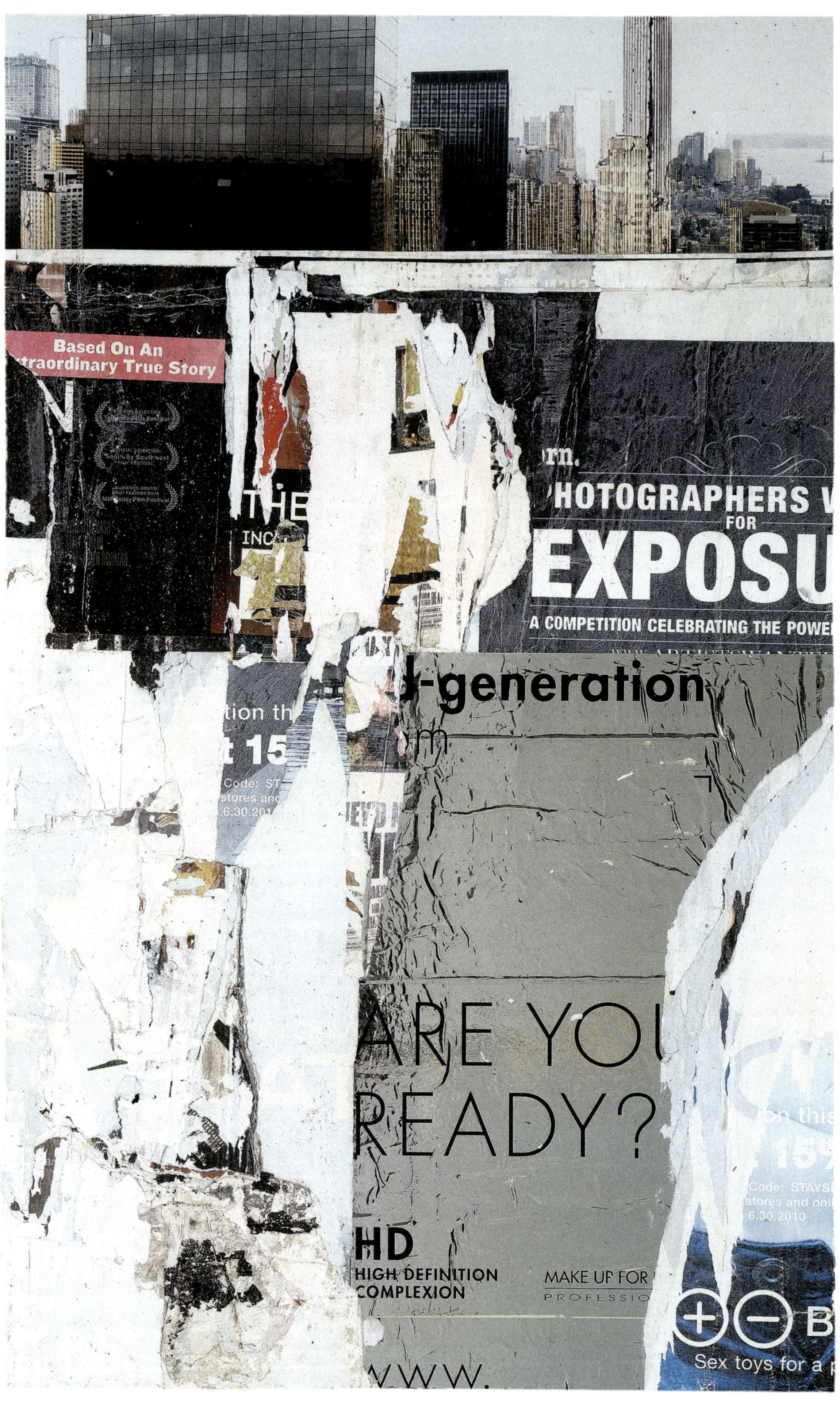

    Are You Ready?   2011, 162 × 97 cm

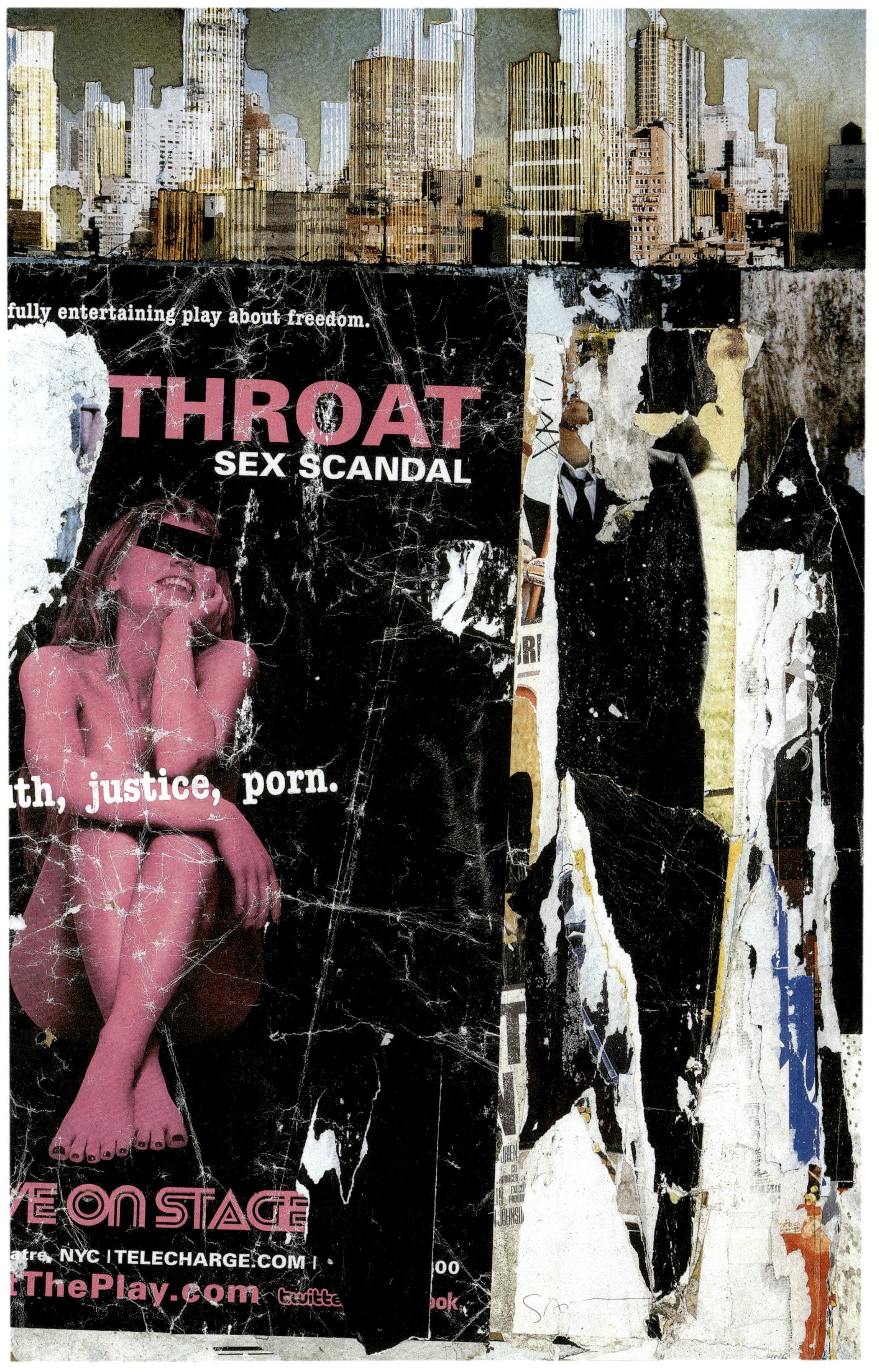

Sex Scandal   2010, 116 × 73 cm

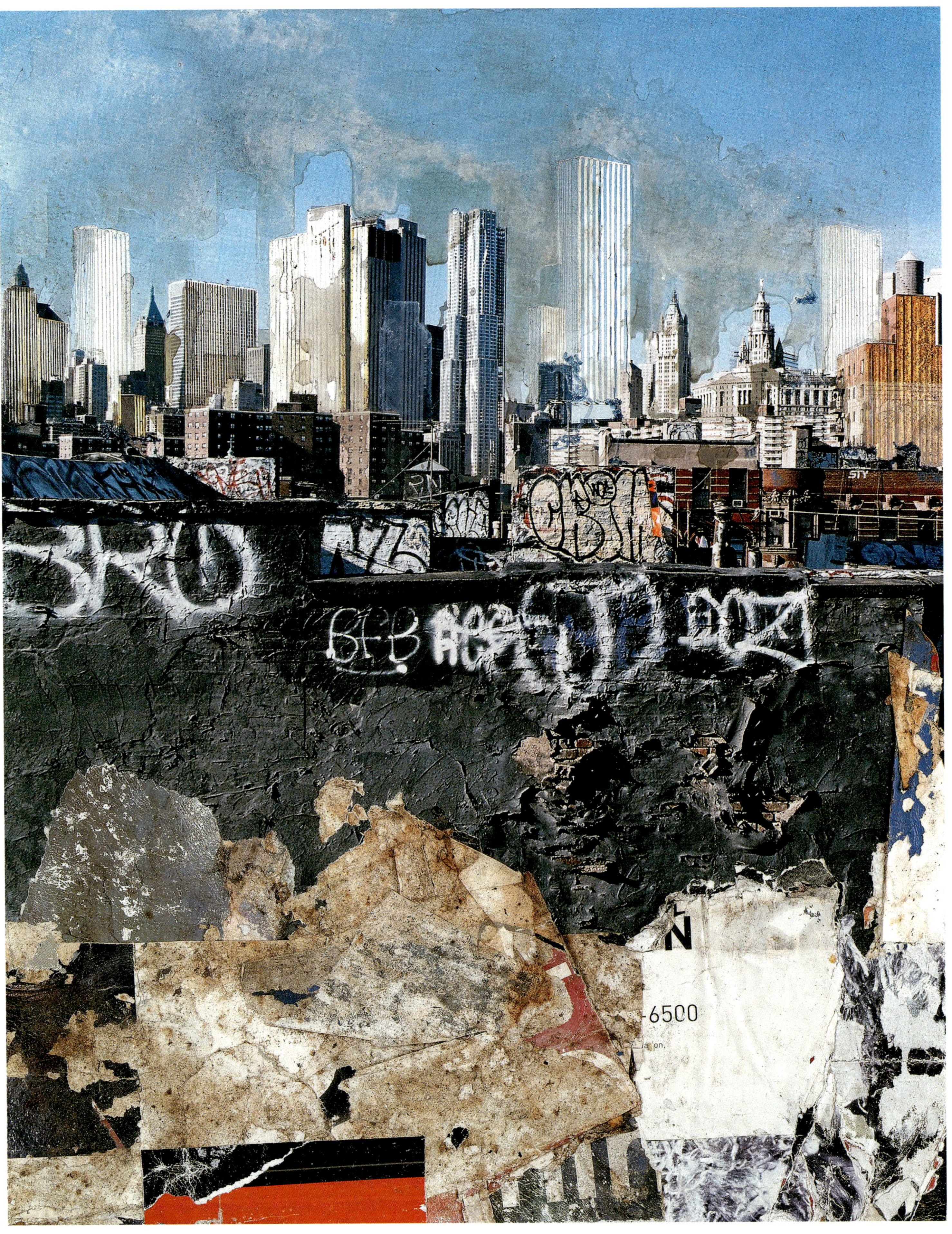

     6500   2011, 65 × 50 cm

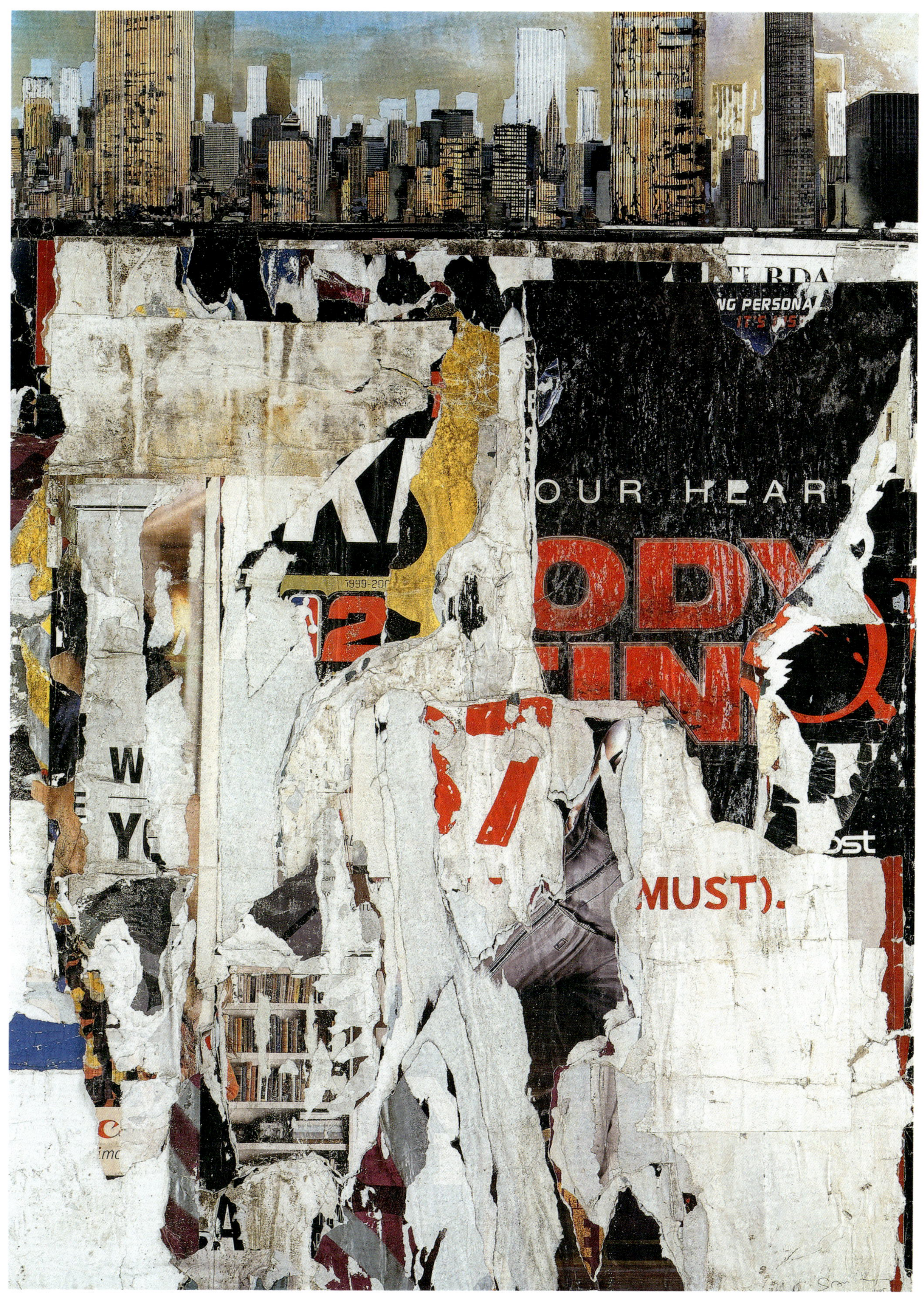

Must   2010, 162 × 114 cm

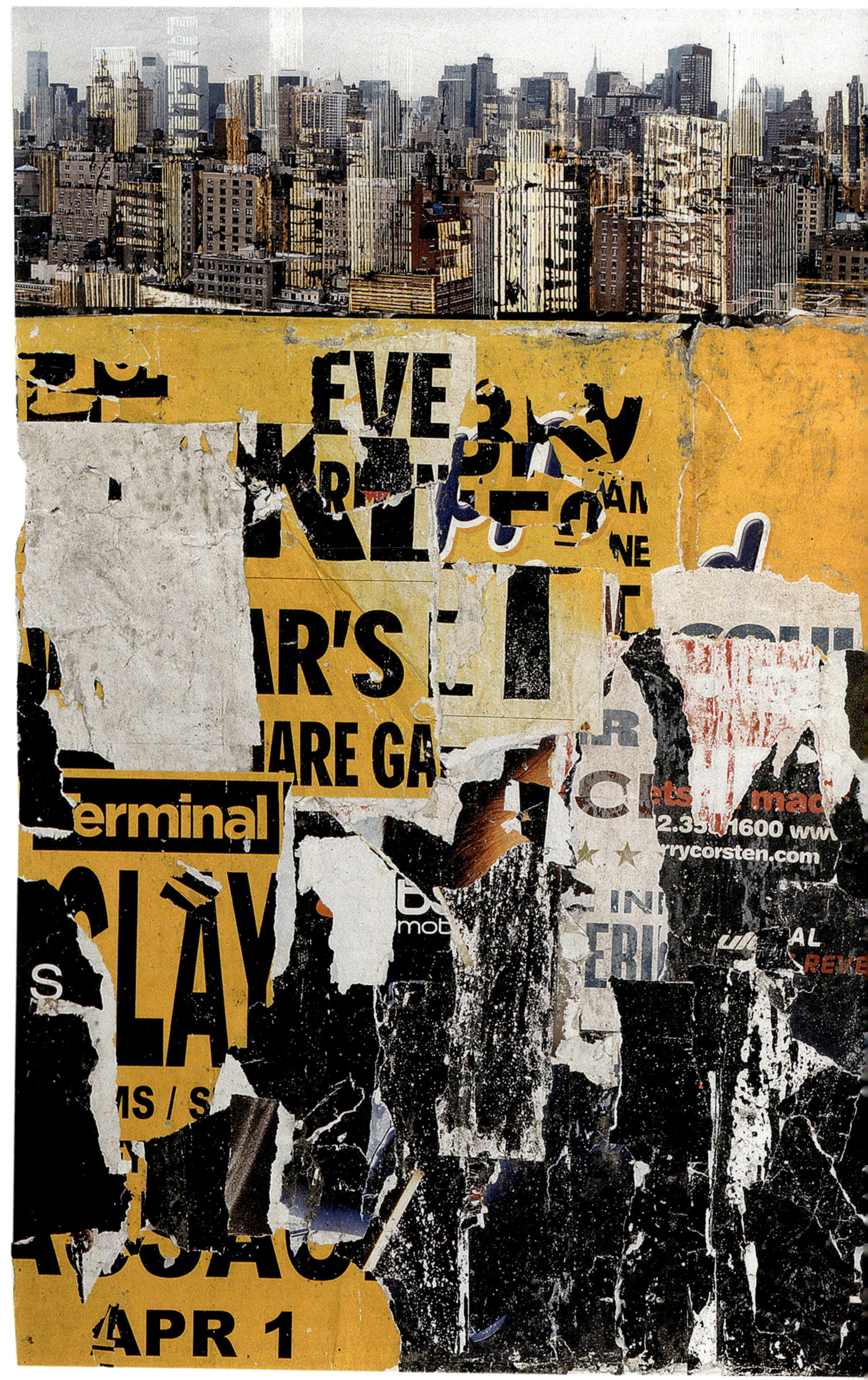
EVE 3 RY
AM NE
AR'S
ARE GA
erminal
SLAV
S
MS / S
APR 1
2.35 1600 ww
rrycorsten.com
B mob
AL
REVE

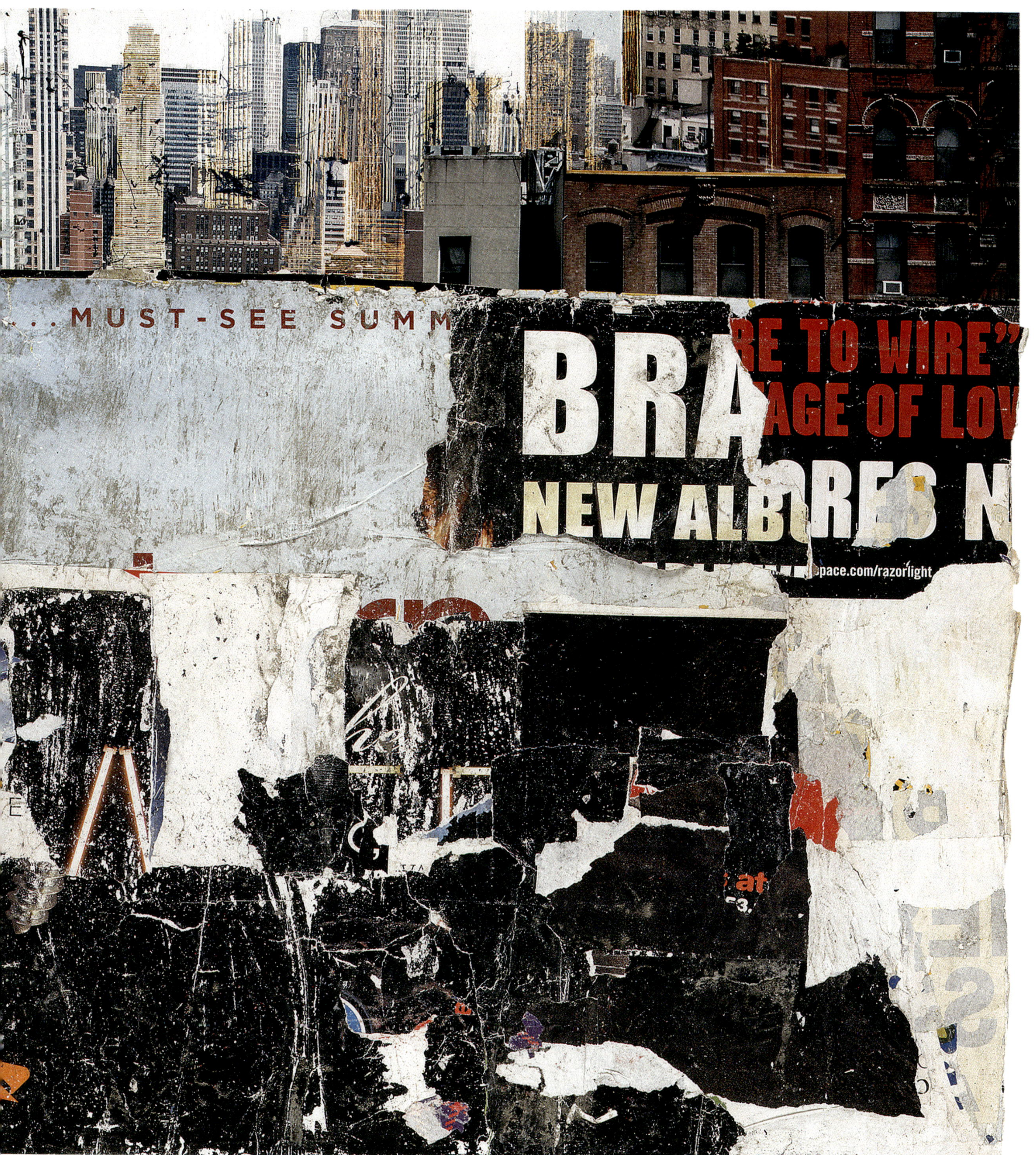

Must See   2010, 124 × 187 cm

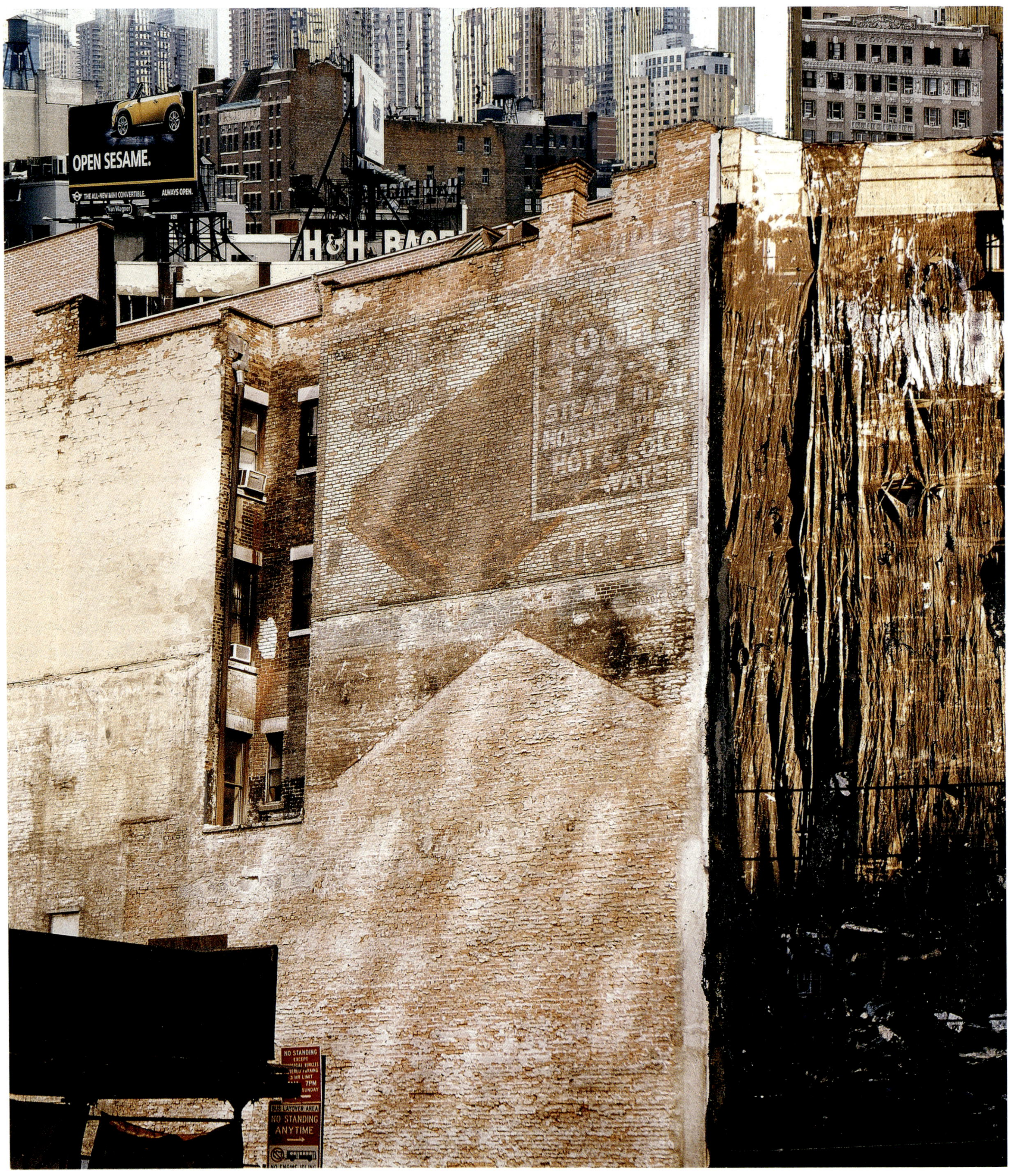

Open Sesame   2010, 110 × 95 cm

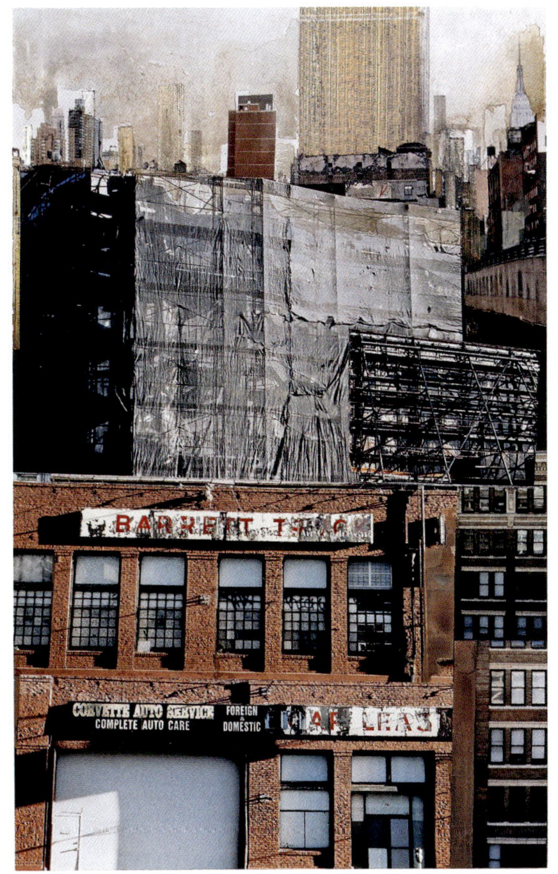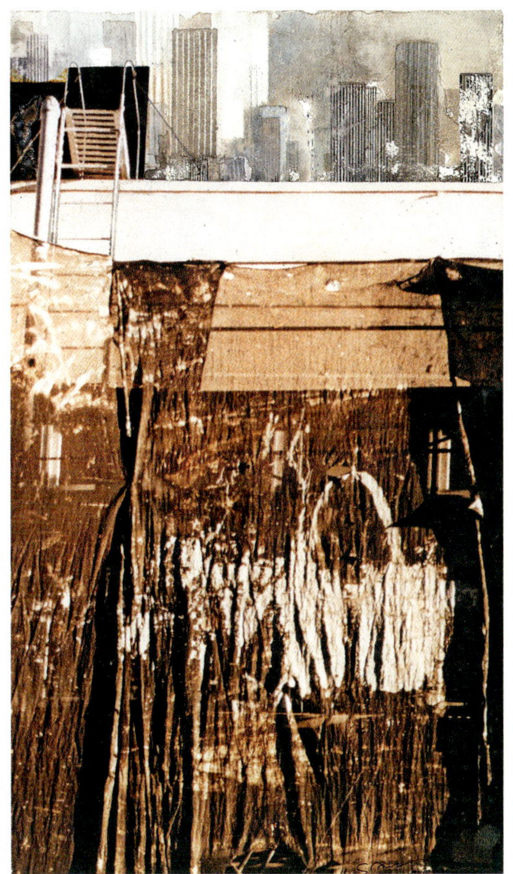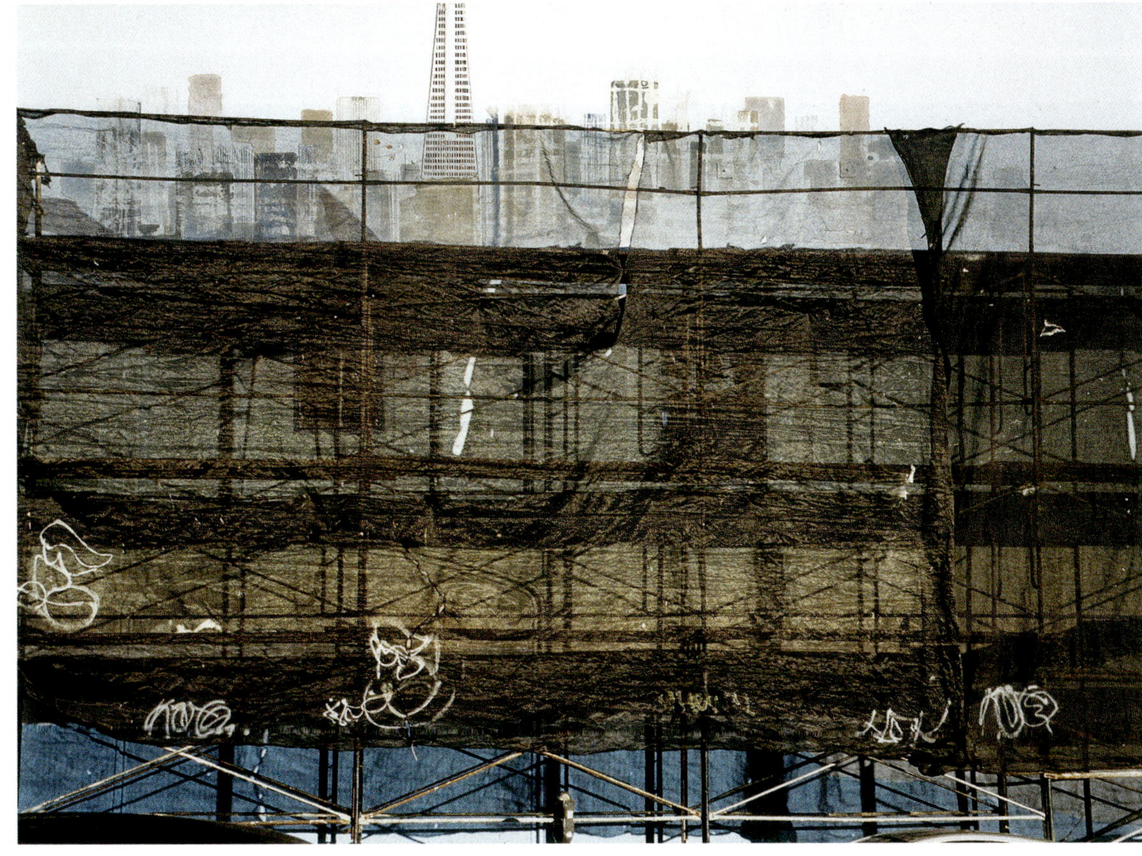

Corvette Auto Service   2010, 130 × 81 cm
SF Protection Cover I | SF Schutzplane I | SF La Bâche I   2010, 46,8 × 27 cm
SF Protection Cover II | SF Schutzplane II | SF La Bâche II   2010, 89 × 130 cm

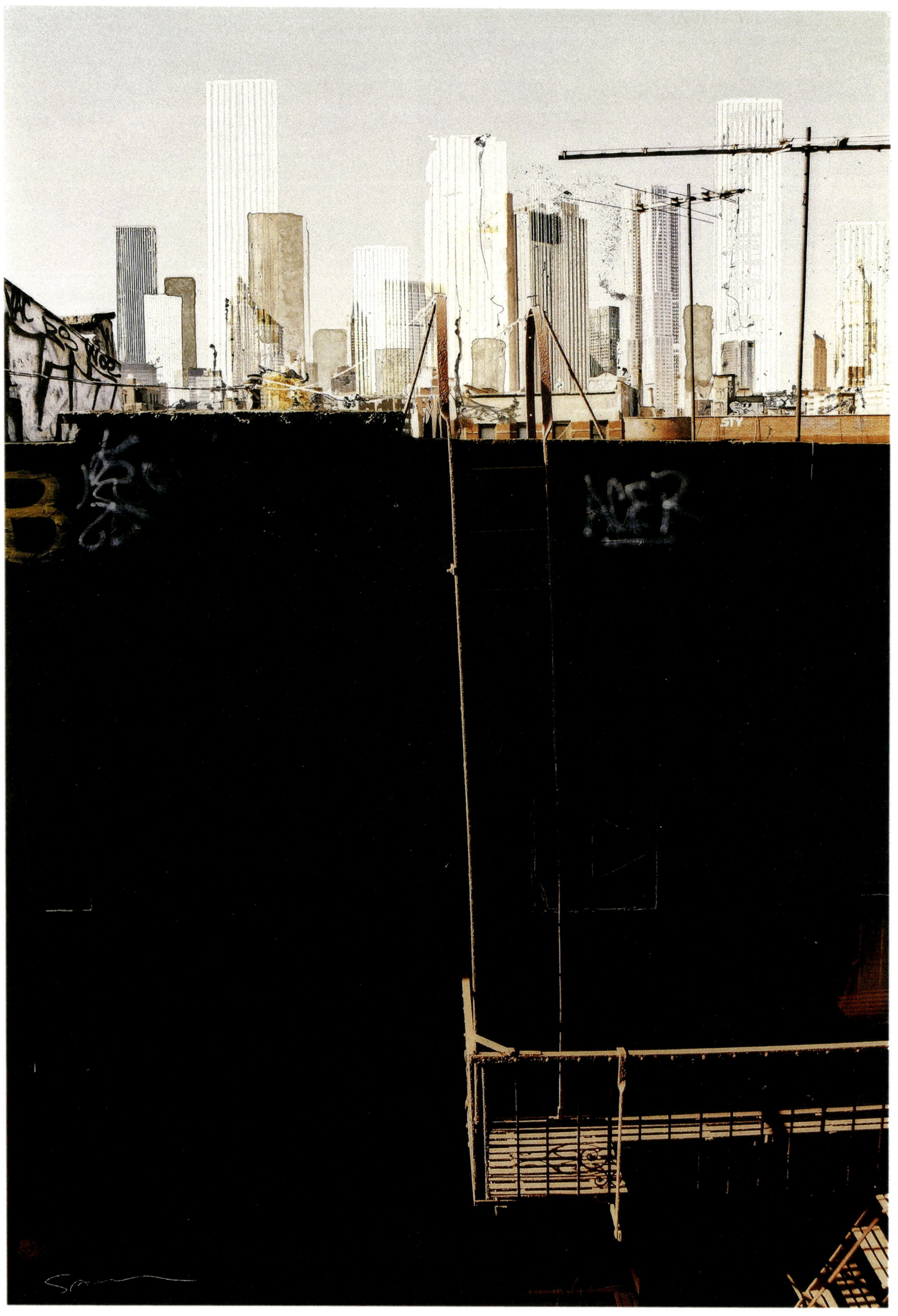

  The Ladder | Die Leiter | L'échelle   2011, 81 × 54 cm

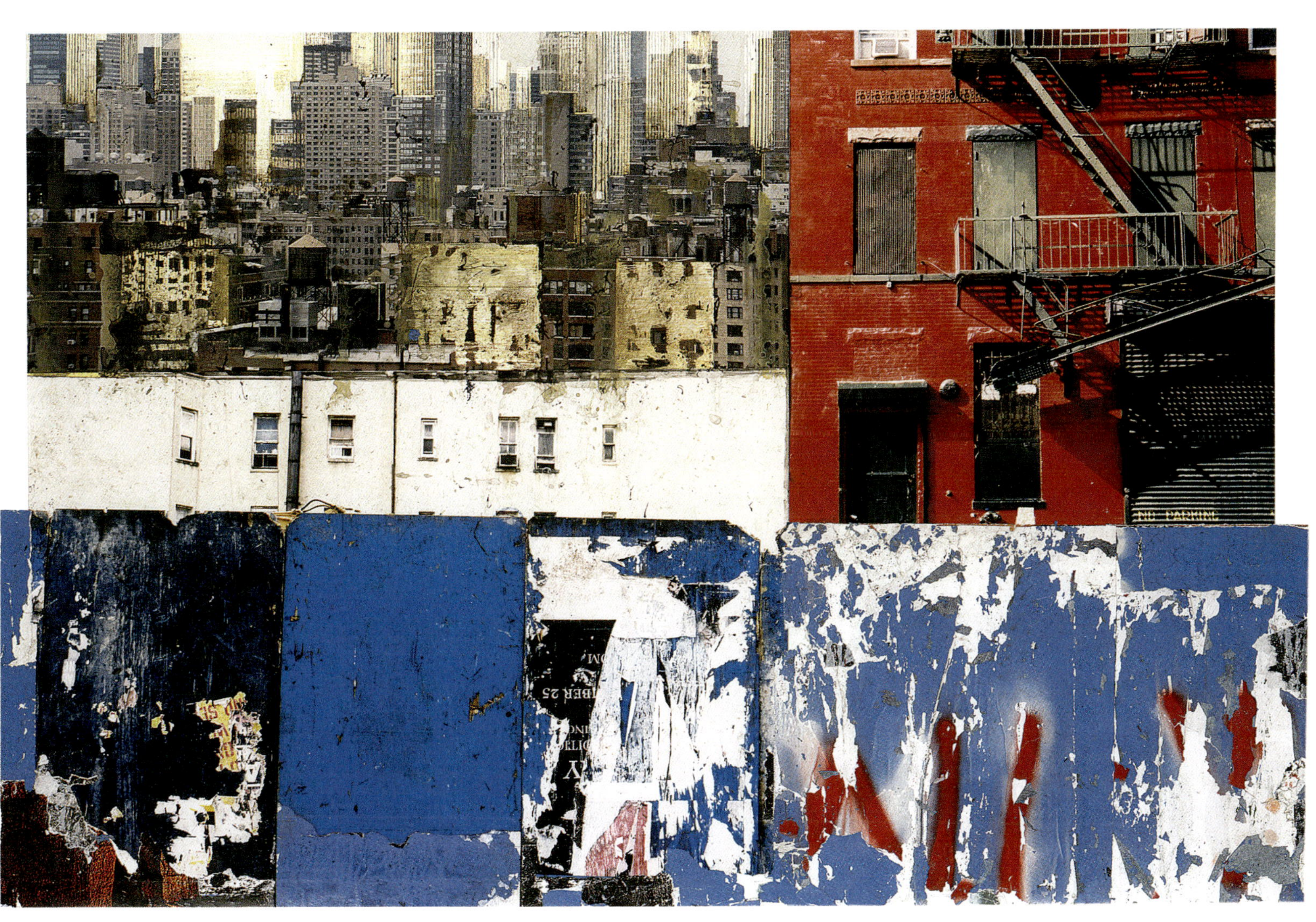

NO PARKING   2009, 89 × 130 cm

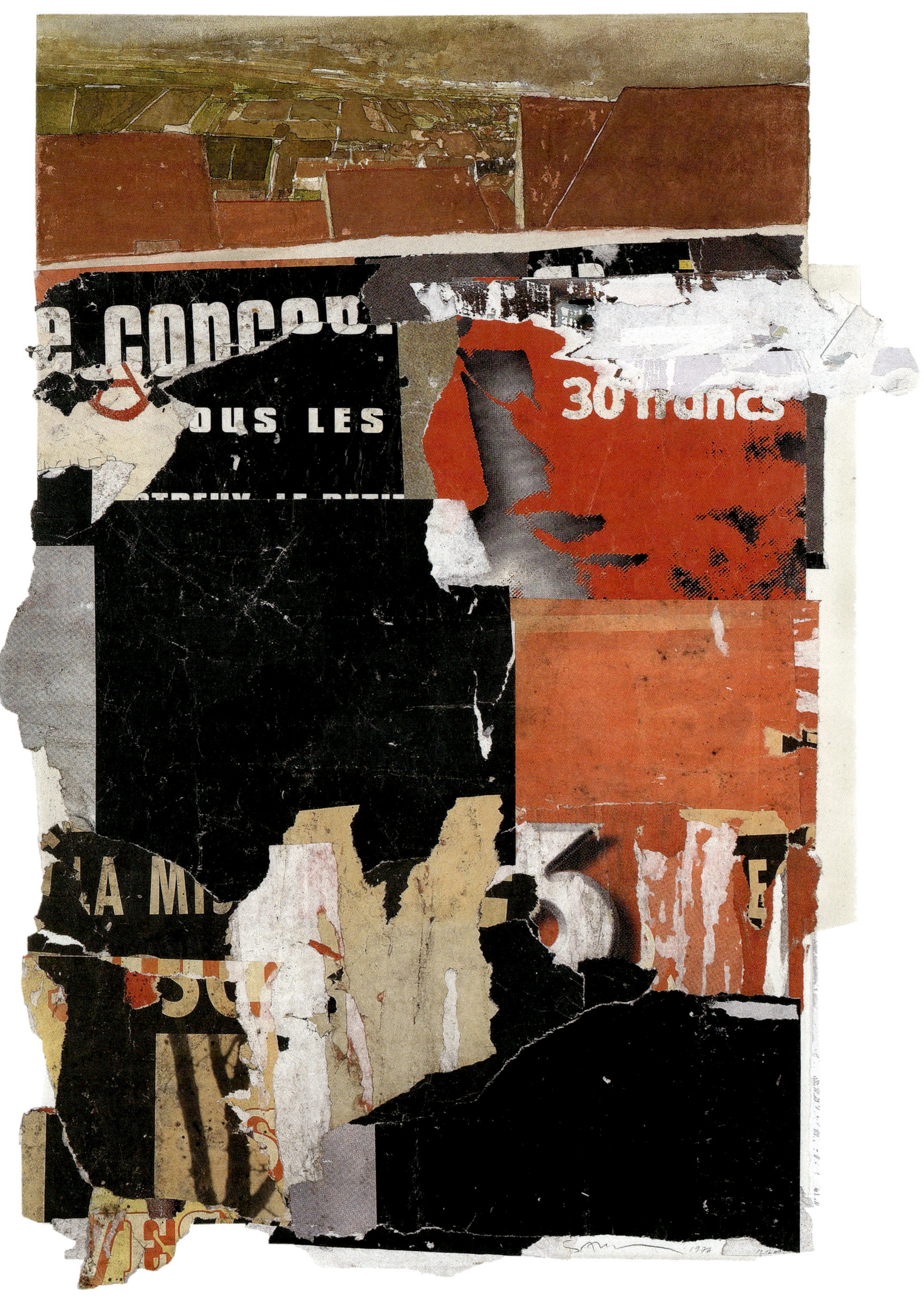

   30 Francs   1976, 79,4 × 57,5 cm

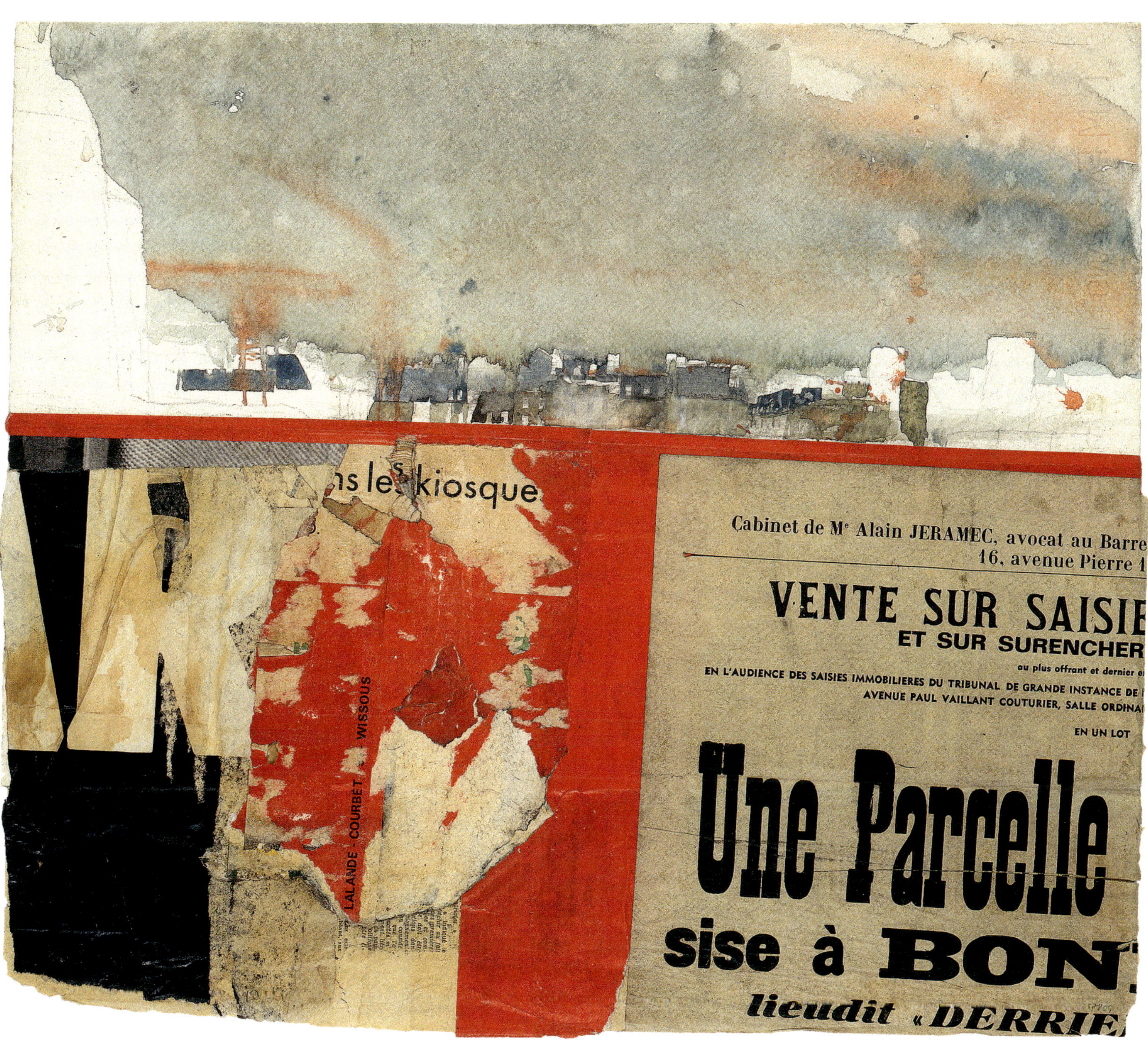

Vente sur saisie (Le trou des Halles) 1978, 43,7 × 48,8 cm

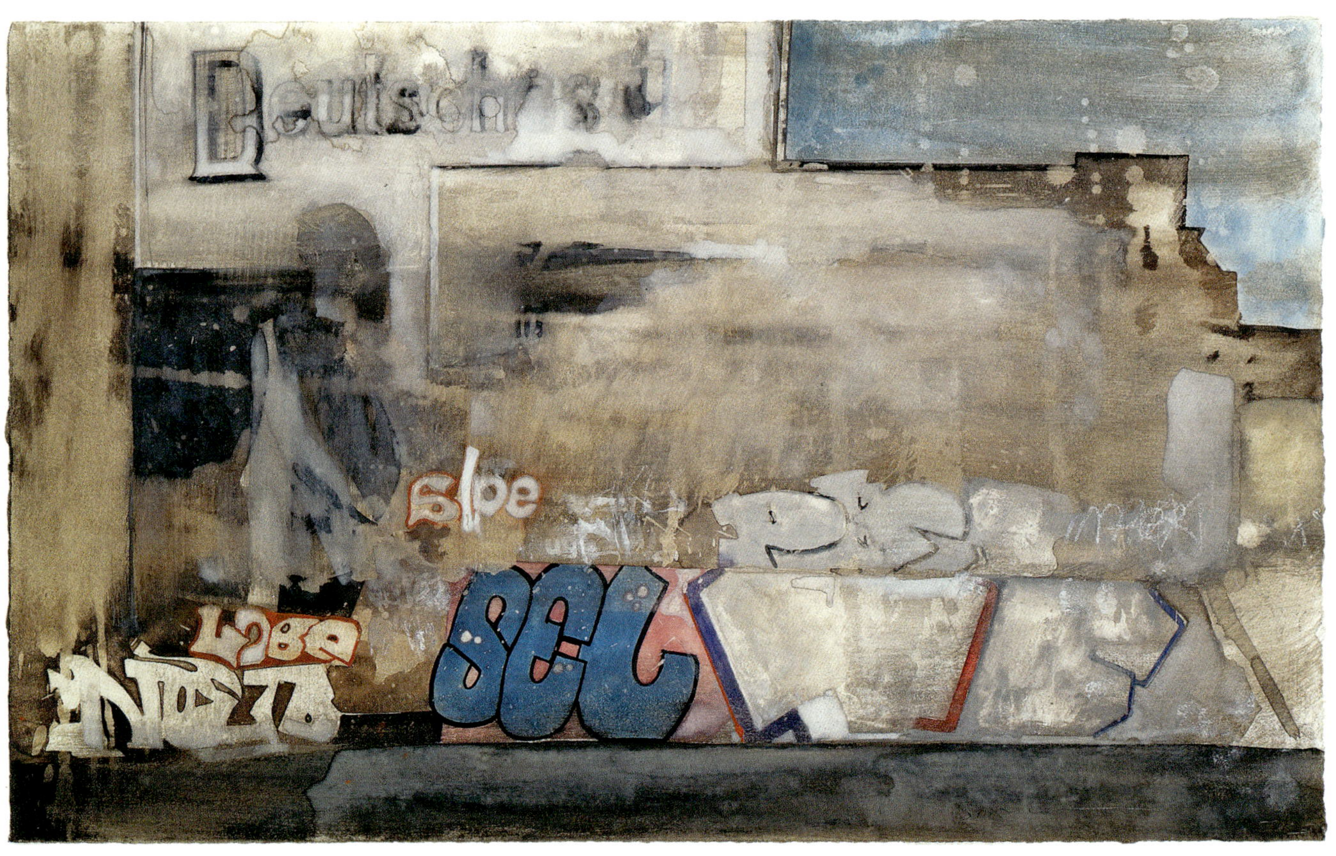

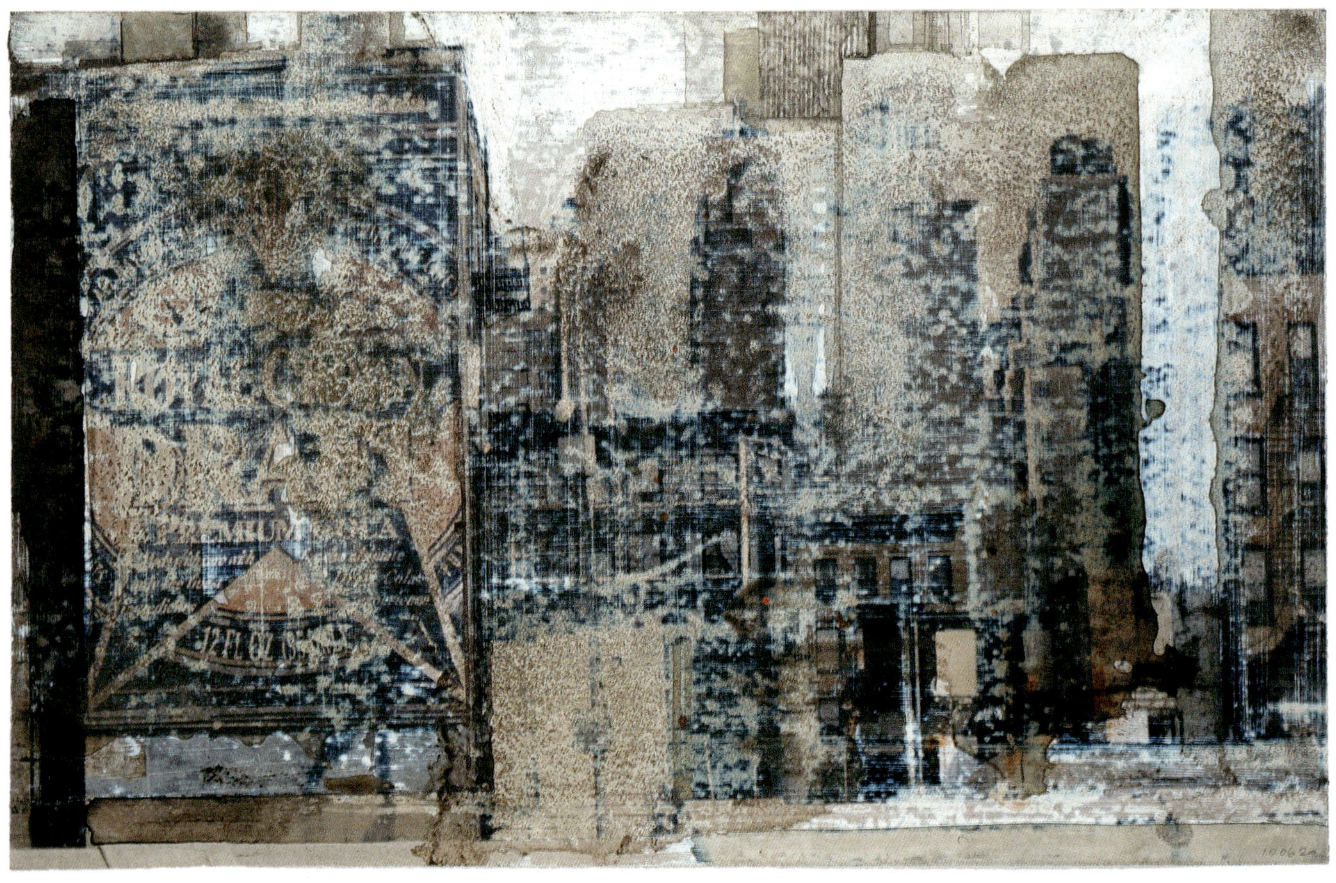

Berlin Wall "Sel" | Berliner Mauer „Sel" | Mur de Berlin «Sel»   1994, 30 × 47,5 cm
Premium   2006, 30,5 × 46,2 cm

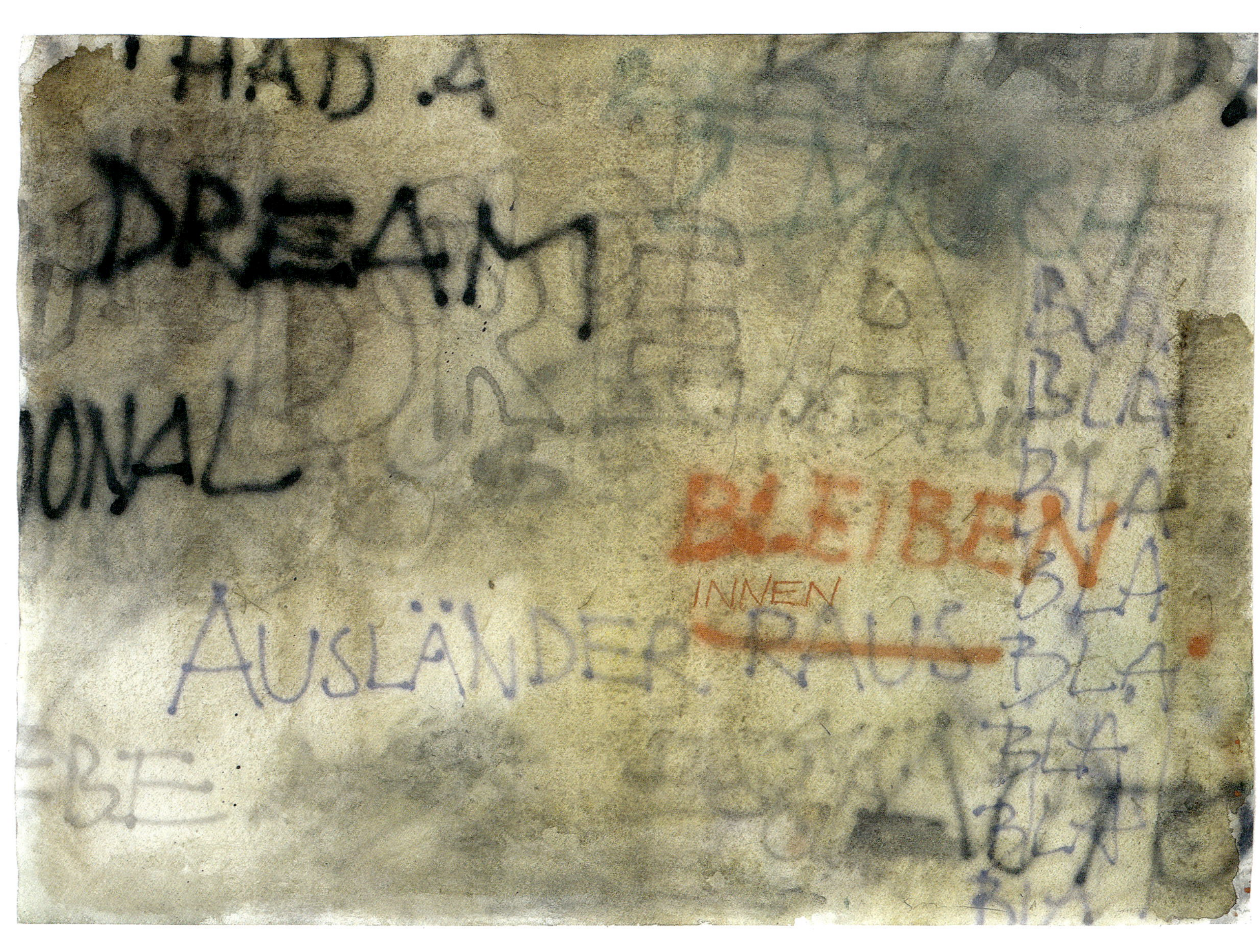

Ausländer„innen" bleiben   1995, 72,4 × 99 cm

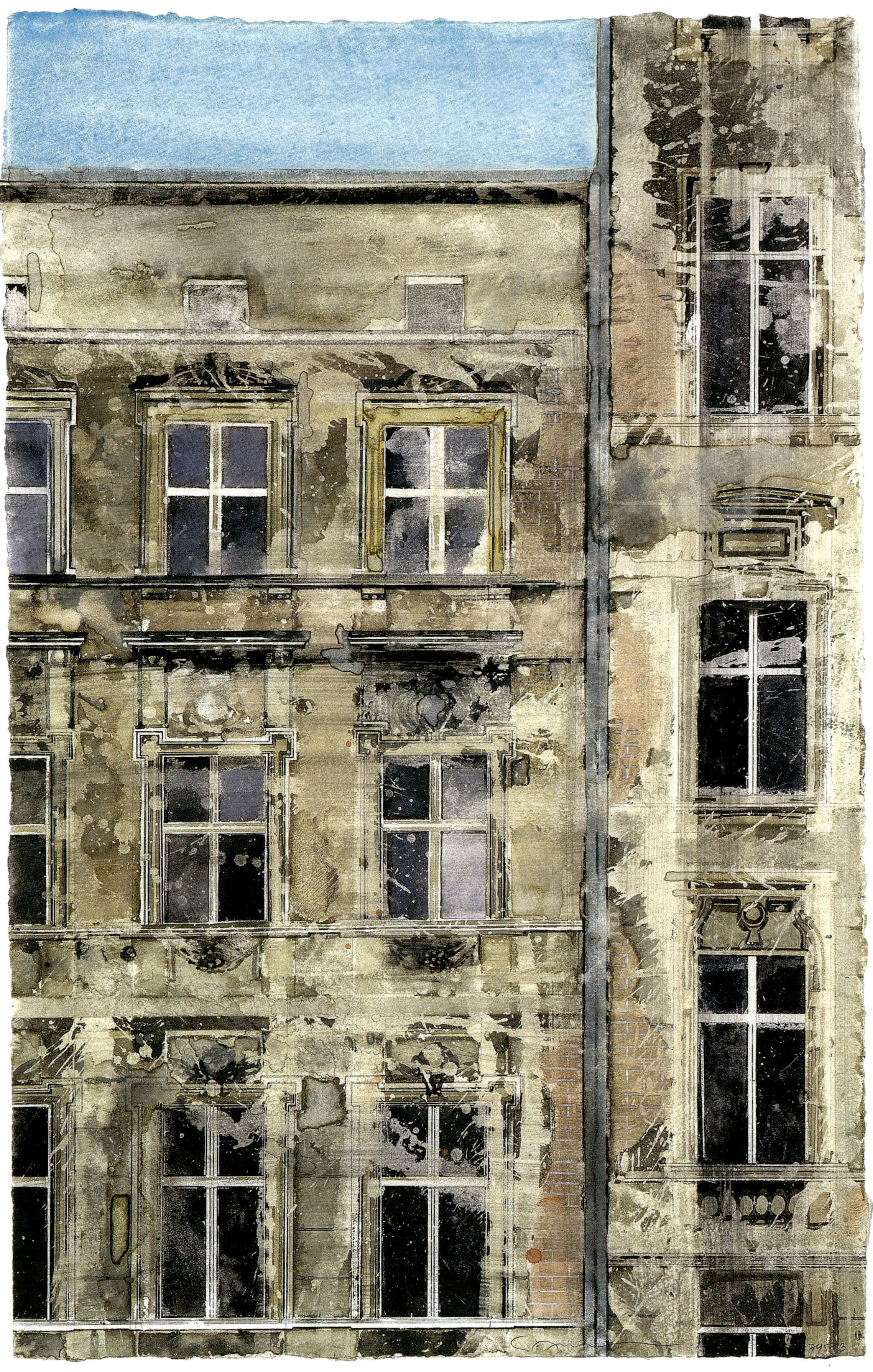

Berlin   1995, 47,4 × 30,5 cm

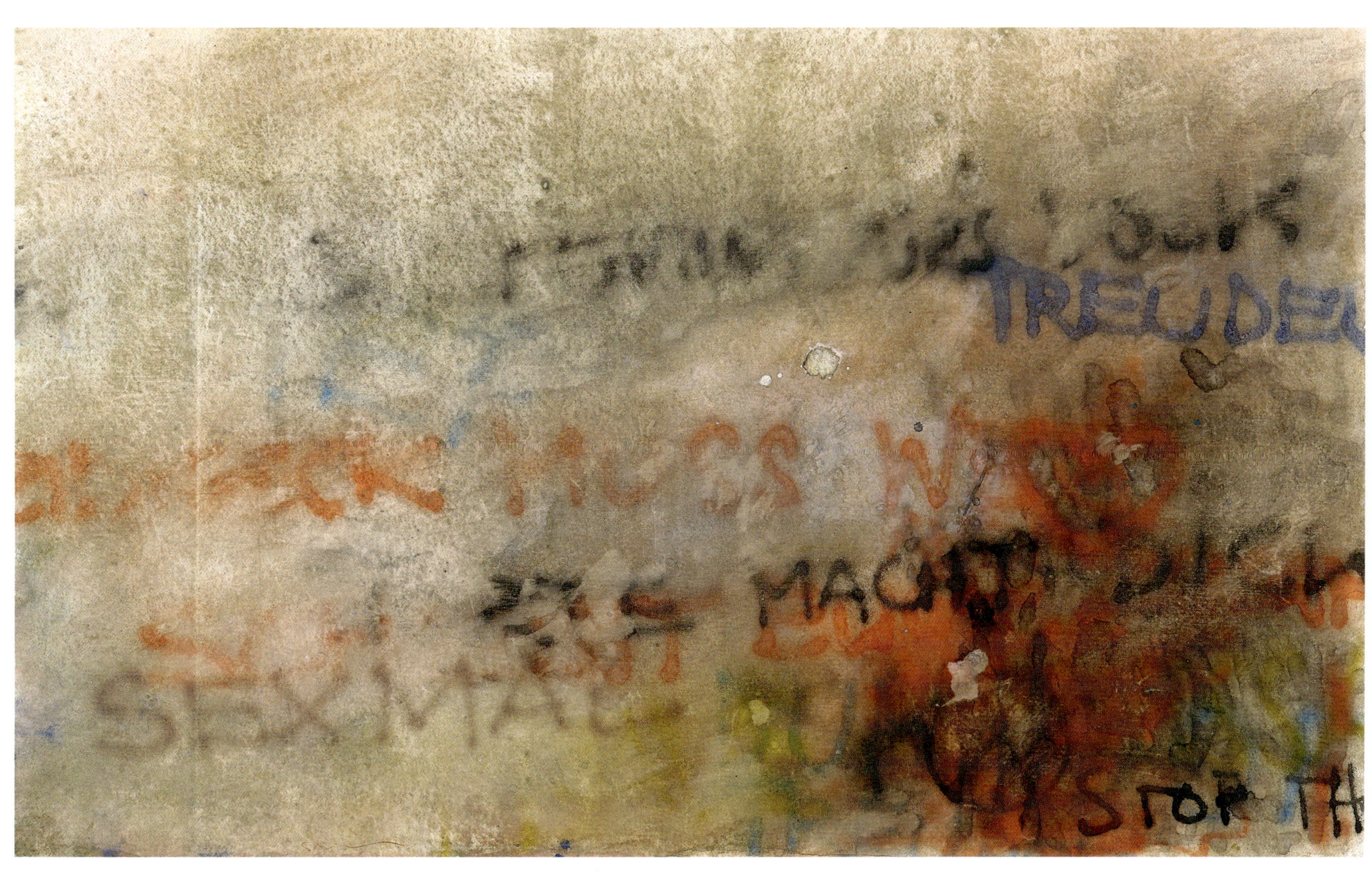

Sexmal   1996, 72,5 × 115,7 cm

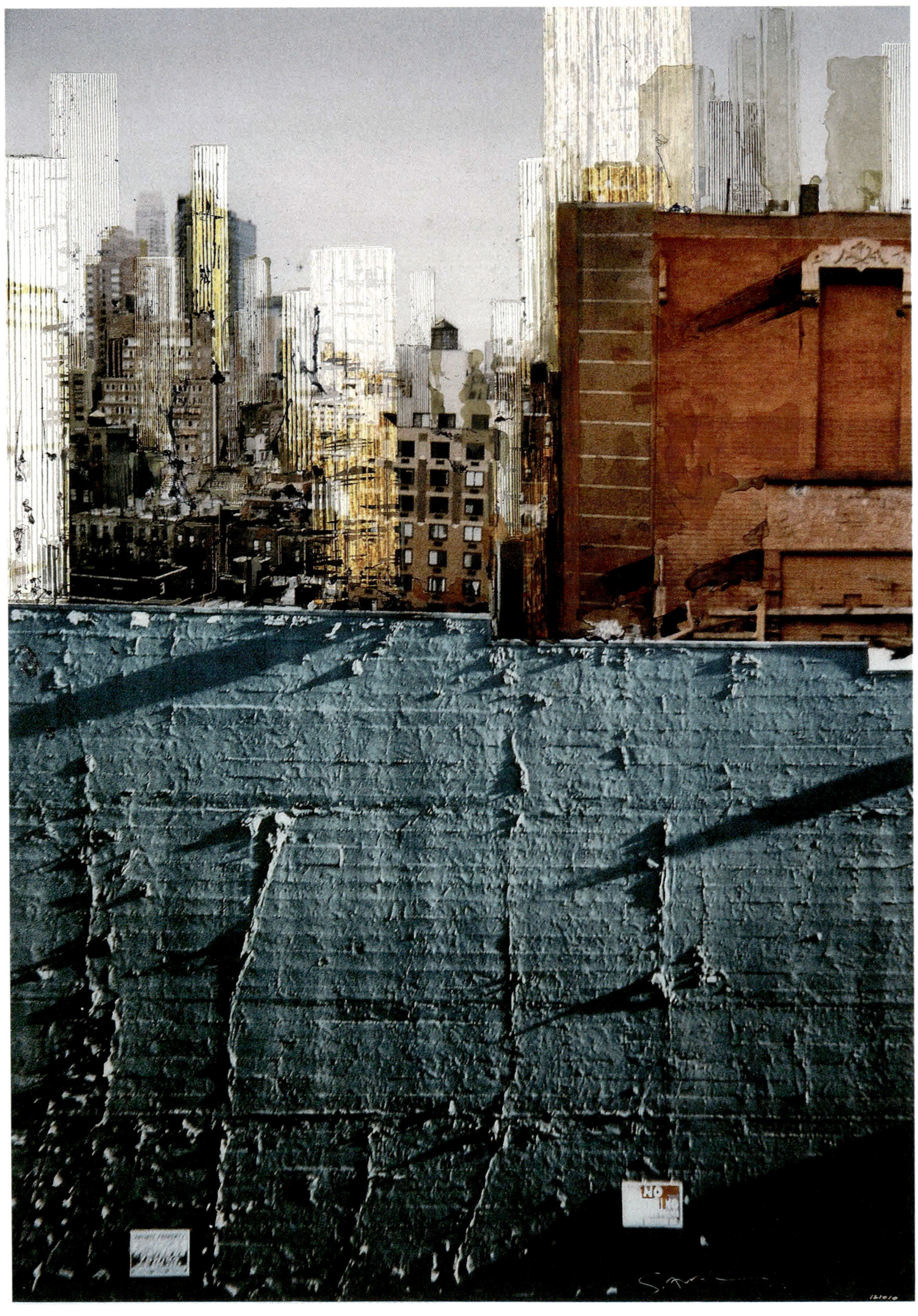

SF Green Wall | SF Grüne Mauer | SF Mur vert   2010, 81 x 60 cm

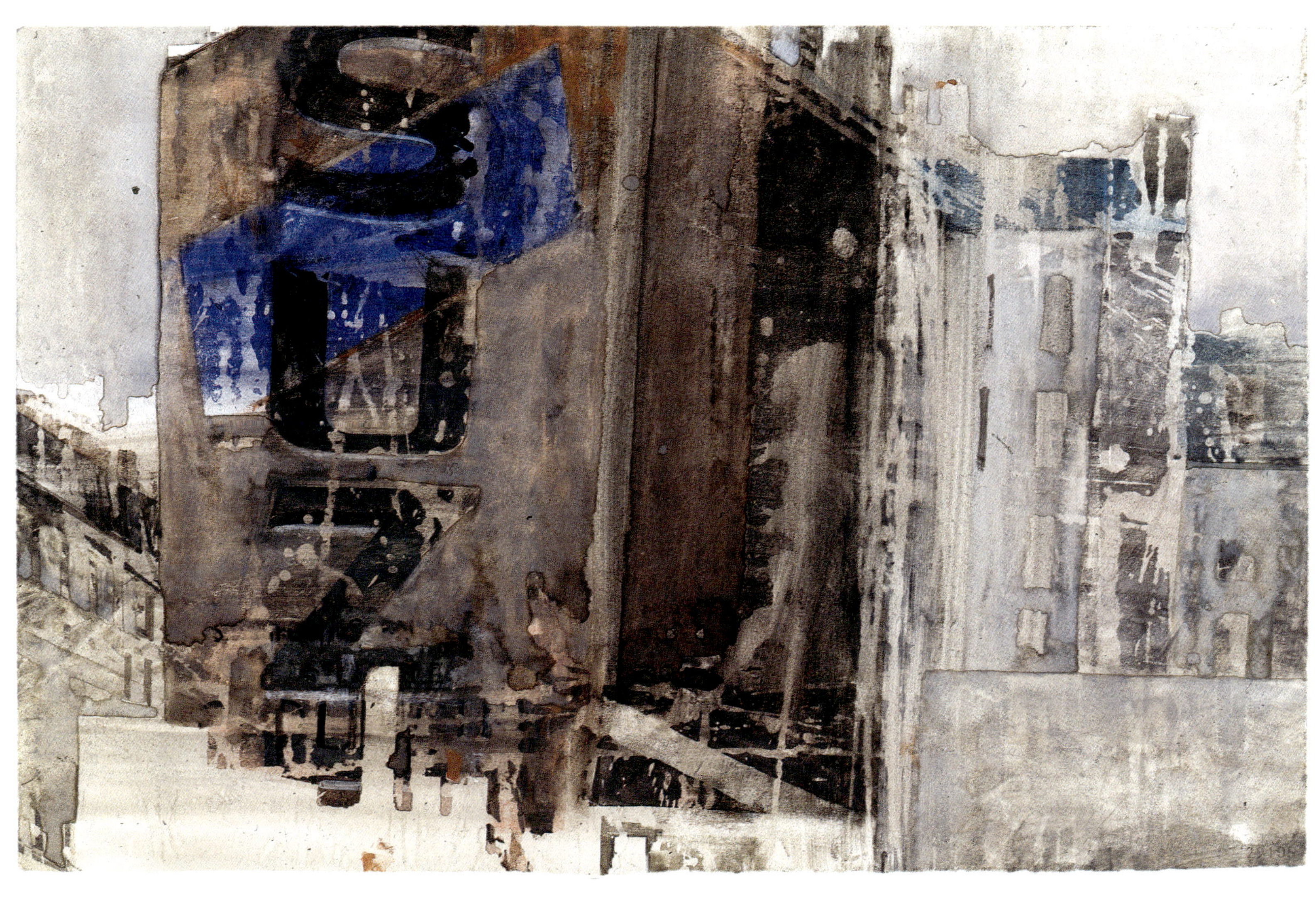

Suze   1991, 33 × 50 cm

Messages
Mitteilungen
Messages

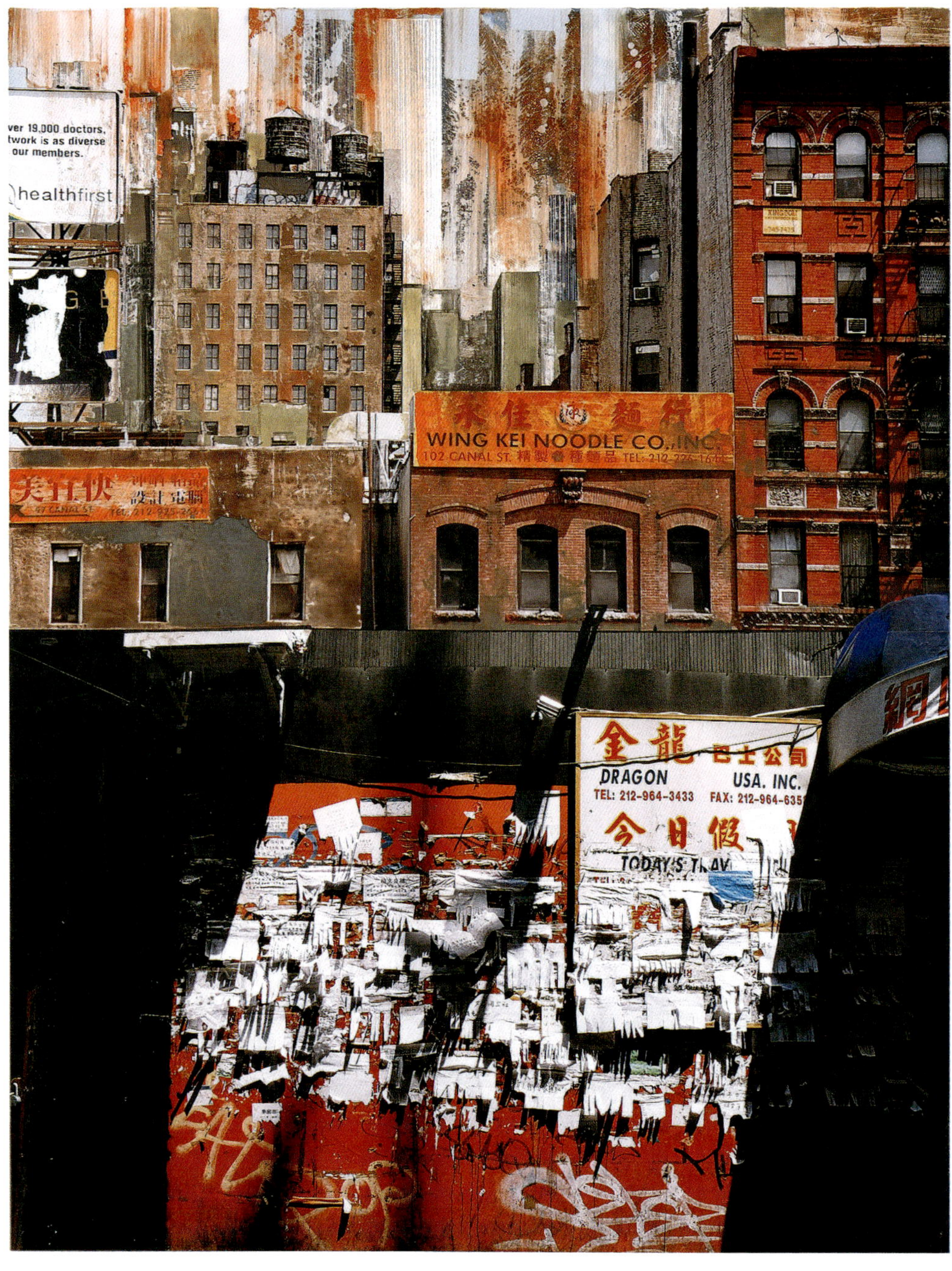

  New York, Chinatown   2010, 169 × 128 cm

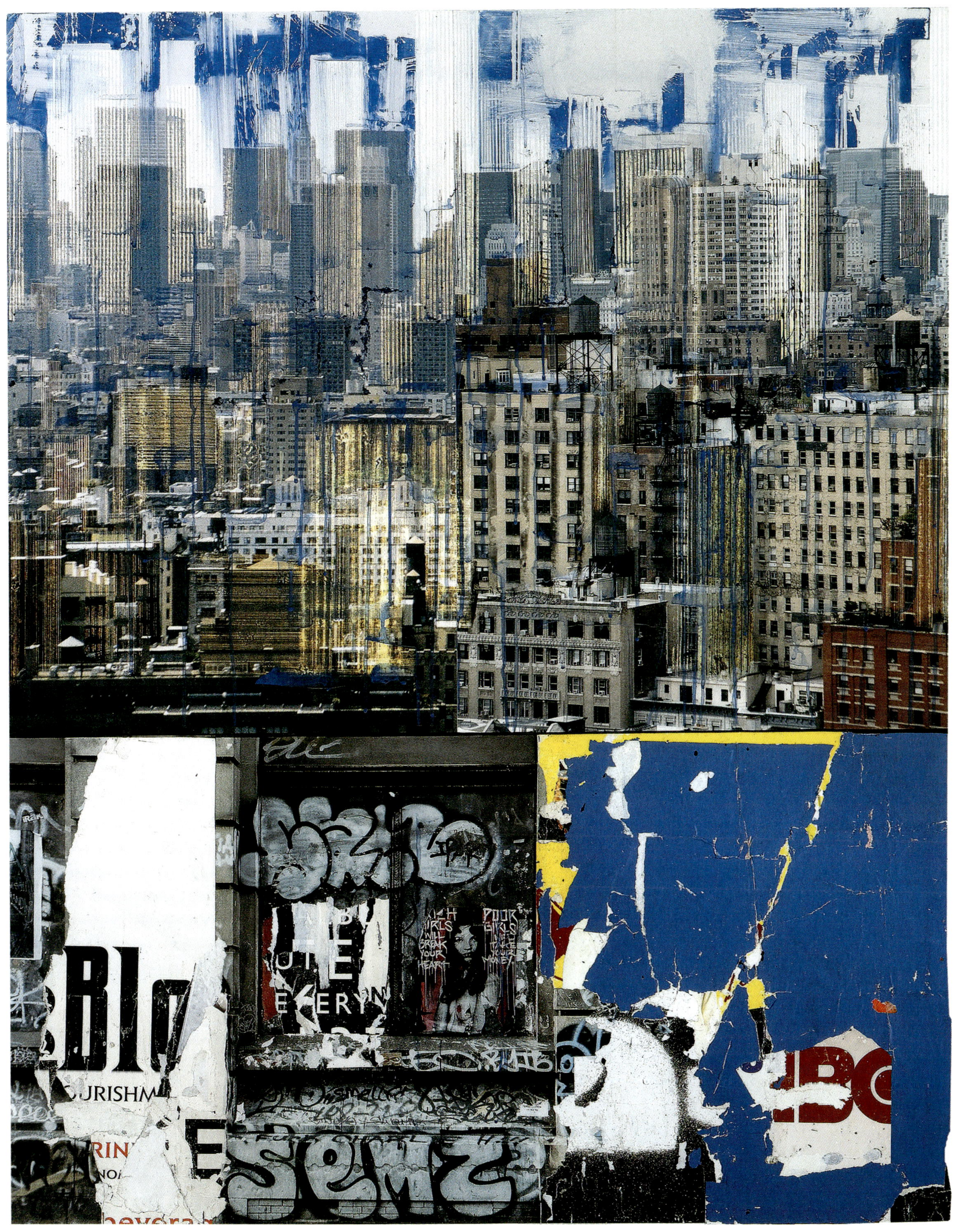

Rich girls will take your heart, Poor girls will take your money   2010, 134 × 104 cm

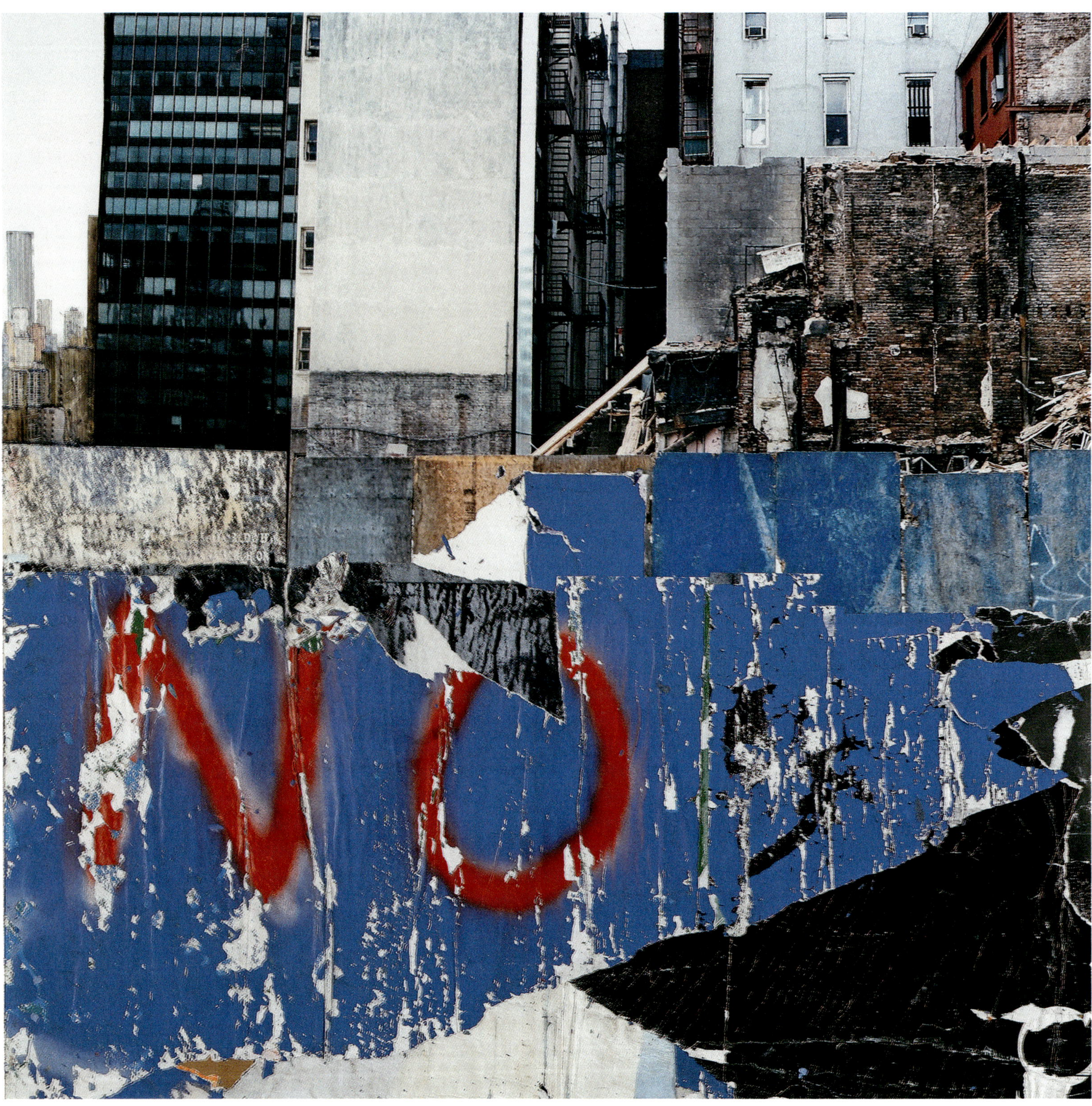

NO   2011, 90 × 90 cm

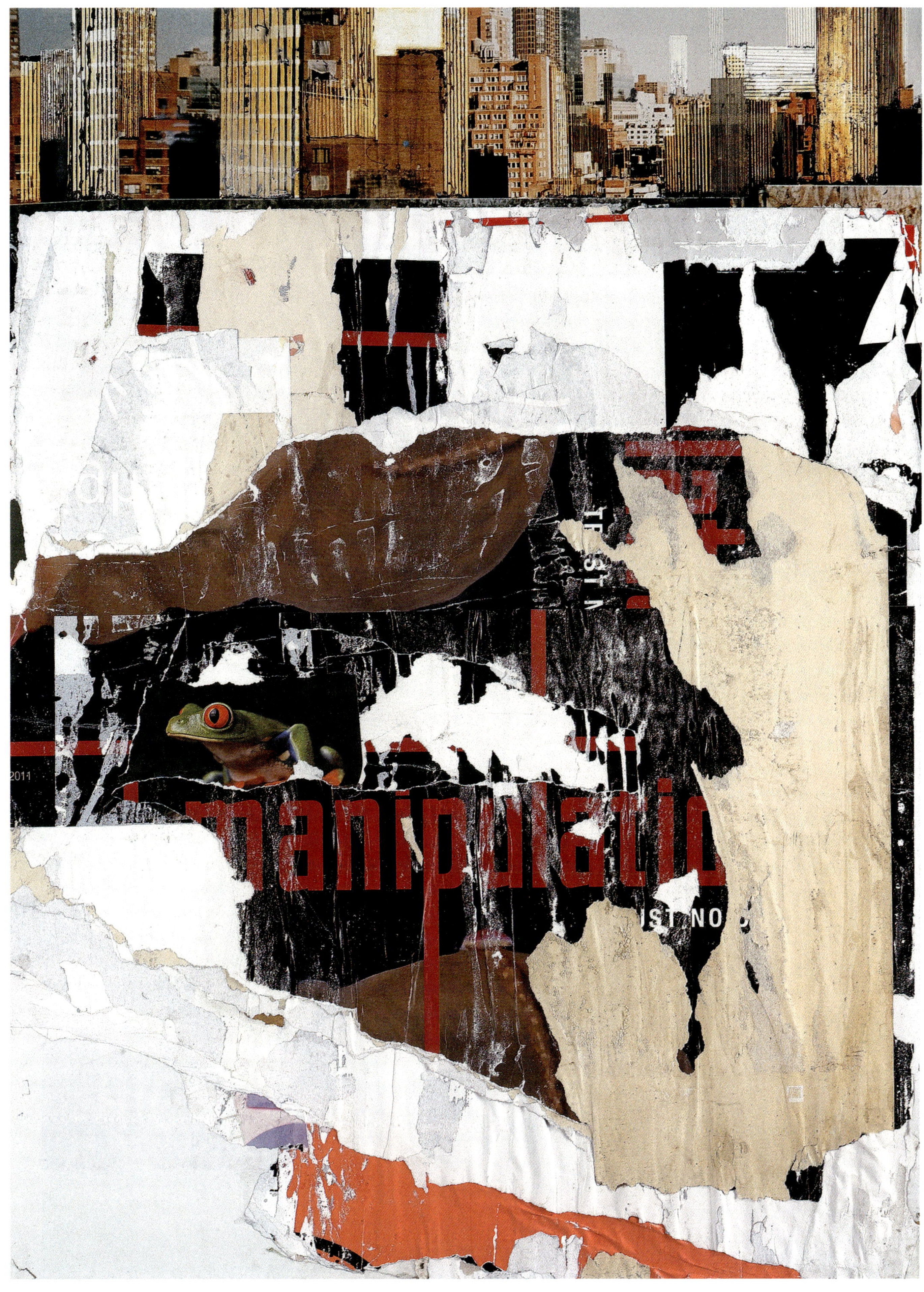

Manipulation, You are observed   2012, 92 × 65 cm

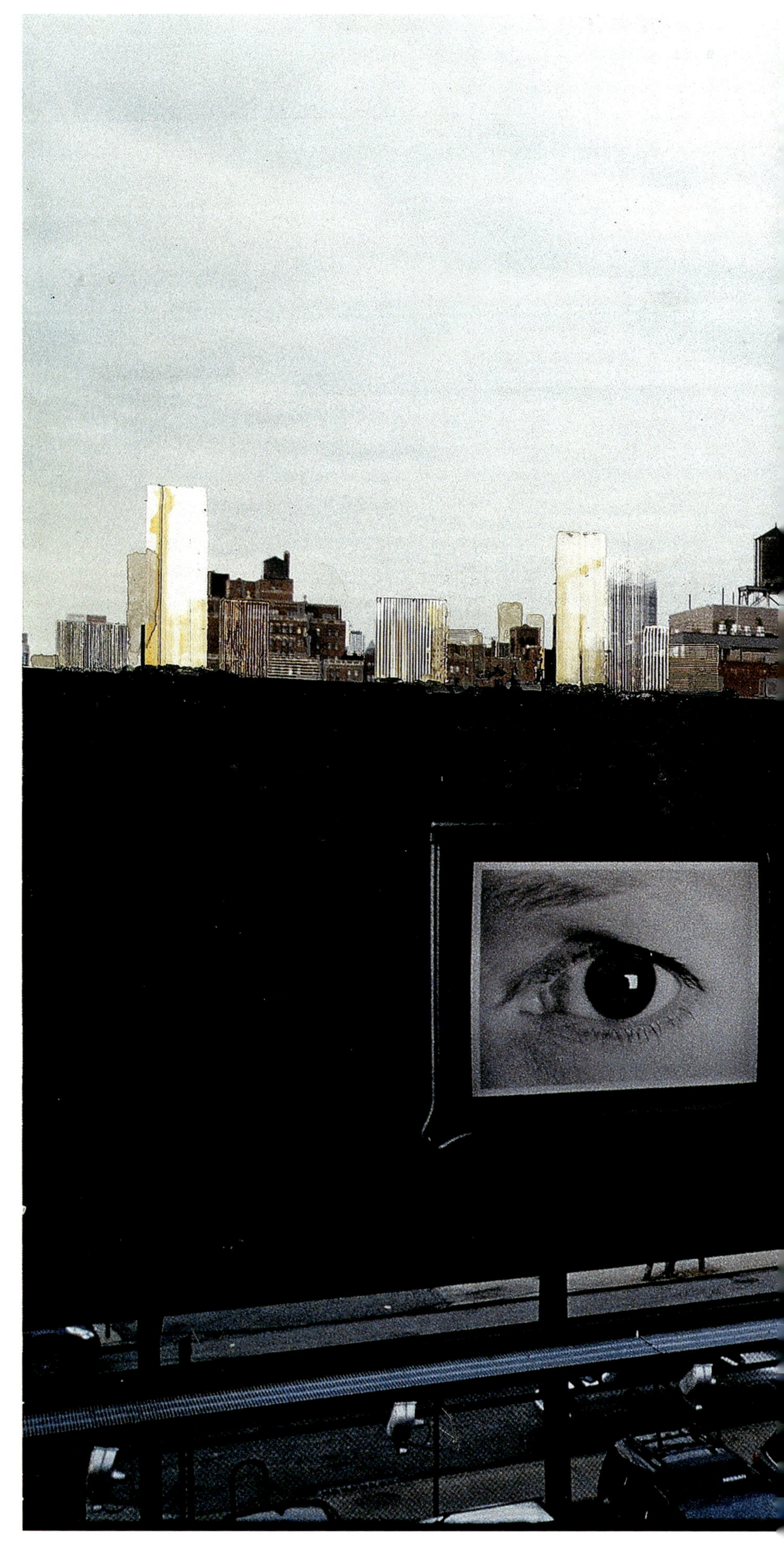

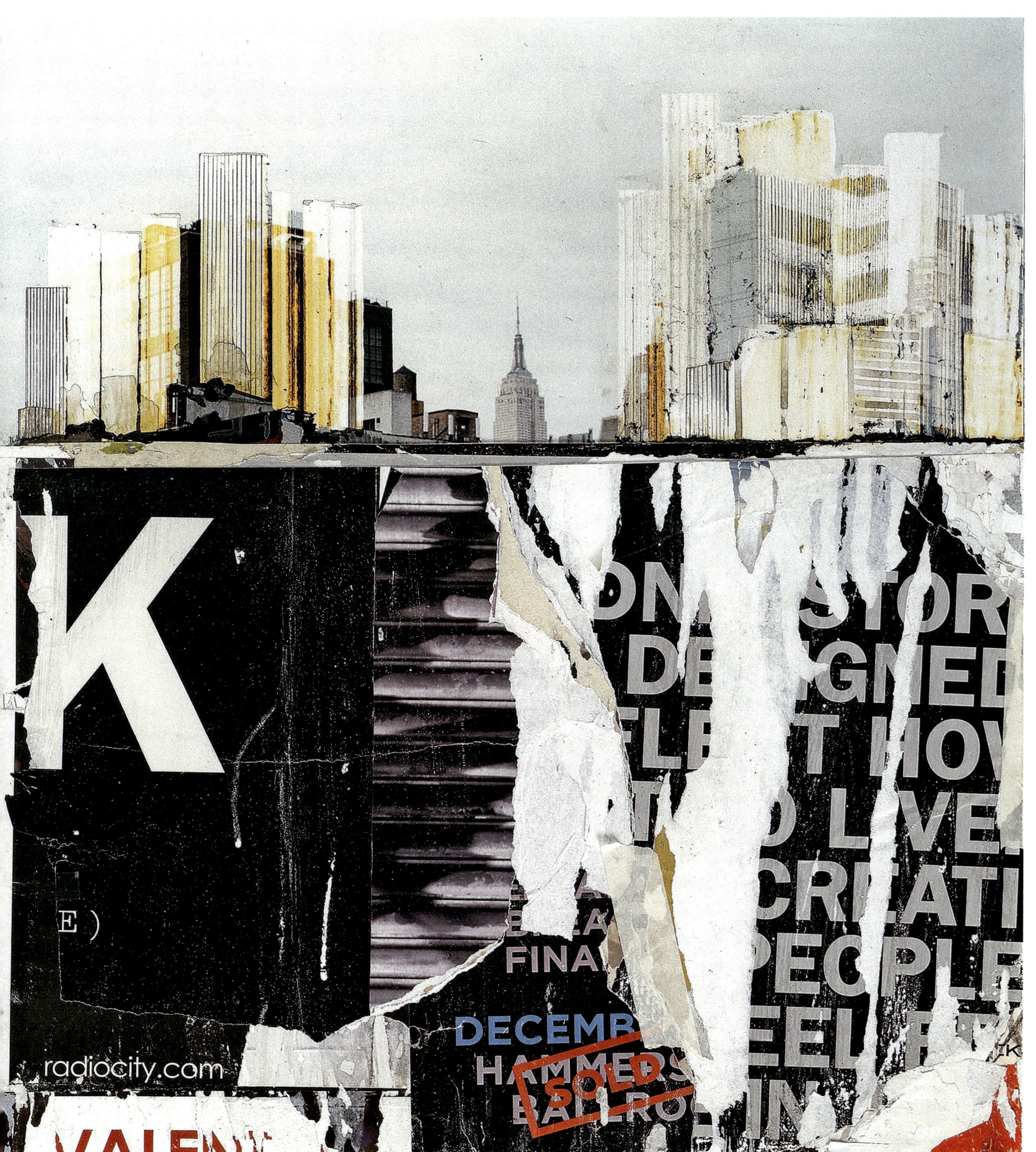
K
radiocity.com
VALEN
DECEMB
HAMMERS
SOLD
FINA
DESIGNED
HO
LIVE
CREATI
PEOPLE

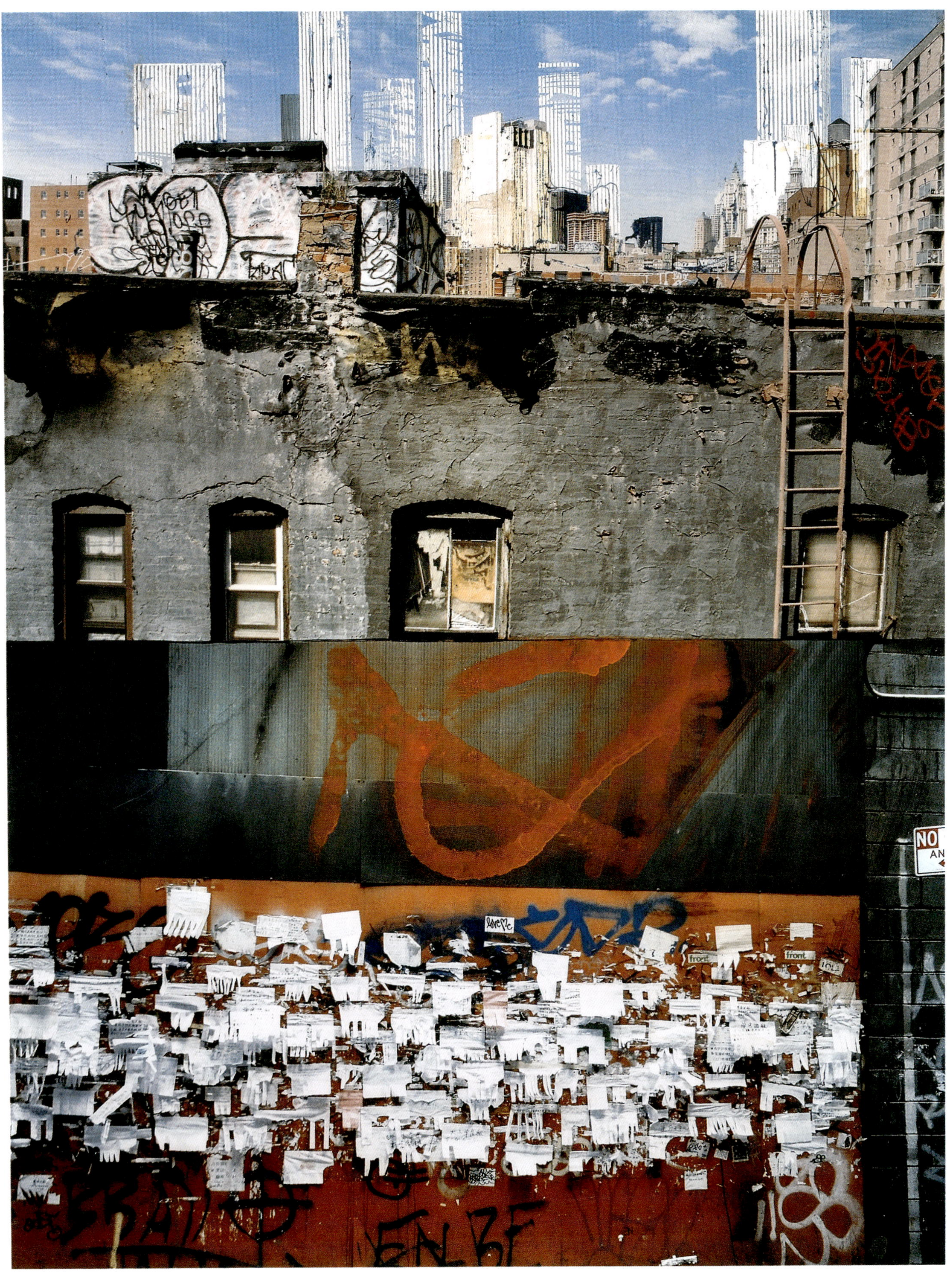

    Love me   2010, 110 × 83 cm

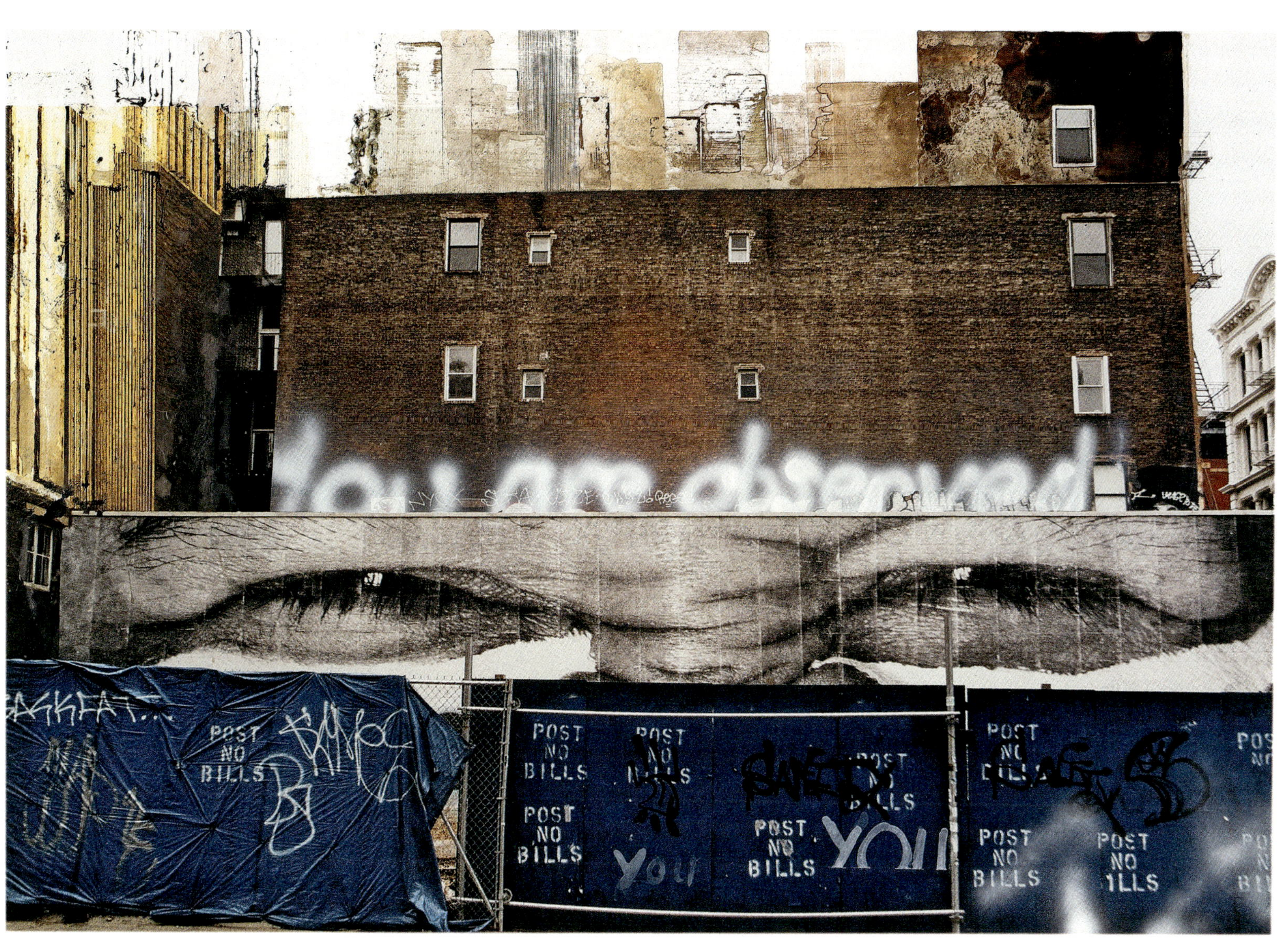

You are observed I   2012, 97 × 130 cm   139

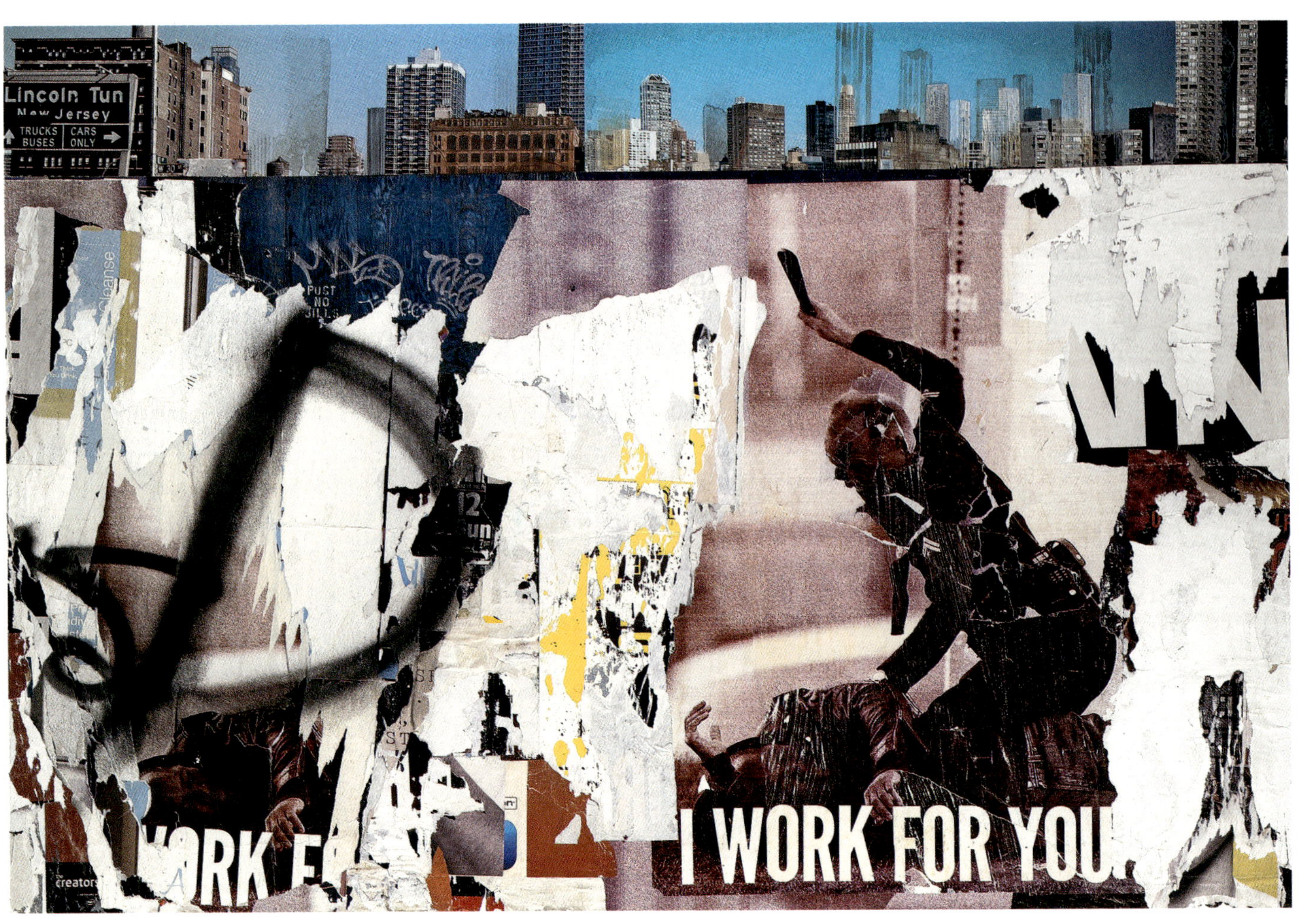

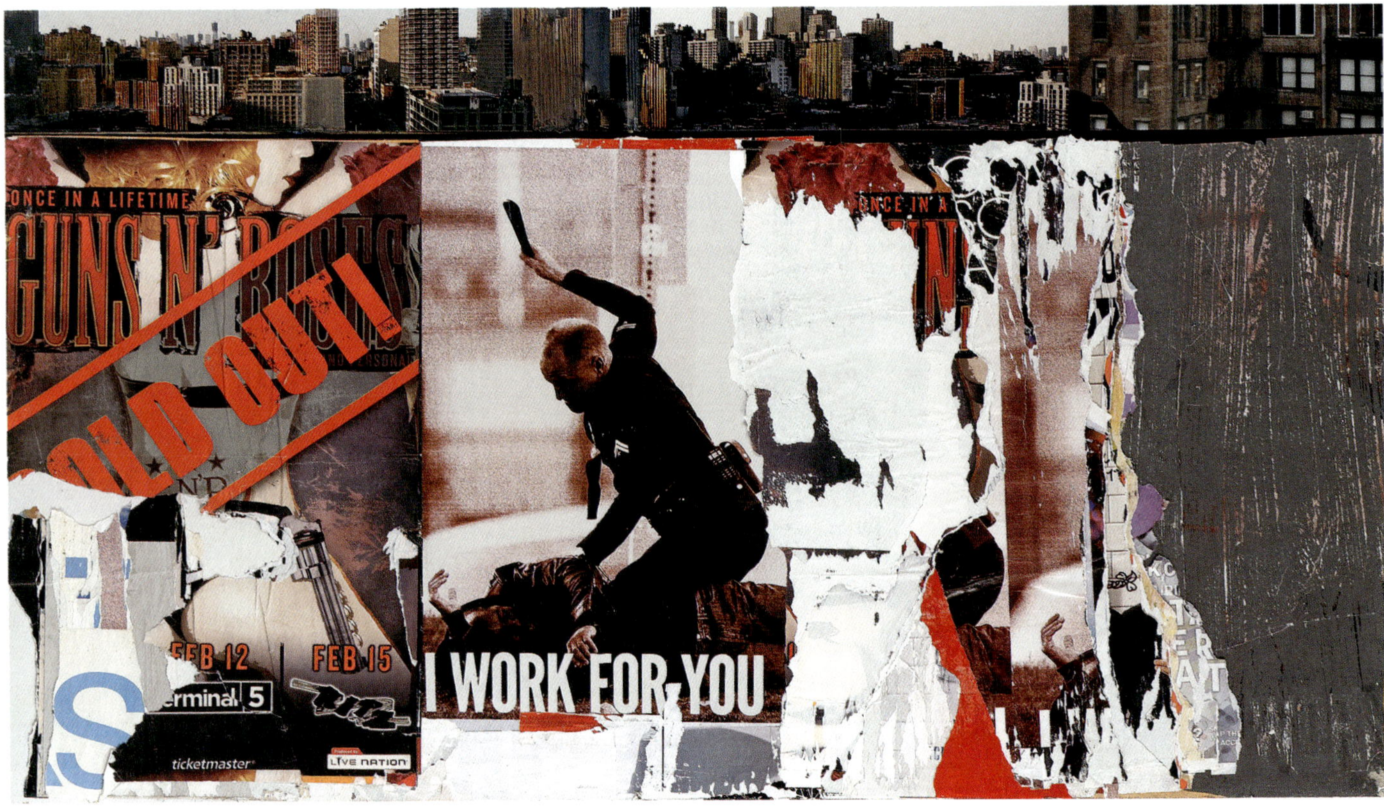

I work for you II   2012, 114 × 162 cm
I work for you I   2012, 114 × 195 cm

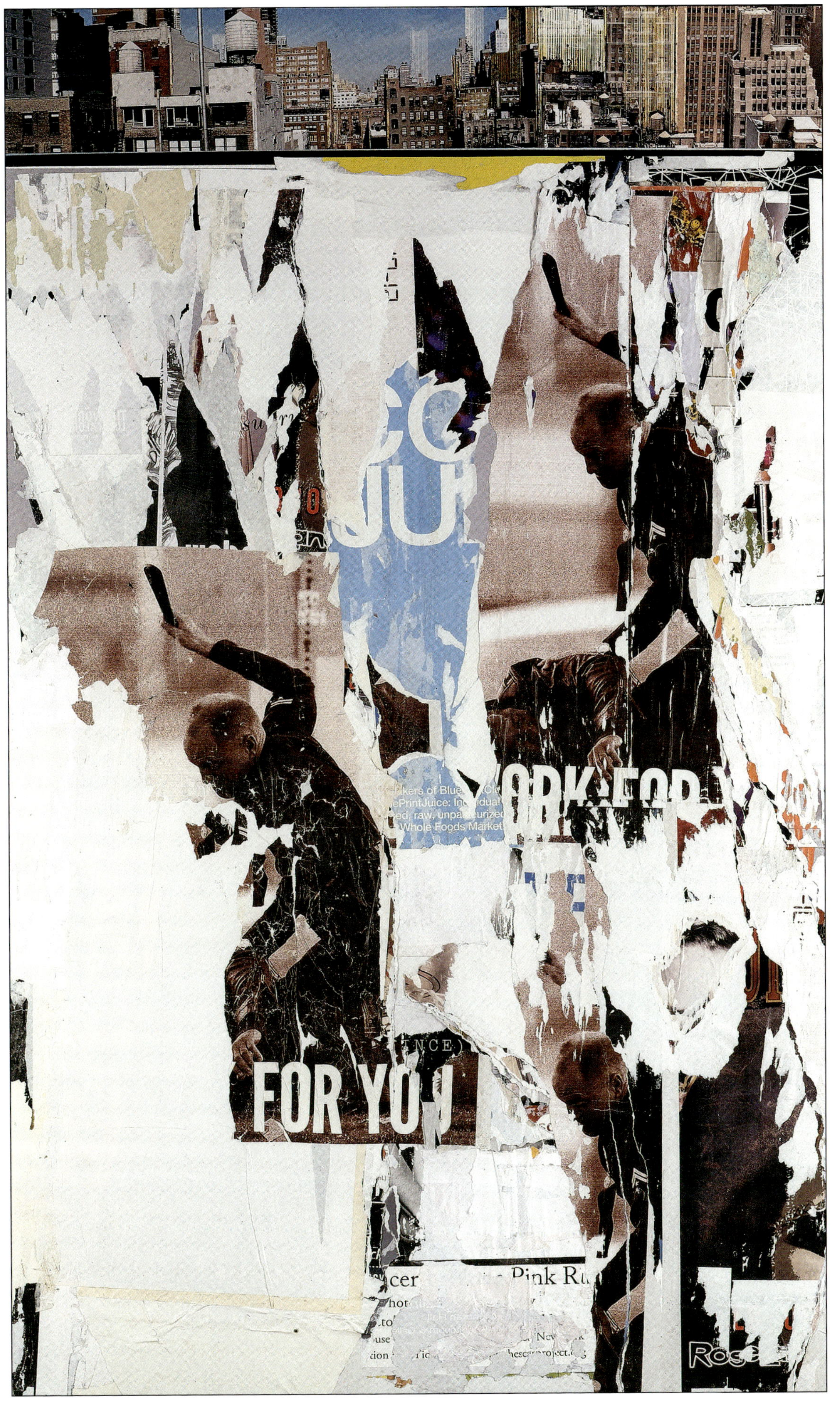

For you   2012, 195 × 114 cm

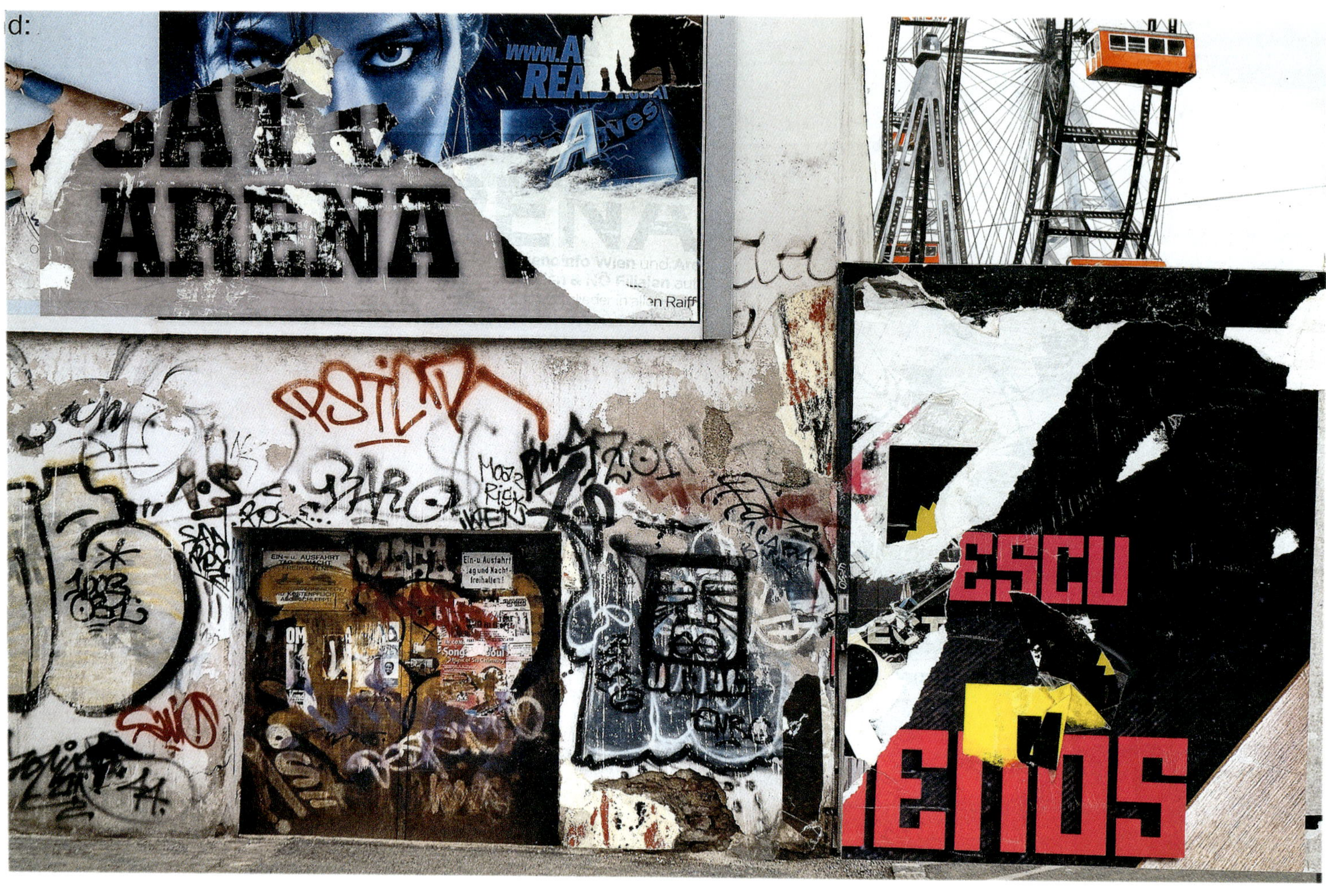

 Vienna, Arena | Wien, Arena | Vienne, Arena   2010, 54 × 81 cm

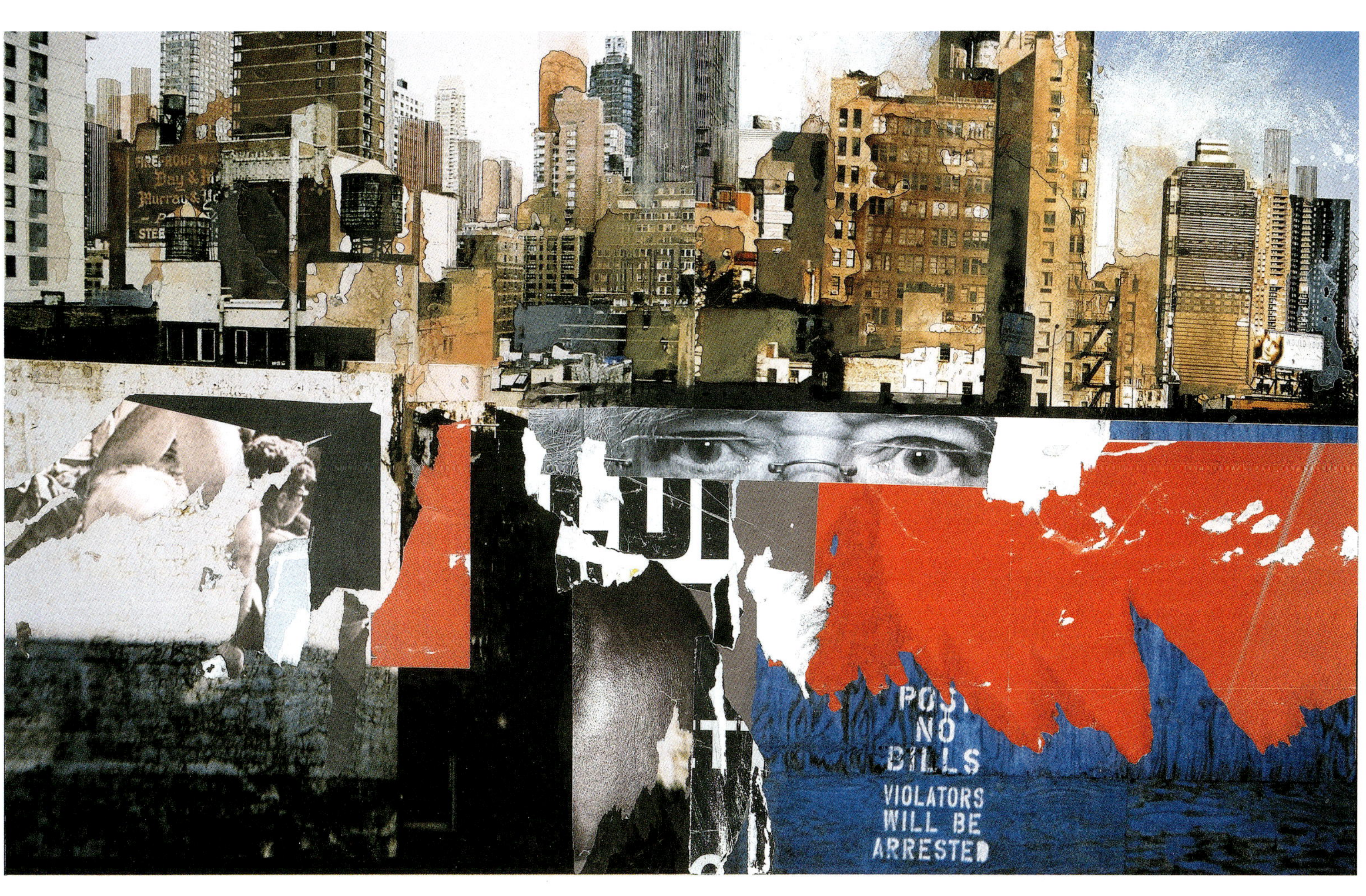

You are observed II   2012, 73 × 116 cm

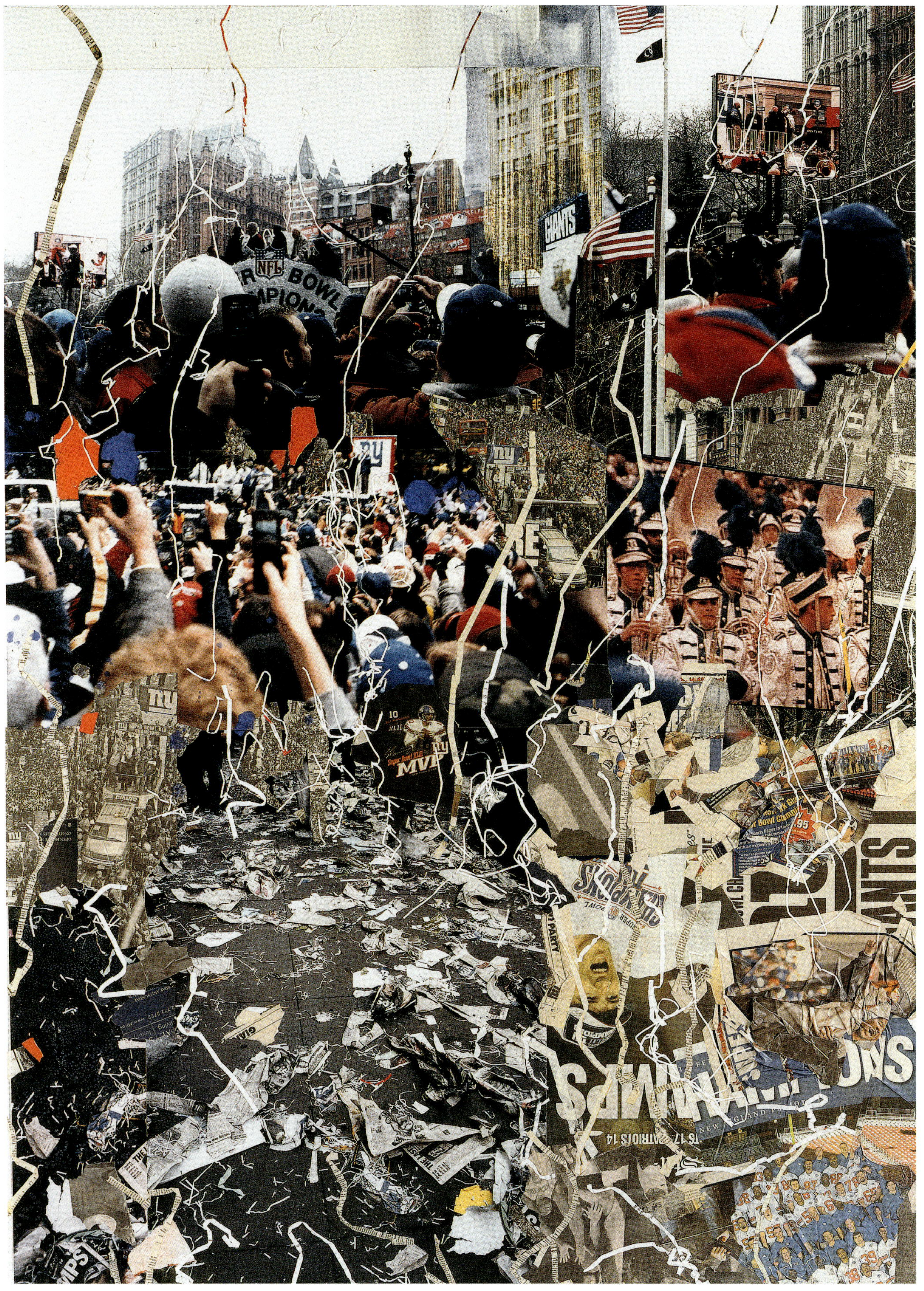

Superbowl I   2008, 162 × 114 cm

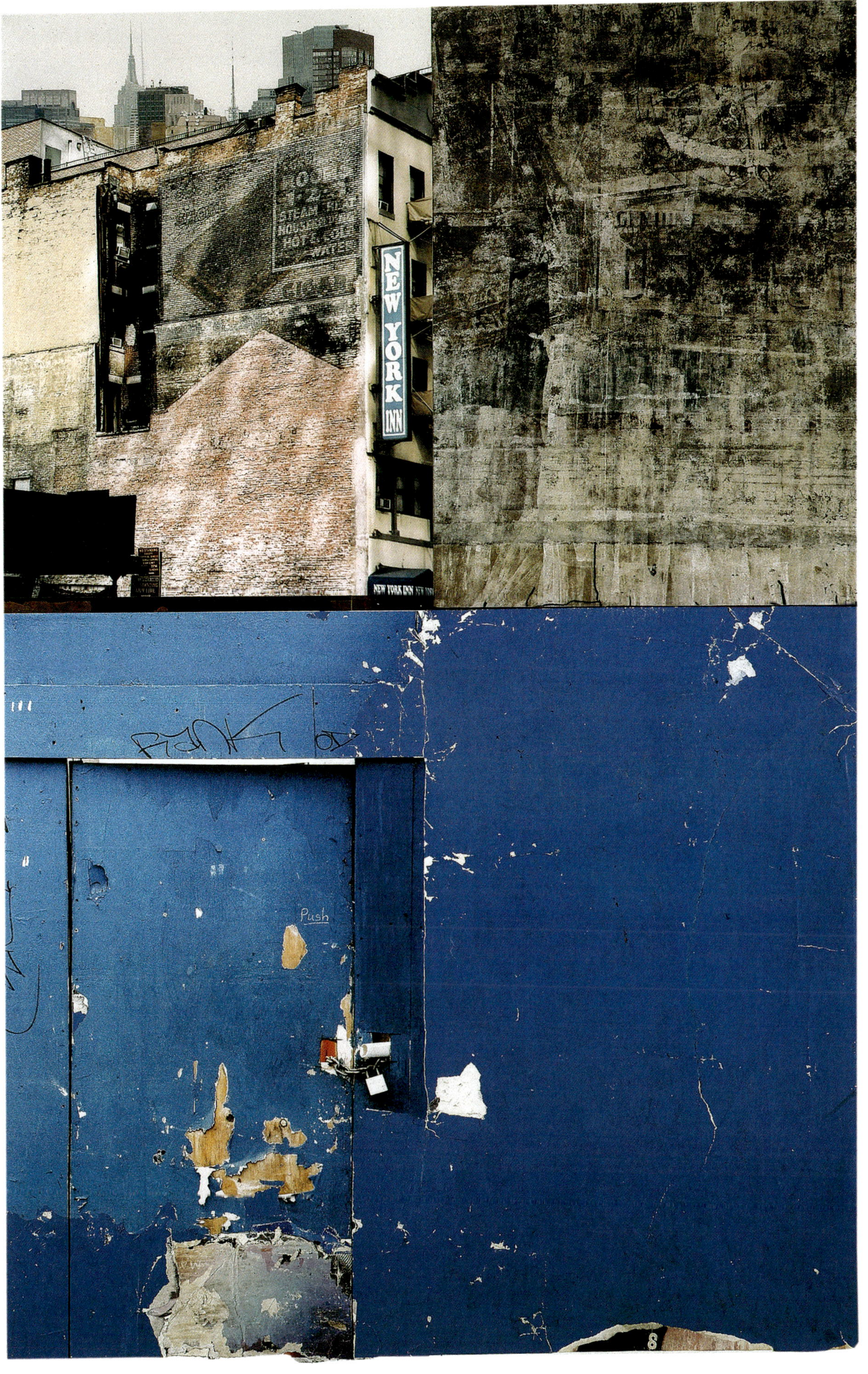

The Message | Die Botschaft | Le message   2009, 162 × 114 cm

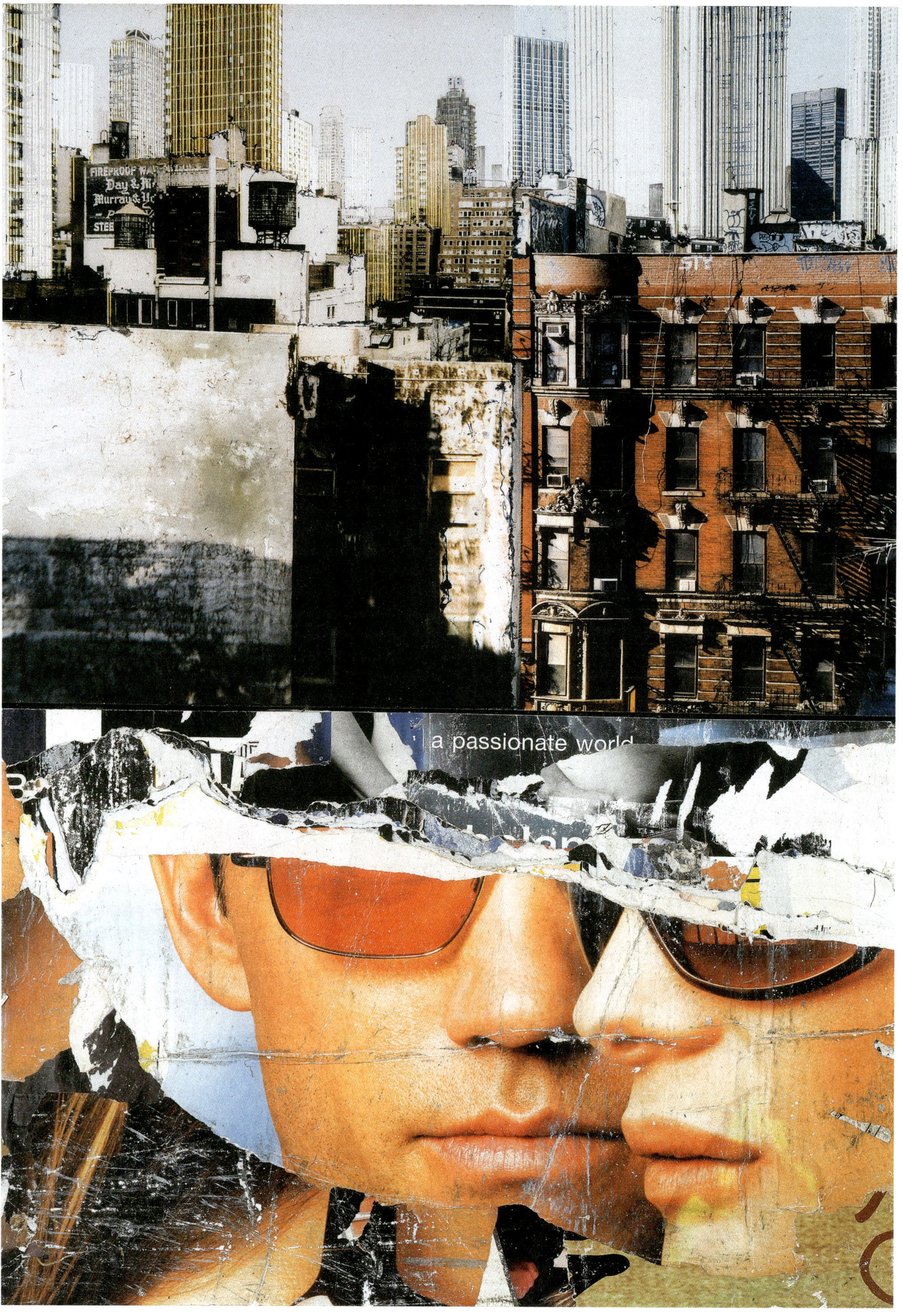

    A Passionate World   2010, 130 × 89 cm

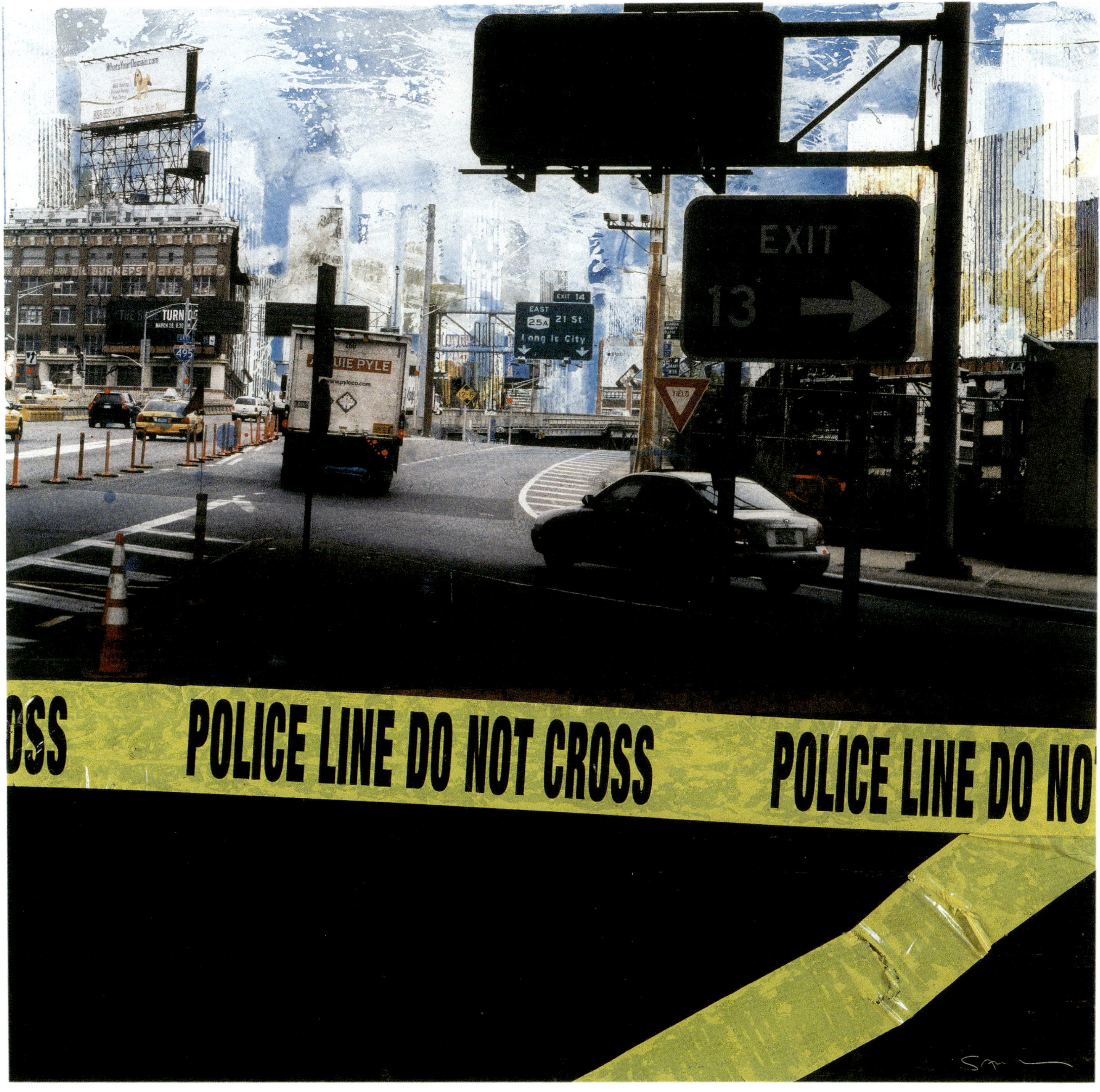

Police Line   2010, 80 × 80 cm

Reflections
Spiegelungen
Reflets

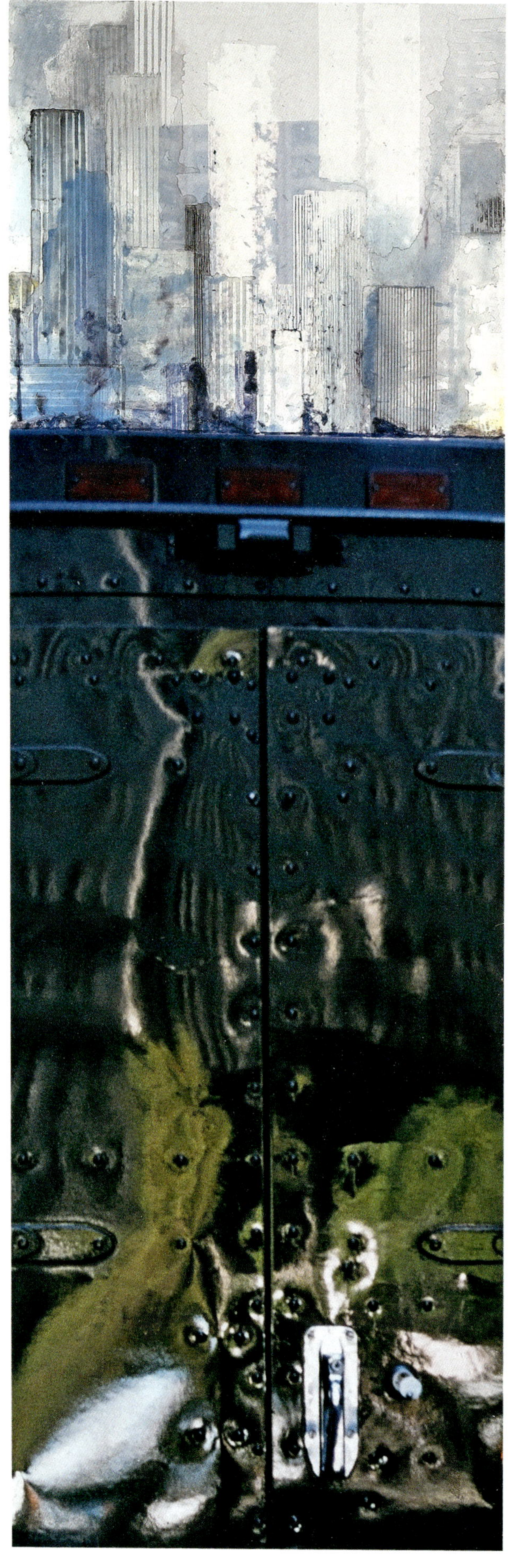

   SF Reflection | SF Spiegelung | SF reflet   2010, 86 × 29,5 cm

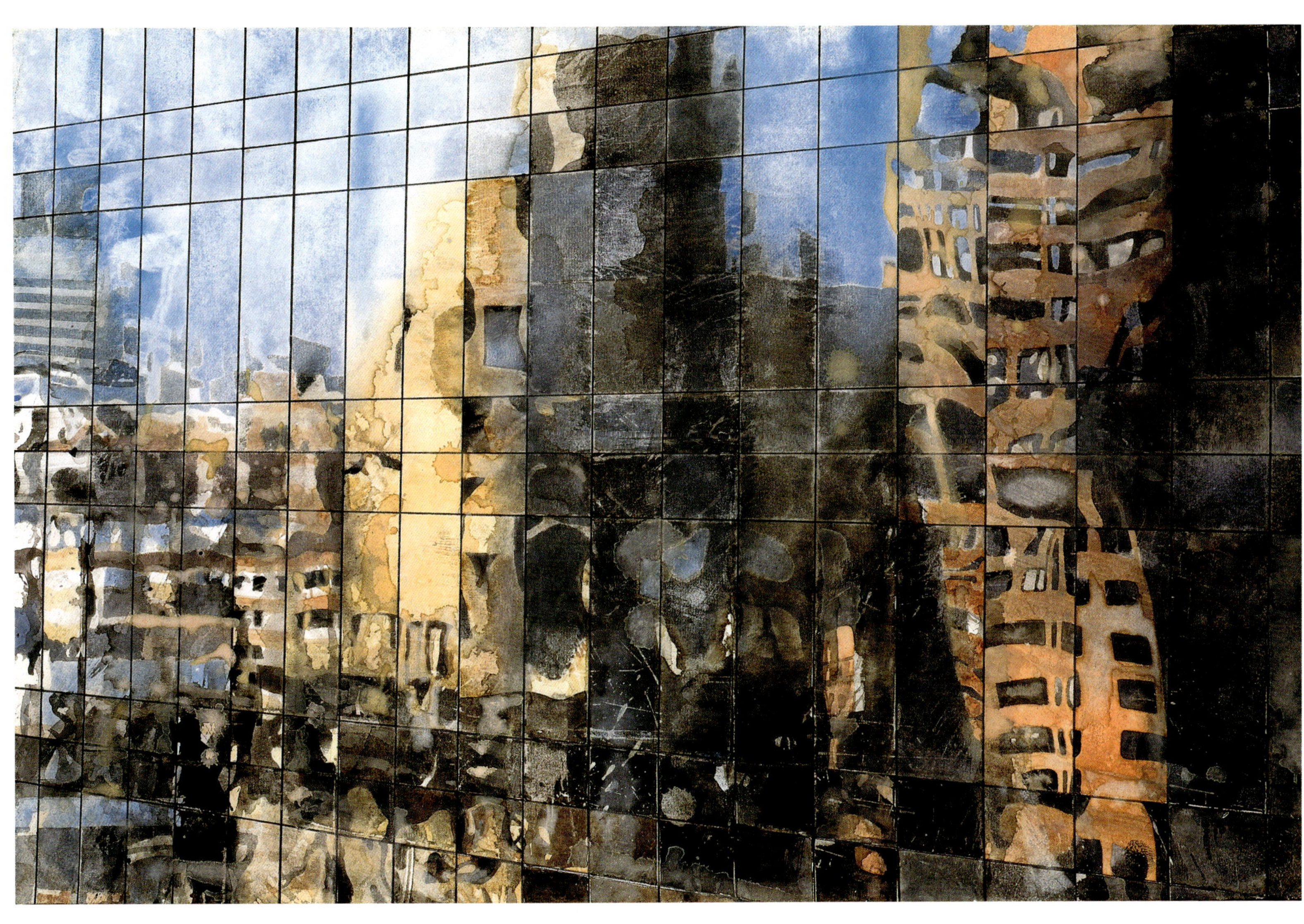

Aerial Reflection   2010, 40 × 57 cm

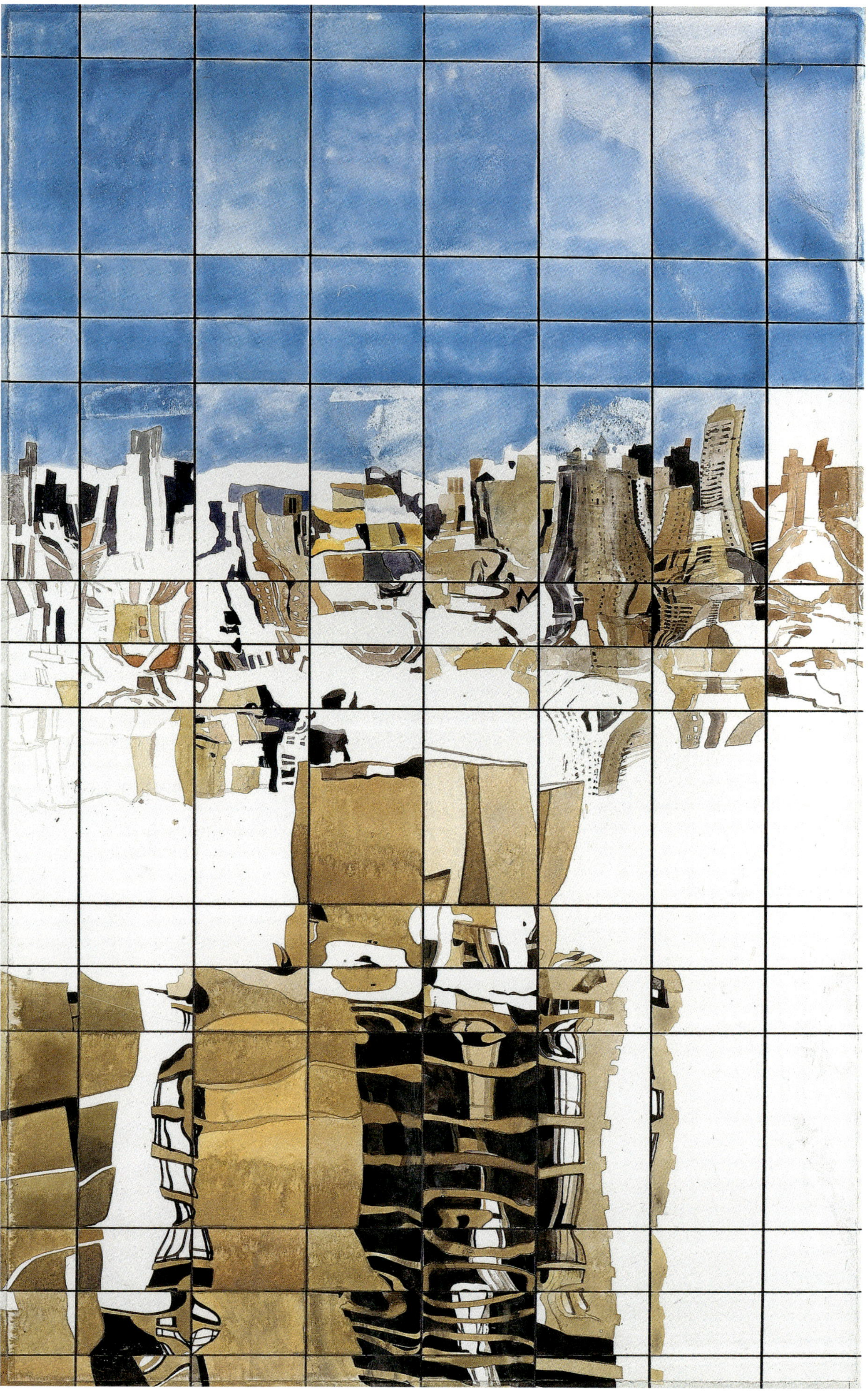

Central Park, Reflection | Central Park, Spiegelung | Central Park, reflet   2010, 100 × 68 cm

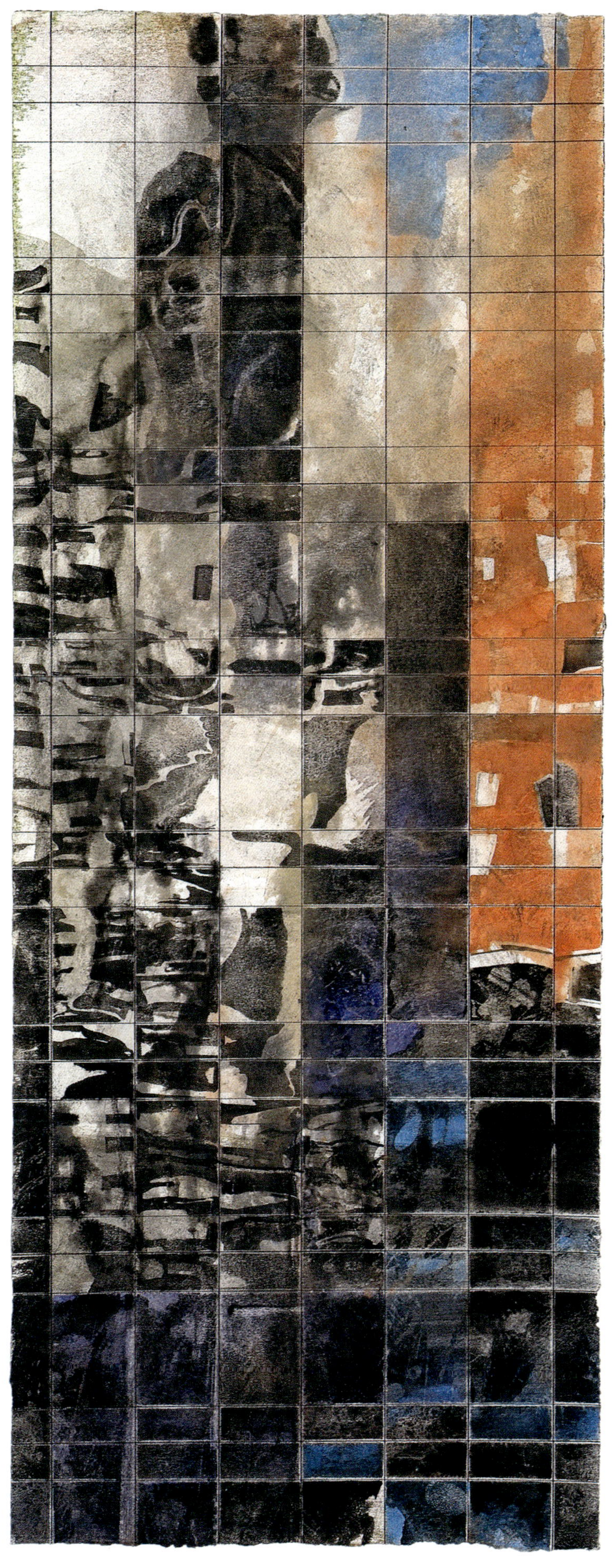

Red Building Reflection   2009, 68,4 × 26,3 cm

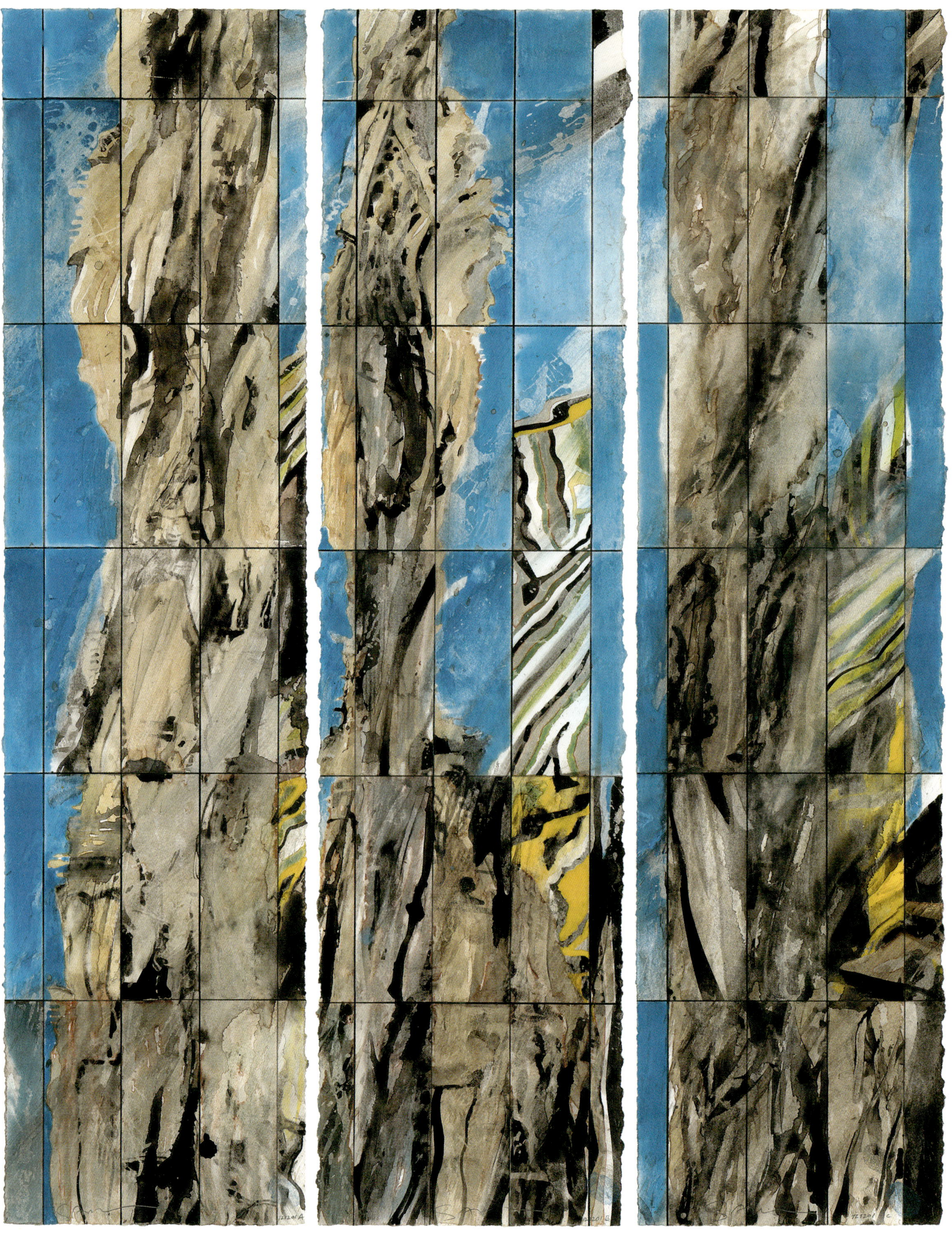

Vienna, Saint Stephen's Cathedral – Reflection | Wien, Stephansdom – Spiegelung | Vienne, Saint-Étienne – reflet   2008, 62,5 × 15,3 cm (3 ×)

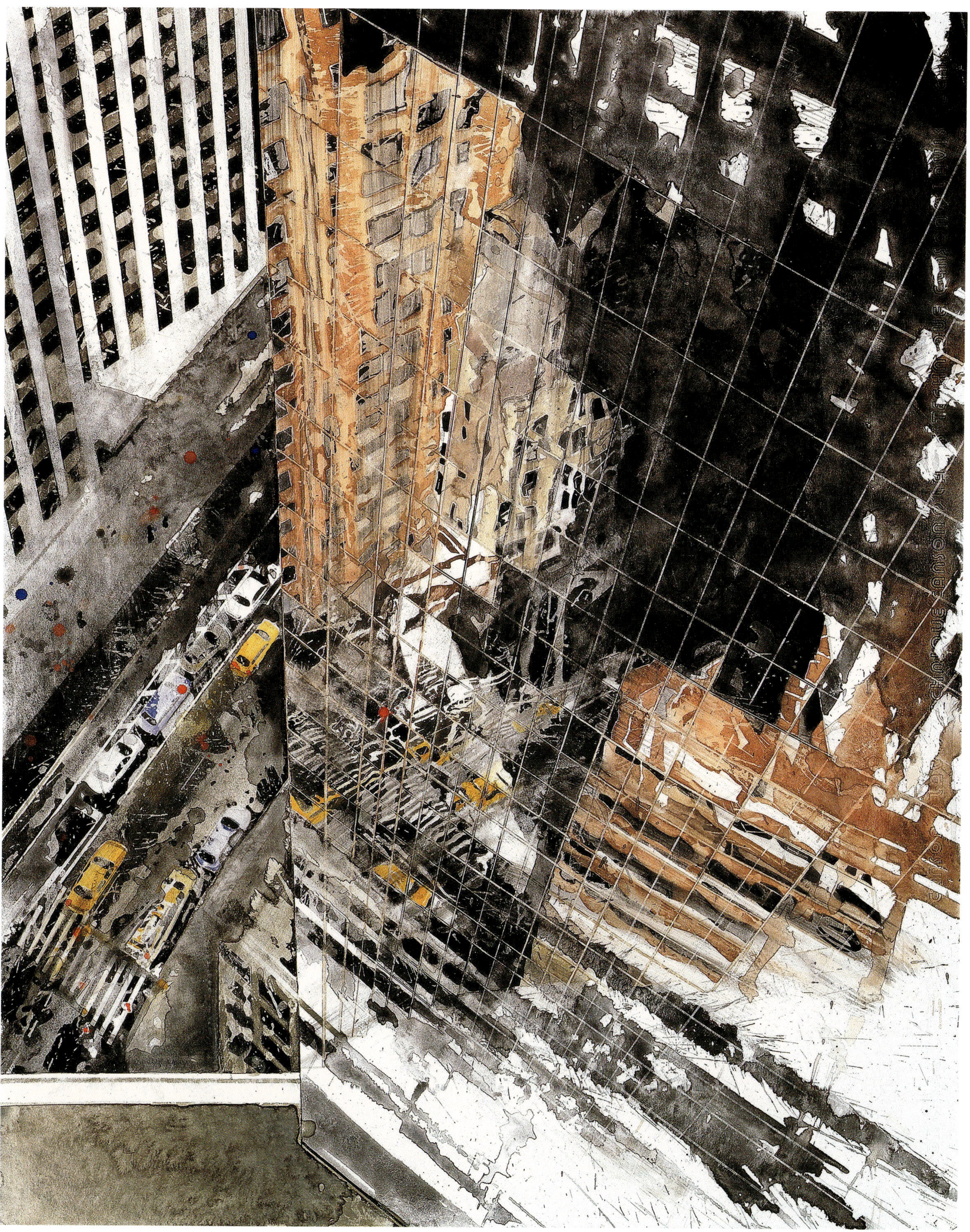

Reflection 7th Avenue | *Spiegelung 7th Avenue* | Reflet 7th Avenue   2012, 64,8 × 50,8 cm

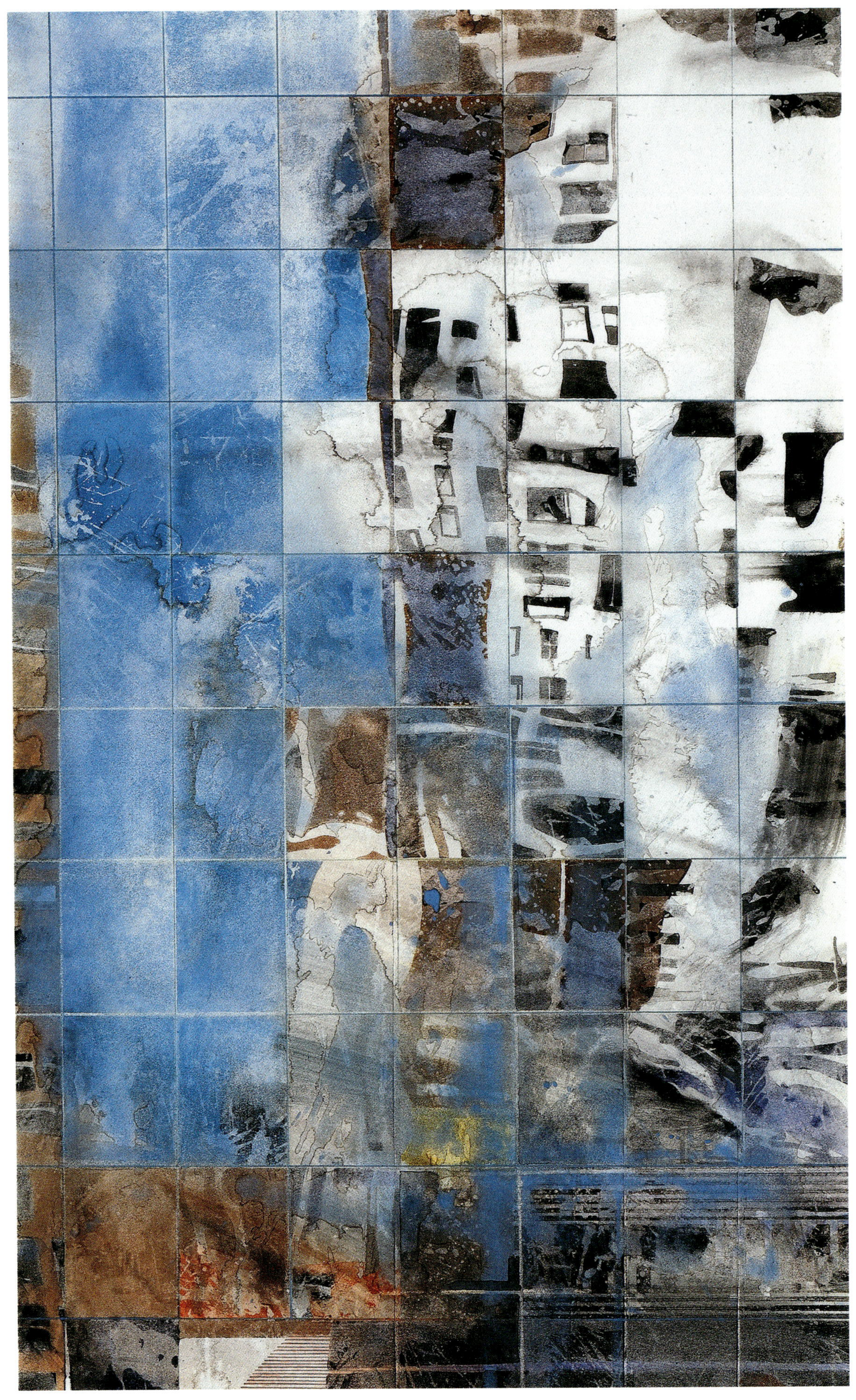

NY Reflection   2009, 46,8 × 29,5 cm

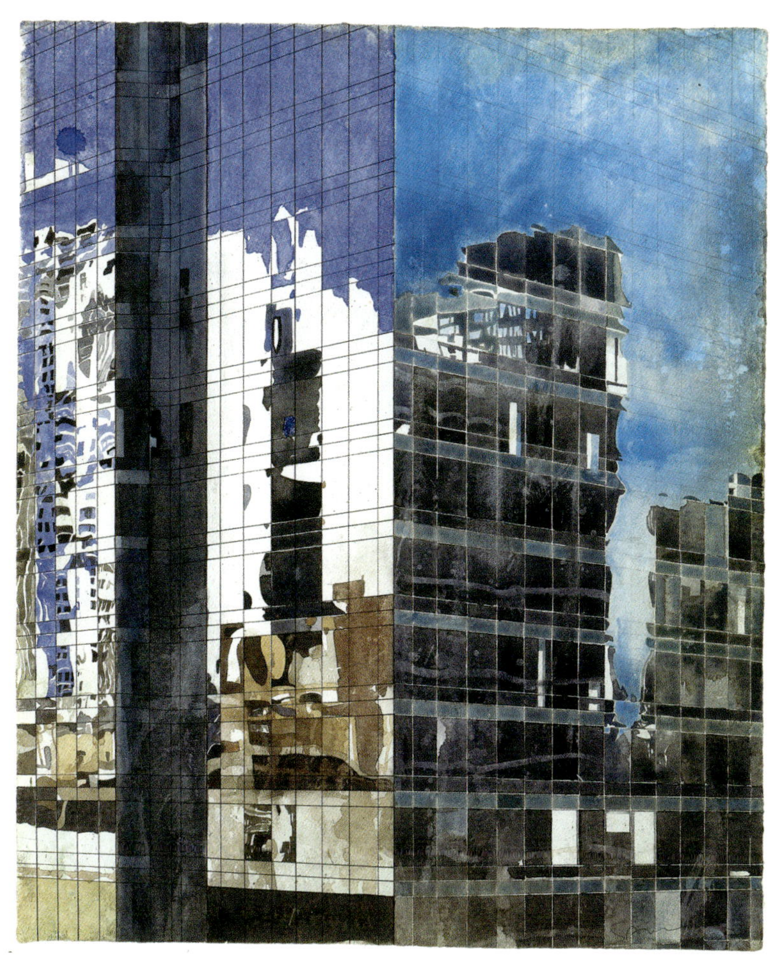

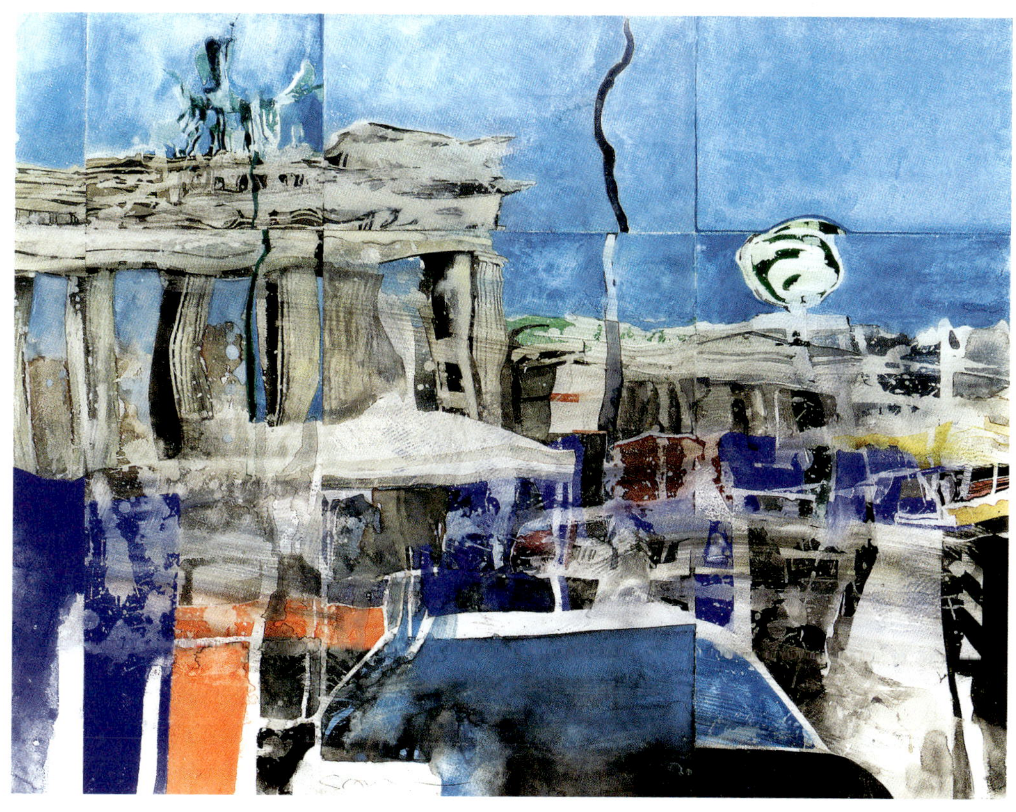

NY Aerial Reflection II   2010, 62,3 × 50,3 cm

Berlin, Brandenburg Gate – Reflection | Berlin, Brandenburger Tor – Spiegelung | Berlin, Porte de Brandenbourg – reflet   1997, 47 × 59,5 cm

Stairs, jalousies
Treppen, Jalousien
Escaliers, stores

   Stairs, Place Vendôme | Treppen, Place Vendôme | Escaliers, Place Vendôme   2010, 73 × 26,7 cm

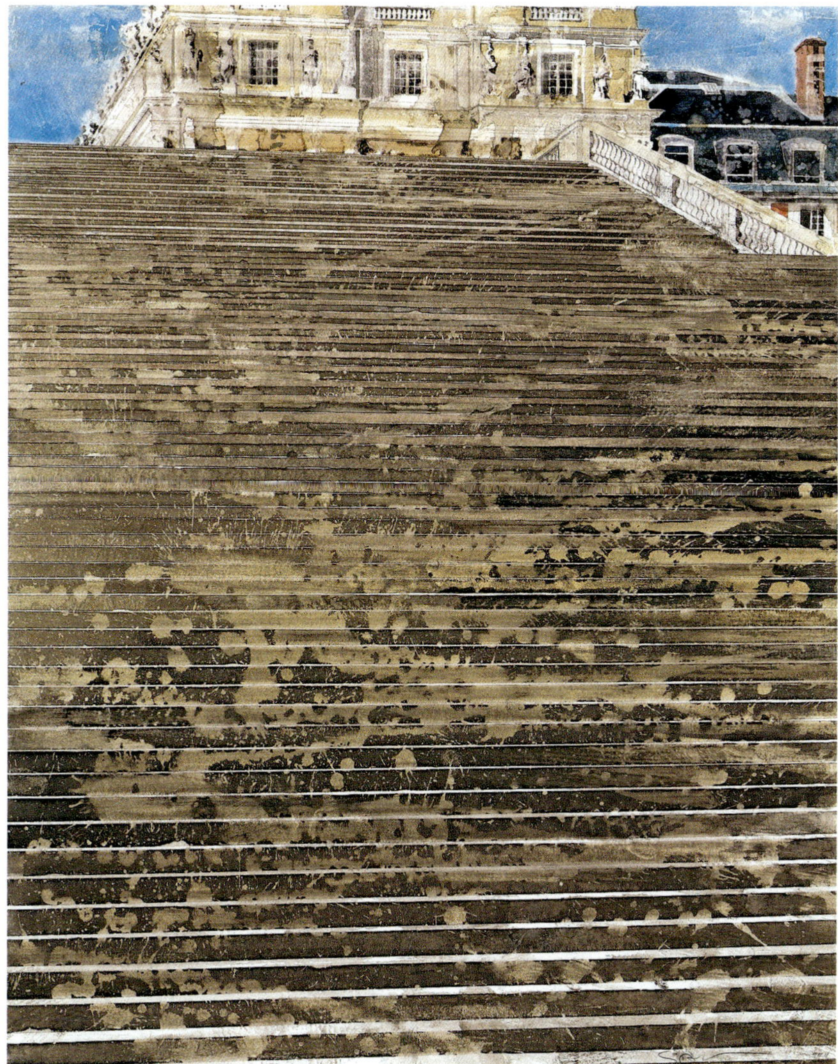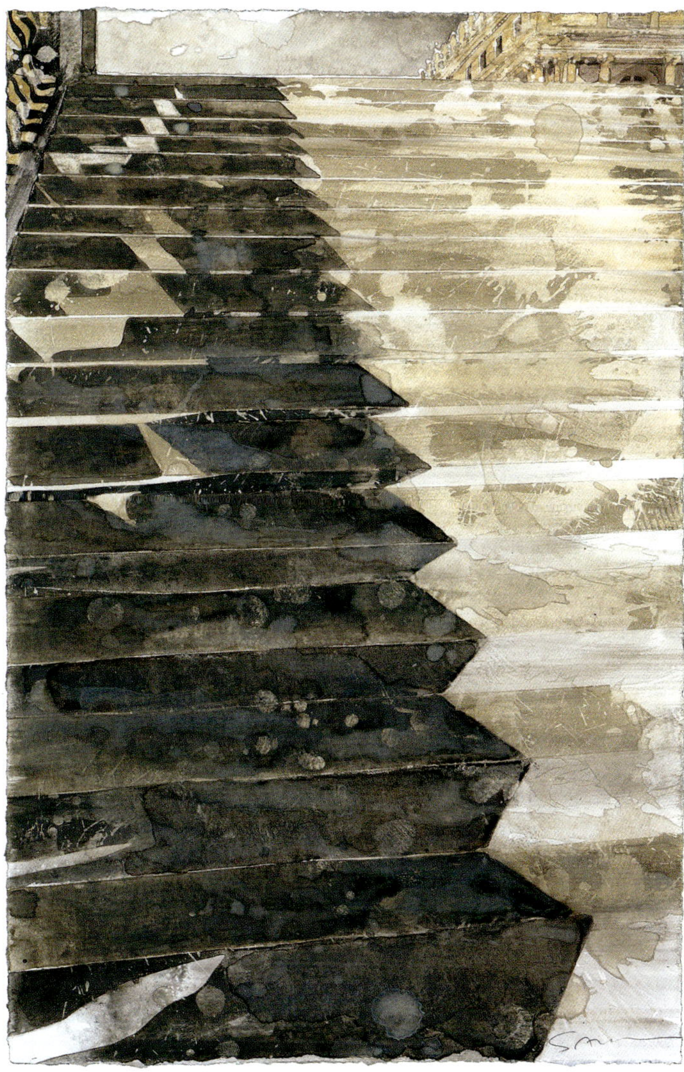

Stairs at Versailles I | Treppen in Versailles I | Escaliers à Versailles I   2010, 64,8 × 50 cm

Shadow on the Steps at Versailles | Schatten auf den Treppen in Versailles | Ombres sur les escaliers à Versailles   2010, 47,7 × 30,4 cm

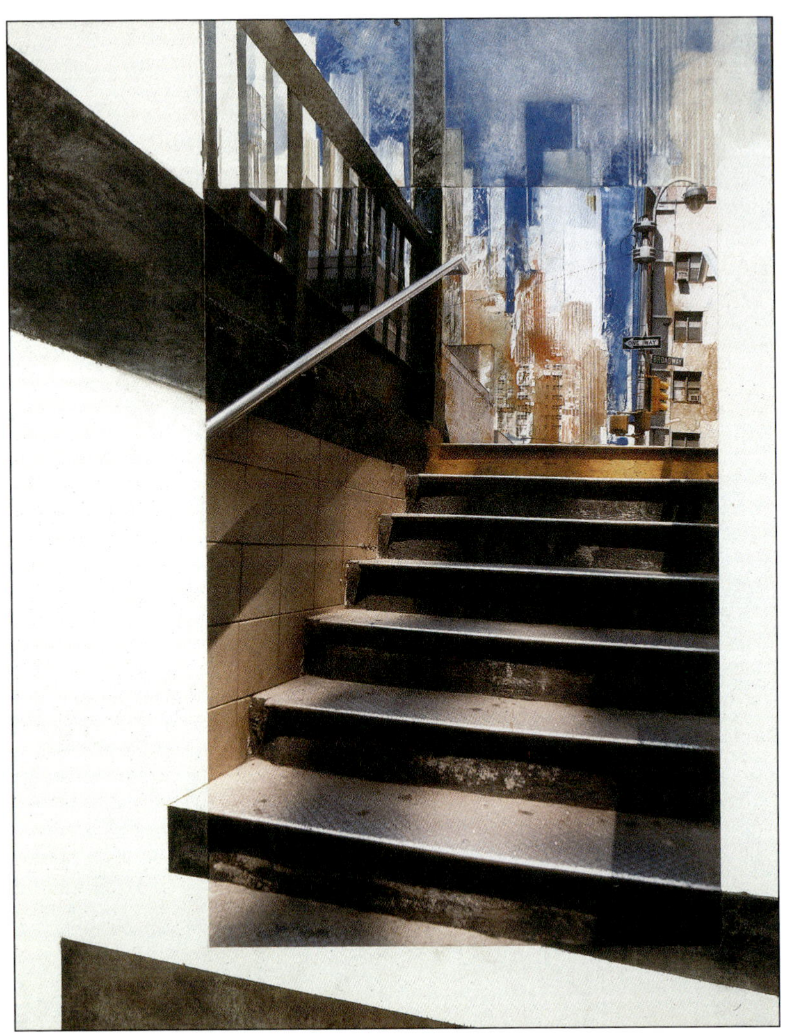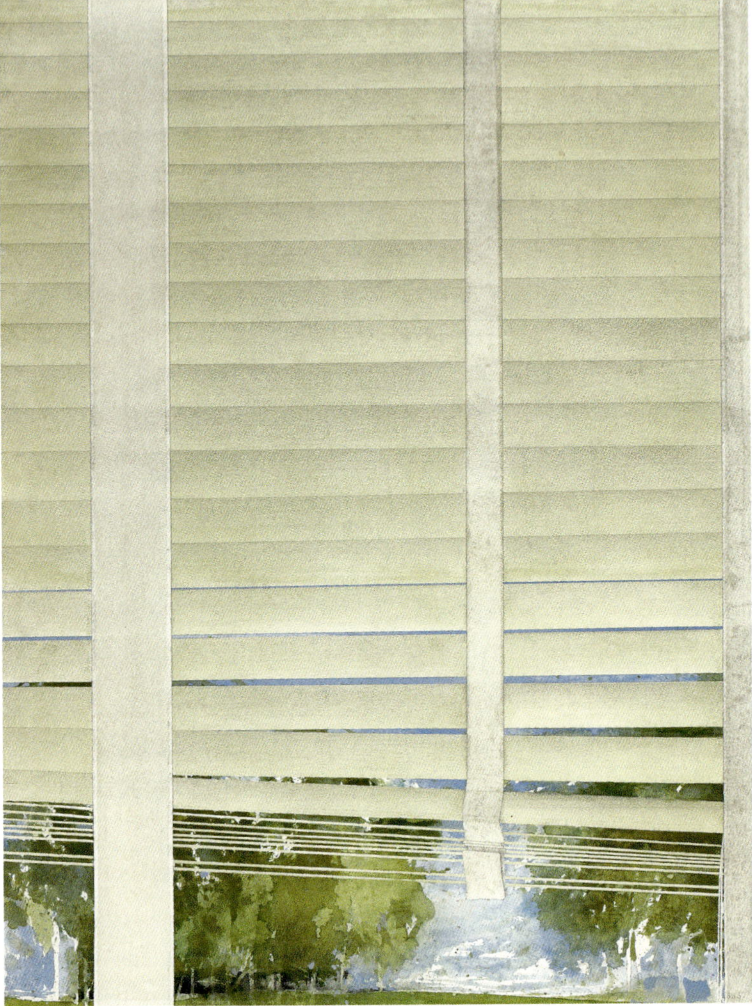

Steps (Broadway) | Treppen (Broadway) | Escaliers (Broadway)   2009, 101 × 76 cm
White Jalousie | Weiße Jalousie | Store blanc   1983, 77,5 × 57 cm

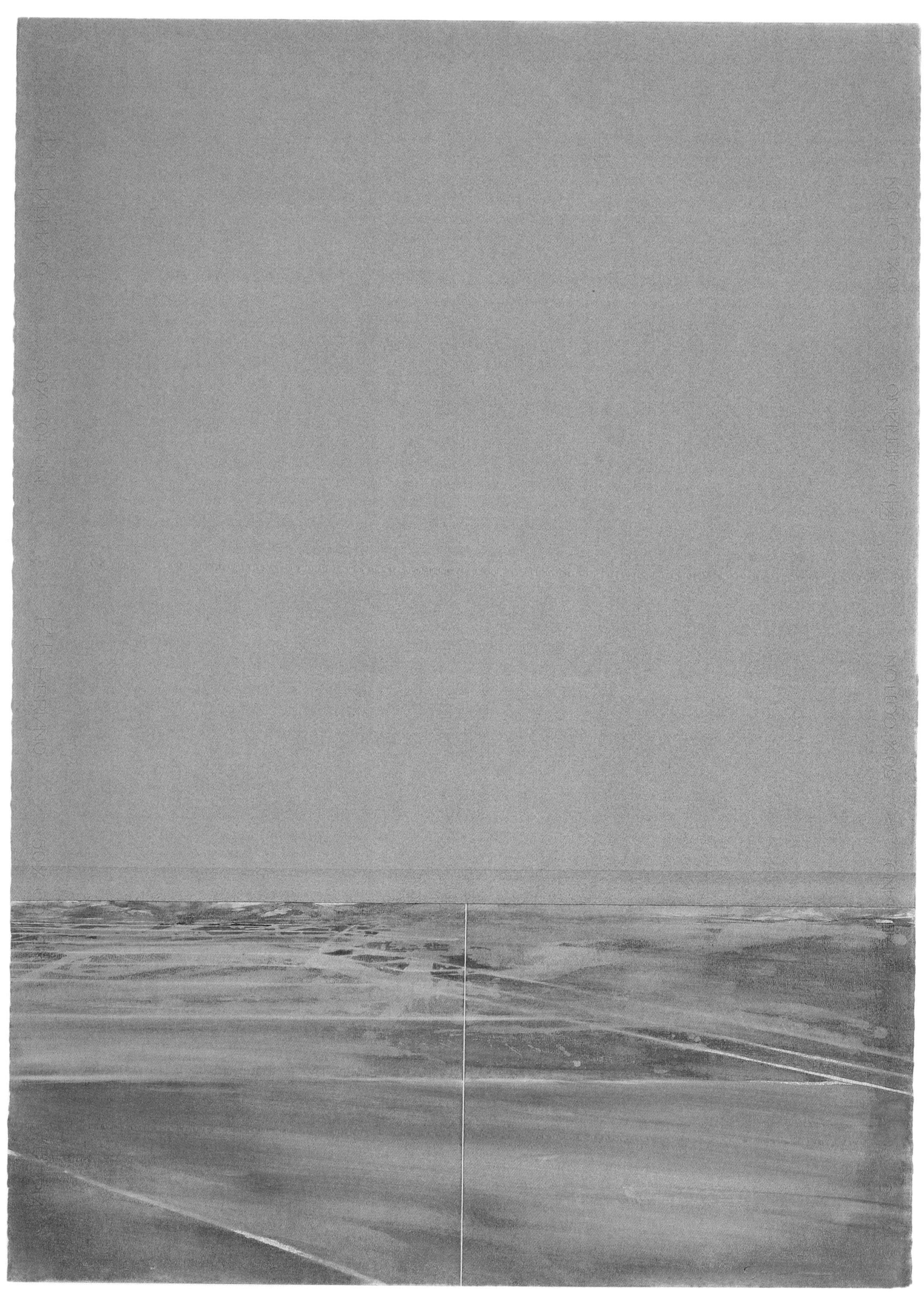

Store ou ciel   1981, 99,7 × 70,8 cm

City Rooftops

Dachlandschaften
Paysages de toits

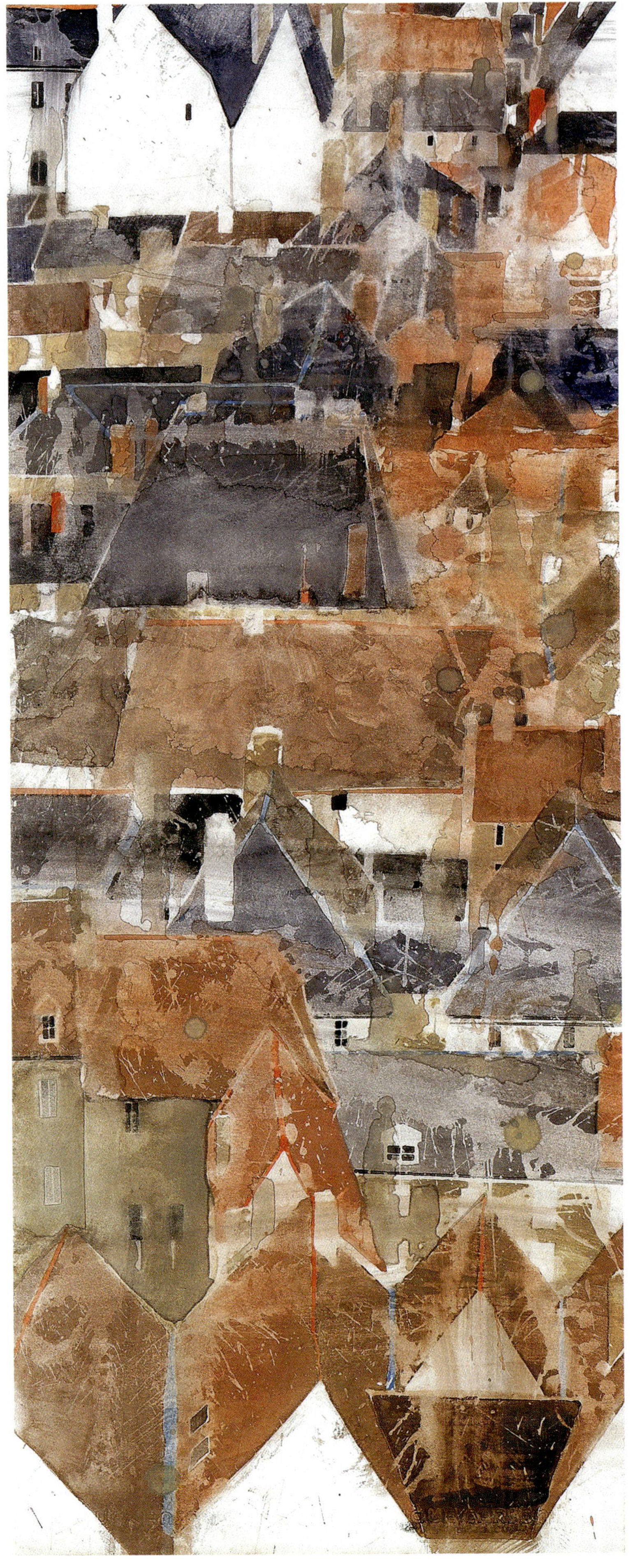

The Rooftops of Chartres | Die Dächer von Chartres | Les toits de Chartres   2010, 75,4 × 29,5 cm

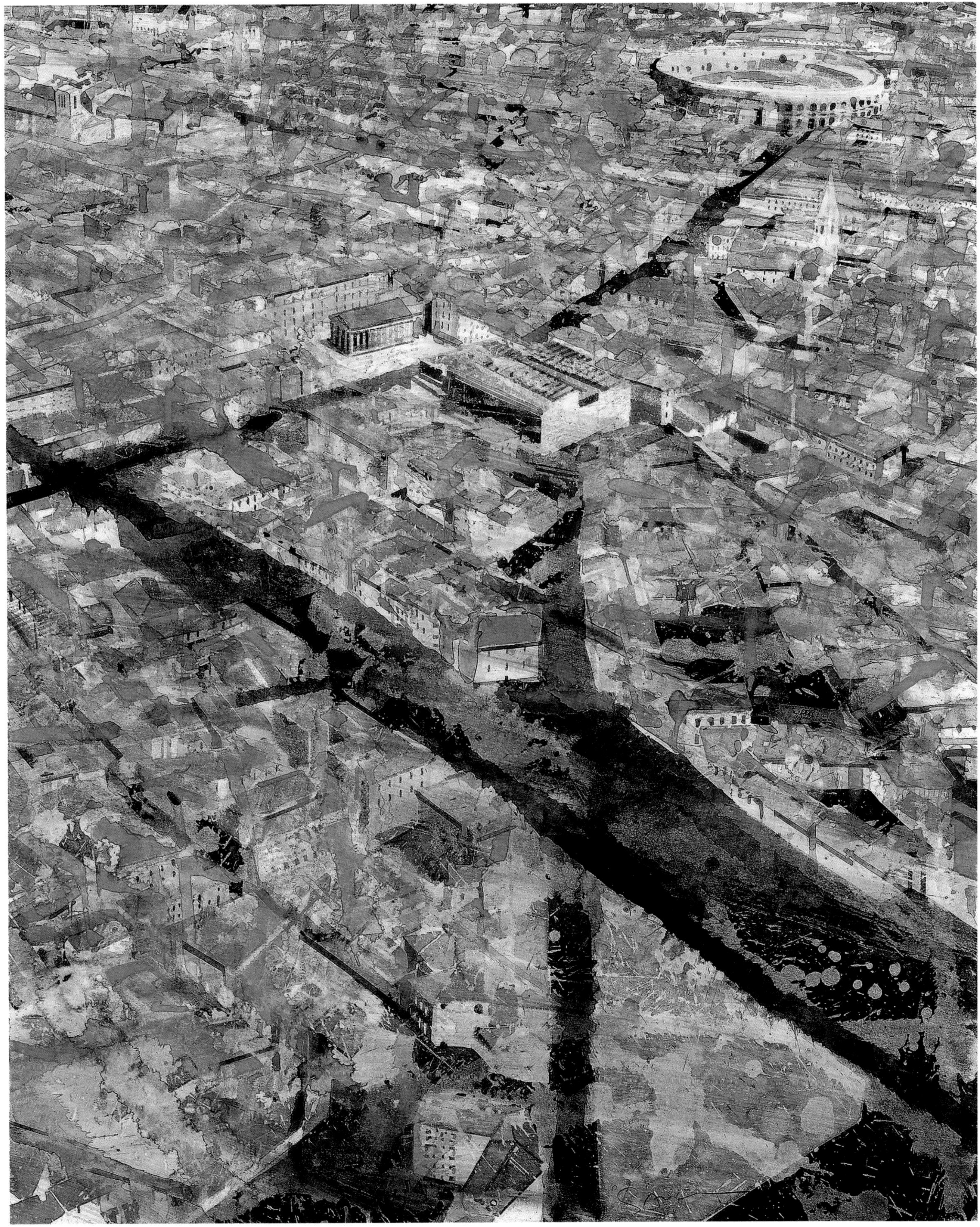

Nîmes, La Maison Carrée   2007, 74 × 61 cm

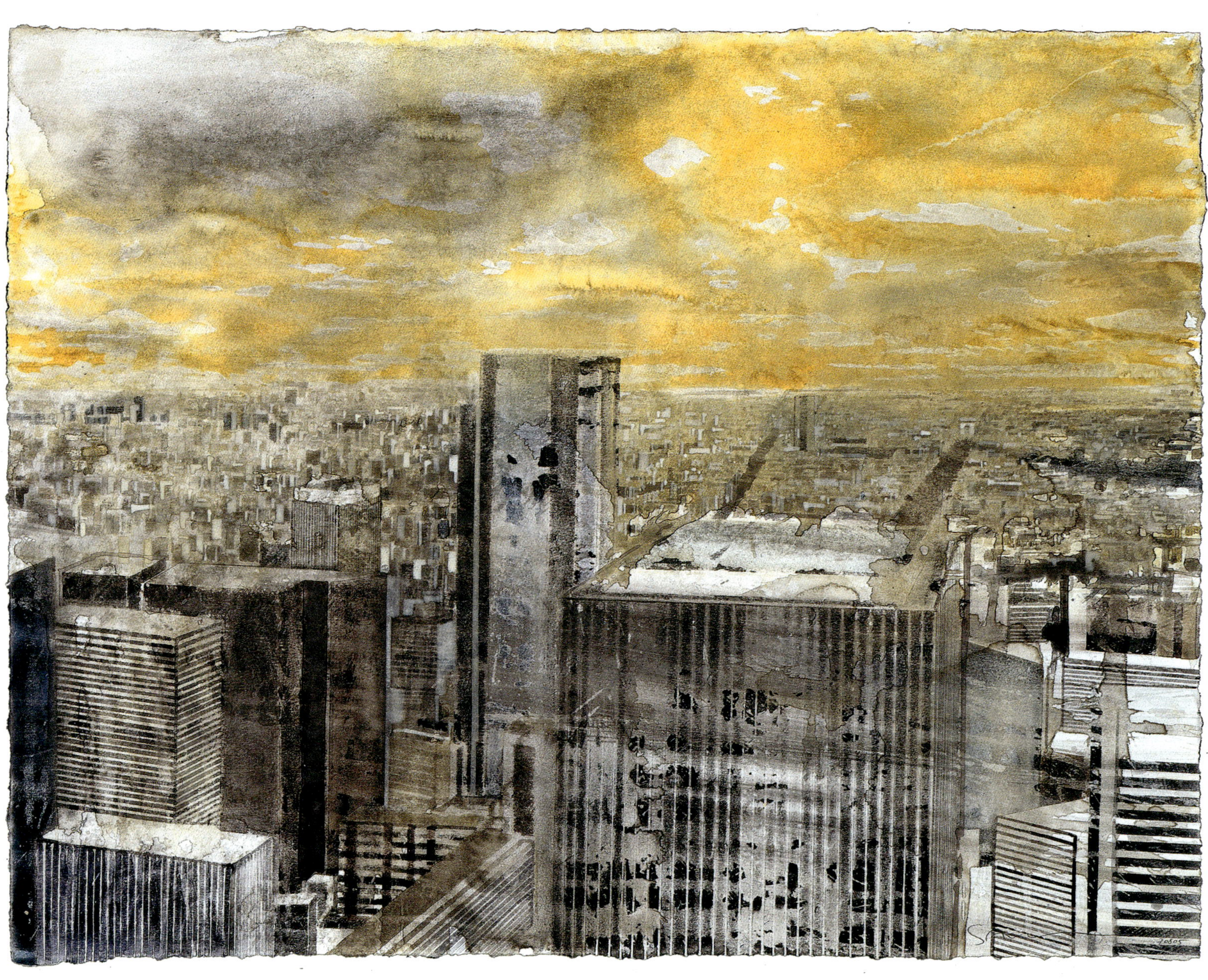

162　　Paris La Défense　2008, 47 × 59,5 cm

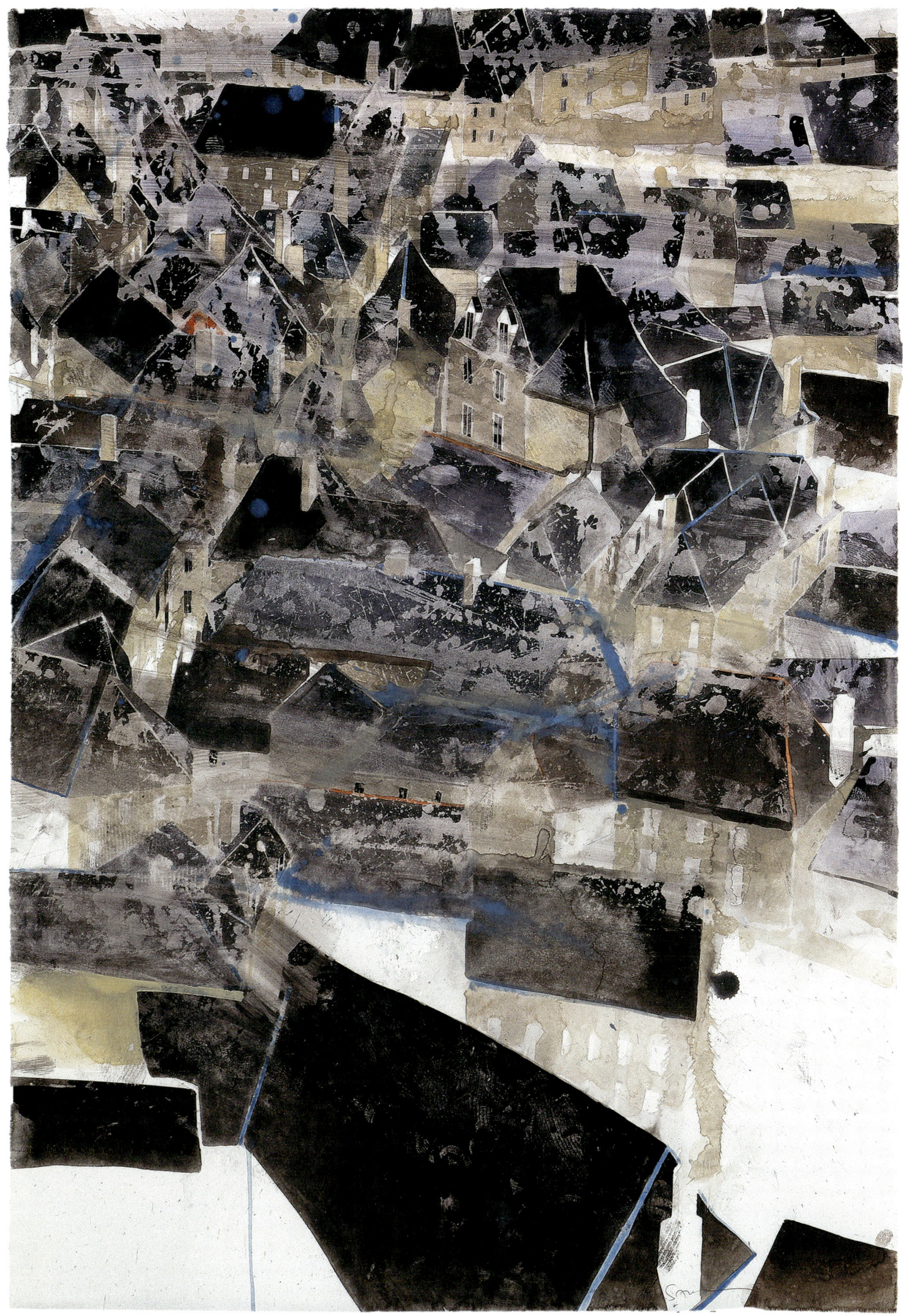

La grande Turenne   2008, 107,8 × 73,4 cm

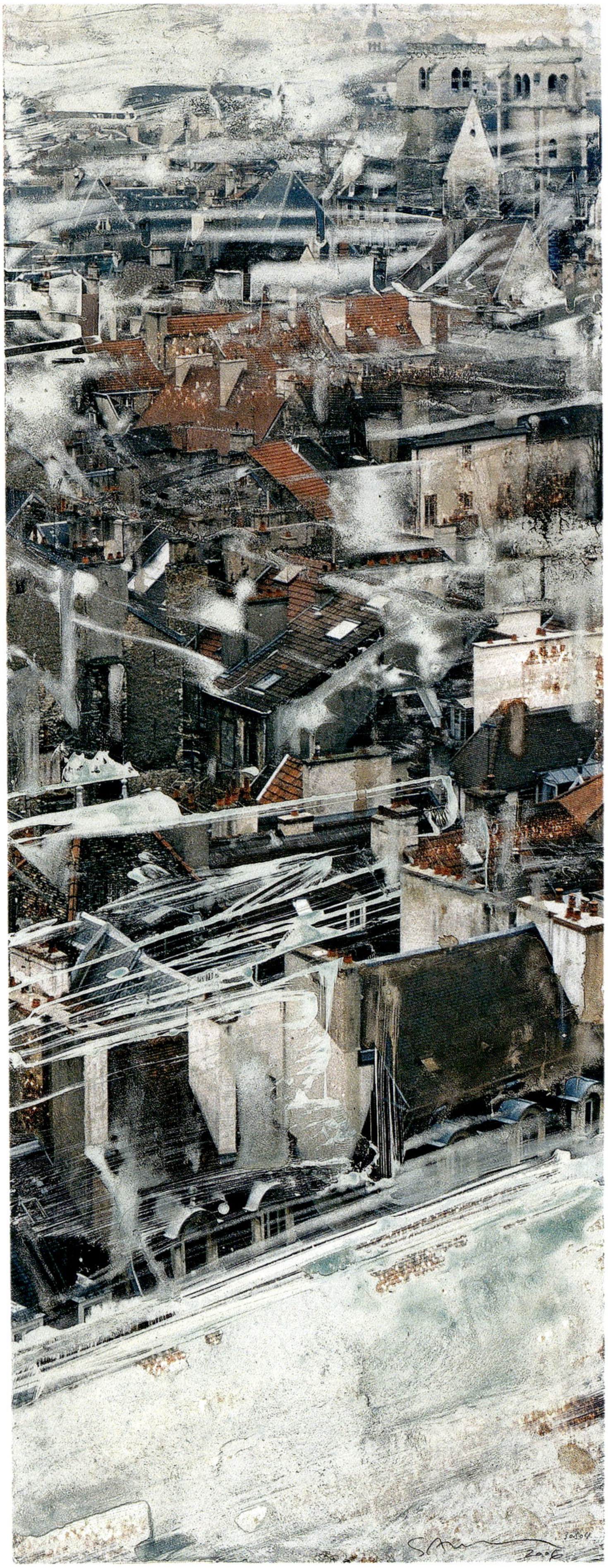

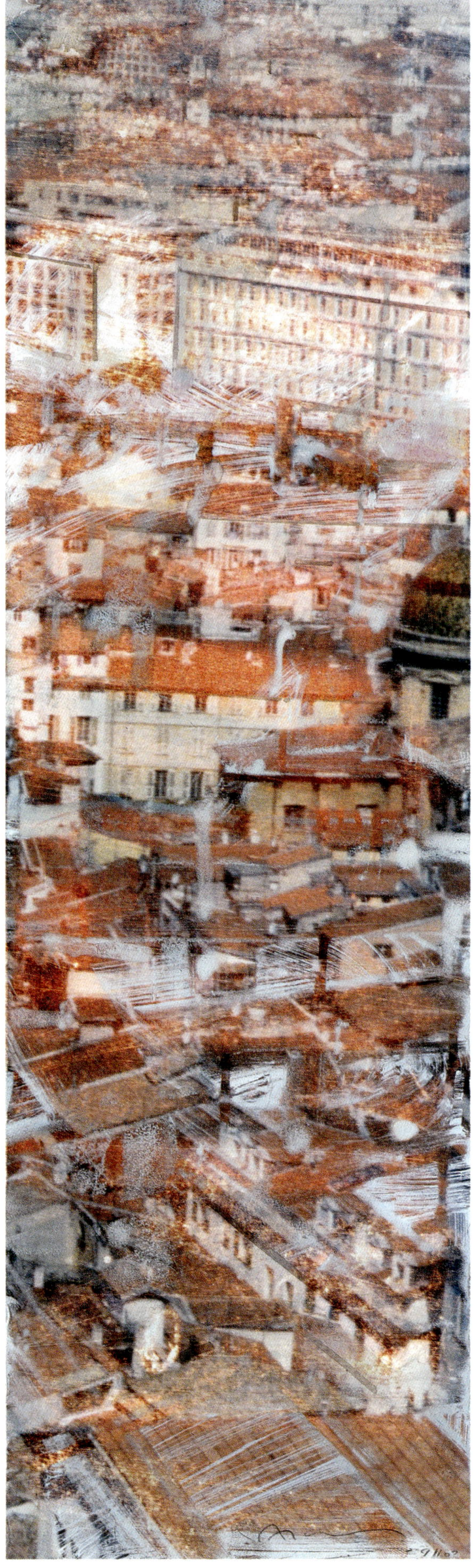

   Dijon   2006, 74,4 × 28,3 cm   Nice   2008, 50,5 × 14,9 cm

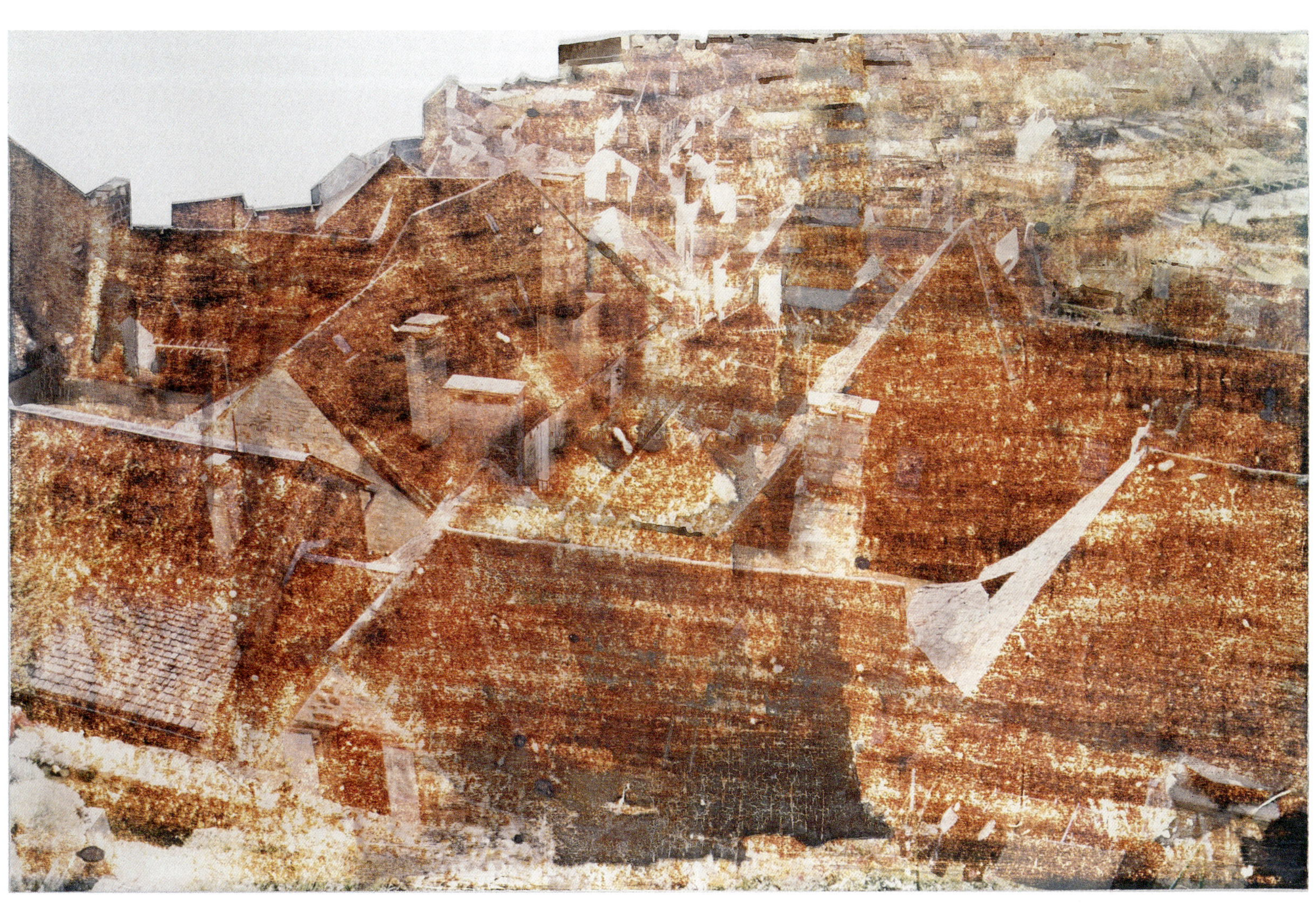

The Rooftops of Beaune | Die Dächer von Beaune | Les toits de Beaune   2004, 50,6 (39,2) × 75,3 cm

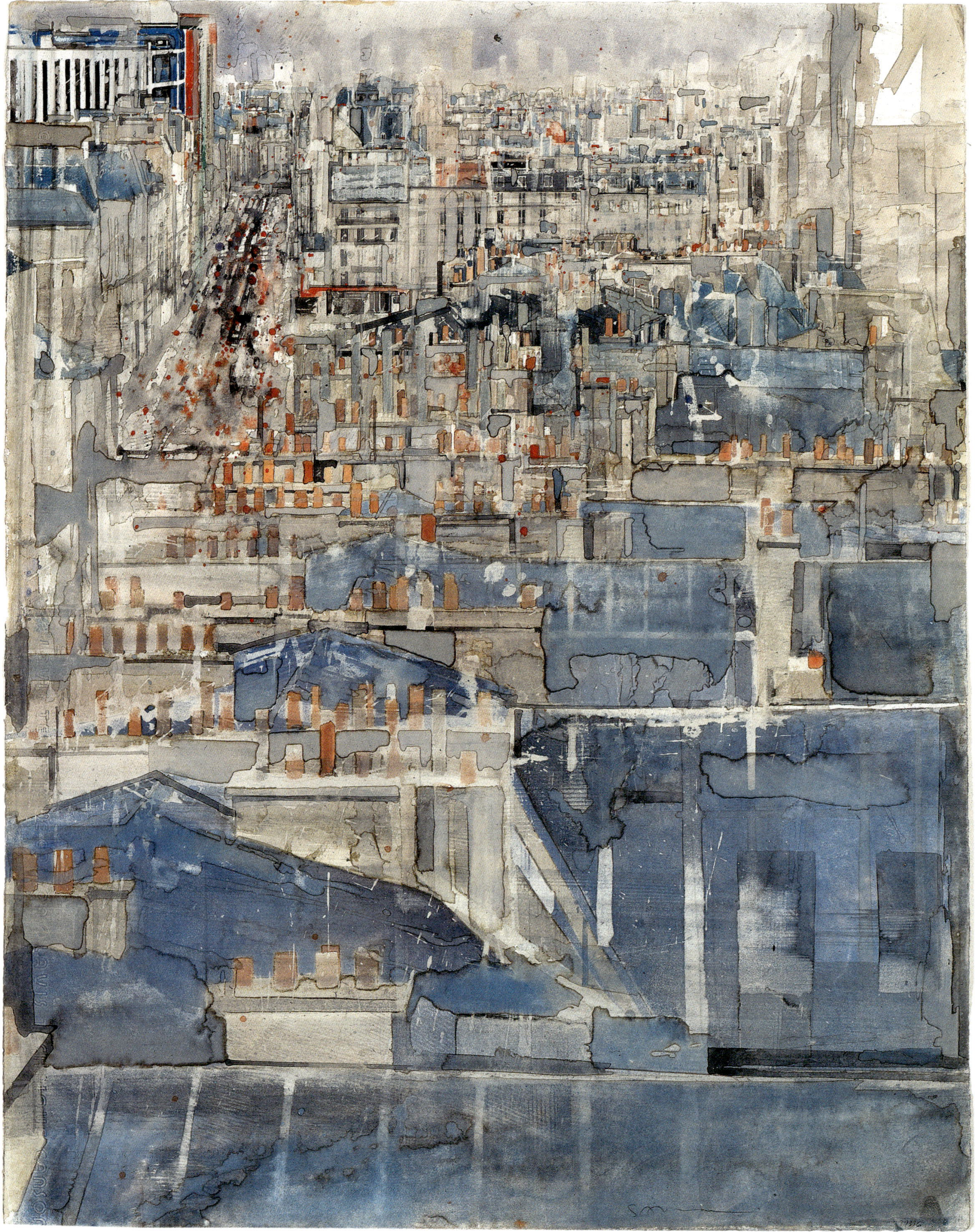

    Paris, Rue du Renard   1993, 63,7 × 49,5 cm

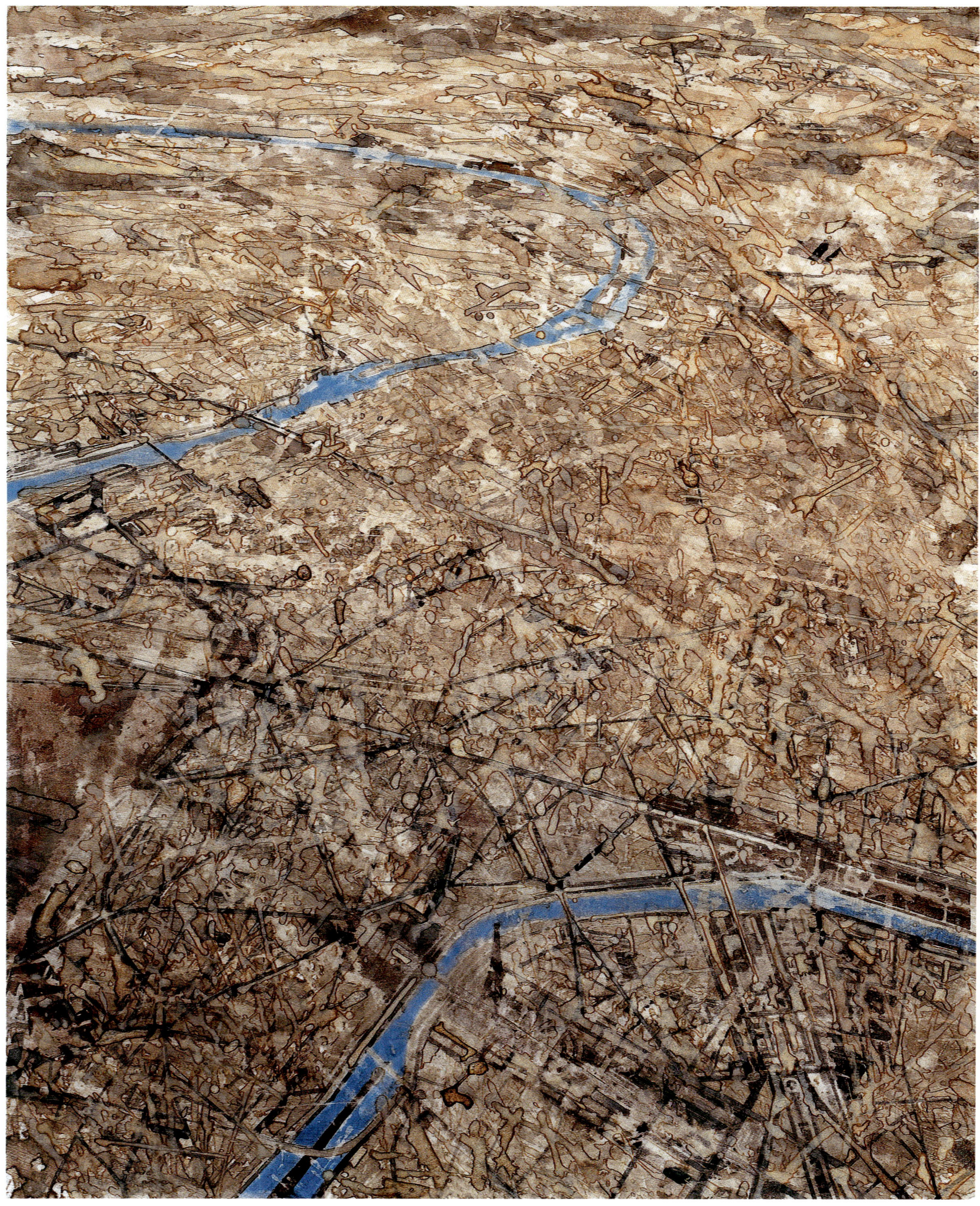

Over Paris | Über Paris | Au-dessus de Paris   2007, 60,1 × 47,8 cm

Cathedrals
Kathedralen
Cathédrales

Has the world lost an architect in Gottfried Salzmann? His most recent works might tempt one to wonder, given how effortlessly he grasps the essential features of complex building structures and masters even the most difficult overlaps. While his urban panoramas clearly indicate a general interest in aspects of construction and geometric patterns, we now recognize a certain fascination with architectural history as well. Although he was strongly attracted by French Gothic cathedral architecture even during his years as a student, he has only recently come to feel equal to the task of dealing adequately with the subject.

In these works, the verticality of Gothic architecture joins with the urge to explore great heights awakened earlier by skyscrapers. Salzmann feels as if under a clear sky in the spheres of lofty vaults. As in a polyphonic composition, he dispenses with all incidental elements, rendering only the pure spatial structure. He is fascinated above all by the configurations of vaulted ceilings and the steep rise of the pillars. As in an exterior, firmly joined structures are dissolved into delicate tonal gradations. Interior space is defined primarily by its vastness, and despite the precision with which it is rendered, it appears governed more by the artist's imagination than by tectonic laws.

While the cathedrals represent a counterpoint to the pulsating street scenes, they allow the eye just as little rest.

Gottfried Salzmann serait-il architecte dans l'âme ? Cette idée nous effleure dès que nous voyons ses tout derniers travaux, tant on y sent la maîtrise des formes architecturales les plus complexes. Les panoramas urbains avaient déjà révélé son intérêt pour la construction et les plans géométriques, mais d'autres éléments s'ajoutent ici qui renvoient à l'histoire de l'architecture. Pendant ses études, déjà, Salzmann avait été très attiré par le gothique des cathédrales françaises et leur élégance inégalée, mais c'est seulement maintenant qu'il se sent à même d'aborder ce thème.

La verticalité du gothique rejoint son envie de hauteur que les gratte-ciel avaient déjà réveillée en lui. Dans les sphères voûtées et aériennes, Salzmann se sent comme en plein air. Comme dans une composition polyphonique, il renonce à tout élément ornemental pour ne retenir que la plus pure structure de l'espace. La configuration des voussures le fascine autant que la raideur des colonnes. Comme en extérieur, la rigueur de l'agencement s'estompe dans des tonalités délicates. L'intérieur devient surtout saisissable dans son envergure ; malgré la précision, il semble davantage obéir à l'imagination de l'artiste qu'aux lois de la tectonique.

Les cathédrales sont un contrepoint aux vues urbaines et trépidantes, mais l'œil n'en trouve pas plus de calme pour autant.

 Bourges Cathedral (detail) | Kathedrale von Bourges (Detail) | Cathédrale de Bourges (détail)   2010, 61 × 48 cm

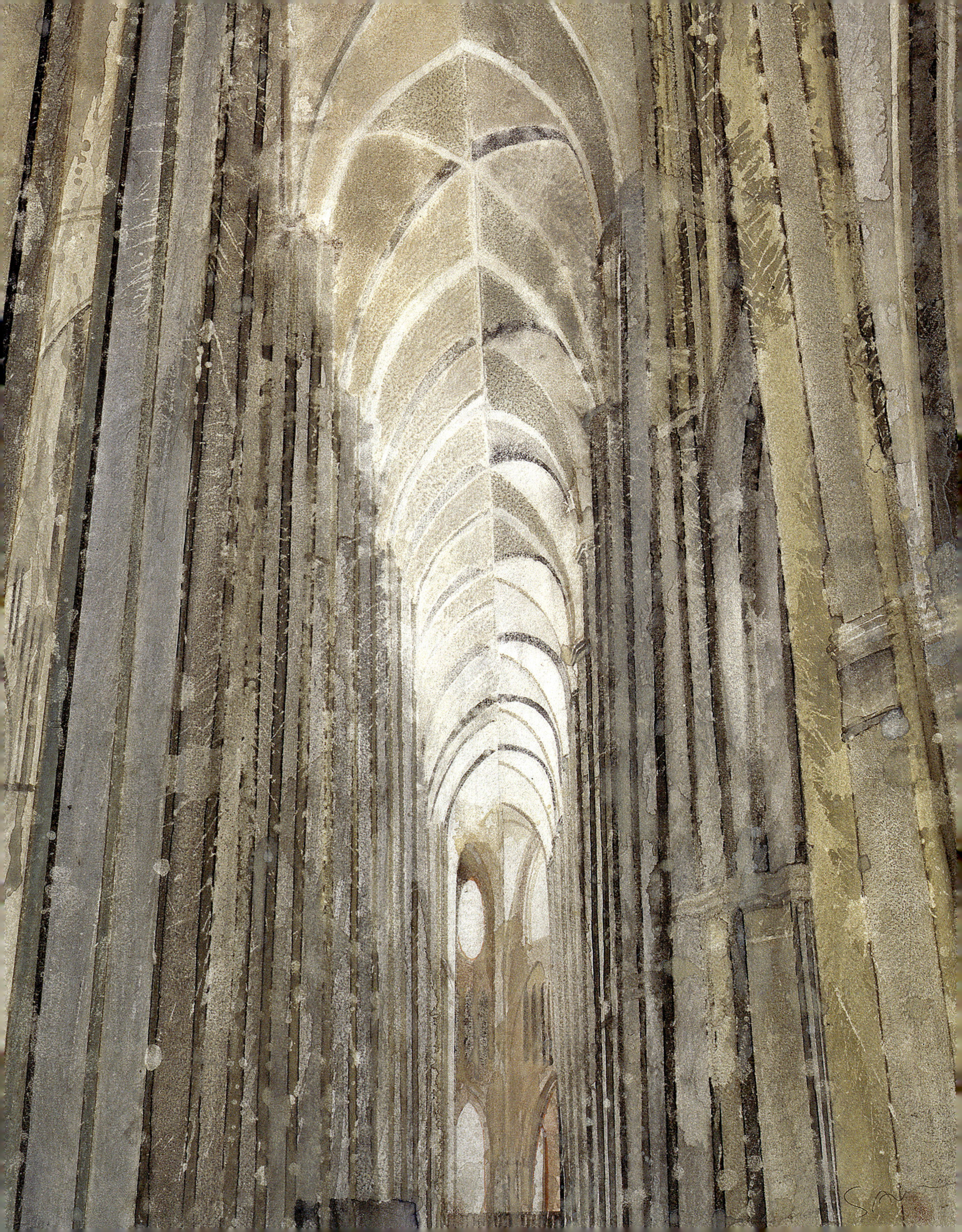

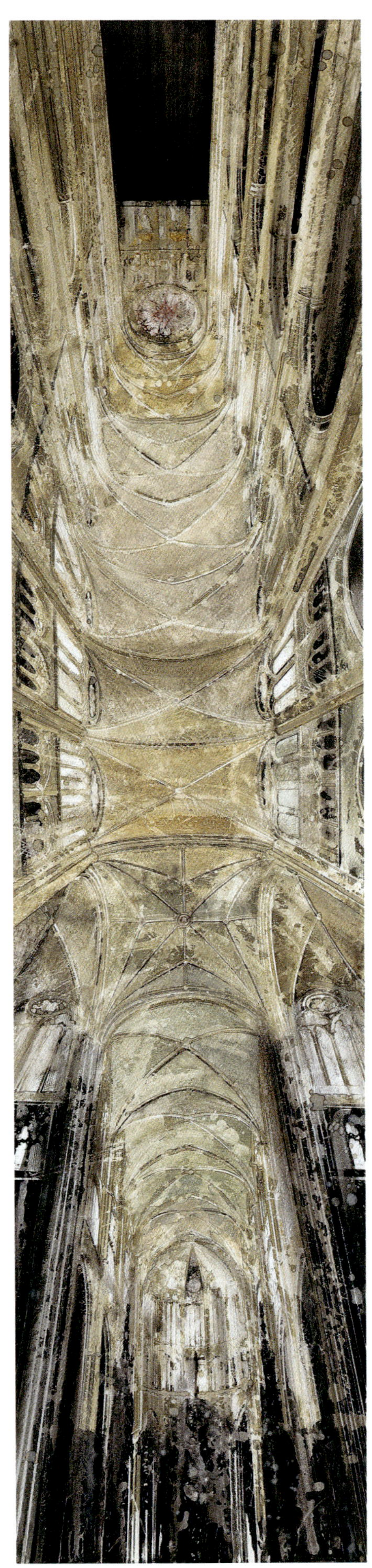

170   The Cathedral | Die Kathedrale | La Cathédrale   2012, 225,3 × 52 cm

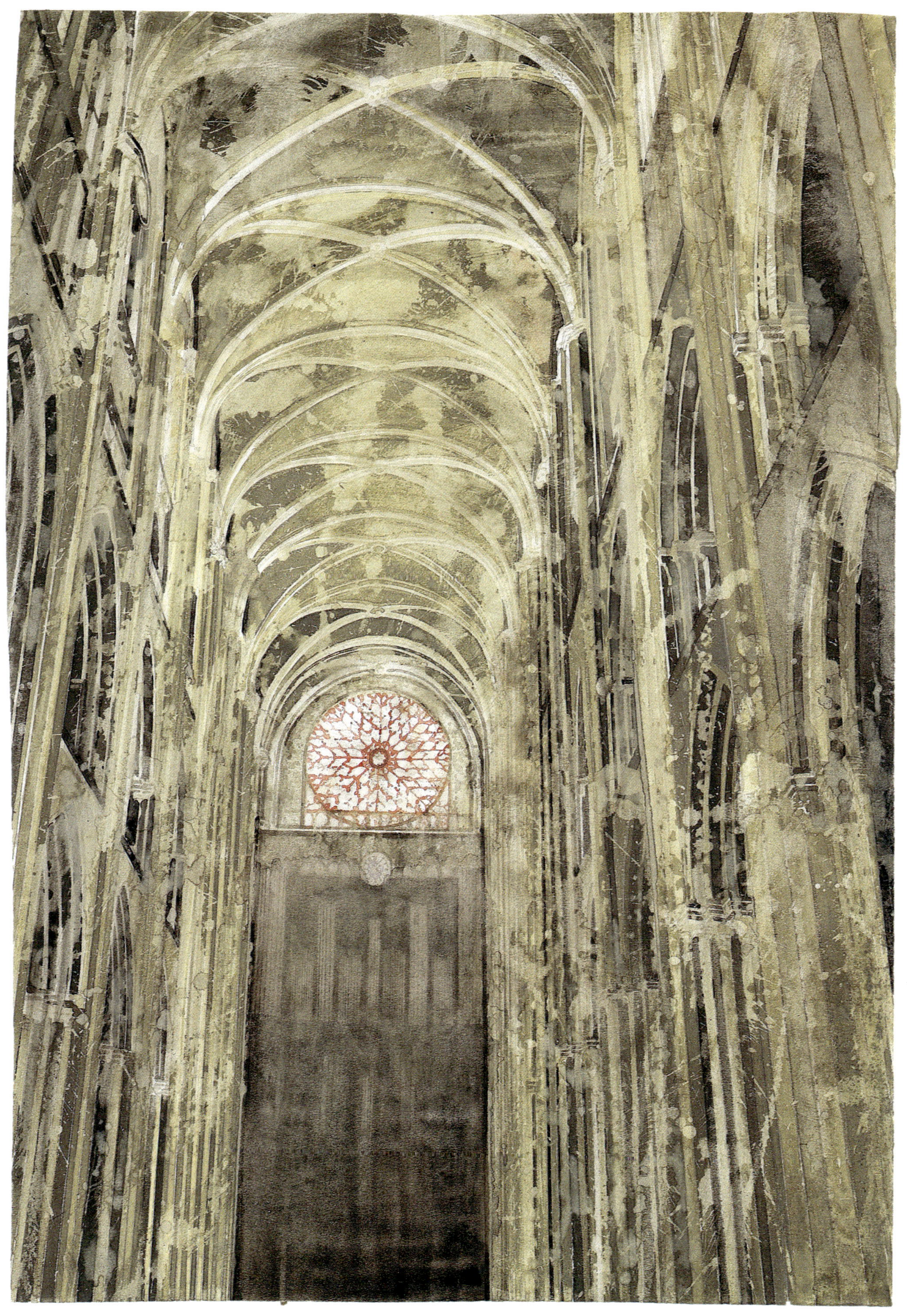

Rouen Cathedral I | Kathedrale von Rouen I | Cathédrale de Rouen I   2011, 92 × 63,3 cm

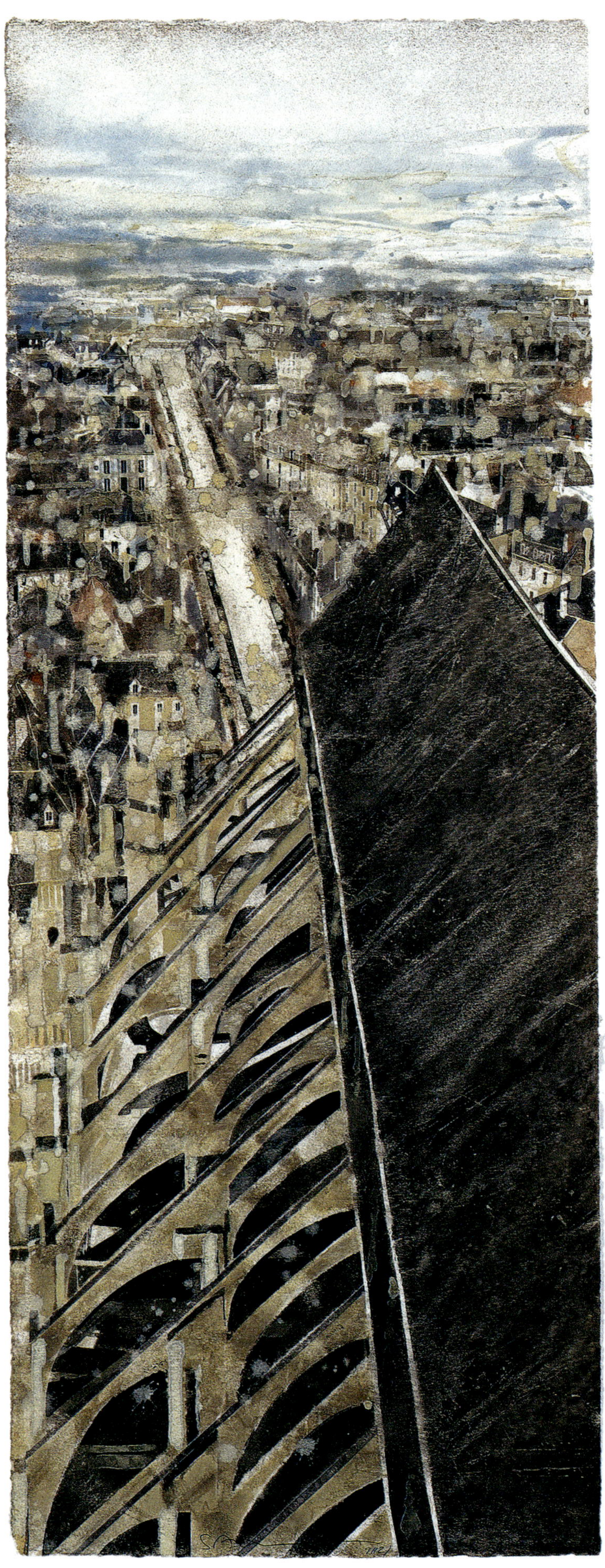

172   Roof of the Bourges Cathedral | *Dach der Kathedrale von Bourges* | Toit de la Cathédrale de Bourges   2010, 68,5 × 26,3 cm

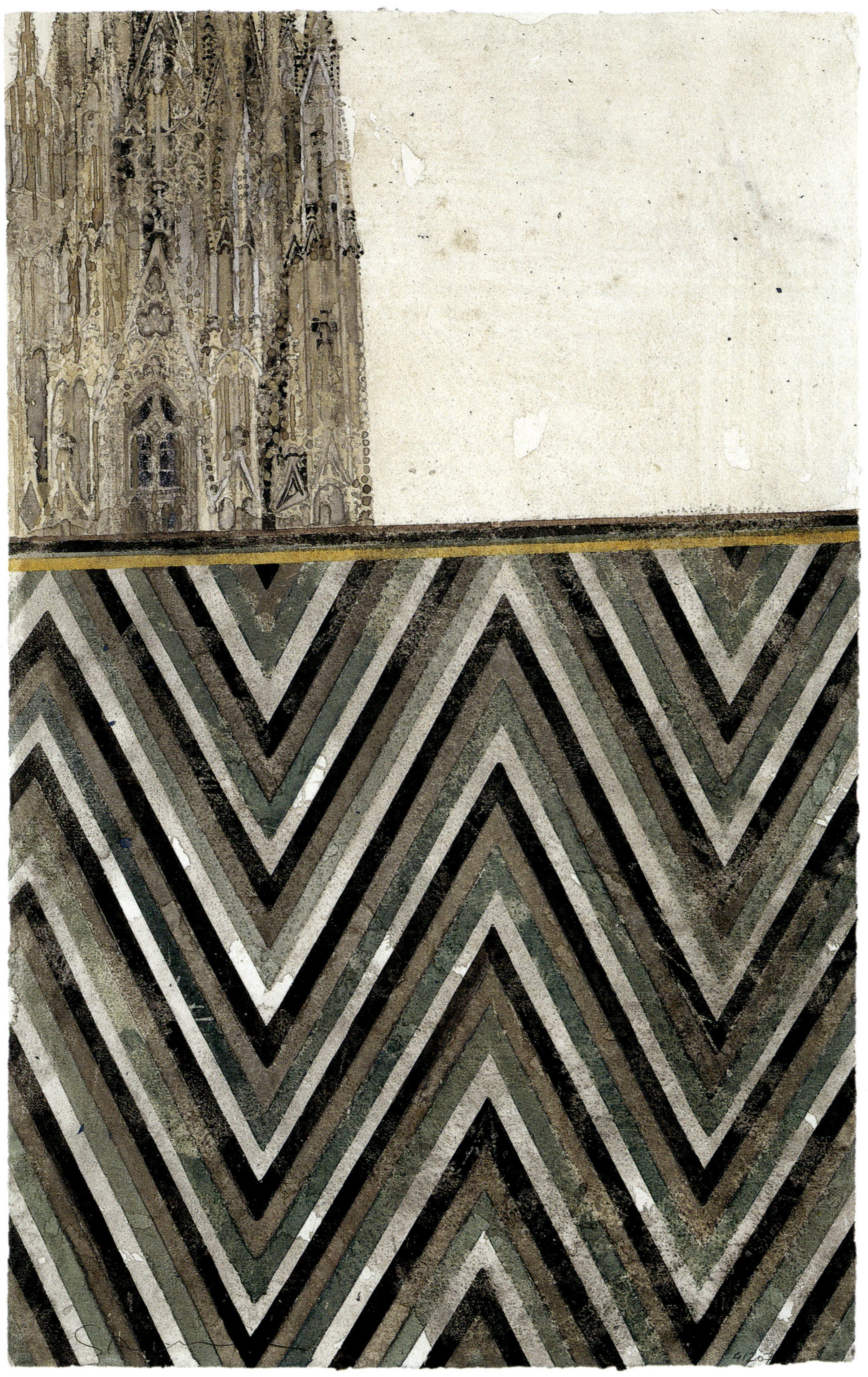

Vienna, Saint Stephen's | | Vienne, Saint-Étienne   2010, 48,9 × 30,7 cm

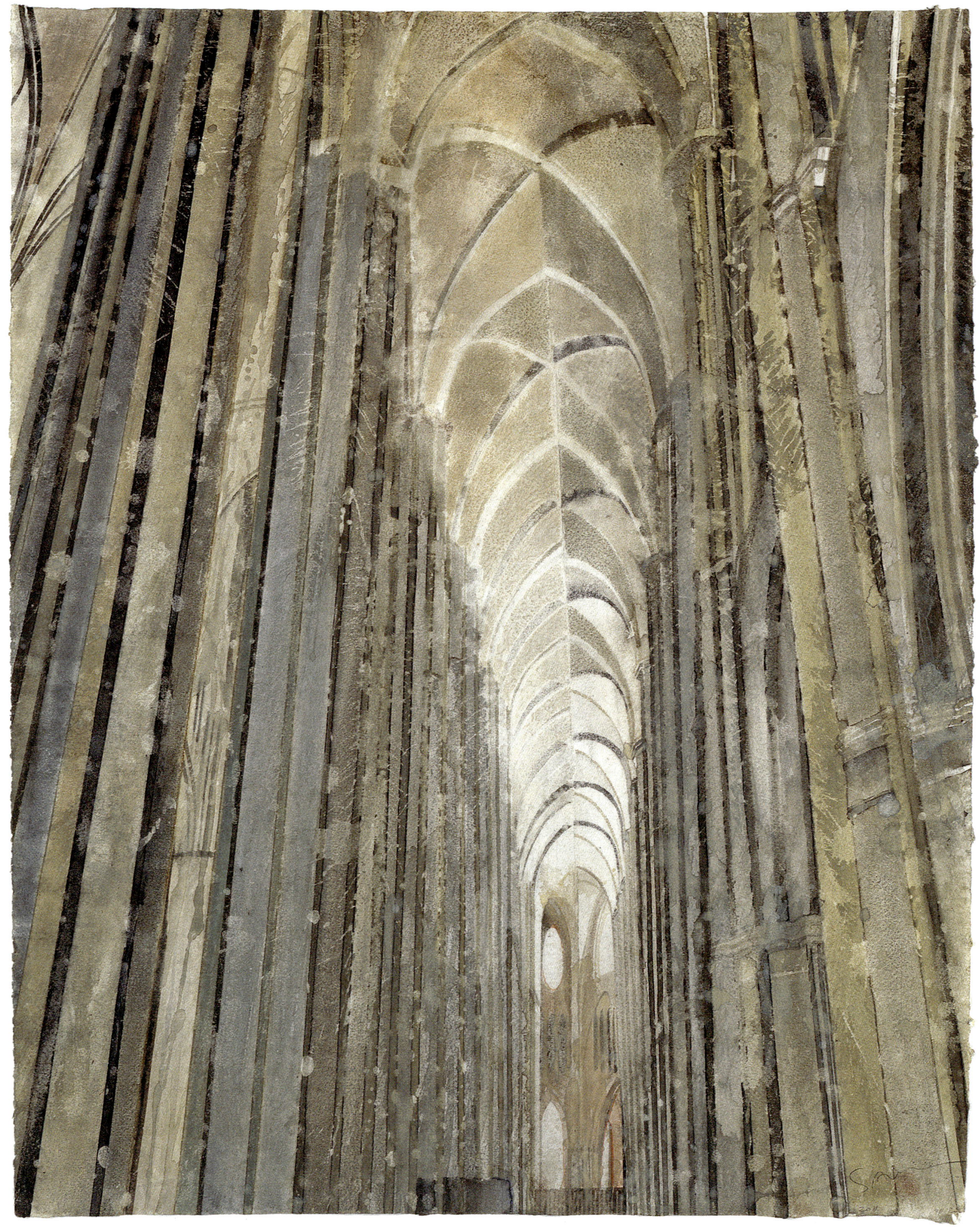

Bourges Cathedral I | Kathedrale von Bourges I | Cathédrale de Bourges I   2010, 61 × 48 cm

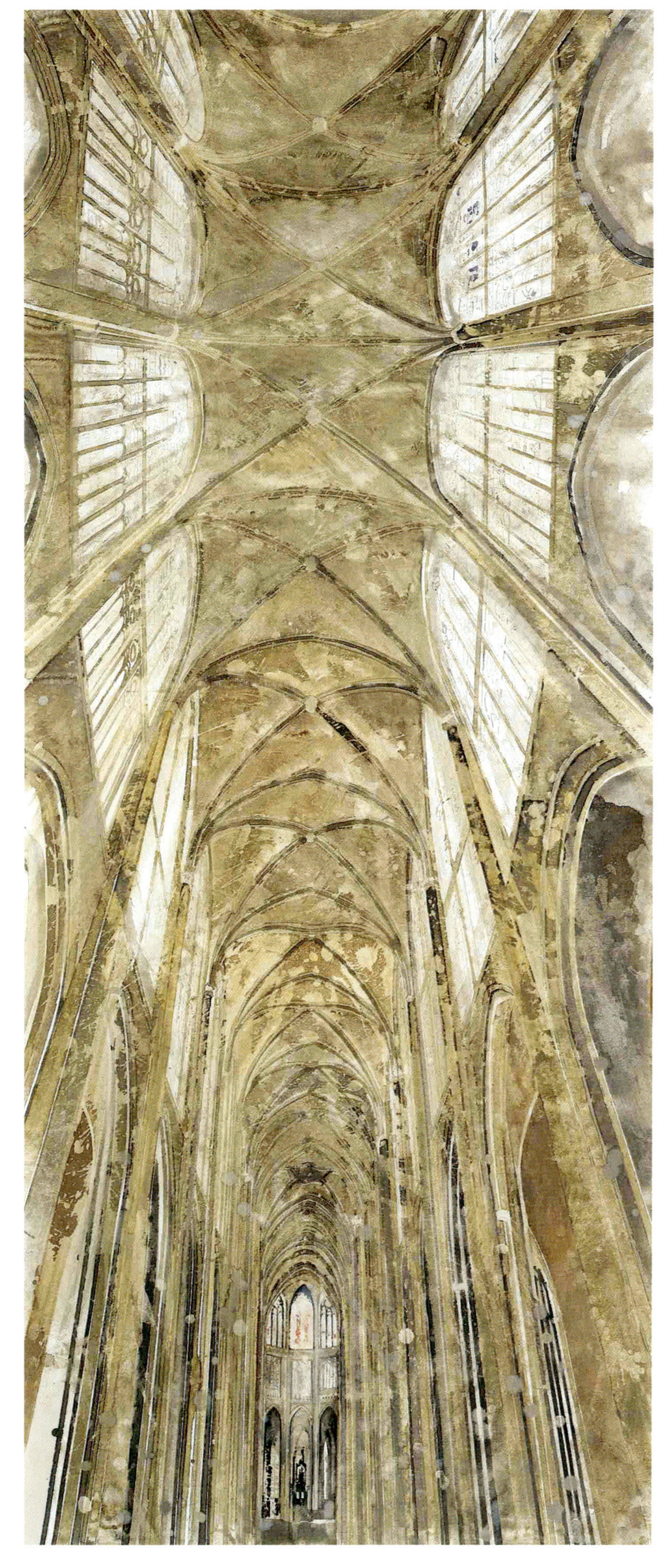

Bourges Cathedral II | Kathedrale von Bourges II | Cathédrale de Bourges II   2012, 151 × 61 cm

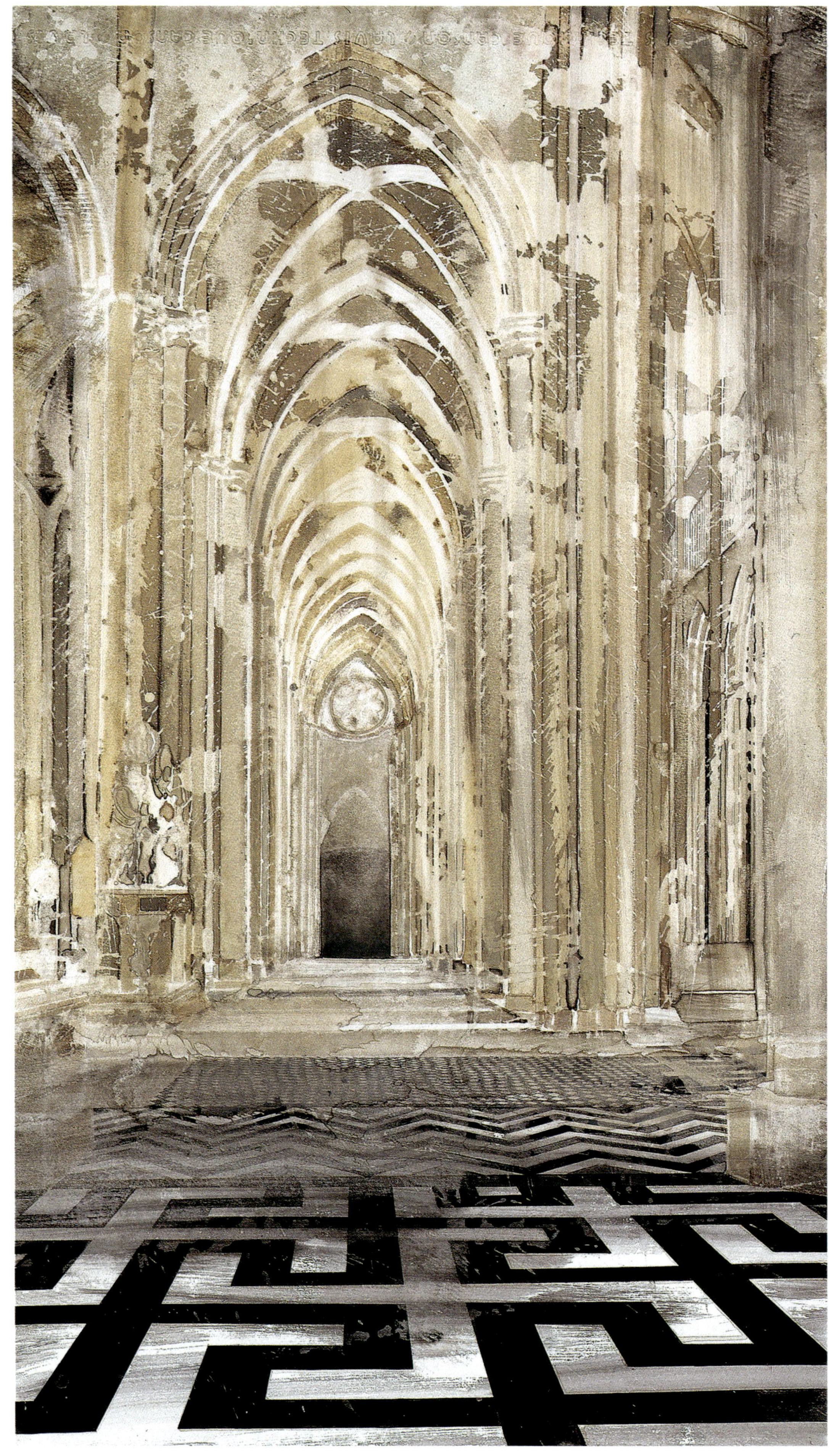

Amiens Cathedral | Kathedrale von Amiens | Cathédrale d'Amiens   2012, 75,8 × 42,9 cm

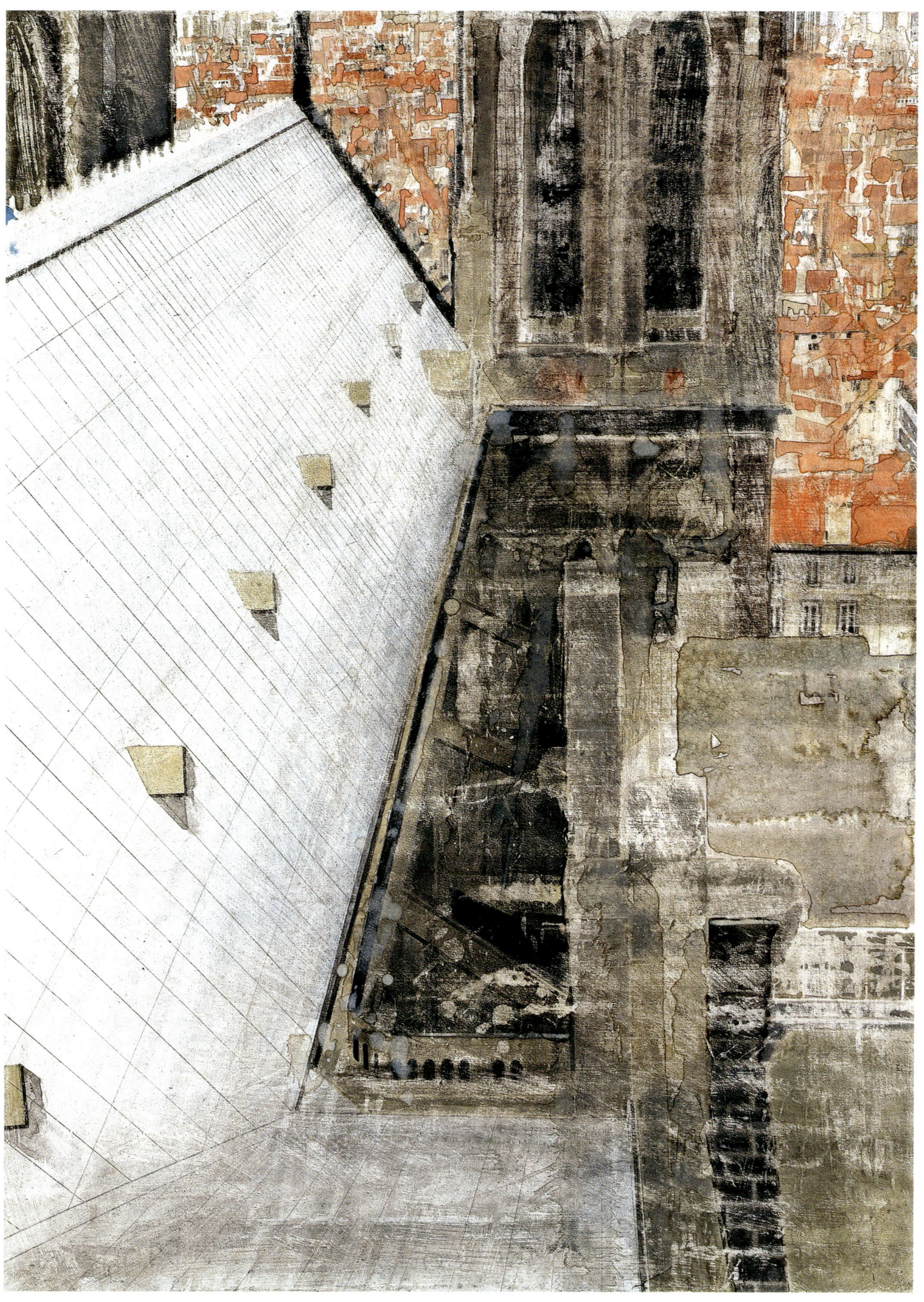

Clermont-Ferrand Cathedral | Kathedrale von Clermont-Ferrand | Cathédrale de Clermont-Ferrand   2010, 70,5 × 50 cm

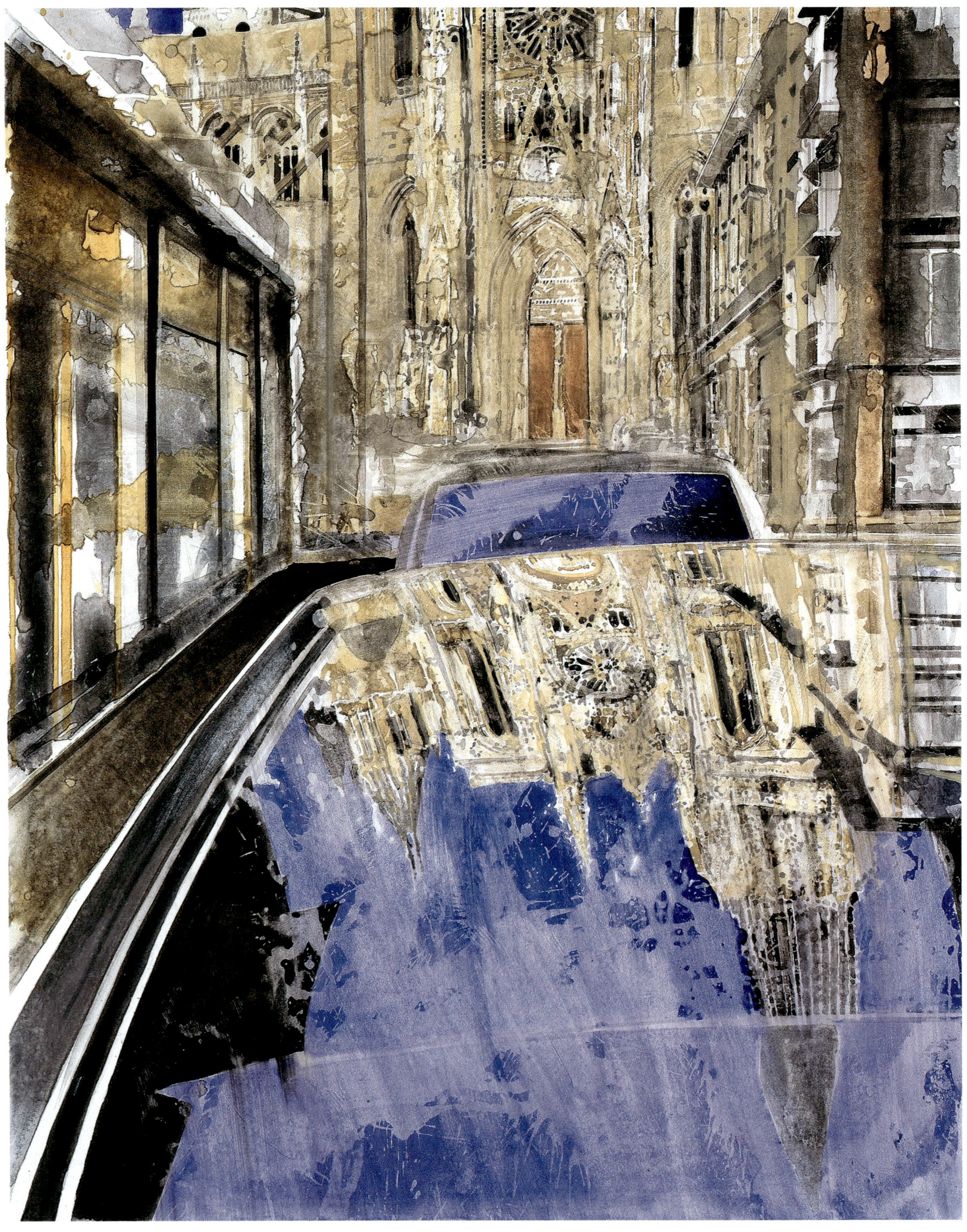

Rouen Cathedral, Reflection I | Kathedrale von Rouen, Spiegelung I | Cathédrale de Rouen, reflet I   2012, 64,8 × 50,9 cm

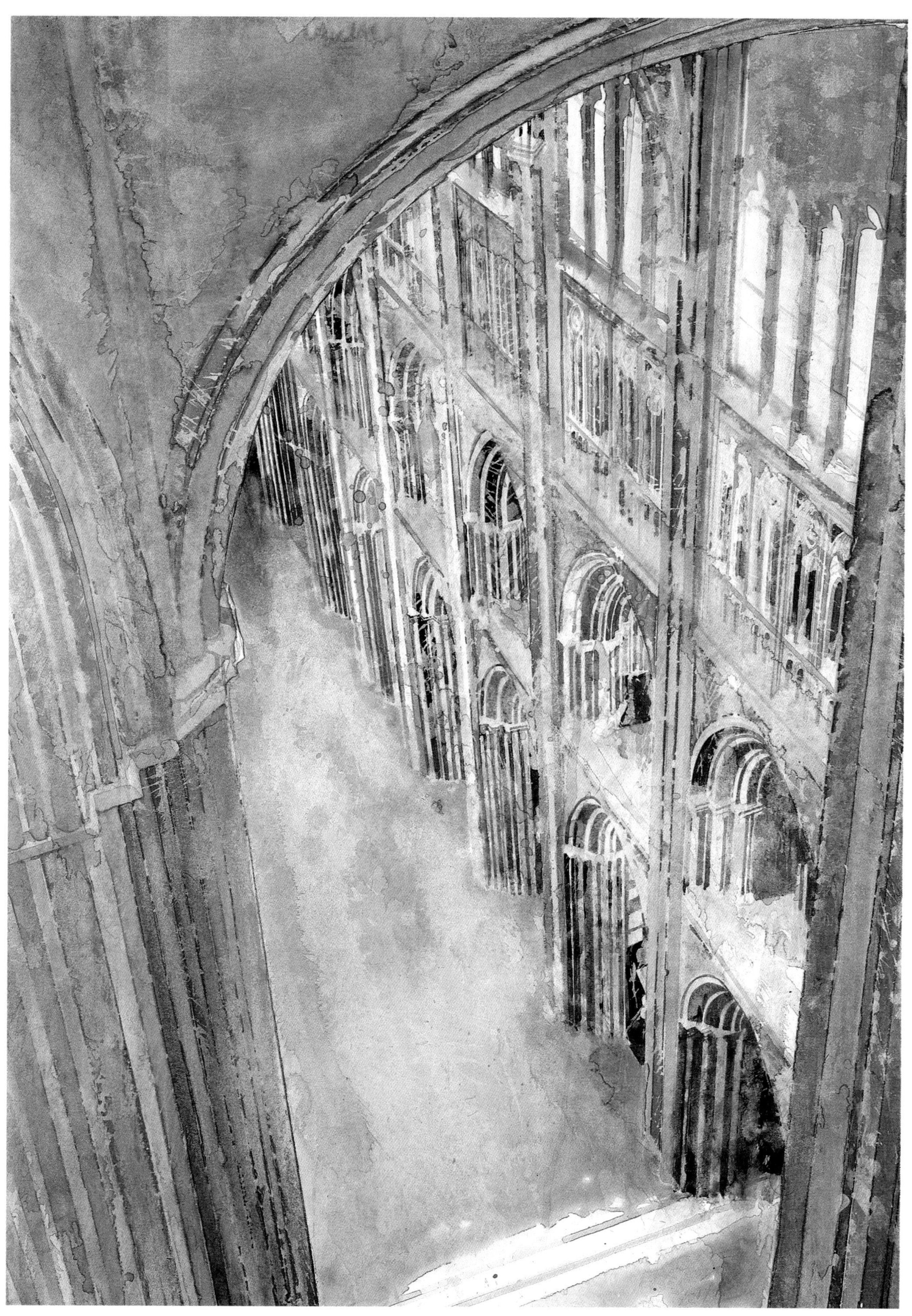

Rouen Cathedral II | Kathedrale von Rouen II | Cathédrale de Rouen II   2012, 70 × 49,6 cm

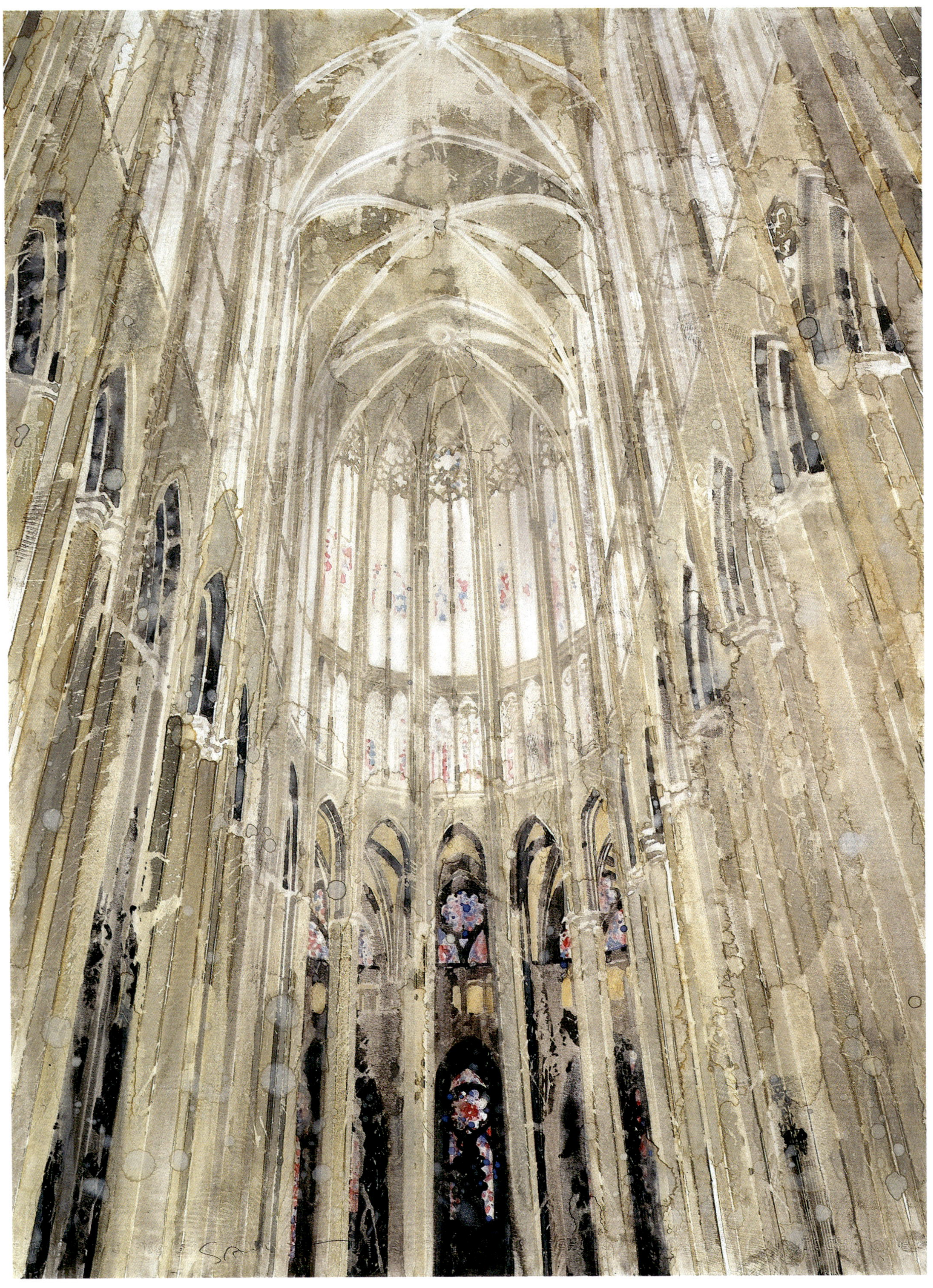

 Beauvais Cathedral II | Kathedrale von Beauvais II | Cathédrale de Beauvais II   2012, 75,8 × 55 cm

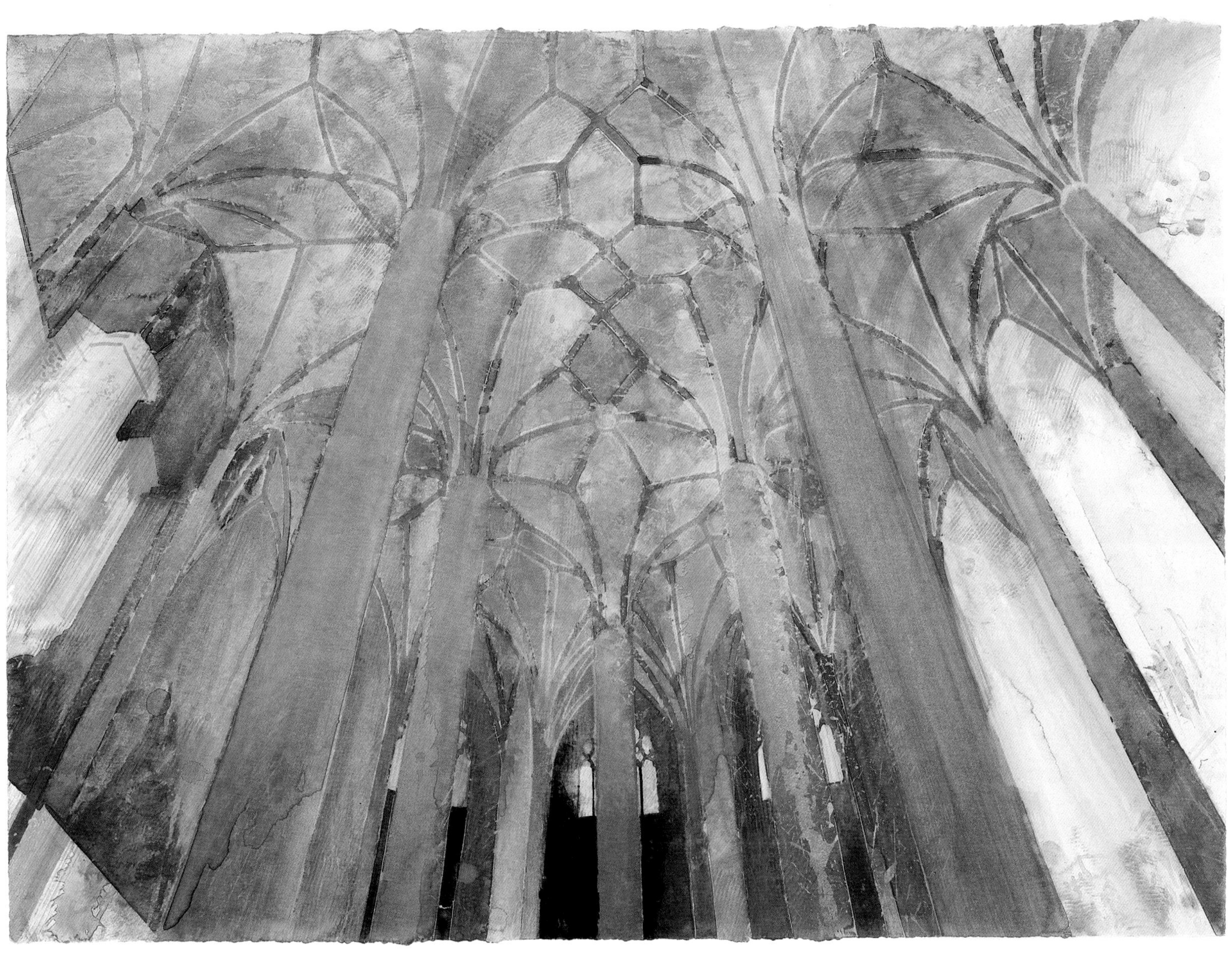

Salzburg, Church of Saint Francis | Salzburg, Franziskanerkirche | Salzbourg, église des Franciscains   2012, 50,5 × 80 cm

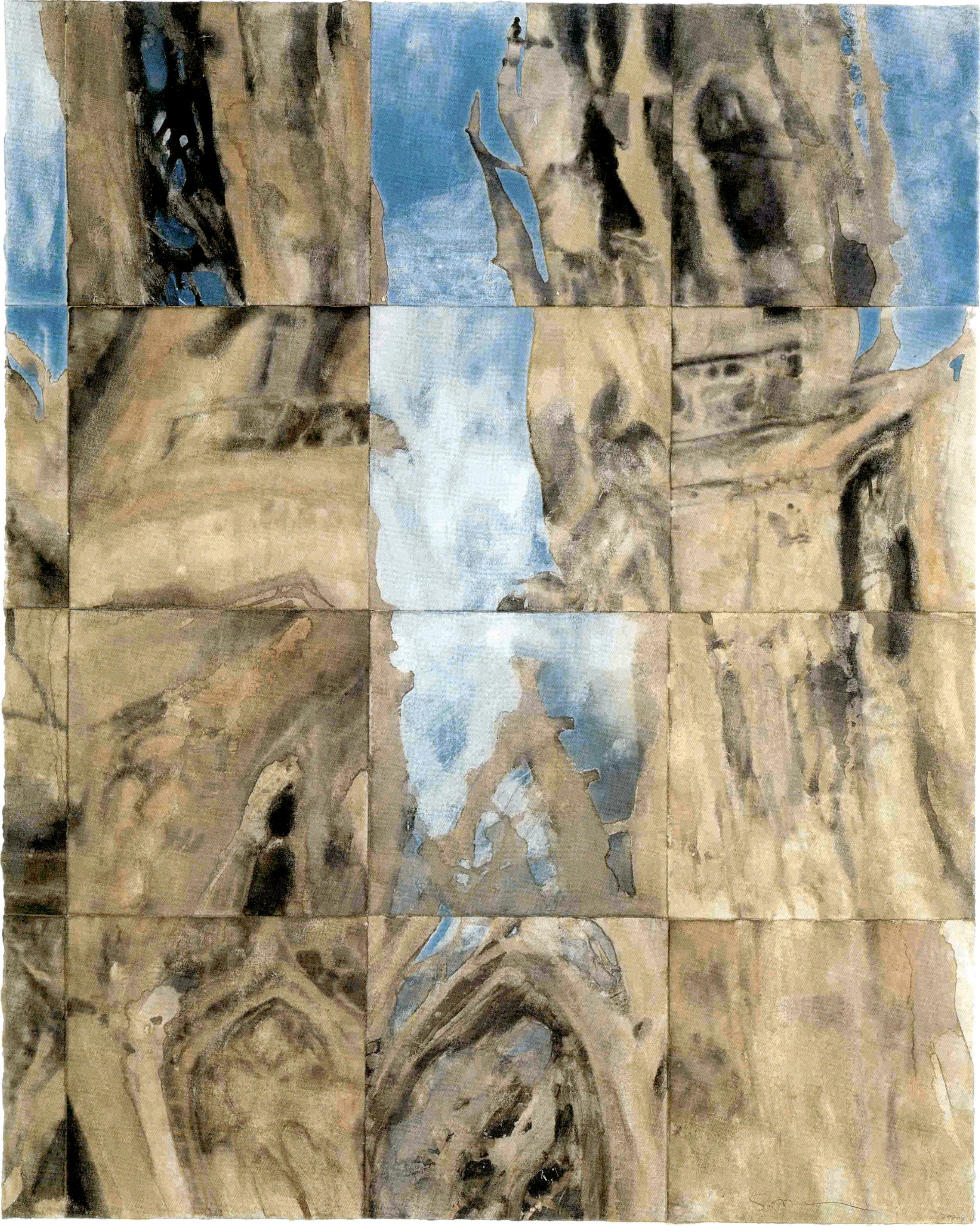

 Rouen Cathedral, Reflection II | Kathedrale von Rouen, Spiegelung II | Cathédrale de Rouen, reflet II   1997, 59,5 × 47,3 cm

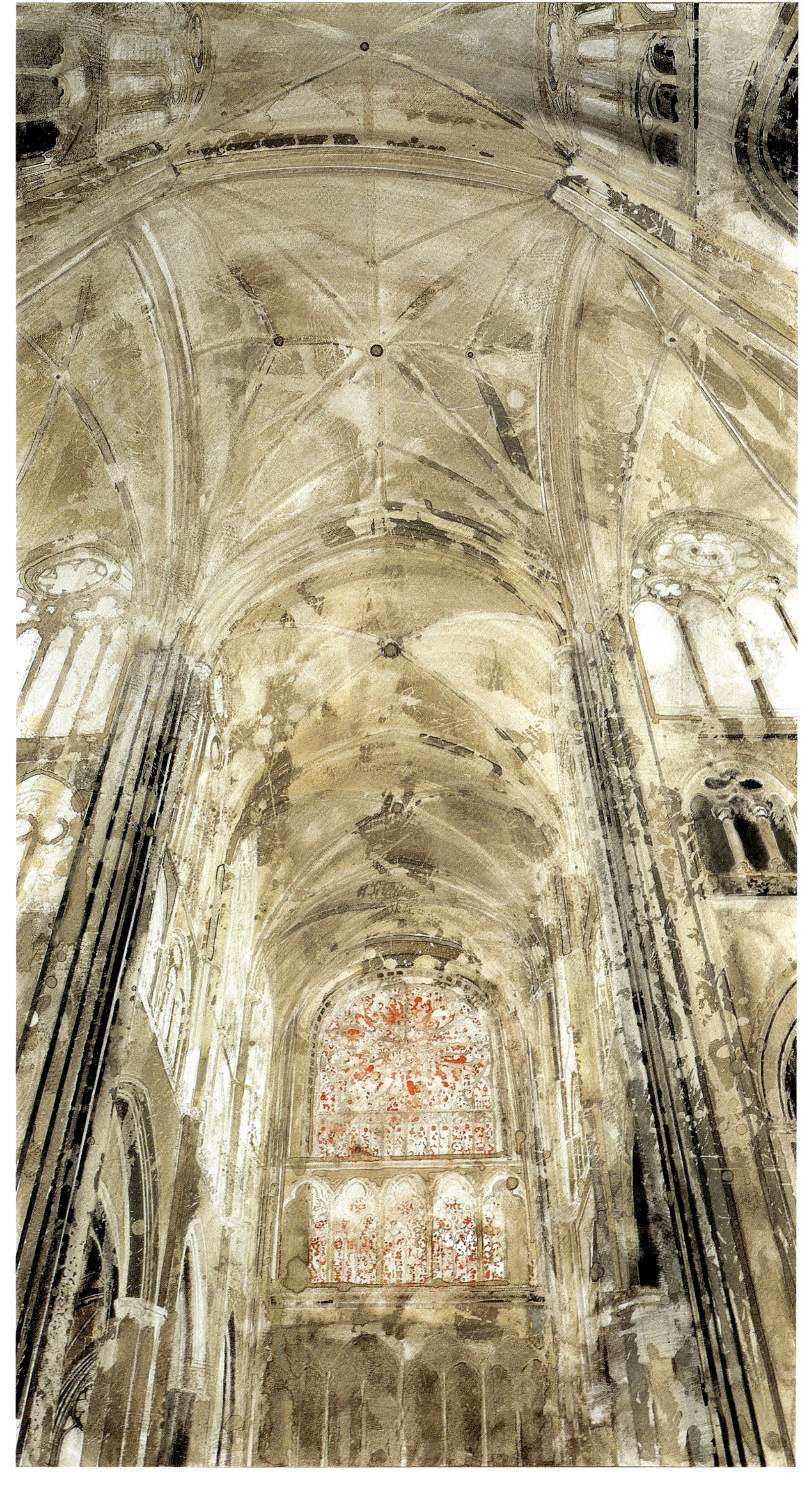

La Rosette   2012, 110 × 59,4 cm

Drawings
Zeichnungen
Dessins

Gottfried Salzmann's work in the medium of drawing reached its most intensive phase some years ago and is regarded by many as one of the highlights of his oeuvre. In contrast to the watercolors, in which Salzmann deals generously with creative stimuli, he relies on reduction in his drawings. In some cases, formal structures are confined to just a few delicate strokes along the outer edge of the picture, while the center is often left entirely empty.

Because it allows for different degrees of pressure or density, charcoal generates a strong atmospheric charge in the transition from representational to abstract form. Even the aspect of gesture, the expressive quality of the artist's style, plays a role in this medium—an exception in Salzmann's oeuvre.

Darkly smoldering, diffuse complexes that often stand for accumulations of plant material, such as masses of leaves, are confronted with sparingly applied individual lines. Having turned his attention to urban themes, he seldom works in the medium of the drawing today. Yet like the often momentary shifts of light and shadow, Salzmann is also capable of capturing on paper the boldly moving forms reflected on a glass surface. He is a specialist in rendering visual phenomena that, although present everywhere, defy fixation.

Die zeichnerische Tätigkeit von Gottfried Salzmann erreichte zu einem schon länger zurückliegenden Zeitpunkt ihr intensivstes Stadium und gehört für viele zu den Höhepunkten seines Schaffens. Anders als beim Aquarell, wo Salzmann mit gestalterischen Reizen nicht sparsam umgeht, setzt er hier auf Reduktion. Manchmal beschränkt sich die Formgebung auf wenige zarte Striche am äußersten Blattrand, während die Mitte oft völlig leer bleibt.

Der Kohlestift mit seinen unterschiedlichen „Anschlagsmöglichkeiten" bzw. Dichtegraden bewirkt eine starke atmosphärische Aufladung im Übergang von gegenständlicher zu abstrakter Formgebung. Sogar das gestische Moment, die Expressivität des Duktus, kommt in diesem Medium ausnahmsweise zum Tragen.

Dunkel schwelende, diffuse Komplexe, die oft für vegetabile Ballungen wie Laubmassen stehen, werden mit betont spärlich gesetzten Einzellinien konfrontiert. Seit sich Salzmann dem urbanen Themenkomplex zugewandt hat, greift er eher selten zum Zeichenstift. So wie den oft augenblicklichen Wechsel von Licht und Schatten unter einem Laubdach versteht Salzmann aber auch die abenteuerlich bewegten Formen, die sich auf einer Glasfläche spiegeln, auf ein Blatt zu bannen. Er ist ein Spezialist für visuelle Phänomene, die allgegenwärtig sind, aber sich der Fixierung entziehen.

Il y a longtemps, déjà, le dessin avait très intensément occupé Gottfried Salzmann et atteint ce que beaucoup considèrent comme un des sommets de son œuvre. À la différence de l'aquarelle, où Salzmann ne ménage pas les moyens artistiques, c'est la réduction qu'il cherche ici. Parfois, la forme se limite à quelques traits tout en finesse, sur le bord extérieur de la feuille, tandis que le centre reste vide.

Le fusain, quant à lui, avec ses diverses « attaques » possibles et sa densité variable, permet de charger davantage l'atmosphère dans le passage du figuratif à l'abstraction. Ce procédé permet aussi par moments de valoriser le gestuel et l'expressivité du trait. Des ensembles diffus, comme dans un sombre crépitement et illustrant souvent des masses feuillues et végétales, se retrouvent face à des lignes isolées, d'une parcimonie affichée. Depuis que Salzmann s'intéresse aux thèmes urbains, il ne recourt plus que rarement au crayon. Mais Salzmann sait aussi bien capter l'alternance rapide de la lumière et de l'ombre sous une canopée qu'il parvient à figer sur la feuille les formes vacillantes que renvoie une surface réfléchissante. Il est le spécialiste des phénomènes visuels omniprésents qui échappent pourtant à tout fixage.

 Patches of Light II (detail) | *Lichtflecken II (Detail)* | *Taches de lumière II (détail)*   1981, 65,3 × 100 cm

  Curtain of Trees I | Baumvorhang I | Rideau d'arbres I   1978, 26,2 × 65,3 cm

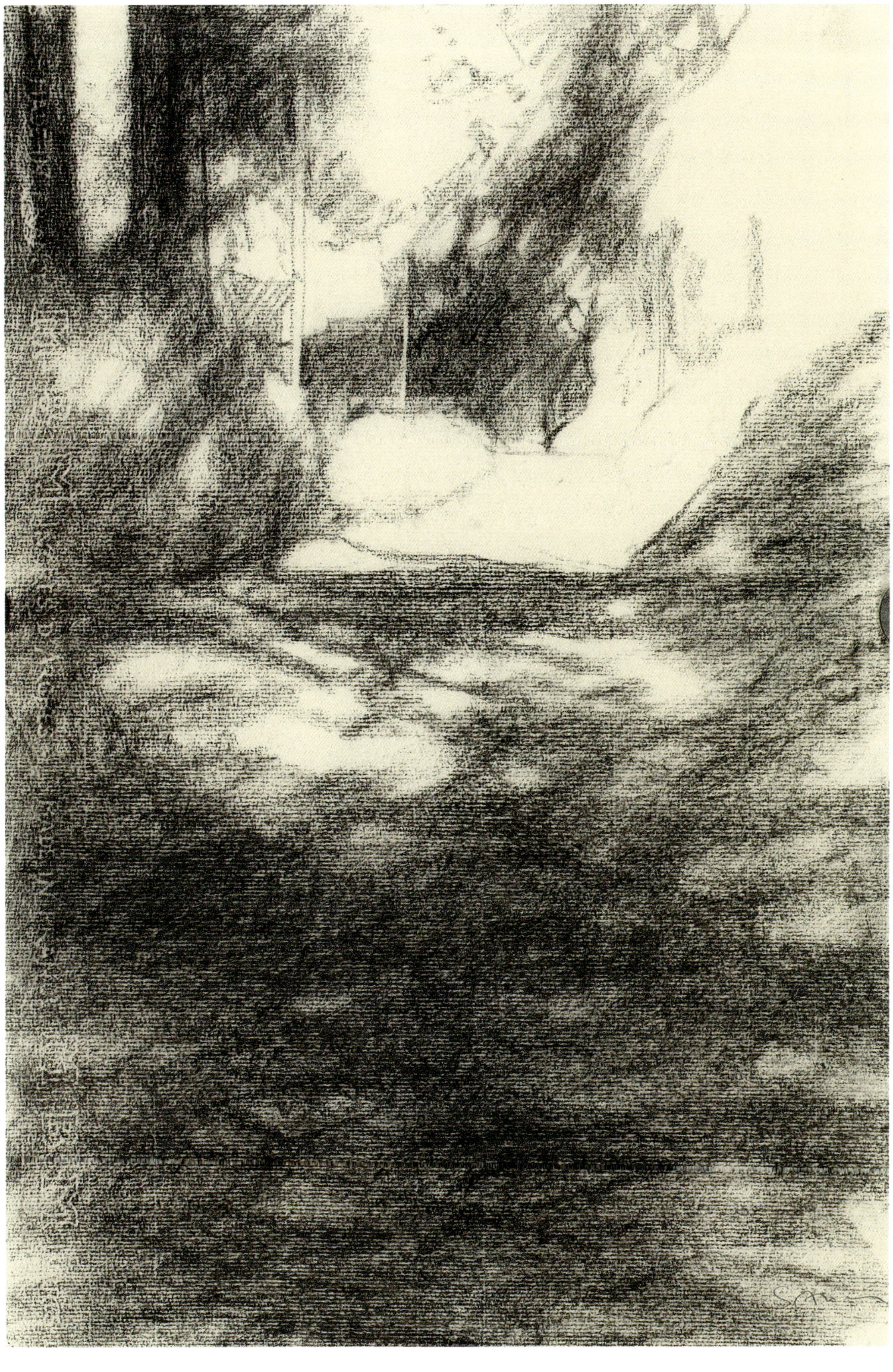

Patches of Light I | Lichtflecken I | Taches de lumière I   1991, 49,9 × 32,6 cm

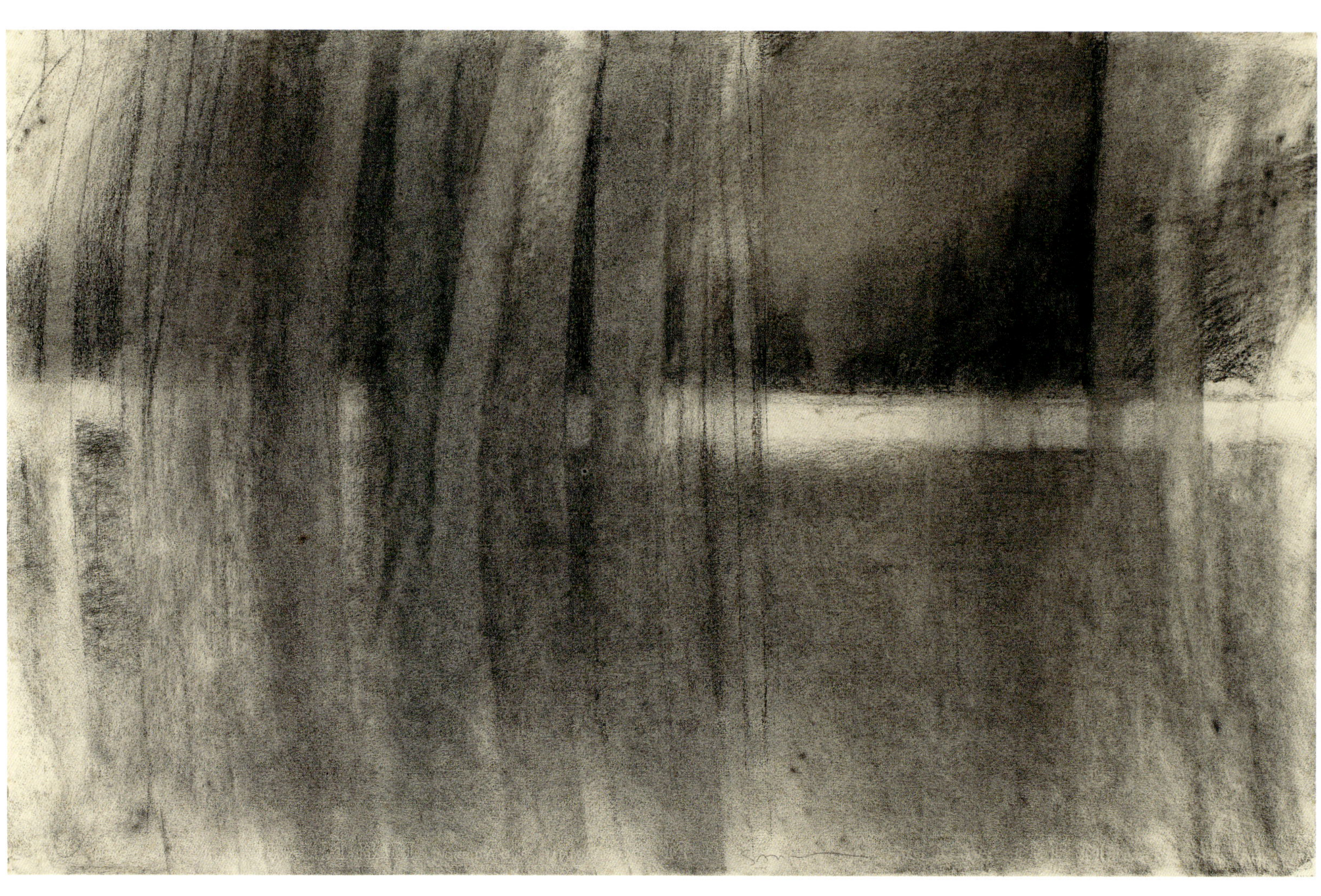

188   Patches of Light II | Lichtflecken II | Taches de lumière II   1981, 65,3 × 100 cm

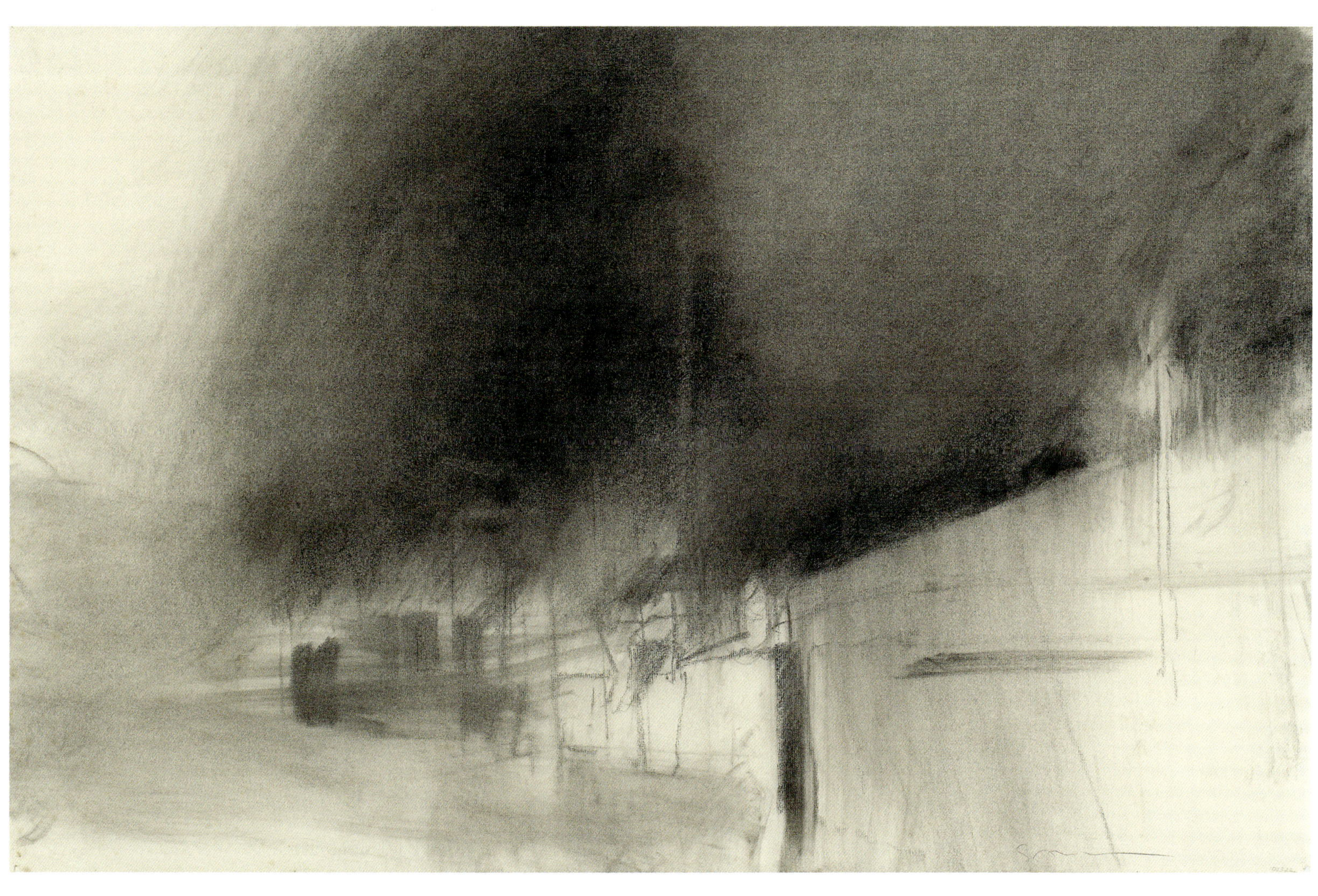

Bordered Trees | Begrenzte Bäume | Rangées d'arbres   1980, 65 × 99 cm

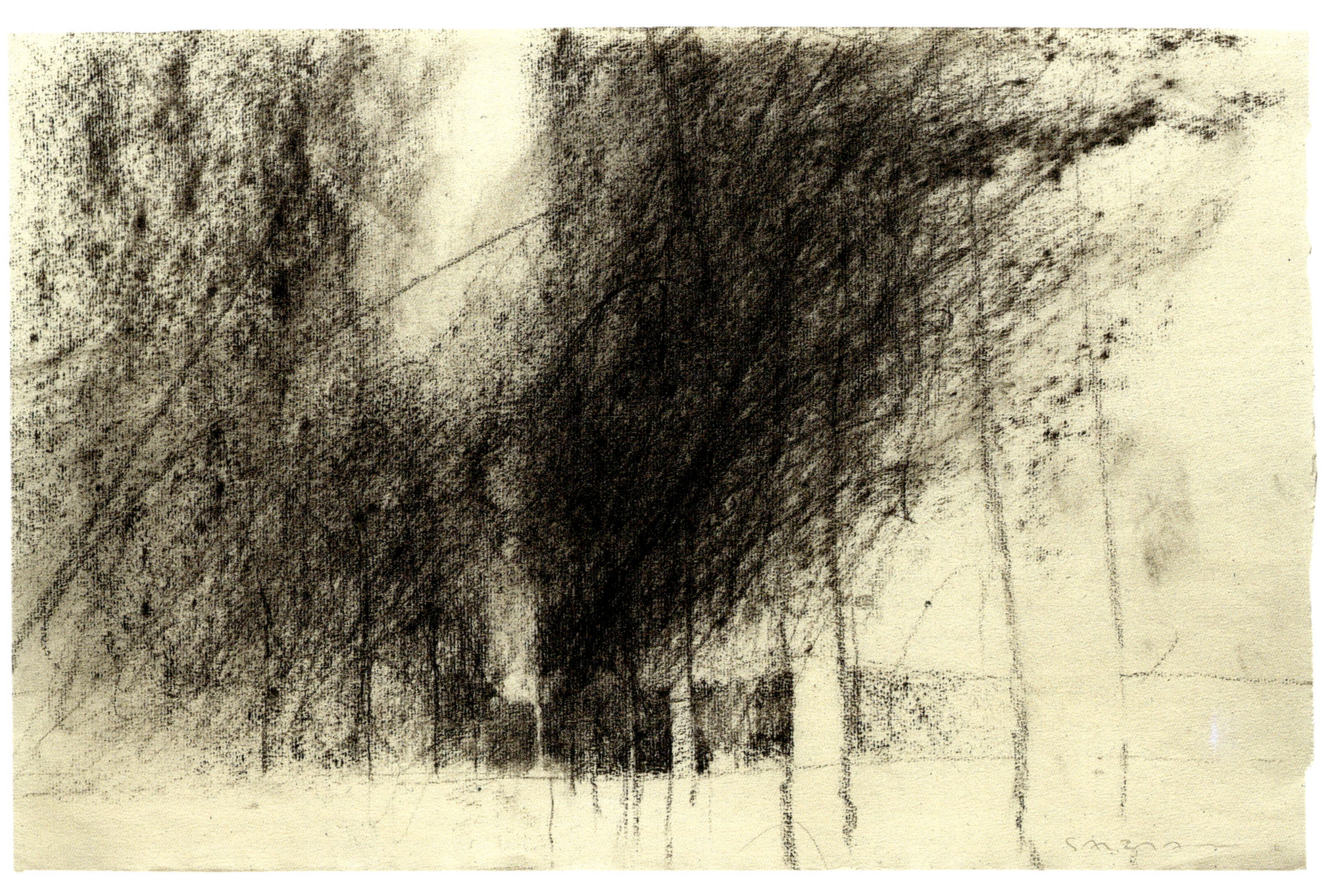

    Allee | Allee | Allée   1981, 33 × 50 cm

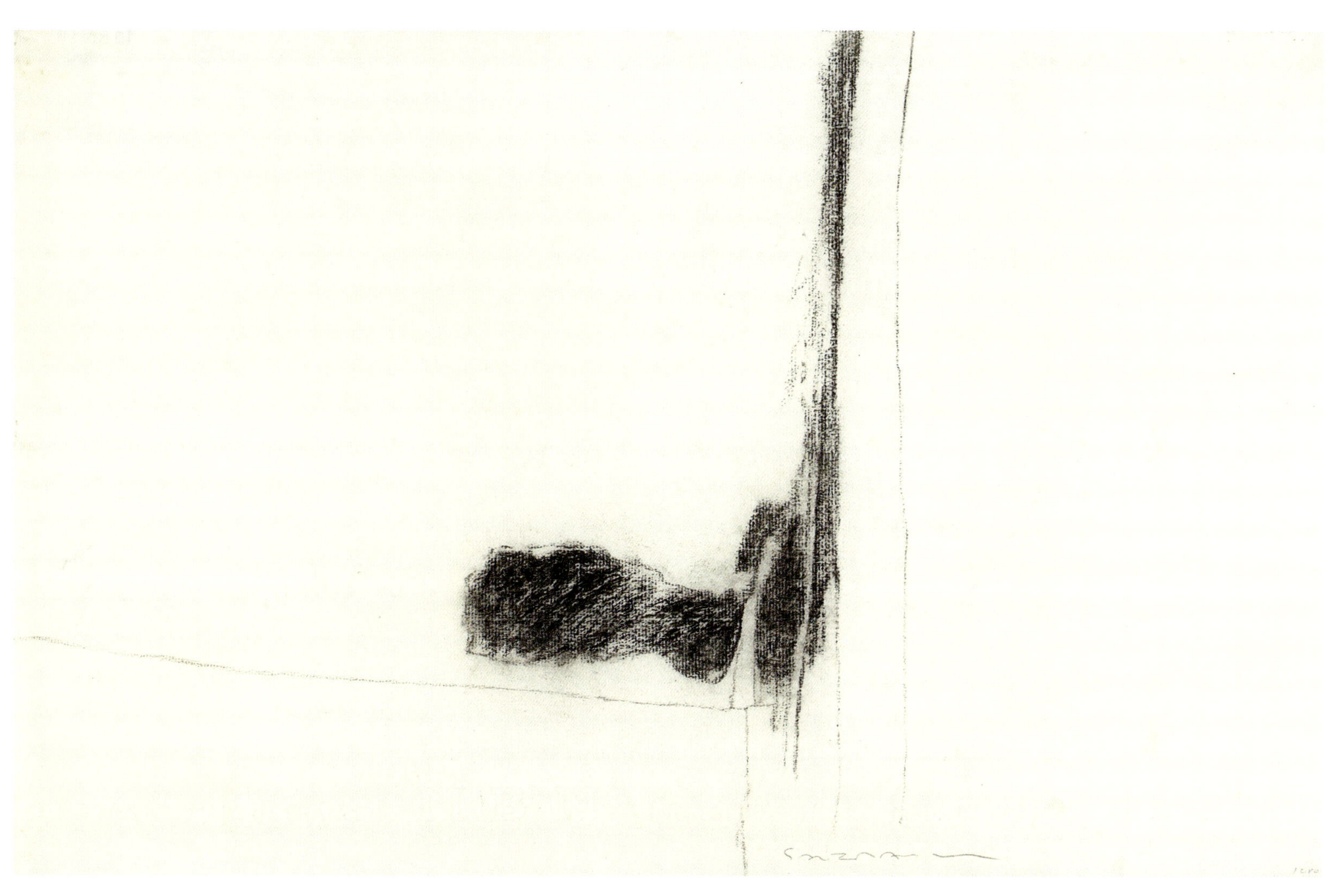

Prints, Photeaufortes
Druckgrafiken, Photeaufortes
Gravures, photeaufortes

When it comes to the use of different techniques in art, it is usually the autonomous and unique character of the corresponding works that is emphasized—in keeping with a dominant position in modernist theory. Gottfried Salzmann is an artist who focuses less on differences and more on similarities and affinities. The fact that some of the effects achievable in watercolor can also be transferred to etching with no loss whatsoever—and in fact may even be intensified—made this graphic technique especially appealing in his eyes.

Salzmann transposed the wipings and hastily executed hatchings of charcoal drawings quite adequately into lithographs, while etching proved more suitable for grainier structures.

As in the art of the watercolor, the pleasure derived from manual procedures and the use of different materials is of essential importance. A more recent original creation is the "photeauforte" technique, in which photography and etching are combined. It produces strikingly concentrated atmospheric effects, while the acid-based etching technique tends to undermine the smooth gloss of the photograph.

Wenn es um die Anwendung verschiedener Techniken geht, wird meist das Eigenständige und Unverwechselbare daran betont – so will es eine dominierende theoretische Position der Moderne. Gottfried Salzmann ist ein Künstler, der weniger auf die Unterschiede als vielmehr auf die Ähnlichkeiten und das Verbindende setzt. Dass sich manche Wirkungen des Aquarells ohne Verluste in die Radierung übersetzen oder vielleicht sogar noch steigern lassen, hat ihn besonders für diese druckgrafische Technik eingenommen.

Die Wischer und zügigen Schraffuren der Kohlezeichnungen setzte Salzmann adäquat in Lithografien um, für körnigere Strukturen eignete sich wiederum die Radierung.

So wie beim Aquarell sind die Lust an manuellen Prozeduren und der Einsatz verschiedener Materialien dabei von essenzieller Bedeutung. Eine jüngere Eigenkreation ist die „Photeauforte"-Technik, die Fotografie und Radierung kombiniert. Sie erzeugt Wirkungen von besonderer atmosphärischer Dichte, wobei die auf Ätzung beruhende Radierung die Glätte des Fotos gewissermaßen unterminiert.

Lorsque l'art recourt à différentes techniques, il est de bon ton d'en souligner l'aspect singulier, unique – ainsi le veulent les positions théoriques dominantes de la modernité. Gottfried Salzmann mise moins sur les différences que sur les ressemblances et les éléments unificateurs. Le fait que certains effets de l'aquarelle puissent être adaptés à l'eau-forte, sans rien y perdre et même au contraire pour s'en trouver rehaussés, l'a particulièrement incité à se tourner vers la technique de la gravure. Salzmann a parfaitement transposé en lithographies les balayages et rapides rainurages des dessins au fusain ; pour les structures plus granuleuses, c'est l'eau-forte qu'il préconise.

Tout comme en aquarelle, le plaisir du procédé manuel et l'utilisation de matériaux divers revêtent une signification essentielle. Récemment, il a ainsi créé la technique de la « photeauforte » qui lui permet d'atteindre à un rendu particulièrement dense de l'atmosphère tout en laissant la morsure du métal éroder en quelque sorte le côté lisse de la photographie.

Trees (detail) | Bäume (Detail) | Arbres (détail)   1987, 80 × 119,5 cm

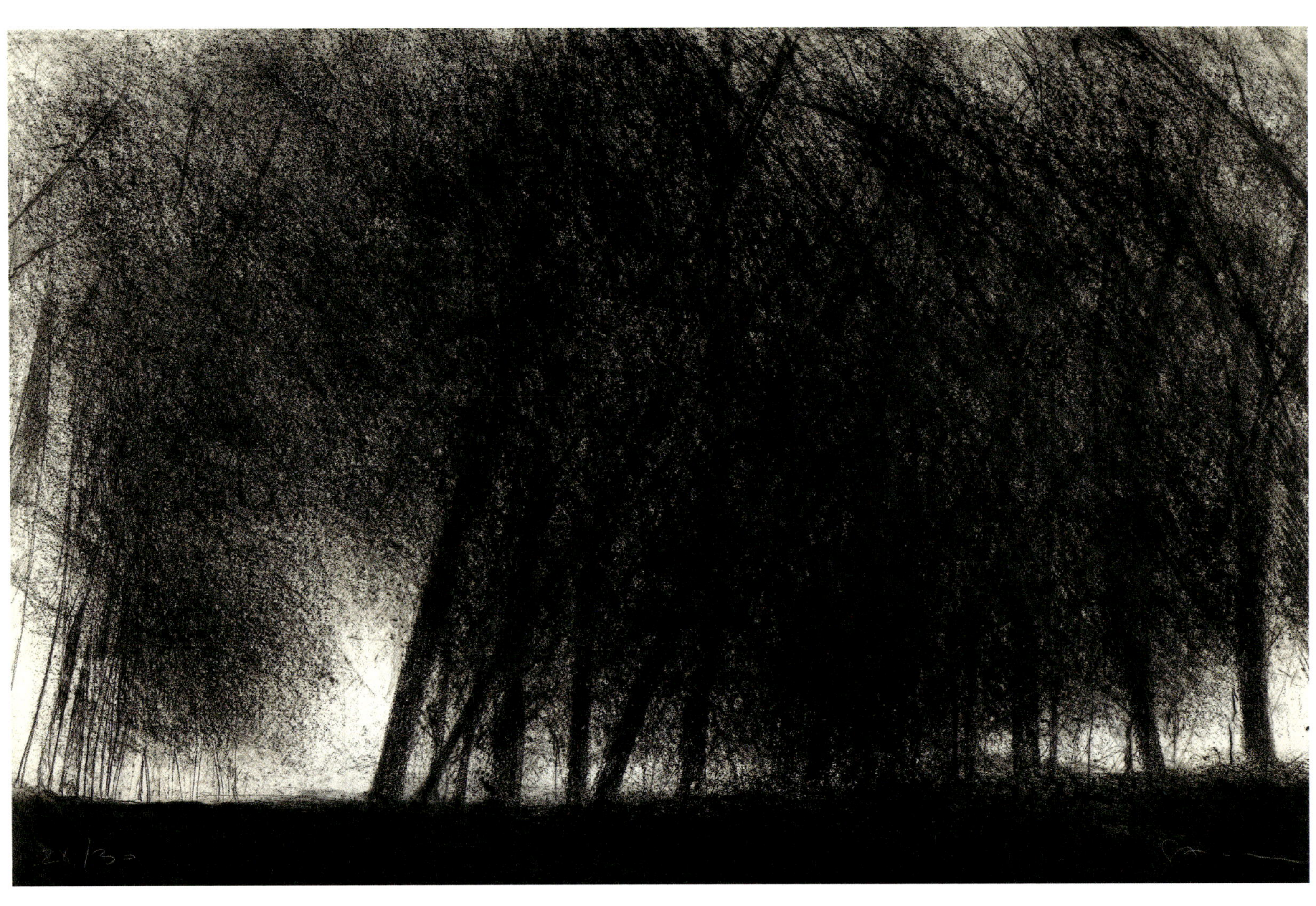

194   Trees | Bäume | Arbres   1987, 80 × 119,5 cm

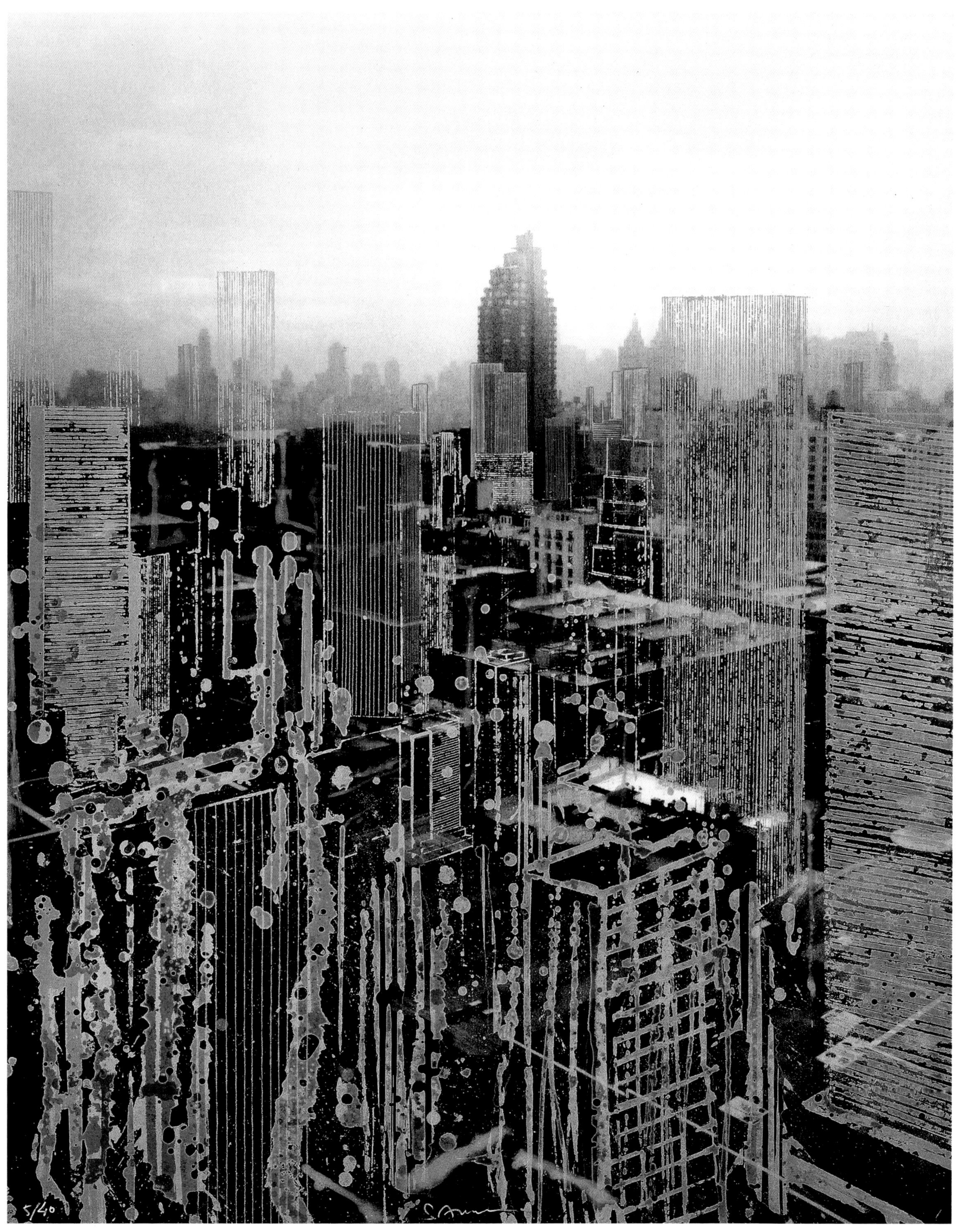

Silver Buildings   2011, 65 × 50 cm

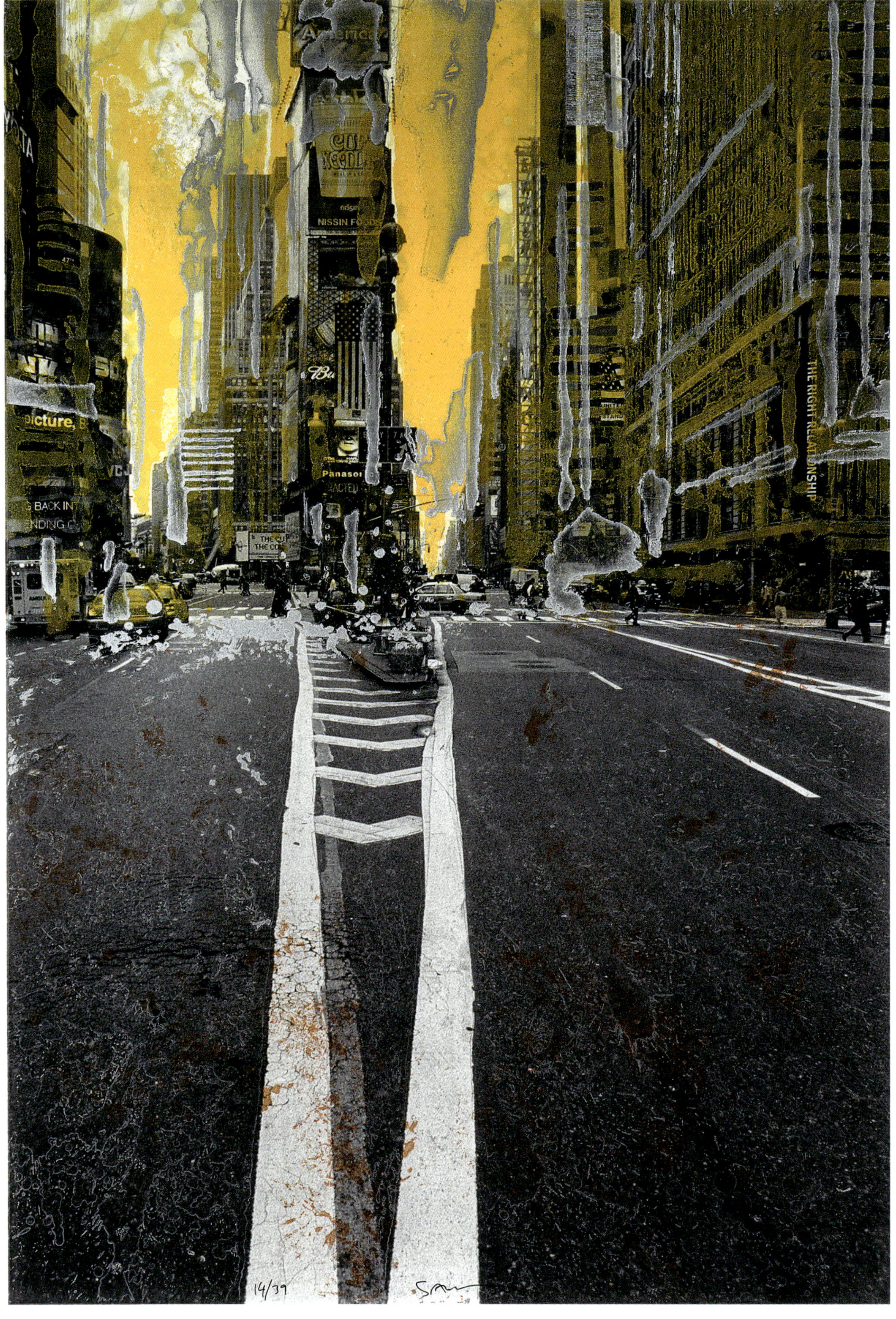

Yellow Times Square | Gelber Times Square | Times Square jaune   2005, 73,5 × 49,3 cm

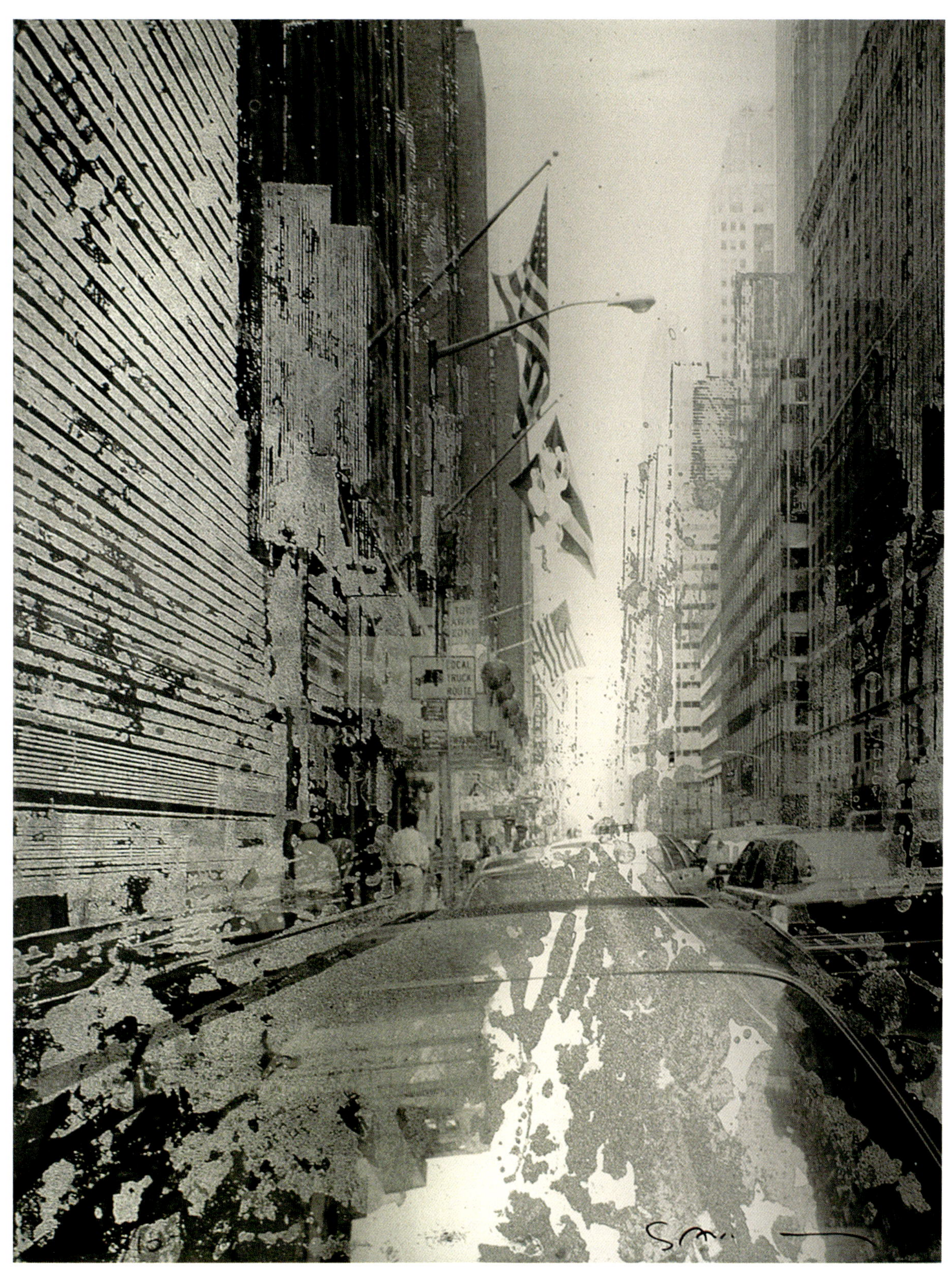

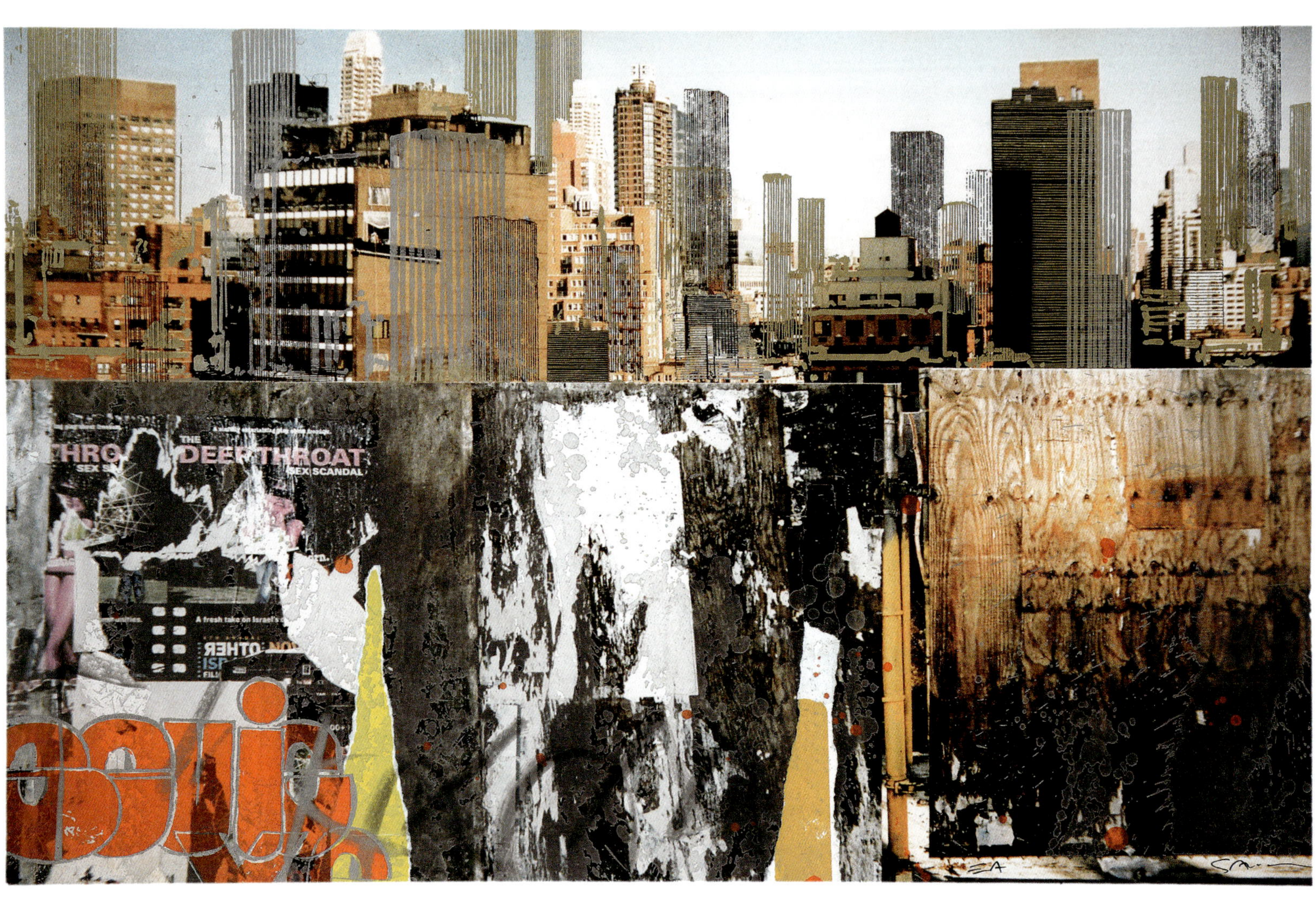

   Deep Throat   2012, 50 × 75 cm

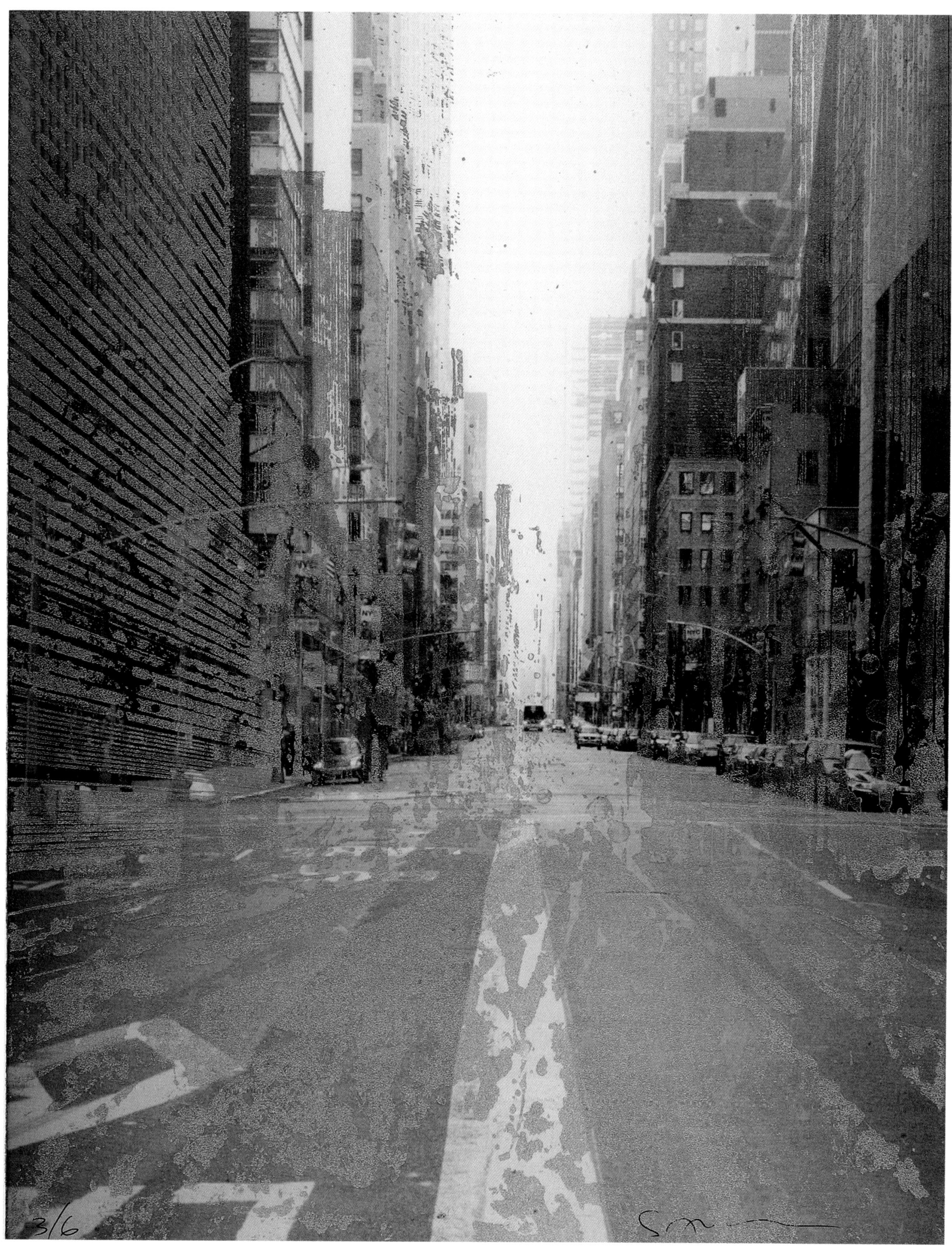

New York: Bus and Fire Lane   2004, 51 × 35 cm

Photographs
Fotografien
Photographies

Gottfried Salzmann's practice of incorporating photography into his art has nothing to do with the recent rise of the medium to fashionability, nor is connected in any way to the current media discourse. His intentions may be compared instead to those of photographers around the turn of the nineteenth to the twentieth century. In the 1970s, he exhibited autonomous photographic works concerned with the theme of the nude. In later years, he took his camera along on his exploratory strolls through the urban landscape. Having combined black-and-white photographs with other techniques in a variety of different ways, he arrived at a point at which the (color) photo assumed a life of its own. As in all of his work, he is concerned here with subtle shifts of context and puzzling perceptual twists, with aesthetic distance, with transparency and the most delicate materiality. Salzmann traces the movements of light on reflective surfaces until all matter is transformed into pure retinal oscillation.

Gottfried Salzmanns Integration der Fotografie in seine künstlerische Arbeit hat nichts mit der rezenten modischen Hochkonjunktur dieses Mediums zu tun und spielt sich auch fern vom aktuellen Mediendiskurs ab. Seine Intentionen sind eher vergleichbar mit denen künstlerischer Lichtbildner der Zeit um 1900. In den siebziger Jahren stellte er selbstständige Fotoarbeiten aus, die sich mit dem Akt beschäftigten, später zog er die Kamera bei seinen urbanen Streifzügen hinzu. Nachdem er das Schwarzweißfoto auf vielfältige Weise mit anderen Techniken kombiniert hat, ist Salzmann an einem Punkt angelangt, an dem sich das (Farb-)Foto wiederum verselbstständigt. Wie immer geht es dabei um subtile Verfremdungen und Verrätselungen der Wahrnehmung, um ästhetische Distanz, um Transparenz und feinste Stofflichkeit. Salzmann spürt den Bewegungen des Lichts auf reflektierenden Oberflächen nach, bis sich alle Materie in reine Netzhaut-Schwingungen verwandelt hat.

Lorsque Gottfried Salzmann intègre la photographie dans son travail artistique, il ne faut y voir aucun effet de mode. Tout ici se joue loin du discours actuel sur les médias. Le dessein de l'artiste serait davantage comparable à celui du photographe de portrait autour de 1900. Dans les années 1970, il a d'ailleurs exposé des œuvres photographiques à part entière sur le thème du nu ; plus tard, l'appareil photo l'a souvent accompagné lors de ses marches urbaines. Après avoir combiné la photographie en noir et blanc avec toutes sortes d'autres techniques, Salzmann est arrivé à un point où c'est désormais la photographie (couleur) qui l'emporte. Distanciations subtiles, ramifications de la perception, recul esthétique, transparence et finesse matérielle sont autant d'effets recherchés par l'artiste. Salzmann est à l'affût des mouvements de la lumière sur les surfaces réfléchissantes jusqu'à ce que toute matière se soit transformée en pures vibrations rétiniennes.

   Times Square VII (detail | Detail | détail) 2009

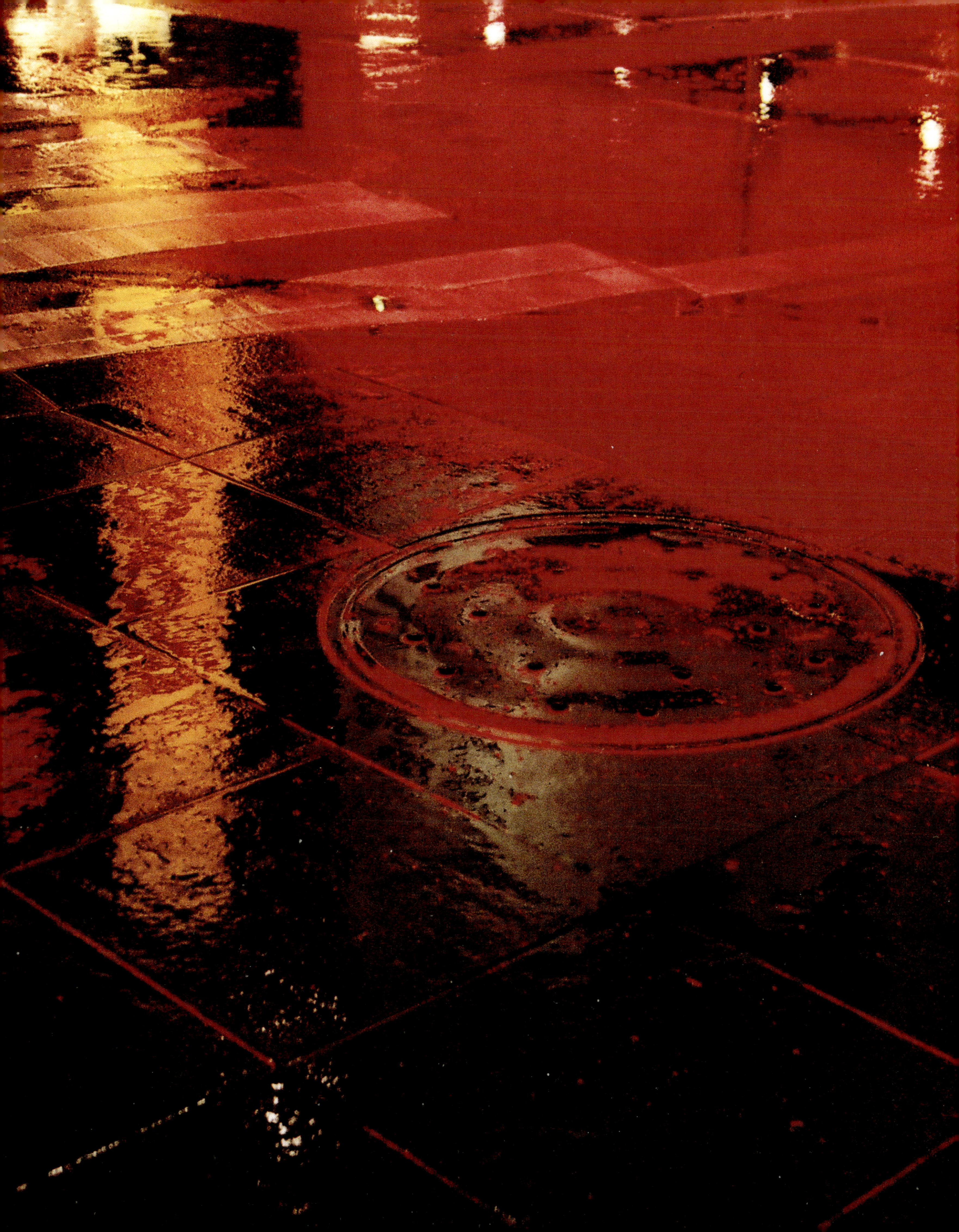

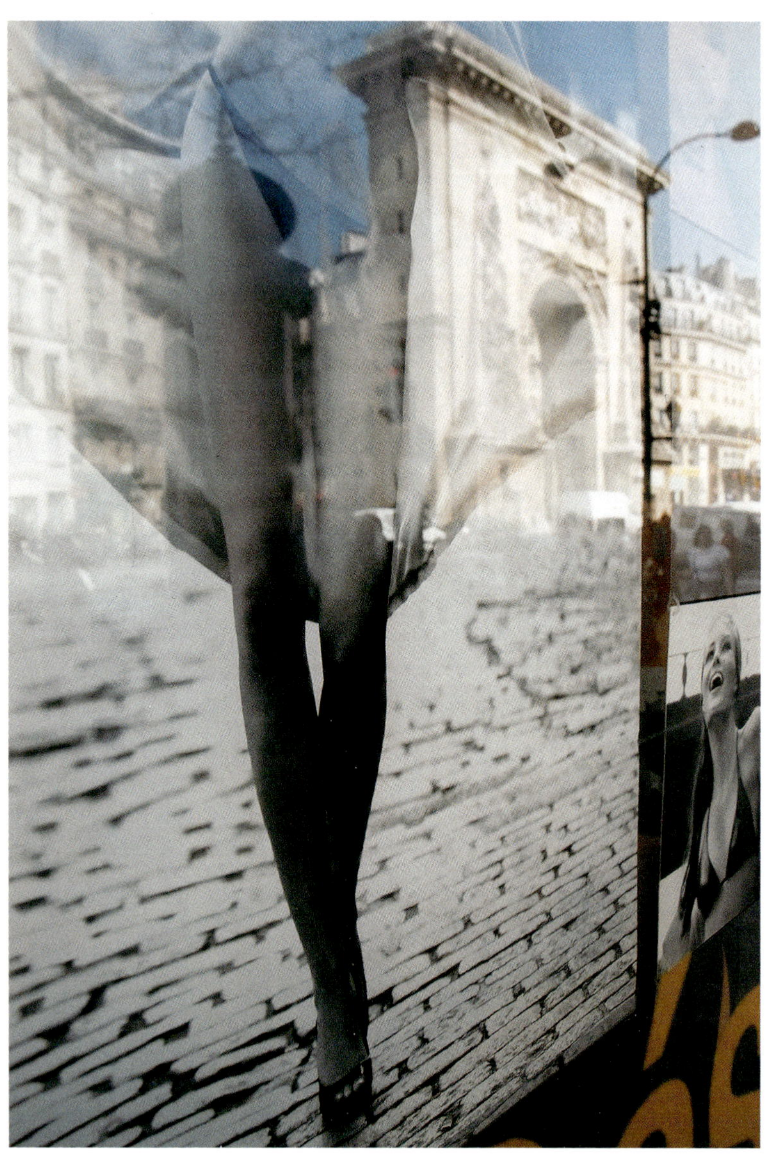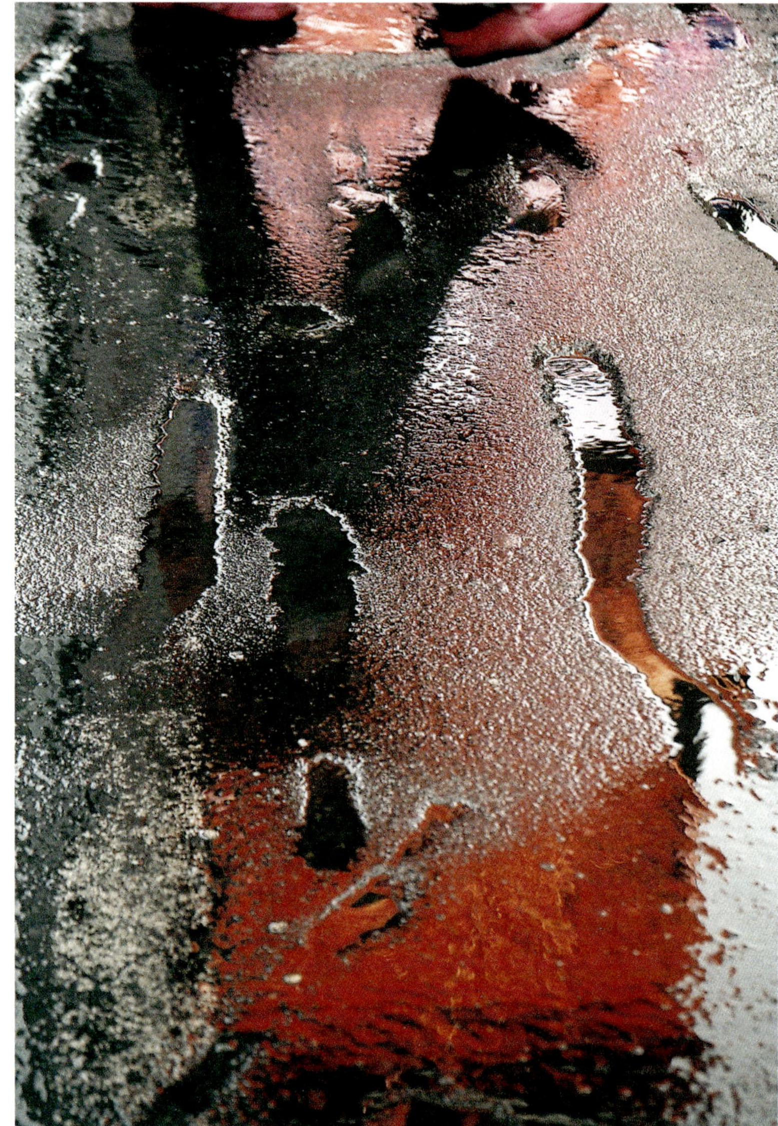

Rue Saint-Denis 2011
Times Square I 2009

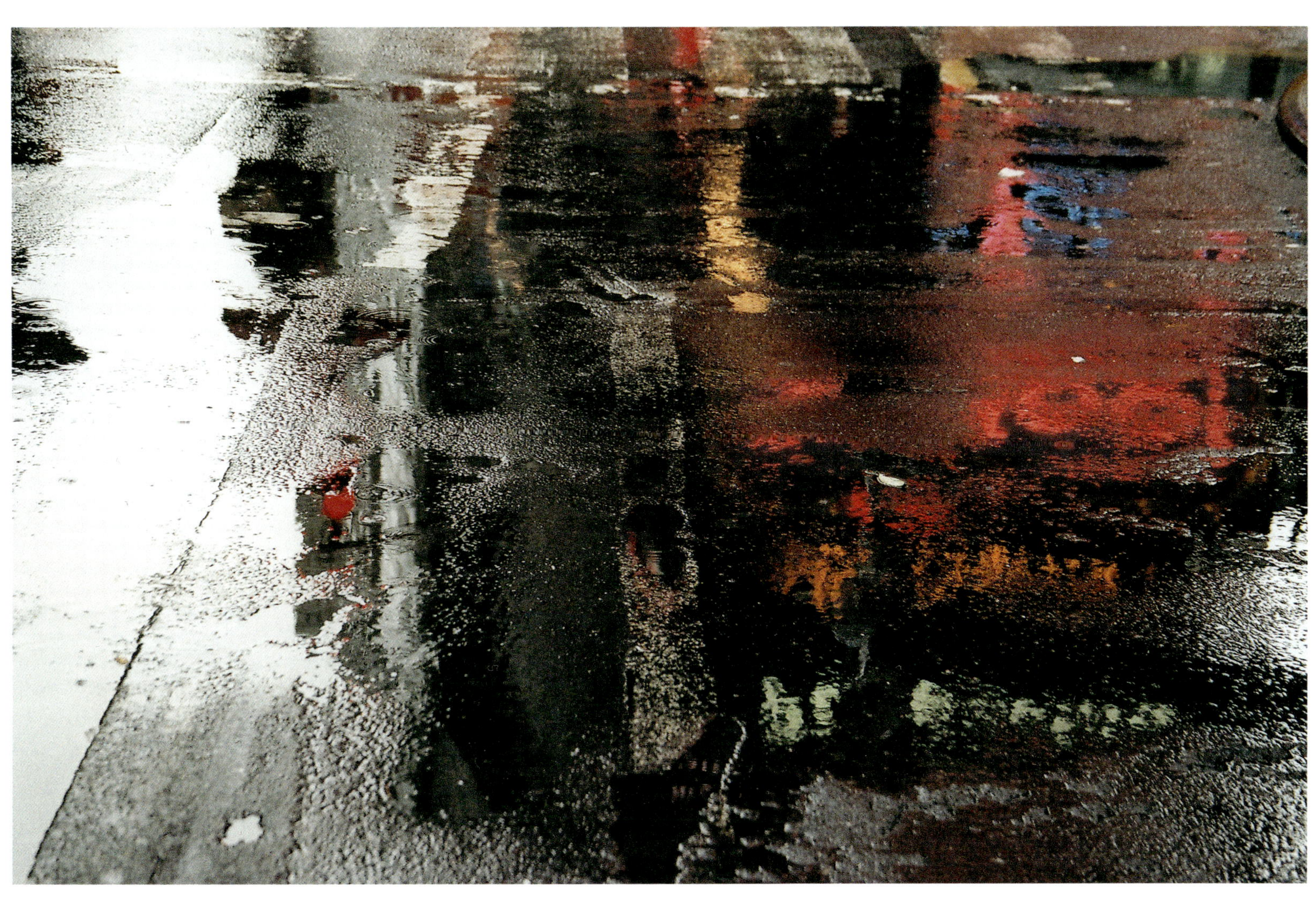

Times Square II   2009   203

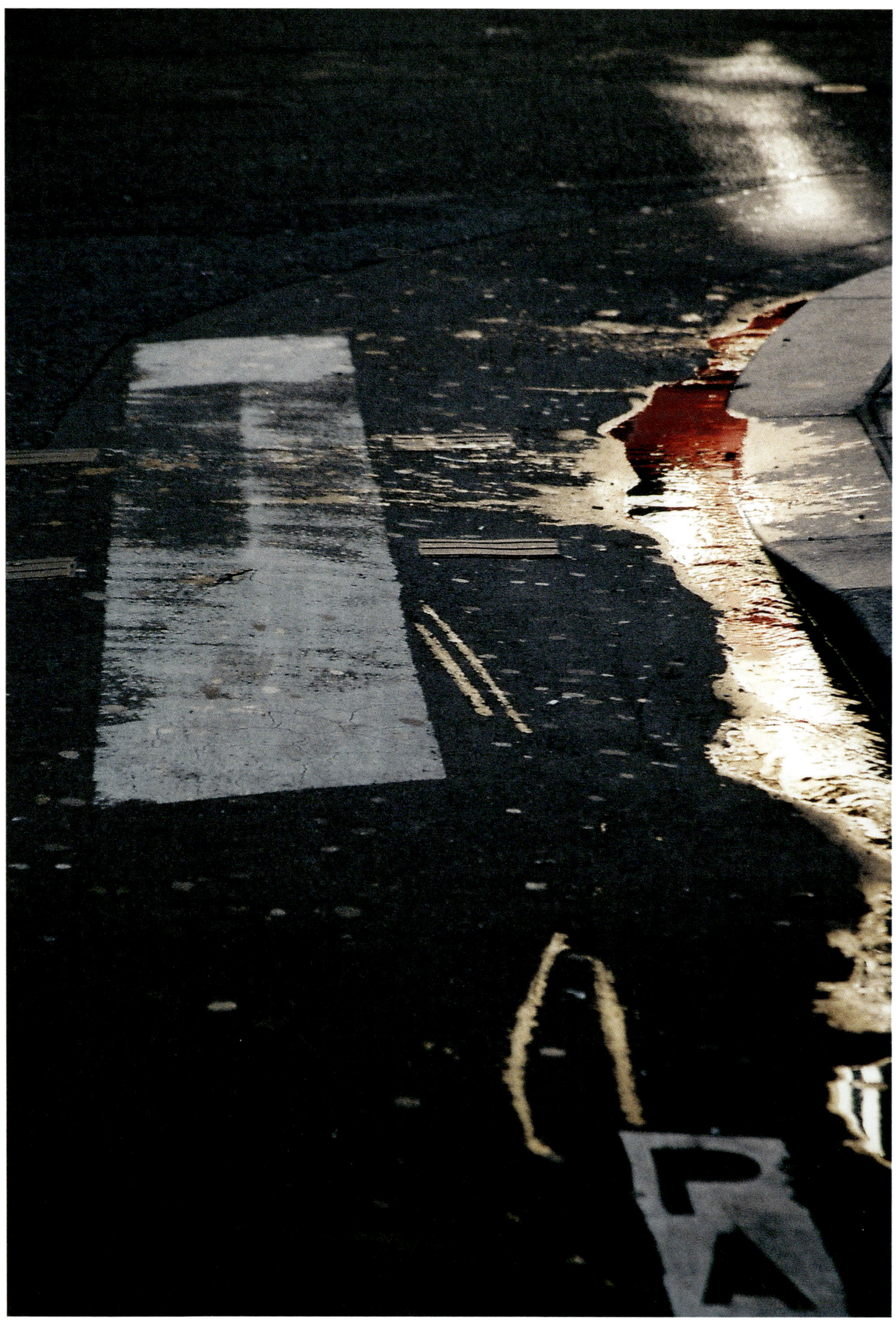

    Times Square III   2009

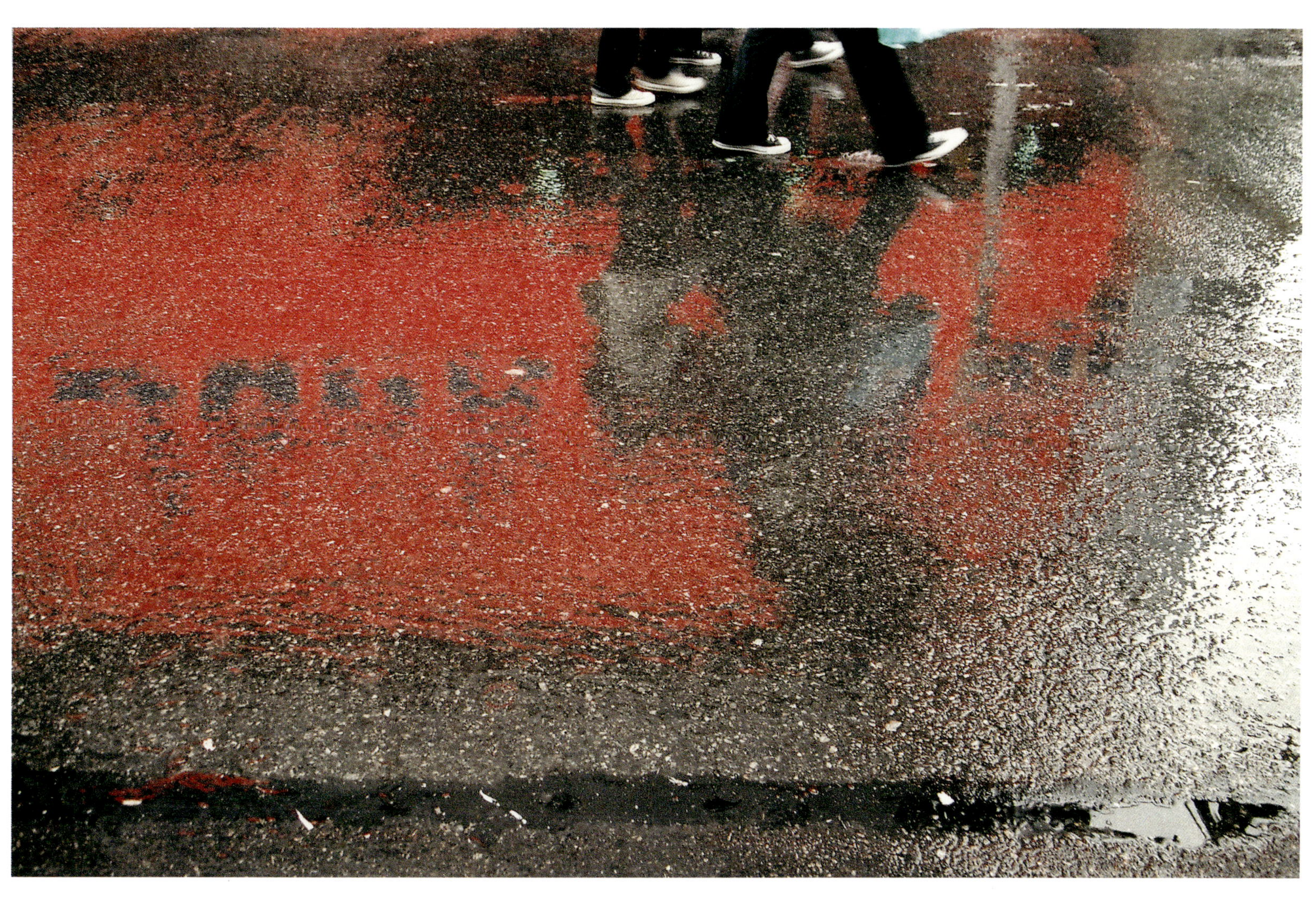

Times Square IV   2009

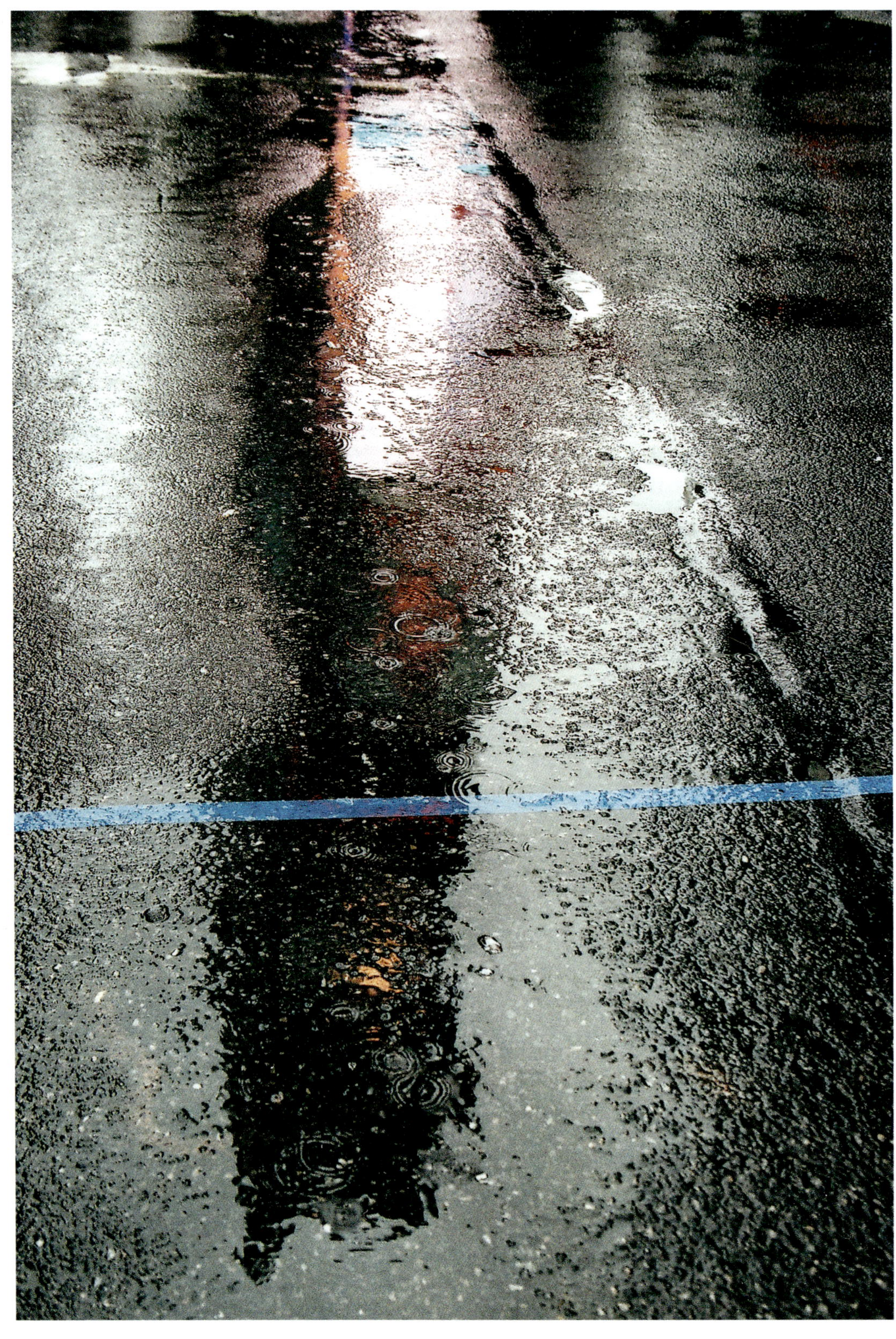

   Times Square V   2009

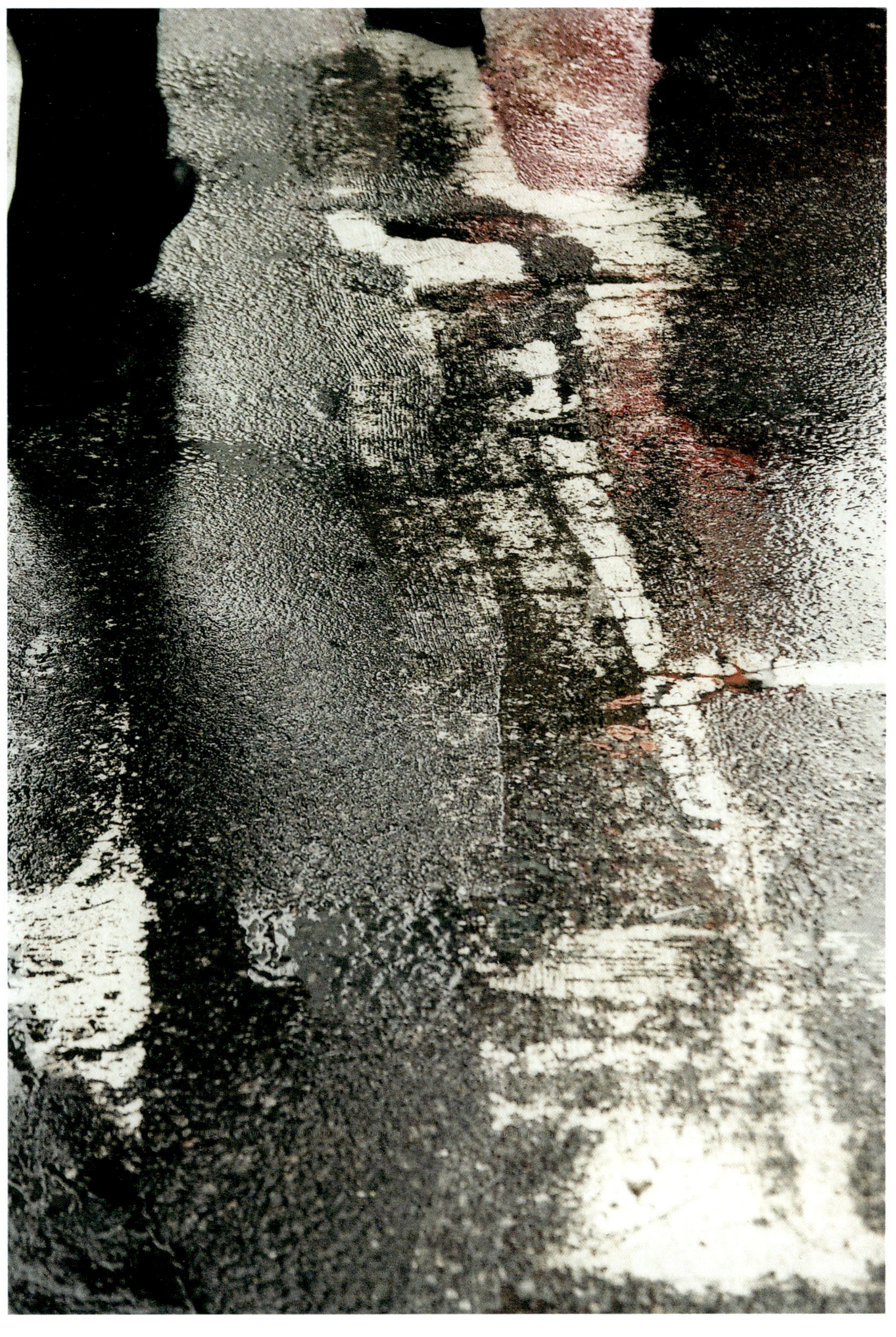

Times Square VI   2009

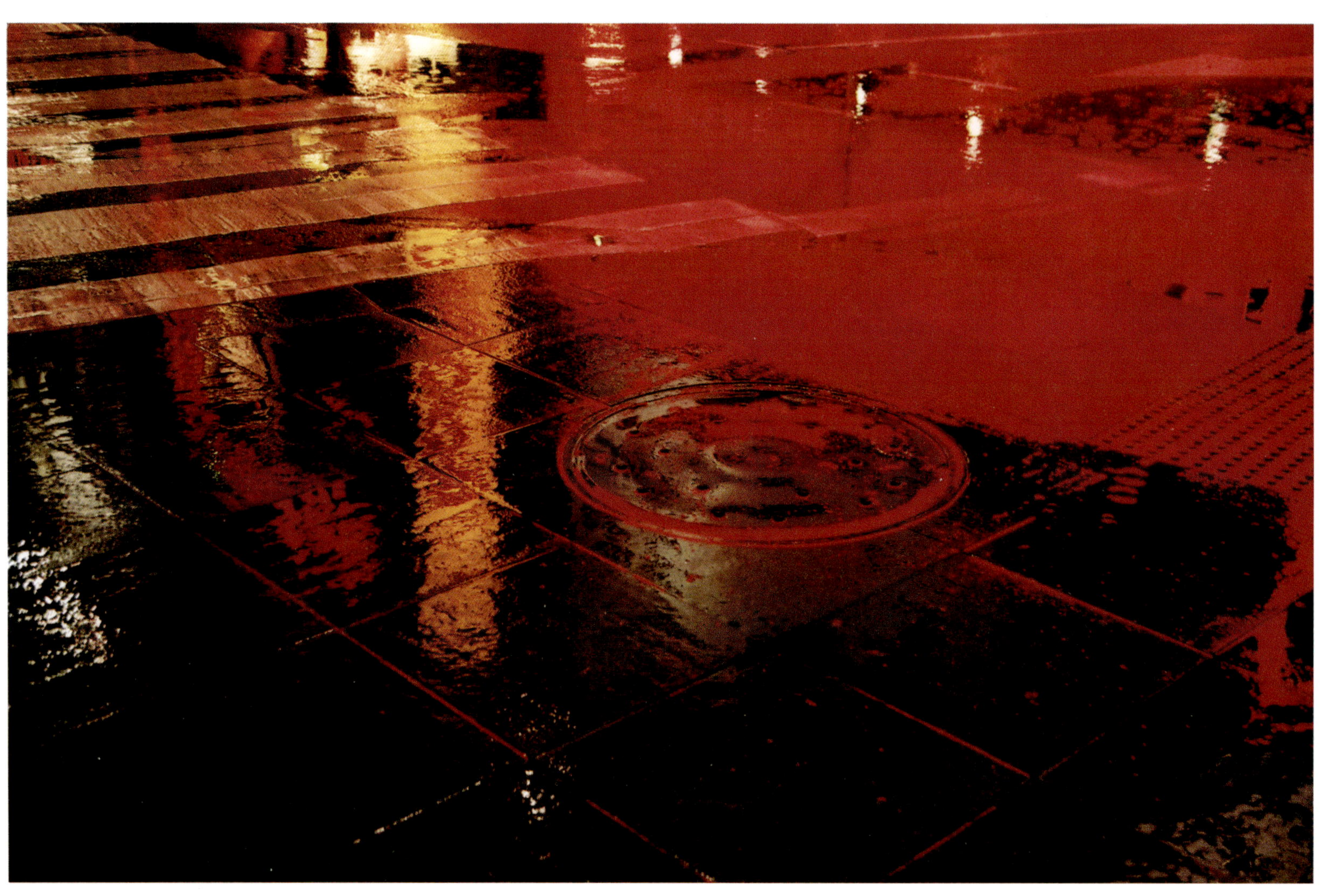

　　Times Square VII　2009

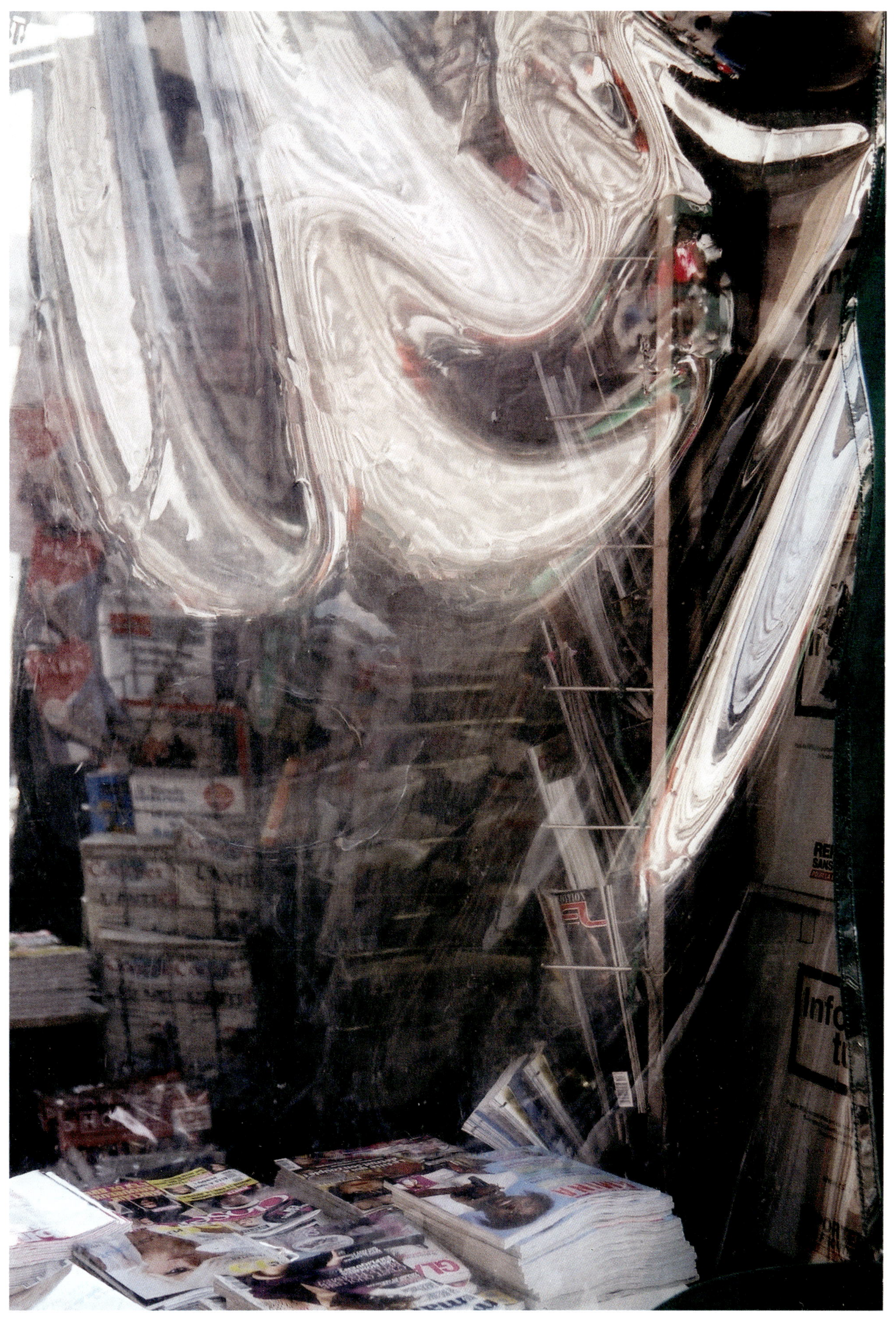

Boulevard Bonne Nouvelle 2011

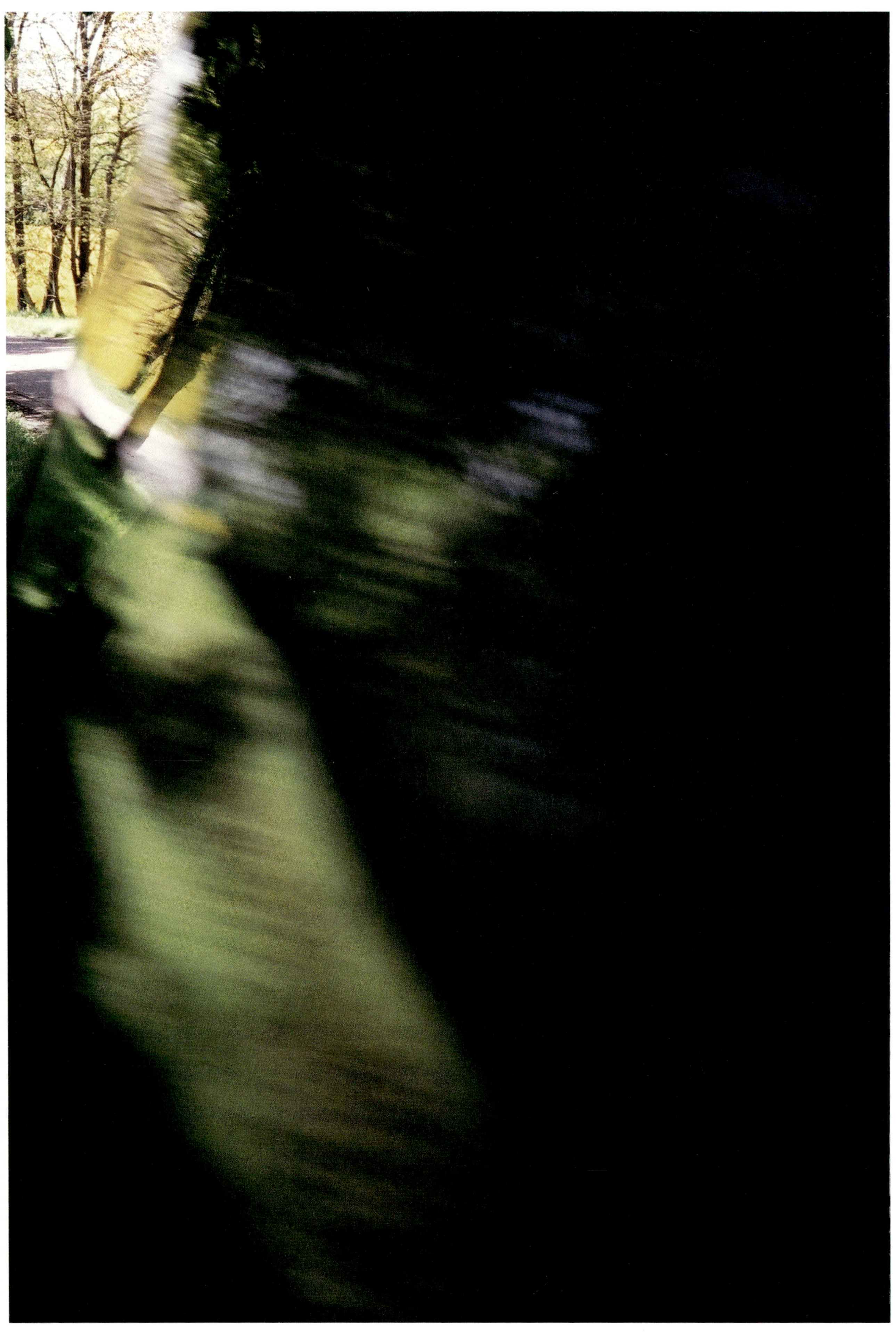

   Avallon   2009

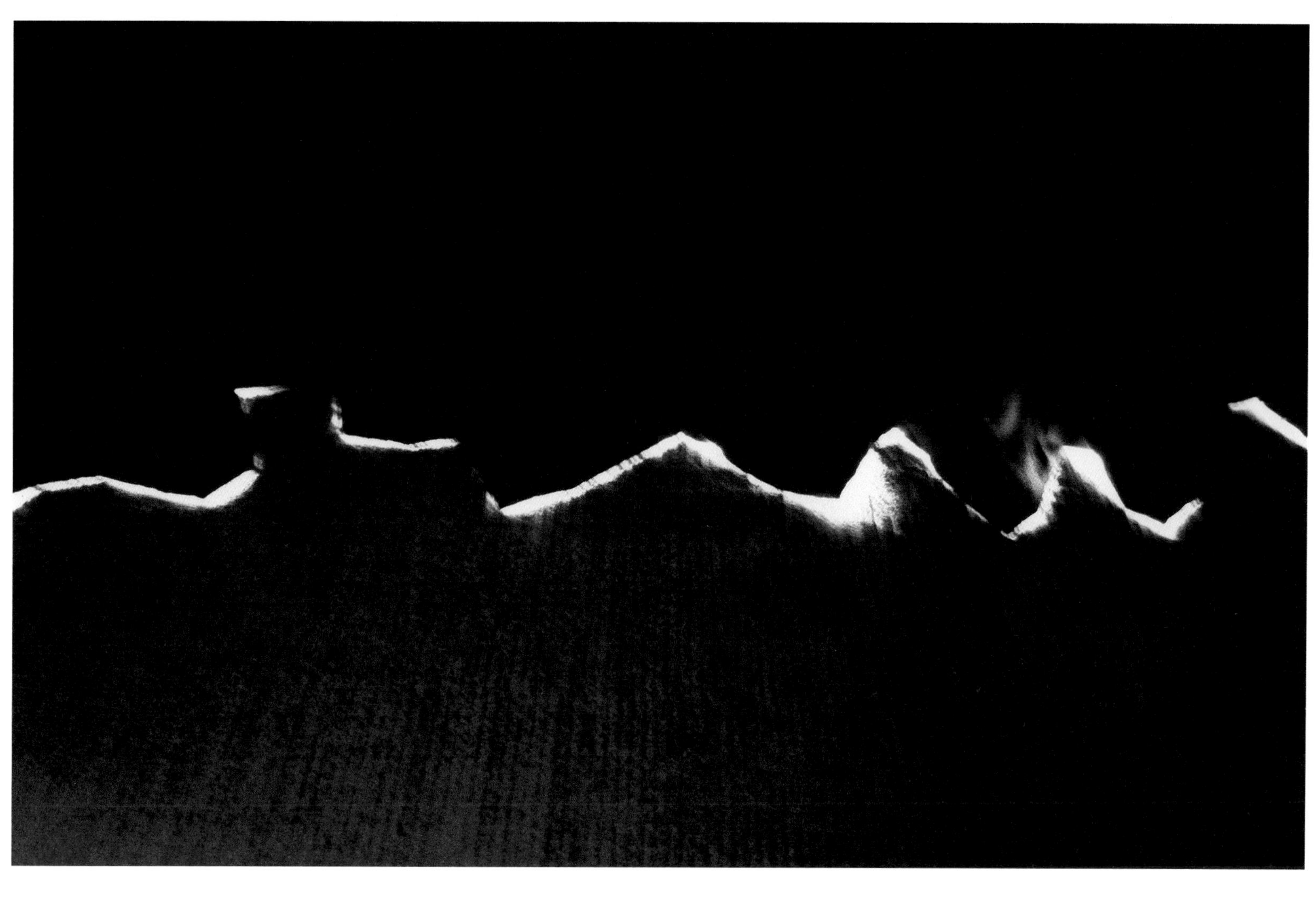

Tarbes   2009

Four-Hand, Nicole Bottet and Gottfried Salzmann | Nicole Bottet und Gottfried Salzmann vierhändig | Quatre mains, Nicole Bottet et Gottfried Salzmann   2007, 65,8 × 52,5 cm

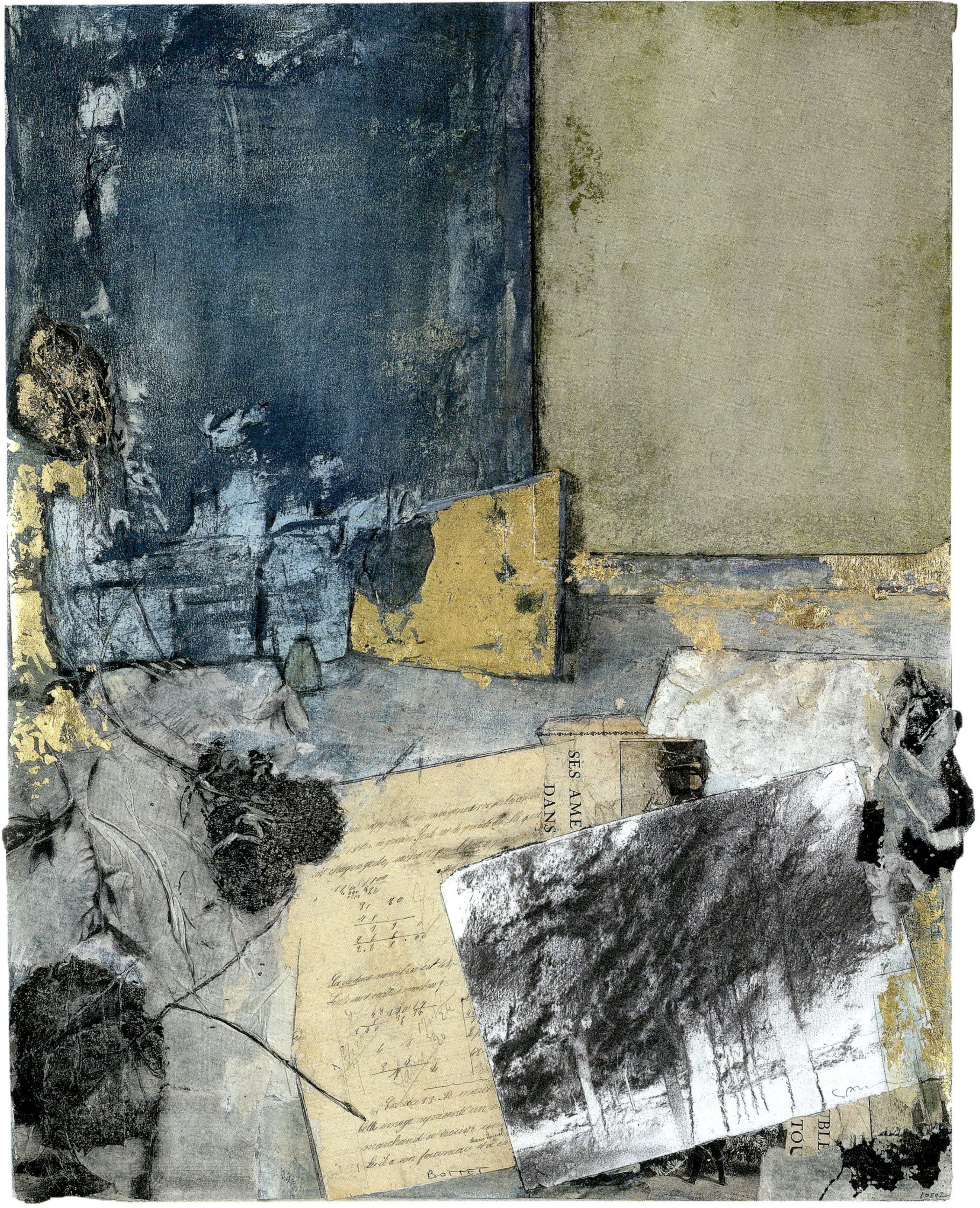

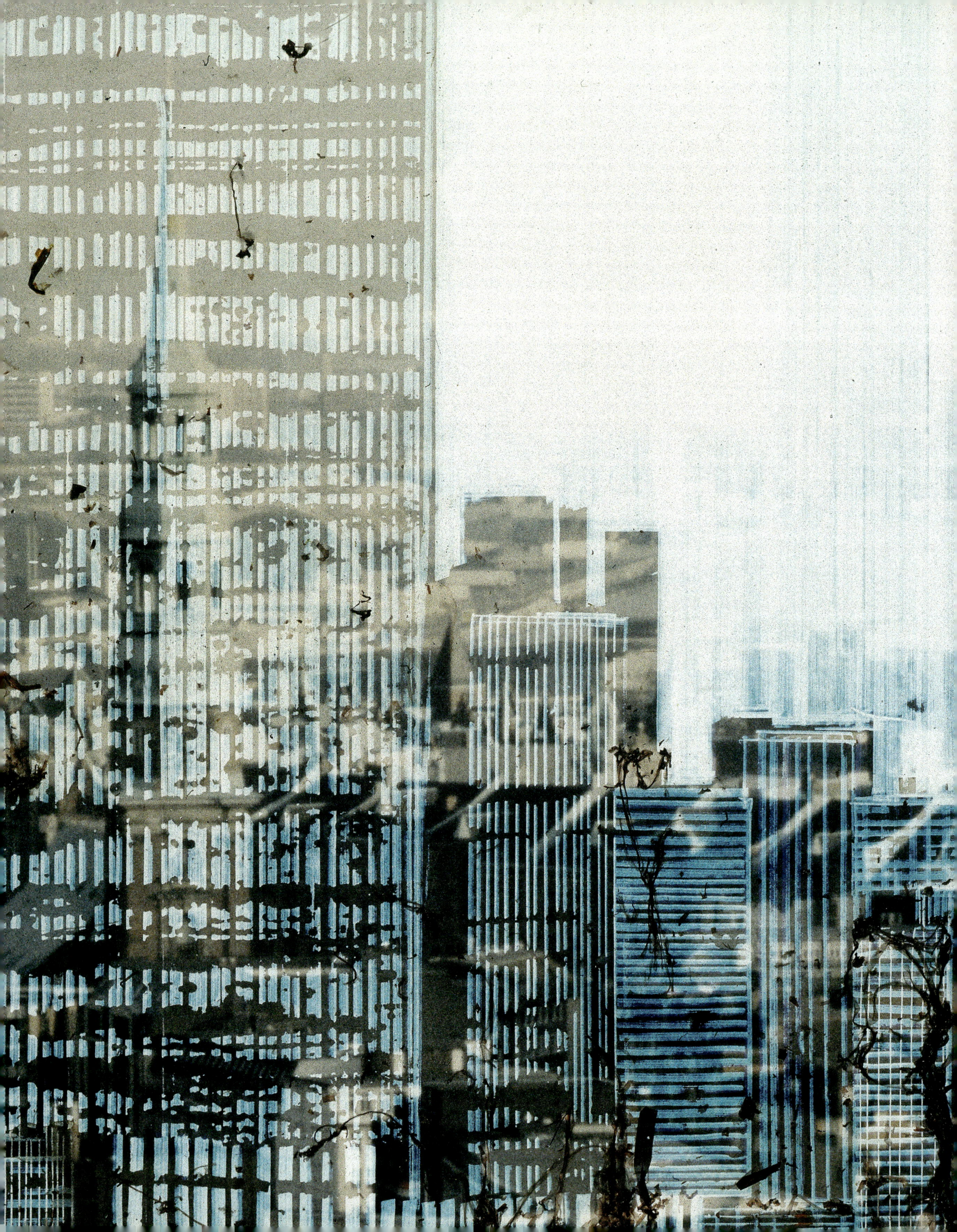

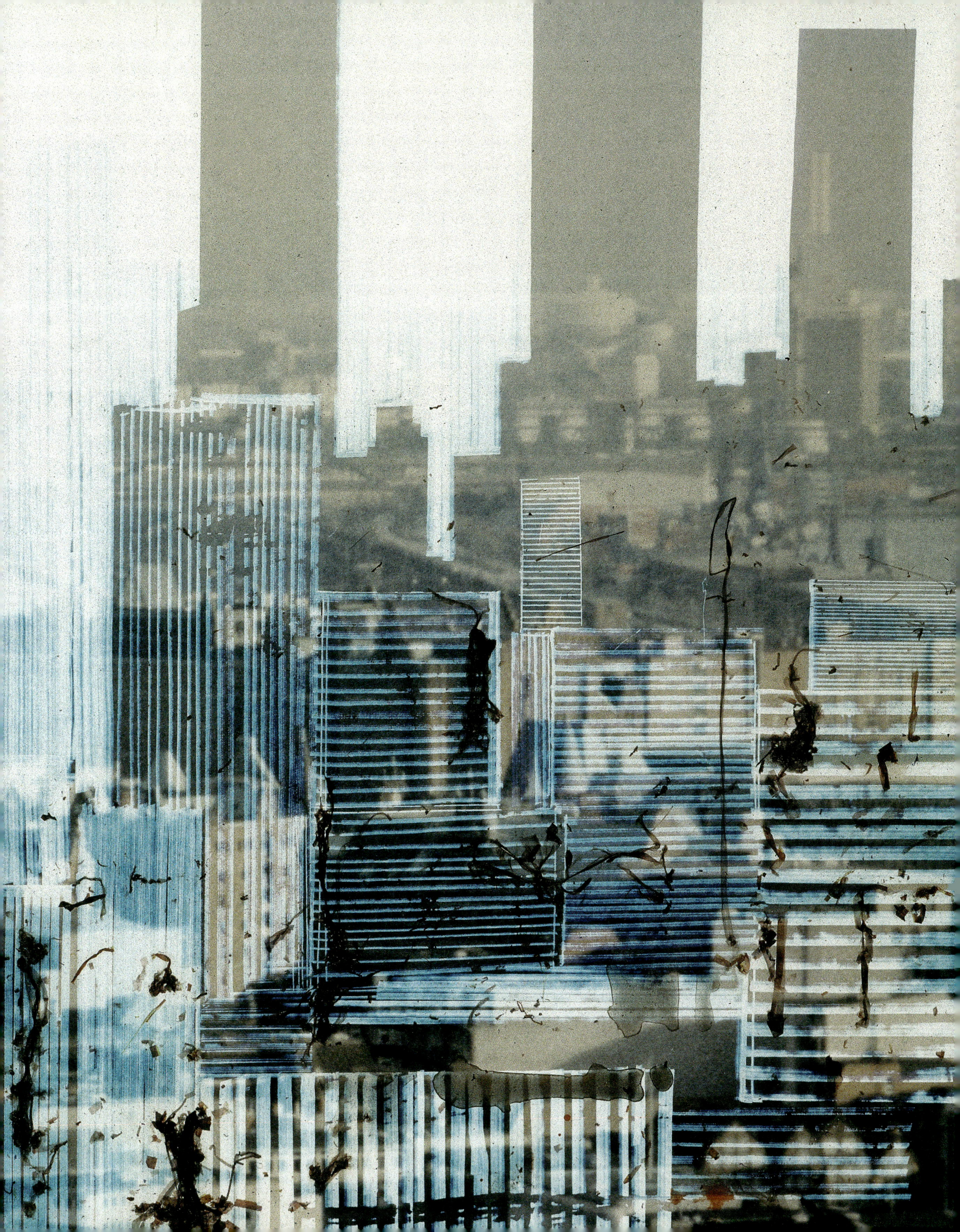

Appendix
Anhang
Appendice

Biography
Biografie
Biographie

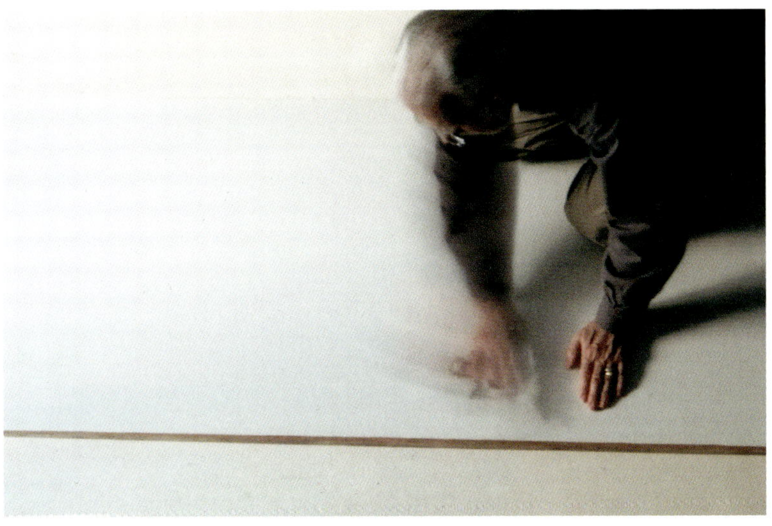

Gottfried Salzmann at work | Gottfried Salzmann bei der Arbeit | Gottfried Salzmann au travail, 2012

1943
Gottfried Salzmann born on February 26 in Saalfelden, Austria
Gottfried Salzmann wird am 26. Februar in Saalfelden, Österreich, geboren
Gottfried Salzmann naît le 26 février à Saalfelden, Autriche

1963–65
Akademie der bildenden Künste, Vienna, Austria | Wien, Österreich | Vienne, Autriche

1965–68
École Nationale Supérieure des Beaux-Arts, Paris, France | Frankreich | France

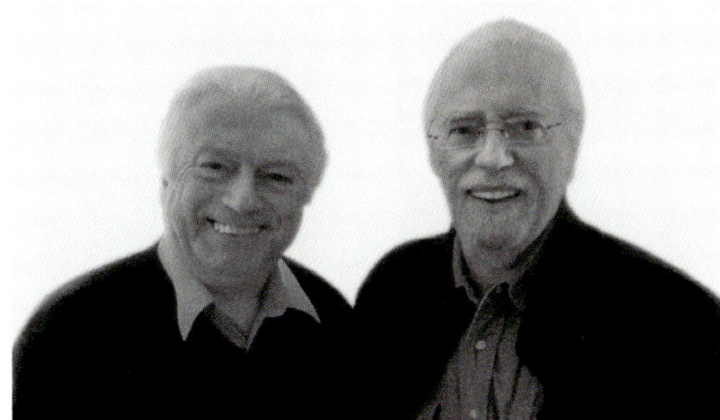

Dr. Staindl with | mit | avec Gottfried Salzmann, 2012

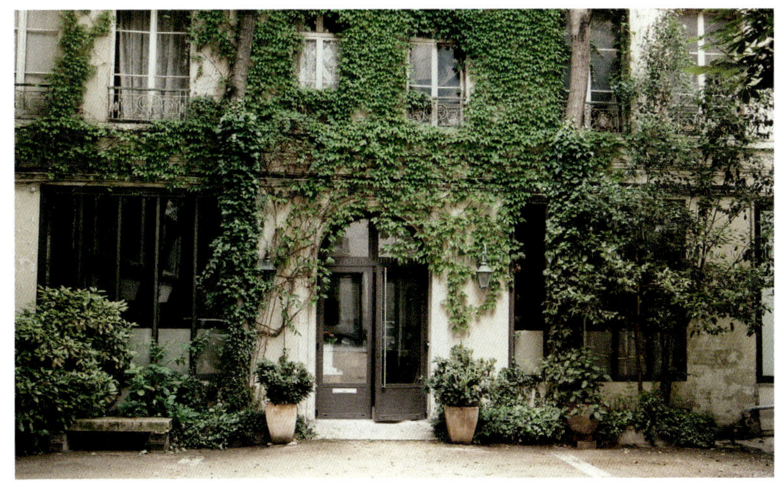

Gottfried Salzmann's studio in Paris, France | Gottfried Salzmanns Atelier in Paris, Frankreich | Atelier de Gottfried Salzmann à Paris, France, 2012

Museum Exhibitions
Ausstellungen in Museen
Expositions dans les musées

2012
Oberösterreichisches Landesmuseum, Linz:
Kubin Haus Zwickledt, Zwickledt, Austria |
Österreich | Autriche

2006
*Opening of the Gottfried Salzmann
Room* | *Eröffnung des Gottfried-Salzmann-
Saals* | *Ouverture de la Salle Gottfried
Salzmann*, Salzburg Museum, Salzburg,
Austria | Salzburg, Österreich | Salzbourg,
Autriche

2003
Salzburg Museum, Salzburg, Austria |
Salzburg, Österreich | Salzbourg, Autriche

2001–2002
Musée de Saint-Maur, La Varenne, France |
Frankreich | France

1998
Palais Bénédictine, Fécamp, France |
Frankreich | France

1997
Prieuré de Saint-Cosme, Tours, France |
Frankreich | France

1996
Centre d'Art Contemporain, Rouen, France |
Frankreich | France (with | mit | avec
Nicole Bottet)

1993
Musée de la Seita, Paris, France |
Frankreich | France

1991
Oberösterreichisches Landesmuseum, Linz,
Austria | Österreich | Autriche
Metropolitan Museum, Manila, Philippines |
Manila, Philippinen | Manille, Philippines
Museum der Moderne Rupertinum, Salzburg,
Austria | Salzburg, Österreich | Salzbourg,
Autriche

1987
Städtische Sammlungen Schweinfurt,
Schweinfurt, Germany | Deutschland |
Allemagne

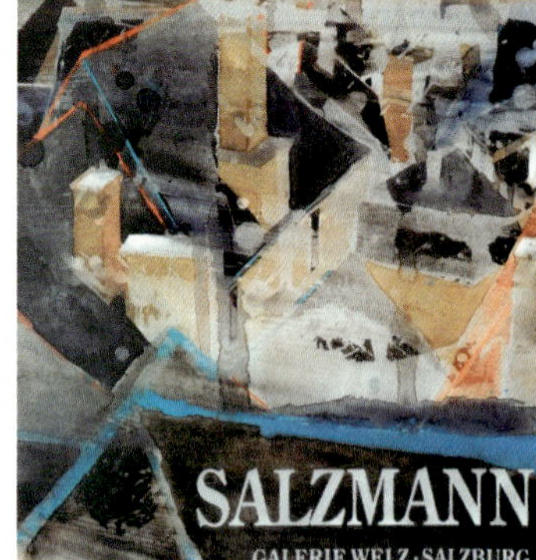

Poster for the exhibition at Welz Gallery, Salzburg,
Austria, 2005 | Plakat zur Ausstellung in der Galerie
Welz, Salzburg, Österreich, 2005 | Affiche pour
l'exposition à la Galerie Welz, Salzbourg, Autriche, 2005

1982
Albertina Museum (Prunkräume),
Vienna, Austria | Wien, Österreich |
Vienne, Autriche

1973
Maison de la Culture, Amiens, France |
Frankreich | France

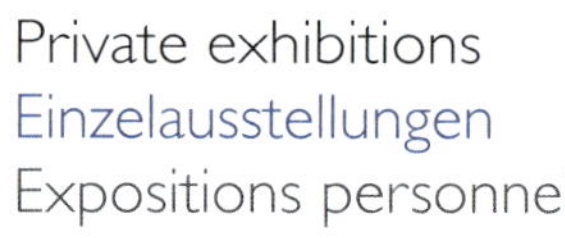

Private exhibitions
Einzelausstellungen
Expositions personnelles

More than 300 private exhibitions in Europe,
the USA, and Asia | Mehr als 300 Einzel-
ausstellungen in Europa, den USA und
Asien | Plus de 300 expositions personnelles
en Europe, USA et Asie

Gottfried Salzmann exhibition | Ausstellung |
exposition, Franklin Bowles Galleries, New York, 2012

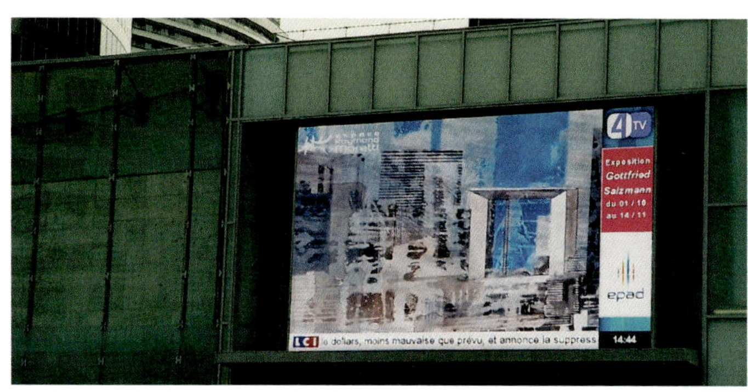

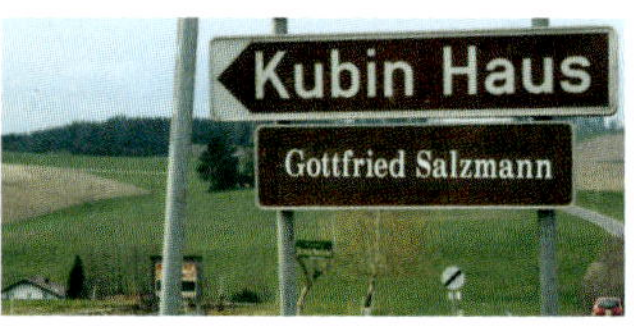

Exhibition in Zwickeldt, Austria,
at the Kubin Haus, 2012 | Aus-
stellung in Zwickeldt, Österreich
im Kubin Haus, 2012 | Exposition
à Zwickeldt, Autriche au Kubin
Haus, 2012

Digital billboard for the exhibition at La Défense, Paris,
France, 2008 | Digitales Werbeplakat für die Ausstel-
lung in La Défense, Paris, Frankreich, 2008 | Panneau
d'affichage numérique pour l'exposition à la Défense,
Paris, France, 2008

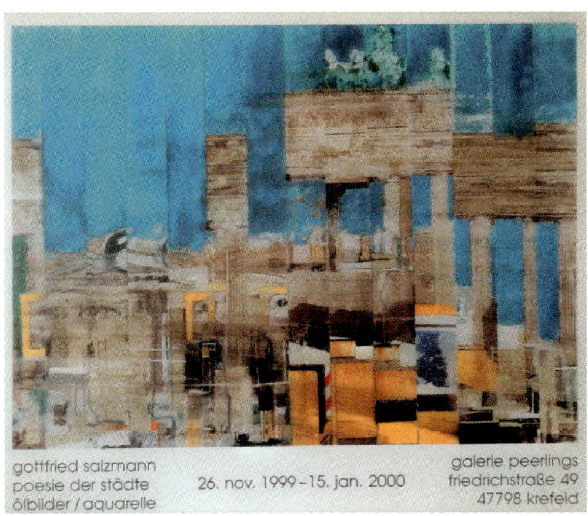

Poster for the exhibition at Peerlings Gallery, Krefeld, Germany, 1999 | Plakat zur Ausstellung in der Galerie Peerlings, Krefeld, Deutschland, 1999 | Affiche pour l'exposition à la Galerie Peerlings, Krefeld, Allemagne, 1999

Albertina Museum, Vienna, Austria | Wien, Österreich | Vienne, Autriche
Museum der Moderne, Salzburg, Austria | Salzburg, Österreich | Salzbourg, Autriche
Salzburg Museum, Salzburg, Austria | Salzburg, Österreich | Salzbourg, Autriche
Oberösterreichisches Landesmuseum, Linz, Austria | Österreich | Autriche
Museum Essl, Kunst der Gegenwart, Klosterneuburg, Austria | Österreich | Autriche
Musée de la Ville de Paris, Paris, France | Frankreich | France

Poster for the exhibition at Rupertinum, Salzburg, Austria, 1991 | Plakat zur Ausstellung Rupertinum, Salzburg, Österreich, 1991 | Affiche pour l'exposition à Rupertinum, Salzbourg, Autriche, 1991

Bibliothèque Nationale de Paris, Paris, France | Frankreich | France
Museum Séoul, Korea | Seoul, Korea | Séoul, Corée
Musée Jenisch, Vevey, Switzerland | Schweiz | Suisse
Kunstmuseum, Vaduz, Liechtenstein
Metropolitan Museum, Manila, Philippines | Manila, Philippinen | Manille, Philippines
Sammlung Leopold, Vienna, Austria | Wien, Österreich | Vienne, Autriche
Strabag Kunstforum, Vienna, Austria | Wien, Österreich | Vienne, Autriche
Musée de Montbéliard, Montbéliard, France | Frankreich | France
Leopold Hoesch Museum, Düren, Germany | Deutschland | Allemagne
Museum Ferdinandeum, Innsbruck, Austria | Österreich | Autriche
SL Green Reality Corporation, New York, USA
AIG/American International Group, Inc. New York, USA
Bain Capital Asia, LLC, Hong Kong, China
etc.

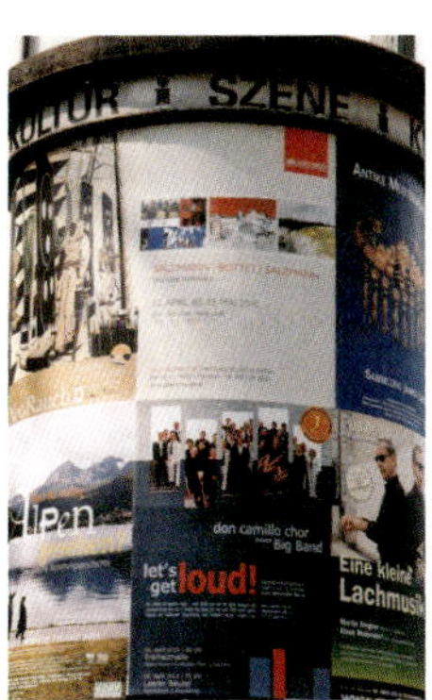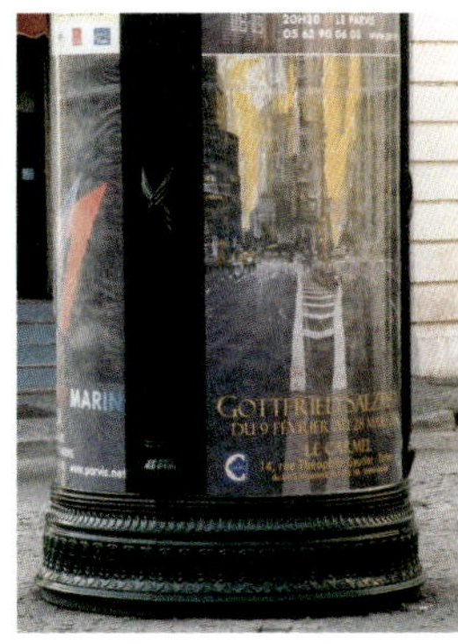

left | links | à gauche: Poster for the exhibition Salzmann | Bottet | Salzmann – Eine Künstlerfamilie at Anna Maria Burger Gallery, Munich, Germany, 2010 | Plakat zur Ausstellung Salzmann | Bottet | Salzmann – Eine Künstlerfamilie in der Galerie Anna Maria Burger, München, Deutschland, 2010 | Affiche pour l'exposition Salzmann | Bottet | Salzmann – Eine Künstlerfamilie à la Galerie Anna Maria Burger, Munich, Allemagne, 2010

right | rechts | à droite: Poster for the exhibition at Le Carmel, Tarbes, France, 2009 | Plakat zur Ausstellung in Le Carmel, Tarbes, Frankreich, 2009 | Affiche pour l'exposition au Carmel, Tarbes, France, 2009

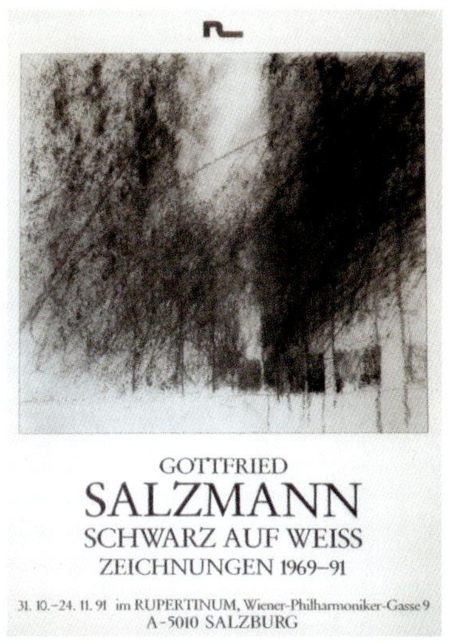

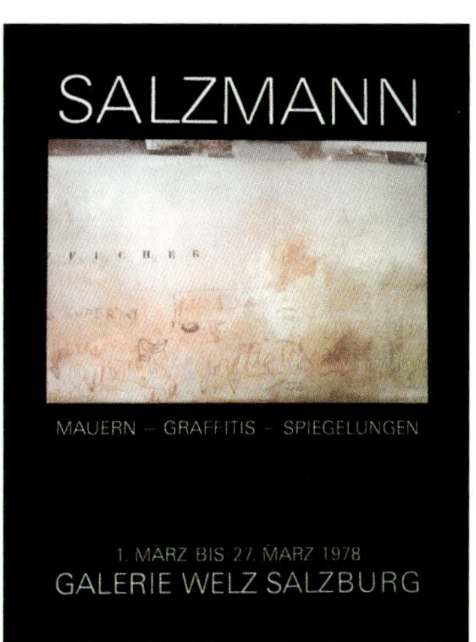

Poster for the exhibition at Welz Gallery, Salzburg, Austria, 1978 | Plakat zur Ausstellung in der Galerie Welz, Salzburg, Österreich, 1978 | Affiche pour l'exposition à la Galerie Welz, Salzbourg, Autriche, 1978

Poster for the exhibition at Albertina Museum Vienna, Austria, 1982 | Plakat zur Ausstellung in der Albertina, Wien, Österreich, 1982 | Affiche pour l'exposition au Musée Albertina, Vienne, Autriche, 1982

2012
Gottfried Salzmann. Orchestrating the Accidental
Franklin Bowles Galleries, New York / San Francisco, USA. Exhibition catalog | Katalog | catalogue

2011
Gottfried Salzmann
Texts by | Texte von | Textes : Anne de la Roussière. Galerie Arcturus, Paris, France | Frankreich | France. Exhibition catalog | Katalog | catalogue

2010
Gottfried Salzmann. On the Streets
Franklin Bowles Galleries New York, USA. Exhibition catalog | Katalog | catalogue

2009
Gottfried Salzmann. City Life
Franklin Bowles Galleries, New York, USA. Exhibition catalog | Katalog | catalogue

2008
Gottfried Salzmann
Texts by | Texte von | Textes : Patrick Devedjian, Bernard Bled. Paris La Défense – on the 50th anniversary of the La Défense district | Anlässlich des 50. Jahrestags von La Défense | À l'occasion des 50 ans de La Défense, Paris, France | Frankreich | France. Exhibition catalog | Katalog | catalogue Espace Raymond Moretti

Gottfried Salzmann. One Man's View
Franklin Bowles Galleries, New York, USA. Exhibition catalog | Katalog | catalogue

2006
Gottfried Salzmann. Urban Perspectives
Franklin Bowles Galleries, New York, USA. Exhibition catalog | Katalog | catalogue

Salzmann
Texts by | Texte von | Textes : Pascale Bonafoux, Nicolaus Schaffer. Preface by | Vorwort von | préface de Klaus Albrecht Schröder, Chief Conservator at the Albertina | Chefkonservator der Albertina | Conservateur en chef du Musée Albertina, Vienna, Austria | Wien, Österreich | Vienne, Autriche. Édition Thalia, Paris, France | Frankreich | France

Gottfried Salzmann
Texts by | Texte von | Textes : Jacques Desage. Galerie Arcturus, Paris, France | Frankreich | France. Exhibition catalog | Katalog | catalogue

2004
Gottfried Salzmann. ART PARIS 2004
Galerie Arcturus, Paris, France | Frankreich | France. Exhibition catalog | Katalog | catalogue

Gottfried Salzmann. Reflections
Texts by | Texte von | Textes : Jean Audigier. Franklin Bowles Galleries, New York, USA. Exhibition catalog | Katalog | catalogue

2003
Gottfried Salzmann. Salzburg, Paris, New York: Arbeiten 1967–2002
Texts by | Texte von | Textes : Erich Marx, Nikolaus Schaffer. Salzburg Museum, Salzburg, Austria | Salzburg, Österreich | Salzbourg, Autriche. Exhibition catalog | Katalog | catalogue

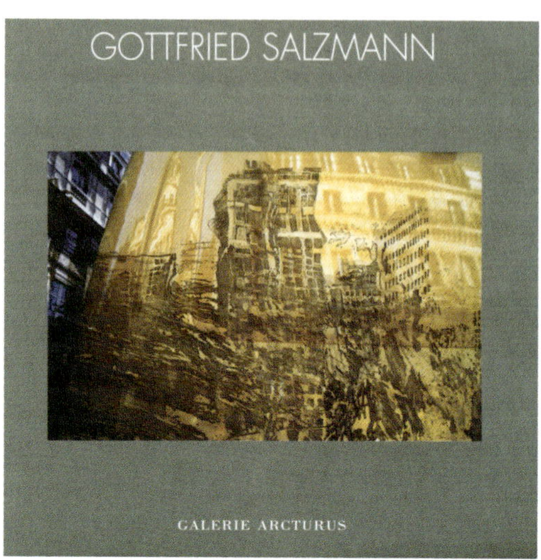

Exhibition catalog | Katalog | catalogue, Galerie Arcturus, Paris, France | Frankreich | France, 2003

Gottfried Salzmann. Hinterglasbilder 1970 – 1977
Texts by | Texte von | Textes : Peter Weiermair. Galerie Maier, Innsbruck, Austria | Österreich | Autriche. Exhibition catalog | Katalog | catalogue

2001
Gottfried Salzmann, Regards sur 30 ans de création
Texts by | Texte von | Textes : Bernadette Boustany, Nicole Bottet. Musée de Saint-Maur, La Varenne, France | Frankreich | France. Exhibition catalog | Katalog | catalogue

2000
Salzmann. L'Aquarelle, PAYSAGES ET VILLES DE L'IDÉE INITIALE À L'AQUARELLE PURE
Texts by | Texte von | Textes : Gottfried Salzmann. Callwey, Munich, Germany | München, Deutschland | Munich, Allemagne

1999
Salzmann. Poesie der Städte | Poésie de la Ville
Texts by | Texte von | Textes : Heinz Spiel-
mann, Nicole Bottet, Gottfried Salzmann.
Verlag Galerie Peerlings, Krefeld, Germany |
Deutschland | Allemagne

1998
Salzmann. Spiegelungen | Reflets
Texts by | Texte von | Textes : Otto Breicha.
Verlag Galerie Welz, Salzburg, Austria |
Salzburg, Österreich | Salzbourg, Autriche

Salzmann. Villes et Reflets
Texts by | Texte von | Textes : Gérard
Matthias, Nicole Bottet. Palais Bénédictine,
Fécamp, France | Frankreich | France.
Exhibition catalog | Katalog | catalogue

1997
*Salzmann. Magique et magistral –
Magisch und Meisterhaft*
Texts by | Texte von | Textes : Marc Hérissé.
Galerie Lochte, Hamburg, Germany |
Deutschland | Allemagne. Exhibition
catalog | Katalog | catalogue

Salzmann, Les Villes
Texts by | Texte von | Textes : Marc Hérissé.
Le Prieuré de Saint-Cosme, Tours, France |
Frankreich | France. Exhibition catalog |
Katalog | catalogue

1995
Salzmann. Paris, Berlin, New York
Texts by | Texte von | Textes : Roland Flak,
Nicole Bottet. Galerie Flak, Paris, France |
Frankreich | France. Exhibition catalog |
Katalog | catalogue

1993
*L'Aquarelle Aujourd'hui: Abrahami,
Levine, Salzmann, Szafran*
Musée-Galerie de la Seita, Paris, France |
Frankreich | France. Exhibition catalog |
Katalog | catalogue

*Salzmann. Wasser-Spiegelung |
Autour de l'eau*
Texts by | Texte von | Textes : Nicole Bottet.
Verlag Galerie Welz, 1993; new edition |
Neuauflage | réédition 1995, Salzburg,
Austria | Salzburg, Österreich | Salzbourg,
Autriche

1991
Gottfried Salzmann – Städte/Landschaften
Texts by | Texte von | Textes : Erich R.
Heller. Oberösterreichische Landesmuseen,
Linz, Austria | Österreich | Autriche.
Exhibition catalog | Katalog | catalogue

1988
Salzmann – Städte | Cities | Villes
Texts by | Texte von | Textes : Bernard
Denvir. Verlag Galerie Welz, Salzburg,
Austria | Salzburg, Österreich | Salzbourg,
Autriche

1982
Salzmann
Texts by | Texte von | Textes : Walter
Koschatzky. Neufeld Galerie und Verlag,
Lustenau, Austria, Switzerland |
Österreich, Schweiz | Autriche, Suisse

Salzmann – Zeichnungen | Dessins | Drawings
Texts by | Texte von | Textes : Wieland
Schmied. Verlag Galerie Welz, Salzburg,
Austria | Salzburg, Österreich | Salzbourg,
Autriche

Salzmann Albertina
Texts by | Texte von | Textes : Walter
Koschatzky, Jean-Marie Dunoyer. Albertina,
Vienna, Austria | Wien, Österreich | Vienne,
Autriche. Exhibition catalog | Katalog |
catalogue

1977
Salzmann
Texts by | Texte von | Textes : Walter
Koschatzky. Verlag Galerie Welz, Salzburg,
Austria | Salzburg, Österreich | Salzbourg,
Autriche

Art Fairs | Kunstmessen | Foires

Cologne | Köln | Cologne, Düsseldorf,
Basel | Bâle, Vienna | Wien | Vienne, Paris,
Washington, DC, Los Angeles, Stockholm,
Hong Kong, Geneva | Genf | Genève,
Frankfurt | Frankfurt am Main | Francfort,
Strasbourg | Straßburg | Strasbourg,
Lugano, Ghent | Gent | Gand

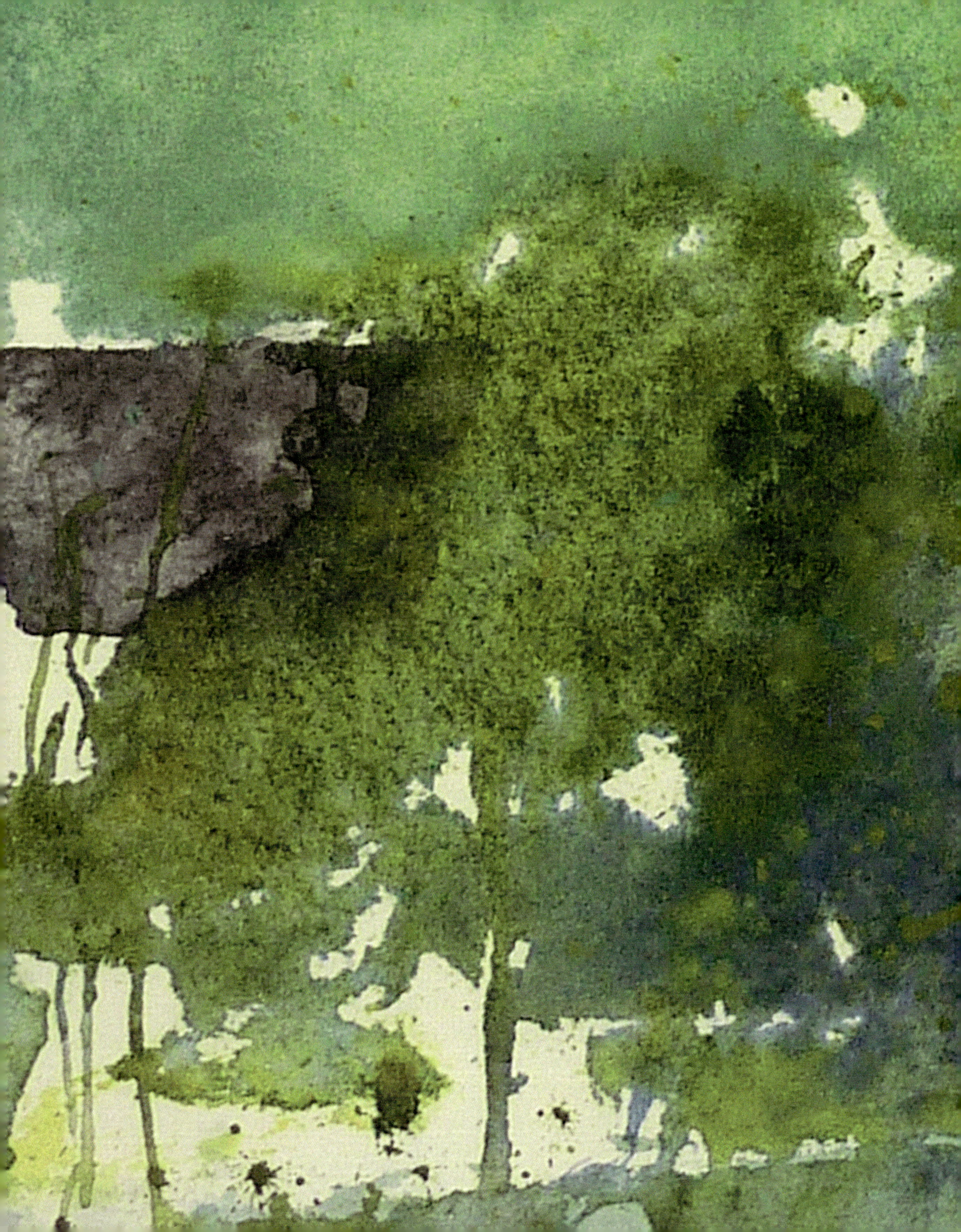

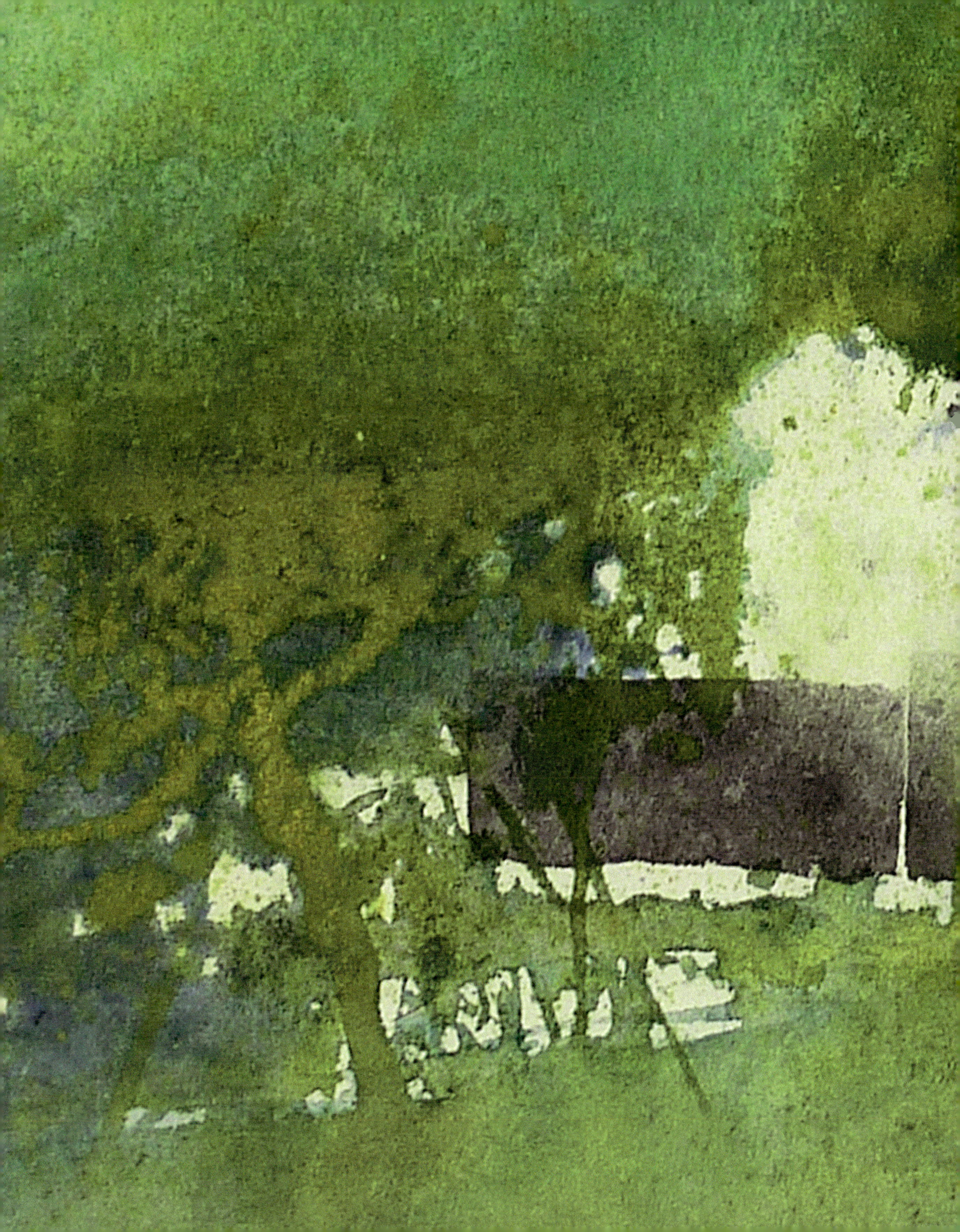

List of Works
Werkverzeichnis
Liste des œuvres

The numbers under the images refer to the respective pages in the book.
Die Zahlen unter den Bildern verweisen auf die entsprechende Seite im Buch.
Le chiffre sous les illustrations renvoie à la page du livre correspondante.

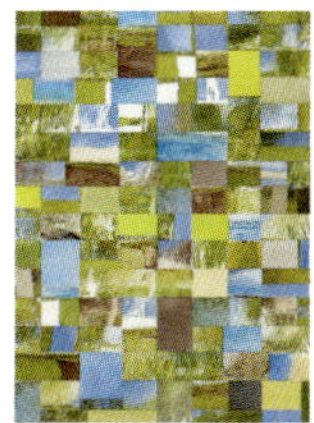

Tagtägliches, 1982

Watercolor, Aquarell, Aquarelle
84,1 × 59,3 cm
Salzburg Museum, Salzburg, Salzbourg

43

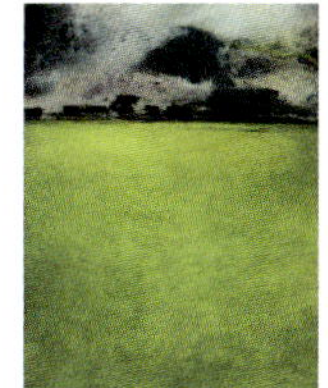

Saint-Palais, 1972

Watercolor, Aquarell, Aquarelle
32,3 × 47,6 cm
Private collection, Gottfried Salzmann,
Privatsammlung, Gottfried Salzmann,
Collection privée Gottfried Salzmann

44

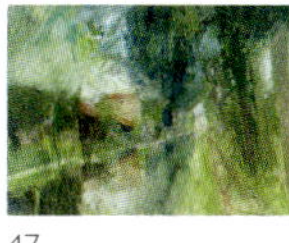

Le Brun des Toits, 1977

Watercolor, Aquarell, Aquarelle
33 × 48 cm
Private collection, Klitzschmüller, near
Hamburg, Privatsammlung Klitzschmüller, bei
Hamburg, Collection privée Klitzschmüller,
près de Hambourg

45

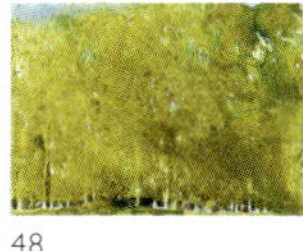

Landscape with Railroad | Landschaft
mit Eisenbahn | Paysage avec voie
ferrée, ca. | ca. | vers 1972

Oil/canvas, Öl/Leinwand, Huile/toile
100 × 73 cm
Salzburg Museum, Salzburg, Salzbourg

46

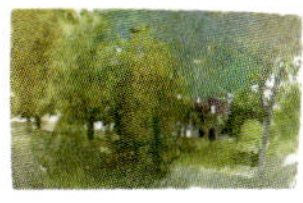

Canal d'Auron, ca. | ca. | vers 1970

Oil/canvas, Öl/Leinwand, Huile/toile
54 × 72,5 cm
Salzburg Museum, Salzburg, Salzbourg

47

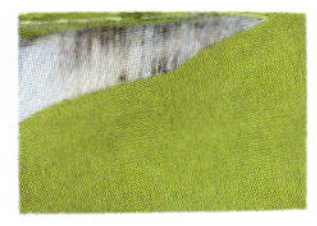

Curtain of Trees | Baumvorhang |
Rideau d'arbres, ca. | ca. | vers 1980

Watercolor/canvas, Aquarell/Leinwand,
Aquarelle/toile
54 × 73,5 cm
Salzburg Museum, Salzburg, Salzbourg

48

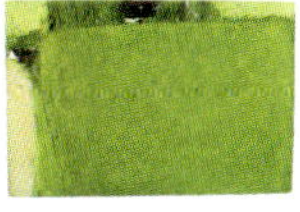

Les Abbés, 1972

Watercolor, Aquarell, Aquarelle
30 × 47 cm
Private collection, Dr. Staindl, Salzburg,
Privatsammlung Dr. Staindl, Salzburg,
Collection privée Dr. Staindl, Salzbourg

49

Triangular Reflection | Dreieck-
spiegelung | Reflet triangulaire, 1980

Watercolor, Aquarell, Aquarelle
35 × 49,8 cm
Private collection, Dr. Staindl, Salzburg,
Privatsammlung Dr. Staindl, Salzburg,
Collection privée Dr. Staindl, Salzbourg

50

Hedge II | Hecke II | Haie II, 1974

Watercolor, Aquarell, Aquarelle
32,7 × 48 cm
Private collection, Dr. Staindl, Salzburg,
Privatsammlung Dr. Staindl, Salzburg,
Collection privée Dr. Staindl, Salzbourg

50

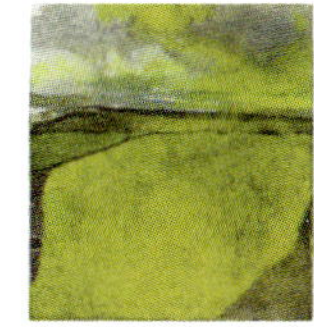

Saint-Martin d'Auxigny, 1972

Watercolor/lithograph, Aquarell/Litho,
Aquarelle/lithographie
22,2 × 19,1 cm
Private collection, Dr. Staindl, Salzburg,
Privatsammlung Dr. Staindl, Salzburg,
Collection privée Dr. Staindl, Salzbourg

51

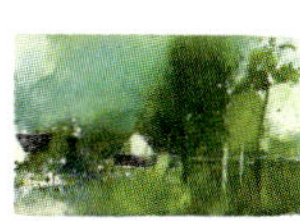

Évecquemont, 1971

Watercolor, Aquarell, Aquarelle
30,8 × 50 cm
Private collection, Dr. Staindl, Salzburg,
Privatsammlung Dr. Staindl, Salzburg,
Collection privée Dr. Staindl, Salzbourg

52

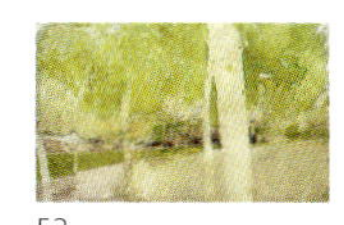

Near Orgeval | Bei Orgeval |
Près d'Orgeval, 1972

Watercolor, Aquarell, Aquarelle
31 × 50 cm

53

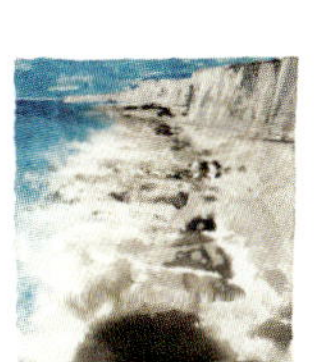

Las Illetas, 1980

Mixed media, Mischtechnik, Technique mixte
37,5 × 49,8 cm
Salzburg Museum, Salzburg, Salzbourg

54

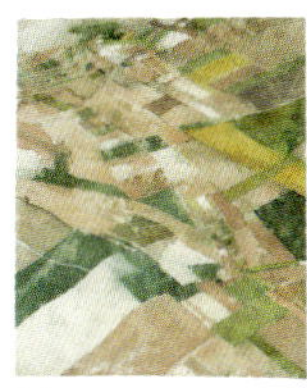

Seacoast Cliffs | Steilküste am
Meer | Falaise du littoral, 1990

Watercolor, Aquarell, Aquarelle
19 × 15 cm
Strabag Kunstforum, Vienna, Wien, Vienne

55

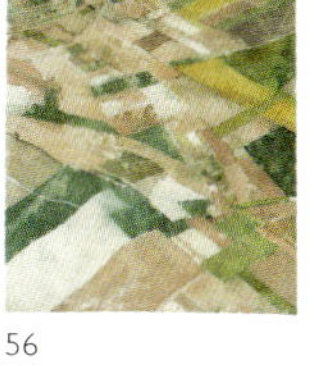

Carpet of Fields | Felderteppich |
Le tapis des champs, 1995

Watercolor, Aquarell, Aquarelle
57,2 × 45,5 cm
Strabag Kunstforum, Vienna, Wien, Vienne

56

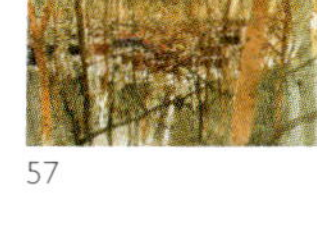

Rooftop Landscape | Dachland-
schaft | Paysage de toits, 1975

Watercolor, Aquarell, Aquarelle
33,3 × 47,7 cm
Private collection, Austria, Privatsammlung,
Österreich, Collection privée, Autriche

57

Troncos Morado, 1972

Watercolor, Aquarell, Aquarelle
38,4 × 58,4 cm
Private collection, E. Coufal, Guadalajara,
Mexico, Privatsammlung E. Coufal, Guada-
lajara, Mexiko, Collection privée E. Coufal,
Guadalajara, Mexique

58

Reflections of Boats in Dieppe |
Bootspiegelung in Dieppe | Reflets
de bateaux à Dieppe, 1985

Watercolor, Aquarell, Aquarelle
23 × 15 cm
Private collection, Dr. Staindl, Salzburg,
Privatsammlung Dr. Staindl, Salzburg,
Collection privée Dr. Staindl, Salzbourg

59

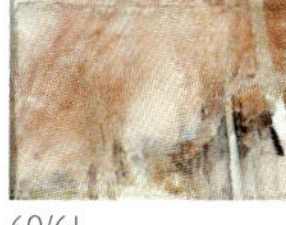

Brouillard IV, 1982

Watercolor, Aquarell, Aquarelle
26,2 × 37,3 cm
Private collection, Dr. Staindl, Salzburg,
Privatsammlung Dr. Staindl, Salzburg,
Collection privée Dr. Staindl, Salzbourg

60/61

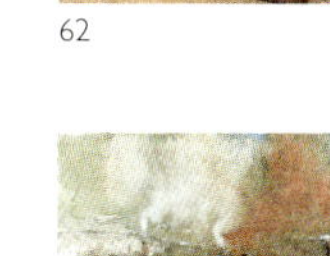

Longwy, 1980

Watercolor, Aquarell, Aquarelle
37,5 × 49,7 cm
Private collection, Austria, Privatsammlung,
Österreich, Collection privée, Autriche

62

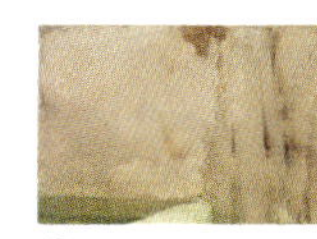

Carling, 1979

Watercolor, Aquarell, Aquarelle
30,7 × 48,2 cm
Private collection, Dr. Staindl, Salzburg,
Privatsammlung Dr. Staindl, Salzburg,
Collection privée Dr. Staindl, Salzbourg

62

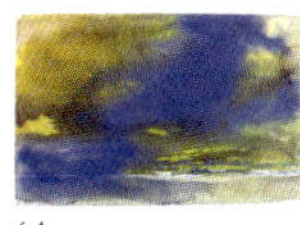

Brouillard III, 1982

Watercolor, Aquarell, Aquarelle
35 × 50,2 cm
Private collection, Gottfried Salzmann,
Privatsammlung, Gottfried Salzmann,
Collection privée Gottfried Salzmann

63

Golden Blue | Goldblau |
Bleu or, 1972

Watercolor, Aquarell, Aquarelle
38,4 × 58,4 cm
Private collection, Dr. Staindl, Salzburg,
Privatsammlung Dr. Staindl, Salzburg,
Collection privée Dr. Staindl, Salzbourg

64

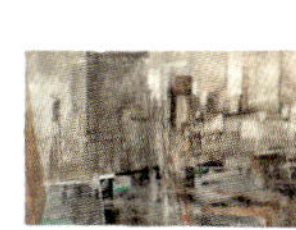

Yellow Sky | Gelber Himmel |
Ciel jaune, 1972

Watercolor, Aquarell, Aquarelle
46 × 48,5 cm
Private collection, Dr. Staindl, Salzburg,
Privatsammlung Dr. Staindl, Salzburg,
Collection privée Dr. Staindl, Salzbourg

65

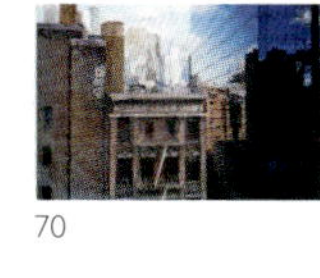

NY 56th Street, 1983

Watercolor, Aquarell, Aquarelle
29,2 × 46,7 cm
Private collection, E. Coufal, Guadalajara,
Mexico, Privatsammlung E. Coufal, Guada-
lajara, Mexiko, Collection privée E. Coufal,
Guadalajara, Mexique

68/69

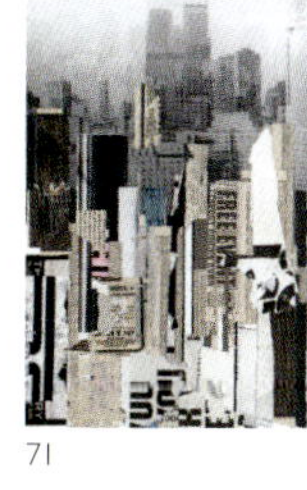

DKS, 2010

Mixed media, photograph/canvas, Mischtechnik, Foto/Leinwand, Technique mixte,
photo/toile
60 × 81 cm

70

Free Event, The Cathedral |
Free Event, Der Dom | Free Event,
La cathédrale, 2011

Mixed media, photograph, collage/canvas,
Mischtechnik, Foto, Collage/Leinwand,
Technique mixte, photo, collage/toile
81 × 54 cm

71

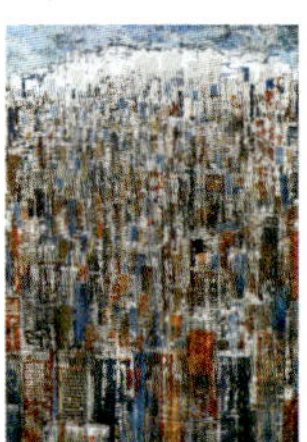

NY Puzzle, 2008

Acrylic, photograph/canvas, Acryl, Foto/
Leinwand, Acrylique, photo/toile
130 × 89 cm
Franklin Bowles Galleries, San Francisco

72

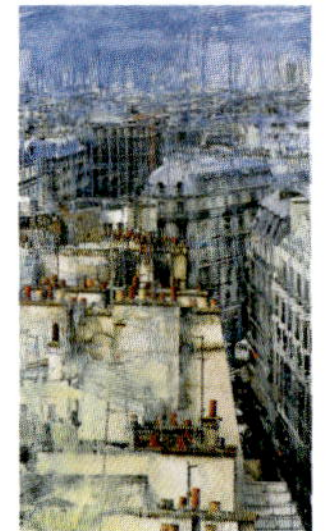

Paris, Chimneys | Paris, Die Kamine |
Paris, Les Cheminées, 2008

Acrylic, photograph/canvas, Acryl, Foto/
Leinwand, Acrylique, photo/toile
95 × 52 cm
Franklin Bowles Galleries, San Francisco

73

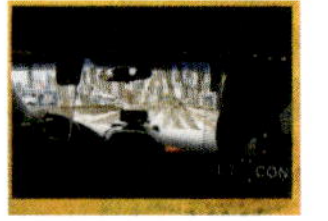

5E31 CON, 2009

Mixed media, photograph/canvas, Mischtechnik, Foto/Leinwand, Technique mixte,
photo/toile
60 × 81 cm
Private collection, Privatsammlung,
Collection privée

74/75

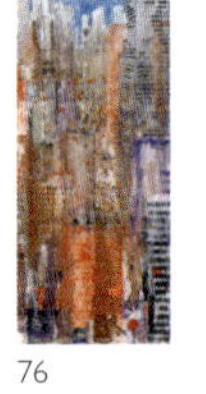

NY I, 2012

Watercolor, Aquarell, Aquarelle
74,3 × 29,3 cm

76

NY II, 2012

Watercolor, Aquarell, Aquarelle
76 × 28 cm

77

NY III, 2012

Watercolor, Aquarell, Aquarelle
75,8 × 28 cm

77

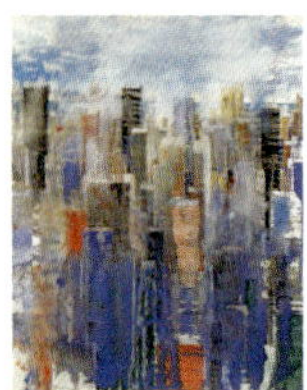

NY, Blue Red Green | NY, Blau Rot
Grün | NY, bleu rouge vert, 2010

Watercolor, Aquarell, Aquarelle
59,5 × 47,2 cm

78

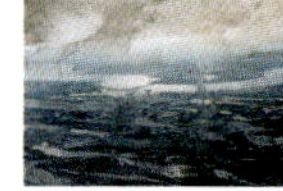

Hamburg over the Elbe | Hamburg
über der Elbe | Hambourg au-dessus
de l'Elbe, 1999

Mixed media, photograph, Mischtechnik, Foto,
Technique mixte, photo
50,5 × 75 cm

79

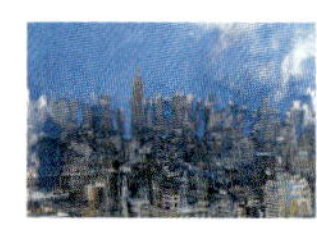

L'arche II, 2008

Mixed media, photograph, Mischtechnik,
Foto, Technique mixte, photo
51 × 38 cm
Franklin Bowles Galleries, San Francisco

80

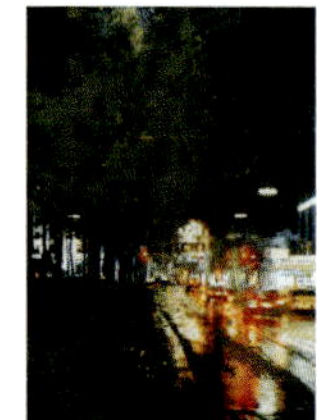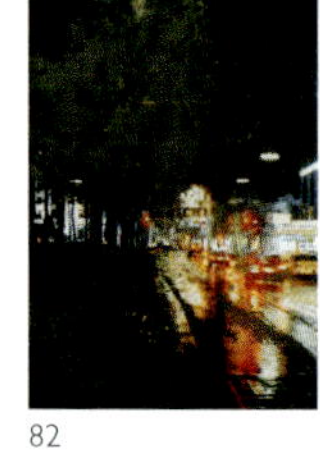

Liquid Sky | Flüssiger Himmel |
Ciel liquide, 2006

Mixed media, photograph, Mischtechnik,
Foto, Technique mixte, photo
50,6 × 75,3 cm
Franklin Bowles Galleries, New York

81

Hamburg by Night | Hamburg bei
Nacht | Hambourg la nuit, 2007

Mixed media, photograph, Mischtechnik,
Foto, Technique mixte, photo
46 × 30,5 cm

82

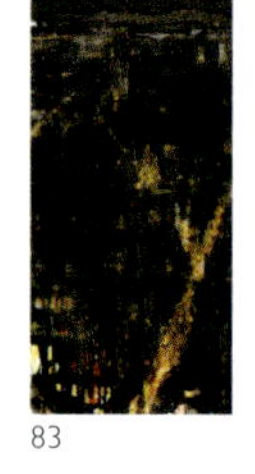

NY by Night | NY bei Nacht |
NY la nuit, 2004

Watercolor, Aquarell, Aquarelle
60 × 26 cm

83

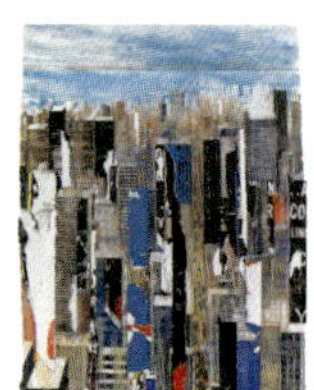

Yellow Buildings, 2009

Mixed media, photograph, Mischtechnik,
Foto, Technique mixte, photo
50,5 × 75,3 cm

84

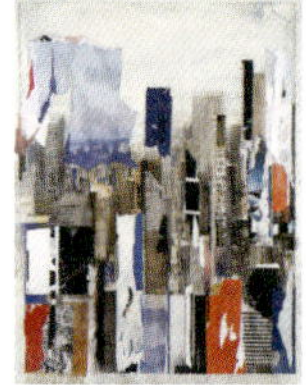

NY Aquacollage, 2011

Watercolor, collage, Aquarell, Collage,
Aquarelle, collage
76,8 × 59,2 cm

85

NY LM, 2012

Collage, watercolor/canvas, Collage,
Aquarell/Leinwand, Collage, aquarelle/toile
76 × 57,5 cm

85

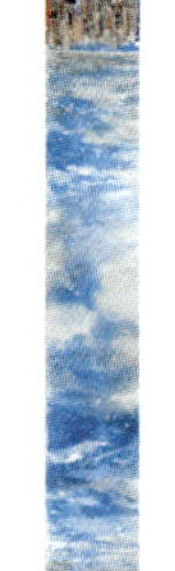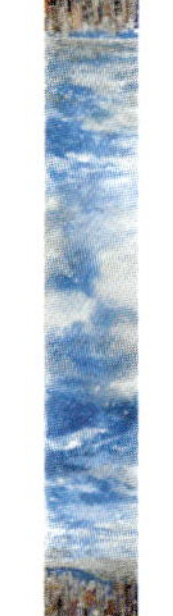

NY East River, 2006

Mixed media, photograph, Mischtechnik,
Foto, Technique mixte, photo
25,3 × 76 cm

86/87

Under the Sky | Unterm Himmel |
Sous le ciel, 2012

Watercolor/canvas, Aquarell/Leinwand,
Aquarelle/toile
500 × 75 cm
Private collection, Gottfried Salzmann,
Privatsammlung Gottfried Salzmann,
Collection privée Gottfried Salzmann

88

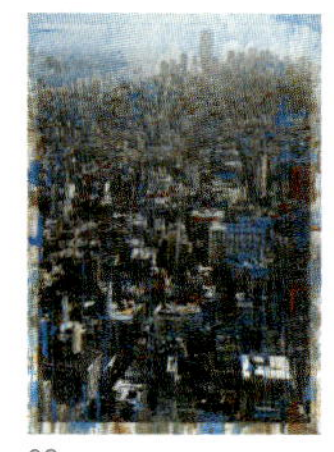

New York, Midtown I, 2001

Acrylic, b/w photograph/canvas, Acryl,
SW-Foto/Leinwand, Acrylique, photo noir
et blanc/toile
131 × 89 cm
Salzburg Museum, Salzburg, Salzbourg

89

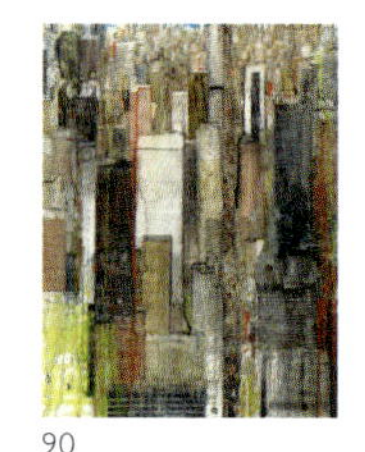

New York, Midtown II, 1995

Watercolor, Aquarell, Aquarelle
74,8 × 55,1 cm
Salzburg Museum, Salzburg, Salzbourg

90

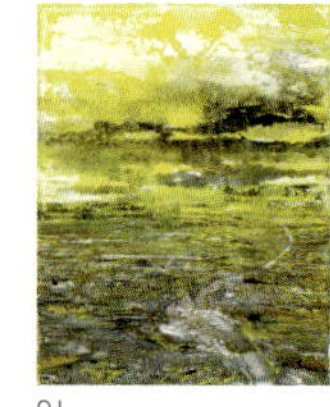

Salzburg from the Air | Salzburg
aus der Flugperspektive | Salzbourg,
perspective aérienne, 2004

Acrylic, photograph/canvas, Acryl, Foto/
Leinwand, Acrylique, photo/toile
124 × 94 cm
Salzburg Museum, Salzburg, Salzbourg

91

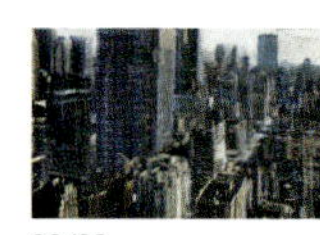

New York, 8th Avenue, 2006

Mixed media, photograph, Mischtechnik,
Foto, Technique mixte, photo
50,6 × 75,8 cm
Salzburg Museum, Salzburg, Salzbourg

92/93

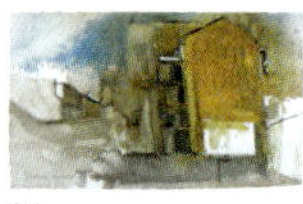

Lion noir, 1969

Watercolor, Aquarell, Aquarelle
30,5 × 49,2 cm
Private collection, Dr. Staindl, Salzburg,
Privatsammlung Dr. Staindl, Salzburg,
Collection privée Dr. Staindl, Salzburg

94

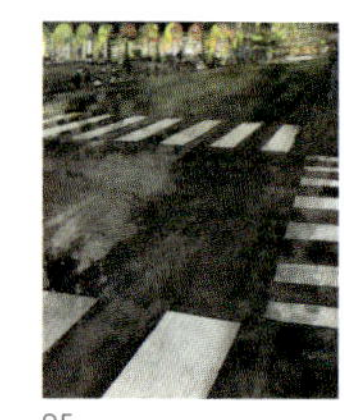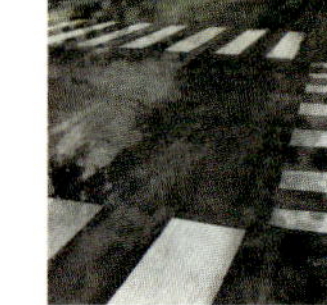

Crosswalk, Paris | Zebrastreifen Paris |
Passage piéton, Paris, 1999

Watercolor, Aquarell, Aquarelle
49,5 × 30,7 cm
Private collection, Dr. Biering, Vienna,
Privatsammlung Dr. Biering, Wien,
Collection privée Dr. Biering, Vienne

95

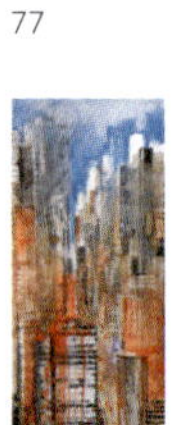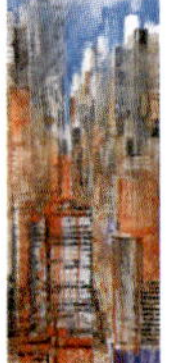

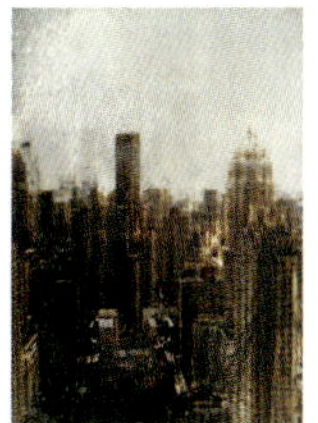

New York, Midtown III, 2006

Mixed media, photograph, Mischtechnik, Foto,
Technique mixte, photo
75,5 × 50,5 cm
Private collection, USA, Privatsammlung, USA,
Collection privée, USA

96

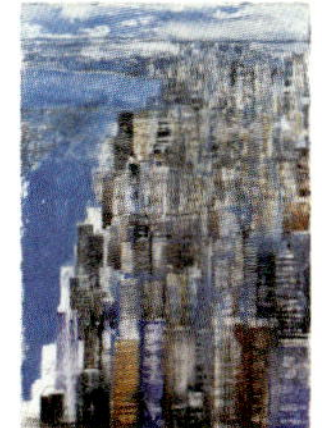

New York: Another Blue Day |
New York: Noch ein blauer Tag |
New York: encore un jour bleu, 2006

Watercolor, Aquarell, Aquarelle
109 × 73 cm
Private collection, USA, Privatsammlung, USA,
Collection privée, USA

97

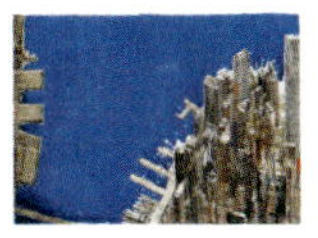

New York before September 11 |
New York vor dem 11. September |
New York avant le 11 septembre, 1998

Watercolor, Aquarell, Aquarelle
47 × 60 cm

98

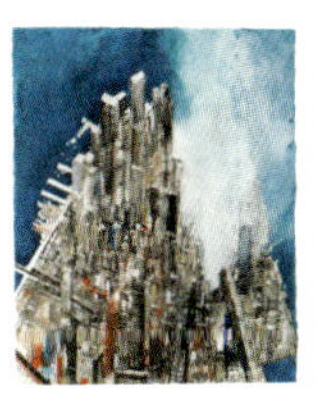

New York, September 11 |
New York 11. September |
New York 11 septembre, 2001

Watercolor, Aquarell, Aquarelle
90 × 72 cm
Strabag Kunstforum, Vienna, Wien, Vienne

99

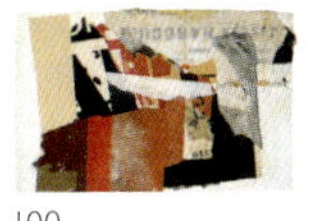

Hardouin, 1967

Collage
32,5 × 50 cm

100

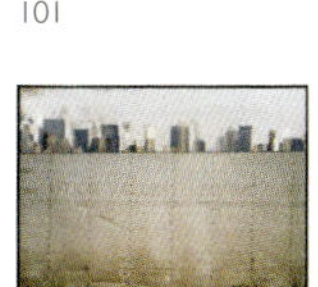

Bach, 1967

Collage
42,2 × 50 cm

101

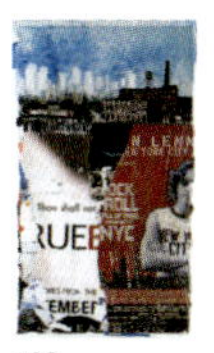

Utica, 2009

Mixed media, photograph/canvas,
Mischtechnik, Foto/Leinwand,
Technique mixte, photo/toile
118 × 131 cm

102

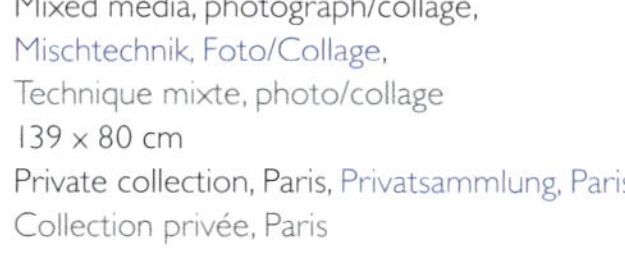

N Lenn, 2010

Mixed media, photograph/collage,
Mischtechnik, Foto/Collage,
Technique mixte, photo/collage
139 × 80 cm
Private collection, Paris, Privatsammlung, Paris,
Collection privée, Paris

103

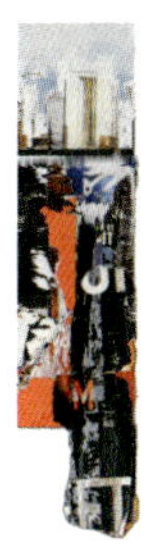

BY, 2011

Mixed media, photograph, collage/wood,
Mischtechnik, Foto, Collage/Holz,
Technique mixte, photo, collage/bois
106 × 29 cm

104

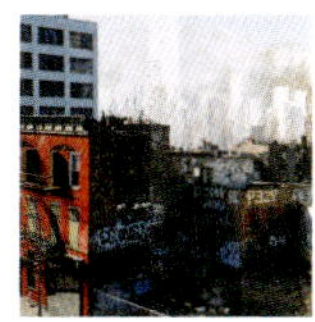

Pezy, 2010

Mixed media, photograph/canvas,
Mischtechnik, Foto/Leinwand,
Technique mixte, photo/toile
78 × 74 cm
Private collection, Alix Narbey, Paris,
Privatsammlung Alix Narbey, Paris,
Collection privée Alix Narbey, Paris

105

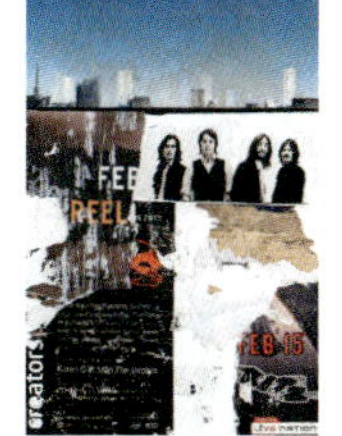

Creators February 15, 2012

Mixed media, photograph, collage/wood,
Mischtechnik, Foto, Collage/Holz,
Technique mixte, photo, collage/bois
81 × 54 cm
Franklin Bowles Galleries, New York

106

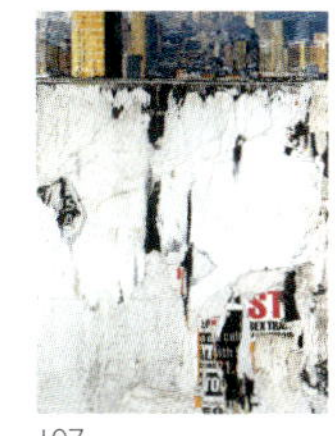

Sextra, 2011

Mixed media, photograph, collage/wood,
Mischtechnik, Foto, Collage/Holz,
Technique mixte, photo, collage/bois
162 × 114 cm

107

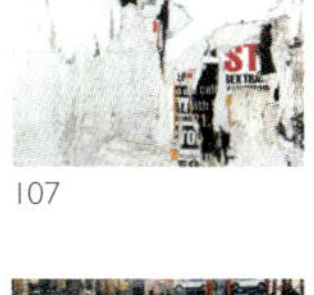

No Dumping, 2010

Mixed media, photograph, collage/wood,
Mischtechnik, Foto, Collage/Holz,
Technique mixte, photo, collage/bois
68 × 130 cm

108/109

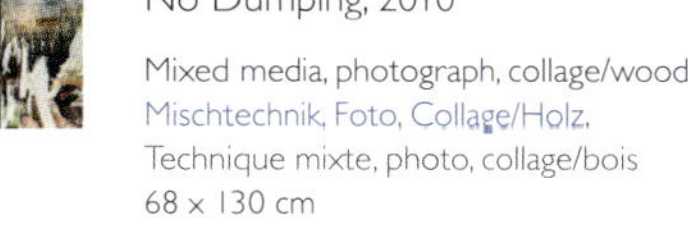

Feb 13, 6:30 pm (The Beatles), 2012

Mixed media, photograph, collage/wood,
Mischtechnik, Foto, Collage/Holz,
Technique mixte, photo, collage/bois
89 × 130 cm
Franklin Bowles Galleries, New York

110

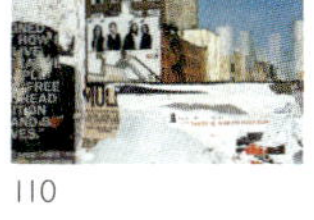

Day Dreaming | Tagträumerei |
Rêverie, 2012

Mixed media, photograph, collage/canvas,
Mischtechnik, Foto, Collage/Leinwand,
Technique mixte, photo, collage/toile
89 × 130 cm

111

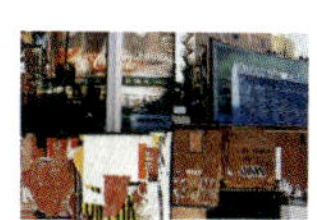

Vienna, Restmüll | Wien, Restmüll |
Vienne, Restmüll, 2009

Mixed media, photograph, collage/canvas,
Mischtechnik, Foto, Collage/Leinwand,
Technique mixte, photo, collage/toile
57 × 178 cm

112/113

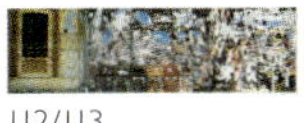

Are You Ready ?, 2011

Mixed media, photograph, collage/wood,
Mischtechnik, Foto, Collage/Holz,
Technique mixte, photo, collage/bois
162 × 97 cm

114

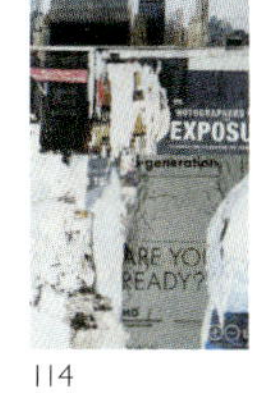

Sex Scandal, 2010

Mixed media, photograph, collage/wood,
Mischtechnik, Foto, Collage/Holz,
Technique mixte, photo, collage/bois
116 × 73 cm

115

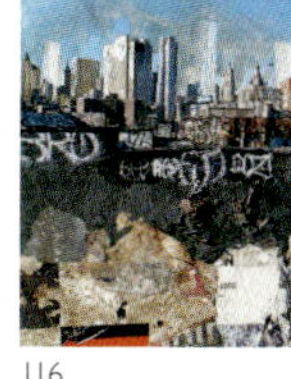

6500, 2011

Mixed media, photograph, collage/wood,
Mischtechnik, Foto, Collage/Holz,
Technique mixte, photo, collage/bois
65 × 50 cm

116

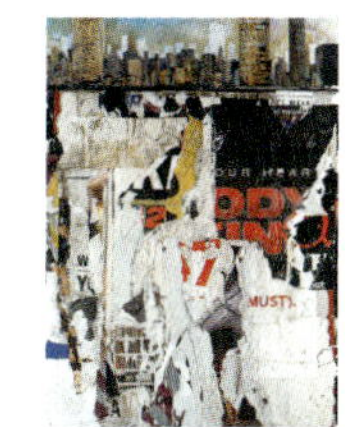

Must, 2010

Mixed media, photograph, collage/wood,
Mischtechnik, Foto, Collage/Holz,
Technique mixte, photo, collage/bois
162 × 114 cm

117

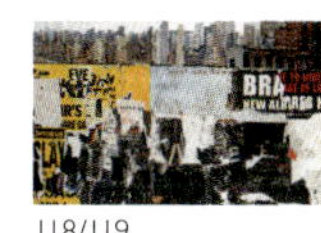

Must See, 2010

Mixed media, photograph, collage/wood,
Mischtechnik, Foto, Collage/Holz,
Technique mixte, photo, collage/bois
124 × 187 cm

118/119

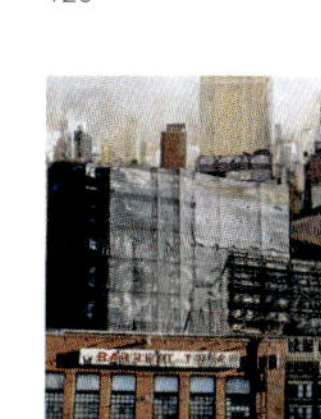

Open Sesame, 2010

Mixed media, photograph, collage/wood,
Mischtechnik, Foto, Collage/Holz,
Technique mixte, photo, collage/bois
110 × 95 cm

120

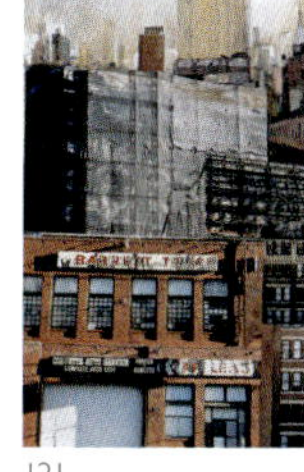

Corvette Auto Service, 2010

Mixed media, photograph/canvas,
Mischtechnik, Foto/Leinwand,
Technique mixte, photo/toile
130 × 81 cm

121

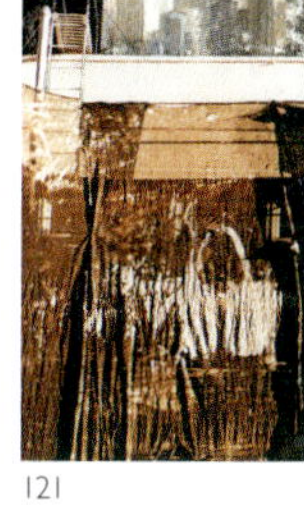

SF Protection Cover I |
SF Schutzplane I | SF La Bâche I, 2010

Mixed media, photograph/canvas,
Mischtechnik, Foto/Leinwand,
Technique mixte, photo/toile
46,8 × 27 cm

121

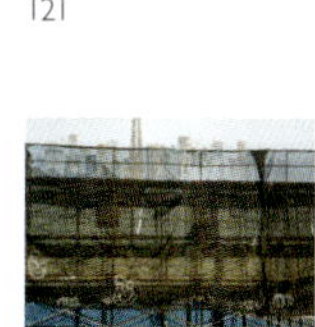

SF Protection Cover II |
SF Schutzplane II | SF La Bâche II, 2011

Mixed media, photograph/canvas,
Mischtechnik, Foto/Leinwand,
Technique mixte, photo/toile
89 × 130 cm

121

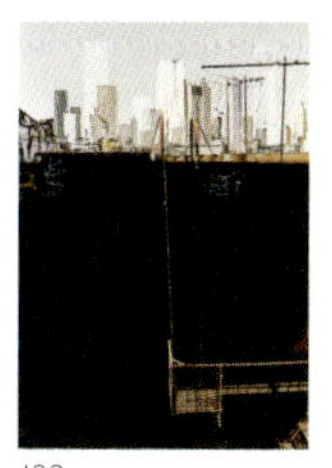

The Ladder | Die Leiter | l'échelle,
2011

Mixed media, photograph/canvas,
Mischtechnik, Foto/Leinwand,
Technique mixte, photo/toile
81 × 54 cm

122

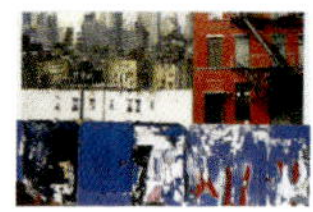

NO PARKING, 2009

Mixed media, photograph/canvas,
Mischtechnik, Foto/Leinwand,
Technique, photo/toile
89 × 130 cm
Galerie für zeitgenössische Kunst, Munich,
München, Munich

123

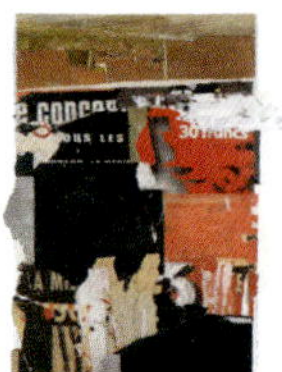
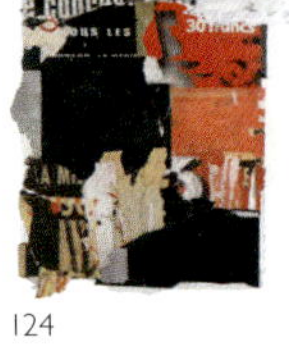

30 Francs, 1976

Collage/watercolor, Collage/Aquarell,
Collage/aquarelle
79,4 × 57,5 cm

124

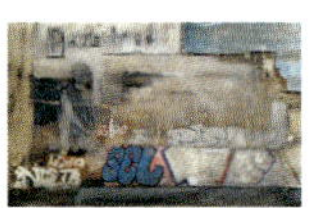

Vente sur saisie (Le trou des Halles),
1978

Collage/watercolor, Collage/Aquarell,
Collage/aquarelle
43,7 × 48,8 cm
Private collection, Nicole Bottet, Paris,
Privatsammlung Nicole Bottet, Paris,
Collection privée Nicole Bottet, Paris

125

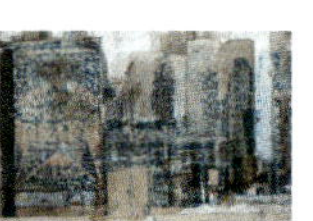

Berlin Wall "Sel" | Berliner Mauer
„Sel" | Mur de Berlin « Sel », 1994

Watercolor, Aquarell, Aquarelle
30 × 47,5 cm

126

Premium, 2006

Mixed media, photograph, Mischtechnik,
Foto, Technique mixte, photo
30,5 × 46,2 cm
Private collection, Nicole Bottet, Paris,
Privatsammlung Nicole Bottet, Paris,
Collection privée Nicole Bottet, Paris

126

Ausländer „innen" bleiben, 1995

Watercolor/canvas, Aquarell/Leinwand,
Aquarelle/toile
72,4 × 99 cm

127

Berlin, 1995

Watercolor, Aquarell, Aquarelle
47,4 × 30,5 cm
Private collection, Nicole Bottet, Paris,
Privatsammlung Nicole Bottet, Paris,
Collection privée Nicole Bottet, Paris

128

Sexmal, 1996

Watercolor, acrylic/canvas, Aquarell, Acryl/
Leinwand, Aquarelle, acrylique/toile
72,5 × 115,7 cm
Salzburg Museum, Salzburg, Salzbourg

129

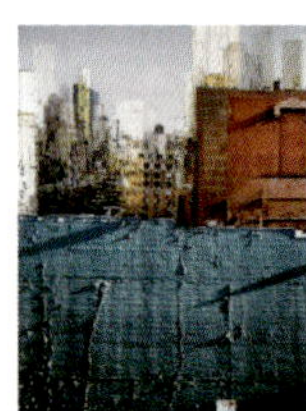

SF Green Wall | SF Grüne Mauer |
SF Mur vert, 2010

Mixed media, photograph/canvas,
Mischtechnik, Foto/Leinwand,
Technique mixte, photo/toile
81 × 60 cm
Franklin Bowles Galleries, San Francisco

130

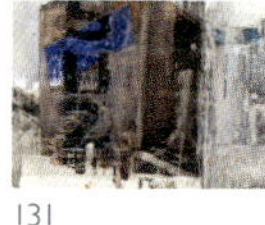

Suze, 1991

Watercolor, Aquarell, Aquarelle
33 × 50 cm
Private collection, Gottfried Salzmann,
Privatsammlung Gottfried Salzmann,
Collection privée Gottfried Salzmann

131

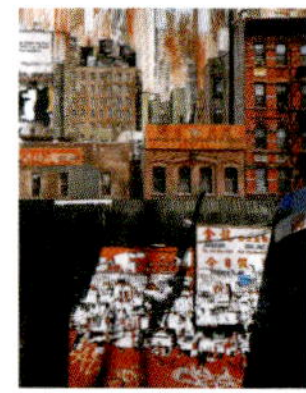

New York, Chinatown, 2010

Mixed media, photograph, collage/canvas,
Mischtechnik, Foto, Collage/Leinwand,
Technique mixte, photo, collage/toile
169 × 128 cm
Private collection, Hong Kong,
Privatsammlung, Hongkong,
Collection privée, Hong Kong

132

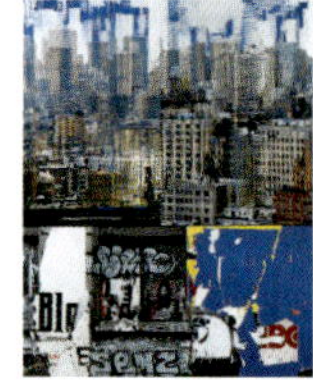

Rich girls will take your heart,
Poor girls will take your money, 2010

Mixed media, photograph, collage/canvas,
Mischtechnik, Foto, Collage/Leinwand,
Technique mixte, photo, collage/toile
134 × 104 cm
Private collection, New York, Privatsammlung,
New York, Collection privée, New York

133

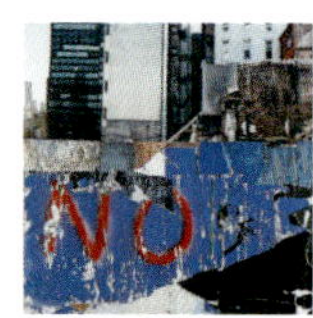

NO, 2011

Mixed media, photograph, collage/wood,
Mischtechnik, Foto, Collage/Holz,
Technique mixte, photo, collage/bois
90 × 90 cm

134

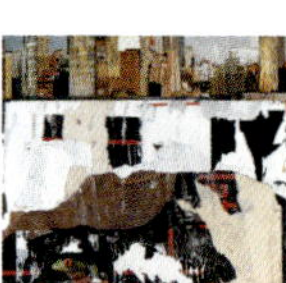

Manipulation, You are observed, 2012

Mixed media, photograph, collage/wood,
Mischtechnik, Foto, Collage/Holz,
Technique mixte, photo, collage/bois
92 × 65 cm

135

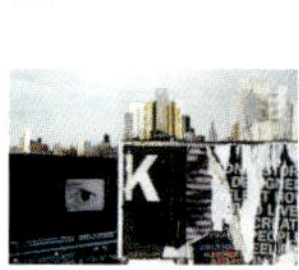

"K" You are observed | „K" You are
observed | « K » You are observed,
2012

Mixed media, photograph, collage/wood,
Mischtechnik, Foto, Collage/Holz,
Technique mixte, photo, collage/bois
81 × 116 cm

136/137

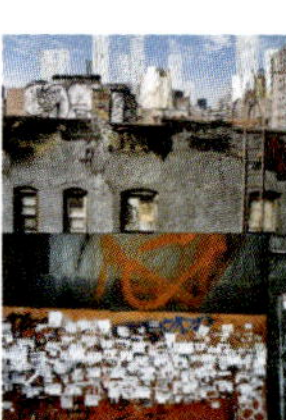

Love me, 2010

Mixed media, photograph, acrylic/canvas,
Mischtechnik, Foto, Acryl/Leinwand,
Technique mixte, photo, acrylique/toile
110 × 83 cm
Franklin Bowles Galleries, New York

138

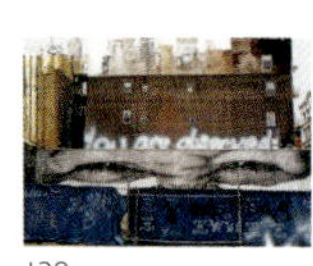

You are observed I, 2012

Mixed media, photograph/canvas,
Mischtechnik, Foto/Leinwand,
Technique mixte, photo/toile
97 × 130 cm

139

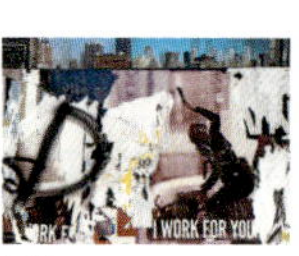

I work for you II, 2012

Mixed media, photograph, collage/wood,
Mischtechnik, Foto, Collage/Holz,
Technique mixte, photo, collage/bois
114 × 162 cm

140

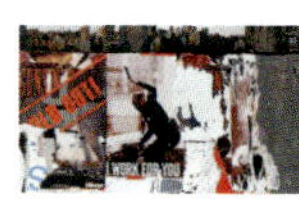

I work for you I, 2012

Mixed media, photograph, collage/wood,
Mischtechnik, Foto, Collage/Holz,
Technique mixte, photo, collage/bois
114 × 195 cm

140

For you, 2012

Mixed media, photograph, collage/wood,
Mischtechnik, Foto, Collage/Holz,
Technique mixte, photo, collage/bois
195 × 114 cm

141

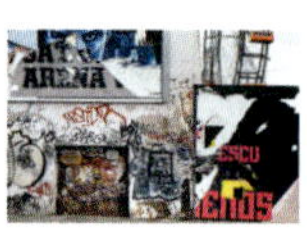

Vienna, Arena | Wien, Arena |
Vienne, Arena, 2010

Mixed media, photograph, collage/wood,
Mischtechnik, Foto, Collage/Holz,
Technique mixte, photo, collage/bois
54 × 81 cm

142

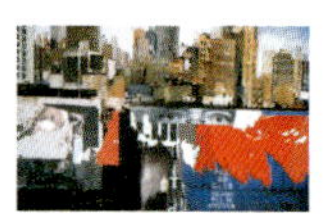

You are observed II, 2012

Mixed media, photograph, collage/wood,
Mischtechnik, Foto, Collage/Holz,
Technique mixte, photo, collage/bois
73 × 116 cm

143

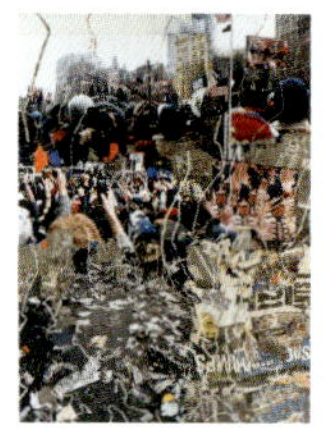

Superbowl I, 2008

Mixed media, photograph, collage/canvas,
Mischtechnik, Foto, Collage/Leinwand,
Technique mixte, photo, collage/toile
162 × 114 cm
Franklin Bowles Galleries, New York

144

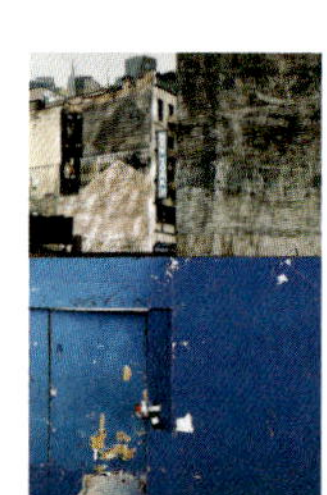

The Message, 2009

Mixed media, photograph, collage/canvas,
Mischtechnik, Foto, Collage/Leinwand,
Technique mixte, photo, collage/toile
162 × 114 cm
Franklin Bowles Galleries, New York

145

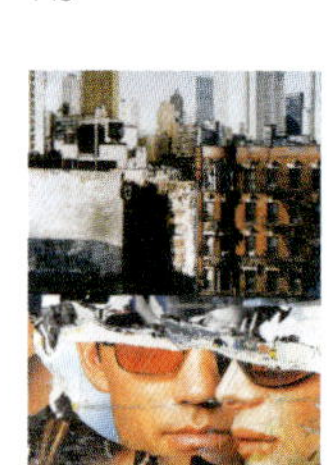

A Passionate World, 2010

Mixed media, photograph, collage/wood,
Mischtechnik, Foto, Collage/Holz,
Technique mixte, photo, collage/bois
130 × 89 cm
Private collection, USA, Privatsammlung, USA,
Collection privée, USA

146

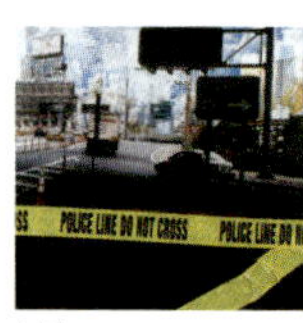

Police Line, 2010

Mixed media, photograph, collage/canvas,
Mischtechnik, Foto, Collage/Leinwand,
Technique mixte, photo, collage/toile
80 × 80 cm
Franklin Bowles Galleries, New York

147

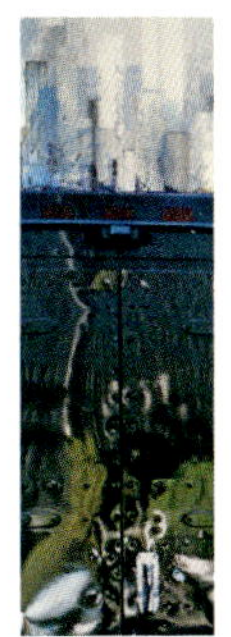

SF Reflection | SF Spiegelung | SF reflet, 2010

Mixed media, photograph/canvas, Mischtechnik, Foto/Leinwand, Technique mixte, phototoile
86 × 29,5 cm

148

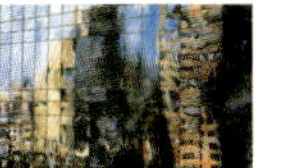

Aerial Reflection, 2010

Watercolor, Aquarell, Aquarelle
40 × 57 cm

149

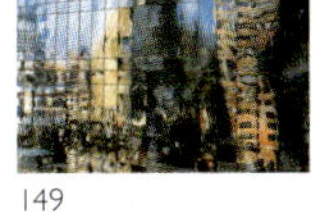

Central Park Reflection | Central Park, Spiegelung | Central Park, reflet, 2010

Watercolor/canvas, Aquarell/Leinwand, Aquarelle/toile
100 × 68 cm

150

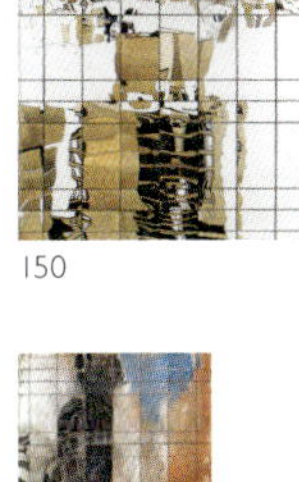

Red Building Reflection, 2009

Watercolor, Aquarell, Aquarelle
68,4 × 26,3 cm

151

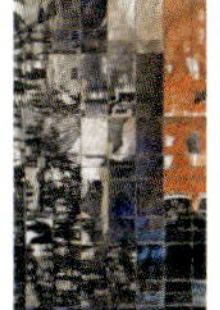

Vienna, Saint Stephen's Cathedral – Reflection | Wien, Stephansdom – Spiegelung | Vienne, Saint-Étienne – reflet, 2008

Watercolor, Aquarell, Aquarelle
62,5 × 15,3 cm (3 ×), triptych | Triptychon | triptyque

152

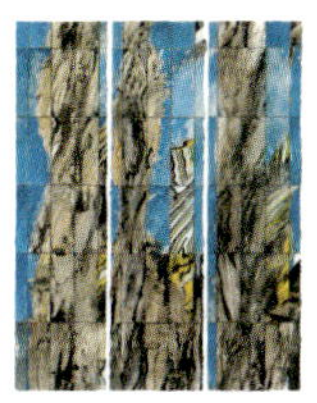

Reflection 7th Avenue | Spiegelung 7th Avenue | Reflet 7th Avenue, 2012

Watercolor, Aquarell, Aquarelle
64,8 × 50,8 cm

153

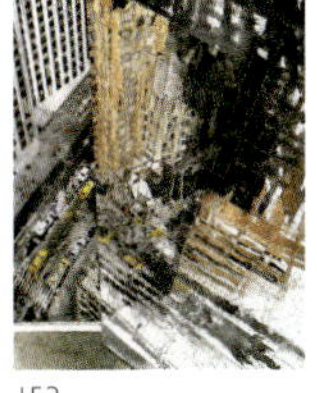

NY Reflection, 2009

Watercolor, Aquarell, Aquarelle
46,8 × 29,5 cm

154

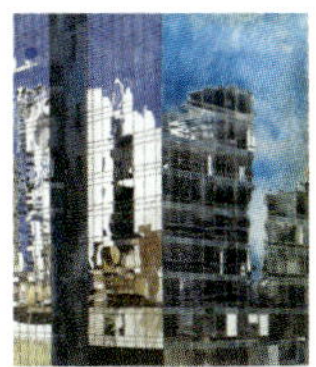

NY Aerial Reflection II, 2010

Watercolor, Aquarell, Aquarelle
62,3 × 50,3 cm

155

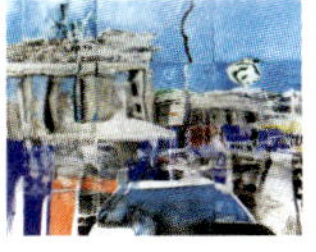

Berlin, Brandenburg Gate – Reflection | Berlin, Brandenburger Tor – Spiegelung | Berlin, Porte de Brandenbourg – reflet, 1997

155

Watercolor, Aquarell, Aquarelle
47 × 59,5 cm
Private collection, Dr. Biering, Vienna, Privatsammlung Dr. Biering, Wien, Collection privée Dr. Biering, Vienne

Stairs, Place Vendôme | Treppen, Place Vendôme | Escaliers, Place Vendôme, 2010

Watercolor, Aquarell, Aquarelle
73 × 26,7 cm

156

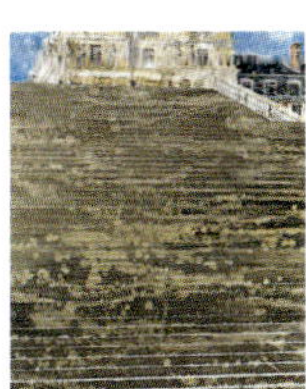

Stairs at Versailles I | Treppen in Versailles I | Escaliers à Versailles I, 2010

Watercolor, Aquarell, Aquarelle
64,8 × 50 cm

157

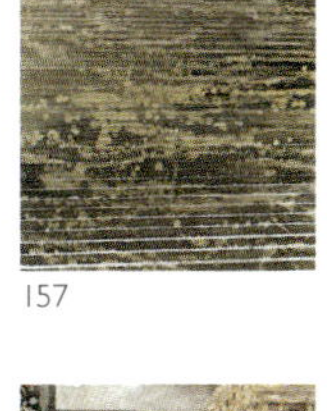

Shadow on the Steps at Versailles | Schatten auf den Treppen in Versailles | Ombres sur les escaliers à Versailles, 2010

Watercolor, Aquarell, Aquarelle
47,7 × 30,4 cm

157

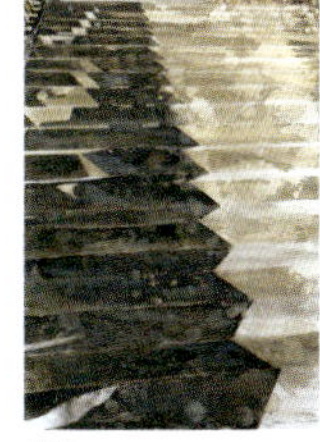

Steps (Broadway) | Treppen (Broadway) | Escaliers (Broadway), 2009

Mixed media, photograph/canvas, Mischtechnik, Foto/Leinwand, Technique mixte, photo/toile
101 × 76 cm

158

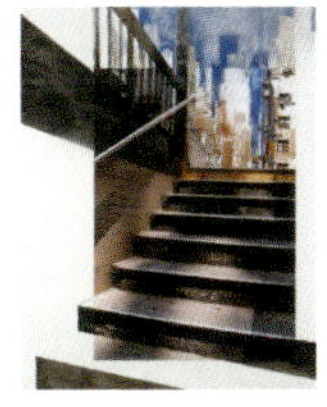

White Jalousie | Weiße Jalousie | Store blanc, 1983

Pencil, watercolor, Bleistift, Aquarell, Crayon, Aquarelle
77,5 × 57 cm
Salzburg Museum, Salzburg, Salzbourg

158

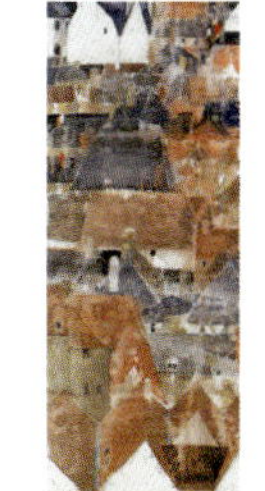

Store ou ciel, 1981

Watercolor, Aquarell, Aquarelle
99,7 × 70,8 cm
Salzburg Museum, Salzburg, Salzbourg

159

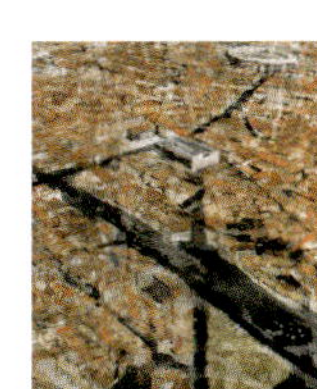

The Rooftops of Chartres | Die Dächer von Chartres | Les toits de Chartres, 2010

Watercolor, Aquarell, Aquarelle
75,4 × 29,5 cm
Galerie Arcturus, Paris

160

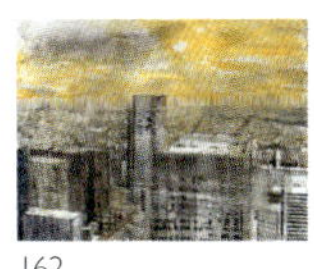

Nîmes, La Maison Carrée, 2007

Watercolor, Aquarell, Aquarelle
74 × 61 cm
Franklin Bowles Galleries, New York

161

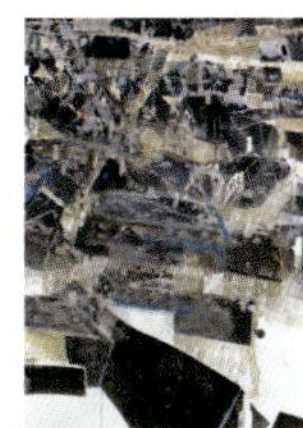

Paris La Défense, 2008

Watercolor, Aquarell, Aquarelle
47 × 59,5 cm

162

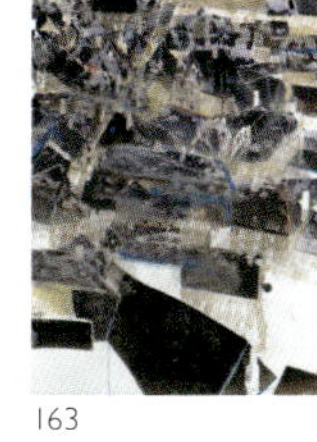

La grande Turenne, 2008

Watercolor, Aquarell, Aquarelle
107,8 × 73,4 cm

163

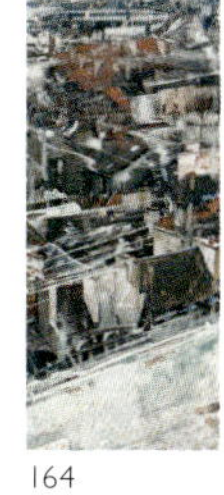

Dijon, 2006

Mixed media, photograph, Mischtechnik, Foto, Technique mixte, photo
74,4 × 28,3 cm

164

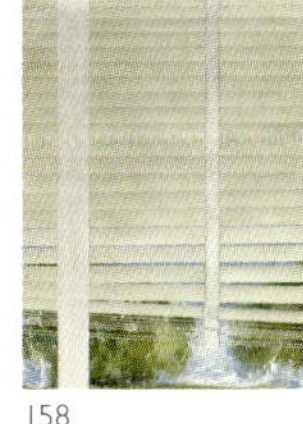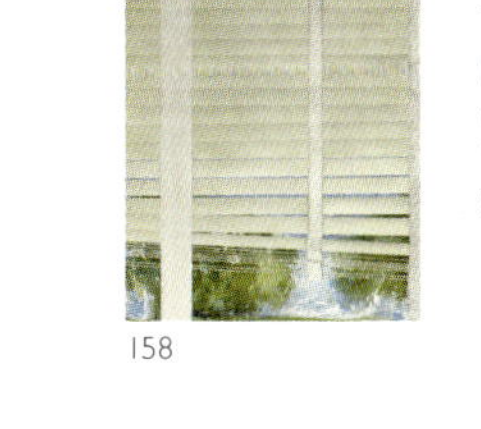

Nice, 2008

Mixed media, photograph, Mischtechnik, Foto, Technique mixte, photo
50,5 × 14,9 cm

164

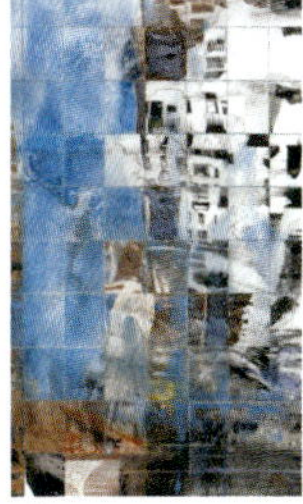

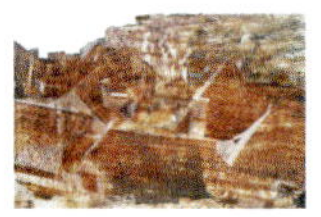
The Rooftops of Beaune |
Die Dächer von Beaune |
Les toits de Beaune, 2004

Mixed media, photograph, Mischtechnik,
Foto, Technique mixte, photo
50,6 (39,2) × 75,3 cm

165

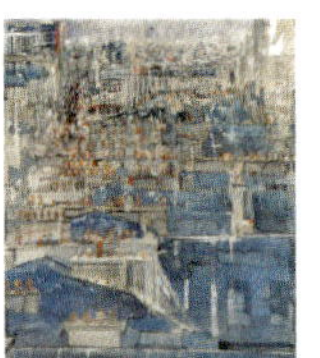
Paris, Rue du Renard, 1993

Watercolor, Aquarell, Aquarelle
63,7 × 49,5 cm
Private collection, Paris, Privatsammlung Paris,
Collection privée, Paris

166

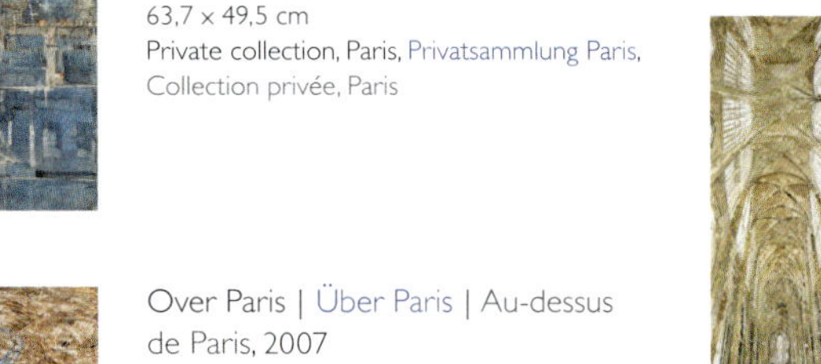
Over Paris | Über Paris | Au-dessus
de Paris, 2007

Watercolor, Aquarell, Aquarelle
60,1 × 47,8 cm
Private collection, USA, Privatsammlung USA,
Collection privée, USA

167

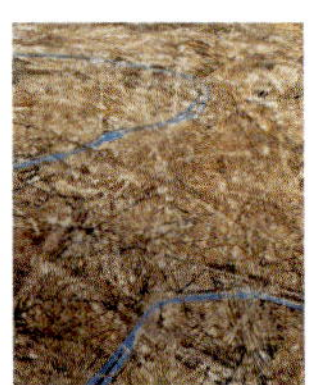

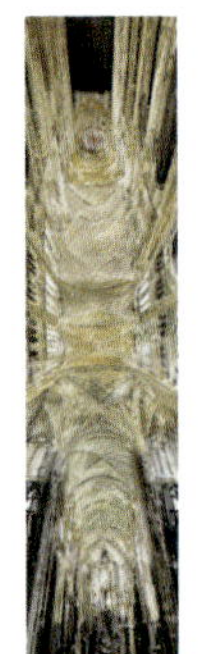
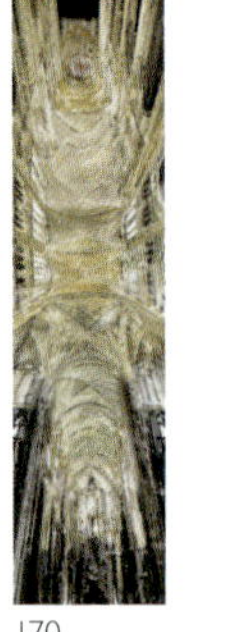
The Cathedral | Die Kathedrale |
La Cathédrale, 2012

Watercolor, Aquarell, Aquarelle
225,3 × 52 cm

170

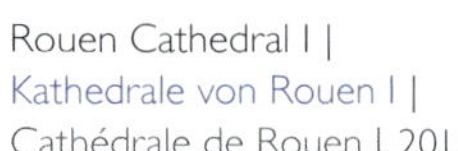
Rouen Cathedral I |
Kathedrale von Rouen I |
Cathédrale de Rouen I, 2011

Watercolor, Aquarell, Aquarelle
92 × 63,3 cm
Franklin Bowles Galleries, New York

171

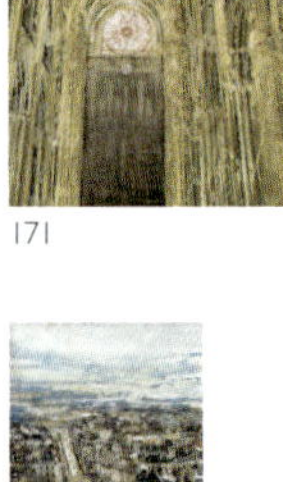
Roof of the Bourges Cathedral |
Dach der Kathedrale von Bourges |
Toit de la Cathédrale de Bourges, 2010

Watercolor, Aquarell, Aquarelle
68,5 × 26,3 cm

172

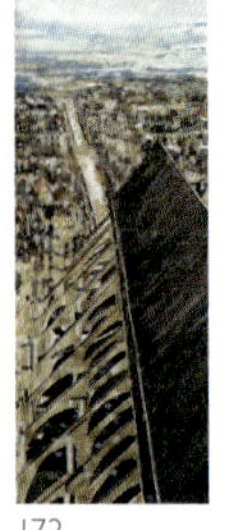
Vienna, Saint Stephen's |
Wien, Stephansdom |
Vienne, Saint-Étienne, 2010

Watercolor, Aquarell, Aquarelle
48,9 × 30,7 cm

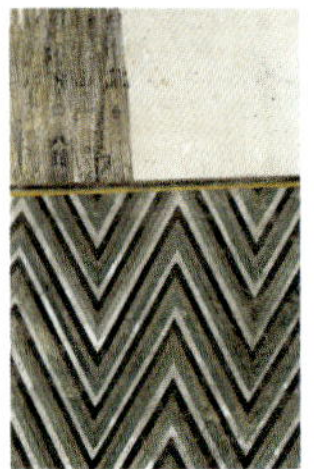

173

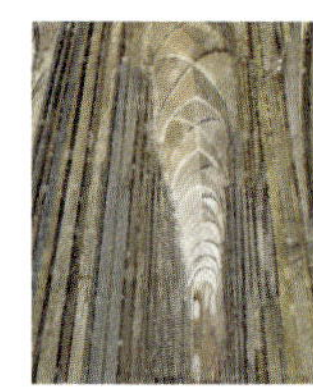
Bourges Cathedral I |
Kathedrale von Bourges I |
Cathédrale de Bourges I, 2010

Watercolor, Aquarell, Aquarelle
61 × 48 cm

174

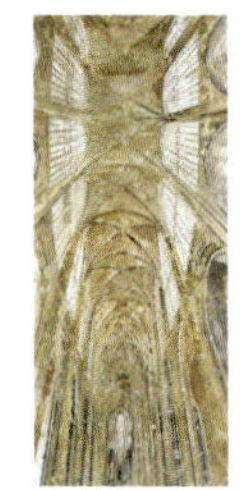
Bourges Cathedral II |
Kathedrale von Bourges II |
Cathédrale de Bourges II, 2012

Watercolor, Aquarell, Aquarelle
151 × 61 cm

175

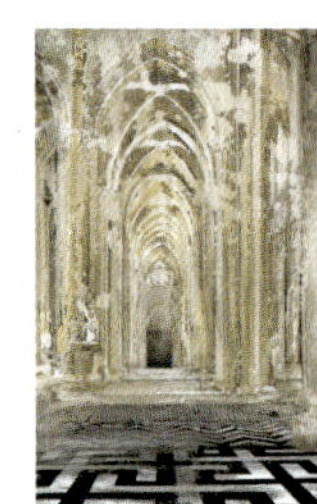
Amiens Cathedral |
Kathedrale von Amiens |
Cathédrale d'Amiens, 2012

Watercolor, Aquarell, Aquarelle
75,8 × 42,9 cm
Franklin Bowles Galleries, New York

176

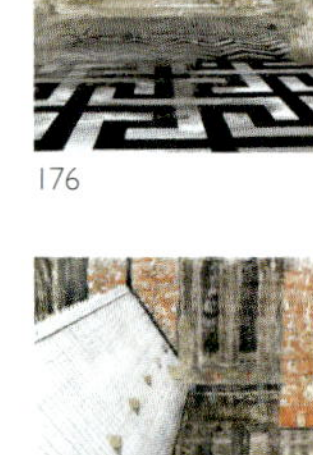
Clermont-Ferrand Cathedral |
Kathedrale von Clermont-Ferrand |
Cathédrale de Clermont-Ferrand,
2010

Watercolor, Aquarell, Aquarelle
70,5 × 50 cm

177

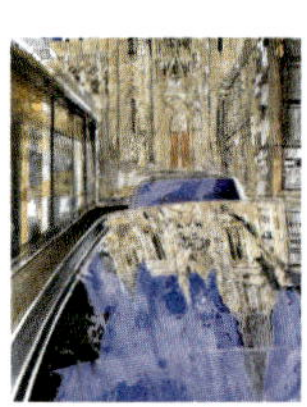
Rouen Cathedral, Reflection I |
Kathedrale von Rouen, Spiegelung I |
Cathédrale de Rouen, reflet I, 2012

Watercolor, Aquarell, Aquarelle
64,8 × 50,9 cm

178

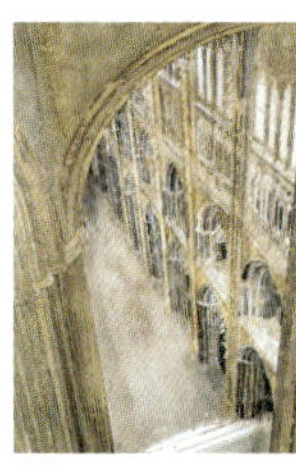
Rouen Cathedral II |
Kathedrale von Rouen II |
Cathédrale de Rouen II, 2012

Watercolor, Aquarell, Aquarelle
70 × 49,6 cm

179

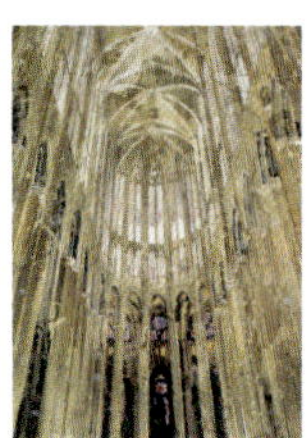
Beauvais Cathedral II |
Kathedrale von Beauvais II |
Cathédrale de Beauvais II, 2012

Watercolor, Aquarell, Aquarelle
75,8 × 55 cm
Franklin Bowles Galleries, New York

180

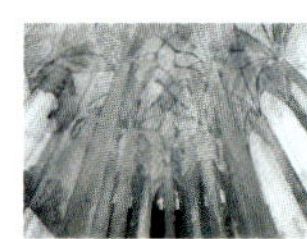
Salzburg, Church of Saint Francis |
Salzburg, Franziskanerkirche |
Salzbourg, église des Franciscains, 2012

Watercolor, Aquarell, Aquarelle
50,5 × 80 cm
Galerie Welz, Salzburg, Salzbourg

181

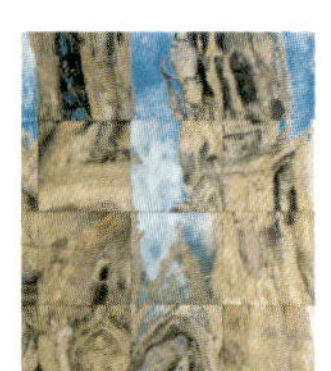
Rouen Cathedral, Reflection II |
Kathedrale von Rouen, Spiegelung II |
Cathédrale de Rouen, reflet II, 1997

Watercolor, Aquarell, Aquarelle
59,5 × 47,3 cm
Private collection, Gottfried Salzmann,
Privatsammlung Gottfried Salzmann,
Collection privée Gottfried Salzmann

182

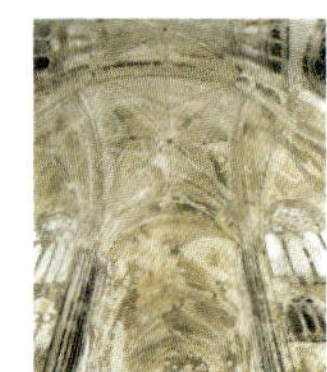
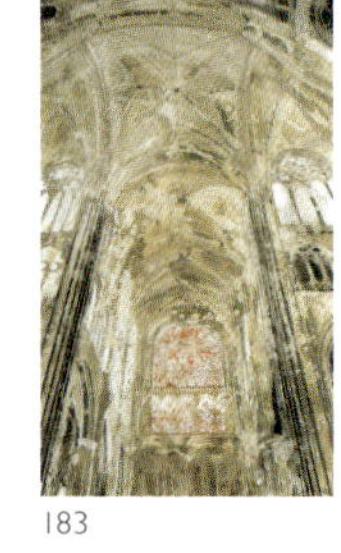
La Rosette, 2012

Watercolor, Aquarell, Aquarelle
110 × 59,4 cm
Franklin Bowles Galleries, New York

183

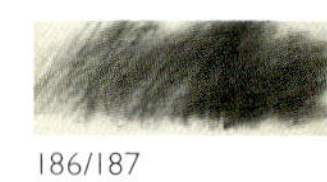
Curtain of Trees I | Baumvorhang I |
Rideau d'arbres I, 1978

Charcoal/paper, Kohle/Papier, Fusain/papier
26,2 × 65,3 cm
Salzburg Museum, Salzburg, Salzbourg

186/187

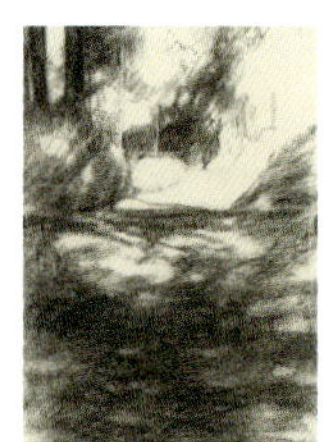
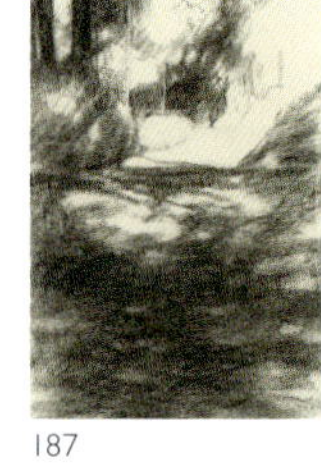
Patches of Light I | Lichtflecken I |
Taches de lumière I, 1991

Charcoal, Kohle, Fusain
49,9 × 32,6 cm
Salzburg Museum, Salzburg, Salzbourg

187

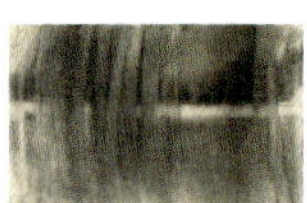
Patches of Light II | Lichtflecken II |
Taches de lumière II, 1981

Charcoal, Kohle, Fusain
65,3 × 100 cm
Salzburg Museum, Salzburg, Salzbourg

188

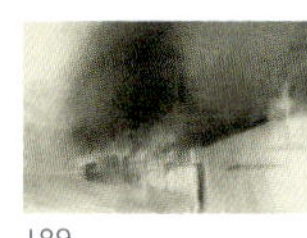
Bordered Trees | Begrenzte Bäume |
Rangées d'arbres, 1980

Charcoal, wiped/paper, Kohle, gewischt/Papier,
Fusain, lavis/papier
65 × 99 cm
Salzburg Museum, Salzburg, Salzbourg

189

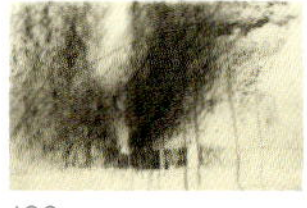
Allee | Allee | Allée, 1981

Charcoal, Kohle, Fusain
33 × 50 cm
Private collection, Dr. Staindl, Salzburg,
Privatsammlung Dr. Staindl, Salzburg,
Collection privée Dr. Staindl, Salzbourg

190

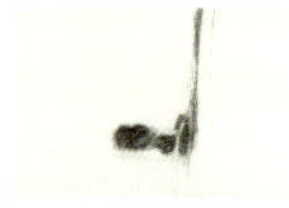
Contrasts | Kontraste | Contrastes,
1980

Charcoal/paper, Kohle/Papier, Fusain/papier
32,5 × 50,1 cm
Salzburg Museum, Salzburg, Salzbourg

191

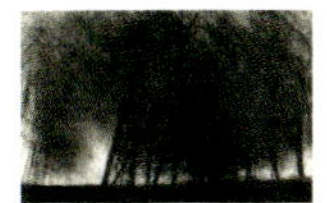

Trees | Bäume | Arbres, 1987

Etching, Radierung, Eau-forte
80 × 119,5 cm
Print | Druck | Taille doucier : Kurt Zein,
Vienna | Wien | Vienne
30 copies | Exemplare | exemplaires

194

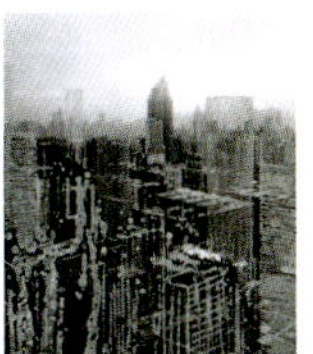

Silver Buildings, 2011

Photeauforte
65 × 50 cm
Print & Edition | Druck & Edition |
Taille doucier & Édition : R.L.D. Paris
40 copies | Exemplare | exemplaires

195

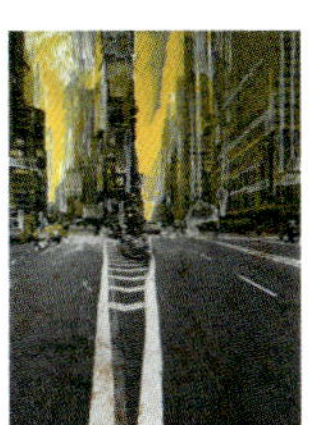

Yellow Times Square | Gelber Times
Square | Times Square jaune, 2005

Photeauforte
73,5 × 49,3 cm
Print | Druck | Taille doucier : R.L.D. Paris,
Edition | Edition | Édition : Verlag Galerie
Peerlings, Krefeld
49 copies | Exemplare | exemplaires

196

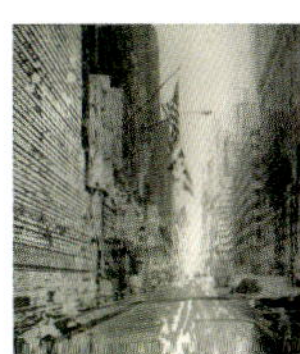

Local Track Route, 2003

Photeauforte
28 × 21 cm
Print | Druck | Taille doucier : R.L.D. Paris
10 copies | Exemplare | exemplaires

197

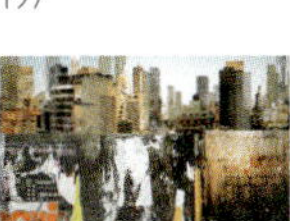

Deep Throat, 2012

Photeauforte
50 × 75 cm
Print | Druck | Taille doucier : R.L.D. Paris,
Edition | Edition | Édition : Verlag Galerie
Peerlings, Krefeld
49 copies | Exemplare | exemplaires

198

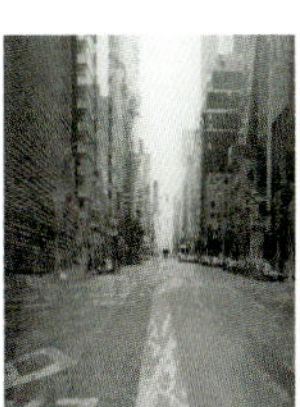

New York: Bus and Fire Lane, 2004

Photeauforte
51 × 35 cm
Print | Druck | Taille doucier : R.L.D. Paris
6 copies | Exemplare | exemplaires

199

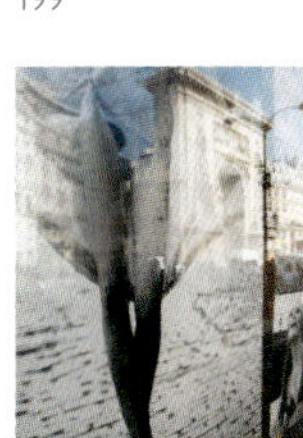

Rue Saint-Denis, 2011

C-Print
Private collection, Gottfried Salzmann,
Privatsammlung Gottfried Salzmann,
Collection privée Gottfried Salzmann

202

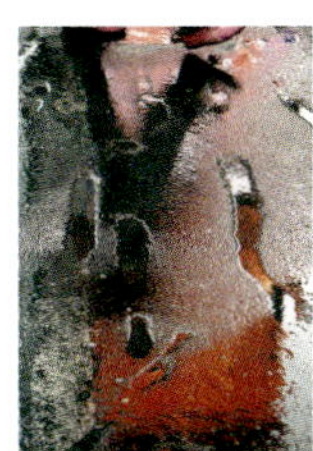

Times Square I, 2009

C-Print
Private collection, Gottfried Salzmann,
Privatsammlung Gottfried Salzmann,
Collection privée Gottfried Salzmann

202

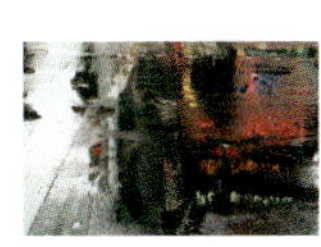

Times Square II, 2009

C-Print
Private collection, Gottfried Salzmann,
Privatsammlung Gottfried Salzmann,
Collection privée Gottfried Salzmann

203

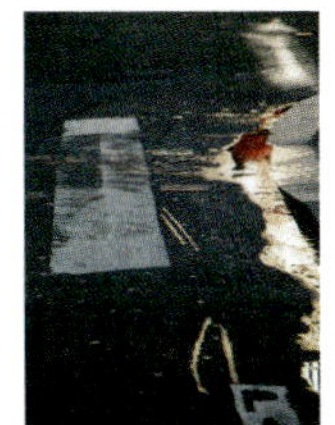

Times Square III, 2009

C-Print
Private collection, Gottfried Salzmann,
Privatsammlung Gottfried Salzmann,
Collection privée Gottfried Salzmann

204

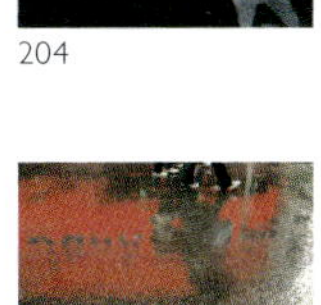

Times Square IV, 2009

C-Print
Private collection, Gottfried Salzmann,
Privatsammlung Gottfried Salzmann,
Collection privée Gottfried Salzmann

205

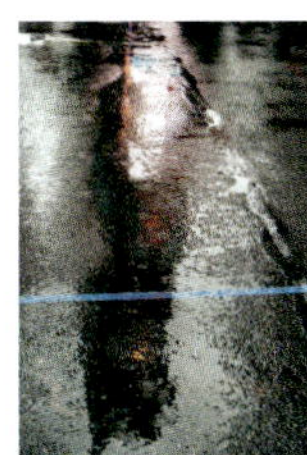

Times Square V, 2009

C-Print
Private collection, Gottfried Salzmann,
Privatsammlung Gottfried Salzmann,
Collection privée Gottfried Salzmann

206

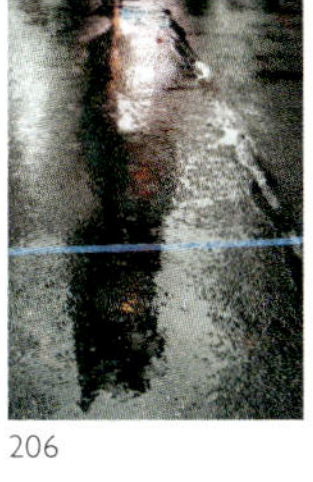

Times Square VI, 2009

C-Print
Private collection, Gottfried Salzmann,
Privatsammlung Gottfried Salzmann,
Collection privée Gottfried Salzmann

207

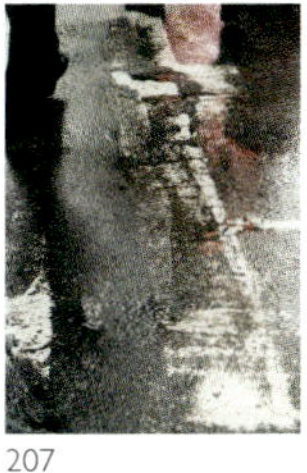

Times Square VII, 2009

C-Print
Private collection, Gottfried Salzmann,
Privatsammlung Gottfried Salzmann,
Collection privée Gottfried Salzmann

208

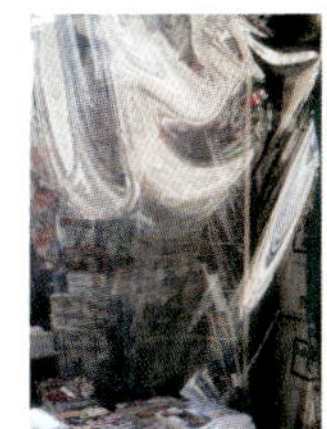

Boulevard Bonne Nouvelle, 2011

C-Print
Private collection, Gottfried Salzmann,
Privatsammlung Gottfried Salzmann,
Collection privée Gottfried Salzmann

209

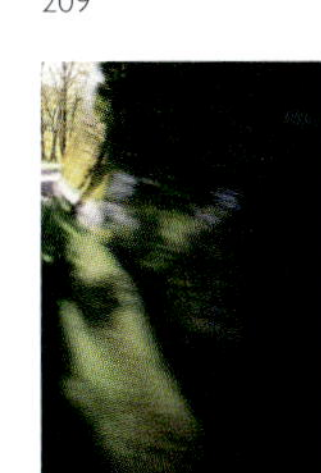

Avallon, 2009

C-Print
Private collection, Gottfried Salzmann,
Privatsammlung Gottfried Salzmann,
Collection privée Gottfried Salzmann

210

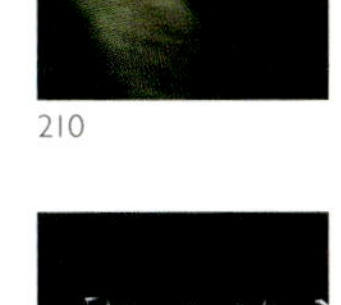

Tarbes, 2009

C-Print
Private collection, Gottfried Salzmann,
Privatsammlung Gottfried Salzmann,
Collection privée Gottfried Salzmann

211

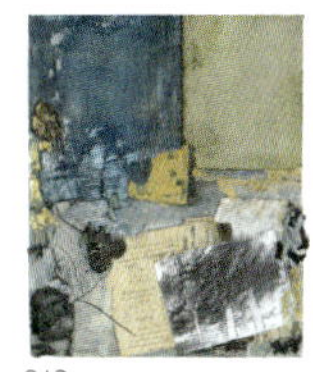

Four-Hand, Nicole Bottet and
Gottfried Salzmann | Nicole Bottet
und Gottfried Salzmann vierhändig |
Quatre mains, Nicole Bottet et
Gottfried Salzmann, 2007

Mixed media, collage, charcoal, gold,
Mischtechnik, Collage, Kohle, Gold,
Technique mixte, collage, fusain, or
65,8 × 52,5 cm

213

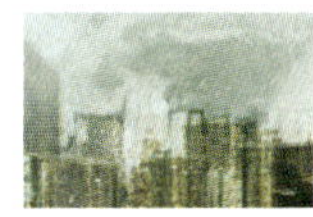

City Corp, 2005

Mixed media, photograph, Mischtechnik,
Foto, Technique mixte, photo
50,7 × 76 cm

8/9

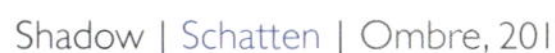

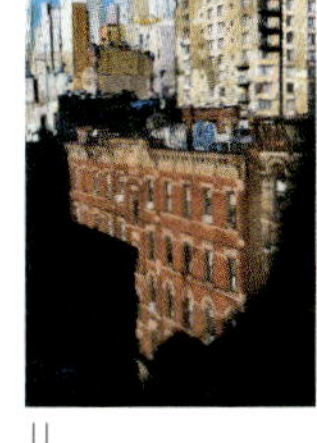

Shadow | Schatten | Ombre, 2011

Mixed media, photograph/canvas,
Mischtechnik, Foto/Leinwand,
Technique mixte, photo/toile
81 × 54 cm

11

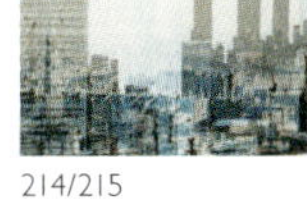

NY Blue Buildings, 2008

Mixed media, photograph, Mischtechnik,
Foto, Technique mixte, photo
49,9 × 76,3 cm

214/215

Published in conjunction with the exhibition | Diese Publikation erscheint anlässlich der Ausstellung | Publié à l'occasion de l'exposition
Gottfried Salzmann

Salzburg Museum, Salzburg, Austria | Salzburg, Österreich | Salzbourg, Autriche

July 21–October 6, 2013 | 21. Juli–6. Oktober 2013 | 21 juillet - 6 octobre 2013

Picture credits | Bildnachweis | Crédits photo :
Jean-Louis Losi : All photos, except for: | Alle Fotografien, außer: | Toutes les photographies, sauf :
Rupert Poschacher : p. | S. | p. 43, 46, 47, 48, 54, 89, 90, 91, 92, 129, 158, 159, 186, 187, 188, 189, 191, 194;
Nieves Salzmann, Nicole Bottet, Dr. Staindl : Private photos | Private Fotos | Photos privées

Cover: Liquid Sky | Flüssiger Himmel | Ciel liquide (p. | S. | p. 81)
p. | S. | p. 1: Brouillard IV (detail | Detail | détail, p. | S. | p. 60)
p. | S. | p. 2: Beauvais Cathedral II | Kathedrale von Beauvais II | Cathédrale de Beauvais II (detail | Detail | détail, p. | S. | p. 180)
p. | S. | p. 4: 6500 (detail | Detail | détail, p. | S. | p. 116)
p. | S. | p. 8: City Corp (detail | Detail | détail, p. | S. | p. 231)
p. | S. | p. 38: Over Paris | Über Paris | Au-dessus de Paris (detail | Detail | détail, p. | S. | p. 167)
p. | S. | p. 40: Nîmes, La Maison Carrée (detail | Detail | détail, p. | S. | p. 161)
p. | S. | p. 214: NY Blue Buildings (detail | Detail | détail, p. | S. | p. 231)
p. | S. | p. 222: Évecquemont (detail | Detail | détail, p. | S. | p. 52)

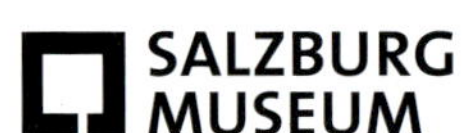 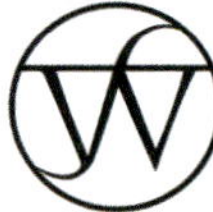 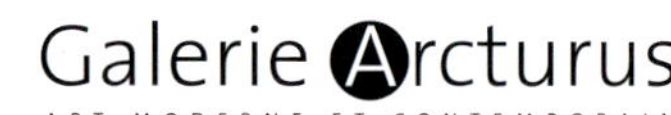 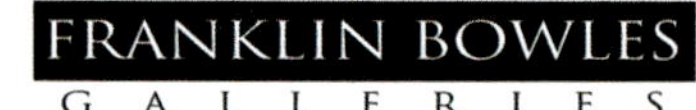 

Prestel Verlag, Munich
A Member of Verlagsgruppe Random House GmbH
Neumarkter Strasse 28
81673 Munich
Tel. +49 (0)89 4136-0
Fax +49 (0)89 4136-2335

www.prestel.de

Prestel Publishing Ltd.
14-11 Wells Street
London W1T 3PD
Tel. +44 (0)20 7323-5004
Fax +44 (0)20 7323-0271

Prestel Publishing
900 Broadway, Suite 603
New York, NY 10003
Tel. +1 (212) 995-2720
Fax +1 (212) 995-2733

www.prestel.com

The Deutsche Nationalbibliothek holds a record of this publication in the Deutsche Nationalbibliografie; detailed bibliographical data can be found under: http://dnb.d-nb.de. / Die Deutsche Nationalbibliothek verzeichnet diese Publikation in der Deutschen Nationalbibliografie; detaillierte bibliografische Daten sind im Internet über http://dnb.d-nb.de abrufbar.

Library of Congress Control Number is available.

British Library Cataloguing-in-Publication Data: a catalogue record for this book is available from the British Library.

Editorial direction | Projektleitung | Direction éditoriale: Eva Dotterweich

Translation | Übersetzung | Traduction: John Southard (German-English | deutsch-englisch | allemand-anglais), Martine Passelaigue (German-French | deutsch-französisch | allemand-français), Bernd Weiß (French-German | französisch-deutsch | français-allemand), Isabel Ollivier (French-English | französisch-englisch | français-anglais)

Copyediting | Lektorat | Suivi: Danko Szabó, Rita Forbes (English | englisch | anglais), Sophie Reinhardt (German | deutsch | allemand), Martine Passelaigue (French | französisch | français)

Design, layout: Rainald Schwarz
Production | Herstellung | Production: Cilly Klotz

Origination | Repro | Photolithographie: Repro Ludwig, Zell am See
Printing and binding | Druck und Bindung | Impression et reliure: Passavia Druckservice GmbH, Passau

ISBN 978-3-7913-5306-7

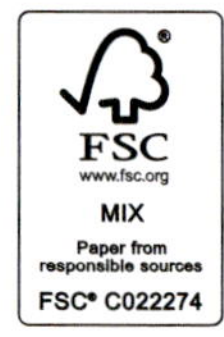

Verlagsgruppe Random House FSC-® N001967
The FSC-certified paper *LuxoArtSamt* was produced by Sappi, Ehingen